Lecture Notes in Computer Science

Commenced Publication in 1973
Founding and Former Series Editors:
Gerhard Goos, Juris Hartmanis, and Jan van Leeuwen

Editorial Board

Andrzej Pelc (Ed.)

Distributed Computing

21st International Symposium, DISC 2007
Lemesos, Cyprus, September 24-26, 2007
Proceedings

 Springer

Volume Editor

Andrzej Pelc
Département d'informatique
Université du Québec en Outaouais
Gatineau, Québec J8X 3X7, Canada
E-mail: pelc@uqo.ca

Library of Congress Control Number: 2007935053

CR Subject Classification (1998): C.2.4, C.2.2, F.2.2, D.1.3, F.1.1, D.4.4-5

LNCS Sublibrary: SL 1 – Theoretical Computer Science and General Issues

ISSN	0302-9743
ISBN-10	3-540-75141-6 Springer Berlin Heidelberg New York
ISBN-13	978-3-540-75141-0 Springer Berlin Heidelberg New York

Springer is a part of Springer Science+Business Media

springer.com

© Springer-Verlag Berlin Heidelberg 2007
Printed in Germany

Typesetting: Camera-ready by author, data conversion by Scientific Publishing Services, Chennai, India
Printed on acid-free paper   SPIN: 12162741   06/3180   5 4 3 2 1 0

Preface

DISC, the International Symposium on Distributed Computing, is an annual forum for presentation of research on all aspects of distributed computing, including the theory, design, implementation and applications of distributed algorithms, systems and networks. The 21st edition of DISC was held during September 24–26, 2007, in Lemesos, Cyprus.

This volume of proceedings begins with abstracts of three invited talks. The keynote speakers of DISC 2007 were: Burkhard Monien from the University of Paderborn, Germany, David Peleg from The Weizmann Institute of Science, Israel, and Michel Raynal from IRISA, Université de Rennes, France.

There were 100 ten-page-long extended abstracts submitted to DISC this year and this volume contains 32 contributions selected by the Program Committee among these 100 submissions. Every submitted paper was read and evaluated by Program Committee members assisted by external reviewers. The final decisions regarding acceptance or rejection of each paper were made during the electronic Program Committee meeting held in June/July 2007. Revised and expanded versions of a few best selected papers will be considered for publication in a special issue of the journal *Distributed Computing*.

The Best Student Paper Award of DISC 2007 was awarded to David Eisenstat for the paper "Fast Robust Approximate Majority" coauthored with Dana Angluin and James Aspnes.

This volume of proceedings also contains nine two-page-long brief announcements (BA). These BAs present ongoing work or recent results whose full description is not yet ready; it is expected that full papers containing those results will soon appear in other conferences or journals. The main purpose of the BA track is to announce ongoing projects to the distributed computing community and to obtain feedback for the authors. Each BA was also read and evaluated by the Program Committee.

This volume concludes with a section devoted to the 20th anniversary of the DISC conferences that took place during DISC 2006, held September 18–20, 2006, in Stockholm, Sweden.

DISC 2007 was organized in cooperation with the University of Cyprus. The main sponsor of DISC 2007 was CYTA - Cyprus Telecommunications Authority. The support of the Cyprus Tourism Organisation, Microsoft (Cyprus) and COST Action 295 DYNAMO is also gratefully acknowledged.

July 2007   Andrzej Pelc

The 2007 Edsger W. Dijkstra Prize in Distributed Computing

The 2007 Edsger W. Dijkstra Prize in Distributed Computing was presented at DISC 2007 for the paper "Consensus in the Presence of Partial Synchrony" by Cynthia Dwork, Nancy Lynch, and Larry Stockmeyer, which appeared in the Journal of the ACM (Vol. 35, No. 2, April, 1988. pages 288–323). A preliminary version appeared in PODC 1984.

This paper introduces a number of practically motivated partial synchrony models that lie between the completely synchronous and the completely asynchronous models, and in which consensus is solvable. It gives practitioners the right tool for building fault-tolerant systems, and contributes to the understanding that safety can be maintained at all times, despite the impossibility of consensus, and progress is facilitated during periods of stability. These are the pillars on which every fault-tolerant system has been built for two decades. This includes academic projects such as Petal, Frangipani, and Boxwood, as well as real-life data centers, such as the Google file system.

In distributed systems, balancing the pragmatics of building software that works against the need for rigor is particularly difficult because of impossibility results such as the FLP theorem. The publication by Dwork, Lynch, and Stockmeyer was in many respects the first to suggest a path through this thicket, and has been enormously influential. It presents consensus algorithms for a number of partial synchrony models with different timing requirements and failure assumptions: crash, authenticated Byzantine, and Byzantine failures. It also proves tight lower bounds on the resilience of such algorithms.

The eventual synchrony approach introduced in this paper is used to model algorithms that provide safety at all times, even in completely asynchronous runs, and guarantee liveness once the system stabilizes. This has since been established as the leading approach for circumventing the FLP impossibility result and solving asynchronous consensus, atomic broadcast, and state-machine replication.

In particular, the distributed systems engineering community has been increasingly drawn towards systems architectures that reflect the basic split between safety and liveness cited above. Dwork, Lynch, and Stockmeyer thus planted the seed for a profound rethinking of the ways that we should build, and reason about, this class of systems. Following this direction are many foundational solutions. First, these include state-machine replication methods such as Lamport's seminal Paxos algorithm and many group communication methods. Another important branch of research that directly follows this work is given by Chandra and Toueg's unreliable failure detector abstraction, which is realized in the eventual synchrony model of this paper. As Chandra and Toueg write: "we argue that partial synchrony assumptions can be encapsulated in the unreliability of failure detectors. For example, in the models of partial synchrony considered in Dwork et al. it is easy to implement a failure detector that satisfies the properties of $\Diamond$W." Finally, the insight by Dwork, Lynch, and Stockmeyer also led to various timed-based models of partial synchrony, such as Cristian and Fetzer's Timed-Asynchronous model and others.

The award committee would like to acknowledge the sincere efforts by the nominators of this work, as well as all other (worthy!) nominations which came short of winning.

The Committee wishes to pay a special tribute via this award to Larry Stockmeyer, who passed away on July 31, 2004. Larry's impact on the field through this paper and many others will always be remembered.

The Committee of the 2007 Edsger W. Dijkstra Prize
in Distributed Computing:

Hagit Attiya
Dahlia Malkhi
Keith Marzullo
Marios Mavronicolas
Andrzej Pelc
Roger Wattenhofer (Chair)

Organization

DISC, the International Symposium on Distributed Computing, is an annual forum for presentation of research on all aspects of distributed computing. It is organized in cooperation with the European Association for Theoretical Computer Science (EATCS). The symposium was established in 1985 as a biannual International Workshop on Distributed Algorithms on Graphs (WDAG). The scope was soon extended to cover all aspects of distributed algorithms as WDAG came to stand for International Workshop on Distributed AlGorithms, and in 1989 it became an annual symposium. To reflect the expansion of its area of interest, the name was changed to DISC (International Symposium on DIStributed Computing) in 1998. The name change also reflects the opening of the symposium to all aspects of distributed computing.

Program Committee Chair
Andrzej Pelc, Université du Québec en Outaouais, Canada

Organizing Committee Chair
Chryssis Georgiou, University of Cyprus, Cyprus

Steering Committee Chair
Alexander Shvartsman, University of Connecticut, USA

Organizing Committee

Chryssis Georgiou	University of Cyprus, Cyprus (Chair)
Marios Mavronicolas	University of Cyprus, Cyprus
Nicolas Nicolaides	Congresswise, Cyprus (Financial Officer)
Anna Philippou	University of Cyprus, Cyprus

Steering Committee

Hagit Attiya	Technion, Israel
Shlomi Dolev	Ben Gurion University, Israel
Pierre Fraigniaud	CNRS and Université Paris 7, France
Rachid Guerraoui	EPFL, Switzerland, (Vice Chair)

Sponsoring Institutions

CYTA - Cyprus Telecommunications Authority

University of Cyprus

Cyprus Tourism Organisation

COST Action 295 DYNAMO

Microsoft

DISC 2007 Webmasters
Chryssis Georgiou, University of Cyprus, Cyprus
Richard Královič, Comenius University, Slovakia

Referees

N. Agmon	M. Elkin	S. L. Horn
M. K. Aguilera	X. Euthimiou	Z. Hu
L. Alvisi	G. Even	R. Kat
H. Attiya	P. Fatourou	L. Katzir
Y. Bartal	H. Fauconnier	D. Kaynar
S. Baswana	A. Fernandez	I. Keidar
A. Beimel	F. Freiling	A. Kinalis
P. Bille	S. Funke	R. Klasing
E. Bortnikov	S. Ganguly	S. Kontogiannis
D. Benjamin Carbajal	P. W. Goldberg	A. Korman
J. Chalopin	O. Goussevskaia	D. R. Kowalski
B. Charron-Bost	R. Guerraoui	R. Královič
I. Chatzigiannakis	T. Harris	D. Krizanc
G. Chockler	Y. Haviv	F. Kuhn
S. Das	D. Hendler	P. Kuznetov
C. Delporte	M. Herlihy	C. Lavault
S. Dolev	E. Hillel	P. Leone
A. Dvir	J.-H. Hoepman	V. Liagkou

M. Liu
A. Lopez-Ortiz
N. Lynch
R. Majundar
D. Malkhi
G. De Marco
E. Markou
T. Mchenry
L. Michael
M. Moir
P. M. Musial
G. Mylonas

N. C. Nicolaou
A. Nisgav
F. Oprea
P. Panagopoulou
D. Pardubska
B. Patt-Shamir
T. Plachetka
G. Prencipe
R. De Prisco
G. Proietti
C. Raptopoulos
E. M. Schiller

G. Shegalov
H. Shpungin
S. Smorodinski
G. Stupp
C. Travers
U. Vaccaro
R. Wattenhofer
T. Wong
Q. Xin
I. Yoffe
S. Zaks
J. Zhang

Table of Contents

Invited Talks

Regular Papers

Brief Announcements

DISC 20th Anniversary

Routing and Scheduling with Incomplete Information

Burkhard Monien and Karsten Tiemann

Faculty of Computer Science, Electrical Engineering, and Mathematics,
University of Paderborn, 33102 Paderborn, Germany
{bm,tiemann}@uni-paderborn.de

Abstract. In many large-scale distributed systems the users have only *incomplete information* about the system. We outline game theoretic approaches that are used to model such incomplete information settings.

1 Introduction

In recent years, combining ideas from game theory and computer science to study distributed systems has become increasingly popular. While most work in this direction assumes that each player is completely informed there are also approaches that allow the more realistic case of incomplete information. Following the concept of *Bayesian decision theory* it is for incomplete information settings usually assumed that a player who does not know relevant parameters of a game is aware of *probability distributions* over the possible outcomes of these parameters. Hence there is a similarity to *stochastic programming* models where probability distributions for the uncertain data of optimization problems are known.

We will now outline two different approaches that are used to handle incomplete information.

2 Harsanyi's Incomplete Information Model

The Nobel laureate Harsanyi [4] introduced in the 1960s an elegant approach that can be used to study non-cooperative games with incomplete information. The *Harsanyi transformation* converts such a game with incomplete information to a game where players have different *types*. In the resulting *Bayesian game*, the players' uncertainty about each other's type is described by a probability distribution over all possible *type profiles*. Each player selects a *strategy* for each of his types. A stable state in which all types of all players minimize their individual cost is called a *Bayesian Nash equilibrium*.

Recently, Harsanyi's approach was used to study a selfish *routing* scenario in *networks* where the players do not know each other's weight. In these so-called *Bayesian routing games*, each type of a player corresponds to some weight. Gairing et al. [2] considered for these games the existence of equilibria, the computation of equilibria, and the so-called *price of anarchy* that measures the worst-possible inefficiency of equilibria with respect to a social welfare measure.

A. Pelc (Ed.): DISC 2007, LNCS 4731, pp. 1–2, 2007.
© Springer-Verlag Berlin Heidelberg 2007

3   Incomplete Information Models Where Every Player Minimizes Its Expected Individual Cost

Another possibility to handle incomplete information is to assume that each player bases his decisions on the *expected values* of unknown parameters. To do so, a player computes the expected values of parameters based on his own *probability distributions* over the possible outcomes of the parameters. Although this approach is popular in the scientific literature we only sketch two models here that are based on this approach.

Expected outcomes of unknown parameters were used for *network routing games* where the players have incomplete information about the edge latency functions. Since each player obtains for each edge his own expected latency function we get games with *player-specific* latency functions [6]. For these games positive and negative results on the existence of equilibria, convergence to equilibria, computation of equilibria, and the price of anarchy are known [3,5,6].

The approach to use expected outcomes for unknown parameters was also used by Dong et al. [1] who developed a *supply chain network model* consisting of manufacturers and retailers where the demands associated with the retail outlets are random. Here every *retailer* maximizes its *expected profit*, which is the difference between the expected revenues, the handling cost, and the payout to the manufacturers. Dong et al. [1] focused on the existence of equilibria, uniqueness of equilibria, and convergence to equilibria.

References

1. Dong, J., Zhang, D., Nagurney, A.: A supply chain network equilibrium model with random demands. European Journal of Operational Research 156(1), 194–212 (2004)
2. Gairing, M., Monien, B., Tiemann, K.: Selfish Routing with Incomplete Information. In: Proceedings of the 17th Annual ACM Symposium on Parallel Algorithms and Architectures, pp. 203–212. ACM Press, New York (2005)Also accepted to Theory of Computing Systems.
3. Gairing, M., Monien, B., Tiemann, K.: Routing (Un-) Splittable Flow in Games with Player-Specific Linear Latency Functions. In: Bugliesi, M., Preneel, B., Sassone, V., Wegener, I. (eds.) ICALP 2006. LNCS, vol. 4051, pp. 501–512. Springer, Heidelberg (2006)
4. Harsanyi, J.C.: Games with Incomplete Information Played by Bayesian Players, I, II, III. Management Science 14, 159–182, 320–332, 468–502 (1967)
5. Mavronicolas, M., Milchtaich, I., Monien, B., Tiemann, K.: Congestion Games with Player-Specific Constants. In: Proceedings of the 32nd International Symposium on Mathematical Foundations of Computer Science (to appear, 2007)
6. Milchtaich, I.: Congestion Games with Player-Specific Payoff Functions. Games and Economic Behavior 13(1), 111–124 (1996)

Time-Efficient Broadcasting in Radio Networks

David Peleg

Department of Computer Science and Applied Mathematics,
The Weizmann Institute of Science, Rehovot 76100, Israel
david.peleg@weizmann.ac.il

As broadcasting is one of the primary functions in radio networks, fast algorithms for performing it are of considerable interest. A radio network consists of stations that can act at any a given time step either as *transmitters* or as *receivers*. Given a deployment of the stations, the reception conditions can be modeled by a graph, where the existence of an edge between two nodes indicates that transmissions of one of them can reach the other, i.e., these nodes can communicate directly. The message transmitted by a node in given time step is delivered in the same time step to all of its neighbors in the graph. A node acting as a receiver in a given step will successfully receive a message if and only if exactly one of its neighbors transmits in that step. If two or more neighbors of a node transmit simultaneously, then a *collision* occurs and none of the messages is heard by the node in that step.

Broadcasting is the following basic communication task. Initially, one distinguished node, called the *source*, has a message which has to be disseminated to all other nodes. Typically, not all stations are within the source's transmission range, hence the source message must be propagated to remote nodes via intermediate ones. The model considered is synchronous, namely, all nodes have individual clocks that tick at the same rate, measuring time steps or *rounds*. The execution time of a broadcasting algorithm in a given radio network is the number of rounds it takes since the first transmission until all nodes of the network have received the source message.

The task of broadcasting in radio networks has been studied in a large variety of different models and under different requirements. Some of the main parameters giving rise to the different variants of the problem are the following.

Collision detection: There are two common models regarding the effect of a collision. The *collision detection* model assumes that a node acting as a receiver can recognize the fact that a collision has occurred. The alternative model is based on the assumption that the receiving node cannot distinguish a collision from background noise, hence it cannot tell whether a collision occurred or no transmissions took place.

Wake-up mode: The broadcasting protocol can be activated at the network stations in accordance to one of the following two models. In the *spontaneous wake up* model, all stations wake up when the source transmits for the first time, i.e., their clocks start simultaneously with the source. Consequently, all nodes may contribute to the efficiency of the broadcasting process by transmitting various preparatory control messages even before they receive the source message. In

A. Pelc (Ed.): DISC 2007, LNCS 4731, pp. 3–4, 2007.
© Springer-Verlag Berlin Heidelberg 2007

contrast, in the *conditional wake up* model, the stations other than the source are initially dormant and do not transmit until they receive a message for the first time and wake up. Thus in this model, the clock of a node starts on the round when it first receives the source message.

Distributed vs. centralized models: In the distributed setting, it is usually assumed that nodes are unaware of the topology of the network and do not know its diameter, its size or other parameters. It is often assumed that the nodes are not even aware of their immediate neighborhood. Networks featuring these characteristics are sometimes called *ad hoc* networks. In contrast, in certain contexts one may be interested in solving the time-efficient broadcasting problem under more favorable conditions, such as full information or assuming a central authority monitoring the broadcasting process. In such cases, it may be possible to pre-compute optimal or near-optimal broadcast schedules.

Topology classes: In addition to the study of general (arbitrary topology) radio networks, some recent interest arose concerning a natural subclass, referred to as *UDG radio networks*, where the network is modeled as a *unit disk graph* (UDG) whose nodes are represented as points in the plane. It is assumed that the transmission devices are capable of transmitting to distance 1, hence two points are joined by an edge if and only if their Euclidean distance is at most 1.

Use of randomness: Both deterministic and randomized broadcasting algorithms were considered in the literature.

The talk will review the literature on time-efficient broadcasting algorithms for radio networks under a variety of models and assumptions.

A Subjective Visit to Selected Topics in Distributed Computing

Michel Raynal

IRISA, Université de Rennes, 35042 Rennes, France
raynal@irisa.fr

After presenting a *personal* view of distributed computing (of course, being personal, this view is partial and questionable), this invited talk will address distributed computing problems that have recently received attention in the literature. For each of them, the talk presents the problem, results from the community, results from the author (and his co-authors), and questions that remain open. The following are among the topics covered in the talk.

Exclude or go fast enough?. The obstruction-free approach consists in designing algorithms that always preserve the safety property and always terminate when the process that issued the operation can execute alone during a "long enough" period of time [7]. It has been shown that the minimal information on failures needed to transform an obstruction-free algorithm into its wait-free counterpart [6] are failure detectors that allows a single process at a time to proceed [5]. This approach requires the processes to *exclude* each other.

The notion of a *timed register* has recently been proposed [9]. Such a register places a timing constraint on each write operation that follows a read operation (on that register). The write succeeds if it occurs "quick enough", otherwise it fails. Such registers allows implementing consensus for any number of processes in systems that satisfy a relatively weak timing assumption. So, this approach demands each process to *go fast enough* between a read of a timed register and the following write on the same timed register.

Each of the previous approaches can be seen as a particular facet of the same scheduling problem. The statement of a general scheduling framework that would unify them seems to be challenging open problem.

Towards a hierarchy of sub-consensus tasks. Asynchronous shared memory systems prone to process crashes defines a land only few parts of which have been explored. But that land has been provided with two main lighthouses: Herlihy's notion of wait-free synchronization (and the associated notion of consensus number) [6], and Gafni's notion of read/write reductions [2]. So, given an asynchronous shared memory system enriched with some base objects, fundamental questions are the following ones: which problems can be wait-free solved? Is there a hierarchy for wait-free subconsensus problems? Is it possible to define a measure (similar to consensus number) for these problems? Etc.

Focusing on the adaptive renaming problem, the talk will present reductions showing that that problem lies exactly in between the set agreement problem and the test-and-set problem, thereby defining a hierarchy of sub-consensus problems [4]. Enriching this hierarchy remains one of the most fundamental challenges of asynchronous computability in presence of failures [2].

A. Pelc (Ed.): DISC 2007, LNCS 4731, pp. 5–6, 2007.
© Springer-Verlag Berlin Heidelberg 2007

An arithmetic of synchronous set-agreement. Synchronous k-set agreement in presence of up to t faulty processes requires $R_{t,f}$ rounds where $R_{t,f} = \min\left(\lfloor\frac{f}{k}\rfloor + 2, \lfloor\frac{t}{k}\rfloor + 1\right)$ rounds (f denoting the number of actual crashes in a run, $0 \le f \le t$). This is a tight bound [1,3]. So, an interesting question is the following: given base objects of some type, how much do they allow bypassing that bound?

The talk will explore the case where the base objects (denoted $[m, \ell]$_SA objects) allow solving the ℓ-set agreement problem among m processes $(m < n)$ [8]. It will present an algorithm that requires $O(\frac{t\ell}{mk})$ rounds (more precisely, $R_{t,f,m,\ell} = \min\left(\lfloor\frac{f}{\Delta}\rfloor + 2, \lfloor\frac{t}{\Delta}\rfloor + 1\right)$, with $\Delta = m\lfloor\frac{k}{\ell}\rfloor + (k \bmod \ell)$). Open problems related to the synchronous set agreement will also be presented.

Acknowledgments

The work described in this talk is not only mine. It mainly results from common works and inflamed discussions with colleagues and friends (Eli Gafni, Rachid Guerraoui, Achour Mostefaoui, Sergio Rajsbaum, Gadi Taubenfeld and Corentin Travers), with whom I additionally share a common view of what are *computing science* and *science*.

References

1. Chaudhuri, S., Herlihy, M., Lynch, N., Tuttle, M.: Tight Bounds for k-Set Agreement. Journal of the ACM 47(5), 912–943 (2000)
2. Gafni, E.: Read-Write Reductions. In: Chaudhuri, S., Das, S.R., Paul, H.S., Tirthapura, S. (eds.) ICDCN 2006. LNCS, vol. 4308, pp. 349–354. Springer, Heidelberg (2006)
3. Gafni, E., Guerraoui, R., Pochon, B.: From a Static Impossibility to an Adaptive Lower Bound: The Complexity of Early Deciding Set Agreement. In: STOC 2005. Proc. 37th ACM Symposium on Theory of Computing, pp. 714–722. ACM Press, New York (2005)
4. Gafni, E., Raynal, M., Travers, C.: Test&Set, Adaptive Renaming and Set Agreement: a Guided Visit to Asynchronous Computability. In: SRDS'07. Proc. 26th IEEE Symposium on Reliable Distributed Systems. IEEE Computer Society Press, Beijing (China) (2007), ftp://ftp.irisa.fr/techreports/2007/PI-1837.pdf
5. Guerraoui, R., Kapałka, M., Kouznetsov, P.: The Weakest Failure Detectors to Boost Obstruction-Freedom. In: Dolev, S. (ed.) DISC 2006. LNCS, vol. 4167, pp. 376–390. Springer, Heidelberg (2006)
6. Herlihy, M.P.: Wait-Free Synchronization. ACM Transactions on Programming Languages and Systems 13(1), 124–149 (1991)
7. Herlihy, M., Luchangco, V., Moir, M.: Obstruction-free synchronization: double-ended queues as an example. In: CDCS '03. Proc. 23rd IEEE Int'l Conference on Distributed Computing Systems I(CDCS '03), pp. 522–529. IEEE Computer Society Press, Los Alamitos (2003)
8. Mostefaoui, A., Raynal, M., Travers, C.: Narrowing Power vs Efficiency in Synchronous Set Agreement. Tech Report # 1836, IRISA, Université de Rennes (France) (2007), ftp://ftp.irisa.fr/techreports/2007/PI-1836.pdf
9. Raynal, M., Taubenfeld, G.: The Notion of a Timed Register and its Application to Indulgent Synchronization. In: SPAA'07. 19th ACM Symposium on Parallel Algorithms and Architectures, pp. 200–207. ACM Press, New York (2007)

Bounded Wait-Free Implementation of Optimally Resilient Byzantine Storage Without (Unproven) Cryptographic Assumptions

Amitanand S. Aiyer[1], Lorenzo Alvisi[1,*], and Rida A. Bazzi[2]

[1] Department of Computer Sciences,
University of Texas at Austin
[2] Department of Computer Sciences,
Arizona State University

Abstract. We present the first optimally resilient, bounded, wait-free implementation of a distributed atomic register, tolerating Byzantine readers and (up to one-third of) Byzantine servers, without the use of unproven cryptographic primitives or requiring communication among servers. Unlike previous (non-optimal) solutions, the sizes of messages sent to writers depend only on the actual number of active readers and not on the total number of readers in the system. With a novel use of secret sharing techniques combined with write back throttling we present the first solution to tolerate Byzantine readers information theoretically, without the use of cryptographic techniques based on unproven number-theoretic assumptions.

1 Introduction

Distributed storage systems in which servers are subject to Byzantine failures have been widely studied. Results vary in the assumptions made about both the system model and the semantics of the storage implementation. The system parameters include the number of clients (readers and writers), the synchrony assumptions, the level of concurrency, the fraction of faulty servers, and the faulty behavior of clients. In the absence of synchrony assumptions, atomic [8] read and write semantics are possible, but stronger semantics are not [7]. We consider implementations with atomic semantics in this paper.

We consider solutions in an asynchronous system of n servers that do not communicate with each other (non-communicating servers) and in which up to f servers are subject to Byzantine failures (f-resilient), any number of clients can fail by crashing (wait-free), and readers can be subject to Byzantine failures. Systems in which servers do not communicate with each other are interesting because solutions that depend on communication between servers tend to have high message complexity, quadratic in the number of servers [10,4].

---

* This work was supported in part by NSF awards CSR—PDOS 0509338 and CyberTrust 043051.

A. Pelc (Ed.): DISC 2007, LNCS 4731, pp. 7–19, 2007.

In the non-communicating servers model, the best previous solution that provides wait-free atomic semantics requires $4f + 1$ servers [3]. That solution (i) requires clients and servers to exchange a finite number of messages and (ii) limits the size of the messages sent by the servers to the readers: the size of these messages is bound by a constant times the logarithm of the number of write operations performed in the system—or, equivalently, by a constant times the size of a timestamp. Unfortunately, this solution allows messages sent to writers to be as large as the maximum number of potential readers in the system, even during times when the number of *actual* readers is small. Recently, and concurrently with our work, a wait-free atomic solution that requires not more than $3f + 1$ servers was proposed, but that solution requires unbounded storage, message of unbounded size, and an unbounded number of messages per read operation [6].

None of these solutions consider Byzantine readers. Byzantine behavior of readers is relevant because wait-free atomic solutions require that readers write to servers [5]. All existing work that considers Byzantine readers uses cryptographic techniques based on unproven number-theoretic assumptions [4,9].

So, the existing results leave open two fundamental questions:

- Is the additional cost of f replicas over the optimal for unbounded solutions required to achieve a bounded wait-free solution?
- Is the use of cryptographic techniques required to tolerate Byzantine readers?

We answer both questions in the negative. We show that tolerating Byzantine readers can be achieved with information-theoretic guarantees and without the use of unproven number-theoretic assumptions. We also show that a bounded wait-free implementation of a distributed storage with atomic semantics is possible for $n = 3f + 1$ (which is optimal). Our solution also bounds the size of messages sent to writers—a significant improvement over Bazzi and Ding's non-optimal solution [3].

To achieve our results, we refine existing techniques and introduce some new techniques. The ideas we refine include *concurrent-reader detection* and *write-back throttling*, originally proposed in the atomic wait-free solution of Bazzi and Ding [3]. In what follows we give a high level overview of the new techniques we introduce.

Increasing resiliency. We increase the resiliency of our solution by introducing a new way by which a reader selects the timestamp of the value it will try to read. Instead of choosing the $f + 1$'st largest among the received timestamps, in our protocol the reader chooses the $2f + 1$'st *smallest*. In fact, we realized that the $f + 1$ largest timestamp worked well for $n = 4f + 1$ simply because, for that value of n, the $f + 1$ largest received timestamp coincides with the $2f + 1$ smallest. We guarantee the liveness of our new selection process by having the reader continuously update the value of the $2f + 1$'st smallest timestamp as it receives responses from new servers.

Bounding message sizes to writers. We bound the sizes of messages sent to servers using three rounds of communication between writers and servers. These rounds occur in parallel with the first two rounds of the write protocol and no server receives a total of more than two messages across the three rounds. In the first round, the writer estimates the number of concurrent readers; in the second and third rounds it determines their identities.

Tolerating Byzantine readers. We use write back throttling combined with secret sharing to tolerate Byzantine readers. The idea is to associate a random secret with each write and share the secret among the servers in such a way that it can only be reconstructed if enough servers reveal their shares. By requiring that a correct server only divulge its share if the write has made sufficient progress, we use a reader's ability to reconstruct the secret as a proof that the reader is allowed to write back. By using secret sharing, we avoid relying on unproven number theoretic assumptions and achieve instead information-theoretic guarantees.

2   Model/Assumptions

The system consists of a set of n replicas (servers), a set of m writers and a set of readers. Readers and writers are collectively referred to as clients. Clients have unique identifiers that are totally ordered. When considering boundedness of the sizes of messages, we assume that a read operation in the system can be uniquely identified with a finite bit string (otherwise any message sent by a reader can be unbounded in size). The identifier consists of a reader identifier and a read operation tag. Similarly write operations are identified by the writer identifier and the timestamp of the value being written. Since timestamps are non-skipping [2], writes can also be represented by finite strings.

Clients execute protocols that specify how *read* and *write* operations are implemented. We assume that clients do not start a new operation before finishing a previous operation. We assume that up to f servers may deviate arbitrarily from the specified protocol (Byzantine) and that the remaining $(n - f)$ servers are correct. We require that the total number of servers n be at least $3f + 1$.

We assume that messages cannot be spoofed. While this is typically enforced in practice using digital signatures, based on public key cryptography, such techniques are not necessarily required to enforce our requirement. We assume FIFO point-to-point asynchronous channels between clients and servers. Servers do not communicate with other servers.

Writers are benign and can only fail by crashing. In Section 3 we also assume that the readers are benign; we relax this assumption in Section 5 where we consider Byzantine readers . When considering Byzantine readers, we make the additional assumption that the channels between the servers and the writers are private i.e. messages sent over these channels cannot be eves-dropped by the adversary.

For our implementation, the probability that a given read operation by a Byzantine reader improperly writes back a value is 2^{-k} where k is a security parameter. We choose k to be sufficiently large so that the probability of failure for all operations is small. If $k = o + k'$ bits, where o is the number of bits required to represent one operation, then the system failure probability is $2^{-k'}$.

Schemes based on public key cryptography, in the best case, also suffer from this negligible small probability of error. If the unproven assumptions that they are based upon do not hold, their probability of error can be significantly larger.

3   Bounded Atomic Register

We present a single-writer protocol that implements a wait-free atomic register using $3f + 1$ replicas where the size and the number of messages exchanged per operation is bounded.

Figures 1–3 present a single-writer-multiple-reader version of the protocol that assumes that the readers are benign. In Section 5 we show how to extend this protocol to handle Byzantine readers. These protocols can also be easily extended to support multiple-writers, using ideas from [3]. We refer the reader to [1] for proofs and a more detailed discussion.

3.1   Protocol Overview

The write operation. The write operation is performed in two phases.

In phase 1, the writer sends the value to all the servers and waits for $(n-f)$ acknowledgements. The writer also initiates, in parallel, the GetConcurrentReaders protocol to detect concurrent readers. The GetConcurrentReaders is a bounded protocol, described in Section 3.3, that detects all read operations which are considered to be active at all the non-faulty servers, when the protocol is executed.

In phase 2, the writer asks all the servers to update their *current timestamp*, and to forward the values that they have to all the concurrent readers detected in phase 1. On receiving $(n - f)$ acknowledgements, the write operation completes.

This two-phase mechanism guarantees that if a non-faulty server updates its current timestamp, then at least $f + 1$ non-faulty servers must have already received the value.

The read operation. To understand the reader's protocol, we consider a simple scenario. The reader starts by requesting second phase information from the servers. Each server replies with the most current timestamp for which it knows that the corresponding write operation reached its second phase. Now, assume that the reader receives replies from all correct servers in response to its request for second phase information. The timestamps returned by these correct servers can be quite different because the reader's requests could reach them at different times and the writer could have executed many write operations during that time. Of special interest is the largest second phase timestamp returned by a correct server. Let us call that timestamp $t_{largest}$. If the writer executes no write operation after its write of $t_{largest}$, then, when the reader receives the second phase response with $t_{largest}$, it can simply request all first phase messages and be guaranteed to receive $f + 1$ replies with identical value v and timestamp $t_{largest}$; at that time, the reader would be able to determine that, by reading v, it would not violate atomic semantics. The reader then writes back the value and then the timestamp in two phases to complete the read operation.

```
write( ) {                              // Phase W2
  inc(ts)                                 send (WRITE_TS, ts, CR) to all
  // Phases W1                              wait for (n − f) acks.
  cobegin {                             }
    writeVal();                         writeVal( ) {
    CR = GetConcurrentReaders()           send (WRITE_VAL, ⟨v, ts⟩) to all
  } coend                                  wait for (n − f) acks.
                                        }
```

Fig. 1. The Writer's Protocol

While this scenario is instructive, it overlooks some complications. For instance, a fast writer might write many values with timestamps larger than $t_{largest}$. Also, the reader does not know when it has received replies from all correct servers. If we assume, for now, that the reader *can* tell when it has received values from all correct servers, then we can solve the problems caused by a fast writer by having the fast writer help the reader to terminate. This is done by having the writer detect concurrent read operations and then have the writer request from the server to *flush out* the written value to concurrent readers. Our solution requires that servers keep the 3 most up to date written values because the detection of concurrent readers is only guaranteed when the writer completely writes a value whose timestamp is larger than $t_{largest} + 1$.

There remains the problem of the reader not knowing when it has received replies from all correct servers. In fact, in response to its request for second phase information, the reader can receive replies only from $n − f$ servers—f of which may be faulty—and it might not be able to terminate based on these responses. We handle this situation by simply *assuming* that these $n − f$ messages are all from correct servers. If they indeed are, then the reader will for sure be able to decide on $t_{largest}$ by requesting the first phase information (it is possible that the reader will be able to decide even if they are not correct). If, however, the reader is unable to decide, then there are other correct servers whose replies are not amongst the $n − f$ replies, and, by waiting long enough, the reader will eventually receive some message from one of those servers. When an undecided reader receives a new message, it recalculates $t_{largest}$ assuming that, with the new messages it received, it must finally have replies from all correct servers: therefore, the reader re-requests the first phase information from all servers. This process continues until the reader indeed receives replies from all correct servers, in which case, it is guaranteed to decide.

Finally, in the above discussion we have assumed that the reader knows what $t_{largest}$ is—in reality, in our protocol the reader can only estimate $t_{largest}$ by using the $2f + 1$'st smallest second phase timestamp. We can show that this is sufficient to guarantee that the reader can decide and that its decision is valid [1].

3.2   Protocol Guarantees

The protocol presented provides atomic semantics. The reader and the writer protocols always terminate and are wait-free.

Boundedness. A solution is amortized bounded if m operations do not generate more than $m \times k$ messages, for some constant k without some servers being

Definitions:
valid($\langle v, ts \rangle$) $\triangleq$ |{ $s : \langle v, ts \rangle \in$ Values[s] }| $\geq f + 1$
notOld($\langle v, ts \rangle$) $\triangleq$ |{ $s : last\_comp[s] \leq ts$}| $\geq 2f + 1$
fwded($\langle v, ts \rangle$) $\triangleq$ |{ $s : fwd[s] = \langle v, ts \rangle$}| $\geq f + 1$

read( ) {
  $\forall s$: last_comp[s] = $\bot$; fwd[s] = $\bot$; Values[s] = $\emptyset$
  // Phase R1
  send (GET_TS) to all

  repeat
    on receive (TS, s, ts) from server s
      last_comp[s] = ts
    on receive (FWD, s, $\langle v, ts \rangle$, Vals) from server s
      fwd[s] = $\langle v, ts \rangle$
      Values[s] = Values[s] $\cup$ Vals
  until (|{$x : last\_comp[x] \neq \bot$}| $\geq n - f$)

  // Phase R2
  send (GET_VAL) to all
  repeat
    on receive (TS, s, ts) from server s
      last_comp[s] = ts
      send (GET_VAL) to all
    on receive (VALS, s, Vals) from server s
      Values[s] = Values[s] $\cup$ Vals
    on receive (FWD, s, $\langle v, ts \rangle$, Vals) from server s
      fwd[s] = $\langle v, ts \rangle$
      Values[s] = Values[s] $\cup$ Vals
  until ($\exists \langle v_C, ts_C \rangle$: fwded($\langle v_C, ts_C \rangle$)
        $\vee$(notOld($\langle v_C, ts_C \rangle$) $\wedge$ valid($\langle v_C, ts_C \rangle$)))

  // Phase R3
  WriteBack(ts_C)
  return $\langle v_C, ts_C \rangle$
}

WriteBack(ts) {
  // Round 1
  send (WBACK_VAL, $\langle v, ts \rangle$) to all
    wait for ($n - f$) acks.
  // Round 2
  send (WBACK_TS, ts) to all
    wait for ($n - f$) acks.
}

Fig. 2. Reader's protocol

Initialization:
READERS := $\emptyset$
RNextVal := $\bot$

server( ) {
  // Write Protocol messages
  on receive (WRITE_VAL, $\langle v, ts \rangle$) from writer
    if (RVal.ts $< ts$)
      (RPrev2 , RPrev , RVal) := (RPrev , RVal, $\langle v, ts \rangle$)
    send WRITE-ACK1 to the writer
  on receive (WRITE_TS, ts, CR) from writer
    if (Rcts$< ts$)
      Rcts:= ts
    for each $r \in CR$:
      send (FWD, s, RVal, { RVal, RPrev , RPrev2 })
        to r
    READERS = READERS \ CR
    send WRITE-ACK2 to the writer
  // Read Protocol messages
  on receive (GET_TS) from reader r:
    READERS .enqueue(r)
    send (TS, s, Rcts) to r
  on receive (GET_VAL) from reader r
    send (VALS, s, { RVal, RPrev }) to r
  // Write back Messages
  on receive (WBACK_VAL, $\langle v, ts \rangle$) from reader r
    wait for (Rcts$\geq ts - 1$)
    if (RVal.ts $< ts$)
      (RPrev2 , RPrev , RVal) := (RPrev , RVal, $\langle v, ts \rangle$)
    send WBACK-ACK1 to r
  on receive (WBACK_TS, ts) from reader r
    wait for (RVal.ts $\geq ts$)
    if (Rcts$< ts$)
      Rcts:= ts
    READERS .remove(r)
    send WBACK-ACK2 to r
  // GetConcurrentReaders Protocol messages
  on receive (GET_ACT_RD_CNT) from writer
    send (RDRS_CNT, s, READERS .size())
      to writer
  on receive (GET_ACT_RDS, count) from writer
    send (READERS, s, READERS [1:count])
      to writer
  on receive (GET_ACT_RDS_INS, A) from writer
    send (RDRS_INS, s, READERS $\cap$ A) to writer }

Fig. 3. Protocol for server s

detected as faulty. In an amortized bounded solution, a client executing a particular operation might have to handle an unbounded number of *late* messages. In a bounded solution a client operation will always handle no more than k messages for some constant k and if more than k messages are received, the faulty behavior of some servers will be detected.

Our solution is amortized bounded. This does not rule out the possibility that a reader receives many unsolicited messages from a server. All we can do in that case is to declare the server faulty and our proof of boundedness does not apply to such rogue servers that are detected to be faulty.

To make the solution bounded for the reader techniques such as [3] can be used.

3.3 Bounded Detection of Readers

The protocol requires that the writer be able to detect ongoing read operations. A writer that invokes GetConcurrentReaders() after all correct servers have started processing a read request r issued by client c_r must be able to identify r (assuming r does not terminate before the end of the execution of the detection protocol).

Definitions:

notLarge(s) $\triangleq$ $|\{x : count[x] \geq count[s]\}| \geq f+1$
GetConcurrentReaders() {
 $\forall s$: readers[s] := $\perp$
 $\forall s$: count[s] := $\perp$
 $\forall s$: sent[s] := false
 union_set := $\perp$
 // Get Active reader count
 send (GET_ACT_RD_CNT) **to** all servers
 // Get Active reader lists from servers with valid count
 repeat
  on receive (RDRS_CNT, s, count) **from** server s
   count[s] = count
   $\forall p$: **if** (notLarge(p) $\wedge$ sent[p] = false)
    send (GET_ACT_RDS) **to** server p
    sent[p] := true
  on receive (READERS, s, R) **from** server s
   if ($\neg$ sent[s] $\vee$ (sent[s] $\wedge$ count[s] $\neq$ $|R|$))
    detect failure of s
   else
    readers[s] := R
 until ($|\{$readers[s] : readers[s] $\neq\perp\}| \geq f+1$)
 union_set := $\cup_s$ readers[s]

 // Get union_set $\cap$ Active reader lists from the rest
 for each (s : sent[s] $\neq true$)
  send (GET_ACT_RDS_INS, union_set) **to** server s
 repeat
  on receive (READERS, s, R) **from** server s
   if ($\neg$ sent[s] $\vee$ (sent[s] $\wedge$ count[s] $\neq$ $|R|$))
    detect failure of s
   else
    readers[s] := R
  on receive (RDRS_INS, s, R) **from** server s
   if (R $\not\subset$ union_set)
    detect failure of s
   else
    readers[s] := R
 until ($|\{s : $readers[$s$] $\neq\perp\}| \geq n-f$)
 CR = $\{x : |\{s : x \in readers[s]\}| \geq (f+1)\}$
 return CR
}

Fig. 4. Bounded detection of readers: Writer code

A simple way to implement the required functionality is for the writer to collect, from all servers, the sets of ongoing read operations (the *active reader operations*) and to identify those among them that appear in at least $f+1$ sets: this is the approach taken in [3]. Because it is possible that some servers may have begun processing read requests that have not yet reached the other servers, faulty servers can send arbitrarily long lists of bogus active operations without being detected as faulty. Our protocol rectifies this problem, and is shown in Figure 4.

Protocol Description. The idea of the protocol is to first estimate the number of active read operations in the system and then accept lists of active reader operations whose size is bounded by this estimate. The difficulty is in ensuring that all genuinely active operations, and only those, are detected. The protocol has two phases. In the first phase, the writer determines a set of servers who are returning a *valid* active list count, i.e. a count of active reader operations that does not exceed the count returned by at least *some* correct server. In the second phase, the writer requests these servers for their active lists, which are known not to be too large.

For servers, whose count is not known to be *valid*, the writer cannot request the active list since it could be too large. However, once the writer has collected $f+1$ active lists from servers with a *valid* count, the writer sends the union of these lists to the remaining servers and only requests for the elements in the server's active list that is present in the union.

On receiving the active sets (or their intersection) from at least $n-f$ servers, the writer computes the set of concurrent readers.

Protocol guarantees. Since the writer only needs to wait for $(n-f)$ responses, this sub-protocol always terminates. The number of messages exchanged in this sub-protocol is bounded as the writer does not send or receive more than two messages to any server. The messages sent in the first two phases are bounded in size because the writer only requests active lists from servers with a *valid* count.

The messages in the third step is also bounded in size, because the size of the computed union set is bounded.

4   Tolerating Byzantine Readers

In a wait-free atomic implementation of replicated storage, readers must write to servers to ensure read-read atomicity [5]. With Byzantine readers, servers need guarantees that the values written by readers are valid. This can be satisfied by having the reader present a proof that a correct server vouches for the value and such a proof can be satisfied by having the reader present evidence that $f + 1$ servers vouch for the value it wants to write back. Traditionally, such vouchers or proofs rely on public key cryptography, which depend on unproven assumptions such as the hardness of factoring, or the hardness of computing discrete logarithms [9].

In general, it is not sufficient for a reader to prove that the value it is writing originated from the writer. For instance, if the reader is expected to write more than one value in some order, then the reader should not write a later value without having completed writing the previous value in the order. Omitting to write some values can in general lead to violations of the protocol's requirements.

With respect to the protocol presented in Section 3, the servers should verify two things:

1. A reader is allowed to write back a value only if it proves that it received the value from a correct server (i.e. by having $f + 1$ servers vouch for the value).
2. A reader is allowed to perform a second round write back of the timestamp only after $f + 1$ correct servers have accepted the first round write back message (i.e. $2f + 1$ servers accepted the first round write back).

With public key cryptography, these proofs can be easily implemented. A server signs messages it sends to a reader and a reader can provide as proof the requisite number of signed messages.

An important observation is that these (signed) messages indicate the progress in terms of the server state and are not specific to the particular read operation. The protocol remains correct even if these proofs are put together from signed messages sent by servers in response to different read operations.

We present a secret-sharing-based approach that can be used to implement these types of proofs. This shows that the (strong) assumption of computationally one-way functions, used by PKIs, is not required for these applications. We believe that our approach can be used not just with the protocol presented in Section 3, but also with other protocols that have a similar structure—however, characterizing such protocols and developing a general framework to replace cryptographic-based techniques with our techniques are left for future work.

4.1   Provably Correct Proofs Using Secret Sharing

Consider the read and write protocols in Figure 5, which are typically part of larger protocols.

Write(*value*, *ts*)
    send (*value*, *ts*) to all
    wait for $n - f$ acks

Read(*ts*)
    send READ_REQUEST to all
    wait for t replies with same value v and timestamp ts
    send v to all
    wait for $n - f$ acks

Fig. 5. Simple client protocols

In the protocol, the reader is attempting to read a value whose timestamp is ts and the writer writes a value whose timestamp is ts (not necessarily the same). The server code corresponding to these two protocols is the obvious one.

As presented, the reader protocol is not guaranteed to terminate and typically, it will be part of a larger protocol that ensures termination. We will not concern ourselves with termination in the remainder of this section.

We would like to transform the two protocols so that correct readers are not affected and faulty readers cannot write back a value that was not written by the writer.

We achieve the transformation by splitting the write operation into two parts. In a first part, the writer sends the value to be written along with some *other information* that we will explain shortly. In the second part of a write operation, the writer sends a message indicating that the first part has finished. The servers process the message with the values, exactly as in the simple protocol, but only when it receives the FINISHED_SENDING_VALUES message. In other words, the values received in the first part are hidden and are not processed (or sent to readers) unless the server knows that the writer finishes the first part. This knowledge can be obtained directly from the writer or indirectly from the reader.

So, we need a way for a reader that received t identical values to convince a correct server that only received a first message from the writer to open the value that the server received from the writer. By doing this, the reader is effectively writing back a value but without having to sign the value. The write back consists of making a hidden value non-hidden. A reader knows that it can write back to all correct servers if it knows that the writer finished the first part and started the second part at some correct server because, in that case, all correct servers will eventually receive the value from the writer which is sent in the first part.

So, the question is how can we provide a proof that the writer made enough progress. This is where the *other information* enter the picture. The main idea is to have the writer associate a randomly generated secret with the value it wants to write. The writer generates this secret, creates shares, and sends these shares to servers before (roughly speaking) starting the actual write operation.

A server which *knows* that the writer has completed the first part and started the second part, is willing to provide the value as well as shares of the secret. The secret is shared such that if (and only if) enough messages are received, the reader will be able to reconstruct the secret. Thus, reconstructing the secret can be used as a proof that the writer made enough progress in its write operation. The details of the secret sharing scheme are given below.

The modified writer and reader protocols are shown in Figure 6.

Each secret is split using the techniques of [11] such that $k.t$ shares are required to reconstruct the secret, where $k > f$. Each server is given $k + 1$

```
Write(value, ts)                              Read(ts)
  generate secret s                             send READ_REQUEST to all
  ∀1 ≤ i ≤ n generate shares sᵢ[1 . . . k + 1]  value_read = ⊥
  ∀1 ≤ i ≤ n send (value, ts, sᵢ[1 . . . k + 1]) to serverᵢ  repeat
  send FINISHED_SENDING_VALUES to all             receive message (v, ts, sᵢ[1 . . . k]) from server i
  wait for n − f replies                          if received ≥ t messages with the same v and ts
                                                    fork {
                                                      send (v, collectedSharesFor(v)) to all
                                                      wait for n − f acks
                                                      value_read = v
                                                    }
                                                until (value_read != ⊥)
```

Fig. 6. Modified client protocols

shares, along with the message that was going to be sent in the simple protocol. After sending these messages to all the servers, the writer sends the FIN-
ISHED_SENDING_VALUES message.

If a read request reaches a server after the server received the FINISHED_
SENDING_VALUES message from the writer, the server sends the value to the
reader along with k of the shares the server received from the writer. One share
is never revealed and is used by servers only for verifying that a reconstructed
secret is correct. Secret sharing ensures that the secret can be reconstructed if
and only if t number of servers give away their shares.

The server now accepts a write back from a reader only if the reader can
provide enough shares that can reconstruct the correct secret at the server. The
server can accept a write back even before receiving the FINISHED_SENDING_
VALUES message. If the server decides to accept the write back message, the
server unhides the message and acts as if it has received a FINISHED_SENDING_
VALUES message directly from the writer.

Note that unlike the case with cryptographic solution in which the reader
could determine locally whether the received signatures are valid, in our protocol the reader needs the cooperation of the servers in order to determine if
the received shares can reconstruct the correct secret. Here, the reader cannot
determine if the proof is going to be valid because it does not have any shares
to verify against. This may cause the write backs to not succeed if there are
not enough correct shares. Also, the shares that enable the reader to write back
might not arrive all at once. The reader might first receive $n − f$ replies that
do not include the crucial shares of some slow correct servers. So, the reader's
protocol would have the reader request verification from servers every time the
reader receives a new share. The reader can finish when it has received enough
identical values and it knows that it can write back.

5   Protocol Tolerating Byzantine Readers

To convert the protocol presented in Section 3 to a Byzantine reader tolerant
protocol, the writer has to perform an extra phase. This extra phase contains
the secrets required for both the phases of the write protocol. So phase 1 and
Phase 2 of the original protocol are replaced with (Phase 1' || Phase 2'), Phase
1", and Phase 2" where the primes and double primes are used to indicate the
transformed phases and the || indicates that the first transformed phases are
executed concurrently.

5.1   The Write Protocol

Before beginning the two phases of the write, the writer generates two random secrets. The writer sends the shares for these secrets, along with the value and timestamp information that it is going to write, to all the servers before initiating the write phases.

The first secret is used to prove that the reader has received $f + 1$ identical values and is split such that $t = f + 1$. The second secret is used to prove that the reader has received $(n - f)$ acknowledgements to the first phase write back and is split such that $t = (n - f)$.

On receiving these shares and information regarding the value and timestamp that is going to be written, the servers hold them separately and do not update any values or timestamps that are used in the original protocol.

After sending these shares and values to all the servers, the writer begins the original write protocol, asking the servers to update the value and then the timestamp. Only on receiving the message from writer to update the value, or on accepting a write back message, will a server update its value and reveal its secret shares. The same holds true for updating the timestamp.

5.2   The Read Protocol

The read protocol is similar to the original read protocol in Section 3. The only difference being that the reader needs to include the collected shares as a proof to be allowed to perform the write back.

As in Section 3, the reader waits to collect $f + 1$ matching responses for an acceptable timestamp. It then tries to write back the value providing as a proof the set of shares collected so far. Retrying each time it receives more shares, or when it can try to write back a different value.

The server will only accept the write back if value being written back matches the value that was initially received from the writer, and the shares can reconstruct the correct secret. If at least one non-faulty server has revealed the value, then all servers will eventually receive the value and the shares sent by the writer to be able to verify the information provided by the reader. Thus valid write backs from correct readers will be eventually accepted.

Moreover, since the servers receive the value from the writer directly, the reader need not send the value along with the write back. It is sufficient to use a lightweight tag, or the timestamp to identify the write [5]. Thus, preventing the servers from having to process large messages from bad readers. For simplicity, we assume that the protocol does not have this optimization.

On accepting the first write back for the value, the server responds with its shares of the second secret. On receiving $(n - f)$ of these responses, the reader proceeds to write back the timestamp in the second phase sending the shares it received in these responses as proof that $(n - f)$ servers have accepted the first phase write back. The reader retries writing back whenever it receives additional shares. When all the correct servers accept the write back value and respond with their shares of the second secret, the reader will have enough correct shares to reconstruct the secret correctly and complete the write back.

Late write backs. One complication is that if a first round write back arrives late at a server, the server might not have the shares to give the reader because the old shares might have been replaced with newer ones due to subsequent writes. If a server that receives a write back message has a current timestamp that is larger than the timestamp being written back, it simply sends a write back acknowledgment, but without the shares (sending $\perp$ for the shares).

The meaning of a write back without shares is that the writer has started the second phase of the write of a value with a higher timestamp. When the reader finishes its first round of write back it will collect $(n - f)$ acknowledgments, some with shares and some without shares, and send these along with its second phase write back. If one of the acknowledgments without shares is from a correct server, then this means that the writer must have started writing a new value and finished the second phase of the write operation for which the reader is sending a second phase write back, and therefore all correct servers will eventually receive the second phase message from the writer and can accept the write back. If none of the acknowledgments without secrets is from a correct server, then the reader will eventually receive either enough secrets (as we argued in the previous paragraph) or one acknowledgment without secrets from a correct server; in either case, the correct reader will be able to finish its second phase write back.

Bounding number of retries. The reader only tries to write back values that have been received from at least $f + 1$ different servers. Since the reader queries the servers for values up to $f + 1$ times and gets up to 2 values from each server in addition to 3 values in the forwarded message, the reader can get up to $2(f + 1) + 3$ different values from each server. Thus a correct reader may only retry writing back a maximum of $\frac{n(2f+5)}{f+1}$ different values. Also, since each value will only be retried $f + 1$ times, the number of messages exchanged due to the retries is still bounded.

Acknowledgements. We thank Allen Clement and Harry Li for their helpful discussions on secret verification.

References

1. Aiyer, A., Alvisi, L., Bazzi, R.A.: Bounded Wait-free Implementation of Optimally Resilient Byzantine Storage without (Unproven) Cryptographic Assumptions. Technical Report TR-07-32, University of Texas at Austin, Department of Computer Sciences (July 2007)
2. Bazzi, R.A., Ding, Y.: Non-skipping timestamps for byzantine data storage systems. In: Guerraoui, R. (ed.) DISC 2004. LNCS, vol. 3274, pp. 405–419. Springer, Heidelberg (2004)
3. Bazzi, R.A., Ding, Y.: Bounded wait-free f-resilient atomic byzantine data storage systems for an unbounded number of clients. In: Dolev, S. (ed.) DISC 2006. LNCS, vol. 4167, pp. 299–313. Springer, Heidelberg (2006)
4. Cachin, C., Tessaro, S.: Optimal resilience for erasure-coded byzantine distributed storage. In: DSN, Washington, DC, USA, pp. 115–124. IEEE Computer Society Press, Los Alamitos (2006)

5. Fan, R., Lynch, N.: Efficient replication of large data objects. In: Fich, F.E. (ed.) DISC 2003. LNCS, vol. 2848, pp. 75–91. Springer, Heidelberg (2003)
6. Guerraoui, R., Vukolic, M.: Refined Quorum Systems. Technical Report LPD-REPORT-2007-001, EPFL (2007)
7. Herlihy, M.: Wait-free synchronization. ACM Transactions on Programming Languages and Systems 13(1), 124–149 (1991)
8. Lamport, L.: On interprocess communication. part i: Basic formalism. Distributed Computing 1(2), 77–101 (1986)
9. Liskov, B., Rodrigues, R.: Byzantine clients rendered harmless. In: Fraigniaud, P. (ed.) DISC 2005. LNCS, vol. 3724, pp. 311–325. Springer, Heidelberg (2005)
10. Martin, J.-P., Alvisi, L., Dahlin, M.: Minimal byzantine storage. In: Malkhi, D. (ed.) DISC 2002. LNCS, vol. 2508, pp. 311–325. Springer, Heidelberg (2002)
11. Tompa, M., Woll, H.: How to share a secret with cheaters. J. Cryptol. 1(2), 133–138 (1988)

A Simple Population Protocol for
Fast Robust Approximate Majority

Dana Angluin[1], James Aspnes[1,*], and David Eisenstat[2,**]

[1] Yale University, Department of Computer Science
{dana.angluin,james.aspnes}@yale.edu
[2] Princeton University, Department of Computer Science
deisenst@cs.princeton.edu

Abstract. We describe and analyze a 3-state one-way population protocol for approximate majority in the model in which pairs of agents are drawn uniformly at random to interact. Given an initial configuration of x's, y's and blanks that contains at least one non-blank, the goal is for the agents to reach consensus on one of the values x or y. Additionally, the value chosen should be the majority non-blank initial value, provided it exceeds the minority by a sufficient margin. We prove that with high probability n agents reach consensus in $O(n \log n)$ interactions and the value chosen is the majority provided that its initial margin is at least $\omega(\sqrt{n \log n})$. This protocol has the additional property of tolerating Byzantine behavior in $o(\sqrt{n})$ of the agents, making it the first known population protocol that tolerates Byzantine agents. Turning to the register machine construction from [2], we apply the 3-state approximate majority protocol and other techniques to speed up the per-step parallel time overhead of the simulation from $O(\log^4 n)$ to $O(\log^2 n)$. To increase the robustness of the phase clock at the heart of the register machine, we describe a consensus version of the phase clock and present encouraging simulation results; its analysis remains an open problem.

1   Introduction

Population protocols [1] model distributed systems in which individual agents are extremely limited, in fact finite-state, and complex behavior of the system as a whole emerges from the rules governing pairwise interaction of the agents. Such models have been defined and used in other fields, for example, statistics, epidemiology, physics and chemistry; understanding their behavior is a fundamental scientific problem. The new perspective we bring as computer scientists is to ask what computational behaviors these systems can exhibit. In addition to fundamental scientific knowledge, answers may provide novel designs for distributed computational systems at many scales.

Chemists have defined a standard model of small molecules in a well-mixed solution, in which the molecules are agents, the state of an agent represents the chemical species of the molecule, and interaction rules specify the probable products of a collision between two molecules; the sequence of collisions is determined by uniform

* Supported in part by NSF grant CNS-0435201.
** Supported in part by a Gordon Y. S. Wu Fellowship and a National Defense Science and Engineering Graduate Fellowship.

A. Pelc (Ed.): DISC 2007, LNCS 4731, pp. 20–32, 2007.

random draws of a pair of agents to interact [4, 5]. In [1] it is shown that this model in principle permits the design of a "computer in a beaker," that is, we can design interaction rules that allow a population of n molecules to simulate the behavior of a register machine with a constant number of registers holding numbers of magnitude $O(n)$ for $poly(n)$ steps with error probability $1/poly(n)$ in parallel time that is a factor of $poly(n)$ larger than the number of simulated instructions. In [2] we have shown that a careful analysis of the properties of epidemics permits us to design a much more efficient simulation, in which the per-step slowdown factor is $O(\log^4 n)$ parallel time.

The register machine of [2] has several shortcomings: it requires an initial configuration with a designated leader, it does not tolerate faults, and $O(\log^4 n)$ is still fairly slow. One goal of this paper is to develop more tools for the design of fast robust population protocols, with improvement of the register machine as a critical testbed. The main tool we develop is our 3-state protocol for approximate majority; this is a protocol that rapidly takes a configuration of x's, y's and b's to a configuration that is all x's or all y's. The final value represents the majority value (among x's and y's) in the initial configuration, provided it exceeds the minority value by a sufficient margin, namely $\omega(\sqrt{n \log n})$. Moreover, we show that is robust to $o(\sqrt{n})$ Byzantine agents, the first population protocol that provably tolerates any Byzantine agents. With a sufficiently redundant representation of register values, this protocol gives a fast comparison operation, which, when combined with other techniques, reduces the slowdown factor of the simulation to $O(\log^2 n)$ parallel time. Though the approximate majority protocol has only 3 states, its analysis is nontrivial; we expect that the protocol and its analysis will find other applications in the design of fast robust population protocols.

The register machine of [2] has at its heart the construction of a phase clock that causes the agents to move together rapidly through a fixed cycle of phases; together meaning that no two agents are more than a very few phases apart, and rapidly meaning the parallel time to complete a cycle is $O(\log n)$. We would like to avoid the need for a designated leader or leaders in the initial configuration to synchronize the phase clock, and we would like the phase clock to be robust. In Section 8 we describe an apparently robust consensus variant of the phase clock, and a protocol to start it from a uniform initial configuration. We give simulation results suggesting that it performs well. However, the problem of analyzing it formally remains open; more tools are necessary.

2   Model

A **population protocol** consists of a finite set of states Q, a finite set of input symbols $X \subseteq Q$, a finite set of output symbols Y, an output function $\gamma : Q \to Y$, and a **joint transition function** $\delta : Q \times Q \to Q \times Q$. A population protocol is executed by a fixed finite **population** of agents with states in Q. For convenience, we assume that each agent has an identity $v \in V$, but agents do not know their own identities or others'.

Initially, each agent is assigned a state according to an **input** $x : V \to X$ that maps agent identities to input symbols. In the general population protocol model, there is an **interaction graph**, a directed graph $G = (V, A)$ without self-loops, whose arcs indicate the possible agent interactions that may take place. (G is directed because we assume that interacting agents are able to break symmetry.) In this paper, G will always be a complete graph.

During each execution step, an arc (v, w) is chosen uniformly at random from A. The "source" agent v is the **initiator**, and the "sink" agent w is the **responder**. These agents update their states jointly according to δ: if v is in state q_v and w is in state q_w, the state of v becomes $\delta_1(q_v, q_w)$, the state of w becomes $\delta_2(q_v, q_w)$, where δ_i gives the ith coordinate of the output of δ. The states of all other agents are unchanged. For any given V, a population protocol **computes** a (possibly partial) function $f : X^V \to Y$ in ℓ steps with error probability ϵ if for all $x \in f^{-1}(Y)$, the configuration $c : V \to Q$ after ℓ steps satisfies the following properties with probability $1 - \epsilon$.

- All agents agree on the correct output: for all $v \in V$, $f(x) = \gamma(c(v))$.
- This remains true with probability 1 in the future.

We are interested in the guarantees one can make about a fixed protocol over a family of functions f defined for all finite populations.

Although we have described the population protocol model in a sequential light, in which each step is a single pairwise interaction, interactions between pairs involving different agents are independent and may be thought of as occurring in parallel. In measuring the speed of population protocols, then, we define 1 unit of **parallel time** to be $|V|$ steps. The rationale is that in expectation, each agent initiates 1 interaction per parallel time unit; this corresponds to the chemists' idealized assumption of a well-mixed solution.

2.1 Byzantine Agents

We extend the basic randomized population protocol model described above to allow Byzantine behavior from some of the agents. In addition to the n normal agents we allow a population to include z Byzantine agents. For each interaction, an ordered pair of agents is selected uniformly at random from the population of normal and Byzantine agents. A Byzantine agent may simulate any normal agent state in an interaction, and its choice of state may depend on both the global configuration and the identity of the specific agent it encounters. The state of Byzantine agents is not meaningful and so is not included in the description of a configuration. We first describe our protocol and analyze its behavior without Byzantine agents.

3 A 3-State Approximate Majority Protocol

We analyze the behavior of the following population protocol with states $Q = \{b, x, y\}$. The state b is the **blank** state. Row labels give the initiator's state and column labels the responder's state.

$$
\begin{array}{cccc}
 & x & b & y \\
x & (x,x) & (x,x) & (x,b) \\
b & (b,x) & (b,b) & (b,y) \\
y & (y,b) & (y,y) & (y,y)
\end{array}
$$

Note that this protocol is **one-way**: every interaction changes at most the responder's state; thus it can be implemented with one-way communication. Only the interactions

xb, yb, xy, and yx change the responder's state; we may think of these as the only interactions that consume energy. The **blank configuration** of all b's is stable, but cannot be reached from any non-blank configuration because no interaction can eliminate the last x or y. The configurations of all x's and all y's are stable, and every non-blank configuration can reach at least one of them.

An intuitive description of the process is that agents in state b are undecided, while initiators in states x and y are attempting to convert responders that they meet to adopt their respective states. Such an initiator immediately converts an undecided responder, but only succeeds in reducing an opposing responder to undecided status. The process may also be thought of as two competing epidemics, x's and y's, with the ability to reverse each other's progress.

In Sections 4 and 5, we show that with high probability this protocol (a) converges from any non-blank configuration to a stable configuration in $O(n \log n)$ interactions; and (b) correctly computes the initial majority x or y value provided $\omega(\sqrt{n \log n})$ more agents carry this value in the starting configuration than carry the opposing value. In Section 6, we show that it can tolerate $o(\sqrt{n})$ Byzantine agents; the formal definition of this property is given there.

4 Convergence

We show that, from any non-blank initial configuration, the 3-state approximate majority protocol converges to either all x tokens or all y tokens within $O(n \log n)$ interactions with high probability. We divide the space of non-blank configurations into four regions: three corners, where most tokens are b, x, or y, and a central region where the tokens are more evenly balanced. We show that the number of interactions in each region is bounded by $O(n \log n)$ w.h.p., by constructing a family of supermartingales of the form $M = e^{aS/n} f(x, y)$ where $a > 0$ is a constant, S counts the number of interactions of a particular type and f is a potential function defined across the entire space of configurations. (We overload x, y and b to denote the number of each token in a configuration.)

Specifically, we let τ_* be the stopping time at which the protocol converges, and let $\tau = \min(\tau_*, kn \log n)$ for some fixed k. Assuming f does not vary too much over the space of configurations, we can use the supermartingale property $E[M_\tau] \leq M_0$ to show that $e^{aS_\tau/n}$ is small, and then use Markov's inequality to get the bound on S_τ. Summing the bounds for each region then gives the total bound on the number of interactions. Though it would seem that truncating at time $kn \log n$ assumes what we are trying to prove, in fact we show that with high probability the total number of interactions is much less than $kn \log n$, implying that we do in fact converge by the given time bound.

The resulting proof requires a careful selection of f. To keep the argument at least locally simple, we construct separate potential functions to bound different classes of operations, based on the type of interaction that occurs and which region of the configuration space it occurs in. The reason for this classification is that the behavior of the protocol is qualitatively different in different regions of the configuration space. When most tokens are blank, the protocol acts like an epidemic, with non-blank tokens rapidly infecting blank tokens. When most tokens carry the same non-blank value, the protocol acts like coupon collector, with the limit on convergence being the time for the few remaining minority tokens to be converted to the majority value. In the central region, where no token type predominates, the protocol acts like a random walk with increasing bias away from the center. Unfortunately, in none of these configurations does the protocol act *enough* like the analogous well-known stochastic processes to permit a direct reduction to previous results, and the behavior in border areas blends smoothly between one form and another. The supermartingale/potential function approach allows separate arguments designed for each region to be blended smoothly together. Unfortunately, this still requires considerable calculation to verify that each potential function does what it is supposed to. In this extended abstract, the detailed calculations are omitted for reasons of space.

The reader may be surprised to find that such a simple protocol requires such a lengthy proof. Despite substantial efforts, we were unable to apply more powerful tools to this problem. Part of the reason is that we are trying to obtain exact asymptotic bounds on a system much of whose interesting behavior occurs when particular tokens are very rare or when the behavior of the protocol is highly random (e.g., with evenly balanced numbers of x and y tokens); this (together with the fact that the corresponding systems of differential equations do not have closed-form solutions) appears to rule out arguments based on classical techniques involving reduction to a continuous process in the limit (e.g., [6,7]). Similarly, approaches based on direct computation of hitting times or eigenvalues of the resulting Markov chain would appear to require substantially more work than a direct potential function argument.

It is possible that such difficulties are an inherent property of randomized population protocols. The ability to construct register machines using such protocols [1,2] suggests that analysis of an arbitrary protocol for arbitrarily large populations quickly enters the realm of undecidability. But we cannot rule out the possibility that a more sophisticated approach might give an easier proof of the convergence rate for the particular protocols we are interested in.

Our results are stated using explicit constant factors. The reader should be warned that in many cases these are gross overestimates, and that from simulation we observe that the expected number of interactions to convergence seems to be less than $4n \log n$ from two challenging initial configurations (see Figure 1.) The first of these, an initial population evenly divided between x and y with no blank tokens, can be shown numerically for reasonably small n to be the configuration that maximizes expected convergence time.

The full convergence bound is stated below.

Theorem 1. *Let τ_* be the time at which $x = n$ or $y = n$ first holds. Then for any fixed $c > 0$ and sufficiently large n,*

$$\Pr\left[\tau_* \geq 6754n \log n + 6759cn \log n\right] \leq 5n^{-c}.$$

Proof. We give here a brief sketch only. First, we show that the potential function $f = \frac{1}{(x-y)^2+2n}$ is reduced by $-\Theta(1/n)$ of its previous value on average conditioned on an xb or a yb interaction, and that it rises by a smaller relative amount conditioned on an xy or a yx interaction. It follows that $f \cdot e^{O(S-\alpha T)/n}$ is a supermartingale, where S

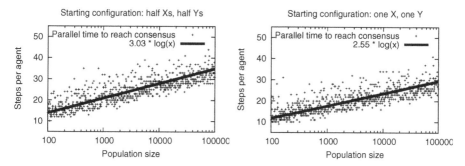

Fig. 1. Simulation results: parallel time of approximate majority from two initial conditions

counts xy and yx interactions, T counts xb and yb interactions, and $\alpha < 1$. The factor of $O(n)$ drop in f between the maximum initial $f = 1/(2n)$ and final $f = 1/(n^2 + 2n)$ allows only a similar expected rise in $e^{(S - \alpha T)/n}$ and thus (with high probability) only an $O(n \log n)$ rise in $S - \alpha T$. Since all but at most $n - 1$ initial blank tokens destroyed in T must have previously been created in S, $T \le S + n$, giving an $O(n \log n)$ bound on, in turn: (a) S alone; (b) $S + T$; (c) all interactions in the central region (where xy, yx, xb, or yb interactions are likely). Separate potential functions are used to bound the remaining interactions in the corners.   □

5   Correctness of Approximate Majority

Not only does the 3-state protocol converge quickly, but it also converges to the dominant non-blank value in its input if there is a large enough initial majority.

Theorem 2. *With high probability, the 3-state approximate majority protocol converges to the initial majority value if the difference between the initial majority and initial minority populations is $\omega(\sqrt{n \log n})$.*

Proof. Without loss of generality, assume that the initial majority value is x. We consider a coupled process (u_t, u'_t) where $u_t = (x_t - y_t)$ and u'_t is the sum of a series of fair ± 1 coin flips. Initially $u'_0 = u_0$. Later values of u'_t are specified by giving a joint distribution on $(\Delta u, \Delta u')$. We do so as follows. Let p be the probability that $\Delta u = 1$ and q the probability that $\Delta u = -1$. Then let

$$(\Delta u, \Delta u') = \begin{cases} (0, 0) & \text{with probability } 1 - p - q, \\ (1, 1) & \text{with probability } \frac{1}{2}(p + q), \\ (1, -1) & \text{with probability } p - \frac{1}{2}(p + q), \\ (-1, -1) & \text{with probability } q. \end{cases}$$

The probability in the third case is non-negative if $p/(p + q) = \Pr[\Delta u = 1 | \Delta u \ne 0] \ge \frac{1}{2}$. This holds as long as $u \ge 0$; should u ever drop to zero, we end the process.

Observe that unless this event happens, we have $u_t \ge u'_t$. We can also verify by summing the cases that Δu rises with probability exactly p and drops with probability exactly q; and that $\Delta u'$ rises or drops with equal probability $\frac{1}{2}(p + q)$. So we have $E[\Delta u'] = 0$ and that $|\Delta u'| \leq 1$, the preconditions for Azuma's inequality.

Theorem 1 shows that the process converges before $O(n \log n)$ interactions with high probability. Suppose the process converges at some time $\tau = O(n \log n)$. Then by Azuma's inequality we have that $|u'_\tau - u'_0| = O(\sqrt{n \log n})$ throughout this interval with high probability. So if $u'_0 = u_0 = \omega(\sqrt{n \log n})$, it follows that $u_0 \geq u'_0 \geq 0$ throughout the execution, and in particular that the process does not terminate before convergence and that u is non-negative at convergence. But this excludes the $y = n$ case, so the process converges to the initial majority value.   □

6 Tolerating Byzantine Agents

In this section, we show that the 3-state approximate majority protocol can tolerate up to $o(\sqrt{n})$ Byzantine agents, computing the correct majority value in $O(n \log n)$ time with high probability despite their interference. However, to do so we must both assume a somewhat larger initial majority, and slightly relax the criterion for convergence.

The issue with convergence is that Byzantine agents can always pull the normal agents out of a converged configuration. For example, if all normal agents are in the x state, any encounter with a Byzantine initiator can shift the normal agent to a b state, and a second encounter can shift it to a y state, even though there are no normal y agents in the population. So we must accept a small number of normal agents that do not have the correct value.

But in fact the situation is worse: if we run long enough, there exists a trajectory with nonzero probability that takes us to the blank configuration, which is stable. So we must also accept a small probability that we reach the blank configuration quickly, and the assurance that we reach it with probability 1 after a very long time. However, we can show that with high probability neither outcome occurs within a polynomial number of steps.

Our technique is to adjust the potential functions used by the non-Byzantine process to account for Byzantine transitions. We then use these adjusted potential functions to show that (a) strong pressure exists to keep the process out of the high-b corner and in the high-x and high-y corners, and (b) the number of interactions (including Byzantine interactions) to reach the x or y corner is still small.

6.1 Biased-Walk Barriers

Let us begin by showing that it is difficult even for Byzantine agents to force the protocol into a configuration with a low value of $v_t = x_t + y_t$.

Observe that if the Byzantine agents attempt to minimize v, v nonetheless increases at each interaction with likelihood proportional to vb and decreases with likelihood proportional to $2xy + zv$. So the probability of an increase conditioned on any change in v is $vb/(vb + 2xy + zv) \geq vb/(vb + v^2/2 + zv) = b/(b + z + v/2) \geq b/n$ provided $z \leq v/2$. For large b and small z this gives a random-walk behavior that is strongly biased upwards.

Suppose $\sqrt{n} \leq v \leq n/8$. Then $b \geq (7/8)n$ and $z = o(\sqrt{n}) \ll v/2$, so $\Pr[\Delta v = 1 | \Delta v \neq 0] \geq 7/8$. We wish to bound the probability starting from some initial v_0

in this range that v reaches $\sqrt{n}$ before it reaches $n/8$. Though the probability that v rises or falls changes over the interval, the position of v can be lower-bounded by the position of a coupled variable v' that moves according to a biased random walk with fixed probability $p = 7/8$ of increasing by 1 and $q = 1/8$ of decreasing by 1. From the standard analysis of the gambler's ruin problem,[1] we have that $(q/p)^{v'_t}$ is a martingale, and thus that the quantity

$$\Pr[v' \text{ reaches } \sqrt{n} \text{ before } n/8](q/p)^{\sqrt{n}} + \Pr[v' \text{ reaches } n/8 \text{ before } \sqrt{n}](q/p)^{n/8}$$

is equal to $(q/p)^{v_0}$. Because $(q/p)^{n/8} = (1/7)^{n/8}$ is exponentially small, it makes sense to ignore the second addend, leaving

$$\Pr[v' \text{ reaches } \sqrt{n} \text{ before } n/8](q/p)^{\sqrt{n}} < (q/p)^{v_0}$$

or

$$\Pr[v' \text{ reaches } \sqrt{n} \text{ before } n/8] < (q/p)^{v_0 - \sqrt{n}}.$$

It follows that if $v_0 \geq \sqrt{n} + c \log_7 n$, then the probability that v drops to $\sqrt{n}$ before reaching $n/8$ is bounded by n^{-c}. Once v reaches $n/8$, further drops to $\sqrt{n}$ become exponentially improbable even conditioned on starting at $v = n/8 - 1$. We thus have:

Lemma 1. *Fix $c > 0$. Let $z = o(\sqrt{n})$ and let $v_0 \geq \sqrt{n} + c \log_7 n$. Then for sufficiently large n, the probability that $v_t \leq \sqrt{n}$ for any $t < e^{n/8} n^{-c}$ is less than $2n^{-c}$.*

Proof. The probability that v reaches $\sqrt{n}$ before reaching $n/8$ for the first time is at most n^{-c}. For each subsequent drop to $n/8 - 1$, there is a probability of at most $(1/7)^{n/8-1-\sqrt{n}} \leq \exp(-n/8)$ that v reaches $\sqrt{n}$ before returning to $n/8$. Since each such excursion below $n/8$ involves at least one interaction, $e^{n/8} n^{-c}$ interactions gives at most an expected n^{-c} drops to $\sqrt{n}$ for a total probability of reaching $v = \sqrt{n}$ bounded by $2n^{-c}$. □

We can apply a similar analysis to the x and y corners, but here the protocol drifts toward the all-x or all-y configuration instead of away from it. Here we track $3y + b$ for the x corner and $3x + b$ for the y corner. Because these functions can change by more than just ± 1, the simple random walk analysis becomes more difficult. Instead, we proceed by showing that $\exp(3y+b)$ is a supermartingale, and bound the probability of moving from $2\sqrt{n}$ to $3\sqrt{n}$ by $\exp(-\sqrt{n})$, the inverse of the change in $\exp 3y + b$.

Formally, we have:

Lemma 2. *Fix $c > 0$. Let $z = o(\sqrt{n})$ and let $3y_0 + b_0 \leq 2\sqrt{n}$. Then for sufficiently large n, the probability that $3y_t + b_t \geq 3\sqrt{n}$ for any $t < e^{\sqrt{n}-1} n^{-c}$ is less than n^{-c}.*

Proof. (Omitted for reasons of space.) □

---

[1] See, for example, [3, §XIV.2].

6.2   Convergence Time with Byzantine Agents

The convergence time is given in the following theorem.

Theorem 3. *Let τ be the time at which $x \geq n - \sqrt{n}$, $y \geq n - \sqrt{n}$, or $v \leq \sqrt{n}$ first holds. Let v_0 be the initial number of x's and y's. Then for any fixed $c > 0$ and sufficiently large n, if $v_0 \geq \sqrt{n} + c \log_7 n$, then*

$$\Pr\left[\tau \geq 6754n \log n + 6759cn \log n \text{ or } v_\tau \leq \sqrt{n}\right] = n^{-c+o(1)}.$$

Proof. (Proof omitted for reasons of space.)   □

Note that once we are in the x or y corner, Lemma 2 tells us that we remain there with high probability for exponential time. So we have a complete characterization of the convergence behavior of the 3-state majority protocol with $o(\sqrt{n})$ Byzantine agents. It is also not hard to see that the proof of Theorem 2 also continues to hold for $z = o(\sqrt{n})$, provided we increase the size of the initial majority to $\omega(\sqrt{n} \log n)$ to compensate for the offset of $o(\sqrt{n} \log n)$ generated by Byzantine interactions.

7   Speeding Up the Register Machine Construction

In this section we show how to use the 3-state approximate majority protocol and other techniques to speed up the register machine construction in [2] so that it has per-step parallel time overhead of $O(\log^2 n)$ instead of $O(\log^4 n)$. The original construction is based on a single agent representing a finite-state controller operating via commands spread by epidemics on register values represented in unary by tokens scattered across the population. A major bottleneck in [2] is the difficulty of carrying out exact comparisons (performed in $O(\log^2 n)$ time using $O(\log n)$ rounds that alternate cancellation with amplification) and of performing subtractions (done in $O(\log^3 n)$ using addition, comparison, and binary search). Our approximate majority protocol gives a simpler and faster implementation of comparison, provided we pad out the register values to avoid near-ties. A further adjustment to the representation gives cheap subtraction.

Because space does not permit us to repeat the description of the original construction here, we refer the reader to [2] for details.

We begin by replacing the original $O(\log^2 n)$ parallel time comparison operation by our new $O(\log n)$ parallel time approximate majority protocol. To ensure that a comparison is correct with high probability, we need to ensure that the register values being compared differ by $\omega(\sqrt{n \log n})$. We guarantee this by having registers hold values that are multiples of $n^{2/3}$; three such registers are sufficient to represent $n = (n^{1/3})^3$ different values, thinking of them as the high, middle and low order **wide-digits** of a number in base $n^{1/3}$. Thus, to compare two wide digits, say A and B, we do an approximate majority comparison of $A + (1/2)n^{2/3}$ with B; if the result is that A is in the majority, then we conclude that $B \leq A$, otherwise that $A < B$. To compare two registers composed of $O(1)$ wide-digits it suffices to proceed digit by digit.

The subtraction operation of [2] requires $O(\log n)$ rounds of binary search where the $O(\log^2 n)$ parallel time comparison operation dominates the cost of each round. Though we could replace these comparisons with our faster comparison operation and reduce the cost of subtraction to $O(\log^2 n)$, we can obtain a still better reduction to $O(\log n)$ parallel time by use the logician's construction of the integers from the natural numbers: the value A in a register is represented by the difference $A_+ - A_-$ of values in two different registers. To compute $C \leftarrow A + B$, we compute $C_+ \leftarrow A_+ + B_+$ and $C_- \leftarrow A_- + B_-$. To compute $C \leftarrow A - B$, we compute $C_+ \leftarrow A_+ + B_-$ and $C_- \leftarrow A_- + B_+$. These operations both take parallel time $O(\log n)$, because addition is already $O(\log n)$ in the previous construction. An additional clock cycle of cancellation keeps the $+$ and $-$ components from overflowing.

For registers with this balanced representation, we must revisit comparison. To compare A with B, we compare $(A_+ + B_-)$ with $(A_- + B_+)$. Since these differ by a multiple of $n^{2/3}$, our previous comparison method works. The result is that subtraction can be done with $O(1)$ additions and comparisons, which gives parallel time of $O(\log n)$.

The most expensive operation in [2] is division by a constant, which is based on $O(\log n)$ rounds of binary search in which subtraction dominates. The improved cost of subtraction immediately reduces the parallel time for division to $O(\log^2 n)$ without any change to the division algorithm.

The remaining issue is how to convert the input values in the registers, which are represented in simple unary, into the wide-digits representation. We use the previous machine operations to create a reference value of magnitude $\Theta(n^{2/3})$ in a register and the usual base-conversion algorithms to extract the wide digits of each input register value and store them multiplied by the reference value; this initialization takes polylogarithmic parallel time [2], after which the per-step overhead of simulating the register machine is $O(\log^2 n)$. Thus, for simulating the register machine specified in [2], we have the following improvement.

Theorem 4. *A probabilistic population of n agents with a designated leader can simulate the steps of the virtual register machine defined in [2], such that the probability that any single step in the simulation fails or takes more than $O(n \log^2 n)$ interactions can be made $O(n^{-c})$ for any fixed c.*

8   A More Robust Phase Clock?

The fault tolerance of the 3-state approximate majority protocol and the inherent redundancy of the wide-digit representation of register values is encouraging: perhaps there is a fast and provably robust version of the register machine construction. However, there is a second component of our register machine that must be made more robust. This is the **phase clock**, a subprotocol used to count off intervals of $\Theta(\log n)$ parallel time so that the leader can estimate when an epidemic has finished propagating.

The phase clock of [2] is a protocol with m states and one designated leader. The state of an agent represents the phase that it is in. A responder in phase i adopts the phase of any initiator in phases $i + 1 \bmod m$ through $i + m/2 \bmod m$, but ignores initiators in other phases. New phases are triggered by the leader agent. When the leader responds to an initiator in its own phase, that leader moves to the next phase. Counting the number of interactions between the event that the leader enters phase 0 until the event that the leader next enters phase 0 as a **round**, it is shown that with high probability each of a polynomial number of rounds takes parallel time $\Theta(\log n)$ with inverse polynomial probability of error. Note that although this protocol also works when given $\Theta(n^{1-\epsilon})$ designated leaders, it requires an initial configuration with the appropriate number of designated leaders, and is not robust to errors.

We now describe (a) a method for quickly starting the phase clock from a uniform initial state, and (b) a consensus variant of the phase clock that appears to be more robust. Our present techniques are not sufficient to analyze the resulting algorithm, so we must make do with simulation results.

Simulation results suggest that the following protocol can start up a phase clock with high probability in $\Theta(\log n)$ parallel time. This protocol is one-way, so for brevity we identify δ with δ_2.

This protocol is the semidirect product of several components. The first component allows us to make approximate coin tosses. The states are $Q_{coin} = \{0,1\}$, with initial value $x_{coin} = 0$, and the transition function is $\delta_{coin}(q,q') = 1 - \pi_{coin}(q)$. Starting from any configuration, this protocol rapidly converges towards an equal proportion of agents in each state. The second component counts the number of consecutive coin values equal to 1 the agent has seen immediately prior, up to a maximum of $\ell > 0$. The states are $Q_{count} = \{0, 1, \ldots, \ell\}$, $x_{count} = 0$, and the transition function $\delta_{count}(q,q') = \pi_{coin}(q)(\min\{\pi_{count}(q') + 1, \ell\})$.

The third component approximates an exponential decay process. There is a parameter $k_1 \leq \ell$. The states are $Q_{decay1} = \{0,1\}$, $x_{decay1} = 1$, and the update function is $\delta_{decay1}(q,q') = [\pi_{count}(q) < k_1]\pi_{decay1}(q')$. The idea is that for all $0 < \alpha < 1$ and $0 < c$, we can find k_1 such that with high probability, there is a period of $cn \log n$ steps where the number of agents with decay1 value of 1 is between 1 and n^α. In this period, using agents with decay1 value of 1 as temporary leaders, we can run a *disposable* phase clock that functions correctly only for a constant number of phases before all the values of decay1 become 0. This phase clock is used to choose a stable leader population of size $\Theta(n^{1-\epsilon})$, which in turn supports a second copy of the phase clock that runs for polynomially many steps.

Our consensus variant of the phase clock from [2] works as follows. In addition to the phases $0, 1, \ldots, \phi-1$, we have a blank "phase". Thus $Q_{phase1} = \{b, 0, 1, \ldots, \phi-1\}$. $x_{phase1} = 0$. If x is a nonblank phase, then let $succ(x) = (x+1) \bmod \phi$ be the successor phase of x. We have

$$\delta_{phase1}(q,q') = \begin{cases} p' & \text{if } p = b \\ p & \text{if } p' = b \\ p' & \text{if } p' = p \neq b \text{ and } \pi_{decay1}(q) = 0 \\ succ(p') & \text{if } p' = p \neq b \text{ and } \pi_{decay1}(q) = 1 \\ p' & \text{if } p, p' \neq b \text{ and } p' = succ(p) \\ p & \text{if } p, p' \neq b \text{ and } succ(p') = p \\ b & \text{otherwise,} \end{cases}$$

where $p = \pi_{phase1}(q)$ and $p' = \pi_{phase1}(q')$. If the phase of the initiator is blank or one behind the responder's, the responder's phase is unchanged. If the phase of the responder is blank, it copies the phase of the initiator. If the phases are non-blank and equal, the responder increments its phase if and only if the initiator has decay value 1 (temporary leader status.) If the initiator's phase is one more than the responder's, the responder increments its phase. In all other cases, the responder sets its phase to blank. In summary, we are following a multiple-valued generalization of the 3-state majority algorithm *except* when the phases are nonblank and within distance 1 of one another. In this case, we revert to behavior like that of the original phase clock.

Once the disposable phase clock is running, it is used to select the real phase clock's leaders. This is accomplished by having another exponential decay process that is re-set by the disposable phase clock each complete cycle. Thus we need a way to detect approximately the onset of each cycle. Our criterion is for each agent to keep a local "maximum" of the phases it has been in, and perform the reset when this maximum wraps around. Formally, $Q_{max} = \{0, 1, \ldots, \phi - 1\}$, $x_{max} = 0$, and

$$\delta_{max}(q, q') = \begin{cases} p' & \text{if } p' \neq b \text{ and } (p' - \pi_{max}(q')) \bmod \phi \leq \phi/2 \\ \pi_{max}(q') & \text{otherwise,} \end{cases}$$

where $p' = \delta_{phase1}(q, q')$. Since the last cycle may be partial, we also need a one-value history for the decay process. Now $Q_{decay2} = \{0, 1\} \times \{0, 1\}$, $x_{decay2} = (1, 1)$, and

$$\delta_{decay2}(q, q') = \begin{cases} (1, y) & \text{if } \delta_{max}(q, q') < \pi_{max}(q') \\ ([\pi_{count}(q) < k_2]y, y') & \text{otherwise,} \end{cases}$$

where $(y, y') = \delta_{decay2}(q')$. The final set of leaders are those agents with $y' = 1$ when the disposable phase clock stops running. A second copy of the consensus phase clock, running from the initial configuration using $y' = 1$ to designate leaders, rapidly converges in simulation to correct robust phase clock behavior when the number of leaders becomes appropriate.

We implemented the disposable phase clock leader election protocol and tried it once on each value of $\lfloor 1.01^n \rfloor$ between 100 and 100000 for integers n, with every agent in the same initial state. There are three parameters to tune: ϕ, k_1, and k_2. The protocol is not very sensitive to the settings of these parameters, but the setting $\phi = 9$, $k_1 = 5$, and $k_2 = 4$ worked better than many others.

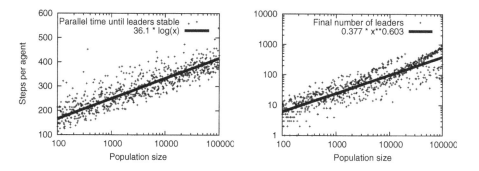

Fig. 2. Simulation results: parallel time of leader election and final number of leaders

The results are depicted in Figure 2. As can be seen, it seems that the protocol generally leaves $\Theta(n^{1-\epsilon})$ leaders and completely converges in $O(\log n)$ time.

Acknowledgments

The second author would like to thank Joanna Ellman-Aspnes for suggestions that helped overcome an obstacle in the proof of the main lemma bounding convergence. The authors would like to thank the DISC 2007 reviewers for their helpful comments.

References

1. Angluin, D., Aspnes, J., Diamadi, Z., Fischer, M.J., Peralta, R.: Computation in networks of passively mobile finite-state sensors. Distributed Computing, 235–253 (2006)
2. Angluin, D., Aspnes, J., Eisenstat, D.: Fast computation by population protocols with a leader. In: Dolev, S. (ed.) DISC 2006. LNCS, vol. 4167, pp. 61–75. Springer, Heidelberg (2006)
3. Feller, W.: An Introduction to Probability and its Applications, 3rd edn., vol. 1. John Wiley and Sons, Chichester (1958)
4. Gillespie, D.T.: Exact stochastic simulation of coupled chemical reactions. Journal of Physical Chemistry 81(25), 2340–2361 (1977)
5. Gillespie, D.T.: A rigorous derivation of the chemical master equation. Physica A 188, 404–425 (1992)
6. Kurtz, T.G.: Approximation of Population Processes. Number 36 in CBMS-NSF Regional Conference Series in Applied Mathematics. Society for Industrial and Applied Mathematics, Philadelphia (1981)
7. Wormald, N.C.: Differential equations for random processes and random graphs. Annals of Applied Probability 5(4), 1217–1235 (1995)

A Denial-of-Service Resistant DHT

Baruch Awerbuch[1,*] and Christian Scheideler[2]

[1] Dept. of Computer Science, Johns Hopkins University, Baltimore, MD 21218, USA
baruch@cs.jhu.edu
[2] Institut für Informatik, Technische Universität München, 85748 Garching, Germany
scheideler@in.tum.de

Abstract. We consider the problem of designing scalable and robust information systems based on multiple servers that can survive even massive denial-of-service (DoS) attacks. More precisely, we are focusing on designing a scalable distributed hash table (DHT) that is robust against so-called past insider attacks. In a past insider attack, an adversary knows *everything* about the system up to some time point t_0 not known to the system. After t_0, the adversary can attack the system with a massive DoS attack in which it can block a constant fraction of the servers of its choice. Yet, the system should be able to survive such an attack in a sense that for *any* set of lookup requests, one per non-blocked (i.e., non-DoS attacked) server, every lookup request to a data item that was last updated *after* t_0 can be served by the system, and processing all the requests just needs polylogarithmic time and work at every server. We show that such a system can be designed.

1 Introduction

On Feb 6 of this year, hackers launched a distributed denial-of-service (DoS) attack on the root servers of the Domain Name System (DNS) [10]. DoS attacks can overwhelm servers with hacker-generated traffic and make them unavailable for legitimate communications. While the attacks significantly slowed the operations of some of the servers, they caused no problems for the overall DNS system because the system shifts work to other root servers if it has trouble with the first ones it tries to reach. This is possible because information is replicated among all root servers, and the root servers together have sufficient bandwidth to handle even major DoS attacks.

In this paper, we consider the problem of designing distributed information systems that are highly resilient against DoS attacks even if every piece of information is not replicated everywhere but only among a small subset of the servers. For distributed information systems that are connected to the Internet, like the DNS system, the servers may be known and therefore open to DoS attacks. There are various forms of DoS attacks. Application-layer DoS attacks, that try

---

* Supported by NSF CCF 0515080, ANIR-0240551, CT-0716676, CCR-0311795, and CNS-0617883.

A. Pelc (Ed.): DISC 2007, LNCS 4731, pp. 33–47, 2007.

to abuse the protocols of the system in order to prevent it from functioning correctly, or network-layer DoS attacks that just aim at overloading servers with junk or faked messages in order to prevent them from processing legal ones. We are interested in designing a scalable information system (i.e., a system in which the data and requests are handled in a scalable way) that can withstand even massive application-layer and network-layer DoS attacks (i.e., the attacker is powerful enough to generate requests or junk that can affect a constant fraction of the servers). Certainly, if the attacker has *complete* knowledge of the information system, then scalability and robustness against massive DoS attacks cannot be achieved at the same time. But what if the attacker only has complete knowledge up to some time step t_0 (that may not be known to the system)? Would it at least be possible to protect everything that was inserted into the system or updated *after* time step t_0? To answer this question, let us first formally define the attack model we will be focusing on in this paper.

1.1 The Past Insider Attack Model

The past insider attack model is motivated by the fact that a large percentage of the security breaches in corporate systems have internal reasons, many of them being caused by human error or negligence or insider attacks. In these cases, the entire system may be temporarily exposed, with potentially severe consequences for its functionality if this exposure is abused.

In the past insider attack model, we assume that an attacker has complete knowledge of the system up to some time step t_0 that is not known to the system. It can use this knowledge to attack the system at any time point after t_0. Given n servers, we allow the attacker to generate any collection of lookup requests it likes, one per non-blocked server, including lookup requests to blocked or non-existing data, and to block any set of ϵn servers for some sufficiently small constant $0 < \epsilon < 1$. The goal is to design a storage strategy for the data and a lookup protocol so that the following conditions are met:

For every data item d, the total space for storing d in the system is by at most a polylogarithmic factor larger than the size of d, and for any set of lookup requests with at most one request per non-blocked server, the following holds:

- *Scalability:* Every server in the system spends at most a polylogarithmic amount of work and time on the requests.
- *Robustness:* Every lookup request to a data item inserted after t_0 (or a non-existing data item) is served correctly.
- *Correctness:* Every lookup request to a data item is served correctly whenever the system is not under a DoS attack.

By "served correctly" we mean that the latest version of the data item is returned to the server requesting it. (We assume that there is a unique way of identifying the latest version such as the version number or a time stamp.)

Note that our model is different from proactive security models in which the adversary can never learn too much about the system within a certain time frame. Approaches for this model aim at protecting *everything* in the system, but this comes at a high price because this means that all the information in the system has to be continuously refreshed, which may not be feasible in practice. We can show that one can protect nearly everything without continuous refreshing, and most importantly, everything that was updated after the security breach is over.

1.2   Towards Robustness Against Past Insider Attacks

Let us have a quick look at the basic approaches for storing data in a distributed system.

- *An explicit data structure such as a distributed search tree or skip graph:* This approach is scalable but has, due to its structure, major problems with correctness and robustness under DoS-attacks.
- *An implicit data structure like a hash table:* The hash table is structureless and therefore has less problems with correctness. It is also scalable, but it is not robust because the adversary knows exactly where the copies of a data item are located and can therefore block these.
- *The random placement of data copies among the servers:* This is not scalable but certainly robust.

Is there a way of combining these approaches in order to achieve scalability, robustness and correctness at the same time? Our main contribution in this paper is to show that a certain hybrid version of a hash table and random placement can achieve this task. More precisely, we will prove the following result.

Theorem 1. *Given n servers, our storage strategy just needs $O(\log^2 n)$ copies per data item so that our lookup protocol can serve any set of lookup requests, one per non-blocked server, in a scalable, robust and correct way, w.h.p. The robustness holds for any DoS attack in which at most ϵn servers are blocked, where $\epsilon > 0$ is a sufficiently small constant.*

In the proof of the theorem, we assume that the servers are completely interconnected since we are only focusing on reliable servers, so there are no scalability problems w.r.t. connectivity.

Although we consider only problems where all lookup requests are given at the beginning, we note that our lookup protocol can also be applied in a scenario where continuously new requests are generated. Furthermore, the correctness condition can be strengthened in a sense that beyond $O(n + D/n^k)$ data items, where D is the total number of data items in the system and k can be an arbitrary constant, all of the data inserted before t_0 can still be accessed by our lookup protocol under a DoS attack, but it can obviously not be guaranteed that everything is still accessible. Using coding strategies (like Reed-Solomon codes), the storage overhead for the data items can be reduced to $O(\log n)$ in Theorem 1. The constant ϵ that we need in our proofs is $\epsilon < 1/144$, but we did not try to optimize constants in this paper.

The beauty of our approach is that, even though it uses much more sophisticated concepts, it is still based on the well-known consistent hashing principle

[5], i.e., the servers are assigned to points in the $[0, 1)$-interval and a data copy mapped to point $x \in [0, 1)$ is stored at the server that is the closest predecessor of x in $[0, 1)$. Thus, it could in principle be used on top of existing DHTs based on consistent hashing such as Chord in order to turn these into highly DoS-resilient DHTs. However, notice that in the scenarios considered in this paper, we can afford a completely interconnected network though most DHT implementations are based on bounded degree overlay networks, which would create an additional vulnerability.

Finally, we remark that we do not address the problem of handling insert requests in this paper but only how to store data in the system in a scalable way so that it can be retrieved despite massive DoS attacks. Managing insert requests is a tricky issue when application- and network-layer DoS attacks are allowed, and we discuss some of the reasons behind that in Section 2.1. Taking this restriction into account, our strategies would work best for archival systems or systems for information retrieval like Google, CiteSeer or Akamai.

1.3 Related Work

The most prominent approach for a scalable information system is to implement a distributed hash table, or DHT. Well-known examples of DHTs are Chord [22], CAN [18], Pastry [3], and Tapestry [24]. Most of the DHT-based systems are based on concepts proposed in two influential papers: a paper by Plaxton et al. on locality-preserving data management in distributed environments [17] and a paper by Karger et al. on consistent hashing and web caching [5]. However, since in both cases the data management is based on hashing, none of these approaches is robust against past-insider attacks.

Various attacks on the data management layer of DHTs have been considered in the past. Most of the work considers the flash crowd scenario in which many peers want to access the same information at the same time. When using a pure DHT design, this can lead to severe bottlenecks. To remove these bottlenecks, various caching strategies have been proposed. Among them are CoopNet [16], Backslash [19], PROOFS [20] in the systems community and [14] in the theory community. However, being able to handle flash crowds is not sufficient to handle arbitrary collections of lookup and insert requests in a scalable way because much worse than having many requests to the *same* data item is to have many requests to *different* data items at the *same* location. Standard combining or caching strategies do not work here, but work on deterministic simulations of CRCW PRAMs (e.g., [11]) turned out come to the rescue here. These concepts allow the design of insert and lookup protocols that are guaranteed to handle *any* set of requests with at most one request per server that can be chosen by an adversary knowing *everything* about the system [2]. Thus, application-layer DoS attacks can be handled but not network-layer attacks since the protocols in [2] are purely hash-based.

There is a vast amount of literature on network-layer DoS attacks (see, e.g. [4,12] for a taxonomy of these DoS attacks). Several authors have explored the use of DHTs to prevent DoS attacks from outsiders (e.g., [8,6,13]). Secure

Overlay Services (SOS) [8], for example, uses a proxy approach based on the Chord network to protect applications against flooding DoS attacks. WebSOS [21] is an implementation of SOS for web servers that makes use of graphical Turing tests, web proxies and client authentication. Mayday [1] generalizes the SOS architecture and analyzes the implications of choosing different filtering techniques and overlay routing mechanisms. Internet Indirection Infrastructure (i3) [9] also uses the Chord overlay to protect applications from direct DoS attacks. Other DoS limiting overlay network architectures have been explored in, e.g., [15,23]. Most of the approaches above use traffic analysis or indirection approaches to make DoS attacks hard, but none of these would be able to survive the attackers considered in this paper since they essentially rely on the ability to protect servers from direct hits of adversarial traffic.

2   A DoS-Resistant DHT

In this section we describe how to store and retrieve information in a scalable and robust way in a DHT of completely interconnected servers. The DHT is based on the consistent hashing principle in a sense that the servers (also called *nodes* henceforth) are given points in the $[0, 1)$-ring and any data copy that is mapped to a point $x \in [0, 1)$ is stored at the node that is the closest predecessor of x in $[0, 1)$. First, we present our data storage strategy. Afterwards, we present and analyze our lookup protocol. For simplicity, we make the following assumptions:

- The number of nodes in the DHT is fixed to n, and n is a power of 2.
- The nodes are numbered from 0 to $n - 1$, and node i is responsible for the interval $[i/n, (i + 1)/n)$ in $[0, 1)$.

Both assumptions can be relaxed (one can imagine, for example, that the nodes are randomly spread in $[0, 1)$ so that the DHT does not need central coordination), but we use them here since they will keep our proofs simple.

2.1   The Storage Strategy

Like in [2], we use $c = \Theta(\log m)$ hash functions, denoted by $h_1, \ldots, h_c$, that map data names to points in the $[0, 1)$ interval, where m represents the size of the universe of all data names, but this is the only feature the approach in this paper has in common with [2].

First, we introduce some notation. We assume that the points in $[0, 1)$ are given in binary form, i.e., point $x \in [0, 1)$ is given as $(x_1, x_2, \ldots) \in \{0, 1\}^*$ with $x = \sum_{i \geq 1} x_i/2^i$. For any two bit sequences $x, y \in \{0, 1\}^*$, $x \circ y$ is the unique point $z \in [0, 1)$ with $(z_1, z_2, \ldots) = (x_1, \ldots, x_{|x|}, y_1, \ldots, y_{|y|})$. For any point $x \in [0, 1)$ and $\ell \in \mathbb{N}$, we call set $T_\ell(x) = \{z \in [0, 1) \mid z = y \circ x \text{ for some } y \in \{0, 1\}^\ell\}$ the set of all points *at distance* ℓ from x. A *route* to x of length ℓ is any sequence of points $R = (z_\ell, z_{\ell-1}, \ldots, z_0)$ with the property that $z_0 = x$ and for every $i > 0$, $z_{i+1} = b \circ z_i$ for some bit $b \in \{0, 1\}$ (which implies that $z_i \in T_i(x)$ for every i). Let $\mathcal{R}_\ell(x)$ be the set of all possible routes of length ℓ to x. A *random* route to

x is a route R chosen uniformly and independently at random from $\mathcal{R}_\ell(x)$ (i.e., z_ℓ is chosen uniformly and independently at random from $T_\ell(x)$).

When a data item d is inserted or updated in the system, we select a random route $R_i = (z_{i,\log n}, z_{i,\log n-1}, \ldots, z_{i,0}) \in \mathcal{R}_{\log n}(h_i(d))$ for every $i \in \{1, \ldots, c\}$. For each distance $j \in \{0, \ldots, \log n\}$, we store $\gamma \log n$ copies of d, for some constant γ that will be determined later. For each of these copies, we select an $i \in \{1, \ldots, c\}$ uniformly and independently at random and store the copy in point $z_{i,j}$ (resp. the node owning that point according to the consistent hashing scheme). Hence, altogether, we store $O(\log^2 n)$ copies of each data item in the system. It would be sufficient for our lookup protocol if instead of storing $O(\log n)$ copies for each data item for each distance j, we use Reed-Solomon or other codes to store each data item in $O(\log n)$ encoded pieces for each distance. That would reduce the overall storage overhead to $O(\log n)$ in Theorem 1, but for simplicity we will just assume that copies of d are stored.

Notice that as long as the set of DoS-attacked nodes is static, our storage strategy could be transformed into an efficient insert protocol together with techniques in [2] to avoid congestion problems. However, for a dynamically changing set of DoS-attacked nodes this is tricky since some non-DoS-attacked nodes are now missing information that is necessary for our lookup protocol to work correctly. A potential countermeasure here could be to delay the execution of the insert protocol at DoS-attacked nodes until the DoS-attack goes away. This requires extra management overhead and complicates the design of the insert protocol, which is why we left it out here.

For the rest of this paper, we will assume that the binary representations of all points are rounded to $\log n$ bits (i.e., the points are multiples of $1/n$, so there is one point for each node). For any $\ell \in \mathbb{N}$ let $\mathcal{T}_\ell = \{T_\ell(x) \mid x \in [0,1)\}$, where we consider the points in $T_\ell(x)$ to be rounded to $\log n$ bits. That is, $|\mathcal{T}_\ell| = n/2^\ell$ and each set in $\mathcal{T}_\ell$ has a size of 2^ℓ.

2.2 The Lookup Protocol

We assume that we are given any collection of lookup requests, one per non-blocked server. The lookup protocol consists of two stages. The first stage is the contraction stage and the second stage is the expansion stage. During the contraction stage, the lookup requests are forwarded along random routes towards the hash values of the requested data items. Each lookup request encountering too many blocked or congested nodes stops and waits for the expansion stage to be executed. During the expansion stage, lookup requests are woken up in a controlled manner, and node sets of exponentially increasing size are explored in order to search for copies of the requested data items until sufficiently many copies have been found or the protocol decides that the item does not exist in the system. We start with the formal description of the contraction stage.

The contraction stage. Each lookup request for some data item d chooses, for each $i \in \{1, \ldots, c\}$ and $j \in \{1, \ldots, \alpha \log n\}$, a random route $R_{i,j} \in \mathcal{R}_{\log n}(h_i(d))$ of length $\log n$ to $h_i(d)$, where α is a sufficiently large constant. Hence, altogether there are $\alpha c \log n$ random routes. For every i, let $Q_{\ell,i}$ be the set of all nodes in the routes $R_{i,j}$ to $h_i(d)$ that belong to $T_\ell(h_i(d))$, and let $Q'_{\ell,i}$ be the non-blocked nodes in $Q_{\ell,i}$.

Initially, all lookup requests are active, and all $i \in \{1, \ldots, c\}$ are active for all lookup requests. Then the contraction stage proceeds in rounds, executed from $\log n$ down to 0. In round r, every active request for some data item d sends a message to all nodes in its set $Q_{r,i}$ for all active i. Each of the nodes $v \in Q'_{r,i}$ replies back to that request. The reply contains the number $m_{v,i}(d)$ of messages it has received from requests to data item d for index i, which is called the *multiplicity* of d at v, and the number $C_{v,i}$ of different data items for which it was contacted by requests for index i, which is called the *congestion* at v. Afterwards, each lookup request checks the following rules:

1. For each active $i \in \{1, \ldots, c\}$ with $|Q'_{r,i}| < (\alpha \log n)/2$, the request deactivates i. If the total number of deactivated i's is at least $c/2$, the request becomes inactive.
2. For each active $i \in \{1, \ldots, c\}$ with $|\{v \in Q'_{r,i} \mid |C_{v,i}| \geq 2\alpha c \log n\}| \geq |Q_{r,i}|/2$, the request deactivates i. If the total number of deactivated i's is at least $c/2$, the request becomes inactive.
3. If there is an active i for which there is a node v in $Q'_{r,i}$ with $m_{v,i}(d) \geq 2\alpha \log n$, the request becomes inactive.

Inactive lookup requests do not participate any further in the contraction stage.

The expansion stage. Each lookup request for some data item d that was active till the end of the previous stage, gets the most up-to-date copy of d from every non-blocked $h_i(d)$, returns the most up-to-date copy among these and finishes.

For the other requests, the expansion stage proceeds in rounds, this time numbered from 1 to $\log n$. In round r, every lookup request for some data item d that got deactivated in a round $r' < r$ and is not finished yet sends a message of the form $(d, r, i, -)$ (where "$-$" is an empty placeholder for a copy of d) to a random node in $Q'_{i,r}$ for each i that was active at the end of that round in the contraction stage. Each node v stores the IDs of the nodes that sent messages to it in S_v and stores the messages it received from them into its active pool of messages A_v, one copy for each $(d, r, i, -)$. If $|A_v| > 3c/\sigma$, then any set of messages is discarded from A_v to get down to $|A_v| = 3c/\sigma$, where the constant σ is chosen as in Lemma 1 below. For any remaining $(d, r, i, -)$ in A_v for which v stores a copy b of d (due to the data storage strategy defined above), $(d, r, i, -)$ is replaced by (d, r, i, b). Afterwards, A_v is managed as a FIFO queue. Every node v in the system executes the following push strategy $O(c \log n)$ many times:

- v dequeues one message (d, r, i, b) from A_v, enqueues it back to A_v and sends a copy of it to a random node in $T_r(h_i(d))$.
- For each message (d, r, i, b) received by v, v first checks whether A_v contains some message (d, r, i, b') in which copy b' is older than b (or empty). If so,

v replaces b' by b. Otherwise, v checks if $|A_v| = 3c/\sigma$. If so, v discards the message. Otherwise, it checks whether it stores a copy b' of d that is younger than b. If so, v inserts (d, r, i, b') into A_v, and otherwise it inserts (d, r, i, b) into A_v.

If after these steps $|A_v| = 3c/\sigma$, then v sends for each node $w \in S_v$ with original message $(d, r, i, -)$ the message $(d, r, i, *)$ back to w, where the "$*$" indicates that v was too congested. Otherwise, v sends (d, r, i, b) in A_v back to w.

Each lookup request that receives at most $c/4$ many $(d, r, i, *)$ messages returns the message (d, r, i, b) with the most up-to-date b (which may also be "$-$" if no copy was found) to whoever generated the request and is finished. Otherwise, it continues to participate in round $r + 1$.

2.3   Robust Hash Functions

In this section, we specify a central property the c hash functions $h_1, \ldots, h_c$ have to satisfy for the lookup protocol to work correctly and efficiently.

Given a set S of data items and a $k \in \mathbb{N}$, we call $F \subseteq S \times \{1, \ldots, c\}$ a k-*bundle* of S if every $d \in S$ has exactly k many tuples (d, i) in F. Given $h_1, \ldots, h_c$ and a distance ℓ, let $\Gamma_{F,\ell}(S) = \bigcup_{(d,i) \in F} T_\ell(h_i(d))$. Let U be the set of all possible (names of the) data items and $\mathcal{H}$ be the collection of hash functions $h_1, \ldots, h_c$, and let $m = |U|$. Given a $0 < \sigma < 1$, we call $\mathcal{H}$ a (k, σ)-*expander* if for any $\ell \le \log n$, any $S \subseteq U$ with $|S| \le \sigma n/2^\ell$, and any k-bundle F of S it holds that $|\Gamma_{F,\ell}(S)| \ge 2^\ell |S|$.

Lemma 1. *Let $0 < \lambda < 1$ be any constant. Then it holds for any $c \ge 8 \log m$ and $\sigma \le 1/24$ that if the functions $h_1, \ldots, h_c$ are chosen uniformly and independently at random, then $\mathcal{H}$ is a $(c/4, \sigma)$-expander with high probability.*

Proof. Suppose that, for randomly chosen functions $h_1, \ldots, h_{2c-1}$, $\mathcal{H}$ is not a $(c/4, \sigma)$-expander. Then there exists an $i \le \log n$ and a set $S \subset U$ with $|S| \le \sigma n/2^i$ and a $c/4$-bundle F of S with $|\Gamma_{F,i}(S)| < 2^i |S|$. We claim that the probability $p_{s,i}$ that such a set S of size s exists is at most

$$\binom{m}{s} \binom{cs}{cs/4} \binom{n/2^i}{s} \cdot \left(\frac{s}{n/2^i}\right)^{cs/4}$$

This holds because there are $\binom{m}{s}$ ways of choosing a subset $S \subset U$. Furthermore, there are $\binom{cs}{cs/4}$ ways of choosing $cs/4$ pairs (d, j) for F and at most $\binom{n/2^i}{s}$ ways of choosing a set W of s sets in $\mathcal{T}_i$ witnessing a bad expansion of the pairs in F. The fraction of collections $\mathcal{H}$ for which the selected pairs (d, j) indeed have the property that $T_i(h_j(d)) \subseteq W$ is equal to $(\frac{s}{n/2^i})^{cs/4}$ because the hash functions $h_1, \ldots, h_c$ are chosen independently and uniformly at random.

Next we simplify $p_{s,i}$. Using the conditions on c and σ in the lemma it holds that

$$\binom{m}{s}\binom{cs}{cs/4}\binom{n/2^i}{s}\cdot\left(\frac{s}{n/2^i}\right)^{cs/4}$$

$$\leq\left(\frac{em}{s}\right)^s(4e)^{cs/4}\left(\frac{en}{s2^i}\right)^s\left(\frac{s2^i}{n}\right)^{cs/4}\;=\;\left[\frac{em}{s}\cdot\left(4e^{1+4/c}\cdot\left(\frac{s2^i}{n}\right)^{1-4/c}\right)^{c/4}\right]^s$$

$$\leq\left[m\cdot\left(4e^{1+4/c}\cdot\sigma^{1-4/c}\right)^{c/4}\right]^s\leq\left[m\cdot\left(\frac{1}{2}\right)^{c/4}\right]^s\leq\frac{1}{m^s}$$

if $c\geq 8\log m$ and m is sufficiently large. Hence, summing up over all possible values of s and i, we obtain a probability of having a bad $c/4$-bundle of at most $(2\log n)/m$, which proves the lemma.   □

We remark that the hash functions have to form a $(c/4,\sigma)$-expander for some constant σ for our lookup protocol to work, but they do not have to be chosen at random. The proof above just illustrates that if they are chosen at random, they will form a $(c/4,\sigma)$-expander w.h.p.

2.4   Analysis of the Lookup Protocol

Next we show that the lookup protocol is correct, robust and efficient, i.e., for every lookup request for some data item d inserted after time t_0 (the threshold in the past insider model), a correct answer will be delivered for any DoS attack under our model, and every node spends only polylogarithmic time and work on the requests in the system. The correctness condition for all other data items is implied by our proofs. First, we prove the correctness of a lookup request given that it finishes in the expansion stage.

Lemma 2. *If a lookup request for some data item d finishes in round r of the expansion stage and d was inserted after t_0, then it returns the most up-to-date version of d.*

Proof. Consider any lookup request for some data item d that finishes in round r of the expansion stage and d was inserted after t_0. This means that it got at most $c/4$ many messages of the form $(d,r,i,*)$. The request only participates in round r of the expansion stage if it was still active at the beginning of round $r-1$ in the contraction stage, which is only the case if it had at least $c/2$ active indices i at the beginning of round $r-1$. These indices were all used in round r of the expansion stage, which means that at the end of that round the request got at least $c/4$ messages back of the form (d,r,i,b) where b is the most up-to-date copy of d that the node contacted by the request in $T_r(h_i(b))$ found. Let I be the set of these indices. From the fact that each $i\in I$ was active at the beginning of round $r-1$ in the contraction stage it follows that in round r of that stage, $Q'_{r,i}\geq(\alpha\log n)/2$ (because otherwise i would have been deactivated in that round). Hence, at least half of the nodes in $Q_{r,i}$ that were sampled from $T_r(h_i(b))$ are non-blocked nodes. Since the nodes in $Q_{r,i}$ were chosen independently at random, it follows from the Chernoff bounds that the total number of blocked nodes in $T_r(h_i(b))$ is at most $2|T_r(h_i(b))|/3$, w.h.p., if α is a sufficiently large constant. We call a $T_r(h_i(b))$ satisfying such a property *non-blocked* in this proof. We can show the following claim.

Claim 1. *For any node v in a non-blocked set $T_r(h_i(b))$ it holds that if after $\phi c \log n$ executions of the push strategy in the expansion stage, where ϕ is a sufficiently large constant, $|A_v| < 3c/\sigma$, then there are lookup requests for less than $3c/\sigma$ data items that sent messages to nodes in $T_r(h_i(b))$ and every entry (d, r, i, b) in A_v stores the most up-to-date copy of d among the non-blocked nodes in $T_r(h_i(b))$ at the end.*

Proof. Can be shown along the lines of existing proofs on random, push-based broadcasting in complete networks (e.g., [7]). □

Hence, the lookup request obtains at least $c/4$ many replies (d, r, i, b) with most up-to-date copies in the respective sets $T_r(h_i(b))$. Since for each $i \in I$ at least a third of the nodes in $T_r(h_i(b))$ are not blocked, w.h.p., the lookup request returns the most up-to-date copy for at least $(c/4) \cdot (2^r/3) = c2^r/12$ of the $c2^r$ nodes in all sets $T_r(h_i(b))$, $i \in \{1, \ldots, c\}$. According to the robust storage strategy, $\gamma \log n$ many most up-to-date copies of d are randomly distributed among these $c2^r$ nodes, and none of these locations is known to the adversary, so the probability that none of these is stored in the at least $c2^r/12$ non-blocked nodes accessed by the request is at most $(1 - 1/12)^{\gamma \log n}$, which is polynomially small if γ is a sufficiently large constant.

We remark that for the data items least recently updated before t_0, at most $f = \max\{n, D/n^k\}$ many of them are bad, w.h.p., in a sense that none of their most up-to-date copies is stored in the at least $c2^r/12$ non-blocked nodes, where D is the number of data items in the system and k can be any constant. This is because there are at most 2^n ways of selecting $c2^r/12$ non-blocked out of at most n considered nodes and $\binom{D}{f}$ ways of selecting bad data items while the probability that these are indeed bad is at most $((1 - 1/12)^{\gamma \log n})^f$. If γ is sufficiently large compared to k, multiplying these terms gives a polynomially small probability. Hence, apart from f data items, the lookup protocol will deliver correct answers also for data items inserted or updated before t_0, w.h.p. □

Next, we look at the robustness and efficiency and will show that within a polylogarithmic time every request finishes, w.h.p. First, we consider the contraction stage. We show that the number of messages sent to any node is polylogarithmic in every round, which implies that every node spends only a polylogarithmic time and work on the contraction stage.

Lemma 3. *For every round r, at most $O(c \log^2 n)$ messages are sent to any node in the system, w.h.p.*

Proof. Consider some fixed node v in some set $T \in \mathcal{T}_r$. First, we bound $m_{v,i}(d)$ for any data item d and index i with $T_r(h_i(d)) = T$. Suppose that $m_{v,i}(d) \geq$

$8\alpha \log n$. Since every request for d chooses the nodes in $Q_{r,i}$ independently at random from the nodes in T, it follows from the Chernoff bounds that the expected number of messages for d at a node in T is at least $6\alpha \log n$, w.h.p. Hence, the expected number of messages for d in $T_{r+1}(h_i(d))$ was at least $3\alpha \log n$, w.h.p. However, in this case it holds for every node $w \in T_{r+1}(h_i(d))$ that $m_{w,i}(d)$ was at least $2\alpha \log n$, w.h.p. Thus, every request for d that was still active at round $r+1$ must have either deactivated i or became inactive. Hence, it must hold for every node $v \in T$ that $m_{v,i}(d) \le 8\alpha \log n$, w.h.p., for any data item d and i with $T_r(h_i(d)) = T$.

A congestion bound of $|C_{v,i}| \le 8\alpha \log n$ can be shown along exactly the same lines. Since there are c different indices i, the total number of messages sent to v is bounded by $c(8\alpha \log n)^2 = O(c \log^2 n)$. $\qquad\square$

Hence, the runtime of the contraction stage and work per node is $O(c \log^3 n)$, w.h.p. Next we analyze the number of different data items for which lookup requests become inactive. This will be important to bound the congestion at the nodes in the expansion phase.

Let D_r be the set of all data items for which there are lookup requests that become inactive in round r. Furthermore, let BC_r be the set of data items with requests that become inactive due to too many inactive indices and MC_r be the set of data items with requests that become inactive due to a too high multiplicity. Certainly, $D_r = BC_r \cup MC_r$. First, we bound BC_r.

Lemma 4. *If $\epsilon < 1/144$, then it holds for every round r that $|BC_r| \le 8\epsilon n/2^r$, w.h.p.*

Proof. For any r and any $T \subseteq \mathcal{T}_r$, we call T *blocked* if the attacker blocks more than a third of its nodes with its DoS attack, and T is called *congested* if more than a third of the nodes in T have a congestion of at least $2\alpha c \log n$. Consider any data item d. We call d *blocked* at round r if at least $c/4$ of its c sets $T_r(h_i(d))$ are blocked, and we call it *weakly blocked* at round r if there are blocked sets $T_{r_1}(h_{i_1}(d)), T_{r_2}(h_{i_2}(d)), \ldots, T_{r_k}(h_{i_k}(d))$ with $r_1, \ldots, r_k \ge r$ and $k = c/4$ and $i_1, \ldots, i_k$ being pairwise different. Similarly, we call d *congested* at round r if at least $c/4$ of its c sets $T_r(h_i(d))$ are congested, and we call it *weakly congested* at round r if there are congested sets $T_{r_1}(h_{i_1}(d)), T_{r_2}(h_{i_2}(d)), \ldots, T_{r_k}(h_{i_k}(d))$ with $r_1, r_2, \ldots, r_k \ge r$ and $k = c/4$ and $i_1, \ldots, i_k$ being pairwise different. In the following, WB_r denotes the set of weakly blocked data items and WC_r the set of weakly congested data items at round r.

Claim 2. *Whenever a request for some data item d deactivates some index i in round r, then $T_r(h_i(d))$ is either blocked or congested, w.h.p.*

Proof. Consider any request for some data item d in round r. Index i is deactivated for that request if

1. there are at least $(\alpha \log n)/2$ nodes in $Q_{r,i}$ that are blocked, or
2. there are at least $(\alpha \log n)/2$ nodes in $Q'_{r,i}$ that are congested.

In the first case, suppose that $T_r(h_i(d))$ is not blocked. Then the probability that $R_{i,j}$ chooses a node in $T_r(h_i(d))$ that is blocked is at most $1/3$ and, hence, the expected number of nodes chosen by the routes $R_{i,1}, \ldots, R_{i,\alpha \log n}$ that are blocked is at most $(\alpha \log n)/3$. Since the nodes are chosen independently at random, it follows from the Chernoff bounds that the probability that at least $(\alpha \log n)/2$ nodes in $Q_{r,i}$ are blocked is polynomially small in n (if the constant α is sufficiently large). Hence, if the request deactivates index i because of at least $(\alpha \log n)/2$ blocked nodes, then $T_r(h_i(d))$ is blocked, w.h.p.

The arguments for the congestion follow along the same lines.   □

Now suppose that a request for data item d becomes inactive at round r due to at least $c/2$ deactivated indices. Then there are at least $c/4$ indices for which condition 1 in the contraction stage is true or at least $c/4$ indices for which condition 2 is true. In the first case, it follows from Claim 2 that d is weakly blocked, and in the second case, it follows from Claim 2 that d is weakly congested, w.h.p. For weakly blocked data items, the following claim holds.

Claim 3. *If s blocked nodes can cause a set of b weakly blocked data items at round r, then a set of $2s$ blocked nodes can cause a set of b blocked data items at round r.*

Proof. Consider item d to be weakly blocked, and let $T_{r_1}(h_{i_1}(d))$, $T_{r_2}(h_{i_2}(d))$, $\ldots, T_{r_k}(h_{i_k}(d))$ be the sets witnessing that with $k = c/4$. Any route through a set $T_{r'}(h_{i'}(d))$ with $r' > r$ can have at most $2^{r'-r}$ sets $T \in \mathcal{T}_r$ it can go through, and each of these sets T has a size of $|T_{r'}(h_{i'}(d))|/2^{r'-r}$. Hence, the number of nodes causing $T_{r'}(h_{i'}(d))$ to be blocked is sufficient to block also all $T \in \mathcal{T}_r$ reachable from $T_{r'}(h_{i'}(d))$. Hence, for any set of b weakly blocked data items, we can turn them into blocked data items when moving the blocking of nodes at distance $r' > r$ to nodes at distance r. Since we have to keep those sets $T_{r'}(h_{i'}(b))$ with $r' = r$ blocked, we have to at most double the number of nodes needed to transform weakly blocked data items into blocked data items.   □

If the adversary can block at most $2\epsilon n$ nodes, then at most $6\epsilon n/2^r$ of the $n/2^r$ sets in $\mathcal{T}_r$ can be blocked, which covers at most $6\epsilon n$ nodes. Suppose the attacker can block a set S of data items in round r. Then there is a $c/4$-bundle F for S. According to Lemma 1, it holds that $|\Gamma_{F,r}(S)| \geq 2^r|S|$ if $|S| \leq \sigma n/2^r$. Since the largest possible size of $\Gamma_{F,r}(S)$ is $6\epsilon n$, it follows that $|S| \leq 6\epsilon n/2^r$, which is less than $\sigma n/2^r$ (so that Lemma 1 implies an upper bound on $|S|$) if $6\epsilon < 1/24$, or $\epsilon < 1/144$. Hence, if the adversary can block at most $2\epsilon n$ nodes, then it can cause at most $6\epsilon n/2^r$ blocked data items in round r. This implies together with Claim 3 that if the adversary can block at most ϵn nodes, then it can cause at most $6\epsilon n/2^i$ weakly blocked data items in round r. Combining this with Claim 2, it follows that if the adversary can block at most ϵn nodes, then $|WB_r| \leq 6\epsilon n/2^r$, w.h.p.

Using the same arguments for congested data items, it also follows that $|WC_r| \leq 6\epsilon n/2^r$, w.h.p. Hence, $|BC_r| \leq |WB_r| + |WC_r| \leq 12\epsilon n/2^r$, w.h.p.   □

Next we bound MC_r.

Lemma 5. *For every round r, $|MC_r| \leq n/2^r$.*

Proof. Suppose that there are ℓ many lookup requests for data item d in round r. Then the expected number of messages per node w.r.t. i in any $T_r(h_i(d))$ is $(\alpha \log n)\ell/2^r$. If $\ell \leq 2^r$, this is at most $\alpha \log n$. Since each message chooses a node independently at random, it follows from the Chernoff bounds that the probability that there is a node in a set $T_r(h_i(d))$ with at least $2\alpha \log n$ messages for d is polynomially small. Hence, if a lookup request for some data item d becomes inactive due to condition 3 of the contraction stage, then d has a multiplicity of at least 2^r, w.h.p. Since there are at most n active requests at round r, it follows that $|MC_r| \leq n/2^r$. □

Combining Lemmas 4 and 5 it follows that $|D_r| \leq 12\epsilon n/2^r + n/2^r \leq 2n/2^r$, w.h.p. Now we are ready to analyze the expansion stage. First, we bound the number of messages sent to a node in each round.

Lemma 6. *For every round r, at most $O(c \log n)$ messages are sent to any node in the system, w.h.p.*

Proof. Only requests that were active in round $r-1$ of the contraction stage will participate in round r of the expansion stage. According to Lemma 3, the number of messages sent to any node in the system in any round of the contraction stage is $O(c \log^2 n)$ w.h.p. Since every lookup request sends out $\alpha c \log n$ messages in the contraction stage but only at most c messages in the expansion stage, it follows that the number of messages sent to any node in the expansion stage is at most $O(c \log n)$, w.h.p. □

The description of the expansion stage and Lemma 6 immediately imply that the runtime and work per node of the expansion stage is at most $O(c \log^3 n)$. Combining this with our bounds for the contraction stage, we get:

Lemma 7. *For any collection of lookup requests, one per non-blocked node, the lookup protocol needs at most $O(c \log^3 n)$ time and work at every node.*

Next, we show that every request will eventually finish in the lookup protocol, w.h.p.

Lemma 8. *For every round r, the number of data items with requests participating in it is less than $3n/2^r$.*

Proof. We prove the lemma by induction on the number of rounds. For round 1, the lemma certainly holds. So consider any round $r \geq 1$ for which the lemma holds. A set $T \in \mathcal{T}_r$ is called *congested* if there are messages for at least $3c/\sigma$ many different data items in T. Since there are requests for less than $3n/2^r$ many data items and the messages for each data item are limited to c sets $T \in \mathcal{T}_r$, there must be less than $\sigma n/2^r$ many sets $T \in \mathcal{T}_r$ that are congested. A data item d is called *congested* if there are at least $c/4$ many indices i for which $T_r(h_i(d))$ is congested. Let S be the set of congested data items. Then there is a $c/4$-bundle F for S. According to Lemma 1, it holds that $|\Gamma_{F,r}(S)| \geq 2^r|S|$ if $|S| \leq \sigma n/2^r$. Since the largest possible size of $\Gamma_{F,r}(S)$ is less than σn, it follows that $|S| < \sigma n/2^r$. As a worst case, we assume that all requests for congested data items will not finish in round r and therefore have to continue in round $r + 1$. These will combine with the requests for at most $n/2^r + 12\epsilon n/2^r$ data items with requests that became inactive in round r of the contraction stage, which gives an upper bound of less than $3n/2^{r+1}$ on the number of data items with requests in round $r + 1$ (given that $\epsilon < 1/144$ and $\sigma \leq 1/24$). $\square$

Hence, in round $r = \log n$, there are at most 3 data items left with requests. In this round, all sets $T_r(h_i(d))$ are equal to the entire node set, so there is no congested node set left. Hence, according to the expansion protocol, every request will finish in that round. Combining this with Lemmas 2 and 7 proves Theorem 1.

3   Conclusions

In this paper we showed that a DHT for scalable data storage and retrieval can be designed that is provably robust against massive application- and network-layer DoS attacks. Certainly, low-level protocols still have to be developed for our operations that work well and correctly in an asynchronous environment. Also, it would be interesting to find out whether adaptations of our strategies are possible to bounded degree DHTs so that they can sustain DoS attacks of a similar magnitude as considered in this paper.

References

1. Andersen, D.G.: Mayday: Distributed filtering for internet services. In: 4th Usenix Symp. on Internet Technologies and Systems (2003)
2. Awerbuch, B., Scheideler, C.: Towards a scalable and robust DHT. In: Proc. of the 18th ACM Symp. on Parallel Algorithms and Architectures (SPAA). ACM Press, New York (2006), http://www14.in.tum.de/personen/scheideler
3. Druschel, P., Rowstron, A.: Pastry: Scalable, distributed object location and routing for large-scale peer-to-peer systems. In: Proc. of the 18th IFIP/ACM International Conference on Distributed Systems Platforms (Middleware 2001). ACM Press, New York (2001)
4. Dittrich, D., Mirkovic, J., Dietrich, S., Reiher, P.: Internet Denial of Service: Attack and Defense Mechanisms. Prentice Hall PTR, Englewood Cliffs (2005)
5. Karger, D., Lehman, E., Leighton, T., Levine, M., Lewin, D., Panigrahi, R.: Consistent hashing and random trees: Distributed caching protocols for relieving hot spots on the World Wide Web. In: Proc. of the 29th ACM Symp. on Theory of Computing (STOC), pp. 654–663. ACM Press, New York (1997)
6. Kargl, F., Maier, J., Weber, M.: Protecting web servers from distributed denial of service attacks. World Wide Web, pp. 514–524 (2001)
7. Karp, R., Shenker, S., Schindelhauer, C., Vöcking, B.: Randomized rumor spreading. In: Proc. of the 41st IEEE Symp. on Foundations of Computer Science (FOCS), pp. 565–574. IEEE Computer Society Press, Los Alamitos (2000)

8. Keromytis, A.D., Misra, V., Rubenstein, D.: SOS: Secure Overlay Services. In: Proc. of ACM SIGCOMM, pp. 61–72. ACM Press, New York (2002)
9. Lakshminarayanan, K., Adkins, D., Perrig, A., Stoica, I.: Taming ip packet flooding attacks (2003)
10. Lawton, G.: Stronger domain name system thwarts root-server attacks. IEEE Computer, 14–17 (May 2007)
11. Mehlhorn, K., Vishkin, U.: Randomized and deterministic simulations of PRAMs by parallel machines with restricted granularity of parallel mamories. Acta Informatica 21, 339–374 (1984)
12. Mirkovic, J., Reiher, P.: A taxonomy of ddos attacks and defense mechanisms. ACM SIGCOMM Computer Communications Review 34(2) (2004)
13. Morein, W.G., Stavrou, A., Cook, D.L., Keromytis, A.D., Misra, V., Rubenstein, D.: Using graphic turing tests to counter automated ddos attacks against web servers. In: Proc. of the 10th ACM Int. Conference on Computer and Communications Security (CCS), pp. 8–19. ACM Press, New York (2003)
14. Naor, M., Wieder, U.: Novel architectures for P2P applications: the continuous-discrete approach. In: Proc. of the 15th ACM Symp. on Parallel Algorithms and Architectures (SPAA). ACM Press, New York (2003)
15. Oikonomou, G., Mirkovic, J., Reiher, P., Robinson, M.: A framework for collaborative ddos defense. In: Jesshope, C., Egan, C. (eds.) ACSAC 2006. LNCS, vol. 4186. Springer, Heidelberg (2006)
16. Padmanabhan, V.N., Sripanidkulchai, K.: The case for cooperative networking. In: Proc. of the 1st International Workshop on Peer-to-Peer Systems (IPTPS) (2002)
17. Plaxton, G., Rajaraman, R., Richa, A.W.: Accessing nearby copies of replicated objects in a distributed environment. In: Proc. of the 9th ACM Symp. on Parallel Algorithms and Architectures (SPAA), pp. 311–320. ACM Press, New York (1997)
18. Ratnasamy, S., Francis, P., Handley, M., Karp, R., Shenker, S.: A scalable content-addressable network. In: Proc. of the ACM SIGCOMM '01. ACM Press, New York (2001)
19. Stading, T., Maniatis, P., Baker, M.: Peer-to-peer caching schemes to address flash crowds. In: Proc. of the 1st International Workshop on Peer-to-Peer Systems (IPTPS) (2002)
20. Stavron, A., Rubenstein, D., Sahn, S.: A lightweight robust P2P system to handle flash crowds. In: Proc. of the IEEE Intl. Conf. on Network Protocols (ICNP). IEEE Computer Society Press, Los Alamitos (2002)
21. Stavrou, A., Cook, D.L., Morein, W.G., Keromytis, A.D., Misra, V., Rubenstein, D.: Websos: An overlay-based system for protecting web servers from denial of service attacks (2005)
22. Stoica, I., Morris, R., Karger, D., Kaashoek, M.F., Balakrishnan, H.: Chord: A scalable peer-to-peer lookup service for Internet applications. In: Proc. of the ACM SIGCOMM '01, ACM Press, New York (2001), See also http://www.pdos.lcs.mit.edu/chord/
23. Yang, X., Wetherall, D., Anderson, T.: A dos-limiting network architecture. In: Proc. of the ACM SIGCOMM. ACM Press, New York (2005)
24. Zhao, B.Y., Kubiatowicz, J., Joseph, A.: Tapestry: An infrastructure for fault-tolerant wide-area location and routing. Technical report, UCB/CSD-01-1141, University of California at Berkeley (2001), See also http://www.cs.berkeley.edu/~ravenben/tapestry

Mobility Versus the Cost of Geocasting in Mobile Ad-Hoc Networks[*]

Roberto Baldoni, Kleoni Ioannidou, and Alessia Milani

Università di Roma *La Sapienza*, Italy
baldoni@dis.uniroma1.it, ioannidu@cs.toronto.edu, milani@dis.uniroma1.it

Abstract. We present a model of a mobile ad-hoc network in which nodes can move arbitrarily on the plane with some bounded speed. We show that without any assumption on some topological stability, it is impossible to solve the geocast problem despite connectivity and no matter how slowly the nodes move. Even if each node maintains a stable connection with each of its neighbours for some period of time, it is impossible to solve geocast if nodes move too fast. Additionally, we give a tradeoff lower bound which shows that the faster the nodes can move, the more costly it would be to solve the geocast problem. Finally, for the one-dimensional case of the mobile ad-hoc network, we provide an algorithm for geocasting and we prove its correctness given exact bounds on the speed of movement.

Keywords: Mobile ad-hoc networks, geocast, speed of movement vs cost of the solution, distributed systems.

1 Introduction

There has been increasing interest in mobile ad-hoc networks with nodes that move arbitrarily on the plane. This is justified by the significance of (wireless) mobile computing in emerging technologies. Current technologies require a stable infrastructure which is used for communication between mobile nodes. Unfortunately, in some cases, such as a military operation or after some physical disaster, a fixed infrastructure cannot exist. For such cases, it is desirable to program the mobile nodes to solve important distributed problems within specific geographical areas and without depending on a stable infrastructure. This is why there has been an increasing interest in studying "geo" related problems in mobile ad-hoc networks such as georouting [1,2], geocasting [3,4,5,6], geoquorums [6], etc.

Geocasting is a variant of the multicast problem [7]. In geocasting, the nodes eligible to deliver a message are the ones that belong to a specific geographical area. Specifications to this problem can be either best effort or deterministic. An implementation of a best effort specification aims to maximize the probability

---

[*] The work described in this paper was partially supported by the Italian Ministry of Education, University, and Research (MIUR) under the ISMANET project and by the European Community under Resist Network of Excellence.

that nodes eligible to deliver the information, they actually deliver it [3,4,5]. Deterministic specifications define a set of nodes and an implementation of such a specification ensures that each of these nodes will deliver the information [6].

When geocasting is solved for mobile ad-hoc networks, the speed of how nodes move becomes an important factor. This is because it can heavily influence, for example, the completion time of the message diffusion in a certain geographical area till making geocasting unsolvable if these speeds are too high. In an extreme (unrealistic) scenario, nodes can move fast enough to ensure that no two neighbours stay connected for enough time to complete the receipt of a message. Geocasting cannot be solved in this scenario even though the topology of the mobile ad-hoc network never disconnects. To our knowledge this relation among problem solvability, the cost of a solution, and mobility has never been investigated.

This paper focuses on geocasting based on deterministic specifications investigating the relation between cost of solving geocasting and mobility. In particular, we firstly provide a model of computation (Section 2) and a specification for the geocasting problem (Section 3) which both take into account (explicitly or implicitly) node mobility. The model makes a distinction between strong and weak connectivity. A system strongly connected has some assurance of topological stability, i.e., there is always a path between every two nodes formed by strong neighbors, where strong neighbors means that they remain neighbors for some period of time. A connected system that does not satisfy the previous property is weakly connected. Our model does not rely on either GPS or synchrony being thus very weak with respect to other models presented in the literature [8]. The geocasting specification is split in three properties: reliable delivery, integrity, and termination. Reliable delivery states that all nodes, which remain for some positive time C within distance d from the location l where the geocast has been issued, will deliver the geocast information. Conversely, integrity defines the minimum distance between the location l and a node in order that the latter does not deliver the geocast information. Termination states that after some period of time C' from geocasting of some information, there will be no more communication related to this geocast.

Hence, a general framework of geocasting algorithms is proposed (Section 3.2), which captures existing geocast algorithms. An algorithm belonging to this framework acts as follows: once a node receives a message (with the geocast information) broadcast by a neighbour, it may repeat a (local) broadcast k times, once every α rounds, depending on some condition. Using this framework in our model several results have been proved: (i) if nodes are weakly connected geocasting cannot be solved no matter how slowly the nodes can move (Theorem 1); (ii) if stronger connectivity holds, then geocasting is still impossible for some bound of node's speed of movement (Theorems 2 and 3); (iii) a tradeoff lower bound that relates the cost of geocasting to the speed of movement of nodes (Theorem 4).

Finally, if the speed is small enough, we show how to solve the geocasting problem in a one-dimensional setting (Section 5). We prove that the time complexity of this algorithm increases with the speed of nodes. The algorithm does not require any knowledge of the topology of the system. These results confirm the intuition that the fastest the nodes move, the more expensive it would be to solve the geocasting problem and if nodes move too fast then no solution can be achieved.

2   A Model for Mobile Ad-Hoc Networks

We consider a system of (mobile) nodes which move with bounded speeds in a continuous manner on the plane. There is no known upper bound on the number of nodes in the system and nodes do not fail. Nodes communicate by exchanging messages over a wireless radio network. To define neighbourhood of nodes, let distance(p, p', t) denote the physical distance between two nodes p and p' at time t. Two nodes p and p' are *neighbours* at some time t, if distance$(p, p', t) < r$, for fixed $r > 0$. We assume that each node can have at most H neighbours at each time.

Nodes do not have access to a global clock, instead they have (not necessarily synchronized) local clocks which run at the same rate. Within a small time period, called a *round*, a node can execute in a sequential and atomic manner receiving at most H messages, broadcasting at most one message, and local computation. To perform a local broadcast of a message m, a node p is provided with a primitive denoted *broadcast*(m). It takes at least one round for a broadcast message m to be received by a node which then generates a *receive*(m) event. For simplicity of presentation, the duration of a round is one time unit (i.e., in $[t, t + i]$, i rounds have elapsed). If *broadcast*(m) is performed by node p at time t then all nodes that remain neighbours of p throughout $[t, t+T]$ receive m by time $t+T$, for some fixed integer $T > 0$. It is possible that some nodes that are neighbours of p at times in $[t, t+T]$ also receive m but no node receives m after time $t+T$. If two or more nodes perform broadcasts concurrently there may be interference and messages may be lost. We assume this to be dealt by a lower level communication layer [9] within the T rounds it takes for a message to be (reliably) delivered to its destination. There is no other way that messages can be lost.

Connectivity. The standard definition of connectivity, called *weak connectivity*, ensures that for every pair of nodes p and p' and every time t, there is at least one path of neighbours connecting p and p' at time t. Weak connectivity allows an adversary to continually change the neighbourhood of nodes and render impossible even the basic task of geocasting (Theorem 1). For this reason, we assume a stronger version, called *strong connectivity*. To define this, first, we introduce the notion of strong neighbours. If there is an upper bound on the speed of nodes, then the closer two neighbours are located to each other, the longer they will remain neighbours. Hence, if nodes are located fairly close, then their connection is guaranteed for some period of time. Formally,

Definition 1 (Strong Neighbours). *Let $\delta_2 = r$ and δ_1 be fixed positive real numbers such that $\delta_1 < \delta_2$. Two nodes p and p' are strong neighbours at some*

time t, if there is a time $t' \leq t$ such that $distance(p, p', t') \leq \delta_1$ and $distance(p, p', t'') < \delta_2$ for all $t'' \in [t', t]$.

Assumption 1 (Strong Connectivity). *For every pair of nodes p and p' and every time t, there is at least one path of strong neighbours connecting p and p' at t.*

Two nodes *strongly connect* when they become strong neighbours and they *lose their connection or disconnect* when they cease being neighbours. By increasing δ_1, the set of strong neighbours of each node either remains the same or increases. This is desirable, because then strong connectivity is not too much stronger than weak connectivity. Therefore, for practical applications, we would like to design algorithms considering values of δ_1 that are as large as possible. Because of this, in this paper, we assume $\delta_1 \geq \frac{\delta_2}{2}$.

Mobility. We assume an upper bound on the speed of node movement which exists in practical situations. Then, Lemma 1 describes some topological stability. Formally,

Assumption 2 (Movement Speed). *It takes at least $T' > 0$ rounds for a node to travel distance $\delta = \frac{\delta_2 - \delta_1}{2}$ on the plane.*

From Definition 1 and Assumption 2, we gain some topological stability in the network, which is formally expressed in the following lemma:

Lemma 1. *If two nodes become strong neighbours at time t, then they remain (strong) neighbours throughout $[t, t + T']$ (i.e., for T' rounds).*

Proof. If p and p' become strong neighbours at time t, then $distance(p, p', t) = \delta_1$. To disconnect, they must move away from each other so that their distance is larger than or equal to δ_2 (traversing in total distance at least 2δ). From assumption 2, this takes at least T' rounds when they travel in opposite directions.

3   The Geocast Problem

The goal of geocasting is to deliver information to nodes in a specific geographical area. The geocast problem can be solved by a geocast service, implemented by a geocast algorithm which runs on mobile nodes. The geocast service supports each mobile node with two primitives: Geocast(I, d) to geocast information I at distance d and Deliver(I) to deliver information I. As illustrated in Figure 1, on each mobile node there is a process running the geocast algorithm and a co-located user of the service which invokes geocast. The geocast algorithm uses *broadcast(m)* and *receive(m)* to achieve communication among neighbours.

Mobile Node

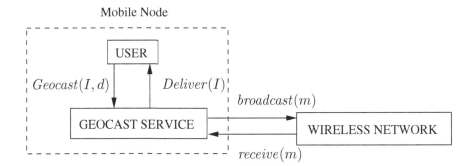

Fig. 1. System Architecture

3.1 A Geocast Specification

The geocast information is initially known by exactly one node, *the source*. If the source performs Geocast(I, d) at time t from location l, then:

Property 1 (Reliable Delivery). There is a positive integer C such that, by time $t+C$, information I is delivered by all nodes that are located at distance at most d away from l throughout $[t, t + C]$.

The following properties rule out solutions which waste resources causing continuous communication or distribution of information I among all nodes.

Property 2 (Termination). If no other node issues another call of geocast then there is a positive integer C' such that after time $t + C'$, no node performs any communication triggered by a geocast (i.e. local broadcast).

Property 3 (Integrity). There is $d' > d$ such that, if a node has never been within distance d' from l, it never delivers I.

3.2 A General Framework for Geocasting Algorithms

We present a framework, (k, α)-Geocast(I, d) for $\alpha \geq 1$, that describes a large class of geocast algorithms. When the source invokes (k, α)-Geocast(I, d), k messages containing I are broadcast, once every α rounds. When a node receives a message containing I, k broadcasts of messages containing I are generated, once every α rounds as long as some condition (described by a boolean function *CHECK*) holds. *CHECK* can be different for each algorithm in this class.

More precisely, for each call of Geocast(I, d), each node p stores a variable $time_{p,I}$, and a boolean variable $flag_{p,I}$, initially set to $\perp$ and 0, respectively. We denote $clock_p$ the current value of the physical clock at p.

When source s executes (k, α)-Geocast(I, d), $time_{s,I}$ is set to $clock_s$ and every α rounds $flag_{s,I}$ is set to 1 (illustrated in Figure 2 (a)). This causes the broadcast of a message m containing information I (illustrated in Figure 2 (b)).

$(k, \alpha) - Geocast(I, d)$ **by** s
1    $time_{s,I} \leftarrow clock_s;$
2   **for** $(i = 1; i + +; i \leq k)$
3   **when** $(clock_s == time_{s,I} + [(i - 1)\alpha)])$
4            $flag_{s,I} \leftarrow 1;$

(a)

when $(flag_{s,I} == 1)$
1    $trigger\langle broadcast(m)\rangle;$ % $I \in m$ %
2    $flag_{s,I} \leftarrow 0;$

(b)

Fig. 2. $(k, \alpha) - Geocast(I, d)$ algorithm performed by the source s

The first time a node p executes $receive(m)$, $time_{p,I}$ gets the value of $clock_p$. Any time p receives a message with information I, if $CHECK$ is true, it sets $flag_{p,I}$ to 1, every α rounds for k times (illustrated in Figure 3 (a)), which in turn causes a broadcast of a message containing I (illustrated in Figure 3 (b)). After each such broadcast, $flag_{p,I}$ is set to 0.

Note that if p receives more than one message containing I within α rounds, only one broadcast is triggered. Hence at most one broadcast happens at p every α rounds. The above is ensured by setting $flag_{p,I}$ to 1 only at certain times as shown in line 7 of Figure 3 (a). In particular, $flag_{p,I}$ is set to 1, k times, starting at the closest time after $t_{p,I}$ that is equal to $time_{p,I} + j\alpha$ (where j is an integer).

upon event $\langle receive(m)\rangle$ **by** p
1    $trigger\langle Deliver(I)\rangle;$ % I is contained in m %
2    $t_{p,I} \leftarrow clock_p;$
3   **if** $(time_{p,I} == \perp)$
4   **then** $time_{p,I} \leftarrow t_{p,I};$
5   **if** $(CHECK)$
6   **then for** $(i = 1; i + +; i \leq k)$
7   **when** $(clock_p == time_{p,I} + [\lceil \frac{t_{p,I} - time_{p,I}}{\alpha} \rceil + (i - 1)]\alpha)$
8                $flag_{p,I} \leftarrow 1;$

(a)

when $(flag_{p,I} == 1)$ **by** p
1    $trigger\langle broadcast(m)\rangle;$ % $I \in m$ %
2    $flag_{p,I} \leftarrow 0;$

(b)

Fig. 3. $(k, \alpha) - Geocast(I, d)$ algorithm performed by node p

4   Impossibility Results

End-to-end communication is impossible if the system remains disconnected. Eventual connectivity [10] ensures the existence of a path between sender and receiver with edges which transmit infinitely many messages if infinitely many messages are sent through. Eventual connectivity is necessary for achieving end-to-end communication in general networks. For our mobile ad-hoc network, we show that it is impossible to solve the geocast problem using algorithms in (k, α) - Geocast under weak connectivity, or under strong connectivity if nodes move too fast. To do so, we relate the speed of movement (which is inversely related to T') to the speed of communication (which is inversely related to T). We also show how the speed of nodes relates to the cost of any (k, α) - Geocast algorithm.

For the following impossibility results, we set $CHECK$ to true because if reliable delivery is impossible when the maximum broadcasts are allowed, it is also impossible for less broadcasts.

The fact that the (k, α) - Geocast class of algorithms contains a large class of natural geocasting algorithms (including existing ones) makes our impossibility results significant for practical applications. We note that the following lower bounds are not necessarily tight.

Theorem 1. *No algorithm in (k, α) - Geocast(I, d) can solve the geocast problem under the weak connectivity assumption no matter how slowly the nodes move.*

Proof. Assume that the maximum speed of the nodes is $v > 0$. Consider a state, s_{pq}, such that all nodes are located on a straight line. The source s is the leftmost node at position l. The only neighbour, p, of s is on its right at distance $r - d_\epsilon$ from l, at position l_1 such that $d_\epsilon \leq \frac{v \min\{\alpha, T\}}{2}$. There is a node q located on the right of p at distance d_ϵ from p at position l_2, as illustrated in Figure 4.

Because $d_\epsilon \leq \frac{v \min\{\alpha, T\}}{2}$, distance $2d_\epsilon$ can be traversed during $\min\{\alpha, T\}$ rounds. From state s_{pq} at time t, node q moves with speed $\frac{2d_\epsilon}{\min\{\alpha, T\}}$ until it reaches location l_1 at time $t + \frac{\min\{\alpha, T\}}{2}$. Then, node p moves away from l with speed $\frac{2d_\epsilon}{\min\{\alpha, T\}}$ until it reaches location l_2 at time $t + \min\{\alpha, T\}$. The state, s_{qp}, reached is the same as s_{pq} if we replace p by q and q by p. Weak connectivity is preserved.

Because the switch between s_{pq} and s_{qp} takes $\min\{\alpha, T\}$ rounds, and according to the algorithm at most one broadcast can be initiated every α rounds, it is possible to create an execution where the source starts a local broadcast either at state s_{pq}, or at state s_{qp} and its neighbourhood changes within $\min\{\alpha, T\}$ rounds. This implies that no node ever delivers I. In particular, if $\alpha > T$ then there can be at most one message broadcast every T rounds and this message will be lost because the neighbourhood changes within $\min\{\alpha, T\} = T$ rounds. Otherwise, $\alpha \leq T$. Since there is at most one message broadcast every α rounds, every such message will be lost because the change in the neighbourhood happens within $\min\{\alpha, T\} = \alpha \leq T$ rounds.

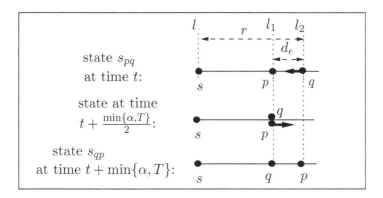

Fig. 4. Proof of Theorem 1

As stated in Section 2, we assumed that $\delta_1 \geq \frac{\delta_2}{2}$ which is reasonable for practical applications. The following results in this section hold given this assumption. Our lower bounds would be stronger if they held for all values of δ_1. This extension would be of theoretical interest and we leave it as future work.

Theorem 2. *No algorithm in (k, α) - Geocast(I, d) can solve the geocast problem if $T' < \frac{T}{4}$ even if strong connectivity holds.*

Proof. Consider a (k, α)-Geocast(I, d) algorithm executed at time t by the source s. We will describe an execution of this algorithm (illustrated in Figure 5) during which no node (other than s) knows information I, violating reliable delivery. Let s_{pq} be the state at time t with the following properties: all nodes are located on a single line; the source, s, is the leftmost node located at position l; the first node, p, located on the right of l is at position l_1 at distance δ_1 from l; the second node, q, located on the right of l is at position l_2 at distance δ_2 from l and at distance $\delta_2 - \delta_1 = 2\delta$ from l_1; all other nodes of the system are located on the right of s at distance at least $\delta_1 + \delta_2$ from l. Node p is the only (strong) neighbour of s. Nodes s and q are the only (strong) neighbours of p, p is the only (strong) neighbour of q located on the left of q at time t, and the remaining (strong) neighbours, Q, of node q are located on its right at distance exactly δ_1. We conclude that strong connectivity holds at state s_{pq}. Assume that, from state s_{pq}, p moves from l_1 to l_2 and q moves from l_2 to l_1 on a straight line with their highest speed. Each of them will traverse a path of distance 2δ and arrive at its destination at time $t + 2T'$ (by the communication speed assumption). Strong connectivity holds throughout $[t, t + 2T']$ because throughout $[t, t + 2T')$, the sets of strong neighbours of every node in the system does not change, and the state, s_{qp}, reached at time $t + 2T'$ is the same as the state at time t if we replace p by q and q by p. If the above movement happens continually, then for any even integer i, we reach state s_{pq} and for any odd integer i, we reach state s_{qp} at time $t_i = t + 2T'i$.

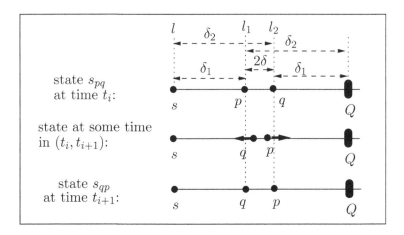

Fig. 5. Proof of Theorem 2

Let t' be a time at which the source s performs a (local) broadcast during its call of (k, α)-Geocast(I, d). We consider the following two cases for $i =$ odd (the proof for $i =$ even is symmetrical):

- There is i such that $t_i = t'$. Because i is odd, the system is in state s_{qp} at time t_i, it reaches state s_{pq} at time t_{i+1}, and $t_{i+1} - t_i = 2T'$. At time t', q is the only neighbour of s. Node q will stop being a neighbour of s at time $t_{i+1} = t_i + 2T' = t' + 2T'$ which happens before time $t' + T$ because $T' < \frac{T}{4}$. Therefore q will not receive the message being broadcast by s at time t'.
- Otherwise, there is i such that $t_i < t' < t_{i+1}$. Because i is odd, the system is in state s_{qp} at time t_i and the only neighbours of s at time t' are p and q. But node q will cease being a neighbour of s at time t_{i+1} and node p will cease being a neighbour of s at time t_{i+2}. The local delivery of the broadcast message completes at time $t' + T$. Node q will not receive the message broadcast at time t' by s because $t' + T > t_i + 2T' = t_{i+1}$. Similarly, p will not receive this message because $t' + T > t_i + 4T' = t_{i+2}$.

In both cases, any node that will become a neighbour of s after time t' will not receive the broadcast message either.

Theorem 3. *No algorithm in (k, α) - Geocast(I, d) can solve the geocast problem if $T' < \frac{\delta T}{\delta_1}$, for a system with unbounded number of nodes even if strong connectivity holds.*

Proof. We describe an execution (illustrated in Figure 6) during which all nodes are placed on a straight line and a node receives a message containing I if and only if it is located on or on the left of the original location, l, of the source $s = p_0$. In this execution, there is a node, q, always located on the right of this position at distance less than d, and hence, never delivers I, violating reliable delivery. Initially, at time $t = t_0$, the nodes are placed on a line on the right of

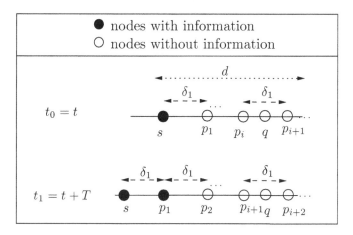

Fig. 6. Proof of Theorem 3

q_0, one every δ_1 distance, with the exception of q. Let p_i be the node located at distance $i\delta_1$ on the right of l at time t_0 (for $i \geq 0$). At time t_0, the only neighbours of p_0 are p_1 and possibly q because, since $\delta_1 \geq \frac{\delta_2}{2}$, all other nodes are at distance at least δ_2 from p_0. Similarly, at time t_0, the only neighbours of p_i (for $i \geq 1$) are p_{i-1}, p_{i+1} and possibly q. All nodes p_i for $(i \geq 0)$ move continually, with speed $\frac{\delta_1}{T}$ towards the left. Note that this is possible because $T' < \frac{T\delta}{\delta_1}$ which implies that $\frac{\delta_1}{T}$ is smaller than the maximum speed (i.e., $\frac{\delta}{T'}$). All other nodes p_i for $i \geq 0$ form a path such that each two consecutive nodes are strong neighbours. Furthermore, q is always a strong neighbour of the first node on its right throughout the execution because their distance is at most equal to δ_1. We conclude that strong connectivity holds.

At time t_0 only p_0 (at location l) knows I. Node p_1 delivers I at time $t_1 = t+T$ when it is at location l. This is because during T rounds, p_1 moves distance $\frac{T\delta_1}{T} = \delta_1$ and it moves towards the left starting from a location at distance δ_1 on the right of l. At time t_1, both p_0 and p_1 will rebroadcast messages with information I. Similarly, node p_i is the rightmost node to deliver I at time $t_i = t + iT$ when at location l. All other nodes that delivered I are on the left of location l at that time. Since q is never a neighbour of any node on or on the left of position l, it will never deliver I.

Theorem 4. *Assuming that $T' > \max\{\frac{1}{4}, \frac{\delta}{\delta_1}\}T$, then if it is possible to solve geocast, it would take more than $(\lfloor \frac{d-\delta_2}{\delta_1 - \frac{T\delta}{T'}} \rfloor + 1)T$ rounds to ensure reliable delivery, using any (k, α)-Geocast(I, d) algorithm for a system with more than $\lfloor \frac{d-\delta_2}{\delta_1 - \frac{T\delta}{T'}} \rfloor$ nodes even if strong connectivity holds.*

Proof. We describe an execution (illustrated in Figure 7) of a geocast algorithm that causes as much rebroadcasting as possible and which cannot guarantee reliable delivery in less than $(\lfloor \frac{d-\delta_2}{\delta_1 - \frac{T\delta}{T'}} \rfloor + 1)T$ rounds. During this execution there

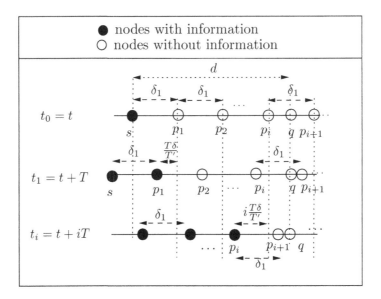

Fig. 7. Proof of Theorem 4

is a node, q, located exactly at distance d from the original location, l, of the source, $s = q_0$. At time t_0, the nodes (other than q) are placed on a line on the right of q_0, one every δ_1 distance. Let p_i be the node at distance $i\delta_1$ on the right of l at time t_0 (for $i \geq 0$). At time t_0, the only neighbours of p_0 are p_1 and possibly q because (since $\delta_1 \geq \frac{\delta_2}{2}$) all other nodes are at distance at least δ_2 from p_0. Similarly, at time t_0, the only neighbours of p_i (for $i \geq 1$) are p_{i-1}, p_{i+1} and possibly q. All nodes p_i for ($i \geq 0$) move continually, with their maximum speed (i.e., $\frac{\delta}{T'}$) towards the left. Strong connectivity holds because, all nodes p_i (for $i \geq 0$, other than q) form a path of strong neighbours and q is a strong neighbour of the first node on its right throughout the execution because their distance is at most equal to δ_1.

At time $t = t_0$ only p_0 knows I. Node p_1 first delivers I at time $t_1 = t + T$ when it is at distance $\delta_1 - \frac{T\delta}{T'}$ on the right of l. Node p_i is the rightmost node to deliver I at time $t_i = t + iT$ when at distance $i\delta_1 - i\frac{T\delta}{T'}$ on the right of l. Node q can only deliver I within T rounds after at least one of its neighbours has delivered I. The earliest this happens is within T rounds after I is delivered by a neighbour of q on its left. This neighbour has to be at distance smaller than δ_2 from q. Hence, reliable delivery cannot happen before time $t_j + T (= t + (j+1)T)$ for the smallest possible j for which $d - (j\delta_1 - j\frac{T\delta}{T'}) < \delta_2$ (i.e., $j > \lfloor \frac{d - \delta_2}{\delta_1 - \frac{T\delta}{T'}} \rfloor$).

Theorem 4 verifies the intuition that the larger the speed of the nodes can be (which is inversely related to T') the more time it would take to solve geocasting.

5   A Geocasting Algorithm

We consider a special case of the mobile ad-hoc model, called *one-dimensional* mobile ad-hoc model, for which the nodes move on a line. Inter-vehicle communication [11] is an application of geocast in this model. For simplicity, the line is straight and horizontal and the locations are real numbers representing points which increase towards the right. We show that $(7, T)$ - Geocast(I, d) works if $T' > 9T$. We attach a counter, $cmsg$, to each message which is set to zero only in the first message broadcast by the source. Each node maintains, in a local counter, the largest counter value it has either received or broadcast. Every time it is ready to broadcast (i.e. its flag is set to 1), it increments its local counter by one and appends this new value to the message. Upon receiving a message with counter $cmsg$, the receiver evaluates $CHECK$ which returns true iff $cmsg \leq 6T(i + 1) + 2T$, where $i = \lfloor \frac{d}{\delta_1 - \frac{6\delta T}{T'}} \rfloor$. Assume that the source $s = q_0$ initiates a call of $(7, T)$ - Geocast(I, d) at time $t = t_0$ from location $l = l_0$. Next, we prove that I propagates from l_0 towards the right of l_0. (For the left of l_0, the proof is symmetrical.) This happens in steps so that within a small period of time, I moves from a node, q_j (at time t_j and location l_j), to another node, q_{j+1} at some large distance away. The proofs of lemmata 2, 3, and 4 used for correctness appear in the full version of the paper [12].

Lemma 2. *If $T' > 9T$ and node q_j delivers I at time t_j when at location l_j then, assuming that CHECK returns true for all nodes throughout $[t_j, t_{j+1}]$, there is a node q_{j+1} which delivers I at time t_{j+1} at location l_{j+1} such that $t_{j+1} - t_j \leq 6T$ and $l_{j+1} - l_j \geq \delta_1 - 6\delta T/T'$.*

Lemma 3. *If $T' > 9T$ and there is a j such that a node p is located in $[l_j, l_{j+1}]$ at some time $t \in [t_j, t_{j+1}]$, then, assuming that CHECK returns true for all nodes throughout $[t_j, t_{j+1}]$, p delivers I by time $t_{j+1} + 2T$.*

Lemma 4. *If a node q stays within distance d from l throughout $[t_0, t_{i+1}]$ for i such that $l + d \in [l_i, l_{i+1}]$, then there is $j \leq i$ such that q is located at some position in $[l_j, l_{j+1}]$ at some time in $[t_j, t_{j+1}]$.*

Theorem 5. *If $T' \geq 9T$, then $(7, T)$ - Geocast(I, d) ensures reliable delivery for $C \leq 6T(i + 1) + 2T$ rounds, where $i = \lfloor \frac{d}{\delta_1 - \frac{6\delta T}{T'}} \rfloor$.*

Proof. During $[t, t + C]$, any node's $CHECK$=true because if geocast starts at time t, then (by induction on time) during $[t, t + C]$, all messages broadcast or received have counters at most equal to C. Then, we show that $C \leq 6T(i + 1) + 2T$, where $i = \lfloor \frac{d}{\delta_1 - \frac{6\delta T}{T'}} \rfloor$. First, we calculate the maximum value that i could take in any execution such that $l_i \leq l + d$ (i.e., $(l + d) \in [l_i, l_{i+1}]$). Next, we show that it suffices that I gets delivered and rebroadcast by a node at location l_{i+1}. From Lemma 2, $l_i - l \geq i(\delta_1 - 6\delta T/T')$. Then $i \leq \lfloor \frac{l_i - l}{\delta_1 - \frac{6\delta T}{T'}} \rfloor$ and because $l_i - l \leq d$, $i \leq \lfloor \frac{d}{\delta_1 - \frac{6\delta T}{T'}} \rfloor$. It remains to calculate C. All nodes that remain within distance d from $l(= l_0)$ throughout $[t, t + C]$, also remain within that distance throughout $[t_0, t_{i+1}]$, (recall that $t = t_0$). If p remains in this area throughout $[t_0, t_{i+1}]$ then from Lemma 4, there is a j such that p is located at some position in $[l_j, l_{j+1}]$ at some time in $[t_j, t_{j+1}]$ for $j \leq i$ and from Lemma 3, p delivers I by time $t_{j+1} + 2T$. Therefore, since $j \leq i$, all nodes within distance d from l deliver I by time $t_{i+1} + 2T = t + C$. By Lemma 2, $t_{i+1} - t \leq 6T(i+1)$ and $C \leq 6T(\lfloor \frac{d}{\delta_1 - \frac{6\delta T}{T'}} \rfloor + 1) + 2T$.

Theorem 6. *If $T' \geq 9T$ then $(7, T)$ - Geocast(I, d) ensures termination for $C' = (6T(i+1) + 2T + 1)T + 8T$ rounds, where $i = \lfloor \frac{d}{\delta_1 - \frac{6\delta T}{T'}} \rfloor$.*

Proof. Every message received causes rebroadcasting of I in a message with counter at least incremented by one and this will happen at least once every T rounds (for at least 7 times). Termination happens within $7T$ rounds from the time after which any message received has counter larger than $6T(i+1) + 2T$, where $i = \lfloor \frac{d}{\delta_1 - \frac{6\delta T}{T'}} \rfloor$. This happens within $(6T(i+1) + 2T + 1)T + T$ rounds, because all messages broadcast after time $(6T(i+1) + 2T + 1)T$ have counters at least equal to $6T(i+1) + 2T + 1$ and all such messages are received within at most another T rounds. Therefore, $C' = (6T(\lfloor \frac{d}{\delta_1 - \frac{6\delta T}{T'}} \rfloor + 1) + 2T + 1)T + 8T$ rounds.

Theorem 7. *If $T' \geq 9T$ then $(7, T)$ - Geocast(I, d) ensures integrity.*

Proof. A broadcast message will be received at least after one round during which any node can traverse distance at most $\frac{\delta}{T'}$. Therefore, if a node broadcasts a message from location l' at time t', then its neighbours receive it the earliest at time $t' + 1$, when at distance less than $\delta_2 + \frac{\delta}{T'}$ away from l'. Then, if the source starts $(7, T)$ - Geocast(I, d) at time t from location l, at time $t + m$, the furthest node that delivers I is at distance less than $m(\delta_2 + \frac{\delta}{T'})$ away from l. By Theorem 6, after time $t + C'$, no node broadcasts messages with information I. Therefore, no node delivers I after time $t + C' + T$. But at time $t + C' + T$, all nodes that have delivered I are within distance less than $(C' + T)(\delta_2 + \frac{\delta}{T'})$ from l. Therefore, if a node remains further than $d' = (C' + T)(\delta_2 + \frac{\delta}{T'})$ from l, it will never deliver I.

6   Related Work

Geocast was introduced by Navas et al. [2,1]. Geocast algorithms for mobile ad-hoc networks [3,7,5,4], unlike our deterministic solution, only provide probabilistic guarantees. This may not suffice. For example, Dolev et al. [6] need deterministic geocast to implement atomic memory. Deterministic solutions are given for multicast [13,14,15] and broadcast [8] for mobile ad-hoc networks. Both solutions in [13,14] consider a finite and fixed number of mobile nodes arranged somehow in logical or physical structures. They divide the nodes into groups each of which has a special node which coordinates message propagation and collects acknowledgments. Moreover, they make the following stronger than necessary assumption: they require that the network topology stabilizes for periods long enough to ensure delivery. Finally, simulation results [16] show that the approach proposed in [13] does not work if nodes move fast. Bounds that allow the algorithms to work correctly are not presented. Chandra et al. [15] provide a broadcasting algorithm and show by experiments that either all or none of the nodes get the message with high probability. Mohsin et al. [8] implement (deterministic) broadcast for a synchronous mobile ad-hoc network with restricted movement patterns. In particular, nodes move on top of a grid such that at the beginning of each round nodes are located at grid points. They assume that all nodes move at the same constant speed and direction of movement cannot change within a round. Finally, nodes need to inform their neighbours about their future moving pattern for short future time periods.

7   Conclusion and Future Work

To the best of our knowledge, this is the first time in which bounds are formally defined on the speed of node movement which make it possible to solve geocasting and relate its time complexity to the speed. This formally verifies that the faster nodes move, the most costly it would be to solve geocasting. Our upper bounds and lower bounds do not match neither for the cost of geocast, nor for the bounds on speed of movement. Although the gap is not large, it would have theoretical interest to match these bounds. We proved our results for the case where $\delta_1 \geq \frac{\delta_2}{2}$. It is unknown whether our lower bounds still hold for $\delta_1 < \frac{\delta_2}{2}$. Another future direction would be to design a geocast algorithm that works for a two-dimensional model including failures.

References

1. Imielinski, T., Navas, J.C.: Gps-based geographic addressing, routing, and resource discovery. Communication of the ACM 42(4), 86–92 (1999)
2. Navas, J.C., Imielinski, T.: Geocast: geographic addressing and routing. In: Proceedings of the 3rd Annual ACM/IEEE International Conference on Mobile Computing and Networking (MobiCom), pp. 66–76. ACM Press, New York (1997)
3. Ko, Y., Vaidya, N.H.: Geotora: a protocol for geocasting in mobile ad hoc networks. In: Proceedings of the 8th International Conference on Network Protocols (ICNP), p. 240. IEEE Computer Society Press, Los Alamitos (2000)
4. Ko, Y., Vaidya, N.H.: Flooding-based geocasting protocols for mobile ad hoc networks. Mobile Network and Application 7(6), 471–480 (2002)
5. Liao, W., Tseng, Y., Lo, K., Sheu, J.: Geogrid: A geocasting protocol for mobile ad hoc networks based on grid. Journal of Internet Technology 1(2), 23–32 (2001)
6. Dolev, S., Gilbert, S., Lynch, N., Shvartsman, A., Welch, J.: Geoquorum: Implementing atomic memory in ad hoc networks. In: Proceedings of the 17th International Conference on Principles of DIStributed Computing (DISC), pp. 306–320 (2003)
7. Boleng, J., Camp, T., Tolety, V.: Mesh-based geocast routing protocols in an ad hoc network. In: Proceedings of the 15th International Parallel & Distributed Processing Symposium (IPDPS), pp. 184–193 (April 2001)

8. Mohsin, M., Cavin, D., Sasson, Y., Prakash, R., Schiper, A.: Reliable broadcast in wireless mobile ad hoc networks. In: Proceedings of the 39th Hawaii International Conference on System Sciences (HICSS), p. 233.1. IEEE Computer Society Press, Los Alamitos (2006)
9. Koo, C., Bhandari, V., Katz, J., Vaidya, N.H.: Reliable broadcast in radio networks: the bounded collision case. In: Proceedings of the 25th Annual ACM Symposium on Principles of Distributed Computing (PODC), pp. 258–264. ACM Press, New York (2006)
10. Ellen, F.: End to end communication. In: Proceedings of the 2nd International Conference On Principles Of Distributed Systems (OPODIS), Hermes, pp. 37–44 (1998)
11. Benslimane, A.: Optimized dissemination of alarm messages in vehicular ad-hoc networks (vanet). In: Proceedings of the 7th IEEE International Conference on High Speed Networks and Multimedia Communications (HSNMC), pp. 655–666 (2004)
12. Baldoni, R., Ioannidou, K., Milani, A.: Mobility versus the cost of geocasting in mobile ad-hoc networks. Technical report, 3/07 MIDLAB - Universit di Roma "La Sapienza" (2007)
13. Pagani, E., Rossi, G.P.: Reliable broadcast in mobile multihop packet networks. In: Proceedings of the 3rd Annual ACM/IEEE International Conference on Mobile Computing and Networking (MobiCom), pp. 34–42. ACM Press, New York (1997)
14. Gupta, S.K.S., Srimani, P.K.: An adaptive protocol for reliable multicast in mobile multi-hop radio networks. In: Proceedings of the 2nd Workshop on Mobile Computing Systems and Applications (WMCSA), p. 111. IEEE Computer Society Press, Los Alamitos (1999)
15. Chandra, R., Ramasubramanian, V., Birman, K.P.: Anonymous gossip: Improving multicast reliability in mobile ad-hoc networks. In: Proceedings of the 21st International Conference on Distributed Computing Systems (ICDCS), pp. 275–283. IEEE Computer Society Press, Los Alamitos (2001)
16. Pagani, E., Rossi, G.P.: Providing reliable and fault tolerant broadcast delivery in mobile ad-hoc networks. Mobile Networks and Applications 4(3), 175–192 (1999)

Self-stabilizing Counting in Mobile Sensor Networks with a Base Station

Joffroy Beauquier, Julien Clement, Stephane Messika, Laurent Rosaz, and Brigitte Rozoy

Univ. Paris Sud, LRI, UMR 8623, Orsay, F-91405, CNRS, Orsay, F-91405

Abstract. Distributed computing must adapt its techniques to networks of mobile agents. Indeed, we are facing new problems like the small size of memory and the lack of computational power. In this paper, we extend the results of Angluin et al (see [4,3,2,1]) by finding self-stabilizing algorithms to count the number of agents in the network. We focus on two different models of communication, with a fixed base station or with pairwise interactions. In both models we decide if there exist algorithms (probabilistic, deterministic, with k-fair adversary) to solve the self-stabilizing counting problem.

1 Introduction

Habitat and environmental monitoring represents a class of sensor network applications with enormous potential benefits both for scientific communities and for society as a whole. The intimate connection with its immediate physical environment allows each sensor to provide localized measurements and detailed information that is hard to obtain through traditional instrumentation. Many environmental projects use sensor networks.

The SIVAM project in Amazonia is related to meteorological predictions, sensors are placed in glacial areas for measuring the impact of the climate evolution, (see [9]), use of sensors is considered in Mars exploration (see [10]) or for detecting the effect of the wind or of an earthquake on a building (see [11]).

A sensor network has been deployed on Great Duck Island (see [8]) for studying the behavior of Leachs Storm Petrels. Seabird colonies are notorious for the sensibility to human disturbance and sensor networks represent a significant advance over traditional methods of monitoring. In [1], Angluin et al. introduced the model of population protocols in connection with distributed algorithms for mobile sensor networks. A sensor is a package containing power supply, processor, memory and wireless communication capacity. Some physical constraints involve limitations of computing or storage capacity and communication. In particular, two sensors have to be close enough to be able to communicate. A particular static entity, the base station, is provided with more computing resources.

The codes in the base station and in the sensors define what happens when two close sensors communicate and how they communicate with the base station. An important assumption made in this model is that the interactions between

A. Pelc (Ed.): DISC 2007, LNCS 4731, pp. 63–76, 2007.

the sensors themselves and between the sensors and the base station are not controlled. Also, a hypothesis of fairness states that in an infinite computation the numbers of interactions between two given sensors or between a particular sensor and the base station are infinite. Eventually the result of the computation is stored at the base station and does not change any more.

This model takes into account the inherent power limitation of the real sensors and also the fact that they can be attached to unpredictably moving supports. For being still more realistic the model should consider the possibility for the sensors to endure failures. Temperature variations, rain, frost, storm, etc. have consequently, in the real world, that some sensors are crashed and that some others are still operating, but with corrupted data.

Most of population protocols do not consider the possibility of failures. The aim of this paper is to perform computation in mobile sensor networks subject to some type of failures. The framework of self-stabilization is particularly well adapted for dealing with such conditions. A self-stabilizing system, after some memory corruptions hit some processors, regains its consistency by itself, meaning that first, (convergence) it reaches a correct global configuration in a finite number of steps and second, (correction) from then its behavior is correct until the next corruption. It is important to note that this model assumes that the code is immutable, e.g, stored in a ROM and then cannot be corrupted. Traditionally self-stabilization assumes that failures are not too frequent (for giving enough time to the system for recovery) and thus the effect of a single global failure is considered. That is equivalent to consider that the system may be started in any possible global configuration. Note that the issue of combining population protocols with self stabilization has been addressed for ring networks in [4] and in a different framework in [6].

In the present work we make the assumption that, if the input variables can be corrupted, as any other variable, first they do not change during the time of the computation and second they are regularly read by the sensor. Then eventually a sensor deals with its correct input values.

In this paper we consider the very basic problem of computing the number of (not crashed) sensors in the system, all sensors being identical (same code, no identifiers), when their variables are arbitrary initialized (but the input value of each sensor is 1). This problem is fundamental, first because the ability of counting makes easier the solution of other problems (many distributed algorithms assume that the size of the network is known in advance) and second because if counting is feasible, sum, difference and test to 0 are too. In practice, one might want to count specific sensors, for example those carried by sick petrels.

We present a study of this problem, under slightly different models. The variations concern the determinism or the randomization of the population protocols. In a sub model, the sensors only communicate with the base station and in another they communicate both between each other and with the base station. According to the different cases, we obtain solutions or prove impossibility results.

2   Motivation and Modelization

Imagine the following scenario : A group of birds (petrels) evolves on an island, carrying on their body a small sensor. Whenever a petrel is close enough to the base station, its sensor interacts with the base station, which can read the value of the sensor, compute, and then write in the petrel sensor memory.

Depending on the hypothesis, the sensors may or may not interact with each other when two petrels approach close enough.

2.1   Mobile Sensor Networks with a Base Station

A mobile sensor network is composed of an base station, and of n undistinguishable mobile sensors (In the sequel we will use the term of petrel, in relation with our motivation example, instead of sensor.)

The network configuration considers the memory content of the base station, a, and the petrels' state, p_i. We denote the network configuration by $(a, p_1, ..., p_n)$ where p_i is the state of the ith petrel. There are two kinds of **events**:

• the meeting of petrel number i with the base station. After that meeting, p_i is changed, according to the protocol, to p'_i, and a to a', depending on (a, p_i) (Note that the transition is independent of i, because petrels are not distinguishable).
• the meeting of petrel number i with petrel number j. After that meeting, p_i and p_j are changed to p'_i and p'_j, depending on (p_i, p_j) (here again, independently of (i, j)).

In the Sensors-To-base-station-Only model (TB for short), only the first kind of event is possible. i.e. the sensors do not interact with each other.
In the petrels-To-Base-station-and-To-Petrels model (TBTP for short), both events are possible: sensors do interact with each other. For deterministic protocols, the last model can be divided into two sub-models, the symmetric (STBTP), resp. the asymmetric one (ATBTP): When two petrels meet, if their state is the same, they have to, resp. they don't have to, change to the SAME state. A probabilistic algorithm can use coin flips and perform an election between meeting petrels to simulate the Asymmetric TBTP model.

2.2   The Problem

The number of petrels is unknown from the base station, which aims at counting them.

We want that, eventually, the *PetrelNumber* variable in the base station is and remains equal to n.

In probabilistic algorithms (we consider non-oblivious daemons, that is, they can decide what is the next event depending on previous results of coin flips), we require that this property is obtained with probability 1.

More generally, our algorithms must be self-stabilizing (see [7]), i.e., whatever the initial configuration (but we initialize the base station), the base station must give the exact number of petrels in the network (with probability 1, for probabilistic algorithms) within a finite number of steps. This requirement does not allow us to make any assumption on the initial configuration (except for the base station), or to reset the value of the sensors.

2.3   Executions, Daemons, Fairness, Rounds

Definition 1 (Execution). *An execution is an infinite sequence* $(C_j)_{j \in \mathbb{N}}$ *(where* $\mathbb{N}$ *denotes the set of non-negative integers) of configurations and an infinite sequence* $(e_j)_{j \in \mathbb{N} \setminus \{0\}}$ *of events such that* C_{j+1} *is obtained after* e_j *occurs on* C_j.

The daemon is the imaginary adversary that chooses the initial configuration and that schedules the possible actions at every step. To solve the problem, the daemon must be fair:

Definition 2 (Fairness). *An execution is fair if every petrel communicates with the base station infinitely often, and, in the TBTP model, if every two petrels communicate with each other infinitely often. (Note that this fairness is weaker than the one used by Angluin et al., which says that a configuration that is reachable infinitely often is eventually reached)*

•*A daemon for a deterministic protocol is fair if every execution is fair.*
•*A daemon for a probabilistic protocol is strongly fair if every execution is fair and it is weakly fair if the measure of the set of the fair executions is one. The distinction between weak and strong fairness is of little importance in this paper.*

Definition 3 (k-fairness). *Let* k *be an integer. An execution is k-fair, if every petrel communicates with the base station at least once in every* k *consecutive events, and, in the TBTP model, if every two petrels communicate with each other in every* k *consecutive events.*
   A daemon is k-fair if the execution is k-fair.
   In this paper when the daemon is k-fair, the value of k *is not assumed to be known by the base station.*

Throughout the paper, the daemon is assumed to be fair, unless it is explicitly assumed to be k-fair.

Definition 4 (Oblivious). *For probabilistic algorithms, a daemon is non-oblivious if the decision of what is the next event can depend on the result of previous coin flips. An oblivious daemon could be able to decide at the start of the execution what the whole sequence of events will be.*

Definition 5 (Rounds). *A round is a sequence of consecutive events, during which every petrel meets the base station at least once, and in the TBTP model, every two petrels meet each other.*
   The first round is the shortest round starting from initial configuration, the second round is the shortest round starting from the end of the first round, and so on.

2.4   Initial Conditions

Throughout the paper, we assume that the petrels are arbitrarily initialized, but that an initial value can be chosen for the base station. This assumption is justified if one thinks of mobile sensors networks as the petrel population and the base station. The existence of a base station and the possibility to initialize it are the main differences between our model and classical sensor networks.

Note that if both the petrels and the base station can be initialized , then the problem is obvious, with only one bit per petrel sensor. Note also that if one can initialize neither the petrels nor the base station, then there is no protocol to count the petrels (unless the daemon is k-fair, see remark 1 in Sec. 3).

Indeed, assume on the contrary that there is such a protocol. Let the daemon repeat the following: it waits till every petrel has met the base station and *Petrel Number* = n (this will eventually happen), then it holds back one particular petrel. When *PetrelNumber* is $n - 1$ (this will eventually happen since the configuration is the same as if there were n petrels), the daemon frees the last petrel.

With such a daemon, *PetrelNumber* will never stabilize so the protocol fails. If the protocol is deterministic, the daemon is fair, if the protocol is probabilistic, it is weakly fair.

It can also be proved that there does not exist any algorithm under a strongly-fair daemon *PetrelNumber* will stabilize with probability 0 although the daemon is strongly-fair.

2.5 Memories

We will not make limitation on the memory size of the base station. (Note: The codes will often use "infinite" arrays (indexed by integers), but only a finite number of register will contain non-0 values. Of course, in practice, arrays will have to be replaced by data structures to keep only the non-0 registers.)

On the other hand, we will make more or less strong assumptions on the memory size of the petrel sensors:

Definition 6 (Size of the petrel sensor memories). *The memory is* **infinite** *if it is unlimited. In particular, it can carry integers as large as needed, which can drift, that is, which can tend to infinity as times passes by. (this has a practical application only if the drift is slow and there are enough bits in the sensors to carry "large"integers). The memory is* **bounded** *if an upper-bound P on the number of petrels is known, and if the number of different possible states of the memory is* $\alpha(P)$ *for some function* α. *The protocol may use the knowledge of P. The memory is* **finite** *if the number of different possible states of the memory is a constant* α.

3 The Petrels-To-Base-Station-Only Model (TB)

In this section, the sensors can only communicate with the base station. People acquainted with classical sensor networks may question the point of such a model. There are two justifications for looking for solutions in that model :

1. Sensors are meant to be small. To implement that model, sensors only need to carry a device so that the base station can read and write in their memories. All the code can be implemented in the base station.

2. The decision to run such algorithms can be made by just changing the code in the base station. This is doable even if the sensors are already away. For example, if an observation made of the petrels, given you the idea to count something new and not forecast, you can use a TB algorithm.

3.1 With Infinite Memory

In this subsection, we assume that the petrel sensors (and the base station) have an infinite memory. In this case, there exist self-stabilizing deterministic algorithms to solve the problem.

The way the first algorithm works is simple. The drift of integers is fast, and convergence is obtained after two rounds. The second one is a little tricky. The drift is slow, but it converges in about P (i.e. the number of petrels) rounds.

```
variables
        [each petrel] number :integer
        [base station] R : array[integers] of booleans, initialized at 0
        [base station] PetrelNumber to maintain as cardinal{i | R[i]=1}
        [base station] LargestNumber : integer initialized at 0
When a petrel p approaches the base station :
        if R[number_p] = 1 then R[number_p] <- 0
        number_p <- LargestNumber
        R[LargestNumber] <- 1
        LargestNumber ++
```

Algorithm 1. For Unbounded Memory

3.2 With Finite or Bounded Memory

Under a fair daemon

In this paragraph we show that if the daemon only respects fairness, there neither exists a deterministic algorithm nor a probabilistic algorithm making it possible for the base station to count the number of sensors present.

Proposition 1. *The daemon is supposed to be fair. If the sensors have a finite memory then, there is no deterministic algorithm solving the counting problem.*

Proof. The idea of this proof is to exhibit two executions resulting from two different initial configurations that will appear to be identical for the base station. The proof is analog to the one of proposition 10, but details are in the full version [5].

Then, it becomes natural to try to build a probabilistic algorithm in order to break the symmetry. Indeed, the daemon has no control on the random, thus we can hope to beat him. Unfortunately, even in this case, there is no solution:

Proposition 2. *Suppose that the daemon is strongly fair and non-oblivious. If the sensors have a finite memory, then there does not exist any probabilistic algorithm solving the counting problem*

```
variables
        [each petrel] number :integer
        [base station] R : array[integers] of booleans, initialized at 0
        [base station] PetrelNumber to maintain as sum{R[i]}
When a petrel p approaches the base station :
        if R[number_p] > 1 then R[number_p] --
        number_p ++
        R[number_p] ++
```

Algorithm 2. For Unbounded Memory

Proof. Let us consider a daemon D with n sensors $(p_1, \ldots, p_n)$ initialized in $I = (x_1, x_2, \ldots, x_n)$.

The sensors' memory being finite, for every petrel p, in particular for the last one, there is a state s and a positive real number η such as :

$$\mathbb{P}\{p \text{ goes infinitely often in } s\} \geq \eta$$

In order to "confuse" the base station, let the daemon D' proceeds as follow with $n + 1$ sensors $(p_1, \ldots, p_n, p_{n+1})$: it puts them in the initial configuration $I = (x_1, x_2, \ldots, x_n, s)$.

There is an integer k_1 such that with D, with probability at least $(1 - \varepsilon)$, if p_n gets in state s infinitely often, then it gets once in state s during the k_1 next events and every sensor has met the base station at least once. The daemon D' holds back the sensor p_{n+1} and for at most k_1 events, lets evolve the other n's as would do daemon D until p_n gets in state s. If k_1 events have been done without p_n getting in state s then D' has lost (note that the daemon may lose either because s does not appear infintely often with D or because the first occurrence of s arrives too late with D). Otherwise D' frees p_{n+1} and holds p_n.

The daemon D' resumes simulating D with p_{n+1} instead of p_n and as in the first step, but with k_1 replaced by k_2 such that the probability is now at least $(1 - \frac{\varepsilon}{2})$ instead of $(1 - \varepsilon)$. The daemon keeps on with that technique, with k_l for the lth step so that the probability is at least $(1 - \frac{\varepsilon}{2^{l-1}})$.

Therefore, D' wins with probability $\eta \prod_{i=0}^{l} (1 - \frac{\varepsilon}{2^i}) > 0$.

In this case, from the point of view of the base station, the execution is indistinguishable from D, so *PetrelNumber* is eventually equal to n which is wrong. So, the base station has a non null probability to lose.

Note that the proofs work with no assumption on n (the number of petrels) which may be equal to 1. Thus the impossibility is proved both for finite and bounded memories.

3.3   A k-Fair Daemon

Under the assumption of fairness, there exists neither a deterministic algorithm nor a probabilistic algorithm. Thus, we have to reduce the capacities of the daemon. If we assume the daemon is k-fair, we will get both deterministic and probabilistic solutions.

Deterministic algorithm
The algorithm 3 is given below.

```
variables
        [each petrel] bit : boolean
        [base station] i, cpt, PetrelNumber : integers
        [base station] bit_A : boolean, initialized at 0
The base station does :
For i from 0 to infinity do
        cpt <- 0
        do 2^i times :
            wait till a petrel p approaches
            if bit_p = bit_A then cpt ++
                                bit_p <- not(bit_p)
        PetrelNumber <- cpt
        bit_A <- not(bit_A)
```

Algorithm 3. Deterministic, k-fair daemon

The convergence time is less than $8k$. The reader may find details in the full version [5]

Remark 1. This algorithm works even if the base station variables are not initialized but a large initial value of i induces a large convergence time.

This deterministic algorithm requires an infinite memory of the base station, due to the drift of 2^i (and of i). This can be avoided by the following probabilistic algorithm.

Probabilistic algorithm, k-fair daemon or oblivious daemon
The algorithm is as follows:

```
variables
        [each petrel] number, color : integer
        [base station] R : array[integers] of [0...2]
                    /* 0 stands for empty, others for colors */
                    initialized at empty
        [base station] PetrelNumber to maintain as card{j | R[j] is non empty}
When a petrel p approaches the base station :
        h <- the minimum integer such that R[h] = empty
        if R[number_p] <> color_P /* including if one of them is 0 */
        then    number_p <- h
        else if h<number_p
            then R[number_p]<-0
                number_p<-h
        color_p <- random{1..2}
        R[number_p] <- color_p
```

Algorithm 4. Probabilistic, k-fair daemon

The proof of convergence is in the full version [5] We obtain a worse time of convergence (possibly exponential) than with the deterministic algorithm but we observe that the base station requires a finite memory.

4 The Petrels-To-Base-Station-And-To-Petrels Model (TBTP)

We recall that P is an upper bound of the number of petrels and $\alpha(P)$ is the number of the different possible states of the memory. In a first section we introduce deterministic algorithms solving the counting problem. Then, in a second part, we get interested in the lowest value $\alpha(P)$ may get.

4.1 Bounded Memory, Algorithms

Proposition 3. *There are deterministic solutions, with $\alpha(P) \geq P$, to the counting problem.*

We are going to exhibit different algorithms. The two first ones concern the ATBTP model and the third one the STBTP model. It is interesting to note that we need more memory in the STBTP model. The question remains open to know what is the minimal memory required in the symmetric case, and if it really needs to be larger than in the asymmetric case. Explanations of the algorithms are in the full version [5]

The ATBTP Model. We propose two algorithms :

- The first one with $\alpha(P) = P + 1$, converges in three rounds.
- The second one with $\alpha(P) = P$, converges in $P + 1$ rounds.

```
variables
        [each petrel] number :integer in [0..P]
        [base station] T : array [1..P] of boolean,
                       initialized at 0 everywhere
        [base station] PetrelNumber to maintain as cardinal{i | T[i]=1 }
When a petrel p approaches the base station :
        if number_p = 0
        then    number_p <- an integer y such that T[y]=0
                T[number_p] <- 1
        else T[number_p] <- 1
When two petrels meet :
        If their numbers are the same
        then the number of one petrel becomes 0
```

Algorithm 5. Deterministic asymmetric algorithm with $\alpha(P) = P + 1$

```
variables
        [each petrel]  number :integer in [1..P]
        [base station] T : array [1..P] of boolean,
                       initialized at 0 everywhere
        [base station] PetrelNumber to maintain as cardinal{i | T[i]=1 }
When a petrel p approaches the base station :
        T[number_p] <- 1
When two petrels meet :
        If their numbers are the same integer x
        then the number of one petrel becomes x+1 mod P
```

Algorithm 6. Deterministic asymmetric algorithm with $\alpha(P) = P$

The STBTP Model. The following symmetric algorithm with $\alpha(P) = 4P$ converges in three rounds:

```
variables
        [each petrel] number :integer in [1..2P]
        [each petrel] Intention : (Keep,GiveUp)
        [base station] T array [1..2P] of (Free,Taken,GivenUp),
                       initialized at Free everywhere
        [base station] PetrelNumber to maintain as cardinal{i | T[i]=Taken }
When a petrel p approaches the base station :
        Depending on Intention_p :
        Keep :   T[number_p] <- Taken  /* even if T[number_p] was GivenUp */
        GiveUp : T[number_p] <- GivenUp
                 number_p <- a y such that T[y] = Free
                 T[number_p] <- Taken
                 Intention_p <- Keep
When two petrels meet :
        If     their numbers are the same integer x
            and their both intentions are Keep
        Then their both intentions change to GiveUp
```

Algorithm 7. Deterministic symmetric algorithm with $\alpha(P) = 4P$

4.2   Bounded Memory, Minimum Value for $\alpha(P)$

We prove in this section there does not exist asymmetric algorithms with $\alpha(P) \leq P - 1$.

The non-existence of algorithms with $\alpha(P) \leq P - 2$ is much easier to prove than the non-existence of algorithms with $\alpha(P) = P - 1$. So let us start with the easier case:

Proposition 4. *There is no deterministic solution, with $\alpha(P) \leq P - 2$, to the counting problem.*

Proof. Assume that there is a solution. Consider an execution E with $P - 1$ sensors $(p_1, \ldots, p_{P-1})$ initialized in the states $(x_1, \ldots, x_{P-1})$. There is a state y

and two petrels p and p' such that infinitely often, p and p' will be simultaneously in state y. Now, as a daemon, perform the following execution E' with P sensors:

Initialize them in $(x_1, \ldots, x_{P-1}, y)$, then repeat the following:

- Hold back petrel p_P and proceed as in E until every petrel but p_P has met each other petrel but p_P, and p and p' are in state y.
- Free p_P, hold back p, proceed as in E with p_P instead of p until p_P has met every other petrel (but p), and p_P and p' are again in state y.
- Free p, hold back p', proceed as in E with p_P instead of p' until p_P has met p, and p_P and p are again in state y.

The daemon is fair, and from the point of view of the base station, E and E' are identical, thus in E', $PetrelNumber$ will stabilize to $P - 1$, as in E, which is a wrong result. This is a contradiction.

We are now going to look to the case where $\alpha(P) = P - 1$.

Proposition 5. *There is no deterministic solution with, $\alpha(P) = P - 1$, to the counting problem.*

Proof. Assume on the opposite that there is such a solution.

Consider an execution E with $P - 1$ sensors $(p_1, \ldots, p_{P-1})$ initialized in the states $(x_1, \ldots, x_{P-1})$.

If there is a state y and two petrels p and p' such that infinitely often, p and p' are simultaneously in state y, then one can conclude as in the previous proof, so we can assume from now on it is not the case.

This implies that eventually, say from instant T, all petrels have distinct states.

This means first, that, in E, from T, the base station never changes the state of a petrel it meets. Second, the rule when two petrels with different states meet must be that they keep their current state (or exchange them, which is of little effect). Thus the protocol rules for meeting petrels are such that the states can change only if the meeting petrels are in the SAME state.

Lemma 1. *There is a state y and a finite piece of execution E_{KL} with P petrels, starting with two petrels in state y and one petrel in each other state, finishing in the same configuration, during which petrels do not meet the base station, and whose first event is the meeting of the two petrels in state y.*

The end of the proof is analog to the proof of proposition 10, but the reader may find the entire proof in the full version [5]

It remains now to prove the key lemma (the detailled proof is in the full version [5]):

Let us introduce two kinds of vectors, the first one for representing the states of all the sensors at a given time, the second one to represent the effect of the meeting of petrels.

Definition 7. *The vector of configuration V_C of configuration C is the vector in $\mathbb{N}^{P-1}$ whose i^{th} coordinate is the number of sensors in the ith state s_i.*

For each state x, let us define $y(x)$ and $z(x)$ to be the states that two petrels' sensors get when they meet while both in state x.

Definition 8. *The vector of variation V_x of state x is $\mathbb{1}_{y(x)} + \mathbb{1}_{z(x)} - 2\mathbb{1}_x$.*

The ith coordinate of V_x represents the variation of the number of sensors in state s_i when two petrels in state x meet, and indeed, if, from a configuration represented by V, two petrels in state x meet, the new configuration is represented by $V + V_x$.

We claim first that there is a non-null linear combination of the vectors of variations, with non-negative integer coefficients, which is null.

To prove the claim, start with P petrels and repeat making two petrels in the same state meet each other (you will always find two such petrels). The vectors of configuration you will get will stay in $Y = \{(q_j)_{1 \le j < P} | q_j \in \mathbb{N}, \sum_j q_j = P\}$ which is finite. So if you let long enough petrels with same state meet, you will encounter twice the same configuration. The set of meetings between the two appearances of that configuration gives you the wanted combination.

More formally: define $(V_{y,i})_{0 \le i} \in Y^{\mathbb{N}}$ and $(V_{w,i})_{1 \le i} \in Z^{\mathbb{N}}$ by induction as follows:
$V_{y,0} = (2, 1, 1, 1, \ldots, 1)$.

Once $V_{y,i}$ is defined, find a coefficient x of $V_{y,i}$ which is at least 2 (there is such a coefficient), then define $V_{y,i+1} = V_{y,i} + V_x$ and $V_{w,i+1} = V_x$. It is easy to check that $V_{y,i+1}$ will be in Y.

Since Y is finite, there are two integers i_1 and i_2, with $0 \le i_1 < i_2 \le card(Y)$ such that $V_{y,i_1} = V_{y,i_2}$. Then $\sum_{i_1 < i \le i_2} V_{w,i}$ fulfills the requirement since $V_{y,i_2} = V_{y,i_1} + \sum_{i_1 < i \le i_2} V_{w,i}$.

That first claim is proved. Let $\sum_x \beta_x V_x$ be such a combination (So, $\forall x, \beta_x \in \mathbb{N}$, $\exists x, \beta_x > 0$, and $\sum_x \beta_x V_x = (0, 0, \ldots, 0)$). For the sake of simplicity, let us assume that our combination minimizes $\sum_x \beta_x$.

Let H be the multi set of vectors of variations where each V_x appears β_x times.

Our second claim is that there is an index y and an ordering $(h_1, h_2, \ldots, h_{card(H)})$ of the elements in H, such that $h_1 = V_y$, and for every $i \in [1, card(H)]$, the $\delta(i)^{th}$ coordinate of $Z_i = (1, 1, \ldots, 1) + \mathbb{1}_y + \sum_{j<i} h_j$ is 2 or more, and no coordinate of Z_i is negative (where $delta(i)$ is the index such that $h(i) = V_{\delta(i)}$).

Proof of the second claim
Let y be an index such that $\beta_y > 0$.

We build the h_i by induction on i : Let $h_1 = V_y$

Assume the h_j's have been built up to $j = i - 1$, let us build h_i, for some $i \in [2, card(H)]$:

Let $Z_i = (1, 1, \ldots, 1) + \mathbb{1}_y + \sum_{j<i} h_j$. Since it is in Y, there is an index x such that $Z_i|_x \ge 2$ (where $M|_v$ denotes the vth coordinate of M). We may assume that $x \ne y$ or $(x = y$ and $Z_i|_x \ge 3)$ (indeed, otherwise, $Z_i = (1, 1, \ldots, 1) + \mathbb{1}_y$, which implies that $\sum_{j<i} h_j = 0$, which contradicts the minimality of $\sum_x \beta_x$ in our combination).

Thus $\sum_{j<i} h_j|_x > 0$, but since $\sum_{h \in H} h|_x = 0$, it means that there is an element in H, not taken yet, whose x^{th} coordinate is negative. This element is V_x for it is the only vector of variations whose x^{th} may be negative. Let $h_i = V_x$. The built sequence $(h_1, h_2, ..., h_{card(H)})$ satisfies the requirement, so the second claim is proved.

The E_{KL} execution is the following:
Start with P petrels, two of them in state y, and one of them in each other state. For i from 1 to $card(H)$, make two petrels in state x_i meet, where x_i is the state such that $V_{x_i} = h_i$ (there are two such petrels thanks to the propriety on Z_i is the second claim)   □

Note on the key lemma:
The upper-bound on the length of E_{KL} given by the proof is $card\{\{(q_j)_{1 \leq j < P} | q_j \in N, \sum_j q_j = P\}$ which is exponential in P. One can wonder if it has to be large, or if there is such an execution E_{KL} of size polynomial in P. The answer is that it might be indeed exponential. Consider the set of states $[0, P-1]$. Take $y = 0$ (that is, start, with two petrels in state 0, and one in each state $i \in [1, P-1]$), and let the protocol be that when two petrels in state i meet, one of them gets in state 0, the other one gets in state $(i+1) \bmod P$.

5   Resume

The TB model

model \ memory	Finite	Bounded	Bounded,k-fair daemon	Unbounded
deterministic	impossible	impossible	Algorithm 3	Algorithm 1-2
convergence time			4k events	depends on which algorithm
probabilistic	impossible	impossible	Algorithm 4	unneeded
convergence time			exponential in k	

The TBTP model

model \ memory	Finite	Bounded,$\alpha(P) < P$	Bounded,$\alpha(P) \geq P$
symmetric deterministic	impossible	impossible	Algorithm 7
convergence time			$\alpha(P) = 4P$, 3 rounds
asymmetric deterministic	impossible	impossible	Algorithm 5 or 6
convergence time			$\alpha(P) = P + 1$, 3 rounds $\alpha(P) = P$, P+1 rounds

6   Final Remarks

In this article, we have studied the problem of self-stabilizing counting in different models of mobile sensor networks. We designed different algorithms depending on the communication model and the class of daemon. We also gave some proof of impossibility. In the cases where no deterministic (symmetric) solutions exist, we proposed probabilistic solutions. The knowledge of the size of a population is at the basis of the solutions of more complex problems, in particular when different types of population are present.

An interesting perspective could be to model the movement of the sensors, by random processes for example, in order to improve our algorithms and to get better bounds for the convergence time.

Acknowledgments. This work was supported by grants from Region Ile-de-France.

References

1. Angluin, D., Aspnes, J., Diamadi, Z., Fischer, M.J., Peralta, R.: Computation in networks of passively mobile finite-state sensors. In: Proc. of 23 Annual Symposium on Principle of Distributed Computing PODC 2004 (2004)
2. Angluin, D., Aspnes, J., Eisenstat, D.: Fast computation by population protocols with a leader. In: Dolev, S. (ed.) DISC 2006. LNCS, vol. 4167, pp. 61–75. Springer, Heidelberg (2006)
3. Angluin, D., Aspnes, J., Eisenstat, D., Ruppert, E.: The computational power of population protocols. In: Proc. of 25 Annual Symposium on Principle of Distributed Computing PODC 2006 (2006)
4. Angluin, D., Aspnes, J., Fischer, M.J., Jiang, H.: Self-stabilizing population protocols. In: Anderson, J.H., Prencipe, G., Wattenhofer, R. (eds.) OPODIS 2005. LNCS, vol. 3974, pp. 103–117. Springer, Heidelberg (2006)
5. Beauquier, J., Clement, J., Messika, S., Rosaz, L., Rozoy, B.: Self-stabilizing counting in mobile sensor networks. In: Technical Report L.R.I, number 1470 (March 2007)
6. Delporte-Gallet, C., Fauconnier, H., Guerraoui, R., Ruppert, E.: When birds die: Making population protocols fault-tolerant. In: Gibbons, P.B., Abdelzaher, T., Aspnes, J., Rao, R. (eds.) DCOSS 2006. LNCS, vol. 4026, pp. 51–66. Springer, Heidelberg (2006)
7. Dolev, S.: Self-Stabilization. MIT Press, Cambridge (2000)
8. Mainwaring, A., Polastre, J., Szewczyk, R., Culler, D., Anderson, J.: Wireless sensor networks for habitat monitoring (2002)
9. Martinez, K., Hart, J.K., Ong, R.: Environmental sensor networks. IEEE Computer 37(8), 50–56 (2004)
10. Ulmer, C., Yalamanchili, S., Alkalai, L.: Wireless distributed sensor networks for in-situ exploration of mars. In: Georgia Institute of Technology and California Institute of Technology, editors, Technical Report (2003)
11. Xu, N., Rangwala, S., Chintalapudi, K.K., Ganesan, D., Broad, A., Govindan, R., Estrin, D.: A wireless sensor network for structural monitoring. In: SenSys '04: Proceedings of the 2nd international conference on Embedded networked sensor systems, pp. 13–24. ACM Press, New York (2004)

Scalable Load-Distance Balancing

Edward Bortnikov, Israel Cidon, and Idit Keidar

Department of Electrical Engineering
The Technion
Haifa 32000
ebortnik@techunix.technion.ac.il
{cidon,idish}@ee.technion.ac.il

Abstract. We introduce the problem of *load-distance balancing* in assigning users of a delay-sensitive networked application to servers. We model the service delay experienced by a user as a sum of a network-incurred delay, which depends on its network distance from the server, and a server-incurred delay, stemming from the load on the server. The problem is to minimize the maximum service delay among all users.

We address the challenge of finding a near-optimal assignment in a scalable distributed manner. The key to achieving scalability is using *local* solutions, whereby each server only communicates with a few close servers. Note, however, that the attainable locality of a solution depends on the *workload* – when some area in the network is congested, obtaining a near-optimal cost may require offloading users to remote servers, whereas when the network load is uniform, a purely local assignment may suffice. We present algorithms that exploit the opportunity to provide a local solution when possible, and thus have communication costs and stabilization times that vary according to the network congestion. We evaluate our algorithms with a detailed simulation case study of their application in assigning hosts to Internet gateways in an urban wireless mesh network (WMN).

Keywords: Local Computation, Distributed Algorithms, Load-Distance Balancing, Wireless Networks.

1 Introduction

The increasing demand for real-time access to networked services is driving service providers to deploy multiple geographically dispersed service points, or servers. This trend can be observed in various systems, such as content delivery networks (CDNs) [12] and massively multiplayer online gaming (MMOG) grids [8]. Another example can be found in wireless mesh networks (WMNs) [2]. A WMN is a large collection of wireless routers, jointly providing Internet access in residential areas with limited wireline infrastructure via a handful of wired gateways. WMNs are envisaged to provide citywide "last-mile" access for numerous mobile devices running media-rich applications with stringent quality of service (QoS) requirements, e.g., VoIP, VoD, and online gaming. To this end, gateway functionality is anticipated to expand, and to deploy application server logic [2].

A. Pelc (Ed.): DISC 2007, LNCS 4731, pp. 77–91, 2007.
© Springer-Verlag Berlin Heidelberg 2007

Employing distributed servers instead of centralized server farms enables location-dependent QoS optimizations, which enhance the users' soft real-time experience. Service responsiveness is one of the most important QoS parameters. For example, in the first-person shooter (FPS) online game [8], the system must provide an end-to-end delay guarantee of below 100ms. In VoIP, the typical one-way delay required to sustain a normal conversation quality is below 120ms [10].

Deploying multiple servers gives rise to the problem of *service assignment*, namely associating each user session with a server or gateway. For example, each CDN user gets its content from some proxy server, a player in a MMOG is connected to one game server, and the traffic of a WMN user is typically routed via a single gateway [2].

In this context, we identify the need to model the service delay of a session as a sum of a *network delay*, incurred by the network connecting the user to its server, and a *congestion delay*, caused by queueing and processing at the assigned server. Due to the twofold nature of the overall delay, simple heuristics that either greedily map every session to the closest server, or spread the load evenly regardless of geography do not work well in many cases. In this paper, we present a novel approach to service assignment, which is based on both metrics. We call the new problem, which seeks to minimize the maximum service delay among all users, *load-distance balancing* (Section 3).

Resource management problems in which the assignment of every user to the closest server leads to unsatisfactory results are often solved centrally. For example, Cisco wireless local area network (WLAN) controllers [1] perform global optimization in assigning wireless users to access points (APs), after collecting the signal strength information from all managed APs. While this approach is feasible for medium-size installations like enterprise WLANs, its scalability may be challenged in large networks like an urban WMN. For large-scale network management, a distributed protocol with local communication is required.

We observe that, however, load-distance-balanced assignment cannot always be done in a completely local manner. For example, if some part of the network is heavily congested, then a large number of servers around it must be harnessed to balance the load. In extreme cases, the whole network may need to be involved in order to dissipate the excessive load. A major challenge is therefore to provide an *adaptive* solution that performs communication to a distance proportional to that required for handling the given load in each problem instance. In this paper, we address this challenge, drawing inspiration from workload-adaptive distributed algorithms [6,14].

In Section 4, we present two distributed algorithms for load-distance balancing, Tree and Ripple, which adjust their communication requirements to the congestion distribution, and produce constant approximations of the optimal cost. Tree and Ripple dynamically partition the user and server space into *clusters* whose sizes vary according to the network congestion, and solve the problem in a centralized manner within every such cluster. Tree does this by using a fixed hierarchy of clusters, so that whenever a small cluster is over-congested and needs to offload users, this cluster is merged with its sibling in the hierarchy, and the problem is solved in the parent cluster. While Tree is simple and guarantees a logarithmic convergence time, it suffers from two drawbacks. First, it requires maintaining a hierarchy among the servers, which may be difficult in a dynamic network. Second, Tree fails to load-balance across the boundaries of the hierarchy. To overcome these shortcomings, we present a second distributed algorithm, `Ripple`, which does not require maintaining a complex infrastructure, and achieves lower costs and better scalability, through a more careful load sharing policy. The absence of a fixed hierarchical structure turns out to be quite subtle, as the unstructured merges introduce race conditions. In the full version of this paper [7], we prove that `Tree` and `Ripple` always converge to solutions that approximate the optimal one within a constant factor. For simplicity, we present both algorithms for a static workload. In Appendix A, we discuss how they can be extended to cope with dynamic workloads.

We note that even as a centralized optimization problem, load-distance balancing is NP-hard, as we show in the full version of this paper [7]. Therefore, `Tree` and `Ripple` employ a centralized polynomial 2-approximation algorithm, `BFlow`, within each cluster. For space limitations, the presentation of `BFlow` is also deferred to the full paper.

Finally, we empirically evaluate our algorithms using a case study in an urban WMN environment (Section 5). Our simulation results show that both algorithms achieve significantly better costs than naïve nearest-neighbor and perfect load-balancing heuristics (which are the only previous solutions that we are aware of), while communicating to small distances and converging promptly. The algorithms' metrics (obtained cost, convergence time, and communication distance) are scalable and congestion-sensitive, that is, they depend on the distribution of workload rather than the network size. The simulation results demonstrate a consistent advantage of `Ripple` in the achieved cost, due to its higher adaptiveness to user workload.

2 Related Work

Load-distance balancing is an extension of the load balancing problem, which has been comprehensively addressed in the context of tightly coupled systems like multiprocessors, compute clusters etc. (e.g., [4]). However, in large-scale networks, simple load balancing is insufficient because servers are not co-located. While some prior work [8,12] indicated the importance of considering both distance and load in wide-area settings, we are not aware of any study that provides a cost model that combines these two metrics and can be analyzed. Moreover, in contrast with distributed algorithms for traditional load balancing (e.g., [11]), our solutions explicitly use the cost function's distance-sensitive nature to achieve locality.

A number of papers addressed geographic load-balancing in cellular networks and wireless LANs (e.g., [5,9]), and proposed local solutions that dynamically adjust cell sizes. While the motivation of these works is similar to ours, their model is constrained by the rigid requirement that a user can only be assigned to a base station within its transmission range. Our model, in which network distance is part of cost rather than a constraint, is a better match for wide-area networks like WMNs, CDNs, and gaming grids. Dealing with locality in this setting is more challenging because the potential assignment space is very large.

Workload-adaptive server selection was handled in the context of CDNs, e.g., [12]. In contrast with our approach, in which the servers collectively decide on the assignment, they chose a different solution, in which users probe the servers to make a selfish choice. The practical downside of this design is a need to either install client software, or to run probing at a dedicated tier.

Local solutions of network optimization problems have been addressed starting from [16] ,in which the question "what can be computed locally?" was first asked by Naor and Stockmeyer. Recently, different optimization problems have been studied in the local distributed setting, e.g., Facility Location [15], Minimum Dominating Set and Maximum Independent Set [13]. While some papers explore the tradeoff between the allowed running time and the approximation ratio (e.g., [15]), we take another approach – namely, the algorithm achieves a *given* approximation ratio, while adapting its running time and communication distance to the workload. Similar methods have been applied in related areas, e.g., fault-local self-stabilizing consensus [14], and local distributed aggregation [6].

3 Definitions and System Model

Consider a set of k servers S and a set of n user sessions U, such that $k \ll n$. The users and the servers reside in some metric space, in which the *network delay* function, $D : (U \times S) \rightarrow \mathbb{R}^+$, captures the network distance between a user and a server.

Consider an assignment $\lambda : U \rightarrow S$ that maps every user to a single server. Each server s has a monotonic non-decreasing *congestion delay* function, $\delta_s : \mathbb{N} \rightarrow \mathbb{R}^+$, reflecting the delay it incurs to every assigned session. For simplicity, all users incur the same load. Different servers can have different congestion delay functions. The service delay $\Delta(u, \lambda)$ of session u in assignment λ is the sum of the two delays:

$$\Delta(u, \lambda) \triangleq D(u, \lambda(u)) + \delta_{\lambda(u)}(|\{v : \lambda(v) = \lambda(u)\}|).$$

Note that our model does not include congestion within the network. Typically, application-induced congestion bottlenecks tend to occur at the servers or the last-hop network links, which can be also attributed to their adjacent servers. For example, in a CDN [12], the assignment of users to content servers has a more significant impact on the load on these servers and their access links than on the congestion within the public Internet. In WMNs, the effect of load on wireless links is reduced by flow aggregation [10], which is applied for increasing the wireless capacity attainable for real-time traffic. The last-hop infrastructure, i.e., the gateways' wireless and wired links, is mostly affected by network congestion [2].

The cost of an assignment λ is the *maximum* delay it incurs on a user:

$$\Delta^M(\lambda(U)) \triangleq \max_{u \in U} \Delta(u, \lambda).$$

The LDB (load-distance balancing) assignment problem is to find an assignment λ^* such that $\Delta^M(\lambda^*(U))$ is minimized. An assignment that yields the minimum cost is called *optimal*. The LDB problem is NP-hard. Our optimization goal is therefore to find a constant approximation algorithm for this problem. We denote the problem of computing an α-approximation for LDB as $\alpha-$LDB.

We solve the $\alpha-$LDB problem in a failure-free distributed setting, in which servers can communicate directly and reliably. The network delay function D and the set of server congestion functions $\{\delta_s\}$ are known to all servers. We concentrate on synchronous protocols, whereby the execution proceeds in phases. In each phase, a server can send messages to other servers, receive messages sent by other servers in the same phase, and perform local computation. This form of presentation is chosen for simplicity, since in our context synchronizers can be used handle asynchrony (e.g., [3]).

Throughout the protocol, every server knows which users are assigned to it. At startup, every user is assigned to the closest server (this is called a NearestServer assignment). Servers can then exchange the user information, and alter this initial assignment. Eventually, the following conditions must hold: (1) the assignment stops changing; (2) all inter-server communication stops; and (3) the assignment solves $\alpha-$LDB for a given α.

In addition to the cost, in the distributed case we also measure for each individual server its *convergence time* (the number of phases that this server is engaged in communication), and *locality* (the number of servers that it communicates with).

4   Distributed LD-Balanced Assignment

In this section, we present two synchronous distributed algorithms, Tree and Ripple, for $\alpha-$LDB assignment. These algorithms use as a black box a centralized algorithm ALG (e.g., BFlow [7]), which computes an r_{ALG}-approximation for a given instance of the LDB problem. They are also parametrized by the *required* approximation ratio α, which is greater or equal to r_{ALG}. Both algorithms assume some linear ordering of the servers, $S = \{s_1, \ldots, s_k\}$. In order to improve communication locality, it is desirable to employ a locality-preserving ordering (e.g., a Hilbert space-filling curve on a plane [17]), but this is not required for correctness.

Both Tree and Ripple partition the network into non-overlapping zones called *clusters*, and restrict user assignments to servers residing in the same cluster (we call these *internal* assignments). Every cluster contains a contiguous range of servers with respect to the given ordering. The number of servers in a cluster is called the *cluster size*.

Initially, every cluster consists of a single server. Subsequently, clusters can grow through merging. The clusters' growth is congestion-sensitive, i.e., loaded areas are surrounded by large clusters. This clustering approach balances between a centralized assignment, which requires collecting all the user information at a single site, and the nearest-server assignment, which can produce an unacceptably high cost if the distribution of users is skewed. The distance-sensitive nature of the cost function typically leads to small clusters. The cluster sizes also depend on α: the larger α is, the smaller the constructed clusters are.

We call a value ε, such that $\alpha = (1+\varepsilon)r_{ALG}$, the algorithm's *slack factor*. A cluster is called ε-*improvable* with respect to ALG if the cluster's cost can be reduced by a factor of $1 + \varepsilon$ by harnessing all the servers in the network for the users of this cluster. ε-improvability provides a local bound on how far this cluster's current cost can be from the optimal cost achievable with ALG. Specifically, if no cluster is ε-improvable, then the current local assignment is a $(1 + \varepsilon)$-approximation of the centralized assignment with ALG. A cluster containing the entire network is vacuously non-improvable.

Within each cluster, a designated *leader* server collects full information, and computes the internal assignment. Under this assignment, a cluster's *cost* is defined as the maximum service delay among the users in this cluster. Only cluster leaders engage in inter-cluster communication. The distance between the communicating servers is proportional to the larger cluster's diameter. When two or more clusters merge, a leader of one of them becomes the leader of the union. Tree and Ripple differ in their merging policies, i.e., which clusters can merge (and which leaders can communicate for that).

4.1   Tree - A Simple Distributed Algorithm

We present a simple algorithm, Tree, which employs a *fixed* binary hierarchy among servers. Every server belongs to level zero, every second server belongs to level one, and so forth (that is, a single server can belong to up to $\lceil \log_2 k \rceil$ levels). For $i \geq 0$ and $l > 0$, server $i \times 2^l$ is a level-l *parent* of servers $2i \times 2^{l-1}$ (i.e., itself) and $(2i+1) \times 2^{l-1}$ at level $l - 1$.

The algorithm proceeds in rounds. Initially, every cluster consists of a single server. During round $l > 0$, the leader of every cluster created in the previous round (i.e., a server at level $l - 1$) checks whether its cluster is ε-improvable. If it is, the leader sends a merge request to its parent at level l. Upon receiving this request from at least one child, the parent server merges all its descendants into a single cluster, i.e., collects full information from these descendants, computes the internal assignment using ALG, and becomes the new cluster's leader. Collecting full information during a merge is implemented through a sending a query from the level-l leader to all the servers in the new cluster, and collecting the replies.

A single round consists of three synchronous phases: the first phase initiates the process with a *"merge"* message (from a child to its parent), the second disseminates the *"query"* message (from a leader to all its descendants), and the third collects the *"reply"* messages (from all descendants back to the leader). Communication during the last two phases can be optimized by exploiting the fact that a server at level $l - 1$ that initiates the merge already possesses full information from all the servers in its own cluster (that is, half of the servers in the new one), and hence, this information can be queried by its parent directly from it. If the same server is both the merge initiator and the new leader, this query can be eliminated altogether.

Fig. 1(a) depicts a sample clustering of Tree where 16 servers reside on a 4×4 grid and are ordered using a a Hilbert curve. The small clusters did not grow because they were not improvable, and the large clusters were formed because their sub-clusters were improvable. Note that the size of each cluster is a power of 2.

Tree guarantees that no ε-improvable clusters remain at the end of some round $1 \leq L \leq \lceil \log_2 k \rceil$, and all communication ceases. We conclude the following (the proof appears in the full paper [7]).

Theorem 1. (Tree's convergence and cost)

1. *If the last communication round is $1 \leq L \leq \lceil \log_2 k \rceil$, then there exists an ε-improvable cluster of size 2^{L-1}. The size of the largest constructed cluster is $\min(k, 2^L)$.*
2. *The final (stable) assignment's cost is an α-approximation of the optimal cost.*

Tree has some shortcomings. First, it requires maintaining a hierarchy among all servers. Second, the use of this static hierarchy leads it to make sub-optimal merges.

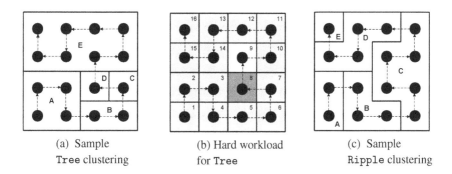

| (a) Sample | (b) Hard workload | (c) Sample |
| Tree clustering | for Tree | Ripple clustering |

Fig. 1. Example workloads for the algorithms and clusters formed by them in a 4×4 grid with Hilbert ordering. (a) A sample clustering $\{A, B, C, D, E\}$ produced by Tree. (b) A hard workload for Tree: $2N$ users in cell 8 (dark gray), no users in cell 9 (white), and N users in every other cell (light gray). (c) A sample clustering $\{A, B, C, D, E\}$ produced by Ripple.

Fig. 1(b) shows an example workload on the network in Fig. 1(a). The congestion delay of each server is zero for a load below $N + 1$, and infinite otherwise. Assume that cell 8 contains $2N$ users (depicted dark gray in the figure), cell 9 is empty of users (white), and every other cell contains N users (light gray). An execution of Tree eventually merges the whole graph into a single cluster, for any value of ε, because no clustering of $s_1, \ldots, s_8$ that achieves the maximum load of at most N (and hence, a finite cost) exists. Therefore, due to the rigid hierarchy, the algorithm misses the opportunity to merge s_8 and s_9 into a single cluster, and solve the problem within a small neighborhood.

4.2 Ripple - An Adaptive Distributed Algorithm

Ripple, a workload-adaptive algorithm, remedies the shortcomings of Tree by providing more flexibility in the choice of the neighboring clusters to merge with. Unlike Tree, in which an ε-improvable cluster always expands within a pre-defined hierarchy, in Ripple, this cluster tries to merge only with neighboring clusters of *smaller* costs. This typically results in better load-sharing, which reduces the cost compared to the previous algorithm. The clusters constructed by Ripple may be therefore highly unstructured (e.g., Fig. 1(c)). The elimination of the hierarchy also introduces some challenges and race conditions between requests from different neighbors.

We first make some formal definitions and present Ripple at a high level. Following this, we provide the algorithm's technical details. Finally, we claim Ripple's properties; their formal proofs appear in the full version of this paper [7].

Overview. We introduce some definitions. A cluster is denoted C_i if its current leader is s_i. The cluster's cost and improvability flag are denoted by $C_i.cost$ and $C_i.imp$, respectively. Two clusters C_i and C_j $(1 \leq i < j \leq k)$ are called *neighbors* if there exists an l such that server s_l belongs to cluster C_i and server s_{l+1} belongs to cluster C_j. Cluster C_i is said to *dominate* cluster C_j if:

Message	Semantics	Size
$\langle$"probe",id,cost,imp$\rangle$	Assignment summary (cost and ε-improvability)	small, fixed
$\langle$"propose",id$\rangle$	Proposal to join	small, fixed
$\langle$"accept",id,λ,nid$\rangle$	Accept to join, includes full assignment information	large, depends on #users

Constants		Value
$L, R,$ Id		0, 1, the server's id

Variable	Semantics	Initial value
LdrId	the cluster leader's id	Id
Λ	the internal assignment	NearestServer
Cost	the cluster's cost	Δ^M(NearestServer)
NbrId[2]	the L/R neighbor cluster leader's id	$\{$Id $- 1,$ Id $+ 1\}$
ProbeS[2]	"probe" to L/R neighbor sent?	$\{$false, false$\}$
ProbeR[2]	"probe" from the L/R neighbor received?	$\{$false, false$\}$
PropR[2]	"propose" from L/R neighbor received?	$\{$false, false$\}$
ProbeFwd[2]	need to forward "probe" to L/R?	$\{$false, false$\}$
Probe[2]	need to send "probe" to L/R in the next round?	$\{$true, true$\}$
Prop[2]	need to send "propose" to L/R?	$\{$false, false$\}$
Acc[2]	need to send "accept" to L/R?	$\{$false, false$\}$

Fig. 2. Ripple's messages, constants, and state variables

1. $C_i.imp =$ true, and
2. $(C_i.cost, C_i.imp, i) > (C_j.cost, C_j.imp, j)$, in lexicographic order (*imp* and cluster index are used to break ties).

Ripple proceeds in rounds. During a round, a cluster that dominates some (left or right) neighbor tries to reduce its cost by inviting this neighbor to merge with it. A cluster that dominates two neighbors can merge with both in the same round. A dominated cluster can only merge with a single neighbor and cannot split. When two clusters merge, the leader of the dominating cluster becomes the union's leader.

Dominance alone cannot be used to decide about merging clusters, because the decisions made by multiple neighbors may be conflicting. It is possible for a cluster to dominate one neighbor and be dominated by the other neighbor, or to be dominated by both neighbors. The algorithm resolves these conflicts by uniform coin-tossing. If a cluster leader has two choices, it selects one of them at random. If the chosen neighbor also has a conflict and it decides differently, no merge happens. When no cluster dominates any of its neighbors, communication stops, and the assignment remains stable.

Detailed Description. Fig. 2 provides a summary of the protocol's messages, constants, and state variables. See Fig. 4 for the pseudo-code. We assume the existence of local functions ALG : $(U, S) \rightarrow \lambda$, $\Delta^M : \lambda \rightarrow \mathbb{R}^+$, and improvable : $(\lambda, \varepsilon) \rightarrow$ {true, false}, which compute the assignment, its cost, and the improvability flag.

In each round, neighbors that do not have each other's cost and improvability data exchange "*probe*" messages with this information. Subsequently, dominating cluster leaders send "*propose*" messages to invite others to merge with them, and cluster leaders that agree respond with "*accept*" messages with full assignment information. More specifically, a round consists of four phases:

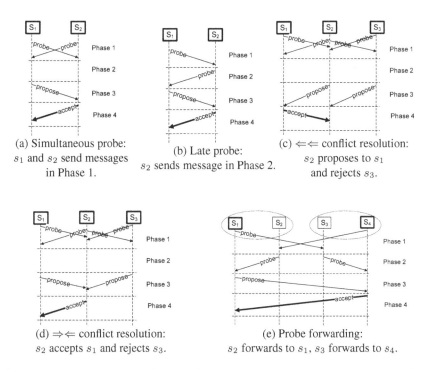

(a) Simultaneous probe: s_1 and s_2 send messages in Phase 1.

(b) Late probe: s_2 sends message in Phase 2.

(c) $\Leftarrow\Leftarrow$ conflict resolution: s_2 proposes to s_1 and rejects s_3.

(d) $\Rightarrow\Leftarrow$ conflict resolution: s_2 accepts s_1 and rejects s_3.

(e) Probe forwarding: s_2 forwards to s_1, s_3 forwards to s_4.

Fig. 3. Ripple's scenarios. Nodes in solid frames are cluster leaders. Dashed ovals encircle servers in the same cluster.

Phase 1 - probe initiation. A cluster leader sends a *"probe"* message to neighbor i if Probe$[i]$ is true (ll. 4–6). Upon receiving a probe from a neighbor, if the cluster dominates this neighbor, the cluster's leader schedules a proposal to merge (line 53), and also decides to send a probe to the neighbor in this direction in the next round (line 55). If the neighbor dominates the cluster, the cluster's leader decides to accept the neighbor's proposal to merge, should it later arrive (line 54). Fig. 3(a) depicts a simultaneous mutual probe. If neither of two neighbors sends a probe, no further communication between these neighbors occurs during the round.

Phase 2 - probe completion. If a cluster leader does not send a *"probe"* message to some neighbor in Phase 1 and receives one from this neighbor, it sends a late *"probe"* in Phase 2 (ll. 14–16). Fig. 3(b) depicts this late probe scenario. Another case that is handled during Phase 2 is probe forwarding. A *"probe"* message sent in Phase 1 can arrive to a non-leader due to a stale neighbor id at the sender. The receiver then forwards the message to its leader (ll. 19–20). Fig. 3(e) depicts this scenario: server s_2 forwards a message from s_1 to s_4, and s_3 forwards a message from s_4 to s_1.

Phase 3 - conflict resolution and proposal. A cluster leader locally resolves all conflicts, by randomly choosing whether to cancel the scheduled proposal to one neighbor, or to reject the expected proposal from one neighbor (ll. 58–68). Figures 3(c) and 3(d) illustrate the resolution scenarios. The rejection is implicit: simply, no *"accept"* is sent.

Finally, the leader sends *"propose"* messages to one or two neighbors, as needed (ll. 28–29).

Phase 4 - acceptance. If a cluster leader receives a proposal from a neighbor and accepts this proposal, then it updates the leader id, and replies with an *"accept"* message with full information about the current assignment within the cluster, including the locations of all the users (line 37). The message also includes the id of the leader of the neighboring cluster in the opposite direction, which is anticipated to be the new neighbor of the consuming cluster. If the neighboring cluster itself is consumed too, then this information will be stale. The latter situation is addressed by the forwarding mechanism in Phase 2, as illustrated by Fig. 3(e). At the end of the round, a consuming cluster's leader re-computes the assignment within its cluster (ll. 70–72). Note that a merge does not necessarily improve the assignment cost, since a local assignment procedure ALG is not an optimal algorithm. If this happens, the assignment within each of the original clusters remains intact. If the assignment cost is reduced, then the new leader decides to send a *"probe"* message to both neighbors in the next round (ll. 73–74).

Ripple's Properties. We now discuss Ripple's properties. Their proofs appear in the full version of this paper [7].

Theorem 2. (Ripple's **convergence and cost**)

1. *Within at most k rounds of* Ripple, *all communication ceases, and the assignment does not change.*
2. *The final (stable) assignment's cost is an α-approximation of the optimal cost.*

Note that the theoretical upper bound on the convergence time is k despite potentially conflicting coin flips. This bound is tight (see [7]). However, the worst-case scenario is not representative. Our case study (Section 5) shows that in realistic scenarios, Ripple's *average* convergence time and cluster size remain flat as the network grows.

For some workloads, we can prove Ripple's near-optimal locality, e.g., when the workload has a single congestion peak:

Theorem 3. (Ripple's **locality**) *Consider a workload in which server s_i is the nearest server for all users. Let C be the smallest non-ε-improvable cluster that includes s_i. Then, the size of the largest cluster constructed by* Ripple *is at most $2|C| - 1$, and the convergence time is at most $|C| - 1$.*

An immediate generalization of this claim is that if the workload is a set of isolated congestion peaks that have independent local solutions, then Ripple builds these solutions in parallel, and stabilizes in a time required to resolve the largest peak.

5   Numerical Evaluation

In this section, we employ Tree and Ripple for gateway assignment in an urban WMN, using the BFlow centralized algorithm [7] for local assignment. We compare our algorithms with NearestServer.

```
 1: Phase 1 {Probe initiation} :
 2:    forall d ∈ {L, R} do
 3:       initState(d)
 4:       if (LdrId = Id ∧ Probe[d]) then
 5:          i ← improvable(Λ, ε)
 6:          send ⟨"probe", Id, Cost, i⟩
                 to NbrId[d]
 7:          ProbeS[d] ← true
 8:          Probe[d] ← false
 9:    forall recv ⟨"probe", id, cost, imp⟩ do
10:       handleProbe(id, cost, imp)

11: Phase 2 {Probe completion} :
12:    if (LdrId = Id) then
13:       forall d ∈ {L, R} do
14:          if (¬ProbeS[d] ∧ ProbeR[d]) then
15:             i ← improvable(Λ, ε)
16:             send ⟨"probe", Id, Cost, i⟩
                    to NbrId[d]
17:    else
18:       forall d ∈ {L, R} do
19:          if (ProbeFwd[d]) then
20:             send the latest "probe" to LdrId
21:    forall recv ⟨"probe", id, cost, imp⟩ do
22:       handleProbe(id, cost, imp)

23: Phase 3 {Conflict resolution & proposal} :
24:    if (LdrId = Id) then
25:       resolveConflicts()
26:    {Send proposals to merge}
27:    forall d ∈ {L, R} do
28:       if (Prop[d]) then
29:          send ⟨"propose", Id⟩ to NbrId[d]
30:    forall recv ⟨"propose", id⟩ do
31:       PropR[dir(id)] ← true

32: Phase 4 {Acceptance or rejection} :
33:    forall d ∈ {L, R} do
34:       if (PropR(d) ∧ Acc[d]) then
35:          {I do not object joining}
36:          LdrId ← NbrId[d]
37:          send ⟨"accept", Id, Λ, NbrId[d̄]⟩
                 to LdrId
38:    forall recv ⟨"accept", id, λ, nid⟩ do
39:       Λ ← Λ ∪ λ; Cost ← Δ^M(Λ)
40:       NbrId[dir(id)] ← nid
41:    if (LdrId = Id) then
42:       computeAssignment()
```

```
43: procedure initState(d)
44:    ProbeS[d] ← ProbeR[d] ← false
45:    Prop[d] ← Acc[d] ← false
46:    ProbeFwd[d] ← false

47: procedure handleProbe(id, cost, imp)
48:    d ← dir(id)
49:    ProbeR[d] ← true
50:    NbrId[d] ← id
51:    i ← improvable(Λ, ε)
52:    if (LdrId = Id) then
53:       Prop[d] ←
             dom(Id, Cost, i, id, cost, imp)
54:       Acc[d] ←
             dom(id, cost, imp, Id, Cost, i)
55:       Probe[d] ← Prop[d]
56:    else
57:       ProbeFwd[d] ← true

58: procedure resolveConflicts()
59:    {Resolve ⇐⇐ or ⇒⇒ conflicts}
60:    forall d ∈ {L, R} do
61:       if (Prop[d] ∧ Acc[d̄]) then
62:          if (randomBit() = 0) then
63:             Prop[d] ← false
64:          else
65:             Acc[d̄] ← false
66:    {Resolve ⇒⇐ conflict}
67:    if (Acc[L] ∧ Acc[R]) conflicts then
68:       Acc[randomBit()] ← false

69: procedure computeAssignment()
70:    Λ' ← ALG(Users(Λ), Servers(Λ))
71:    if (Δ^M(Λ') < Δ^M(Λ)) then
72:       Λ ← Λ'; Cost ← Δ^M(Λ')
73:       forall d ∈ {L, R} do
74:          Probe[d] ← true

75: function dom(id₁, cost₁, imp₁,
                  id₂, cost₂, imp₂)
76:    return (imp₁ ∧
             (imp₁, cost₁, id₁)
                 >
             (imp₂, cost₂, id₂))

77: function dir(id)
78:    return (id < Id) ? L : R
```

Fig. 4. Ripple's pseudo-code: single round

The WMN provides access to a real-time service (e.g., a network game). The mesh gateways, which are also application servers, form a rectangular grid. This topology induces a partitioning of the space into cells. The wireless backbone within each cell is an 16×16 grid of mesh routers, which route the traffic either to the gateway, or to the neighboring cells. The routers apply flow aggregation [10], thus smoothing the impact of network congestion on link latencies. Each wireless hop introduces an average delay of 6ms. The congestion delay of every gateway (in ms) is equal to the load. For example, consider a workload of 100 users uniformly distributed within a single cell, under the NearestServer assignment. With high probability, there is some user close to the corner of the cell. The network distance between this user and the gateway is is 16 wireless hops, incurring a network delay of $16 \times 6\text{ms} \approx 100\text{ms}$, and yielding a maximum service delay close to $100 + 100 = 200\text{ms}$ (i.e., the two delay types have equal contribution).

Every experiment employs a superposition of uniform and peaky workloads. We call a normal distribution with variance R around a randomly chosen point on a plane a *congestion peak*. R is called the *effective radius* of this peak. Every data point is averaged over 20 runs, e.g., the maximal convergence time in the plot is an average over all runs of the maximal convergence time among all servers in individual runs.

Sensitivity to slack factor: We first consider a 64-gateway WMN (this size will be increased in the next experiments), and evaluate how the algorithms' costs, convergence times, and locality depend on the slack factor. The workload is a mix of a uniform distribution of 6400 users with 6400 additional users in ten congestion peaks with effective radii of 200m. We consider values of ε ranging from 0 to 2. The results show that both Tree and Ripple significantly improve the cost achieved by NearestServer (Fig. 5(a)). For comparison, we also depict the theoretical cost guarantee of both algorithms, i.e., $(1 + \varepsilon)$ times the cost of BFlow with global information. We see that for $\varepsilon > 0$, the algorithms' costs are well below this upper bound.

Fig. 5(b) demonstrates how the algorithms' convergence time (in rounds) depends on the slack factor. For $\varepsilon = 0$ (the best possible approximation), the whole network eventually merges into a single cluster. We see that although theoretically Ripple may require 64 rounds to converge, in practice it completes in 8 rounds even with minimal slack. As expected, Tree converges in $\log_2 64 = 6$ rounds in this setting. Note that for $\varepsilon = 0$, Tree's average convergence time is also 6 rounds (versus 2.1 for Ripple) because the algorithm employs broadcasting that involves all servers in every round. Both algorithms complete faster as ε is increased.

Fig. 5(c) depicts how the algorithms' average and maximal cluster sizes depend on ε. The average cluster size does not exceed 2.5 servers for $\varepsilon \geq 0.5$. The maximal size drops fast as ε increases. Note that for the same value of ε, Ripple builds slightly larger maximal-size clusters than Tree, while the average cluster size is the same (hence, most clusters formed by Ripple are smaller). This reflects Ripple's workload-adaptive nature: it builds bigger clusters where there is a bigger need to balance the load, and smaller ones where there is less need. This will become more pronounced as the system grows, as we shall see in the next section.

Sensitivity to network size: Next, we explore Tree's and Ripple's scalability with the network size, for $\varepsilon = 0.5$ and the same workload as in the previous section. We

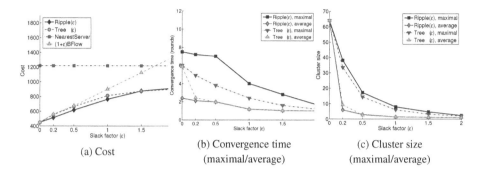

(a) Cost

(b) Convergence time
(maximal/average)

(c) Cluster size
(maximal/average)

Fig. 5. Sensitivity of $\mathtt{Tree}(\varepsilon)$'s and $\mathtt{Ripple}(\varepsilon)$'s cost, convergence time (rounds), and locality (cluster size) to the slack factor, for mixed user workload: 50%uniform/50%peaky (10 peaks of effective radius 200m)

gradually increase the number of gateways from 64 to 1024. Fig. 6 depicts the results in logarithmic scale. We see that thanks to $\mathtt{Ripple}$'s flexibility, its cost scales better than $\mathtt{Tree}$'s, remaining almost constant with the network growth (Fig. 6(a)). Note that $\mathtt{NearestServer}$ becomes even more inferior in large networks, since it is affected by the growth of the expected *maximum* load among all cells as the network expands.

Fig. 6(b) and Fig. 6(c) demonstrate that $\mathtt{Ripple}$'s advantage in cost does not entail longer convergence times or less locality: it converges faster and builds smaller clusters than $\mathtt{Tree}$. This happens because $\mathtt{Tree}$'s rigid cluster construction policy becomes more costly as the network grows (the cluster sizes in the hierarchy grow exponentially).

Sensitivity to user distribution: In the full paper [7], we also study the algorithms' sensitivity to varying workload parameters, like congestion skew and the size of congested areas. We demonstrate that whereas our algorithms perform well on all workloads, their advantage for peaky distributions is most clear. Here too, $\mathtt{Ripple}$ achieves a lower cost than $\mathtt{Tree}$. The algorithms' maximal convergence times and cluster sizes are high only when the workload is skewed.

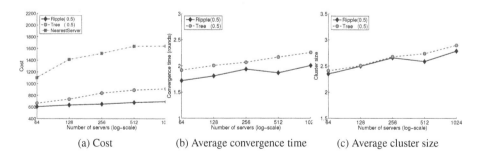

(a) Cost

(b) Average convergence time

(c) Average cluster size

Fig. 6. Scalability of $\mathtt{Ripple}(0.5)$ and $\mathtt{Tree}(0.5)$ with the network's size (log-scale), for mixed workload: 50% uniform/50% peaky (10 peaks of effective radius 200m)

6 Conclusions

We defined a novel load-distance balancing (LDB) problem, which is important for delay-sensitive service access networks with multiple servers. In such settings, the service delay consists of a network delay, which depends on network distance, and a congestion delay, which arises from server load. The problem seeks to minimize the maximum service delay among all users. The $\alpha-$LDB extension of this problem is achieve a desired α-approximation of the optimal solution.

We presented two scalable distributed algorithms for $\alpha-$LDB, Tree and Ripple, which compute a load-distance-balanced assignment with local information. We studied Tree's and Ripple's practical performance in a large-scale WMN, and showed that the convergence times and communication requirements of these algorithms are both scalable and workload-adaptive, i.e., they depend on the skew of congestion within the network and the size of congested areas, rather than the network size. Both algorithms are greatly superior to previously known solutions. Tree employs a fixed hierarchy among the servers, whereas Ripple requires no pre-defined infrastructure, scales better, and consistently achieves a lower cost.

References

1. Cisco Wireless Control System:
   http://www.cisco.com/univercd/cc/td/doc/product/wireless/wcs
2. Akylidiz, I.F., Wang, X., Wang, W.: Wireless Mesh Networks: a Survey. Computer Networks Journal (Elsevier) (March 2005)
3. Awerbuch, B.: On the Complexity of Network Synchronization. J. ACM 32, 804–823 (1985)
4. Barak, A., Guday, S., Wheeler, R.: The MOSIX Distributed Operating System. LNCS, vol. 672. Springer, Heidelberg (1993)
5. Bejerano, Y., Han, S.-J.: Cell Breathing Techniques for Balancing the Access Point Load in Wireless LANs. IEEE INFOCOM (2006)
6. Birk, Y., Keidar, I., Liss, L., Schuster, A., Wolff, R.: Veracity Radius – Capturing the Locality of Distributed Computations. ACM PODC (2006)
7. Bortnikov, E., Cidon, I., Keidar, I.: Scalable Load-Distance Balancing in Large Networks. Technical Report 587, CCIT, EE Department Pub No.1539, Technion IIT (May 2006), http://comnet.technion.ac.il/magma/ftp/LDBalance_tr.pdf
8. Chen, J., Knutsson, B., Wu, B., Lu, H., Delap, M., Amza, C.: Locality Aware Dynamic Load Management form Massively Multiplayer Games. PPoPP (2005)
9. Du, L., Bigham, J., Cuthbert, L.: A Bubble Oscillation Algorithm for Distributed Geographic Load Balancing in Mobile Networks. IEEE INFOCOM (2004)
10. Ganguly, S., Navda, V., Kim, K., Kashyap, A., Niculescu, D., Izmailov, R., Hong, S., Das, S.: Performance Optimizations for VoIP Services in Mesh Networks. JSAC 24(11) (2006)
11. Ghosh, B., Leighton, F.T., Maggs, B., Muthukrishnan, S., Plaxton, G., Rajaraman, R., Richa, A., Tarjan, R., Zuckerman, D.: Tight Analyses of Two Local Load Balancing Algorithms. ACM STOC (1995)
12. Hanna, K.M., Nandini, N.N., Levine, B.N.: Evaluation of a Novel Two-Step Server Selection Metric. IEEE ICNP (2001)
13. Kuhn, F., Moscibroda, T., Nieberg, T., Wattenhoffer, R.: Local Approximation Schemes for Ad Hoc and Sensor Networks. ACM DIALM-POMC (2005)
14. Kutten, S., Peleg, D.: Fault-Local Distributed Mending. J. Algorithms (1999)

15. Moscibroda, T., Wattenhoffer, R.: Facility Location: Distributed Approximation. ACM PODC (2005)
16. Naor, M., Stockmeyer, L.: What can be Computed Locally? ACM STOC(1993)
17. Niedermeyer, R., Reinhardt, K., Sanders, P.: Towards Optimal Locality in Mesh Indexings. In: Chlebus, B.S., Czaja, L. (eds.) FCT 1997. LNCS, vol. 1279, pp. 364–375. Springer, Heidelberg (1997)

A Handling a Dynamic Workload

For the sake of simplicity, both `Tree` and `Ripple` have been presented in a static setting. However, it is clear that the assignment must change as the users join, leave, or move, in order to meet the optimization goal. In this section, we outline how our distributed algorithms can be extended to handle this dynamic setting.

We observe that the clustering produced by `Tree` and `Ripple` is a partition of a plane into regions, where all users in a region are associated with servers in this region. As long as this spatial partition is stable, it can be employed for dynamic assignment of new users that arrive to a region. In a given region, the leader can either (1) re-arrange the internal assignment by re-running the centralized algorithm in the cluster, or (2) leave all previously assigned users on their servers, and choose assignments for new users so as to minimize the increase in the cluster's cost.

`Tree` and `Ripple` can be re-run to adjust the partition either periodically, or upon changes in the distribution of load. Simulation results in Section 5 suggest that the overhead of re-running both algorithms is not high. However, this approach may force many users to move, since the centralized algorithm is non-incremental. In order to reduce handoffs, we would like to avoid a global change as would occur by running the algorithm from scratch, and instead make local adjustments in areas whose load characteristics have changed.

In order to allow such local adjustments, we change the algorithms in two ways. First, we allow a cluster leader to initiate a merge whenever there is a change in the conditions that caused it not to initiate a merge in the past. That is, the merge process can resume after any number of quiet rounds. Second, we add a new cluster operation, *split*, which is initiated by a cluster leader when a previously congested cluster becomes lightly loaded, and its sub-clusters can be satisfied with internal assignments that are no longer improvable. Note that barring the future load changes, a split cluster will not re-merge, since non-improvable clusters do not initiate merges.

This dynamic approach eliminates, e.g., periodic cluster re-construction when the initial distribution of load remains stationary. Race conditions that emerge between cluster-splitting decisions and concurrent proposals to merge with the neighboring clusters can be resolved with the conflict resolution mechanism described in Section 4.2.

Time Optimal Asynchronous Self-stabilizing Spanning Tree

Janna Burman and Shay Kutten

Dept. of Industrial Engineering & Management
Technion, Haifa 32000, Israel
bjanna@tx.technion.ac.il, kutten@ie.technion.ac.il

Abstract. This paper presents an improved and time-optimal self-stabilizing algorithm for a major task in distributed computing- a rooted spanning tree construction. Our solution is decentralized ("truly distributed"), uses a bounded memory and is *not* based on the assumption that either **n** (the number of nodes), or **diam** (the actual diameter of the network), or an existence of cycles in the network are known. The algorithm assumes asynchronous and reliable FIFO message passing and unique identifiers, and works in dynamic networks and for any network topology.

One of the previous time-optimal algorithms for this task was designed for a model with coarse-grained atomic operations and can be shown not to work properly for the totally asynchronous model (with just "read" or "receive" atomicity, and "write" or "send" atomicity). We revised the algorithm and proved it for a more realistic model of totally asynchronous networks.

The state in the presented algorithm does not stabilize until long after the required output does. For such an algorithm, an increased asynchrony poses much increased hardness in the proof.

1 Introduction

A system that reaches a legal state starting from an arbitrary one is called *self-stabilizing* [15]. The *stabilization time* is the time from the moment of the faults till the system reaches a legal state.

The task of a directed spanning tree construction requires the marking, in each node, of some of the node's edges such that the collection of marked edges forms a tree. Moreover, we mark in each node the edge leading to its parent on the tree. Given a spanning tree, most of the major tasks for distributed network algorithms become much easier, including the tasks of reset, broadcast, topology learning and updating, mutual exclusion, voting, committing, querying, scheduling, leader election, and others.

In this extended abstract, we directly address only the task of constructing a spanning tree with **diam** height in $O(\mathbf{diam})$ time, but this, together with the method of [9], also yield an $O(\mathbf{diam})$ time reset algorithm. In the context of self stabilization, it was observed that a self stabilizing reset protocol can translate

A. Pelc (Ed.): DISC 2007, LNCS 4731, pp. 92–107, 2007.
© Springer-Verlag Berlin Heidelberg 2007

a non-self stabilizing protocol into a self stabilizing one [4,9,6,7]. Another application of a reset protocol is to translate protocols that use unbounded event counters (e.g. sequence numbers of messages) to use bounded ones [8]. These applications of the reset simplify protocols' design.

An optimal self stabilizing algorithm for constructing a spanning tree was presented in [7]. As opposed to some previous protocols, it was not based on the assumption that either **n** (the number of nodes) or **diam** (the actual diameter of the network) or an existence of cycles in the network were known. It used a bounded memory. For that, it assumed that *some* bound on the diameter was known. This bound may have been very large, but it did not affect the time complexity which was $O(\textbf{diam})$. The effect of the bound on the size of the memory was only polylogarithmic.

The algorithm of [7], however, was designed for a model with a coarse-grained atomicity. That is, it assumed that a node could read a value of a variable written by a neighbor, and also perform an operation based on that read value in one atomic step. Only after both actions, could the neighbor change the value of its own variable. We show a scenario where that algorithm does not yield a correct result in a totally asynchronous model, that is, when an atomic operation contains either a read, or a write, but not both.

In this paper, we modify the algorithm of [7] so that it functions correctly also in a fully asynchronous environment. We kept the main algorithmic ideas of [7], while adding a few tricks that may prove useful in translating also other such protocols. The main contribution of this paper is in the proof that the algorithm after the changes is correct for the more realistic *asynchronous send/receive atomicity* model (similar to "Atomic Read/ Atomic Write" model, but for a message passing model).

Note, that combining the algorithm in [7] with some existing efficient transformer (e.g. [10] or [26]) to refine the atomicity would not have yielded optimal stabilization times in our case. When such a transformer is combined with a coarse-grained atomicity algorithm, a resulted fine-grained atomicity algorithm suffers from a reduction in concurrency due to the mutual exclusion procedures used in the implementation of the transformer. This loss of concurrency results in a higher than a constant delay (up to $\Omega(n)$) between two successive atomic step executions by a particular process.

Numerous self stabilizing reset and spanning tree algorithms that were less efficient than [7] also appeared. We mention some of them below. Many (starting with [17]) championed the claim that a self stabilizing algorithm should use fine-grained atomic operations. We did not see how to use the methods used in [17] (for making their $O(\textbf{n})$ time algorithm work under fine-grained atomicity) to make the algorithm of [7] also work for fine-grained atomicity. We note that moving from a coarse-grained atomicity to fine-grain atomicity of operations is even impossible for some tasks in some models, and for other tasks it is tricky. This is especially tricky for the algorithm of [7], since the latter keeps multiple trees that do not stabilize in the required time $O(\textbf{diam})$, although the output in their algorithm does stabilize in $O(\textbf{diam})$ time in the coarse-grained operations model. The proof requires us to reason about these not yet stabilized trees (to show that they do not prevent also the output tree from stabilizing in $O(\mathbf{diam})$ time). Proving a property of a not yet stabilized tree is made more difficult by the asynchronicity. It would have been much easier to prove that some condition holds for a node in a tree if it was certain (as it is in a coarse-grain atomicity model) that this node has not lost its parent or children without yet knowing about the loss. The current paper makes this necessary step from coarse-grained atomicity to asynchronous networks for the major tasks it solves.

Other related work. Due to the lack of space, we give here a somewhat limited survey of the related work for the well-studied problem of a spanning tree construction. A thorough survey is deferred to the full paper [12].

In [3], a spanning tree construction algorithm with the stabilization time of $O(\mathbf{n}^2)$ (where $\mathbf{n}$ is unknown) is given. In [18], a randomized spanning tree protocol is given implicitly, with the expected stabilization time of $O(\mathbf{diam} \cdot \log \mathbf{n})$, where $\mathbf{diam}$ is unknown. (If $\mathbf{n}$ is known in advance then the stabilization time is $O(\mathbf{diam})$). In [5], the time complexity is $O(\mathbf{diam})$ (where $\mathbf{diam}$ is unknown), but the memory space (and the length of a message) is not bounded. In [2] and [19,13,14], generic self-stabilizing solutions solving also the task of a spanning tree construction are given. These papers present algorithms for weaker models (with unidirectional communication links and even with unreliable communications in [13,14]), but the time-optimal stabilization is not achieved in them. In [20], an algorithm for maintaining a spanning tree for a *completely connected topology* stabilizes in $O(log\mathbf{n}/loglog\mathbf{n})$ with high probability. In [24], a completely connected topology is assumed too, but the model is weaker than in [20]. In [25], a self-stabilizing algorithm for a minimum spanning tree construction is presented for an asynchronous message-passing reliable network. The time complexity in [25] depends on $\mathbf{n}$ (and hence, cannot be time-optimal). In addition, that algorithm of [25] requires a bound on the time that it takes to travel over a path of $\mathbf{n}$ nodes in the network. In [23] and [1], spanning tree algorithms for ad hoc networks with larger than $O(\mathbf{diam})$ stabilization times are given. For an additional survey one can refer to [21]. Finally, we note that the algorithm presented in this paper can be combined with some hierarchial structure (e.g. [22]) to improve the stabilization time in some favorable settings (see [22]), but not in the worst case.

1.1 Notations and Model of Computation

System Model. The system topology is represented by an undirected graph $G = (V, E)$, where nodes represent processors and edges represent communication links. Each node has a unique identifier denoted by *ID*. The number of the nodes is denoted by $\mathbf{n} = |V|$. The actual diameter of the graph is denoted by $\mathbf{diam}$. We assume that there is a known upper bound on the diameter of the network, denoted by D and called the *bound*. This upper bound serves only for the purpose of having finite space protocols, and does not appear in the time complexity. For $v \in V$, we define $N(v) = \{u \mid (v, u) \in E\}$, called the *neighbors* of v. We assume that the topology is dynamically changing- node/link addition or removal are possible (and modeled as faults). We consider an *asynchronous message passing network* model. The message delivery time can be arbitrary, but for the purpose of time analysis only, we assume that each message is delivered in at most one time unit. On each link, messages are delivered in the same order as they have been sent. The number of messages that may be in transit on any link in each direction and at the same time is bounded by some parameter B (independent of the network size). It is necessary, as shown in [16], for self stabilization.

We adopt the usual definitions of the following: a *local state* of a node (an assignment of values to the local variables and the program counter); a *global state* of a system (the cross product of the local states of all the nodes, plus the contents of the links); the semantics of protocol actions (possible atomic (computation) steps and their associated state changes); an *execution* of a protocol P (a possibly infinite sequence of global states in which each element follows from its predecessor by the execution of a single atomic step of P).

Informally, a distributed system allows the processors to execute steps concurrently; however, when processors execute steps concurrently, we assume that there is no influence of these concurrent steps on each other. To catch this formally, we assume that at each given time, only a single processor executes a step. Each step consists of an internal computation and a single communication operation: a *send* or *receive*. Every state transition of a process is due to a communication step execution (including the following local computations). Let us call this the *send/receive atomicity* network model.

Fault Model. The *legality predicate* (defined on the set of global states) of our protocol becomes true when the collection of internal variables of the nodes defines a spanning tree with **diam** height, rooted at the minimal *ID* node. A protocol is called *self-stabilizing* if starting from a state with an arbitrary number of faults (or from an arbitrary state) such that no additional faults hit the system for "long enough", the protocol reaches a *legal* global state eventually and remains in legal global states thereafter. When this happens, we say that the *stabilization* has occurred. The maximum number of time units that takes to reach the stabilization is called the *stabilization time* of the protocol.

2 The Algorithm

Due to the fine-grained communication atomicity, we use the notion of *base* and *image* variables. Each node v has a set of internal variables it writes to- the base variables. Consider some base variable of v, var_v. Every neighbor u of v maintains an internal copy of var_v in its corresponding image variable $\text{var}_u[v]$ at u. The copies get their values from **InfoMsg** messages sent from v to u repeatedly. Node u reads $\text{var}_u[v]$ for algorithm computations. By then, this copy can have a different value then var_v at v, if v has changed it meanwhile. This is the main difficulty encountered by the current paper, as opposed to [7].

2.1   Ideas Adopted from [7]

The algorithm runs multiple versions of the Bellman-Ford's algorithm ([11], see Rule 1 bellow). When running a single version alone, a stabilized tree results (this was observed by [17] for their algorithm which is similar to Bellman-Ford's, and by [7] and others for Bellman-Ford's algorithm itself). The stabilized tree is rooted at the minimal ID node in the network and the stabilization occurs in $O(D)$ time when D is given. This is similar e.g. to [6,17]. Therefore, if the bound parameter D is close to the actual diameter **diam**, Rule 1 is close to optimal. Unfortunately, typically, a hardwired bound will be much larger than the actual diameter, to accommodate for extreme cases, and to have room for scaling up the network size. Nevertheless, coming up with *some* bound is pretty easy. Hence, $\log D + 1$ versions are run in parallel. Each version i, $0 \leq i \leq \log D$, executes the Bellman-Ford version with bound parameter 2^i. Versions with "large enough" bound parameters 2^i (the "higher versions") will stabilize to a desired spanning tree in $O(2^i)$ time. However, the other versions (the "lower versions") can stabilize only in $\Theta(\mathbf{n})$ as demonstrated in [7]. The trick there was that one does not need the smaller i versions to stabilize. One only needs them to detect and inform each node that the version has not yet constructed the required spanning tree which contains all the nodes. This is done by the standard technique of a broadcast over a tree. That is, each version i maintains at each node two bits: `up_cover` and `down_cover`. Using the `up_cover` bit, nodes report towards the root that the version tree has not yet spanned all the nodes; this information is propagated up the tree by having each node take a logical *and* of the `up_cover` bits of its children repeatedly. The purpose of the `down_cover` bit is to disseminate this fact down the tree, by having each node copy the `down_cover` bit of its parent repeatedly. See Rule 2.

Then, each node v selects its output by finding the minimum i such that `down_cover`$_v = 1$ for version i. The tree edges of that version are the output of the combined protocol.

A Counter Example. In the sequel we mention some problems that prevent one from using the solution of [7] in the weaker model we address in this paper. This is demonstrated in [12], because of the lack of space here. We just mention here that the problems manifest in the trees that have not stabilized yet, when the output was supposed to have stabilized already. In an asynchronous network, such a not yet stabilized tree may "pretend" successfully to have stabilized, and to cover the network.

2.2   Revising the Algorithm

Now, we introduce three mechanisms we incorporate in the new algorithm to make the ideas above also work in the weaker model we use.

• **Non-stabilization Detector:** The algorithm of [7] propagated up a tree the information that a node in that tree has a neighbor not in the tree. This information turned out to be unstable, causing the counter example mentioned above. Hence, we augment the above with a new notion of local "non-stabilization detector": if it looks as if any of the neighbors of a node v may still have to change its state, then v observes that the current configuration is not yet stable, and propagates this observation upwards. Below, we give the formal definition of this idea- the `consistent`$_v$ predicate for each node v (see Def. 1). Now, in contrast with the previous solution, the definitions of the rules for the `up_cover` and `down_cover` bits use the `consistent` predicate. They are given in Rule 2.

• **Strict Communication Discipline:** We adopt this module as is from [4] (see Sec. 2.3 below). The main *property of the discipline* is that before a node v may change any of its base variables, all its neighbors "know" the value of v's base variables (see Lem. 3). The proof of Lem. 4 uses this property heavily.

• **Local Reset:** We use this mechanism to ensure the following. Whenever a node v changes the values of its tree variables (line 6, Fig. 1), no neighbor u considers v as its parent (that is, $\mathtt{par}_u \neq v$). Note, that in our model this is not a condition that v can check directly, since by the time v reads u's variables, u may have changed them. We found this property very useful in several places in the proof. For example, whenever a node joins a tree on some specific path called a *legal branch* (see Def. 4), it joins initially with `up_cover` $= 0$ (Lem. 7). This helps to prove that even though the lower versions trees do not stabilize (at least, not in $O(\mathbf{diam})$ time), their `up_cover` does stabilize to zero (Lem. 8). Lines 6-11 (Fig. 1) implement the local reset mechanism.

Intuitively, the main difficulty the revised algorithm overcomes is the following. Consider a branch of a tree whose nodes have a root value of v, however, they are disconnected from v. (A formal definition of this structure we call a "sprig" will follow (Def. 3).). Note, that v does exist. This phenomena is different than branches of a tree of a ghost root- that is, branches with nodes whose root variable contains an *ID* of a node that does not exist. The latter branches disappear by time $T_{valid} = O(2^i)$ for version i (see Def. 2 and Obs. 1), but new sprigs can be created by the lower versions of the algorithm up until time $\Omega(\mathbf{n})$. We needed the above revisions in the algorithm to show that the sprigs do not confuse themselves to have `up_cover` $= 1$ (Lem. 10). Nor do they confuse the nodes of the legal tree of v (nodes that are indeed connected (via a chain of parent markings) to v where v is the value of their root variable). See Lem. 8.

2.3 Algorithm Details

Variables. Graph property variables are represented using a **boldface font**, as in $\mathbf{dist}(v, u)$, which denotes the true distance in the graph between nodes v and u. Protocol variables are represented using `teletype font`. The variables appearing and manipulated in the code of Fig. 1 are local protocol variables of process v. The subscript v of each variable in the figure emphasizes that fact.

Each node $u \in V$ sends a set of values of its internal variables (its *base variables*) periodically to all its neighbors by an `InfoMsg`$_u$ message. Each neighbor v of u copies these values to its local copies (to simplify the code, we omit this simple operation from the algorithm code, but we assume it is performed for each message receive event). The copy of a variable $\mathtt{var_u}$ at v (an *image variable* of u at v) is denoted by $\mathtt{var_v}[u]$. Node u does not send its neighbors any of its image variables.

Note, that for each $v \in V$, in addition to $N(v)$, we use a variable $\mathtt{Nlist}_v$ which is a local list of node identities such that the incident link from v to each node u in the list is believed to be operational and the processor at each such node u is also believed to be up.

A detailed verbal explanation of all the variables appears in [12].

Communication Discipline. Every node sends the $\mathtt{InfoMsg}$ messages repeatedly, using the communication discipline mentioned above. We treat the discipline as being embodied by a lower layer process. Whenever any $\mathtt{InfoMsg}$ arrives at some node v, the discipline (layer) copies the content of the message into the appropriate image variables. Then, the communication discipline can decide either to pass the message to the higher level algorithm or to discard it. If it decides to pass the message, we say that $\mathtt{InfoMsg}$ is *accepted* (then, this message is processed according the code in Fig. 1). Otherwise, we say that $\mathtt{InfoMsg}$ is *received* (and no further processing takes place). Note, that in both cases, v copies the message content (*receives* $\mathtt{InfoMsg}$). For the complexity analysis, we define a *time step*, which is the maximum time for a message to get accepted (it is equivalent to 3 time units). Lem. 3 states the communication discipline property formally.

Algorithm Formal Definition. The formal code for version i of the algorithm in node v appears in Fig. 1; it applies Rules 1 and 2 below. In each iteration, node v outputs its tree edges according to the lowest version in v for which $\mathtt{up\_cover} = 1$.

Rule 1. *(Bellman-Ford with IDs and Bound Parameter* D *(used in [11,17,6] for a single version)) Let v be a node.*
1. $\mathtt{r}_v \leftarrow \min\{\mathtt{ID}_v, \mathtt{r}_v[u]\}$ *where* $u \in \mathtt{Nlist}_v$ *and* $\mathtt{d}_v[u] < $ D.
2. $\mathtt{d}_v \leftarrow \begin{cases} 1 + \min\{\mathtt{d}_v[u] \ : u \in \mathtt{Nlist}_v \text{ and } \mathtt{r}_v = \mathtt{r}_v[u]\}, \text{ if } \mathtt{r}_v \neq \mathtt{ID}_v \ , \\ 0, \hfill \text{ if } \mathtt{r}_v = \mathtt{ID}_v \ . \end{cases}$

Definition 1. *(Used in Rule 2 below)*
- *The* parent *of a node v, denoted* $\mathtt{par}_v$, *is (supposed to be) the smallest ID neighbor u of v for which $\mathtt{r}_v = \mathtt{r}_v[u]$ and $\mathtt{d}_v[u] = \mathtt{d}_v - 1$, if $\mathtt{r}_v \neq v$. Otherwise, if $\mathtt{r}_v = v$, the parent of v is* null.
- *The* children *of v, denoted* $\mathtt{child}_v$, *are the set* $\{u \mid \mathtt{par}_v[u] = v\}$.
- *Given a node v, the predicate* consistent$_v$ *is defined by*
$$\bigwedge_{u \in \mathtt{Nlist}_v} (\mathtt{r}_v[u] = \mathtt{r}_v) \wedge (|\mathtt{d}_v[u] - \mathtt{d}_v| \leq 1) \wedge$$
$$(u = \mathtt{par}_v \Longleftrightarrow u \text{ is the minimal ID node such that } \mathtt{d}_v - \mathtt{d}_v[u] = 1) \wedge$$
$$(\mathtt{d}_v[u] - \mathtt{d}_v = 1 \Longrightarrow \mathtt{par}_v[u] \leq v)$$
- *Node v is a* consistent *node, if* consistent$_v$ = true.

Rule 2
Calculate par_v, child_v, *and* consistent_v *such that they conform to Def. 1.*

$$
\text{up\_cover}_v \leftarrow \begin{cases} \text{consistent}_v, & \text{if } \text{child}_v = \emptyset \\[2mm] \bigwedge_{u \in \text{child}_v} \text{up\_cover}_v[u], & \text{if } \text{child}_v \neq \emptyset \wedge \text{consistent}_v \\[2mm] 0, & \text{otherwise} \end{cases}
$$

$$
\text{down\_cover}_v \leftarrow \begin{cases} \text{down\_cover}_v[\text{par}_v] \wedge \text{consistent}_v, & \text{if } r_v \neq v \\[1mm] \text{up\_cover}_v \wedge \text{consistent}_v, & \text{if } r_v = v \end{cases}
$$

Procedure Send()   (* sending InfoMsg_v *)
1 Send $\text{InfoMsg}_v \equiv [\, r_v, d_v, \text{par}_v, \text{local\_reset}_v, \text{up\_cover}_v, \text{down\_cover}_v \,]$ to Nlist_v

Procedure LocalReset()   (* performing a local reset *)
2 $r_v \leftarrow v$, $d_v \leftarrow 0$, $\text{down\_cover}_v \leftarrow \text{up\_cover}_v \leftarrow 0$, $\text{local\_reset}_v \leftarrow \textbf{true}$
3 *Send()*

Do forever:
4 *Send()*   (* this line is executed atomically *)

Upon accepting $\text{InfoMsg}_v[u]$ *message from neighbor* $u \in \text{Nlist}_v$
                    (* the following is executed atomically (not including reception) *)

5 Use Rules 1, 2 to calculate temporary variables as follows:
   a temporary variable $\textbf{t\_var}_v$ for each var_v computed in the rules.

                                     (* tree changes generate a local reset *)
6 if $[\, \neg \text{local\_reset}_v \wedge (\text{par}_v \neq \textbf{t\_par}_v \vee r_v \neq \textbf{t\_r}_v \vee d_v \neq \textbf{t\_d}_v) \,] \bigvee$
                                     (* reset propagates down the tree *)
7      $[\, \exists u \in \text{Nlist}_v : \text{local\_reset}_v[u] \wedge u = \text{par}_v \,] \bigvee$
                                     (* local reset not yet completed *)
8      $[\, \text{local\_reset}_v \wedge \exists u \in \text{Nlist}_v : \text{par}_v[u] = v \,] \bigvee$
                                     (* candidate parent reset not yet completed *)
9      $[\, \text{local\_reset}_v \wedge \textbf{t\_par}_v \neq \textbf{null} \wedge \text{local\_reset}_v[\textbf{t\_par}_v] \,] \,]$
   then
10   *LocalReset()*
11   *return*
   end if
                    (* a local reset exit (if local_reset_v switches from **true** to **false**) *)
12 $\text{local\_reset}_v \leftarrow \textbf{false}$

13 Update each variable var_v by the value of the temporary variable $\textbf{t\_var}_v$.
14 *Send()*

Fig. 1. Algorithm for version i at node v

3   Preliminary Analysis

In the following analysis, we prove stabilization assuming that there are no faults or topological changes after some time $t_0 = 0$ (at least till the time when algorithm reaches a global legal state).

From now on, let us consider the execution of the algorithm after time $t = 2$ (2 *time steps* after time t_0). It is easy to see that after 2 time steps, no damaged (by faults) messages exist in the network and at least one authentic InfoMsg message has been *accepted* at each node from each neighbor.

Definition 2. *Consider a node $v \in V$ and some time T.*
- *Let T_{valid} be time $t_0 + 2 + 2^i$.*
- *Node v is a* root node, *if $r_v = \mathrm{ID}_v \ (\equiv v)$.*
- *If $r_v \notin \{\mathrm{ID}_u | u \in V\}$, then r_v is a* ghost root.
- *Let $u \in N(v)$. If at time T, $\mathrm{var}_u[v] = \mathrm{var}_v$, we say that node u knows the value of var_v at T.*
- *The* depth *of v is $\mathrm{depth}(v) \stackrel{\mathrm{def}}{=} \max\{\mathrm{dist}(v, u) \mid u \in V\}$.*
- *Let us denote by v_{min} the node with the minimum ID that exists in the network.*
- *Let us denote by a* local reset operation *of node v an invocation of the LocalReset() procedure at line 10 of the algorithm code.*
- *Assume that node v performs a local reset operation at time T. We denote by a* local reset exit *the first time after time T when v executes line 12 of the algorithm code.*
- *Let us denote by a* local reset mode *the state of node v between a local reset operation and the subsequent local reset exit at v.*

Lem. 1 is a rather known property of Bellman-Ford's algorithm. Its proof, as well as some of the following proofs, due to the lack of space, appear in [12].

Lemma 1. *Starting from any initial assignments of the d and r variables, for any node v, after t time steps, $d_v \geq min(t, \mathrm{dist}(r_v, v))$.*

The following observation follows from Lem. 1 and Rule 1-1. (Note, that for every ghost root v, $\mathrm{dist}(r_v, v) = \infty$.)

Observation 1. *After time T_{valid}, for every node v, r_v is not a ghost root and $d_v \geq \mathrm{dist}(v, r_v)$.*

Definition 3. *Let $0 \leq k \leq n - 1$. Let $v, x_j \in V$ for each $0 \leq j \leq k$.*
- *A* parent path *of v to x_0 is a path of nodes $(x_0, x_1, x_2, \ldots, x_k = v)$ such that for each j, $r_{x_j} = r_v$ and for each $1 \leq j \leq k$, $\mathrm{par}_{x_j} = x_{j-1}$.*
- *We say that v is a* descendant *of x_0 and x_0 is an* ancestor *of v.*
- *A* connection path *of v is a parent path of v to $r_v = x_0$ such that x_0 is a root node. Let us denote a connection path of v (to x_0) by $\mathbf{C}_v(x_0)$.*
- *Node v is* connected *(to node x_0) if there is a connection path of v (to x_0).*
- *Let $r_v = x_0$. If node v has no connection path, node v is* disconnected *(from node x_0).*
- *Let a* sprig *of v be a maximal set of nodes $X \subset V$ that satisfies the following*

conditions: (1) $v \notin X$; (2) $\forall x \in X$, $\mathbf{r}_x = v$ and x is disconnected; (3) Every ancestor or descendant x of any $x_0 \in X$ is in X.
- *Let us denote some sprig A of v at time t by $A_v(t)$.*

The following is one of our main lemmas. Informally, we found it harder to ensure properties for sprigs than for legal trees. We use the following lemma to show a property of sprigs that is somewhat similar to the property of the $\mathbf{d}$ values in a legal tree (shown in Lem. 1). Informally, the lemma shows that a node's $\mathbf{d}$ is high if it remains in the same sprig for a long time (an "old" sprig). This may not hold for a node who leaves one sprig (having a high $\mathbf{d}$) and joins another (with a lower $\mathbf{d}$). Such a leave and join may happen even very late in the execution since new sprigs may be created very late in the execution. However, we handle such "new" sprigs later.

Lemma 2. *Consider nodes $v, u \in V$. Let $t \le 2^i$ and $t_1 > 2$. Let α be the following set of assumptions on u: (1) node u is disconnected from $\mathbf{r}_u = v$; (2) node u does not change its $\mathbf{r}_u$ value. If α holds for u during the whole time interval $[t_1, t_1 + 2t]$, then at time $t_1 + 2t$, $\mathbf{d}_u \ge t$.*

Proof: By induction on the time t. For $t = 0$, the lemma holds since $\mathbf{d}_u \ge 0$ always. Assume, that the lemma holds for $t = k$ for every node. For $t = k + 1$, assume that α holds for some node u for the time interval $[t_1, t_1 + 2(k+1)]$. By Def. 3, node u is disconnected and is not a root. Hence, $\mathbf{par}_u \ne \mathbf{null}$. When α holds, node u cannot change its $\mathbf{par}_u$. Otherwise, the condition at line 6 must hold beforehand and then, u must perform a local reset and assign $\mathbf{r}_u \leftarrow u$ (becoming a root) in line 2- a contradiction to α. Hence, for some node $w \in \mathbf{Nlist}(u)$, $w = \mathbf{par}_u$ throughout $[t_1, t_1 + 2k + 2]$.

Let δ be an $\mathbf{InfoMsg}$ message sent by w at time t_{sent} and accepted at u at time t_{rcv} such that δ is the last such message accepted at u by time $t_1 + 2k + 2$. By our model assumptions on communication links , $t_{rcv} \ge t_1 + 2k + 1$. Hence, δ is sent by w at $t_{sent} \ge t_1 + 2k$. Clearly, α holds at w during $[t_1, t_{sent}]$, otherwise it would not have held in u during $[t_1, t_{rcv}]$ since in that case, either u would have been connected (if w would have been connected) or some $\mathbf{InfoMsg}_w$ and line 6 of the algorithm would have caused u to perform a local reset and become a root, violating α. Hence ,by the induction hypothesis, $\mathbf{d}_w \ge k$ at time $t_1 + 2k$.

Moreover, if $\mathbf{d}_w$ is changed at w in $[t_1, t_{sent}]$, then $\mathbf{InfoMsg}_w$ stating this fact and line 6 of the algorithm would have caused u to perform a local reset and become a root, violating α. Thus, $\mathbf{d}_w$ stays unchanged during $[t_1, t_{sent}]$. Hence, $\mathbf{d}_w \ge k$ during the whole interval $[t_1, t_{sent}]$ and $\mathbf{d}_u[w] \ge k$ at u during the whole of $[t_1, t_1 + 2k + 2]$. Now, since $\mathbf{par}_u = w$ during whole $[t_1, t_1 + 2k + 2]$, by Rule 1, $\mathbf{d}_u = \mathbf{d}_u[w] + 1$ during whole this interval. Thus, at time $t_1 + 2k + 2$, $\mathbf{d}_u = \mathbf{d}_u[w] + 1 \ge k + 1$. Hence, the lemma holds for $t = k + 1$ too. ∎

The following lemma is ensured by the communication discipline, which we assume for the algorithm (Sec. 2.3). The lemma is proved in [7]- Lem. 4.2 (we reworded it somewhat).

Lemma 3. *[7] If at some time T, after time $t_0 + 2$, some node v changes any of its base variables, then, at time T, $\forall u \in \mathbf{Nlist}(v)$, for every base variable $\mathbf{var}_v$*

of v, $\text{var}_u[v] = \text{var}_v$ (u's image variable of var_v equals var_v at time T; or in other words, node u knows the value of var_v at time T).

The following lemma can be proven for our algorithm, but not for the previous one [7]. This proved to be a major reason why our algorithm can function in the atomic send / atomic receive model.

Lemma 4. *Assume that at some time T, some node u with $\text{par}_u \neq w$ assigns $\text{par}_u \leftarrow w$. Then, at time T, $\forall v \in \text{Nlist}(u)$, $\text{par}_v \neq u$.*

Proof: (see Fig. 2) To prove the lemma, we assume, by way of contradiction, that some neighbor v of u assigns[1] $\text{par}_v \leftarrow u$ before or at time T and $\text{par}_v = u$ holds till time T inclusively.

To assign a new value to par_u, node u must execute line 13 at time T (also see line 5 and Rule 2). This requires that just before that, u was at a local reset mode and performed a local reset exit at line 12. Since u changes a base variable at time T, by Lem. 3, every neighbor v' of u (and v in particular) knows at time T that u is in a local reset mode ($\text{local\_reset}_{v'}[u] = \textbf{true}$). Let time T^* be the first time when v assigns $\text{local\_reset}_v[u] \leftarrow \textbf{true}$ such that $\text{local\_reset}_v[u]$ stays true until T inclusively. Recall, that we consider the execution of the algorithm after time t=2. Thus, due to line 9, it is guaranteed that v does not *change* its parent pointer to point at u (v cannot perform $\text{par}_v \leftarrow u$) throughout $[T^*, T]$. (A local reset operation and then its exit must precede any tree structure base variables change at any node; but, a local reset exit is impossible at v in $[T^*, T]$, since the condition at line 9 holds throughout this time interval.)

Let T^x be the time when v sends message InfoMsg_v x that is the last one to be *received* by u from v before time T. This message must cause u to set $\text{par}_u[v] \neq u$, otherwise, by the condition at line 8, u cannot become a descendant of w at time T. Hence, at time T^x, $\text{par}_v \neq u$ holds at v. Thus, and due to the guarantee of the time interval $[T^*, T]$ that we have shown above, we must assume that v assigns $\text{par}_v \leftarrow u$ (at line 13) in the time interval (T^x, T^*). When this happens, v sends an InfoMsg_v ($= y$) (line 14) with this new information ($\text{par}_v = u$) to u.

Recall, that by Lem. 3, node u learns at some time $T^* < T^{**} < T$ that its neighbor v knows that u is in a reset mode (at T^{**}, u learns that $\text{local\_reset}_v[u] = \textbf{true}$). Clearly, for u, to learn this, a message of the communication discipline should be sent from v at or after time T^* and should be received at u before time T. Let z be such a message. We proved above that message y is sent before T^*. Hence, and because of the FIFO assumption for each link, message y is *received* at u before message z, and thus, before time T^{**} and before T. Since InfoMsg message y is sent after InfoMsg message x, it should arrive at u after x, but we have assumed above that x is the last InfoMsg to be received from v just before time T. Thus, $y = x$ - a contradiction since these messages bear different information about the value of par_v. ∎

---

[1] The algorithm calculates the **par** pointers by invoking Rule 2 at line 5 and then assigns them at line 13 (Fig.1).

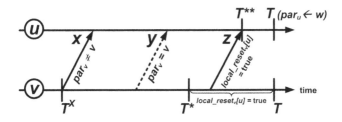

Fig. 2. Illustration for the proof of Lem. 4

4   Analysis of the Lower Version Case ($2^i < \text{depth}(v_{min})$)

In this section we prove for every node in every lower version that down_cover $= 0$ holds in $O(2^i)$ time steps and remains thereafter. First, we prove this for legal trees and then for sprigs. To prove this for legal trees, we use the notion of a *legal branch*. There may be several shortest pathes between two nodes, however, only one of them is a *legal branch* as defined in the following definition. (This matches the way parent pointers are chosen by the algorithm. See Def. 1.)

Definition 4. *Let $u, v \in V$.*
- *Node u is foreign to node v if after time T_{valid}, $\mathbf{r}_u \neq v$ always.*
- *Let u be foreign to v. A legal branch $\mathbf{R}_v(u)$ of v via u is a shortest path between v and u $(x_1 = v, x_2, \ldots, x_k = u)$ s.t. $1 \leq k \leq \text{dist}(v, u) + 1$ and for each $2 \leq j \leq k$, x_{j-1} is the smallest ID neighbor of x_j with $\text{dist}(v, x_{j-1}) = \text{dist}(v, x_j) - 1$. Denote the length of $\mathbf{R}_v(u)$ by $|\mathbf{R}_v(u)|$.*

Lemma 5. *If $2^i < \text{depth}(v_{min})$, then after time T_{valid}, for each node v, there exists a node u such that u is foreign to v and either (1) $\text{dist}(v, u) = 2^i + 1$ or (2) $\text{dist}(v, u) < 2^i + 1$ and $v > u$.*

Definition 5. *Let $v, w \in V$.*
- *Let $f_v = u$ for some u as defined in Lem. 5.*
- *A zero path of node v, denoted by $\mathbf{Z}_v$, is a maximal parent path of nodes $\{x | \exists \mathbf{C}_x(v) \wedge x \in \mathbf{R}_v(f_v)\}$. A fringe node of $\mathbf{Z}_v$ is $w \in \mathbf{Z}_v$ which is the furthest node (in the number of hops) from v. Then, we also denote a zero path of v by $\mathbf{Z}_v(w)$ and its length by $|\mathbf{Z}_v(w)|$ (or $|\mathbf{Z}_v|$).*

Note, that every root node has a zero path (possibly containing only a root). A zero path may change dynamically in time. Nodes may join and leave a zero path. A zero path may "disappear" (if a root node stops to be a root) and "reappear" (if a node becomes a root again). The set of a zero paths stabilizes only in $\Omega(\mathbf{n})$ in some cases. Yet, by the following lemmas 6 to 8, we show that up_cover $= 0$ holds at every node of every zero path that exists after a certain time that is $O(2^i)$ time after the starting time t_0. The proofs of lemmas 6 - 8 establish an induction on the order of the nodes on a zero path, starting from a fringe node neighboring to a foreign node and proceeding to the root. This induction shows that up_cover stabilizes fast to zero over each legal tree (one that has a root, as opposed to a sprig that is disconnected from its root). Let us comment that we needed to introduce the notion of a legal branch for these proofs. Moreover, we needed to add the check (in the consistent predicate, in Rule 2) that a branch is indeed legal when up_cover is updated. The proofs of lemmas 6 - 8 appear in [12].

Lemma 6. *Let* $v, u \in V$ *and let* u *be a fringe node of* $\mathbf{Z}_v$ *(a zero path of* v*), at some time* T *after* T_{valid}*. Then, if* u *stays a fringe node of* $\mathbf{Z}_v$*, in at most 1 time step, at time* $T \leq T1 \leq T + 1$*,* up_cover$_u \leftarrow 0$*.*

Lemma 7. *Let* $v, u \in V$ *and assume that* u *joins a* $\mathbf{Z}_v$ *(a zero path of* v*) at some time* T *after* T_{valid} *(*u *was not in* $\mathbf{Z}_v$ *just before* T*). Then, at time* T*,* up_cover$_u \leftarrow 0$*.*

Lemma 8. *Let* $v, u, x \in V$ *and* $\mathbf{Z}_v(x)$ *be a zero path of* v*. Let* $u \in \mathbf{Z}_v(x)$ *be such that* $\mathbf{dist}(v, u) = \mathbf{dist}(v, f_v) - j$ *(for some* $1 \leq j \leq \mathbf{dist}(v, f_v) \leq 2^i + 1$*). Then, after* $T_{valid} + j$ *time steps,* up_cover$_u = 0$*.*

Let T_{ccover} be the time that is $T_{valid} + 2 \cdot 2^i$ time steps after time t_0. By lemmas 8 and 4 and Rule 2, it is easy to show that down_cover also stabilizes fast to zero on legal trees. Thus, Lem. 9 also follows.

Lemma 9. *After* T_{ccover} *time for any connected node* $u \in V$ *the following holds:* down_cover$_u = 0$*.*

To conclude the analysis for versions for which $2^i \leq \mathbf{depth}(v_{min})$, we need to show that for every node u that is *disconnected* from $\mathbf{r}_u$ (u is a sprig node), down_cover$_u = 0$ holds in $O(2^i)$ time steps and remains such thereafter too. First, let us formalize all the possible modifications that a sprig can encounter. Note, that there may exist several sprigs of v at the same time.

Definition 6. *Consider a sequence of events in the execution, and let* t_j *be the time of the* j*-th event in the sequence. Consider some sprig* $A_v(t_j)$*. At time* t_{j+1}*, we consider sprigs that are non-empty and that have non-empty intersection of nodes with the original sprig* $A_v(t_j)$*. That is, we consider all the possible modifications of* A_v *at time* t_{j+1}*:*
(1) Sprig $A_v(t_{j+1}) \neq \emptyset$ *is one of the following:*
– $A_v(t_j)$*.*
– $A_v(t_j) \cup \{x\}$ *(a join of node) for some* $x \notin A_v(t_j)$*. Note, that by Lem. 4,* x *has no descendants at* t_{j+1}*. (Also, w.l.o.g., no two events happen at the same time.)*
– $A_v(t_j) \setminus \{y\}$ *(a loss of node) for some* $y \in A_v(t_j)$*.*
(2) Non-empty sprigs $A1_v(t_{j+1}), A2_v(t_{j+1}), \cdots$ *such that* $A1_v(t_{j+1}) \cup A2_v(t_{j+1}) \cup \cdots \{z\} = A_v(t_j)$ *(a split of sprig* A_v*) for some node* z *who left sprig* A_v *at* t_j*.*

Lemma 10. *Let* $u \in V$ *be disconnected from* $\mathbf{r}_u$ *at some time after* $T_{ccover} + 2 \cdot 2^i + 1$*. Then,* down_cover$_u = 0$*.*

Proof: Any disconnected node u belongs to some sprig. Let $\mathbf{r}_u \equiv v$. Only two kinds of sprigs exist after time T_{ccover} by Obs. 1:

(1) The old sprigs- these that already exist at T_{ccover}. We consider them old even when they get modified later. Moreover, if $A_v(t_j)$ is an old sprig at some time $t_j \geq T_{ccover}$, then any resulting sprig $A_v(t_{j+1})$ (see Def. 6) at time $t_{j+1} > t_j$ is an old sprig too.

(2) The new sprigs- those that are newly created after T_{ccover} by the following event. Let $w \in V$ be a root node and X be a set of the nodes connected to w (X is a tree rooted at w). When some node $x \in X$ (not a leaf node) leaves X, a new sprig (or sprigs) of w is (or are) created. When a new sprig gets modified, the resulting sprig (or sprigs) is (or are) considered a new sprig (or sprigs).

First, let us consider a set of the old sprigs Φ after T_{ccover}. We show that after at most $2 \cdot 2^i + 1$ time steps $\Phi = \emptyset$. By Lem. 2, in at most $2 \cdot 2^i$ time steps, for any disconnected node $x \in B \in \Phi$, $\mathsf{d}_x \geq 2^i$. Hence, x leaves sprig B in at most additional 1 time step by Rule 1-1, if x has not left sprig B before that. Any node $y \notin B \in \Phi$ that joins sprig B, assigns $\mathsf{d}_y \leftarrow \mathsf{d}_y[z] + 1$ for $z \in B$ such that $\mathsf{par}_y \leftarrow z$. Thus, by this and Lem. 2, for any $x \in B \in \Phi$, at time $T_{ccover} + 2t$, $\mathsf{d}_x \geq t$. Hence, after at most $T_{ccover} + 2 \cdot 2^i + 1$, $\Phi = \emptyset$.

Finally, let us consider a new sprig A that is newly created at some time $T > T_{ccover}$. By Lem. 9, at time T for each $x \in A$, $\mathsf{down\_cover}_x = 0$. After time T sprig A can change in time: split or join/loose nodes. Note, that no sprig has a root node and thus, by Rule 2, the $\mathsf{down\_cover}_x$ bit is calculated by $\mathsf{down\_cover}_x \leftarrow (\mathsf{down\_cover}_x[\mathsf{par}_x] \wedge \mathsf{consistent}_x)$. Hence, a split or a loss of nodes cannot switch the $\mathsf{down\_cover}$ bit (from 0 to 1) at the resulting sprig/s. Now, consider the case that some node $y \notin A$ joins A. Node y becomes a child of some node $x \in A$. At that time, by Lem. 4, a local reset exit occurs at y (line 12) and then, at line 13, node y assigns $\mathsf{par}_y \leftarrow x$ and by Rule 2, adopts the $\mathsf{down\_cover}_{\mathsf{par}_y}$ which is 0 as shown above. Thus, any node that joins A adopts 0 in its $\mathsf{down\_cover}$ (recall that by Lem. 4, it joins alone).

Hence, after time $T_{ccover} + 2 \cdot 2^i + 1$, only new sprigs exist (beside legal trees) and every disconnected node u in such a sprig has $\mathsf{down\_cover}_u = 0$.   ∎

5   Analysis of the Higher Version Case ($2^i \geq \mathbf{depth}(v_{min})$)

Lem. 11 is important to prove the stabilization of the higher versions (Lem. 12). Specifically, it helps to show that a local reset mode in each node has finite duration.

Lemma 11. *Assume a node v performing a local reset operation at some time T.*
(1) Then, in at most 2 time steps after time T, unless the condition of line 9 holds, v performs line 12 of the algorithm (a local reset exit occurs at v).
(2) During the local reset mode at v (starting at time T and till the local reset exit at v), $\mathsf{up\_cover}_v = 0$ and $\mathsf{down\_cover}_v = 0$.

Lemma 12. *If $2^i \geq \mathbf{depth}(v_{min})$, then version i stabilizes in $O(2^i)$.*

Lemma 13. *If $2^i \geq \mathbf{depth}(v_{min})$, then in $O(2^i)$ time, at every node v, $\mathsf{down\_cover}_v = 1$ for version i.*

Lem. 12 above establishes that there exists some higher version that stabilizes at time $O(\mathbf{diam})$. Lem. 13 establishes that in this version down_cover ← 1. Hence, the algorithm can output the tree this version produces. Recall that Sec. 4 shows that in lower versions down_cover stabilizes to zero. All these establish the following theorem.

Theorem 1. *In $O(\mathbf{diam})$ time units, the algorithm produces a shortest paths tree rooted at the minimal* ID *node in the network.*

The proofs (see [12]) in this section are rather similar to the proofs for the higher versions in [7] except for one important point. The local reset we use here has the potential to destabilize these versions. We show that a local reset always ends. Moreover, since a local reset is transferred to children, not to parents, the reset does not destabilize the tree rooted in the minimal *ID* node.

References

1. Abbas, S., Mosbah, M., Zemmari, A.: Distributed Computation of a Spanning Tree in a Dynamic Graph by Mobile Agents. In: IEEEIS'06 (2006)
2. Afek, Y., Bremler-Barr, A.: Self-stabilizing Unidirectional Network Algorithms by Power-Supply. In: SODA'97 (1997)
3. Afek, Y., Kutten, S., Yung, M.: Memory-Efficient Self-Stabilizing Protocols for General Networks. In: van Leeuwen, J., Santoro, N. (eds.) Distributed Algorithms. LNCS, vol. 486. Springer, Heidelberg (1991)
4. Afek, Y., Kutten, S., Yung, M.: The Local Detection Paradigm and its Applications to Self-Stabilization. In: TCS' 97, vol. 186(1–2) (1997)
5. Aggarwal, S., Kutten, S.: Time Optimal Self-stabilizing Spanning Tree Algorithms. In: Shyamasundar, R.K. (ed.) Foundations of Software Technology and Theoretical Computer Science. LNCS, vol. 761. Springer, Heidelberg (1993)
6. Arora, A., Gouda, M.G.: Distributed Reset. In: Veni Madhavan, C.E., Nori, K.V. (eds.) Foundations of Software Technology and Theoretical Computer Science. LNCS, vol. 472. Springer, Heidelberg (1990)
7. Awerbuch, B., Kutten, S., Mansour, Y., Patt-Shamir, B., Varghese, G.: Time Optimal Self-stabilizing Syncronization. In: STOC'93 (1993)
8. Awerbuch, B., Patt-Shamir, B., Varghese, G.: Bounding the Unbounded. In: IN-FOCOM'94 (1994)
9. Awerbuch, B., Patt-Shamir, B., Varghese, G.: Self-stabilization by Local Checking and Correction. In: FOCS'91 (1991)
10. Beauquier, J., Datta, A.K., Gradinariu, M., Magniette, F.: Self-stabilization Local Mutual Exclution and Daemon Refinement. In: Herlihy, M.P. (ed.) DISC 2000. LNCS, vol. 1914. Springer, Heidelberg (2000)
11. Bellman, R.: On routing problem. Qurterly of Applied Mathematics 16(1), 87–90 (1958)
12. Burman, J., Kutten, S.: Time Optimal Asynchronous Self-stabilizing Spanning Tree (extended version), http://tx.technion.ac.il/~bjanna/
13. Delaët, S., Ducourthial, B., Tixeuil, S.: Self-stabilization with r-operators in Unreliable Directed Networks. TR 1361, LRI (2003)
14. Delaët, S., Ducourthial, B., Tixeuil, S.: Self-stabilization with r-operators revised. In: JACIC (2006)

15. Dijkstra, E.W.: Self-stabilization in spite of Distributed Control. Comm. ACM 17, 643–644 (1974)
16. Dolev, S., Israeli, A., Moran, S.: Resource Bounds for Self-stabilizing Message Driven Protocols. In: PODC'91 (1991)
17. Dolev, S., Israeli, A., Moran, S.: Self-stabilization of Dynamic Systems Assuming Only Read/Write Atomicity. DC 7, 3–16 (1994)
18. Dolev, S., Israeli, A., Moran, S.: Uniform Dynamic Self-stabilizing Leader Election (extended abstract). In: Toueg, S., Kirousis, L.M., Spirakis, P.G. (eds.) Distributed Algorithms. LNCS, vol. 579. Springer, Heidelberg (1992)
19. Ducourthial, B., Tixeuil, S.: Self-stabilization with r-operators. DC 14(3), 147–162 (2001)
20. Garg, V.K., Agarwal, A.: Distributed Maintenance of A Spanning-Tree Using Labeled Tree Encoding. In: Cunha, J.C., Medeiros, P.D. (eds.) Euro-Par 2005. LNCS, vol. 3648. Springer, Heidelberg (2005)
21. Gärtner, F.C.: A Survey of Self-Stabilizing Spanning-Tree Construction Algorithms. TR, EPFL (October 2003)
22. Gärtner, F.C., Pagnia, H.: Time-Efficient Self-stabilizing Algorithms Through Hierarchical Structures. In: Huang, S.-T., Herman, T. (eds.) SSS 2003. LNCS, vol. 2704. Springer, Heidelberg (2003)
23. Gupta, S.K.S., Srimani, P.K.: Self-stabilizing Multicast Protocols for Ad Hoc Networks. JPDC 63(1) (2003)
24. Herault, T., Lemarinier, P., Peres, O., Pilard, L., Beauquier, J.: Self-stabilizing Spanning Tree Algorithm for Large Scale Systems. TR 1457, LRI (August 2006)
25. Higham, L., Liang, Z.: Self-stabilizing Minimum Spanning Tree Construction on Message-Passing Networks. In: Welch, J.L. (ed.) DISC 2001. LNCS, vol. 2180. Springer, Heidelberg (2001)
26. Nesterenko, M., Arora, A.: Stabilization-Preserving Atomicity Refinement. J. Parallel Distrib. Comput. 62(5), 766–791 (2002)

Rendezvous of Mobile Agents in Unknown Graphs with Faulty Links

Jérémie Chalopin[1,*], Shantanu Das[2], and Nicola Santoro[3]

[1] LaBRI Université Bordeaux 1, Talence, France
chalopin@labri.fr
[2] School of Information Technology and Engineering, University of Ottawa, Canada
shantdas@site.uottawa.ca
[3] School of Computer Science, Carleton University, Canada
santoro@scs.carleton.ca

Abstract. A group of identical mobile agents moving asynchronously among the nodes of an anonymous network have to gather together in a single node of the graph. This problem known as the (asynchronous anonymous multi-agent) rendezvous problem has been studied extensively but only for networks that are safe or fault-free. In this paper, we consider the case when some of the edges in the network are dangerous or faulty such that any agent travelling along one of these edges would be destroyed. The objective is to minimize the number of agents that are destroyed and achieve rendezvous of all the surviving agents. We determine under what conditions this is possible and present algorithms for achieving rendezvous in such cases. Our algorithms are for arbitrary networks with an arbitrary number of dangerous channels; thus our model is a generalization of the case where all the dangerous channels lead to single node, called the *Black Hole*. We do not assume prior knowledge of the network topology; In fact, we show that knowledge of only a "tight" bound on the network size is sufficient for solving the problem, whenever it is solvable.

1 Introduction

1.1 The Problem

Consider a networked environment, modelled as a simple connected graph, in which operate a set of mobile computational entities, called agents or robots. A central problem in such systems is the so called *rendezvous* (or *gathering*) problem which requires the agents to meet together in a single node of the network. This problem has been extensively studied in the literature (see, for example, [1,3,10,15,17,19,23]) under a variety of models with different assumptions on the identity of the network nodes and/or of the agents (anonymous or distinct labels), the existence of timing bounds on the agents' actions (synchronous or asynchronous), the intercommunication mechanisms (whiteboards

---

* Supported in part by grant ANR-06-SETI-015-03 awarded by the Agence Nationale de la Recherche.

A. Pelc (Ed.): DISC 2007, LNCS 4731, pp. 108–122, 2007.

or pebbles/tokens), the amount and type of memory, etc. In spite of their widely different models, the existing studies on the rendezvous problems share the common assumption that the environment where the agents operate is safe.

Unlike previous studies on the rendezvous problem, we consider the case when the environment where the rendezvous must take place, is not safe. In our model, some of the edges in the graph are harmful for the agents; specifically, any agent that attempts to traverse any such an edge (from either direction) simply disappears, without leaving any trace. The location of the unsafe links are initially unknown to the agents; we only assume that the unsafe links do not disconnect the network. Notice that if all the edges incident to a node u are unsafe, then node u can never be reached by any agent and is equivalent to a *black hole*, i.e., a node that destroys any incoming agent (e.g., [8,9,11,12,13,18]). In other words, the black hole model is just a specific case of the model considered in this paper.

We investigate the problem in a very weak (and thus computationally difficult) setting: the network nodes do not have distinct identities (i.e., the network is anonymous), the agents are identical, and their actions (computations and movements) take a finite but otherwise unpredictable amount of time.

The only previous result for rendezvous in faulty networks was in the case of the ring network containing two unsafe links leading to a single node—the black hole [13]. Our investigation is thus a generalization of these studies to networks of arbitrary topology that contain faults at arbitrary locations.

1.2   Our Results

In this paper we provide a full characterization of the rendezvous problem of asynchronous anonymous agents in anonymous networks with unsafe links. Assuming that the safe part of the network is connected, any port on a safe node which leads to an unsafe part of the network, is called a faulty link. We present the following results in this paper:

- We first show that, if there are τ unsafe links in the network and k agents, then it is not possible, in general, for k' agents to rendezvous if $k' > k - \tau$.
- We then prove that the rendezvous of $k-\tau$ agents is deterministically possible only when the network is *covering minimal*. Even in this case, rendezvous is not possible if the agents do not know the size of the network or at least a tight upper bound. In fact, we prove that a loose upper bound $n \leq B_n \leq 2n$ is not sufficient.
- We then show that this result is tight. In fact, we present an algorithm, RDV that requires only the knowledge of a tight upper bound B on the number of nodes n, such that $n \leq B < 2n$. This algorithm allows rendezvous of $k - \tau$ agents in networks where such a rendezvous is possible; the rendezvous occurs with explicit termination for each surviving agent.
- The total number of moves made by the agents during the execution of algorithm RDV is $O(m(m + k))$ where m is the number of edges in G. We prove that this cost is optimal; in fact, we show that solving rendezvous of $k - \tau$ agents in networks where it is solvable, requires at least $\Omega(m(m + k))$ moves, even when the network topology is known a priori.

– Finally we show that, there exists no *effective* algorithm for *maximal* rendezvous, i.e. there does not exist an algorithm that when executed on any arbitrary network achieves the rendezvous of as many agents as deterministically possible on that network.

Due to the limitations of space, the proofs of some lemmas and theorems have been omitted; These can be found in the full paper.

1.3   Related Work

The problem of *Rendezvous* has been extensively studied mostly using randomized methods (see [1] for a survey). Among deterministic solutions to rendezvous, Yu and Yung [23] and Dessmark et al. [10] presented algorithms for agents with distinct labels. In the anonymous setting, the problem has been studied under different models (synchronous or asynchronous), using either whiteboards [3] or, pebbles/tokens [19]. Some of the recent studies have focussed on minimizing the memory required by the agents for rendezvous([15,17]).

Most of these solutions are designed for anonymous graphs (i.e. graphs where nodes do not have distinct identities) which present the most challenging (i.e. computationally difficult) situations. The issue of computability in anonymous graphs, have been studied by many authors including Angluin [2], Yamashita and Kameda [22], Mazurkiewicz [20], Sakamoto [21], and Boldi and Vigna [4]. Most of these studies have concentrated on the problem of symmetry-breaking or leader election which is in fact, closely related (and sometimes equivalent [7]) to the rendezvous problem for mobile agents. However, all the above results are restricted to safe or fault-free networks.

Recently attention has focused on designing mobile agent protocols for networks which are faulty, in particular, where there is a black hole, that is a harmful network site that destroys any visiting agent. The research on such networks have concentrated on locating the black hole. In asynchronous systems, this has been studied under two different methods—using whiteboards [11,12] or using tokens [14] to mark edges. The objective here is minimizing the number of agents that fall into the black hole and the number of moves. In the case of synchronous agents, the objective is to minimize the time taken by the surviving agents to locate the black hole [9,18]. The general case of multiple black holes has been considered only by Cooper et al. [8]. All these problems assume that the team of agents start from the same node, i.e. they are co-located. When the agents start from distinct nodes, it is very difficult to gather the agents while avoiding the black hole nodes. This has been studied earlier only in the case of ring networks containing a single black hole, by Dobrev et al. [13], where the authors give solutions to rendezvous and near-gathering assuming the knowledge of topology and the size of the network.

2   The Model and Definitions

2.1   The Model

The environment is modelled by the tuple $(G, \xi, p, \lambda, \eta)$ where G is an undirected connected graph, ξ is a set of agents and p specifies the initial placement of the

agents in the graph G (i.e. $\forall A \in \xi, p(A) = v : v \in V(G)$). The number of
nodes is denoted by $n = |V(G)|$ and the number of agents is denoted by $k = |\xi|$.
The agents can move from one node to its adjacent node by traversing the edge
connecting them. The edges incident to a node v are locally oriented i.e. they are
labelled as $1, 2, \ldots, d(v)$, where $d(v)$ is the degree of node v. Notice that each edge
$e = (u, v)$ has two labels, one for the link or port at node u and another for the
link at node v. The edge labelling of the graph G is specified by $\lambda = \{\lambda_v : v \in V\}$,
where for each vertex u, $\lambda_u : \{(u, v) \in E : v \in V\} \rightarrow \{1, 2, 3, \ldots, d(u)\}$ defines
the labelling on its incident edges. For any edge (u, v) we use $\lambda(u, v)$ to denote
the pair $(\lambda_u(u, v), \lambda_v(u, v))$.

The function $\eta : E(G) \rightarrow \{0, 1\}$ denotes which edges are safe/faulty. An edge
$e \in E(G)$ is safe if $\eta(e) = 1$ and faulty otherwise. The faults are permanent, so
any edge that is faulty at the start of the algorithm remains so until the end and
no new faulty edge appears during the execution of the algorithm.

The node from where an agent A starts the algorithm (i.e. the initial location)
is called the *homebase* of agent A. The agents are all identical (i.e. they do
not have distinct names or labels) and they execute the same algorithm. An
agent may enter the system at any time and at any location, and on entry, an
agent immediately starts its individual execution of the algorithm. The system
is totally asynchronous, such that every action performed by an agent takes a
finite but otherwise unpredictable amount of time. As in previous papers on
the subject, we assume that the agents communicate by reading and writing
information on public whiteboards locally available at the nodes of the network.
Thus, each node $v \in G$ has a whiteboard (which is a shared region of its memory)
and any agent visiting node v can read or write to the whiteboard. Access to
the whiteboard is restricted by fair mutual exclusion, so that, at most one agent
can access the whiteboard of a node at the same time, and any requesting agent
will be granted access within finite time. An agent that is granted access to the
whiteboard at node v, is allowed to complete its activity at that node before
relinquishing access to the whiteboard (i.e. access control is non preemptive).

Note that it is not necessary for two agents A and B traversing the same edge
$e = (u, v)$ of the graph, to arrive at node v in the same order in which they left
node u. However, using the whiteboards at the nodes, it is easy to implement
a first-in first-out (FIFO) strategy such that agents traversing an edge can be
assumed to have reached their destination in order (i.e. an agent cannot overtake
another while traversing an edge). For the rest of this paper, we shall assume
this FIFO property; this will simplify the description of our algorithms.

2.2 Directed Graphs and Coverings

In this section, we present some definitions and results related to directed graphs
and their coverings, which we use to characterize those network where rendezvous
is possible. A directed graph(digraph) $D = (V(D), A(D), s_D, t_D)$ possibly having
parallel arcs and self-loops, is defined by a set $V(D)$ of vertices, a set $A(D)$ of
arcs and by two maps s_D and t_D that assign to each arc two elements of $V(D)$:
a source and a target (in general, the subscripts will be omitted). A digraph D is

strongly connected if for all vertices $u, v \in V(D)$, there exists a path between u and v. A *symmetric* digraph D is a digraph endowed with a symmetry, that is, an involution $Sym : A(D) \rightarrow A(D)$ such that for every $a \in A(D)$, $s(a) = t(Sym(a))$. A bidirectional network can be represented by a strongly connected symmetric digraph, where each edge of the network is represented by a pair of symmetric arcs. In this paper, we consider digraphs where the vertices and the arcs are labelled with labels from a recursive label set L and such digraphs will be denoted by (D, μ_D), where $\mu_D : V(D) \cup A(D) \rightarrow L$ is the labelling function. In general, the label on an arc a would be a pair (x, y) and the labelling μ_D should satisfy the property that if $\mu_D(a) = (x, y)$ then $\mu_D(Sym(a)) = (y, x)$, for every arc $a \in D$.

A *digraph homomorphism* γ between the digraph D and the digraph D' is a mapping $\gamma : V(D) \cup A(D) \rightarrow V(D') \cup A(D')$ such that if u, v are vertices of D and a is an arc such that $u = s(a)$ and $v = t(a)$ then $\gamma(u) = s(\gamma(a))$ and $\gamma(v) = t(\gamma(a))$. A homomorphism from (D, μ_D) to (D', μ'_D) is a digraph homomorphism from D to D' which preserves the labelling, i.e., such that $\mu'_D(\gamma(x)) = \mu_D(x)$ for every $x \in V(D) \cup A(D)$.

We now define the notion of graph coverings, borrowing the terminology of Boldi and Vigna[5]. A *covering projection* is a homomorphism φ from D to D' satisfying the following: (i) For each arc a' of $A(D')$ and for each vertex v of $V(D)$ such that $\varphi(v) = v' = t(a')$ there exists a unique arc a in $A(D)$ such that $t(a) = v$ and $\varphi(a) = a'$. (ii) For each arc a' of $A(D')$ and for each vertex v of $V(D)$ such that $\varphi(v) = v' = s(a')$ there exists a unique arc a in $A(D)$ such that $s(a) = v$ and $\varphi(a) = a'$.

The *fibre* over a vertex v' (resp. an arc a') of D' is the set $\varphi^{-1}(v')$ of vertices of D (resp. the set $\varphi^{-1}(a')$ of arcs of D).

If a covering projection $\varphi : D \rightarrow D'$ exists, D is said to be a *covering* of D' via φ and D' is called the base of φ. A symmetric digraph D is a *symmetric covering* of a symmetric digraph D' via a homomorphism φ if D is a covering of D' via φ such that $\forall a \in A(D), \varphi(Sym(a)) = Sym(\varphi(a))$. A digraph D is *symmetric-covering-minimal* if there does not exist any graph D' not isomorphic to D such that D is a symmetric covering of D'.

The notions of coverings extend to labelled digraphs in an obvious way: the homomorphisms must preserve the labelling. Given a labelled symmetric digraph (H, μ_H), the *minimum base* of (H, μ_H) is defined to be the labelled digraph (D, μ_D) such that (i) (H, μ_H) is a symmetric covering of (D, μ_D) and (ii) (D, μ_D) is symmetric covering minimal.

The following results on digraph coverings were proved in [5].

Property 1. Given two non-empty strongly connected digraphs D, D', each covering projection φ from D to D' is surjective; moreover, all the fibres have the same cardinality. This cardinality is called the *number of sheets* of the covering.

Property 2. If the digraph (H, μ_H) is a covering of (D, μ_D) via φ, then any execution of an algorithm $\mathcal{P}$ on (D, μ_D) can be lifted up to an execution on

(H, μ_H), such that at the end of the execution, for any $v \in V(H)$, v would be in the same state as $\varphi(v)$.

2.3 Definitions and Properties

Given any deterministic (distributed) algorithm $\mathcal{P}$ and a network $(G, \xi, p, \lambda, \eta)$, the order in which the various actions are performed by the agents defines an *execution* of the algorithm on the network $(G, \xi, p, \lambda, \eta)$. We define the *synchronous* execution of an algorithm $\mathcal{P}$ to be the particular execution where all agents start executing at exactly the same time and every action taken by any agent takes exactly one unit of time.

We define the *extended-view* of the network $(G, \xi, p, \lambda, \eta)$ as the labelled digraph (H, μ_H) such that, H consists of two disjoint vertex sets V_1 and V_2 and a set of arcs $\mathcal{A}$ as defined below:

- $V_1 = V(G)$;
- $\mu_H(v) = |\{A \in \xi : p(A) = v\}|, \forall v \in V_1$;
- For every safe edge $e = (u, v) \in E(G)$, there are two arcs $a_1, a_2 \in \mathcal{A}$ such that $s(a_1) = t(a_2) = u$, $s(a_2) = t(a_1) = v$, and $\mu_H(a_1) = (\lambda_u(e), \lambda_v(e))$, $\mu_H(a_2) = (\lambda_v(e), \lambda_u(e))$.
- For every faulty edge $e = (u, v)$, there are vertices u' and $v' \in V_2$ with $\mu_H(u') = \mu_H(v') = -1$ and arcs $(u, u'), (u', u), (v, v')$ and $(v', v) \in \mathcal{A}$ with labels $(\lambda_e(u), 0), (0, \lambda_e(u)), (\lambda_e(v), 0),$ and $(0, \lambda_e(u))$ respectively;

Here, the vertices in V_1 represent the (safe) nodes of the network and the vertices in V_2 represent (imaginary) Black-Holes. The label on a *safe* vertex v denotes the number of agents that started from the corresponding node, whereas the label on a *black-hole* vertex is always -1. Intuitively, the *extended-view* can be thought of as a canonical representation of the network.

The following results follow from the definition of the *extended-view* of a network and the Properties 1 and 2.

Lemma 1. *For any deterministic algorithm $\mathcal{P}$, a synchronous execution of $\mathcal{P}$ on the network $(G, \xi, p, \lambda, \eta)$ is equivalent to a synchronous execution of algorithm $\mathcal{P}$ on the extended-view (H, μ_H), such that the final state of any node in G is exactly same as the state of the corresponding vertex in H.*

Lemma 2. *If the extended view of two networks have same minimum-base (D, μ_D) then all nodes in the two networks which belong to the pre-image of a vertex $v \in D$ would always be in the same state, during a synchronous execution of any algorithm $\mathcal{P}$.*

3 Impossibility Results

In this section, we determine some necessary conditions for solution to the rendezvous problem. In the following, whenever the extended-view of a network is symmetric-covering minimal, we shall say the network is *minimal*.

Lemma 3. *In a network containing τ dangerous links and k dispersed agents, τ agents may die while executing any algorithm for rendezvous. Thus, it is not always possible to rendezvous more than $k - \tau$ agents even if the network topology is known to the agents.*

Lemma 4. *It is impossible to rendezvous $k - \tau$ agents in a network whose extended-view is not symmetric-covering minimal.*

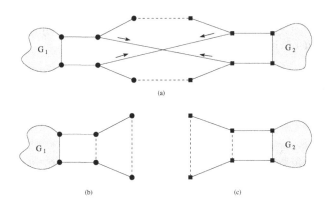

Fig. 1. The network in (a) cannot be distinguished from the networks in (b) and (c) due to the slow edges. (The slow edges are marked by arrows and the dashed lines represent faulty edges).

In the next section, we show how to solve rendezvous of $k - \tau$ agents in any network that is minimal. Thus, we have a complete characterization of networks where rendezvous of $k - \tau$ agents is possible. However, solution to rendezvous requires at least some prior knowledge about the network, as we show below. Notice that since the network is asynchronous, an agent may take an arbitrarily long time to traverse some edge. Thus, a *slow* edge (i.e. one which the agents take a long time to traverse) is indistinguishable from a faulty edge. During the execution of an algorithm, the presence of slow edges may divide the network into two equal parts (for example, see Figure 1) and in such cases, it is not possible for the agents to terminate the algorithm unless an accurate estimate of network size is available.

Lemma 5. *It is impossible to solve rendezvous (with termination detection) of $k - \tau$ agents even in minimal networks if the agents know only an upper bound B on the number of nodes n such that $n \le B \le 2n$.*

The algorithm presented in this paper works only for networks which are minimal. We say that an algorithm $\mathcal{P}$ is an universally *effective* algorithm for rendezvous of $w > 1$ agents if, when executed on any network where rendezvous of w agents is possible, algorithm $\mathcal{P}$ always succeeds in achieving rendezvous within a finite time. We have the following negative result on the existence of such an algorithm.

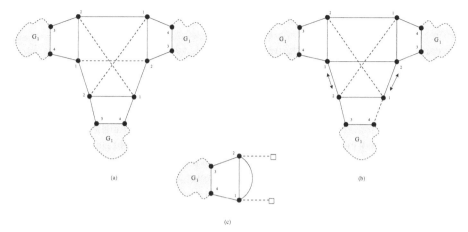

Fig. 2. The networks in (a) and (b) have same topology but differ in the location of faulty edges (shown by dashed lines). (c) The minimum base for the network in (a).

Lemma 6. *There does not exist any universally effective algorithm for rendezvous of $1 < w \leq k$ agents even if the network topology is known a-priori to the agents.*

Proof. Consider the two networks shown in Figure 2(a) and (b). Each network has the same topology and there are three faulty edges in each (but their locations are different). In the network of Figure 2(b) there are two edges (marked by arrows) which are very slow. Since slow edges edges can not be distinguished from faulty edges, the agents would not be able to determine whether they are in the first network or the second. Thus any rendezvous algorithm $\mathcal{P}$ (that terminates within a finite time) must achieve the same result in both networks. Notice that the first network has an extended view which is not minimal (the minimum base is shown in Figure 2(c)). Since algorithm $\mathcal{P}$ must fail to achieve rendezvous in the first network, it must also fail in the second one, even though it is possible to rendezvous in the second network. Thus algorithm $\mathcal{P}$ is not *effective*.

4 Solution Protocol

In this section we present an algorithm for solving Rendezvous in faulty networks, using the knowledge of only an upper bound B on the network size, such that $n \leq B < 2n$. As shown in the previous section, there is no effective algorithm for Rendezvous in faulty networks. Our algorithm always works for any network whose extended-view is covering minimal, achieving the rendezvous of the maximum number of agents possible (i.e. $k - \tau$ agents). We also analyze the complexity of our algorithm and show that it is optimal in terms of the number of moves made by the agents.

Theorem 1. *For solving rendezvous of $(k - \tau)$ agents in an arbitrary network $(G, \xi, p, \lambda, \eta)$ without any knowledge other than the size of the network, the agents need to make at least $\Omega(m(m + k))$ moves in total.*

4.1   The Algorithm for Rendezvous

We can ensure that no more than one agent dies while traversing the same link, using the *cautious walk* technique as in [13]. At each node, all the incident edges are considered to be unexplored in the beginning. Whenever an agent A at a node u has to traverse an unexplored edge $e = (u, v)$, agent A first marks link $\lambda_u(e)$ as "Being Explored" and if it is able to reach the other end v successfully, it immediately returns to node u and re-marks the link $\lambda_u(e)$ as "safe". During the algorithm we follow the rule that no agent ever traverses a link that is marked "Being Explored". This ensures no more than τ agents may die during the algorithm.

We now briefly describe our algorithm for rendezvous (Algorithm RDV). Due to the space constraint, we present only an oversimplified version of the algorithm without the minor technical details. The complete pseudo-code for the algorithm can be found in the full paper.

At any stage of the algorithm, there are teams of agents, each team possessing a *territory* which is a connected acyclic subgraph of G (disjoint from other territories). Each team of agents tries to expand its territory until it spans a majority of the nodes. Once a team is able to acquire more than half the nodes of the network, it wins and agents from all other teams join the winning team to achieve rendezvous.

Initially each territory consists of only the starting node(homebase) of an agent (all agents that start from that node are in this team). Note that if an agent on start-up, finds that its homebase has already been acquired by some other team, it simply joins this team. The algorithm proceeds in a series of exploring and competing rounds. In an exploring round, the team of agents try to expand its territory by exploring new edges and acquiring new nodes. On the other hand, in the competing round a team tries to defeat another team and conquering their territory. The competition between two teams occurs by comparison using the tuple $(j, Code)$ where j is the round number and Code is an encoding of the territory(and its immediate neighborhood).

The territory of each team is a rooted tree and the information stored in the root defines the status of the agents in the team (e.g. whether they are in an exploring round or competing round). Every other node in the tree stores a pointer to its parent in the tree. The status of the root can either INIT-EXPLORE, INIT-COMPETE, COMPETE, LOST, or END.

Only one agent in a team can be competing state (this is called the active agent and all others are passive). When a team is in exploring round, the active agent initiates the exploration and thereafter every agent may participate in the exploration. Each agent explores one unexplored edge and if it succeeds in reaching the other side, it reports this to the root of the tree and the tree is updated accordingly. If the edge connects to a node that is already explored (by another agent or the same agent) then it is marked as tree edge (T-edge) and the new node becomes part of the tree. Otherwise it is marked as non-tree edge (NT-edge).

In the algorithm below, T refers to the tree representing the territory to which the agent belongs. The root of T is denoted by r and Root_Status(T) is the status of the root as written on the whiteboard of r (A copy of T is also stored on the whiteboard). A node u is called a *neighbor* of the tree T if there is a NT-edge between u and some node in T. Each agent starts in *active* state, but may become *passive* or *finished*. The following steps are executed by an agent A:

Algorithm RDV

$< T, rNum > :=$ **Initialize**;
While (Status(A) $\neq$ finished) {
    Case(Status(A) is active and Root_Status(T) is INIT-EXPLORE) {
        If ($|T| > B/2$) **terminate**;
        InitExplore;
        If (Root_Status(T) = LOST) become passive and exit Case;
        Set Root_Status(T) to EXPLORE and become Passive;
    }
    Case(Status(A) is passive) {
        While(Root_Status(T) $\notin$ { EXPLORE, INIT-EXPLORE, END })
            Sleep until woken up;
        If(Root_Status(T) is END) become finished and exit;
        Explore an unexplored edge and go back to r to update T;
        If(Root_Status(T) is EXPLORE) // i.e. no active agents
          become active and set Root_Status(T) to INIT-COMPETE
    }
    Case(Status(A) is active and Root_Status(T) is INIT-COMPETE) {
        do{ $T_{OLD} := T$;
          InitCompete($rNum$);
          If (Root_Status(T) = LOST) become passive and exit Case;
          Result = **Compete**($rNum$); $rNum := rNum + 1$;
        }While($T_{OLD} \neq T$);
        If(Root_Status(T) $\neq$ LOST) Root_Status(T):= INIT-EXPLORE;
    }
}

PROCEDURE *Initialize*: If the homebase of the agent is already part of a tree, then the agent joins this team in passive state. Otherwise, it initializes the tree with only the homebase node and then starts the algorithm in active state with $rNum = 1$.

PROCEDURE *InitExplore*: The agent initiates a new exploring round by traversing T writing "EXPLORE" on every node and waking up as many agents as needed for exploration (more precisely, it wakes-up x agents where x is the number of unexplored edges currently incident to T, unless less than x agents are available in T—in which case it wakes-up everyone).

PROCEDURE *InitCompete*(j): The agent initiates the competing round j by traversing T, writing $(COMPETE, j)$ on each node also assigning labels to the nodes in T. Next, it reads the labels written on the neighboring nodes and constructs an encoding of T and its neighbors, called CODE (this is used for comparisons). Finally it writes the CODE on every node in T.

PROCEDURE *Compete*(j): During this procedure, agent A competes with each node u that is neighbor of T, until it wins or loses. If u is marked END, agent A terminates after writing END on every node of T, waking up any sleeping agents and merging with the tree containing u. Else, if u is in a bigger competing round or in the same competing round with a larger Code, then agent A loses (i.e. it becomes passive and goes back to its root to sleep). Otherwise if u is in exploring round or in a smaller competing round or same round but has smaller Code, then Invade(u) is invoked to determine if the result of the competition is win or loss.

PROCEDURE *Invade*(u): The agent attempts to acquire the tree containing node u. The agent follows the father-links from u to reach the current root r_u of u. At node r_u it uses the usual comparison criteria and if r_u is bigger or equal, then it loses (i.e. it becomes passive and goes back to its root to sleep). Otherwise it wins and it acquires the Tree rooted at r_u, by reversing the father-links in the path from r_u to v where v is the node in the agent's territory from where it started the Invade procedure.

PROCEDURE *terminate*: The agent writes END on all nodes in T and then writes Root_Status(T)=END at the root of T; The agent now becomes finished and locally terminates.

4.2   Analysis of the Algorithm

Theorem 2. *Algorithm RDV correctly solves Rendezvous for $k - \tau$ agents in any network whose extended view is symmetric-covering minimal.*

This result follows from the following lemmas:

Lemma 7. *During the algorithm RDV, the following holds: (i) Each territory is a Tree. (ii) The territories are disjoint. (iii) There is at most one active agent in each territory.*

Proof. (i) Initially each territory is a tree by construction; addition of a new edge does not create cycles because only tree edges are added. When two trees are merged, one is 'larger' than other and the active agent of the larger tree performs the merging by changing the father-links and updating the root. (Notice that there can not be two active agents in a territory.) Thus the merged territory is a tree. (ii) Each tree is a rooted tree and every node contains a pointer to its parent in the tree. Thus, a node cannot belong to two trees. (iii) Initially an agent becomes active only when it successfully constructs T and writes it at the root node. Thus, due to the mutual exclusion property of the whiteboards, there is only one active agent initially in the tree (all other agents in the same tree must start in passive state). A passive agent can become active only when there are no active agents in the tree.

Lemma 8. *There is no deadlock in the algorithm RDV.*

Proof. Notice that as long as there is some active agent, the algorithm progresses. In each tree T, there is at least one active agent unless root-status is EXPLORE. Suppose the root-status of every tree is EXPLORE, then each agent is currently exploring some unexplored edge. There are only τ faulty links in the network and $k > \tau$, so at least one of the exploring agents must return safely from the exploration. This agent now becomes active.

Lemma 9. *(i) If the network is minimal, then exactly one node has Root-Status(T) = END. (ii) When one node has Root-Status(T) = END, every alive agent in G eventually joins this tree. (iii) $(k - \tau)$ agents eventually become finished and reach the node having Root-Status(T)= END.*

Proof. (i) First notice that due to the constraint on the bound B, only one Tree T can have a size greater than $B/2$. Due to Lemma 7, the trees are disjoint and each has a unique root. Thus, at most one node may have Root-Status(T)=END. We now show that at least one node eventually reaches Root-Status(T)=END. A team of agents in tree T stops expanding its Tree only when either Root-Status(T)=END or, all the trees neighboring T have the same CODE and round number. In the later case, the team starts an exploring round. Notice that there must exist a Tree T which has some non-faulty edges incident to it that are either unexplored or being explored (otherwise the network is either disconnected or, not minimal). So one of these edges would be added to T. Thus the size of T would keep increasing until it contains more than $B/2$ nodes and Root-Status(T) = END.

(ii) Every agent either dies or reaches a node labelled "END". All nodes that are labelled "END" are part of the same tree.

(iii) Due to the use of *cautious walk*, at most τ agents may die. Thus each of the surviving agent eventually reaches a node v labelled "END" and goes to the root of this tree which is the node having Root-Status(T)=END.

We now analyze the cost of algorithm RDV. We first count the number of competing rounds and exploring rounds performed during the algorithm.

Lemma 10. *There are $O(m + k)$ competing rounds. The number of exploring rounds is at most the number of competing rounds.*

Proof. A new competing round is started whenever T is expanded, i.e. the new territory T contains one more edge or one more agent than the previous territory T_{OLD}. Thus there can be at most (m+k) competing rounds. After every exploring round completes, there is one competing round. So, the number of exploring rounds can not be more than the number of competing rounds.

Lemma 11. *The agents make at most $O(n(m+k))$ moves in the all the exploring rounds combined.*

Proof. The Procedure InitExplore() makes $|T|$ moves in a tree T. Only one agent (the active one) in every tree executes this procedure. So, this accounts for $O(n)$

moves per exploring round and $O(n(m + k))$ moves in total. Other than that, every passive agent that is woken up makes $O(n)$ moves to go to an unexplored edge, explore it and report it to the root. Since each unexplored edge will be explored once (or at most twice), this cost can be counted per newly explored edge. Thus, this accounts for $O(n.m)$ moves.

Lemma 12. *The agents make at most $O(m(m + k))$ moves in all the competing rounds combined.*

Proof. Only the active agent in a tree participates in the competing round. During procedure InitCompete every edge in G is traversed a constant number of times; this accounts for $O(m)$ moves per round. Similarly O(m) moves are made per round during procedure Compete, for the comparisons with each neighbor. Each execution of Invade() takes $O(n)$ moves, because only tree-edges are traversed and no edge is traversed twice. Whenever an agent execute Invade(), it either wins or loses. A losing agent never competes again, so the total contribution from losing agents is $O(k.n)$. Edges traversed by the wining agents are disjoint, so this accounts for O(n) moves per round.

Due to the above lemmas and Theorem 1, we have the following result:

Theorem 3. *The moves complexity of algorithm RDV is $O(m(m + k))$. Thus algorithm RDV is optimal.*

5   Conclusions

We considered the problem of rendezvous of mobile agent in a faulty network and showed that it is possible to rendezvous at most $k - \tau$ in any network containing k dispersed agents and τ faulty links. We determined the condition under which this is possible and gave an algorithm for solving the problem under this condition. The algorithm we presented is optimal in terms of the total number of moves made by the agents and requires no prior information about the network topology (except the size). Moreover, we showed that it is impossible to have an *effective* algorithm for rendezvous, one that always achieves the rendezvous of as many agents as possible in any given network.

Notice that the only information needed by our algorithm is a strict upper bound on the number of nodes. We assumed that the faulty links do not disconnect the network. In the case of a disconnected network, we can still rendezvous the agents in a connected component if we know a good bound on its size. For example, if the component contains a majority of the nodes (i.e. more than half of them), then original network size can be used as the bound. In this case, if τ is equal to the number of outgoing edges from the component then we can rendezvous $k' - \tau$ agents where k' agents are initially located in this component. For networks containing a single black hole (which does not disconnect the network), our algorithm can be used to rendezvous $k - d_{BH}$ agents where d_{BH} is the degree of the black-hole.

For the results in this paper, we considered two optimization criteria —minimizing the number of agents that are destroyed and the number of moves taken by the surviving agents to rendezvous. It would be interesting to also consider the optimization of whiteboard memory or agent memory when solving the rendezvous problem in faulty networks.

References

1. Alpern, S., Gal, S.: The Theory of Search Games and Rendezvous. Kluwer, Dordrecht (2003)
2. Angluin, D.: Local and global properties in networks of processors. In: STOC '80. Proc. 12th ACM Symp. on Theory of Computing, pp. 82–93. ACM Press, New York (1980)
3. Barrière, L., Flocchini, P., Fraigniaud, P., Santoro, N.: Rendezvous and Election of Mobile Agents: Impact of Sense of Direction. Theory of Computing Systems 40(2), 143–162 (2007)
4. Boldi, P., Vigna, S.: An effective characterization of computability in anonymous networks. In: Welch, J.L. (ed.) DISC 2001. LNCS, vol. 2180, pp. 33–47. Springer, Heidelberg (2001)
5. Boldi, P., Vigna, S.: Fibrations of graphs. Discrete Math. 243, 21–66 (2002)
6. Chalopin, J., Das, S., Santoro, N.: Rendezvous of Mobile Agents in Anonymous Networks with Faulty Channels. Technical Report TR-2007-02, University of Ottawa (2007)
7. Chalopin, J., Godard, E., Métivier, Y., Ossamy, R.: Mobile agents algorithms versus message passing algorithms. In: Shvartsman, A.A. (ed.) OPODIS 2006. LNCS, vol. 4305. Springer, Heidelberg (2006)
8. Cooper, C., Klasing, R., Radzik, T.: Searching for black-hole faults in a network using multiple agents. In: Shvartsman, A.A. (ed.) OPODIS 2006. LNCS, vol. 4305, pp. 320–332. Springer, Heidelberg (2006)
9. Czyzowicz, J., Kowalski, D., Markou, E., Pelc, A.: Searching for a black hole in synchronous tree networks. Combinatorics, Probability and Computing (to appear, 2007)
10. Dessmark, A., Fraigniaud, P., Kowalski, D., Pelc, A.: Deterministic rendezvous in graphs. Algorithmica 46, 69–96 (2006)
11. Dobrev, S., Flocchini, P., Prencipe, G., Santoro, N.: Mobile agents searching for a black hole in an anonymous ring. Algorithmica (to appear, 2007)
12. Dobrev, S., Flocchini, P., Prencipe, G., Santoro, N.: Finding a black hole in an arbitrary network: optimal mobile agents protocols. Distributed Computing (to appear, 2007)
13. Dobrev, S., Flocchini, P., Prencipe, G., Santoro, N.: Multiple agents rendezvous in a ring in spite of a black hole. In: Papatriantafilou, M., Hunel, P. (eds.) OPODIS 2003. LNCS, vol. 3144, pp. 34–46. Springer, Heidelberg (2004)
14. Dobrev, S., Flocchini, P., Kralovic, R., Santoro, N.: Exploring a dangerous unknown graph using tokens. In: Proc. of 5th IFIP International Conference on Theoretical Computer Science (TCS'06) (2006)
15. Gasieniec, L., Kranakis, E., Krizanc, D., Zhang, X.: Optimal memory rendezvous of anonymous mobile agents in a unidirectional ring. In: Wiedermann, J., Tel, G., Pokorný, J., Bieliková, M., Štuller, J. (eds.) SOFSEM 2006. LNCS, vol. 3831, pp. 282–292. Springer, Heidelberg (2006)

16. Godard, E., Métivier, Y., Muscholl, A.: Characterization of classes of graphs recognizable by local computations. Theory of Computing Systems 37(2), 249–293 (2004)
17. Klasing, R., Markou, E., Pelc, A.: Gathering asynchronous oblivious mobile robots in a ring. In: Asano, T. (ed.) ISAAC 2006. LNCS, vol. 4288, pp. 744–753. Springer, Heidelberg (2006)
18. Klasing, R., Markou, E., Radzik, T., Sarracco, F.: Hardness and approximation results for black hole search in arbitrary networks. Theoretical Computer Science (to appear, 2007)
19. Kranakis, E., Krizanc, D., Markou, E.: Mobile agent rendezvous in a synchronous torus. In: Correa, J.R., Hevia, A., Kiwi, M. (eds.) LATIN 2006. LNCS, vol. 3887, pp. 653–664. Springer, Heidelberg (2006)
20. Mazurkiewicz, A.: Distributed enumeration. Inf. Processing Letters 61(5), 233–239 (1997)
21. Sakamoto, N.: Comparison of initial conditions for distributed algorithms on anonymous networks. In: PODC '99. Proc. 18th ACM Symposium on Principles of Distributed Computing, pp. 173–179. ACM Press, New York (1999)
22. Yamashita, M., Kameda, T.: Computing on anonymous networks: Parts I and II. IEEE Trans. Parallel and Distributed Systems 7(1), 69–96 (1996)
23. Yu, X., Yung, M.: Agent rendezvous: A dynamic symmetry-breaking problem. In: Meyer auf der Heide, F., Monien, B. (eds.) ICALP 1996. LNCS, vol. 1099, pp. 610–621. Springer, Heidelberg (1996)

Weakening Failure Detectors for k-Set Agreement Via the Partition Approach

Wei Chen[1], Jialin Zhang[2,*], Yu Chen[1], and Xuezheng Liu[1]

[1] Microsoft Research Asia
{weic,ychen,xueliu}@microsoft.com
[2] Center for Advanced Study
Tsinghua University
zhanggl02@mails.tsinghua.edu.cn

Abstract. In this paper, we propose the partition approach and define several new classes of partitioned failure detectors weaker than existing failure detectors for the k-set agreement problem in both the shared-memory model and the message-passing model. In the shared-memory model with $n + 1$ processes, for any $2 \le k \le n$, we first propose a partitioned failure detector $\Pi\Omega_k$ that solves k-set agreement with shared read/write registers and is strictly weaker than Ω_k, which was conjectured to be the weakest failure detector for k-set agreement in the shared-memory model [19]. We then propose a series of partitioned failure detectors that can solve n-set agreement, yet they are strictly weaker than Υ [10], the weakest failure detector ever found before our work to circumvent any asynchronous impossible problems in the shared-memory model. We also define two new families of partitioned failure detectors in the message-passing model that are strictly weaker than the existing ones for k-set agreement. Our results demonstrate that the partition approach opens a new dimension for weakening failure detectors related to set agreement, and it is an effective approach to check whether a failure detector is the weakest one or not for set agreement. So far, all previous candidates for the weakest failure detectors of set agreement have been disproved by the partitioned failure detectors.

Keywords: Failure detector, partitioned failure detectors, k-set agreement.

1 Introduction

Failure detector abstractions are first proposed by Chandra and Toueg in [3] to circumvent the impossibility result of consensus [9], and have since become a powerful technique to encapsulate system conditions needed to solve many distributed computing problems. Among them the problem of k-set agreement has received many attention from the research community. Informally, in k-set agreement each process proposes some value and eventually all correct processes (those

---

* This work was supported in part by the National Natural Science Foundation of China Grant 60553001, and the National Basic Research Program of China Grant 2007CB807900,2007CB807901.

A. Pelc (Ed.): DISC 2007, LNCS 4731, pp. 123–138, 2007.

that do not crash) decide on at most k different values [4]. It has been shown that k-set agreement cannot be solved in asynchronous systems when k or more processes may crash [1,12,20]. In recent years, a number of studies have focused on failure detectors for solving k-set agreement problem [21,18,11,16,17,19,10,7]. These studies form the collective effort in the pursuit of the weakest failure detector for k-set agreement, a goal yet to be reached. A particular candidate Ω_k was conjectured to be the weakest failure detector for wait-free k-set agreement [19] in the shared-memory model.

Consider distributed shared-memory model with $n + 1$ processes. In a very recent paper [10], Guerraoui et.al define a new class of failure detectors Υ and show that among a wide range of failure detectors defined as *eventually stable failure detectors*, Υ is the weakest one necessary to solve *any* impossible problem in shared-memory distributed systems, and Υ solves the n-set agreement problem. The Υ failure detector disproves the conjecture on Ω_k for the case of $k = n$. For a general k, a generalized Υ^k is proposed to solve k-set agreement, but only when at most k processes may crash, so it does not disprove the conjecture on Ω_k for wait-free k-set agreement.

The eventually stable failure detectors encompass most failure detectors known to solve distributed decision tasks in the shared-memory model prior to [10], as the authors claimed. Therefore, as the title of their paper says, indeed Υ is the weakest failure detector ever found that solves any impossible problem in distributed computing.

In this paper, we introduce a new breed of failure detectors — *partitioned failure detectors* — that could be made strictly weaker than Ω_k and Υ but are still strong enough to solve the set agreement problem. Our motivation is based on the following observation: In k-set agreement when $k > 1$, different processes may decide on different values, and thus it is possible that processes may be partitioned to different components, each of which decides on different values but together they still decide on at most k values. In other words, k-set agreement (with $k > 1$) exhibits the partition nature. The partitioned failure detectors are defined by consistently applying a method that captures the partition nature to weaken existing failure detectors, for which we called the *partition approach*.

In the partition approach, failure detectors partition the processes into multiple components and only processes in one of the components (called a *live component*) are required to satisfy all safety and liveness properties (of an existing failure detector), while processes in other components only need to satisfy safety properties. Since those processes in non-live components may generate quite arbitrary failure detector outputs, intuitively the partitioned failure detectors are a new breed that does not fall into the eventually stable failure detectors covered by [10].

We study the partitioned failure detectors in both the shared-memory model and the message-passing model. In the main part of this paper, we apply the partition approach to failure detectors Ω_k and Υ in the shared-memory model to define weaker failure detectors. More specifically, we first define a new class of failure detectors $\Pi\Omega_k$ by applying static partitions to Ω_k. We show that $\Pi\Omega_k$

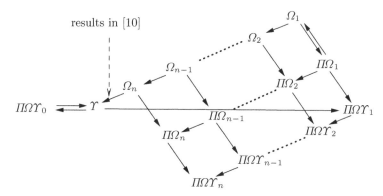

Fig. 1. Relationship diagram for failure detectors in the shared-memory model ($n \geq 3$). If $A \to B$, then A can be transformed into B. If there is no directed path from A to B, then A cannot be transformed into B (Footnote 1 contains the only exception).

is strong enough to solve k-set agreement with shared read/write registers but it is not comparable with Υ, for all $k = 2, 3, \ldots, n$. One direct consequence is that $\Pi\Omega_k$ is strictly weaker than Ω_k (because Ω_k is stronger than Υ), which disproves the conjecture that Ω_k is the weakest failure detector for wait-free k-set agreement in the shared-memory model for any $k \geq 2$. Moreover, $\Pi\Omega_k$ is the first failure detector class that solves k-set agreement (for generic k) but is incomparable with Υ. For example, even though failure detector $\Pi\Omega_2$ solves 2-set agreement, it is not stronger than Υ.

Next, we define failure detectors weaker than Υ but are still strong enough to solve n-set agreement. We achieve this by mixing some of the properties of $\Pi\Omega_k$ and Υ and define another class of partitioned failure detectors $\Pi\Omega\Upsilon_k$. We show that for any $1 \leq k \leq n$, $\Pi\Omega\Upsilon_k$ can still solve n-set agreement but it is strictly weaker than both $\Pi\Omega_k$ and Υ. Moreover, as k increases, the strength of $\Pi\Omega\Upsilon_k$ is strictly weakened. Hence, we find a family of n different failure detector classes strictly weaker than Υ, which is the weakest one ever found before our work.

Figure 1 characterizes the exact relationship among all failure detectors we proposed in this paper for the shared-memory model and the previously defined ones Ω_k and Υ. Note that every nonexistent directed path in the figure corresponds to an impossible transformation from the source class to the destination class, with only one exception.[1] Since Υ is already very weak, one can imagine that it would be very delicate to define the new partitioned failure detectors and prove that they are incomparable to or strictly weaker than Υ. Indeed, the definitions of failure detectors are subtle, and the proofs of the impossible transformations are the most delicate and technically involved.

We also apply the partition approach to failure detectors $\Omega_k \times \Sigma$ in the message-passing model, where Σ is the class of quorum failure detectors needed to work with Ω_k to solve k-set agreement in the message-passing model. We

---

[1] The exception is the following problem that is still open: Can $\Pi\Omega_k$ be transformed into $\Pi\Omega\Upsilon_{k-1}$ for any $k \geq 2$? However, we have proven that $\Pi\Omega_{k+1}$ cannot be transformed into $\Pi\Omega\Upsilon_{k-1}$ for any $k \geq 2$.

define two new families of partitioned failure detectors that are strictly weaker than $\Omega_k \times \Sigma$ but are strong enough to solve k-set agreement in the message-passing model. These partitioned failure detectors are different from the ones in the shared-memory model in that they integrate the partition of quorums in their definitions. Moreover, one family of failure detectors incorporates dynamic splitting of partitions, while all failure detectors in the shared-memory model are statically partitioned.

Our results not only show a number of new failure detectors that are strictly weaker than existing ones such as Ω_k and Υ, but more importantly, they demonstrate the power of the partition approach: The partition approach opens a new dimension for weakening various failure detectors related to set agreement, and it is an effective approach to check whether a failure detector could be the weakest one solving set agreement or not. Using the approach, we have successfully shown that (1) Ω_k is not the weakest failure detector for k-set agreement in the shared-memory model for any $k \geq 2$; (2) Υ is not the weakest failure detector for n-set agreement in the shared-memory model; and (3) $\Omega_k \times \Sigma$ is not the weakest failure detector for k-set agreement in the message-passing model for any $k \geq 2$. So far, all failure detectors that were considered as the candidates for the weakest failure detectors for set agreement have been disproved using our partition approach. Therefore, we believe that partitioned failure detectors demonstrate the flexibility in achieving set agreement, and it is important to use the partition approach as an effective research tool in our pursuit to the ultimate weakest failure detectors for set agreement.

The rest of the paper is organized as follows. Section 2 provides the shared-memory model used in our paper. Section 3 defines $\Pi\Omega_k$ and shows how it solves k-set agreement. Section 4 defines $\Pi\Omega\Upsilon_k$. Section 5 provides a central place to show the relationship among all failure detectors in the shared-memory model as captured by Figure 1. Section 6 summarizes the results in the message-passing model. We conclude the paper in Section 7. Further results including some k-set agreement algorithms and all correctness proofs are covered by two technical reports [7,5] on message-passing model and shared-memory model, respectively.

2   Model

We consider asynchronous shared-memory distributed systems augmented with failure detectors. Our model is the same as the model in [10], which is based on the models of [13,14,2]. We provide the necessary details of the model below.

We consider a system with $n+1$ processes $P = \{p_1, p_2, \ldots, p_{n+1}\}$ where $n \geq 1$. Let $\mathcal{T}$ be the set of global time values, which are non-negative integers. Processes do not have access to the global time. A *failure pattern* F is a function from $\mathcal{T}$ to 2^P, such that $F(t)$ is the set of processes that have failed by time t. Failed processes do not recover, i.e., $F(t) \subseteq F(t+1)$ for all $t \in \mathcal{T}$. Let $correct(F)$ denote the set of *correct processes*, those that do not crash in F. A process is *faulty* if it is not correct. A *failure detector history* H is a function from $P \times \mathcal{T}$ to an output range $\mathcal{R}$, such that $H(p, t)$ is the output of the failure detector module of process

$p \in P$ at time $t \in \mathcal{T}$. A *failure detector* $\mathcal{D}$ is a function from each failure pattern to a set of failure detector histories, representing the possible failure detector outputs under failure pattern F.

Processes communicate with each other by writing to and reading from shared atomic registers. A deterministic algorithm A using a failure detector $\mathcal{D}$ is a collection of $n + 1$ deterministic automata, one for each process. Processes execute by taking *steps*. In each step, a process p: (a) reads from a shared register to obtain a value, or writes a value to a shared register, or queries its failure detector module, based on its current local state; and (b) transitions its current state to a new state, based on its current state, the value returned from the read or from the failure detector module, and the algorithm automaton on p. Each step is completed at one time point t, but the process may crash in the middle of taking its step. A *run* of algorithm A with failure detector $\mathcal{D}$ under a failure pattern F is an infinite sequence of steps such that every correct process takes an infinite number of steps and no faulty process takes any step after it crashes.

We say that a failure detector class $\mathcal{C}_1$ is *weaker than* a failure detector class $\mathcal{C}_2$, if there is a transformation algorithm T such that using any failure detector $\mathcal{D}_2 \in \mathcal{C}_2$, algorithm T implements a failure detector $\mathcal{D}_1 \in \mathcal{C}_1$. By implementing $\mathcal{D}_1$ we mean that for any run of algorithm T with failure detector $\mathcal{D}_2$ under a failure pattern F, T generates the outputs of $\mathcal{D}_1$ as a distributed variable $\mathcal{D}_1$-*output* such that there exists failure detector history $H \in \mathcal{D}_1(F)$ and $H(p, t) = \mathcal{D}_1$-*output*(p, t) for all $p \in P$ and all $t \in \mathcal{T}$, where $\mathcal{D}_1$-*output*(p, t) is the value of the variable $\mathcal{D}_1$-*output* on p at time t. If $\mathcal{C}_1$ is weaker than $\mathcal{C}_2$, we denote it as $\mathcal{C}_1 \preceq \mathcal{C}_2$ and also refer to it as $\mathcal{C}_2$ can be transformed into $\mathcal{C}_1$. if $\mathcal{C}_1 \preceq \mathcal{C}_2$ and $\mathcal{C}_2 \not\preceq \mathcal{C}_1$, we say that $\mathcal{C}_1$ is *strictly weaker than* $\mathcal{C}_2$ and denote it as $\mathcal{C}_1 \prec \mathcal{C}_2$. If $\mathcal{C}_1 \preceq \mathcal{C}_2$ and $\mathcal{C}_2 \preceq \mathcal{C}_1$, we say that $\mathcal{C}_1$ and $\mathcal{C}_2$ are equivalent and denote it as $\mathcal{C}_1 \equiv \mathcal{C}_2$.

In k-set agreement with $1 \leq k \leq n$, each process proposes a value, and makes an irrevocable decision on one value. It needs to satisfy the following three properties: (1) *Validity*: If a process decides v, then v has been proposed by some process. (2) *Uniform k-Agreement*: There are at most k different decision values. (3) *Termination*: Eventually all correct processes decide.

Two related failure detector classes are Ω_k and Υ. Failure detectors in Ω_k output a subset of P of size at most k, and there is a time after which all processes always output the same nonempty set, which contains at least one correct process. Failure detectors in Υ also output a subset of P, and there is a time after which all processes always output the same nonempty set, which is not exactly the set of correct processes.

3   Failure Detector $\Pi\Omega_k$

3.1   Specification of $\Pi\Omega_k$

The class of partitioned failure detectors $\Pi\Omega_k$ is obtained by applying static partitions to Ω_k, as explained below. The output of $\Pi\Omega_k$ for process p is a tuple $(isLeader, lbound, cid)$, where $isLeader$ is a boolean value indicating whether this process is a leader or not, $lbound$ is a non-negative integer indicating the upper bound on the number of possible leaders in p's partitioned component, and *cid* is a component ID drawn from an ID set $\mathcal{I}$ or is a special value $\perp \notin \mathcal{I}$. The *cid* output indicates the component the process belongs to and could be $\perp$ for an initial period before the failure detector decides on a partition.

For a failure detector output x, we use $x.v$ to denote the field v of x, where v could be *isLeader*, *lbound*, or *cid* in the case of $\Pi\Omega_k$. We say that a process p is an *eventual leader* (under a failure pattern F and a failure detector history H) if p is correct and there is a time after which the *isLeader* output on p is always *True*.

A *partition* of P is $\pi = \{P_1, \ldots, P_s\}$, where $s \geq 1$ and P_i's are non-empty subsets of P such that they do not intersect with one another and their union is P. For a process p, we use $\pi[p]$ to denote the partitioned component that contains p. For a component $P_j \subseteq P$ (under a failure pattern F and a failure detector history H), we define $lbound(P_j) = \max\{H(p,t).lbound \mid t \in \mathcal{T}, p \in P_j \setminus F(t)\}$,[2] and $Leaders(P_j) = \{p \in P_j \cap correct(F) \mid \exists t, \forall t' > t, H(p,t').isLeader = True\}$. The value $lbound(P_j)$ is the maximum *lbound* value among processes in component P_j, while $Leaders(P_j)$ is the set of eventual leaders in P_j.

A failure detector $\mathcal{D}$ is in the class $\Pi\Omega_k$ if for any failure pattern F and any failure detector history $H \in \mathcal{D}(F)$, there exists a partition $\pi = \{P_1, \ldots, P_s\}$ of P, such that the following properties hold. First, the *cid* output needs to satisfy these properties:

($\Pi C1$) The *cid* outputs on all correct processes eventually always output non-$\perp$ values. Formally, $\exists t_0 \in \mathcal{T}, \forall p \in correct(F), \forall t \geq t_0, H(p,t).cid \neq \perp$.

($\Pi C2$) The non-$\perp$ *cid* outputs distinguish different components. Formally, $\forall t_1, t_2 \in \mathcal{T}, \forall p_1 \notin F(t_1), \forall p_2 \notin F(t_2), (H(p_1,t_1).cid \neq \perp \land H(p_2,t_2).cid \neq \perp) \Rightarrow ((H(p_1,t_1).cid = H(p_2,t_2).cid) \Leftrightarrow (\pi[p_1] = \pi[p_2]))$.

Next, the *isLeader* and *lbound* outputs satisfy the following set of safety and liveness properties. The safety property is:

($\Pi\Omega 1$) The sum of the maximum *lbound* outputs in all partitioned components does not exceed k. Formally, $\sum_{j=1}^{s} lbound(P_j) \leq k$.

The liveness part specifies that there exists one partitioned component P_j such that:

($\Pi\Omega 2$) Eventually *lbound* outputs by all processes in P_j are the same. Formally, $\exists t_0 \in \mathcal{T}, \forall t_1, t_2 \geq t_0, \forall p_1 \in P_j \setminus F(t_1), \forall p_2 \in P_j \setminus F(t_2), H(p_1,t_1).lbound = H(p_2,t_2).lbound$.

($\Pi\Omega 3$) Eventually the *isLeader* outputs on any correct process in P_j do not change. Formally, $\exists t_0 \in \mathcal{T}, \forall t > t_0, \forall p \in P_j \setminus F(t), H(p,t).isLeader = H(p,t_0).isLeader$.

($\Pi\Omega 4$) There is at least one eventual leader. Formally, $|Leaders(P_j)| \geq 1$.

($\Pi\Omega 5$) The number of eventual leaders is eventually bounded by the *lbound* outputs. Formally, $\exists t_0 \in \mathcal{T}, \forall t \geq t_0, |Leaders(P_j)| \leq H(p,t).lbound$.

---

[2] As a convention, $\max \emptyset = 0$.

We call a component that satisfies the liveness properties ($\Pi\Omega$2–5) a *live component*, and other components *non-live components*. Let $k_i = lbound(P_i)$. Intuitively, each component P_i has a failure detector with the safety properties of Ω_{k_i} restricted to P_i,[3] while at least one component P_j also satisfies all liveness properties of Ω_{k_j}. Intuitively, this is to guarantee that when running a k-set agreement algorithm with $\Pi\Omega_k$, each component P_i may decide on at most k_i values, so with ($\Pi\Omega$1) there are at most k decisions, while the live component P_j can make progress and decide eventually.

The strength of $\Pi\Omega_k$ is fully characterized by Figure 1. We defer to Section 5 as a central place to study and compare the strength of all proposed failure detectors and avoid repetitions. We summarize the strength of $\Pi\Omega_k$ comparing with Ω_k and Υ in the following theorem.

Theorem 1. *The followings hold regarding the strength of $\Pi\Omega_k$. (1) $\Pi\Omega_1 \equiv \Omega_1$. (2) $\Pi\Omega_k \prec \Omega_j$ for all $k \geq 2$, $j \geq 1$, and $k \geq j$. (3) $\Pi\Omega_k \npreceq \Omega_j$ and $\Omega_j \npreceq \Pi\Omega_k$ for all $k \geq 2$ and $k < j \leq n$. (4) $\Pi\Omega_k \prec \Pi\Omega_{k-1}$ for all $k \geq 2$. (5) $\Pi\Omega_k \npreceq \Upsilon$ and $\Upsilon \npreceq \Pi\Omega_k$, for all $k \geq 2$.*

The key result is that $\Pi\Omega_k$ is incomparable with Υ for all $k \geq 2$. Therefore, $\Pi\Omega_k$ is a new class of failure detectors that is strictly weaker than Ω_k, but is strong enough to solve k-set agreement in shared-memory systems with arbitrary failure patterns. It is the only class known (to our best knowledge) that solves k-set agreement with arbitrary failure patterns and is strictly weaker than Ω_k and is incomparable with Υ.[4]

3.2   Solving k-Set Agreement with $\Pi\Omega_k$

The algorithm using $\Pi\Omega_k$ to solve k-set agreement is based on an extension of the k–*converge* algorithm presented in [21]. The original k–*converge* algorithm forces every participant to use the same value of "k". With $\Pi\Omega_k$ failure detectors, we need processes in each component to try to converge on some decisions, the number of which is bounded by the *lbound* output of the failure detector. Therefore we extend the k–*converge* algorithm by moving "k" into the parameter of the routine and rename the routine to *converge*(). We adjust the specification of *converge*() as follows.

Routine *converge*() takes in three parameters: ℓ is the upper bound on the number of values can be committed (this parameter corresponds to the "k" in k–*converge*), p is the process identifier, and v is the input value of the process. It outputs a pair (c, v'), where c is a boolean and v' is one of the input value. When p outputs (c, v'), we say that p picks v', and if $c = True$, we say that p commits to v'. The routine satisfies the following properties: (1) C-Termination: Every correct process picks some value. (2) C-Validity: If a process p picks value

---

[3] In [6] we show that a variation of failure detectors that output *isLeader* and *lbound*, named Ω_k'', is equivalent to Ω_k failure detectors.

[4] The Υ^k failure detector proposed in [10] only solves k-set agreement in systems with at most k failures.

Shared variables:
    Register D, initially $\perp$
    $converge()$ instances: $converge[\,][\,]$

Output of failure detector $\Pi\Omega_k$ on process p_i:
    $isLeader_i$, $lbound_i$, cid_i

Code for process p_i:
```
1   v ← the input value of p_i
2   repeat
3       cid ← cid_i
4   until cid ≠ ⊥
5   r ← 0
6   repeat
7       c ← False
8       if isLeader_i = True then
9           r ← r + 1
10          (c, v) ← converge[cid][r](lbound_i, i, v)
11      if c = True then
12          D ← v; return (D)
13  until D ≠ ⊥
14  return (D)
```

Fig. 2. k-set agreement algorithm using $\Pi\Omega_k$

v, then some process q invoked $converge()$ with parameter v. (3) C-Agreement: If a process p commits to a value, then at most ℓ_{max} values are picked, where ℓ_{max} is the maximum ℓ that processes pass into $converge()$. (4) Convergence: If all processes use the same value in the ℓ parameter ($\ell > 0$), and if there are no more than ℓ distinct input values, then every process that picks a value commits. The first two properties are the same as in [21], while the last two properties are adjusted to accommodate different input values of ℓ. Although the interface and the specification are changed, the algorithm is exactly the same as in [21], and the proof only needs some minor adjustment. The algorithm and its proof are included in [5].

Based on the $converge()$ routine, we provide an algorithm to solve k-set agreement using $\Pi\Omega_k$ in Figure 2. The algorithm is straightforward. We use cid output of failure detectors to isolate each component and make sure only processes in the same component could run the same instance of $converge()$ routine. Within a component, only those processes with $isLeader$ output being $True$ can run $converge()$ instances. Each $converge()$ instance only uses the output of the previous $converge()$ instance as the input, which is important to guarantee the safety of the algorithm. In any $converge()$ instance if some process p commits to a value v, then p writes v to a shared variable D and decides on v, and eventually all correct processes will see a non-$\perp$ D value and decide. The following theorem summarizes the correctness of the algorithm.

Theorem 2. *Algorithm in Figure 2 solves k-set agreement using failure detectors in $\Pi\Omega_k$, for any $k \geq 1$.*

Proof. It's obvious that k-set *Validity* holds.

For *Uniform k-Agreement*, we only need to consider decisions made in line 12, since decisions made in line 14 do not generate new decision values. Consider every component P_i. If some process decides in line 12, we consider the earliest such decision, say by a process $p \in P_i$. Process p decides v because it commits to v in an instance $converge[cid][r]()$. By the *C-Agreement* property of $converge()$, at most ℓ_{max} values can be picked in this $converge[cid][r]()$ instance, where ℓ_{max} is the maximum *lbound* values in the input of this instance. Since the algorithm guarantees for any $r' > r$, instances $converge[cid][r']()$ only uses the values picked in instance $converge[cid][r]()$, we know that there are at most ℓ_{max} values can be decided in line 12 by processes in component P_i. By definition, $\ell_{max} \leq lbound(P_i)$. Then, by property ($\Pi\Omega 1$), there are at most k values that can be decided. So Uniform k-Agreement holds.

For k-set *Termination*, first by property ($\Pi C2$) all correct processes eventually exit the loop in lines 2–4. In the live component P_j that satisfies ($\Pi\Omega 2$–5), eventually there is at least one correct process and at most ℓ processes in P_j invoking $converge()$, where ℓ is the eventually converged *lbound* output value. Moreover, all these processes invoke $converge()$ with the same first parameter value ℓ. Thus, the *C-Termination* and *Convergence* properties guarantee that all correct processes in P_j eventually commit to some value in some $converge()$ instance. Therefore, eventually D is written. Once D is written, all correct processes eventually decide. □

4   Failure Detector $\Pi\Omega\Upsilon_k$

After defining $\Pi\Omega_k$, our next step is to find a mixture of $\Pi\Omega_k$ and Υ such that the new failure detectors are weaker than both and are still strong enough to solve n-set agreement. Since we know that $\Pi\Omega_k$ and Υ are not comparable, it immediately means that the new failure detectors are strictly weaker than both $\Pi\Omega_k$ and Υ. This leads us to the discovery of failure detectors $\Pi\Omega\Upsilon_k$.

The output of $\Pi\Omega\Upsilon_k$ for process p is a tuple $(S, lbound, cid)$, where S is a subset of P that informally matches the output of Υ, and *lbound* and *cid* outputs have the same value range and same informal meaning as the ones in $\Pi\Omega_k$. For a component P_j, let $correct(P_j) = correct(F) \cap P_j$, the set of correct processes in P_j (under a failure pattern F).

A failure detector $\mathcal{D}$ is in the class $\Pi\Omega\Upsilon_k$ if for any failure pattern F and any failure detector history $H \in \mathcal{D}(F)$, there exists a partition $\pi = \{P_1, \ldots, P_s\}$ of P, such that the following properties hold. The *cid* properties and safety properties are the same as $\Pi\Omega_k$, namely ($\Pi C1$), ($\Pi C2$), and ($\Pi\Omega 1$). The liveness part specifies that there exists one partitioned component P_j such that ($\Pi\Omega 2$) of $\Pi\Omega_k$ and the following property hold:

($\Pi\Upsilon 1$) P_j contains at least one correct process, and eventually all correct processes in P_j output the same $S \subseteq P_j$ such that S is not the set of correct processes in P_j and either $S \neq \emptyset$ or the number of correct processes is bounded by the eventual *lbound* output. Formally, $correct(P_j) \neq \emptyset \wedge \exists S_0 \subseteq$

$P_j, S_0 \neq correct(P_j), \exists t_0, (\forall p \in correct(P_j), \forall t > t_0, (H(p,t).S = S_0 \wedge (S_0 \neq \emptyset \vee |correct(P_j)| \leq H(p,t).lbound)))$.

We call a component that satisfies the liveness properties $(\Pi\Omega 2)$ and $(\Pi\Upsilon 1)$ a *live component*, and other components *non-live components*. Intuitively, in the live component P_j, the S output behaves almost the same as the output of Υ, except that S may eventually stabilize to $\emptyset$, in which case the number of correct processes in P_j must be bounded by the eventual *lbound* output. This mixture is important in making $\Pi\Omega\Upsilon_k$ strictly weaker than Υ. In particular, $\Pi\Omega\Upsilon_0$ is well-defined since *lbound* outputs could always be 0. However, in $\Pi\Omega\Upsilon_0$ the above mixture of requirements on S and on *lbound* is gone, and we will show that $\Pi\Omega\Upsilon_0$ is equivalent to Υ (the proof is not straightforward though).

The follow theorem summarizes the results on the strength of $\Pi\Omega\Upsilon_k$ comparing with $\Pi\Omega_k$ and Υ, which is captured in Figure 1 and will be studied in Section 5. The key result is that $\Pi\Omega\Upsilon_k$ is strictly weaker than Υ for any $k \geq 1$, and as k increases, its strength is strictly weakened. Therefore, we found a new family of n classes of failure detectors that are all strictly weaker than Υ. It not only shows that Υ is not the weakest failure detector ever, but also suggests that there are still quite some room under Υ to fit in non-trivial failure detectors.

Theorem 3. *The followings hold regarding the strength of $\Pi\Omega\Upsilon_k$. (1) $\Pi\Omega\Upsilon_0 \equiv \Upsilon$. (2) $\Pi\Omega\Upsilon_k \prec \Pi\Omega\Upsilon_{k-1}$ for all $k \geq 1$. (3) $\Pi\Omega_j \npreceq \Pi\Omega\Upsilon_k$ for all $1 \leq k \leq n$ and $1 \leq j \leq n$. (4) $\Pi\Omega\Upsilon_k \preceq \Pi\Omega_j$ for all $k \geq j \geq 1$. (5) $\Pi\Omega\Upsilon_k \npreceq \Pi\Omega_j$ for all $j \geq k + 2$ and $k \geq 1$.*

The algorithm that solves n-set agreement using $\Pi\Omega\Upsilon_k$ is based on the algorithm using Υ in [10], with modifications to (a) isolate the algorithm for each individual component; (b) obtain the size of each component; and (c) deal with the case that $S = \emptyset$ in the live component. The full algorithm and its proof are included in [5].

5   Comparing Failure Detectors

This section is the central place to show all the results captured in Figure 1 and stated in Theorems 1 and 3. Since Υ is already a very weak failure detector, one can imagine that it would be a subtle and delicate task to show that under Υ there are still such structure in which a series of failure detectors have various strengths. Indeed, besides those obvious transformations, other results on possible or impossible transformations are quite delicate and require subtle techniques to prove them (and a few of them are still open). These proofs really show the subtle relationship between the failure detectors. Unfortunately, due to the space constraint, we can only include the full proofs in [5]. To compensate, we provide intuitive ideas and proof outlines for some key proofs.

5.1   Possible Transformations

For possible transformations, we need to prove all the arrows in Figure 1. Most transformations are obvious from the failure detector definitions.

Lemma 1. *(1)* $\Pi\Omega_k \preceq \Pi\Omega_{k-1}$; *(2)* $\Pi\Omega\Upsilon_k \preceq \Pi\Omega\Upsilon_{k-1}$; *(3)* $\Pi\Omega_k \preceq \Omega_k$; *(4)* $\Pi\Omega\Upsilon_k \preceq \Upsilon$.

Proof. The first two parts hold directly by the definition of failure detectors. The last two parts hold because we can treat Ω_k and Υ as a special case of partitioned failure detectors with only a single component P. $\qquad\square$

Lemma 2. $\Pi\Omega\Upsilon_k \preceq \Pi\Omega_k$ *for all $k \geq 1$.*

Proof Outline. For the transformation from $\Pi\Omega_k$ to $\Pi\Omega\Upsilon_k$, the idea is for each component to come up with the set of at most *lbound* leaders, then the S output of $\Pi\Omega\Upsilon_k$ is the complement of the leader set with respect to the component, and *lbound* and *cid* outputs of $\Pi\Omega\Upsilon_k$ are copied from $\Pi\Omega_k$. The key is that for a live component, the leader set stabilizes and contains at least one correct process. Therefore, its complement S cannot be the set of correct processes. Moreover, if $S = \emptyset$, it means that all processes in the component are eventual leaders, in which case the *lbound* must be at least the number of correct processes in the component. The transformation still needs to solve the problem of estimating the membership of each component, which is addressed in the full transformation algorithm and its proof in [5]. $\qquad\square$

Lemma 3. *(1)* $\Omega_1 \preceq \Pi\Omega_1$; *(2)* $\Upsilon \preceq \Pi\Omega\Upsilon_0$

The transformations for the above lemma are not straigthforward [5].

5.2 Impossible Transformations

Proving the impossible transformations is the critical step to establish the results of this paper. For these proofs, it is sometimes convenient to view it as an adversary trying to defeat any possible transformations. The adversary can (a) see the current output generated by a transformation; (b) manipulate the outputs of the failure detector to be transformed; (c) schedule the executions of processes; and (d) crash processes to prevent the transformation from succeeding.

Among all the impossible transformations captured by the non-existent directed path in Figure 1, several of them are critical ones, meaning that their impossibility implies the rest impossible transformations. This is based on the fact that if we show that $\mathcal{C}_1 \not\succeq \mathcal{C}_2$, then for all $\mathcal{C}_3 \preceq \mathcal{C}_1$ and all $\mathcal{C}_4 \succeq \mathcal{C}_2$, we have $\mathcal{C}_3 \not\succeq \mathcal{C}_4$. The following lemma shows one such critical impossible transformations.

Lemma 4. $\Pi\Omega_2$ *cannot be transformed into* Υ, *i.e.,* $\Pi\Omega_2 \not\succeq \Upsilon$.

Proof Outline. We know that Ω_n can be transformed to Υ easily by taking the complement of the Ω_n output. The reason that this transformation cannot be adapted to $\Pi\Omega_k$ is that $\Pi\Omega_k$ allows a live component P_j in which all processes are eventual leaders and *lbound* stabilizes to $|P_j|$. If we take the complement of the leader set in P_j with respect to P_j we get an empty set. The proof explores this basic idea.

In the case of $\mathit{\Pi\Omega}_2$, suppose for a contradiction that there is a transformation T from $\mathit{\Pi\Omega}_2$ to $\varUpsilon$. The adversary constructs a run in which the $\mathit{\Pi\Omega}_2$ has a partition $\pi = \{P_1, P_2\}$, where $P_1 = \{p\}$. It sets *lbound* of every process to 1 and p's *isLeader* always to *True*, making P_1 a live component of $\mathit{\Pi\Omega}_2$. It will manipulate the *isLeader* outputs for processes in P_2 to create a contradiction. Whenever the S output of $\varUpsilon$ in P stabilizes to some subset S_i, the adversary suppresses all processes in $P \setminus S_i$ (i.e., prohibit these processes from taking any steps) for long enough time to force T to stabilize the S output to a different set $S_{i+1} \neq S_i$, because S_i appears to be the exact set of correct processes. Once T changes the S output, the adversary releases the suppressed processes so that they take some steps, and then it repeats the procedure for S_{i+1}, and so on. The adversary can keep doing so because $P \setminus S_i$ contains either p or some process in P_2, and thus it can always set *isLeader* of some process in $P \setminus S_i$ to *True* without violating the $\mathit{\Pi\Omega}_2$ requirement. The result is that the adversary forces T into an infinite run in which the S output never stabilizes, a contradiction.   □

Lemma 4 implies that for all $\mathit{\Pi\Omega}_k$ with $k \geq 2$, $\mathit{\Pi\Omega}_k$ cannot be transformed into $\varUpsilon$. This is the first key result. Moreover, because $\mathit{\Pi\Omega}_k$ can be transformed into $\mathit{\Pi\Omega\varUpsilon}_k$, Lemma 4 further implies that $\mathit{\Pi\Omega\varUpsilon}_k$ is strictly weaker than $\varUpsilon$, the second key result of the paper. Next lemma shows another key result of the paper.

Lemma 5. *$\varUpsilon$ cannot be transformed into $\mathit{\Pi\Omega}_n$ when $n \geq 2$.*

Proof Outline. Suppose there is a transformation T. If the partition of $\mathit{\Pi\Omega}_n$ generated by transformation T contains only a single component, then the proof is the same as proving $\varUpsilon$ cannot be transformed into Ω_n in [10]. If the partition of $\mathit{\Pi\Omega}_n$ has at least two components, let P_1 be one of the components. The adversary first sets the $\varUpsilon$ output to $P \setminus P_1$, and then repeatedly suppress the leader processes in all components that are potentially live components for $\mathit{\Pi\Omega}_n$ (these are called *quasi-live components* in the proofs), the purpose of which is to construct an infinite run in which there is no live component. The only way the transformation can counter this measure is by setting the *lbound* outputs of processes in P_1 to $|P_1|$. But the adversary can counter this again by crashing all processes in P_1, setting $\varUpsilon$ output to P_1, and re-apply the suppression technique. The result is a run in which no live component exists. The key is that the adversary need to wait until the *lbound* output on P_1 is at least the size of a component to crash the component. This guarantees that the transformation cannot set *lbound* on $P \setminus P_1$ to $|P \setminus P_1|$ to defeat the adversary.   □

Lemma 4 and 5 establish that $\varUpsilon$ and $\mathit{\Pi\Omega}_k$ with $k \geq 2$ are not comparable. Together with the possible transformations of Lemma 2, they immediately imply that $\mathit{\Pi\Omega\varUpsilon}_k$ is strictly weaker than both $\varUpsilon$ and $\mathit{\Pi\Omega}_k$ for any $k \geq 2$.

Next lemma summarizes all other critical impossible transformations proven so far. The proofs to these results are technically involved and can be found in [5].

Lemma 6. *The following results hold: (1) $\Omega_k \not\succeq \mathit{\Pi\Omega}_{k-1}$ for any $k \geq 2$. (2) $\mathit{\Pi\Omega\varUpsilon}_k \not\succeq \mathit{\Pi\Omega\varUpsilon}_{k-1}$ for any $k \geq 1$. (3) $\mathit{\Pi\Omega}_{k+1} \not\succeq \mathit{\Pi\Omega\varUpsilon}_{k-1}$ for any $k \geq 2$.*

In conclusion, Theorem 1 is implied by Lemma 1(1)(3), Lemma 3(1), Lemma 4, Lemma 5 and Lemma 6(1). Theorem 3 is implied by Lemma 1(2)(4), Lemma 3(2) and Lemma 6(2)(3).

There are still an open problem left before we can completely characterize all relationships in Figure 1. It is whether $\Pi\Omega_k$ can be transformed into $\Pi\Omega\Upsilon_{k-1}$ for any $k \geq 2$. We conjecture that this transformation is impossible. If so, Figure 1 is indeed a full characterization of all relationships.

6   Results in the Message-Passing Model

Partition approach can also be applied in the message-passing model to define weaker failure detectors for k-set agreement. We briefly summarize some of the results we obtained in the message-passing model. The complete results are included in [7].

In the message-passing model, it is shown in [17] that besides Ω_k a majority of correct processes is required to solve k-set agreement. The majority requirement can be generalized to the class of *quorum failure detectors* Σ defined in [8]: a failure detector in Σ outputs a set of processes called quorum such that: ($\Sigma1$) any two quorums intersect; and ($\Sigma2$) eventually all quorums contain only correct processes. Thus, we applied the partition approach to the class of failure detectors $\Omega_k \times \Sigma$ to define weaker failure detectors.[5]

We first applies static partitions to $\Omega_k \times \Sigma$ and define Π_k, which is similar to $\Pi\Omega_k$ but replacing the *cid* output with the quorum output. More specifically, the output of a failure detector $\mathcal{D}$ in Π_k for process p is a tuple (*isLeader*, *lbound*, *Quorum*), where *isLeader* is a Boolean value indicating whether this process is a leader, *lbound* is a non-negative integer indicating the upper bound on the number of possible leaders in p's partitioned component, and *Quorum* $\subseteq P$. A failure detector $\mathcal{D}$ is in the class Π_k if for any failure pattern F and any failure detector history $H \in \mathcal{D}(F)$, there exists a partition $\pi = \{P_1, \ldots, P_s\}$ of P, such that H satisfies the following set of safety and liveness properties. The safety properties are ($\Pi\Omega1$) as for $\Pi\Omega_k$ and the following two properties related to the quorum outputs:

($\Pi\Sigma1$) The quorum output of a process p is always contained within p's partitioned component. Formally, $\forall t \in \mathcal{T}, \forall p \notin F(t), H(p,t).Quorum \subseteq \pi[p]$.

($\Pi\Sigma2$) The quorum outputs in the same partitioned component always intersect. Formally, $\forall t_1, t_2 \in \mathcal{T}, \forall p_1 \notin F(t_1), \forall p_2 \notin F(t_2), \pi[p_1] = \pi[p_2] \Rightarrow H(p_1,t_1).Quorum \cap H(p_2,t_2).Quorum \neq \emptyset$.

The liveness part specifies that there exists one partitioned component P_j such that the properties ($\Pi\Omega2$–5) of $\Pi\Omega_k$ hold plus the following:

($\Pi\Sigma3$) Eventually the quorum outputs by all processes in P_j contain only correct processes. Formally $\exists t_0 \in \mathcal{T}, \forall t \geq t_0, \forall p \in P_j \setminus F(t), H(p,t).Quorum \subseteq correct(F)$.

---

[5] Given two classes of failure detectors $\mathcal{C}_1$ and $\mathcal{C}_2$, class $\mathcal{C}_1 \times \mathcal{C}_2$ is the cross-product of the two, i.e., $\mathcal{C}_1 \times \mathcal{C}_2 = \{(\mathcal{D}_1, \mathcal{D}_2) \mid \mathcal{D}_1 \in \mathcal{C}_1, \mathcal{D}_2 \in \mathcal{C}_2\}$.

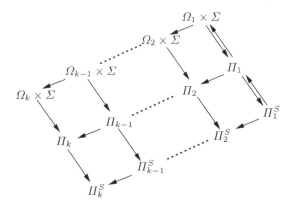

Fig. 3. Relationship diagram for failure detectors in the message-passing model. All failure detector classes in the diagram can be used to solve k-set agreement ($n \geq 2k - 2$ is required to show that transformations from $\Omega_k \times \Sigma$ to Π_{k-1}^S and stronger classes are impossible).

From the definition, we can see that Π_k follows the partition approach and is a static partitioning of $\Omega_k \times \Sigma$: each component P_i has a failure detector with all the safety properties of $\Omega_{k_i} \times \Sigma$ resticted to P_i where $k_i = lbound(P_i)$ and $\sum k_i \leq k$, while at least one component P_j also satisfies all liveness properties of $\Omega_{k_j} \times \Sigma$.

Next we further weaken Π_k by allowing dynamic splitting of components during the run, which leads to the definition of Π_k^S. Failure detectors in Π_k^S output a tuple (*isLeader, lbound, Quorum, cid*). Informally, a failure detector in Π_k^S allows partitioned components to further split during the run, but it uses *cid* to differenciate different components and requires the quorum outputs in a component after the splitting intersects with all quorum outputs before the splitting. The formal definition is included in [7].

With the new families of failure detectors $\{\Pi_z\}_{1 \leq z \leq k}$, and $\{\Pi_z^S\}_{1 \leq z \leq k}$, we compare their strengths with $\{\Omega_z \times \Sigma\}_{1 \leq z \leq k}$. Based on a siginificant amount of proof work, we summarize their relationship with a nice lattice structure shown in Figure 3. Several important results are summarized by the lattice. First, as we expected Π_k weakens $\Omega_k \times \Sigma$,[6] and Π_k^S further weakens Π_k for all $k > 1$. Second, even failure detectors in Π_2 with just two components is not strong enough to be transformed into $\Omega_k \times \Sigma$, and even failure detectors in Π_2^S with only one dynamic split is not strong enough to be transformed into Π_k. This shows that partitioning and dynamic splitting are indeed efficient techniques that weaken failure detectors. Third, for all $z \geq 2$, none of the classes $\Omega_z \times \Sigma$, Π_z, and Π_z^S can be transformed into $\Omega_{z-1} \times \Sigma$, Π_{z-1}, or Π_{z-1}^S. In fact, using a result in [17] we further show that $\Omega_z \times \Sigma$, Π_z, and Π_z^S are not strong enough to solve $(z - 1)$-set agreement. In [7], we further show that the lattice structure

---

[6] Actually, Π_k weakens Σ in all cases, and weakens Ω_k in most cases.

in Figure 3 still holds (under certain mild assumptions) even if we assume that a majority of processes are correct in the system model.

Finally, we design a new algorithm in the message-passing model that solves k-set agreement using Π_k^S. The algorithm is based on the Paxos algorithm structure [15], but has significant new additions with much more complicated proofs to deal with the subtleties introduced by dynamic splittings of partitioned failure detectors.

7 Concluding Remarks

In [5] we further demonstrate the partition approach by defining a new failure detector $\Pi\Upsilon$, which is the result of applying the approach directly to Υ. We show that $\Pi\Upsilon$ is enough to solve n-set agreement but is strictly weaker than Υ. $\Pi\Upsilon$ is stronger than $\Pi\Omega\Upsilon_{n-1}$ but is incomparable with $\Pi\Omega\Upsilon_k$ for $k \leq n - 2$.

We have shown that the partition approach is effective in weakening a number of failure detectors for k-set agreement. However, the partition approach proposed is still an informal method, and sometimes it requires ad-hoc adjustments. One future direction is to see how the approach and the partitioned failure detectors can be formally treated. In particular, it would be interesting to see if one could formally define a general class of partitioned failure detectors and define the weakest failure detectors among all partitioned failure detectors for k-set agreement.

The discovery of failure detectors even weaker than Υ may suggest that the conjecture made in [10] that n-set agreement is the minimum decision task in terms of minimum information required might not be true. This is another research direction to see if there is any other decision task strictly weaker than n-set agreement in terms of failure information needed to solve the problem.

References

1. Borowsky, E., Gafni, E.: Generalized FLP impossibility result for t-resilient asynchronous computations. In: Proceedings of the 25th ACM Symposium on Theory of Computing, pp. 91–100. ACM Press, New York (1993)
2. Chandra, T.D., Hadzilacos, V., Toueg, S.: The weakest failure detector for solving consensus. Journal of the ACM 43(4), 685–722 (1996)
3. Chandra, T.D., Toueg, S.: Unreliable failure detectors for reliable distributed systems. Journal of the ACM 43(2), 225–267 (1996)
4. Chaudhuri, S.: More choices allow more faults: Set consensus problems in totally asynchronous systems. Information and Computation 105(1), 132–158 (1993)
5. Chen, W., Chen, Y., Zhang, J.: On failure detectors weaker than ever. Technical Report TR-2007-50, Microsoft Research (May 2007)
6. Chen, W., Zhang, J., Chen, Y., Liu, X.: Failure detectors and extended Paxos for k-set agreement. Technical Report TR-2007-48, Microsoft Research (May 2007)
7. Chen, W., Zhang, J., Chen, Y., Liu, X.: Partition approach to failure detectors for k-set agreement. Technical Report TR-2007-49, Microsoft Research (May 2007)

8. Delporte-Gallet, C., Fauconnier, H., Guerraoui, R., Hadzilacos, V., Kouznetsov, P., Toueg, S.: The weakest failure detectors to solve certain fundamental problems in distributed computing. In: Proceedings of the 23rd ACM Symposium on Principles of Distributed Computing, pp. 338–346. ACM Press, New York (2004)
9. Fischer, M.J., Lynch, N.A., Paterson, M.S.: Impossibility of distributed consensus with one faulty process. Journal of the ACM 32(2), 374–382 (1985)
10. Guerraoui, R., Herlihy, M., Kouznetsov, P., Lynch, N., Newport, C.: On the weakest failure detector ever. In: Proceedings of the 26th ACM Symposium on Principles of Distributed Computing. ACM Press, New York (2007)
11. Herlihy, M., Penso, L.D.: Tight bounds for k-set agreement with limited scope accuracy failure detectors. Distributed Computing 18(2), 157–166 (2005)
12. Herlihy, M., Shavit, N.: The topological structure of asynchronous computability. Journal of the ACM 46(6), 858–923 (1999)
13. Herlihy, M.P., Wing, J.M.: Linearizability: A correctness condition for concurrent objects. ACM Trans. Prog. Lang. Syst. 12(3), 463–492 (1990)
14. Jayanti, P.: Robust wait-free hierarchies. J. ACM 44(4), 592–614 (1997)
15. Lamport, L.: The part-time parliament. ACM Transactions on Computer Systems 16(2), 133–169 (1998)
16. Mostefaoui, A., Rajsbaum, S., Raynal, M.: The combined power of conditions and failure detectors to solve asynchronous set agreement. In: Proceedings of the 24th ACM Symposium on Principles of Distributed Computing, pp. 179–188. ACM Press, New York (2005)
17. Mostefaoui, A., Rajsbaum, S., Raynal, M., Travers, C.: Irreducibility and additivity of set agreement-oriented failure detector classes. In: Proceedings of the 25th ACM Symposium on Principles of Distributed Computing, pp. 153–162. ACM Press, New York (2006)
18. Mostefaoui, A., Raynal, M.: k-set agreement with limited accuracy failure detectors. In: Proceedings of the 19th ACM Symposium on Principles of Distributed Computing, pp. 143–152. ACM Press, New York (2000)
19. Raynal, M., Travers, C.: In search of the holy grail: Looking for the weakest failure detector for wait-free set agreement (Invited talk). In: Shvartsman, A.A. (ed.) OPODIS 2006. LNCS, vol. 4305, pp. 1–17. Springer, Heidelberg (2006)
20. Saks, M., Zaharoglou, F.: Wait-free k-set agreement is impossible: The topology of public knowledge. SIAM Journal on Computing 29(5), 1449–1483 (2000)
21. Yang, J., Neiger, G., Gafni, E.: Structured derivations of consensus algorithms for failure detectors. In: Proceedings of the 17th ACM Symposium on Principles of Distributed Computing, pp. 297–306. ACM Press, New York (1998)

Amnesic Distributed Storage

Gregory Chockler[1], Rachid Guerraoui[2,*], and Idit Keidar[3]

[1] IBM Haifa Research Lab, Haifa, Israel
chockler@il.ibm.com
[2] School of Computer and Communication Sciences,
EPFL, CH-1015, Lausanne, Switzerland
rachid.guerraoui@epfl.ch
[3] Department of Electrical Engineering,
The Technion – Israel Institute of Technology

Abstract. Distributed storage algorithms implement the abstraction of a shared register over distributed base objects. We study a specific class of storage algorithms, which we call *amnesic*: these have the pragmatic property that old values written in the implemented register might be eventually forgotten, i.e., they are not permanently kept in the storage and might be overwritten in the base objects by more recent values. This paper precisely captures this property and argues that most storage algorithms are amnesic. We establish a fundamental impossibility of an amnesic storage algorithm to implement a robust register abstraction over a set of base objects of which at least one can fail arbitrarily, even if only in a responsive manner, unless readers are allowed to write to the base objects. Our impossibility helps justify the assumptions made by practical robust storage algorithms. We also derive from this impossibility the first sharp distinction between *safe* and *regular* registers. Namely, we show that, if readers do not write, then no amnesic algorithm can implement a regular register using safe registers.

1 Introduction

Storage is a critical aspect of modern computing systems. Today, there is strong interest in distributed storage architectures, either server-based or in the form of storage area networks *(SANs)*, which leverage the technological advances in networks of attached commodity disks to provide increased storage space, availability, and disaster recovery. At the heart of a distributed storage architecture lies an algorithm that implements the *read* and *write* operations of a register abstraction over several underlying base objects, sometimes called servers. Such distributed storage algorithms constitute an active area of research. A major challenge addressed by these algorithms is to ensure that (high-level) *read* and *write* implementations tolerate asynchrony, contention, and failures.

We study in this paper the fundamental limitations of a specific class of storage algorithms, which we define precisely and call *amnesic*. As we explain

---

* Part of this work was conducted when the author was on sabbatical at MIT CSAIL.

A. Pelc (Ed.): DISC 2007, LNCS 4731, pp. 139–151, 2007.

later (Section 5), most previously suggested storage algorithms are amnesic, e.g., [15,6,13,17,2,16,8,11,12,3], although the notion has never been specifically highlighted. Roughly speaking, an *amnesic* storage algorithm is one that eventually forgets old values previously stored in the implemented register after some sequence of new values is written. For instance, an algorithm that stores in base objects the last k values written in the implemented register, for some $k \geq 0$, e.g., [6,13,2,3], is amnesic, because a sequence of k new writes erases all previously stored values. On the other hand, an algorithm that stores the entire history of values written in the base objects, (where values are drawn from an unbounded domain), e.g., [10], is not amnesic. In this sense, amnesia can be seen as a restriction on an algorithm's space consumption, although it is not explicitly formulated this way. Instead, we capture the notion of amnesia in an abstract way in terms of *reachable configurations* of a distributed storage algorithm (Section 3).

Our motivation for refraining from an explicit space restriction is twofold. First, we are interested in algorithms that manipulate potentially unbounded value domains, such as integers, or files. Although in every execution, such an algorithm's space consumption is finite (and depends on the sizes of the written values), it is inherently unbounded. Second, many practical algorithms employ monotonically increasing timestamps [17,14,18,2,10,3,12], which are considered pretty cheap in practice. Thus, the classical concept of *bounded memory* is inadequate for reasoning about many interesting algorithms. We further note that the concept of bounded memory, by itself, does not capture "reasonable" space restrictions. For example, it does not preclude an algorithm that manipulates a large but finite domain (e.g., files of size 1KB), from storing all the (2^{8192}) values in its domain if they were all written at some point. Focusing on amnesic algorithms with unbounded domains provides an abstract way to rule out such algorithms, without precluding the use of increasing timestamps.

We establish in this paper (Section 4) a fundamental limitation on amnesic storage algorithms. We prove that it is impossible for an amnesic storage algorithm to *robustly* implement a register abstraction using a set of distributed (failure-prone) base objects, when readers do not write to the base objects. Underlying our impossibility lies the notion of *robustness*. In short, we consider as *robust* an algorithm that implements a live regular register [15] in the presence of contention, asynchrony, and arbitrary (Byzantine) failures of base objects [13,5,4]. Our impossibility holds if at least one base object can fail in a responsive yet arbitrary manner (R-Arbitrary failure [13]) among an arbitrarily large set of atomic base objects. (A fortiori, the result also holds if a base object may fail in a non-responsive arbitrary (NR-arbitrary) manner). Such arbitrary failures capture software bugs or malicious intrusions, which cannot be ruled out when the service is geographically disperse. We do not require that the algorithm tolerate process failures, which also strengthens our impossibility result.

The assumption that readers do not write is important for large systems with many readers. Whereas it is reasonable for storage servers to communicate using an authenticated channel with a single trusted writer and to assume it not to be malicious[1], a storage that is accessible to a large population of readers cannot typically trust all of them (authenticating all readers to prevent storage corruption might be infeasible). Hence, a more feasible alternative is to disallow the readers to modify the base object states, which is the assumption under which our impossibility is proven.

Given the vast amount of work on practical robust storage, our impossibility result may come as a surprise. In fact, our result does not imply that practical robust storage is unattainable, but rather justifies *why* previous solutions have had to employ authentication [8,17,19], store unbounded histories [10], have servers actively push updates to clients [18], give up on liveness in some situations [2], allow readers to write [3,11], or implement safe registers instead of regular ones [13,17,2,12] (see Section 5).

Our impossibility indeed holds if the implemented register needs to be regular but not if it needs to be safe. In a sense, regularity conveys an important aspect of robustness in the face of concurrency: no value can be returned if it was not written. Since many amnesic robust storage solutions implement safe registers [13,17], we can use our impossibility to derive the first sharp line between safe and regular semantics. We prove that there is no amnesic implementation of a regular register with an unbounded domain from safe ones, if readers do not write (Section 6). The line we draw between safety and regularity is analogous to the celebrated sharp line drawn by Lamport between atomicity and regularity [15], which states that no *bounded memory* algorithm can implement an *atomic* register using *regular* ones, if the readers do not write [15]. No such separation between safety and regularity has ever been established. We identify such a separation by replacing the notion of *bounded* algorithm in Lamport's formulation with our alternative notion of *amnesic* algorithm.

To summarize, this paper makes the following contributions:

- We define the notion of *amnesia*, capturing a pragmatic property of many storage algorithms.
- We prove the *impossibility* of devising a storage algorithm that is *robust* and *amnesic* without allowing readers to write.
- We derive the first sharp distinction between *safe* and *regular* register semantics.

2   Model

2.1   Shared Memory Model

We consider an asynchronous shared memory system consisting of a finite collection of processes interacting through n base objects $O_1, \ldots, O_n$. The term *base* objects is used to distinguish these from the higher level object abstraction implemented by the shared memory algorithm.

---

[1] With a compromised writer, the stored information is rendered meaningless anyway, regardless of any distributed storage algorithm's actions [17,19].

We consider storage algorithms that tolerate at least one arbitrary failure of a base objects. We focus on a weak form of such failures, called *responsive arbitrary (R-Arbitrary)* [13]. This means that the base objects always respond to an invocation, but may respond with an arbitrary value. This assumption strengthens our impossibility result, which directly applies to the more severe *non-responsive arbitrary (NR-Arbitrary)* [13] failures.

Processes are sequential in their ways of invoking high-level operations. That is, after invoking a high-level operation, and until it obtains a response, a process does not invoke a new high-level operation. After invoking a high-level operation, a process might invoke a sequence of low-level operations. We do not assume these low-level invocations to be sequential. That is, a process might invoke several operations on low-level base objects concurrently.

The solution must be *live* in the sense that every high-level operation must eventually complete. We do not require the algorithm to terminate in the presence of process failures, i.e., it does not have to be *wait-free*.

2.2   Registers

We study more specifically storage algorithms that deterministically implement the abstraction of a *register*, which is accessed using *Read()* and *Write()* operations. If the base objects are also registers, we denote their (low-level) operations as *read()* and *write()*, to avoid confusion with the high-level operations. To strengthen our impossibility result, we restrict our attention to storage algorithms that emulate a *single-writer single-reader (SWSR)* register: that is, the emulated register is only writable by a single process (the *writer*), and is read by a single process (the *reader*). The result a fortiori holds for multi-writer multi-reader registers. We assume an infinite value domain V from which the parameters of the *Write()* operation can be arbitrarily chosen by the writer. When it completes, *Write()* simply returns an *Ok* indication. A *Read()* operation does not have any input parameter, and returns a value from V upon completion.

The sequential specification of a register stipulates that a read should return the last value written. When read and write operations may overlap, several semantics have been defined [15]: A register is called *safe* if every read operation that does not overlap any write operation returns the register's value when the read was invoked, i.e., the latest written value or the initial value of the register if no value was written. A register is *regular* if it is safe and every read operation that overlaps some write operations returns either one of the values written by overlapping writes or the register's value before the first overlapping write is invoked. A register is *atomic* if it is regular and if, for any two write operations W and W' with respective input values v and v' such that W' is invoked after W returns, and any two read operations R and R' such that R' is invoked after R returns, if R' returns v, then R does not return v'. To strengthen our impossibility result, we will allow base objects to be atomic.

2.3   Configurations

In this paper, we are only interested in the states of base objects, and not of processes. Therefore, by slight abuse of terminology, we define a *configuration* to be a set of states of all the correct base objects (and not the processes). Basically, the system starts from an initial configuration and each atomic step of the algorithm, e.g., a low-level *write()* on a base object, leads the system to a new configuration. The execution of a high-level operation involves several atomic steps that lead the system from a configuration C to another configuration C'. The assumption that the reader does not write means that $C' = C$ in case no *Write()* is invoked.

We say that a configuration C' is *write-reachable* from a configuration C if there is a sequence S of *Write()* operations that, when executed without overlapping with any other high-level operation, leads the system to C'. If all input parameters of the *Write()* operations of sequence S are from a set $V' \subset V$, we say that C' is *write-reachable* from C *using* V'.

3 Amnesic Storage Algorithms

We introduce in this section the notion of an *amnesic storage algorithm*. We characterize this notion in terms of configurations and write-reachability.

Intuitively, a storage algorithm is amnesic if all but a finite number of configurations reached by the algorithm can be eventually *erased* if a sufficient number of different values are written after them. In short, erasing a configuration C', itself obtained from some configuration C, means reaching a new configuration C'' (after writing a sufficient number of different values) that makes it impossible to tell whether C' was indeed reached. That is, C'' could be reached directly from C without going through C'. The sequence that reaches C'' from C' is in a sense an *eraser* sequence. An observer of C'' does not know whether C' occurred or not.

To preclude the trivial case where erasing a configuration is always performed by the very same sequence, i.e., some sort or *reset* sequence, we require that the configuration C'' could be obtained from C by using values from *any* infinite subset of values. Notice that we do not require that *any* sufficiently long sequence erases every configuration. Yet, our definition is rather weak because we simply require that every configuration has an eraser sequence using any infinite subset of values: such a weak definition strengthens our impossibility result. Formally,

Definition 1 (Amnesic Storage). *A storage algorithm A is amnesic if in every execution of A in which infinitely many different values are written, there is a point t, so that for every configuration C reached from point t onward, every configuration C1 write-reachable from C, and every infinite subset of values $V' \subset V$, there is a configuration C2 that is write-reachable from both C and C1 using V'.*

We say that (see Figure 1) t is the *amnesia point*, $C2$ is an *eraser configuration* of $C1$ from C using V'; the sequence of *Writes()* used to reach $C2$ from $C1$ is an *eraser sequence* of $C1$ from C using V'; the sequence used to reach $C2$ from C is a *bypass sequence* of $C1$ from C using V'.

Clearly, an algorithm that recalls the entire history of written values in the base registers is not amnesic. On the other hand, an algorithm that stores in all

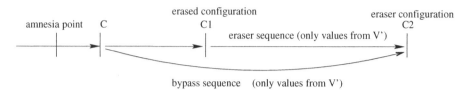

Fig. 1. Amnesia

base registers the last k values written in the high-level register is amnesic. The eraser sequence $S2$ simply needs to be of size k and from V'. The amnesia point captures a situation where an algorithm initially stores some finite number of values forever, but eventually, (at the amnesia point), its storage is "exhausted" and it cannot store additional values forever. To be non-amnesic, an algorithm with an infinite domain needs to be able to recall (in the sense that they cannot be erased) infinitely many configurations that it visited.

It is important to notice here that storage algorithms can also record timestamps while being amnesic. Consider for instance an algorithm that stores in the base registers the last k values written, as well as the total number of values written. Consider a configuration $C1$ obtained after writing i values, starting from an initial configuration C. An eraser sequence using some infinite subset V' consists of k new different *Write()* invocations with parameters from V', and a bypass sequence consists of $i + k$ different *Write()* invocations with parameters from V', the latter k being the same as for the eraser sequence.

Note that violating amnesia does not directly translate to excessive storage requirements. An algorithm may be able to represent some property of an unbounded history in a bounded way, much like a finite-state automaton can recall that an unbounded string belongs to some regular language[2]. Nevertheless, we are unaware of any previous *storage* algorithm that employs such a succinct representation, and so our impossibility result has broad applicability.

4   Impossibility of Amnesic Robust Storage

In this section, we establish the impossibility of devising a storage algorithm that is at the same time *amnesic* and *robust* when readers do not write. Recall that in our context, a storage algorithm is *robust* if (a) at least one base object can suffer an (R-arbitrary) failure; (b) the implemented register is *regular*, i.e., tolerates contention; (c) every invoked high-level operation terminates, including in the presence of contention.

4.1   Simplifications

As we assume that only the writer of the implemented register can modify the base objects, these are also, without loss of generality, single-writer registers, with the same writer as that of the implemented register. Still without loss of generality, since we preclude the reader from writing, we can assume that:

---

[2] We are grateful to Prasad Jayanti for pointing this out.

1. Every high level *Read()* invocation translates into a finite series of concurrent read invocations of all base objects O_1, O_2, .., O_n.
2. The set of configurations obtained after performing any sequence S of *Write()* operations without any overlapping *Read()* is the same as if this sequence was invoked concurrently with this *Read()*. Recall that our definition of configurations only includes base object states.

4.2   Overview of the Impossibility Proof

To prove our impossibility, we proceed by contradiction. More specifically, we assume that there is an amnesic robust storage algorithm A that implements a register over an infinite domain V and we exhibit a scenario where A violates the regularity of the register.

We show that A violates regularity by having the reader return a value that was never written to the implemented register. Not surprisingly, this value is obtained from a low-lever read of the faulty base register. Our scenario has the reader unable to distinguish the response of the faulty base register from the response of a correct one, precisely because A is amnesic, and readers do not write. The proof then goes through three steps:

- *Step 1.* (Using the amnesia assumption.) We construct an execution E, which we call an *amnesic* execution, where sequences of *Write()* operations erase each other in turn, using n different subsets of value domains, $V_1, \ldots, V_n$. We will argue that every amnesic storage algorithm can generate such an execution.
- *Step 2.* (Using the assumption that readers do not write.) We next construct a slight modification E' of E, where the reader samples one base register after each sequence above has erased the previous configuration. No matter how many samples are taken, the reader still cannot obtain evidence of any written value from more than one base register, because the evidence is continuously erased. Finally, the reader returns some value v_i from some subset V_i, for which it saw evidence in some base register O_i.
- *Step 3.* (Using robustness.) Finally, we construct an execution E_i' in which no value from V_i is written, bypassing the configurations where values from V_i are stored. In E_i', O_i incurs an R-arbitrary failure, and returns the same values as in E'. Since the reader cannot distinguish E_i' from E', it returns v_i, which was never written.

4.3   Impossibility

Theorem 1. *No storage algorithm can be amnesic and robust if a single base register can suffer a responsive arbitrary failure and readers do not write.*

Proof (Proof of Theorem 1.). We assume a storage algorithm A that deterministically implements the abstraction of a register with an infinite value domain V, using a collection of n base objects $O_1, \ldots, O_n$. We assume by contradiction that A is robust and amnesic.

We partition V into $n + 1$ infinite subsets $V_0, V_1, \ldots, V_n$. (The intersection of every two subsets is empty, and the union of all subsets is V).

Step 1. We construct an infinite execution of A, E, which we call an *amnesic execution* (see Figure 2). E goes through the infinite sequence of configurations:

$$C_{1,1}, \ldots, C_{1,n}, C_{2,1}, \ldots, C_{2,n}, \ldots, C_{j,1}, \ldots, C_{j,n}, \ldots$$

such that for every $i \in \{1, .., n\}$, there is an execution E_i such that (a) E_i is the subsequence of E obtained by omitting all the configurations $C_{k,i}$, $k > 0$. (That is, configurations $C_{k,i}$ for all k are skipped.) And (b) no value from V_i is ever written in E_i.

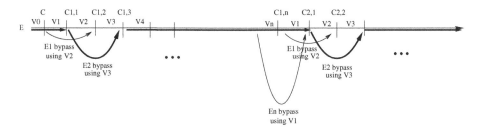

Fig. 2. Amnesic execution E; execution E2 (bypassing V_2) highlighted

We construct E recursively as follows. We perform a series of *Writes()* of different values from V_0 until the algorithm reaches an amnesia point at some configuration C. Then we apply a *Write()* of a single value from V_1. We denote the resulting configuration $C_{1,1}$. Then we use the assumption that the storage algorithm is amnesic and apply to $C_{1,1}$ a sequence that erases $C_{1,1}$ from C using V_2. We denote the resulting configuration by $C_{1,2}$. Then we use again the assumption that the storage algorithm is amnesic and apply to $C_{1,2}$ a sequence that erases $C_{1,2}$ from $C_{1,1}$ using V_3. We denote the resulting configuration by $C_{1,3}$. And so forth recursively. We apply to $C_{j,k}$ a sequence that erases $C_{j,k}$ from $C_{j,k-1}$ using V_{k+1}, where $C_{j,n+1} = C_{j+1,1}$ and $V_{n+1} = V_1$. The resulting execution E is infinite and can be generated from every amnesic storage algorithm.

In addition, for every $1 \leq i \leq n$, execution E_i is constructed, also recursively, as follows (see Figure 2). Up to $C_{1,i-1}$, E_i is exactly like E and hence no *Write()* uses any value from V_i. Configuration $C_{1,i+1}$ is then (directly) reached from $C_{1,i-1}$ via the bypassing sequence of $C_{1,i}$ from $C_{1,i-1}$ using values from V_{i+1}. Then we continue as in E until $C_{2,i-1}$, at which point we execute the bypass sequence of $C_{2,i}$ from $C_{2,i-1}$. And so forth: we apply the same sequence as in E to reach $C_{j,k}$ from $C_{j,k-1}$ for $k \neq i$, and for i, we apply the bypass sequence of $C_{j,i}$ from $C_{j,i-1}$ to reach $C_{j,i+1}$ from $C_{j,i-1}$. It is easy to see that properties (a) and (b) above hold for every E_i, for $i \in \{1, .., n\}$.

Step 2. We now construct an execution E' interleaving a single *Read()* with the sequences of *Write()* operations involved in E. Remember that, without loss of generality, we assume that every *Read()* implementation consists of a sequence of concurrent invocations of all base objects. The interleaving in execution E' is constructed as follows. *Read()* is invoked when the base objects are in configuration $C_{1,1}$. The reader returns from the kth *read()* of base object O_j when the system is in configuration $C_{k,j}$. For instance, the reader returns from the first *read()* of the first base object, O_1, when the system is in configuration $C_{1,1}$, then from the first *read()* of the second base object, O_2, when the system is in configuration $C_{1,2}$.

By the assumption that the reader does not write, execution E' can also be generated by every amnesic storage algorithm. By our liveness assumption, the *Read()* eventually returns a value. Since the *Read()* is invoked after the first write from V_1, by regularity, it returns a value v_i from some V_i for $0 < i \leq n$.

Step 3. We now make use of our assumption of robustness to derive a contradiction. We construct execution E'_i, which is the same as E_i, with two exceptions:

1. For every $j \neq i$, as in E', we apply the kth *read()* of base object O_j when the system is in configuration $C_{k,j}$.
2. The kth *read()* of base object O_i occurs during the kth bypass.
3. O_i returns the same response to its kth *read* invocation in E'_i as in in execution E'.

Execution E'_i can also be generated by every amnesic storage algorithm with base object O_i failing in an arbitrary way. Executions E' and E'_i look the same to the reader (by construction), which then returns a value v_i from V_i in E'_i. But no value from V_i is written in E'_i, contradicting regularity.

5 Amnesic Algorithms and Circumventing the Impossibility

Our impossibility justifies certain assumptions and design decisions made by existing storage algorithms. In this section, we illustrate the importance of the notion of amnesia, by showing that the majority of reliable storage algorithms in the literature are amnesic, and discuss how existing algorithms circumvent our impossibility result.

First note that every bounded memory algorithm is by definition trivially amnesic, because no infinite sub-domains of its domain exist. Since our impossibility result only applies to algorithms that can store values from unbounded domains, it is more interesting to consider algorithms that can manipulate such domains. Interestingly, most bounded memory algorithms in the literature can be easily extended to support unbounded domains. For example, Jayanti et al. [13] present an emulation of a safe register from ones that can suffer NR-Arbitrary faults. Although originally described as a bounded memory algorithm, it does not make any use of the domain size, and only stores values from the domain. Hence, this algorithm can easily work with an unbounded domain, where in each execution, it consumes storage as required for representing the values written in that execution. This algorithm circumvents our impossibility result by implementing only safe storage.

Lamport [15] presents a bounded memory algorithm for implementing a wait-free regular register from safe bits, with readers that do not write. Given the existence of robust safe register emulations [13,17,2], had this algorithm manipulated unbounded domains, it would have contradicted our impossibility. However, this algorithm is aware of its value domain and makes heavy use of this knowledge– it stores one bit for each value in the value domain of the register. The algorithm works as follows: a write operation of the ith value in the domain changes the ith bit to 1, and subsequently writes 0 in bits $i-1, i-2, \ldots, 1$. The reader reads the bits $1, 2, 3, \ldots$ until it encounters a 1 in some bit i, at which point it stops reading and returns i. We observe that neither the reader nor the writer ever accesses a bit higher than the one pertaining to the largest written value. Therefore, this algorithm too can be extended to unbounded domains, e.g., integers, by allocating the ith bit the first time a value greater or equal to i is written. Despite its exponential storage requirements, the resulting algorithm is also amnesic, since writing a single value larger than all previously written ones is an eraser sequence. So how does this algorithm circumvent our impossibility result? We observe that the extended algorithm no longer ensures liveness, because if the writer writes an infinite monotonically increasing sequence of values (an *amnesic* sequence), the reader can "trail" the writer, and never encounter a 1 in any register. Thus, even such exponential storage does not save us from the impossibility.

Many algorithms that store unbounded timestamps are also amnesic, including the classical ABD [6] algorithm, which tolerates only crash failures of base objects, and the safe register emulations of [17,2,12]. Other amnesic algorithms provide atomic semantics (which are stronger than regular) either by assuming a stronger model where data is self-verifying (and hence cannot be forged by base objects), or by having readers write [17,16,8,11,3].

It is also possible to circumvent our impossibility with amnesic algorithms by providing weaker (non-terminating in case of contention) termination guarantees [2]. Specifically, Abraham et al. [2] propose a termination condition called *finite writes (FW)*, which guarantees progress only in executions with a finite number of writes, and present a amnesic storage algorithm implementing a regular FW-terminating register.

A few algorithms circumvent our impossibility by forgoing amnesia. These include the Pasis system [10], which achieves atomic semantics. It circumvents our impossibility by having authenticated readers that are allowed to modify the data stored at the base registers (storage nodes). The storage nodes also keep all versions of data that have been written in the execution, and are therefore, not amnesic. To prevent storage exhaustion, the system implements a garbage collection mechanism, which works well in practice, but, as the authors point out in [9], might fail to terminate in some scenarios.

Martin et al. [18], as well as Bazzi and Ding [7] also provide atomic semantics. They assume storage servers (instead of base registers) that communicate with each other, and a subscription model whereby storage servers push writer updates to subscribed clients. Since theoretically, there is no bound on the number of messages in the reliable push channel in an asynchronous system, these algorithms are also not amnesic. This approach nevertheless, is a viable design alternative in the settings where servers are available and the number of clients is limited.

6   Sharp Separation Between Regularity and Safety

Many amnesic robust storage solutions implement safe registers [13,17,2]. This maybe surprising, as safe and regular semantics are commonly believed to be "equivalent", justified by the existence of known bounded memory reductions from regular registers to safe ones. In particular, Lamport [15] presents a bounded memory algorithm for emulating a regular register from safe ones, in which readers do not write. The algorithm assumes a bounded value domain and its storage requirements, as well as the number of memory accesses in the algorithm, are notoriously high (proportional to the number of possible values the regular register can hold).

The following theorem is an immediate corollary of Theorem 1 and the existence of amnesic storage algorithms that implement a t-tolerant wait-free safe register (with unbounded value domains) from a collection of n base registers up to t of which can suffer arbitrary failures [13,17,2].

Theorem 2. *If readers do not write, it is impossible to implement a live regular register from safe ones with an amnesic algorithm and an infinite domain.*

Interestingly, Lamport has proved the following [15] :

> If readers do not write, it is impossible to implement an atomic register from regular ones with a bounded algorithm.

Thus, Lamport has shown that in *bounded memory* implementations, disallowing readers to write draws a sharp line between regularity and atomicity, but not between safety and regularity.

Hence, our result shows that, when one considers amnesic with infinite value domain instead of bounded memory, the same sharp line does exist between regularity and safety.

7   Concluding Remarks

The observation that no existing storage algorithm with reasonable space requirements that is regular, live in the presence of contention, and does not require readers to write, or preclude arbitrary faults of base registers was made by Abraham et al. [1]. They conjectured that, roughly speaking, if readers do not write, then the storage size grows linearly with the number of values written over the execution's time span. The difficulty in proving this conjecture stems from the lack of appropriate definitions, since the classical notion of bounded memory cannot capture "linear growth" in storage requirements. Our notion of *amnesic* memory is an attempt to capture practical limitations on the information an algorithm recalls about its history, and gives an explanation to the observation that led to this conjecture. An interesting direction for future work may be providing a concrete lower bound on the space requirements of robust storage algorithms that are not amnesic. In addition, we believe that more impossibilities and fine grained distinctions could be obtained if one reconsiders bounded memory restrictions with our amnesic notion in mind.

Acknowledgments

We thank Ittai Abraham, Lorenzo Alvisi, Faith Ellen, Eli Gafni, Prasad Jayanti, Nancy Lynch, Dahlia Malkhi, Jean-Philippe Martin, Michel Raynal, and Marko Vukolić for many fruitful discussions on robust storage algorithms.

References

1. Abraham, I., Chockler, G., Keidar, I., Malkhi, D.: Private communication (2002)
2. Abraham, I., Chockler, G., Keidar, I., Malkhi, D.: Byzantine Disk Paxos: Optimal resilience with byzantine shared memory. Distributed Computing 18(5), 387–408 (2004)
3. Abraham, I., Chockler, G., Keidar, I., Malkhi, D.: Wait-free regular storage from byzantine components. Information Processing Letters (IPL) 101(2), 60–65 (2007)
4. Afek, Y., Greenberg, D.S., Merritt, M., Taubenfeld, G.: Computing with faulty shared objects. Journal of the ACM 42(6), 1231–1274 (1995)
5. Afek, Y., Merritt, M., Taubenfeld, G.: Benign failures models for shared memory. In: Schiper, A. (ed.) Distributed Algorithms. LNCS, vol. 725, pp. 69–83. Springer, Heidelberg (1993)
6. Attiya, H., Bar-Noy, A., Dolev, D.: Sharing memory robustly in message-passing systems. Journal of the ACM 42(1), 124–142 (1995)
7. Bazzi, R.A., Ding, Y.: Non-skipping Timestamps for Byzantine Data Storage Systems. In: Guerraoui, R. (ed.) DISC 2004. LNCS, vol. 3274, pp. 405–419. Springer, Heidelberg (2004)
8. Cachin, C., Tessaro, S.: Optimal resilience for erasure-coded Byzantine distributed storage. In: DSN 2006. Intl. Conference on Dependable Systems and Networks, pp. 115–124 (June 2006)
9. Goodson, G., Wylie, J., Ganger, G., Reiter, M.: Efficient byzantine-tolerant erasure-coded storage. Technical Report CMU-PDL-03-104, Parallel Data Laboratory, CMU (December 2003)
10. Goodson, G., Wylie, J., Ganger, G., Reiter, M.: Efficient byzantine-tolerant erasure-coded storage. In: DSN-2004. The International Conference on Dependable Systems and Networks (June 2004)
11. Guerraoui, R., Levy, R.R., Vukolic, M.: Lucky read/write access to robust atomic storage. In: DSN, pp. 125–136. IEEE Computer Society Press, Los Alamitos (2006)
12. Guerraoui, R., Vukolić, M.: How Fast Can a Very Robust Read Be? In: PODC'06. 25th ACM Symposium on Principles of Distributed Computing. ACM Press, New York (2006)
13. Jayanti, P., Chandra, T., Toueg, S.: Fault-tolerant wait-free shared objects. Journal of the ACM 45(3), 451–500 (1998)

14. Lakshmanan, S., Ahamad, M., Venkateswaran, H.: Responsive security for stored data. IEEE Trans. on Parallel and Distributed Systems 14(19), 818–828 (2003)
15. Lamport, L.: On interprocess communication – Part II: Algorithms. Distributed Computing 1(2), 86–101 (1986)
16. Liskov, B., Rodrigues, R.: Byzantine clients rendered harmless. In: Fraigniaud, P. (ed.) DISC 2005. LNCS, vol. 3724. Springer, Heidelberg (2005)
17. Malkhi, D., Reiter, M.: Byzantine quorum systems. Distributed Computing 11(4), 203–213 (1998)
18. Martin, J.-P., Alvisi, L., Dahlin, M.: Minimal byzantine storage. In: Proceedings of the 16th International Symposium on Distributed Computing (DISC) (October 2002)
19. Rodrigues, R., Liskov, B.: Rosebud: A Scalable Byzantine-Fault-Tolerant Storage Architecture. Technical Report MIT-LCS-TR-932, MIT Laboratory for Computer Science (2004)

Distributed Approximations for Packing in Unit-Disk Graphs*

Andrzej Czygrinow[1] and Michał Hańćkowiak[2]

[1] Department of Mathematics and Statistics
Arizona State University
Tempe, AZ 85287-1804, USA
andrzej@math.la.asu.edu
[2] Faculty of Mathematics and Computer Science
Adam Mickiewicz University, Poznań, Poland
mhanckow@amu.edu.pl

Abstract. We give a distributed approximation algorithm for the vertex-packing problem in unit-disk graphs. Given a graph H, the algorithm finds in a unit-disk graph G a collection of pairwise disjoint copies of H of size which is approximately equal to the packing number of H in G. The algorithm is deterministic and runs in a poly-logarithmic number of rounds in the message passing model.

1 Introduction

Distributed complexity of vast majority of graph-theoretic problems is still far from well understood. In contrast to the sequential or parallel model of computations, the distributed model has resisted efficient solutions for even the most simple graph-theoretic problems. Consider, for example, the maximal independent set problem. A trivial sequential solution for the problem exists, a non-trivial deterministic PRAM algorithm is known (Small-spaces derandomization procedure of Luby [L86]) but the distributed complexity of the maximal independent set problem is still an outstanding open problem. As distributed complexity of many graph-theoretic problems seems very hard to be determined in general graphs, it is natural to consider important sub-classes of graphs. In this paper, we will consider a class of unit-disk graphs and give an efficient distributed approximation algorithm for the vertex-packing problem. The algorithm is purely deterministic and finds a solution of value which is within $(1 - o(1))$ of the optimal.

Many different distributed models can be considered (see Peleg [P00]) each capturing different aspect of distributed computations. Here, we will work in the distributed message-passing model of computations (see for example Linial [L92]) in which the underlying network forms a graph with vertices which correspond to computational units and edges that correspond to communication links between the units. The computations are synchronized and proceed in rounds. In a single round each vertex can send messages to its neighbors, can receive messages from

---

* This work was supported by grant N206 017 32/2452 for years 2007-2010.

A. Pelc (Ed.): DISC 2007, LNCS 4731, pp. 152–164, 2007.

its neighbors, and can perform local computations. In this model the emphasis on the extent to which local computations can be used to determine a global function of the network. The global function considered in this paper comes from the vertex-packing problem. In this problem, we are given a graph H of a fixed size and want to find a maximum number of vertex-disjoint copies of H in the underlying network G. More formally, let G be graph on $|G|$ vertices and let H be a graph on a fixed (independent of G) number of vertices. An L-packing of H in G is a collection of pairwise vertex-disjoint subgraphs $H_1, H_2, \ldots, H_L$ of G such that each H_i is isomorphic to H. The packing number of H, $\nu_H(G)$, is the largest L such that an L-packing of H in G exists. Finding $\nu_H(G)$ is a classical problem in graph theory with many important special cases. In particular, the size of a maximum matching in graph G is equal to $\nu_{K_2}(G)$.

1.1   Model and Notation

As noted before, we will consider the message-passing synchronized distributed model of computations from [L92]. In addition, we assume that vertices in the network have unique identifiers which are in the set $\{1, \ldots, m\}$ where m is a polynomial in $|G|$ and is globally known. The underlying topology of the network will be of a unit-disk graph which is commonly used to model mobile ad-hoc networks. A graph $G = (V, E)$ is called a *unit-disk graph* if there is an injective function $f : V \to R^2$ such that $\{u, v\} \in E$ if and only if $||f(u) - f(v)||_2 \leq 1$. Although the fact that G is a unit-disk graph is critical for our analysis, we will assume that no information (including the Euclidean distance) about a geometric representation of G is available to nodes. Finally, we will use the graph-theoretic notation and terminology from [D05]. In particular, we will denote by $|G|$ the number of vertices of G and by $||G||$ the number of edges.

1.2   Results

We give a distributed approximation algorithm for the packing problem in unit-disk graphs. The algorithm is deterministic, runs in a poly-logarithmic number of rounds, and does not use any information about a geometric representation of the unit-disk graph. Let H be a graph and let G be a unit-disk graph. Given k and H, the algorithm finds in a poly-logarithmic number of rounds a collection of pairwise vertex-disjoint subgraphs $H_1, \ldots, H_L$ of G with $L \geq (1 - O(1/\log^k |G|))\nu_H(G)$ (Theorem 3). The algorithm extends the clustering procedure from [CH06b] by adopting it to a more general class of graphs than the one considered in [CH06b]. Specifically, we will consider the so-called (C, q)-bounded growth graphs (see Definition 1 on page 155) which arise naturally when considering certain auxiliary graphs of a unit-disk graph. In [CH06b] a clustering algorithm for $(C, 2)$-bounded growth graphs with C constant is given. Here, we found it necessary to generalize the procedure from [CH06b] to (C, q)-bounded growth graphs for which q is constant but C may depend on $|G|$. The algorithm essentially works as follows. First a maximal independent set is found. The set is used to partition the graph into clusters of two types: the large clusters that contain many vertices and the other clusters. In the large clusters copies of H are packed greedily into subgraphs induced by $N[v]$. The packing problem in the rest of the graph is reduced to the problem of approximating a maximum independent set in a special graph. We argue that error made in both of the above parts is small and prove that there exists a solution to the packing problem of value which approximates the optimal with the property that every copy of H is either entirely contained in large clusters or is contained in the rest of the graph.

1.3   Related Work

Studying distributed message passing approximation algorithms for unit-disk graphs was initiated by Kuhn et. al. in [KMNW05b] where efficient approximations for the Maximum Independent Set (MaxIS) Problem and the Minimum Dominating Set (MDS) Problem are given. Research described in the series of papers [KMW05], [KMNW05b], and [KMNW05a] is the main motivation for our work here. Continuing the program of Kuhn et. al., we recently gave distributed approximations for two additional problems, the Minimum Connected Dominating Set (MCDS) Problem and the Maximum Matching (MM) Problem (see [CH06b]). All of the above results indicate that distributed poly-logarithmic approximations are fairly easy to find if the underlying graph has the unit-disk graph topology. The second motivation for our study comes from the recent work [CH06a] and [CHS06] in which distributed approximations for MaxIS Problem, MM Problem, and MDS Problem in planar and minor-closed families of graphs are given. The vertex-packing problem is another important problem which admits a distributed approximation in unit-disk graphs. Although minor-closed families of graphs provide different challenges than unit-disk graphs, we also hope that some of the techniques developed in this paper will prove useful in attacking the packing problem for such families of graphs. It is possible that the running time of our packing algorithm can be improved but it seems unlikely that the poly-log bound can be beaten as for example in the case of general graphs, it is shown in [KMW04] that required to achieve a constant or a poly-logarithmic approximation ratio for an inclusion maximal matching is at least $\Omega(\sqrt{\log |G|/\log\log |G|})$ or $\Omega(\log \Delta/\log\log \Delta)$, where Δ denotes the maximum degree of the graph.

1.4   Organization

In the next section we will give our modified clustering algorithm. The algorithm and its analysis follows the pattern of the corresponding discussion in in this [CH06b]. In Section 3, we will present the main result of the paper, a distributed algorithm which yields an almost exact approximation of the vertex-packing problem in unit-disk graphs.

2   Clustering Algorithm

We shall start with the following basic property of unit-disk graphs. Although very rudimentary, the property is a key to our clustering and packing algorithms.

A geometric representation of a unit-disk graph G is an injective function $f :$ $V(G) \rightarrow R^2$ such that two distinct vertices u, v from $V(G)$ form an edge in G if and only if $||f(u) - f(v)||_2 \leq 1$.

Lemma 1. *Let G be a unit-disk graph and let k be a positive integer. For any independent set I in G and any geometrical representation f of G, the number of vertices from $f(I)$ which are contained in a ball in R^2 of radius k is at most $4(k + 0.5)^2$.*

2.1   Clustering Algorithm

Our algorithm for unit-disk graphs uses a small modification of the clustering procedure from [CH06b] which in turn is based on the ruling set algorithm from [AGLP89]. In [CH06b] it is shown that the clustering procedure works in the so-called $(C, 2)$-bounded growth graphs (see Definition 1) where C is a constant. Here, we will need a modification of this algorithm which works in a more general class of graphs. Recall that the distance between two vertices u, v in a graph G, $d_G(u, v)$, is the length of the shortest path in G joining u with v.

Definition 1. *A graph G has a (C, q)-bounded growth if for every vertex v in G and every nonnegative integer m,*

$$|\{u \in V(G) : d_G(u, v) \leq m\}| \leq Cm^q + 1.$$

In our applications q will always be a fixed constant, C however will depend on the graph G. In fact, to get a desired approximation error we will set $C :=$ $\Theta(\log^l |G|)$ for a fixed constant l. Algorithm from [CH06b] uses the ruling forest technique from [AGLP89] and relies on the $(C, 2)$-bounded growth property. We will show that a modification of the algorithm from [CH06b] yields a generalization which is can be applied to the packing problem. The performance of the modified algorithm is summarized in the next theorem.

Theorem 1. *Let q be a fixed constant. There is a distributed algorithm which given a (C, q)-bounded growth graph G with identifiers in $\{1, \ldots, m\}$, $|G| \leq m$, and $0 < \epsilon = \epsilon(|G|) \leq 1$ finds a partition $(V_1, \ldots, V_s)$ of $V(G)$ such that the following two properties are satisfied.*

- *The number of edges between different partition classes is $O(\epsilon C|G|)$ and*
- *For $i = 1, \ldots, s$, the diameter of $G[V_i]$ is $O\left(\frac{\log C + \log 1/\epsilon}{\epsilon}\right)$.*

The algorithm runs in $O\left(C\left(\frac{\log C + \log 1/\epsilon}{\epsilon}\right)^{q+1} \log^{q+1} m \log 1/\epsilon\right)$ rounds.

The algorithm from Theorem 1 is the procedure CLUSTERING which we will describe shortly. The algorithm is based on the ruling set procedure of Awerbuch et. al. [AGLP89]. A *D-ruling set* in a graph $G = (V, E)$ is a subset S of V that has two properties:

- For any two distinct vertices s, s' from S, the distance (in G) between s and s' is at least D.

– For any vertex $v \in V$ there is a vertex $s \in S$ such that the distance between s and v is at most $D \log |G|$.

There is an easy distributed algorithm which finds a D-ruling set in any graph.

Theorem 2 ([AGLP89]). *Let G be a graph such that identifiers of vertices from $V(G)$ are in $\{1, \ldots, m\}$ where m is globally known and is a polynomial in $|G|$. There is a distributed algorithm which finds in G a D-ruling set in $O(D \log |G|)$ rounds.*

Our algorithm uses parameters ϵ, D, and F (used in CLUSTERING) and assumes that graph G has the (C, q)-bounded growth. Parameter q is assumed to be constant, C and ϵ can depend on $|G|$. For $0 < \epsilon < 1$ and C, let l_* be the smallest positive integer with the property

$$(1 + \epsilon)^{l_*} \geq C l_*^q + 1. \tag{1}$$

It is easy to check that when q is constant and ϵ is small then

$$l_* = O\left(\frac{\log C + \log 1/\epsilon}{\epsilon}\right). \tag{2}$$

In addition, let D be such that

$$D > 2l_*. \tag{3}$$

In the next two procedures we will find a clustering of a graph which has a (C, q)-bounded growth. First procedure is essentially one iteration of the main algorithm. We will denote by $N(U)$ the set of vertices in G which are at distance at most one of a vertex from U.

CLUSTERSET
Input: Constant q. Graph $G = (V, E)$ which has (C, q)-bounded growth and such that identifiers of V are bounded by m. Parameters: $0 < \epsilon < 1$ (arbitrary) and D which satisfies (3).
Output: A family of subsets of V.

(1) Find a D-ruling set $\{v_1, v_2, \ldots, v_l\}$ in G.
(2) For every v_i in parallel:
    (a) Let $U_i := \{v_i\}$, $N_i := N(U_i) \setminus U_i$.
    (b) while $|N_i| \geq \epsilon |U_i|$
        • $U_i := U_i \cup N_i$, $N_i := N(U_i) \setminus U_i$.
(3) Return $U_1, U_2, \ldots, U_l$.

We shall start the analysis of CLUSERSET with the following property of the D-ruling set obtained in step one.

Lemma 2. *The number of vertices in the D-ruling set obtained in step one of CLUSTERSET is at least*

$$|G|/(CD^q \log^q |G| + 1).$$

Proof. Let $\{v_1, v_2, \ldots, v_l\}$ denote the ruling set obtained in step one. For every v_i consider the set W_i of vertices in G which are within distance $D \log |G|$ of v_i. From Definition 1, $|W_i| \leq C D^q \log^q |G| + 1$. Since v_i's form a D-ruling set we have $|G| \leq |\bigcup_{i=1}^{l} W_i|$. Thus

$$|G| \leq l(C D^q \log^q |G| + 1).$$

In the next two lemmas we will show that each of U_i's has small diameter and more importantly the total number of edges that intersect different U_i's is small.

Lemma 3. *Let l_* be such that inequality (1) holds and let $\{v_1, v_2, \ldots, v_l\}$ be the ruling set from step one. Then for every $i = 1, \ldots, l$,*

$$\max_{u \in U_i} d_G(v_i, u) \leq l_*.$$

Proof. Let $U_i^{(l)}$ denote the set U_i in the lth iteration of the while loop from step 2(b). Then $|U_i^{(0)}| = 1$ and in the lth iteration $|U_i^{(l)}| \geq (1 + \epsilon)^l$. On the other hand, by Definition 1, $|U_i^{(l)}| \leq C l^q + 1$. Consequently, if l_* is the smallest positive integer such that $(1 + \epsilon)^{l_*} \geq C l_*^q + 1$ then $l \leq l_*$ and so for any $u \in U_i$, the distance $d_G(v_i, u) \leq l_*$.

Lemma 4. *Sets $U_1, U_2, \ldots, U_l$ returned by CLUSTERSET are pair-wise disjoint. In addition, if $e(U_i, V \setminus U_i)$ denotes the number of edges between U_i and $V \setminus U_i$ then*

$$\sum_{i=1}^{l} e(U_i, V \setminus U_i) = O(C\epsilon \sum_{i=1}^{l} |U_i|).$$

Proof. From Lemma 3 for every $u \in U_i$, $d_G(v_i, u) \leq l_*$ and so if $U_i \cap U_j$ is non-empty then the distance between v_i and v_j is at most $2l_*$ which contradicts the fact that v_i, v_j are in the D-ruling set with $D > 2l_*$ by (3). To prove the second part, note that for every U_i returned in step 3, the set $N_i = N(U_i) \setminus U_i$ is such that $|N_i| < \epsilon|U_i|$. Since G has the maximum degree of at most C, the number of edges between U_i and N_i is $C\epsilon|U_i|$.

Recall that identifiers of V are in set $\{1, \ldots, m\}$. We finally note that the running time of CLUSTERSET is $O\left(D \log m + \frac{\log C + \log 1/\epsilon}{\epsilon}\right)$.

Lemma 5. *The number of rounds of CLUSTERSET is $O\left(D \log m + \frac{\log C + \log 1/\epsilon}{\epsilon}\right)$.*

Proof. There are $O(D \log m)$ rounds to find the D-ruling forest in step 1. This is followed by $l_* = O\left(\frac{\log C + \log 1/\epsilon}{\epsilon}\right)$ iterations in step 2.

Our main clustering procedure will call CLUSTERSET repeatedly. In each call, sets $U_1, \ldots, U_l$ are obtained and vertices in $\bigcup U_i$ are deleted from the graph G. Finally, after trimming G with repeated application of CLUSTERSET, the remaining vertices will form one-element clusters.

CLUSTERING

Input: Constant q. Graph $G = (V, E)$ which has (C, q)-bounded growth and such that the identifiers of V are positive integers which are less than or equal to m.
Parameters: $0 < \epsilon < 1$ (arbitrary), D (must satisfy (3)), F (arbitrary).
Output: A partition $\mathcal{P}$ of V.

(1) Repeat F times:
   (a) Call CLUSTERSET in G. Add all sets U_i obtained from CLUSTERSET to family $\mathcal{P}$.
   (b) Delete from G vertices from $\bigcup U_i$ and edges incident to these vertices.
(2) For every vertex left in G create a set which contains only this vertex and add it to $\mathcal{P}$. Return $\mathcal{P}$.

We will analyze CLUSTERING in the next two lemmas.

Lemma 6. *Let* $\mathcal{P} = (V_1, \ldots, V_t)$ *be a partition of* V *returned by* CLUSTERING. *The number of edges of* $G = (V, E)$ *connecting vertices from different* V_i*'s is*

$$O\left(\left(\left(1 - \frac{1}{CD^q \log^q |G| + 1}\right)^F + \epsilon\right) C|G|\right).$$

Proof. First note that since G is a graph with a maximum degree $O(C)$, $\|G\| = O(C|G|)$. Consider sets added to $\mathcal{P}$ in iterations from step 1. Edges with exactly one endpoint in these sets are deleted in step 1(b) and by Lemma 4, the number of them is $O(C\epsilon|G|)$. The remaining edges which must be counted are the edges of G from step two. To estimate these, we note that by Lemma 2, the number of vertices in this graph is $O\left(\left(1 - \frac{1}{CD^q \log^q |G| + 1}\right)^F |G|\right)$. Consequently, the number of edges of G connecting vertices from different V_i's is $O\left(\left(\left(1 - \frac{1}{CD^q \log^q |G| + 1}\right)^F + \epsilon\right) C|G|\right)$.

Lemma 7. CLUSTERING *runs in* $O\left(F\left(D \log m + \frac{\log C + \log 1/\epsilon}{\epsilon}\right)\right)$ *rounds.*

Proof. There are F iterations of step 1, in which, by Lemma 5, the sets are found in $O\left(D \log m + \frac{\log C + \log 1/\epsilon}{\epsilon}\right)$ rounds.

Proof of Theorem 1. Let $D := 2l_* + 1 = O\left(\frac{\log C + \log 1/\epsilon}{\epsilon}\right)$ and let $F := \lceil(\log 1/\epsilon)CD^q \log^q m\rceil$. Then, by Lemma 7, the number of rounds is

$$O\left(F\left(D \log m + \frac{\log C + \log 1/\epsilon}{\epsilon}\right)\right) = O\left(C \log 1/\epsilon \left(\frac{\log C + \log 1/\epsilon}{\epsilon}\right)^{q+1} \log^{q+1} m\right).$$

The number of edges which connect different clusters is $O(\epsilon C|V|)$ by Lemma 6 and the diameter of each cluster is $O(l^*)$ by Lemma 3 which by (1) is $O\left(\frac{\log C + \log 1/\epsilon}{\epsilon}\right)$.

3 Main Algorithm

3.1 Properties of Vertex-Packing in Unit-Disk Graphs

Let $G = (V, E)$ be a unit-disk graph and let H be a fixed connected graph with $h = |H|$. An L-packing of H in G is a collection $\{H_1, \ldots, H_L\}$ of pairwise vertex-disjoint subgraphs of G such that each H_i is isomorphic to H. Let $\nu_H(G)$ be the maximum integer L such that there exists an L-packing of H in G. In this section, we will give a distributed algorithm which given a constant k finds in a poly-logarithmic number of rounds a collection of L subgraphs $H_1, \ldots, H_L$ of G such that each H_i is isomorphic to H and

$$L \geq (1 - O(1/\log^k |G|))\nu_H(G).$$

A starting point to the algorithm is a maximal independent set in G which can be found using the procedure from [KMNW05a] which gives an auxiliary graph $Aux(G)$. Properties of this auxiliary graph will be useful when proving some facts about an optimal packing of H in G.

Definition 2 (Auxiliary graph). *Let $I = \{v_1, \ldots, v_z\}$ be a maximal independent set in graph $G = (V, E)$, H be a graph with $h = |H|$, and l be a fixed positive number. Let V_i be the set of neighbors of v_i such that if $w \in V_i$ then v_i is the neighbor of w in I with the least identifier, that is*

$$V_i = \{w \in N(v_i) : ID(v_i) = \min\{ID(a) : a \in N(w) \cap I\}\},$$

and let $\bar{V}_i = V_i \cup \{v_i\}$. Let

$$\mathcal{B} = \{i : |\bar{V}_i| \geq 2h^3 \log^l |G|\}, \mathcal{S} = \{i : |\bar{V}_i| < 2h^3 \log^l |G|\},$$

and

$$B = \bigcup_{i \in \mathcal{B}} \bar{V}_i, S = \bigcup_{i \in \mathcal{S}} \bar{V}_i.$$

In addition, let $Aux(G)$ be the graph $(\mathcal{W}, \mathcal{E})$ with $\mathcal{W} = \{1, \ldots, z\}$ and $\{i, j\} \in \mathcal{E}$ whenever $i \neq j$ and there is an edge in G between a vertex from $\bar{V}_i$ and a vertex from $\bar{V}_j$.

Clearly, we have
$$|B| \geq 2h^3 |\mathcal{B}| \log^l |G|$$

and because G is a unit-disk graph, for every i, the subgraph induced by $\bar{V}_i$ is a union of at most five cliques. As a result, for every $i \in \mathcal{B}$ we can pack H's greedily in V_i's as long as the number of vertices is at least $5(h - 1) + 1$. Consequently we can pack at least $(2h^3 \log^l |G| - 5(h - 1) + 1)/h \geq h^2 \log^l |G|$ vertex-disjoint copies of H in $G[\bar{V}_i]$.

In addition, from Lemma 1, we see that $Aux(G)$ has the $(C, 2)$-bounded growth with $C = 48$.

Lemma 8. *$Aux(G)$ has $(48, 2)$-bounded growth.*

In particular, the maximum degree of $Aux(G)$ is at most 48 and the number of vertices in $Aux(G)$ which are within distance h of $\mathcal{B}$ is at most $48h^2 + 1$.

We first observe that it is possible to obtain an almost optimal solution to the packing problem with the property that every copy of H is either disjoint with all $\bar{V}_i$ with $i \in \mathcal{B}$ or is entirely contained in some $\bar{V}_i$ with $i \in \mathcal{B}$.

Lemma 9. *Let $H_1, \ldots, H_L$ be an L-packing of a connected graph H in G with $L = \nu_H(G)$. There exists an M-packing $H'_1, \ldots, H'_M$ of H in G with the following properties.*

1. *For every $i = 1, \ldots, M$, either $V(H'_i) \subseteq \bar{V}_j$ for some $j \in \mathcal{B}$ or $V(H'_i) \cap \bar{V}_j = \emptyset$ for every $j \in \mathcal{B}$.*
2. *$M \geq (1 - O(1/\log^l |G|))\nu_H(G)$.*

Proof. We will call a vertex H-saturated by a packing if it is contained in a copy of H from the packing and we call the vertex H-free otherwise. We start with and optimal L-packing $H_1, \ldots, H_L$ and modify it as follows. For every $i = 1, \ldots, L$ if there is a $j \in \mathcal{B}$, with $0 < |V(H_i) \cap \bar{V}_j| < |V(H_i)|$ then delete H_i from the packing. In the next step, for every $j \in \mathcal{B} \cup \mathcal{S}$ if there are at least $5h$ H-free vertices in $\bar{V}_i$ then pack as many copies of H in $G[\bar{V}_i]$ as possible. This will result in an M-packing $H'_1, \ldots, H'_M$ of H with at most $5h - 1$, H-free vertices in every $\bar{V}_j$. Now we count vertices which were H-saturated in the first packing and are H-free in the second packing. Since we deleted copies of H that had at least one vertex in B, the vertices of such H's are contained in $\bar{V}_j$'s which are within distance h (in $Aux(G)$) of $\mathcal{B}$. As all these $\bar{V}_j$'s will have the property that there are at most $5h - 1$, H-free vertices in $\bar{V}_j$ in the second packing, the number of vertices which are H-saturated in the first packing and are H-free in the second is at most

$$(5h - 1)|\mathcal{B}|(48h^2 + 1) = O(h^3|\mathcal{B}|).$$

As a result, $M \geq L - O(h^2|\mathcal{B}|)$. On the other hand,

$$L \geq h^2|\mathcal{B}| \log^l |G|$$

as we can pack at least $h^2 \log^l |G|$ copies of H in each $\bar{V}_i$. Thus

$$M \geq (1 - O(1/\log^l |G|))\nu_H(G).$$

We will now turn our attention to the set S from Definition 2 and we extract a few useful properties of $G[S]$. Obviously as an induced subgraph of G, $G[S]$ is a unit-disk graph. In addition, the maximum degree, Δ_S, of $G[S]$ satisfies

$$\Delta_S < 96h^3 \log^l |G|. \tag{4}$$

However much more is true, in fact $G[S]$ must have the $(48(\Delta_S + 1), 2)$-bounded growth. Let $B_G(v, r)$ be the set of vertices in G which are within distance r in G of v. If for some r and v, $|B_{G[S]}(v, r)| > 48(\Delta_S + 1)r^2 + 1$ then the graph induced by $B(v, r)$ contains an independent set with more than $48r^2$ vertices. However all vertices from $B_{G[S]}(v, r)$ must be contained in Euclidean ball of radius r around v in any geometrical representation of $G[S]$ which contradicts Lemma 1. Although the fact that $G[S]$ has bounded growth is an indication of the direction the algorithm will take, we need to consider a different auxiliary graph.

Definition 3. *Let $G = (V, E)$ be a unit-disk graph and let H be a connected graph on h vertices. Let $\mathcal{G}_H$ be the h-uniform hypergraph with the vertex set V and hyperedge on the set $U \subset V$ if and only if $|U| = h$ and H is a subgraph of $G[U]$. In addition, let $G^c = (W, F)$ be the graph obtained from $\mathcal{G}_H$ by setting $W = E(\mathcal{G}_H)$ and connecting $e, f \in W$ by an edge when $e \neq f$ and $e \cap f \neq \emptyset$.*

Any packing of H in $G[S]$ corresponds to an independent set in $G[S]^c$. Consequently to approximate an optimal packing in G it is enough to approximate a maximum independent set in $G[S]^c$. To do the latter we will again use the bounded growth property.

Lemma 10. *Graph $G[S]^c$ has $(M, 2h)$-bounded growth with $M < h(48(\Delta_S + 1)h^2)^h$.*

Proof. Let e be a vertex in $G[S]^c$ and let m be a nonnegative integer. To estimate $|B_{G[S]^c}(e, m)|$ we first observe that vertices from $G[S]$ which are contained in f's with $f \in B_{G[S]^c}(e, m)$ are within distance hm of any vertex which is contained in e. Consequently the number of such vertices is at most $48(\Delta_S + 1)(hm)^2 + 1$. The number of hyperedges on this vertex set is therefore less than $(48(\Delta_S + 1)(hm)^2 + 1)^h$ which is Mm^{2h} for $M < h(48(\Delta_S + 1)h^2)^h$.

3.2   Algorithm

Our algorithm proceeds in two main steps. In the first step, we find a maximal independent set $I = \{v_1, \ldots, v_l\}$ in a unit-disk graph G using the procedure from [KMNW05a]. Set I leads via Definition 2 to sets $\bar{V}_i$ and to B and S. Lemma 9 implies that it is enough to approximate a packing of H with the property that every copy of H is either entirely contained in B or in S. Finding a packing in $G[B]$ is trivial and follows again from Lemma 9. Finding a packing in $G[S]$ requires clustering and an approximation of a maximum independent set in $G^c[S]$. We will first give a procedure that finds an approximation of a maximum independent set in a (C, q)-bounded growth graph.

APPROXMAXIS
Input: Constants q, and l (positive integer). $G = (V, E)$ which has (C, q)-bounded growth and which identifiers are bounded by m, number $K = K(|G|)$.
Output: An independent set I in G.

(1) Let $\epsilon := \frac{1}{C^2 K}$. Use the algorithm from Theorem 1 to find a partition $\mathcal{P}$ of G.
(3) For every set $P \in \mathcal{P}$, let $\bar{P}$ be the set obtained from P by deleting all vertices in P which have a neighbor in $V \setminus P$. In parallel, for each $P \in \mathcal{P}$, find a maximum independent set I_P in $G[\bar{P}]$.
(4) Return $\bigcup_P I_P$.

Lemma 11. *Let G be a (C,q)-bounded growth graph with identifiers which are in $\{1,\ldots,m\}$. Algorithm* APPROXMAXIS *finds an independent set I in G with*

$$|I| \geq (1 - \Theta(1/K))\alpha(G)$$

where $\alpha(G)$ is the size of a maximum independent set in G. The algorithm runs in

$$O\left(C\left(\frac{\log C + \log 1/\epsilon}{\epsilon}\right)^{q+1} \log^{q+1} m \log 1/\epsilon\right)$$

rounds, where $\epsilon = 1/(C^2 K)$.

Proof. First note that $I = \bigcup_P I_P$ returned by the algorithm is an independent set. Let I^* be an independent set in G of size $\alpha(G)$. For every $P \in \mathcal{P}$,

$$|I_P| \geq |I^* \cap \bar{P}|. \tag{5}$$

Then

$$|I| + |V(G) \setminus \bigcup_P \bar{P}| \geq \sum_P |I^* \cap \bar{P}| + |V(G) \setminus \bigcup_P \bar{P}| \geq |I^*| = \alpha(G). \tag{6}$$

Finally, $|V(G) \setminus \bigcup_P \bar{P}| \leq \epsilon C |V(G)|$ and since $\Delta(G) \leq C$ we have $(C+1)\alpha(G) \geq |V(G)|$. Therefore, as $\epsilon = \frac{1}{C^2 K}$,

$$|V(G) \setminus \bigcup_P \bar{P}| \leq \Theta(\alpha(G)/K). \tag{7}$$

By (6) and (7),

$$|I| \geq (1 - \Theta(1/K))\alpha(G).$$

To establish the time complexity, note that by Theorem 1, the partition $\mathcal{P}$ is found in

$$O\left(C\left(\frac{\log C + \log 1/\epsilon}{\epsilon}\right)^{q+1} \log^{q+1} m \log 1/\epsilon\right)$$

rounds. The diameter of each graph $G[P]$ is at most $O\left(\frac{\log C + \log 1/\epsilon}{\epsilon}\right)$ and each I_i can be found locally in $diam(G[P])$ rounds.

APPROXPACKINGUDG
Input: Constant k. Unit-disk graph $G = (V, E)$, and graph H on a fixed number of vertices h.
Output: Packing of H in G.

(1) Call Kuhn et. al. algorithm from [KMNW05a] to find a maximal independent set in G. Consider the sets $\bar{V}_1, \ldots, \bar{V}_s$ and B, S given in Definition 2 with $l := k$.
(2) For every $v_i \in B$ find an optimal packing of H in $G[\bar{V}_i]$.

(3) Consider graph $G^c[S]$. Set $C := h(48(96h^3 \log^k |G| + 1)h^2)^h$ and let $q = 2h$. Call APPROXMAXIS in $G^c[S]$ with $K := \log^k |G|$ to find an independent set I in $G^c[S]$.
(4) For each $i \in I$, add the hyperedge of $\mathcal{G}_H$ (copy of H) which corresponds to i to the packing.

Theorem 3. *For given k and graph H, algorithm* APPROXPACKINGUDG *finds in a unit-disk graph G an M-packing of H with*

$$M \geq \left(1 - O(1/\log^k |G|)\right) \nu_H(G)$$

where $\nu_H(G)$ is the packing number of H in G. The algorithm runs in $\log^{O(kh^2)} |G|$ rounds.

Proof. From Lemma 9 there is an M-packing of H in G with $M \geq (1 - O(1/\log^k |G|))\nu_H(G)$ and such that every copy of H is either entirely contained in $\bar{V}_j$, for some $j \in \mathcal{B}$, or does not intersect any of $\bar{V}_j$'s with $j \in \mathcal{B}$. Let M_B be the number of copies of H in this packing which are contained in $\bar{V}_j$, for some $j \in \mathcal{B}$ and let M_S be the number of remaining copies of H. Then $M = M_B + M_S$ and the number of copies of H, sol_B, found in the step 2 of the algorithm is such that

$$sol_B \geq M_B. \tag{8}$$

Any copy of H counted by M_S is entirely contained in $G[S]$. Therefore, $M_H \leq \alpha(G^c[S])$ as any independent set in $G^c[S]$ gives a packing of H in $G[S]$ and any packing of H in $G[S]$ gives an independent set in $G^c[S]$.

By Lemma 10, $G^c[S]$ has $(L, 2h)$-bounded growth with $L < h(48(96h^3 \log^k |G| + 1)h^2)^h$. As $K = \log^k |G|$, by Lemma 11, APPROXMAXIS finds in $G^c[S]$ an independent set I of size

$$|I| \geq (1 - \Theta(1/\log^k |G|))\alpha(G^c[S]).$$

Therefore,

$$sol_S = |I| \geq (1 - \Theta(1/\log^k |G|))\alpha(G^c[S]) \geq (1 - \Theta(1/\log^k |G|))M_S. \tag{9}$$

Consequently, by (8) and (9), the number of copies of H in our solution is at least

$$sol_B + sol_S \geq (1 - \Theta(1/\log^k |G|))M \geq (1 - \Theta(1/\log^k |G|)) \left(1 - O(1/\log^k |G|)\right) \nu_H(G)$$

and so

$$sol_B + sol_S \geq (1 - O(1/\log^k |G|))\nu_H(G).$$

To prove the time complexity, note that identifiers of V are bounded by a polynomial in $|G|$. In addition h and k are fixed constants, $K = O(\log^k |G|)$, $C = O(\log^{kh} |G|)$, $\epsilon = 1/(C^2 K)$, and $q = 2h$ is constant. Therefore, APPROX-PACKINGUDG runs in $\log^{O(kh^2)} |G|$ rounds.

References

[AGLP89]   Awerbuch, B., Goldberg, A.V., Luby, M., Plotkin, S.A.: Network Decomposition and Locality in Distributed Computation. In: Proc. 30th IEEE Symp. on Foundations of Computer Science, pp. 364–369 (1989)

[CH06a]   Czygrinow, A., Hańćkowiak, M.: Distributed almost exact approximations for minor-closed families. In: 14th Annual European Symposium on Algorithms (ESA), pp. 244–255 (2006)

[CH06b]   Czygrinow, A., Hańćkowiak, M.: Distributed approximation algorithms in unit disc graphs. In: Dolev, S. (ed.) DISC 2006. LNCS, vol. 4167, pp. 385–398. Springer, Heidelberg (2006)

[CHS06]   Czygrinow, A., Hańćkowiak, M., Szymańska, E.: Distributed approximation algorithms in planar graphs. In: Calamoneri, T., Finocchi, I., Italiano, G.F. (eds.) CIAC 2006. LNCS, vol. 3998, pp. 296–307. Springer, Heidelberg (2006)

[D05]   Diestel, R.: Graph Theory, 3rd edn. Springer, Heidelberg (2005)

[DW04]   Dai, F., Wu, J.: An Extended Localized Algorithm for Connected Dominating Set Formation in Ad Hoc Wireless Networks. IEEE Transactions on Parallel and Distributed Systems 15(10), 908–920 (2004)

[DPRS03]   Dubhashi, D., Mei, A., Panconesi, A., Radhakrishnan, J., Srinivasan, A.: Fast Distributed Algorithms for (Weakly) Connected Dominating Sets and Linear-Size Skeletons. In: Proc. of the ACM-SIAM Symposium on Discrete Algorithms (SODA), pp. 717–724 (2003)

[KMW04]   Kuhn, F., Moscibroda, T., Wattenhofer, R.: What Cannot Be Computed Locally! In: Proceedings of 23rd ACM Symposium on the Principles of Distributed Computing (PODC), pp. 300–309 (2004)

[KMW05]   Kuhn, F., Moscibroda, T., Wattenhofer, R.: On the Locality of Bounded Growth. In: 24th ACM Symposium on the Principles of Distributed Computing (PODC), Las Vegas, Nevada, USA, pp. 60–68 (2005)

[KMNW05a]   Kuhn, F., Moscibroda, T., Nieberg, T., Wattenhofer, R.: Fast Deterministic Distributed Maximal Independent Set Computation on Growth-Bounded Graphs. In: 19th International Symposium on Distributed Computing (DISC), Cracow, Poland, pp. 273–287 (September 2005)

[KMNW05b]   Kuhn, F., Moscibroda, T., Nieberg, T., Wattenhofer, R.: Local Approximation Schemes for Ad Hoc and Sensor Networks. In: 3rd ACM Joint Workshop on Foundations of Mobile Computing (DIALM-POMC), Cologne, Germany, pp. 97–103 (2005)

[L92]   Linial, N.: Locality in distributed graph algorithms. SIAM Journal on Computing 21(1), 193–201 (1992)

[L86]   Luby, M.: A simple parallel algorithm for the maximal independent set problem. SIAM J. Comput. 15(4), 1036–1053 (1986)

[PR01]   Panconesi, A., Rizzi, R.: Some Simple Distributed Algorithms for Sparse Networks. Distributed Computing 14, 97–100 (2001)

[P00]   Peleg, D.: Distributed Computing: A Locality-Sensitive Approach. SIAM (2000)

From Crash-Stop to Permanent Omission: Automatic Transformation and Weakest Failure Detectors

Carole Delporte-Gallet[1], Hugues Fauconnier[1], Felix C. Freiling[2],
Lucia Draque Penso[2], and Andreas Tielmann[1],[⋆]

[1] Laboratoire d'Informatique Algorithmique, Fondements et Applications (LIAFA),
University Paris VII, France
[2] Laboratory for Dependable Distributed Systems,
University of Mannheim, Germany

Abstract. This paper studies the impact of omission failures on asynchronous distributed systems with crash-stop failures. We provide two different transformations for algorithms, failure detectors, and problem specifications, one of which is weakest failure detector preserving. We prove that our transformation of failure detector Ω [1] is the weakest failure detector for consensus in environments with crash-stop and permanent omission failures and a majority of correct processes. Our results help to use the power of the well-understood crash-stop model to automatically derive solutions for the general omission model, which has recently raised interest for being noticeably applicable for security problems in distributed environments equipped with security modules such as smartcards [2,3,4].

1 Introduction

Message omission failures, which have been introduced by Hadzilacos [5] and been refined by Perry and Toueg [6], put the blame of a message loss to a specific process instead of an unreliable message channel. Beyond the theoretical interest, omission models are also interesting for practical problems like they arise from the security area: Assume that some kind of trusted smartcards are disposed on untrusted processors. If these smartcards execute trusted algorithms and are able to sign messages, then it is relatively easy to restrict the power of a malicious adversary to only be able to drop messages of the trusted smartcards or to stop the smartcards themselves. Following this approach, omission models have lead to the development of reductions from security problems in the Byzantine failure model [7] such as fair-exchange [4,3], and secure multiparty computation [2] to well-known distributed problems in the general omission model, such as consensus [8], where both process crashes and message omissions may take place. Apart from that, omission failures can model overflows of local message buffers in typical communication environments.

[⋆] Work was supported by grants from Région Ile-de-France.

A. Pelc (Ed.): DISC 2007, LNCS 4731, pp. 165–178, 2007.

The message omission and crash failures are considered here in asynchronous systems. Due to classical impossibility results concerning problems as consensus [9] in asynchronous systems, following the failure detector approach [10], we augment the system with oracles that give information about failures.

The extension of failure detectors to more severe failure models than crash failures is unclear [11], because in these models failures may depend on the scheduling and on the algorithm. As it is easy to transform the general omission model into a model with only permanent omissions using standard techniques like the piggybacking of messages, we consider only permanent omissions and crashes. This means that if an omission failure occurs, then it occurs permanently. In this model, precise and simple definitions for failure detectors can easily be deduced from the ones in the crash-stop model.

To provide the permanent omission model with the benefits of a well-understood system model like the crash-stop model, we give automatic transformations for problem specifications, failure detectors, and algorithms such that algorithms designed to tolerate only crash-stop failures can be executed in permanent omission environments and use transformed failure detectors to solve transformed problems. Specifically, we give two transformations. At first, one that works in every environment, but that transforms uniform problems into problems with only limited uniformity, and at second one that works only with a majority of correct processes, but transforms uniform crash-stop problems into their uniform permanent omission counterpart. An interesting point is the fact that the transformation of the specification gives for most of the classical problems the standard specification in the message omission and crash failure model. For example, from an algorithmic solution A of the consensus problem with a failure detector $\mathcal{D}$ in the crash-stop model, we automatically get $A' = trans(A)$, an algorithmic solution of the consensus problem using $\mathcal{D}' = trans(\mathcal{D})$ in the message omission and crash failure model.

Moreover, our first transformation preserves also the "weaker than" relation [1] between failure detectors. This means that if a failure detector is a weakest failure detector for a certain (crash-stop) problem, then its transformation is a weakest failure detector for the transformed problem. We can use this to show that our transformation of failure detector Ω [1] is the weakest failure detector for (uniform) consensus in an environment with permanent omission failures and a majority of correct processes. It is interesting to note that this transformed version of Ω can be implemented in partially synchronous models using some weak timing assumptions [12].

The problem of automatically increasing the fault-tolerance of algorithms in environments with crash-stop failures has been extensively studied before [13,14,15,16]. The results of Neiger and Toueg [14], Delporte-Gallet et al. [15], and Bazzi and Neiger [16] assume in contrast to ours synchronous systems and no failure detectors. Neiger and Toueg [14] propose several transformations from crash-stop to send omission, to general omission, and to Byzantine faults. Delporte-Gallet et al. [15] transform round-based algorithms with broadcast primitives into crash-stop-, general omission-, and Byzantine-tolerant algorithms. Asynchronous systems are considered by Basu, Charron-Bost and Toueg [13] but in the context of link failures instead of omission failures and also without failure detectors. The types of link failures that are considered by Basu, Charron-Bost and Toueg [13] are eventually reliable and fair-lossy links. Eventually reliable links can lose a finite (but unbounded) number of messages and fair-lossy links satisfy that if infinitely many messages are sent over it, then infinitely many messages do not get lost. To show our results, we extend the system model of Basu, Charron-Bost and Toueg [13] such that we can model omission failures, failure patterns, and failure detectors. Another definition for a system model with crash-recovery failures, omission failures, and failure detectors is given by Dolev et al. [17]. In this model, the existence of a fully connected component of processes that is completely detached from all other processes is assumed and only the processes in this component are declared to be correct.

To the best of our knowledge, this is the first paper that investigates an automatic transformation to increase the fault tolerance of distributed algorithms in asynchronous systems augmented with failure detectors.

We organize this paper as follows. In Section 2, we define our formal system model, in Section 3, we define our general problem and algorithm transformations, in Section 4 we state our theorems, and finally, in Section 5, we summarize and discuss our results. Due to the lack of space, we omit some parts of the proofs here. They can be found elsewhere [18].

2   Model

The asynchronous distributed system is assumed to consist of n distinct fully-connected processes $\Pi = \{p_1, \ldots, p_n\}$. The asynchrony of the system means, that there are no bounds on the relative process speeds and message transmission delays. To allow an easier reasoning, a discrete global clock $\mathcal{T}$ is added to the system. The system model used here is derived from that of Basu, Charron-Bost and Toueg [13]. It has been adapted to model also failure detectors and permanent omission failures.

Algorithms. An *algorithm A* is defined as a vector of *local algorithm modules* (or simply *modules*) $A(\Pi) = \langle A(p_1), \ldots, A(p_n) \rangle$. Each local algorithm module $A(p_i)$ is associated with a process $p_i \in \Pi$ and defined as a deterministic infinite state automaton. The local algorithm modules can exchange messages via send and receive primitives. We assume all messages to be unique.

Failures and Failure Patterns. A *failure pattern $\mathcal{F}$* is a function that maps each value t from $\mathcal{T}$ to an output value that specifies which failures have occurred up to time t during an execution of a distributed system. Such a failure pattern is totally independent of any algorithm. A *crash-failure pattern* $C : \mathcal{T} \rightarrow 2^{\Pi}$ denotes the set of processes that have crashed up to time t ($\forall t : C(t) \subseteq C(t+1)$).

Additionally to the crash of a process, it can fail by not sending or not receiving a message. We say that it *omits* a message. The message omissions do not occur because of link failures, they model overflows of local message buffers or the behavior of a malicious adversary with control over the message flow of certain processes. It is important that for every omission, there is a process responsible for it. As we already mentioned, we consider only permanent omissions and leave the treatment of transient omissions over to the underlying asynchronous communication layer. Intuitively, a process has a permanent send omission if it always fails by not sending messages to a certain other process after a certain point in time. Analogously, a process has a permanent receive omission if it always fails by not receiving messages from a certain other process after a certain point in time. The permanent omissions are modeled via a send- and a receive-omission failure pattern: $O_S : \mathcal{T} \to 2^{\Pi \times \Pi}$ and $O_R : \mathcal{T} \to 2^{\Pi \times \Pi}$. If $(p_s, p_d) \in O_S(t)$, then process p_s has a permanent send-omission to process p_d after time t. If $(p_s, p_d) \in O_R(t)$, then process p_d has a permanent receive-omission to process p_s after time t. All the failure patterns defined so far can be put together to a single failure pattern $\mathcal{F} = (C, O_S, O_R)$.

With such a failure pattern, we define a process to be *correct*, if it experiences no failure at all. We assume that at least one process is correct. A process p is crash-correct ($p \in cr.\text{-}correct(\mathcal{F})$) in $\mathcal{F}$, if it does not crash. An *in-connected* process is a process that is crash-correct and receives all messages from a correct process (possibly indirectly) and an *out-connected* process is a process where a correct process receives all messages from it (also possibly indirectly). If a process p is in-connected and out-connected in a failure pattern $\mathcal{F}$, then we say that p is *connected* in $\mathcal{F}$ ($p \in connected(\mathcal{F})$). This means that between connected processes there is always reliable communication possible. With a simple relaying algorithm, every message can eventually be delivered. Note that it is nevertheless still possible that connected processes receive messages from disconnected processes or disconnected processes receive messages from connected ones. The difference between connected and disconnected processes is that the former are able to send and to receive messages to/from correct processes and therefore are able to communicate in both directions. It is easy to see that $crash\text{-}correct(\mathcal{F}) \supseteq connected(\mathcal{F}) \supseteq correct(\mathcal{F})$.

We say that a failure pattern $\mathcal{F}'$ is an *omission equivalent extension* of another failure pattern $\mathcal{F}$ ($\mathcal{F} \leq_{om} \mathcal{F}'$), if the set of crash-correct processes in $\mathcal{F}$ is at all times equal to the set of connected processes in $\mathcal{F}'$ and there are no omission failures in $\mathcal{F}$. We define an *environment* $\mathcal{E}$ to be a set of possible failure patterns. $\mathcal{E}^f_{c.s.}$ denotes the set of all failure patterns where only crash-stop faults occur and at most f processes crash. $\mathcal{E}^f_{p.o.}$ denotes the set of all failure patterns where crash-stop and permanent omission faults may occur and at most f processes are not connected (clearly, $\mathcal{E}^f_{c.s.} \subseteq \mathcal{E}^f_{p.o.}$).

Failure Detectors. A failure detector provides (possibly incorrect) information about a failure pattern [10]. Associated with each failure detector is a (possibly infinite) range $\mathcal{R}$ of values output by that failure detector. A *failure detector history FDH with range* $\mathcal{R}$ is a function from $\Pi \times \mathcal{T}$ to $\mathcal{R}$. $FDH(p, t)$ is the value of the failure detector module of process p at time t. A *failure detector* $\mathcal{D}$ is a function that maps a failure pattern $\mathcal{F}$ to a *set* of failure detector histories with range $\mathcal{R}$. $\mathcal{D}(\mathcal{F})$ denotes the set of possible failure detector histories permitted by $\mathcal{D}$ for the failure pattern $\mathcal{F}$. Note that a failure detector $\mathcal{D}$ is specified as a function of the failure pattern $\mathcal{F}$ of an execution. However, an implementation of $\mathcal{D}$ may use other aspects of the execution such as when messages are arrived and executions with the same failure pattern $\mathcal{F}$ may still have different failure detector histories. It is for this reason that we allow $\mathcal{D}(\mathcal{F})$ to be a set of failure detector histories from which the actual failure detector history for a particular execution is selected non-deterministically.

Take failure detector Ω [1] as an example. The output of the failure detector module of Ω at a process p_i is a *single* process, p_j, that p_i currently considers to be *crash-correct*. In this case, the range of output values is $\mathcal{R}_\Omega = \Pi$. For each failure pattern $\mathcal{F}$, $\Omega(\mathcal{F})$ is the set of all failure detector histories FDH_Ω with range $\mathcal{R}_\Omega$ that satisfy the following property: There is a time after which all the crash-correct processes always trust the same crash-correct process:

$$\exists t \in \mathcal{T}, \exists p_j \in cr.\text{-}correct(\mathcal{F}), \forall p_i \in cr.\text{-}correct(\mathcal{F}), \forall t' \geq t : FDH_\Omega(p, t') = p_j$$

The output of failure detector module Ω at a process p_i may change with time, i.e. p_i may trust different processes at different times. Furthermore, at any given time t, processes p_i and p_j may trust different processes.

A local algorithm module $A(p_i)$ can access the current output value of its local failure detector module using the action *queryFD*.

Histories. A *local history of a local algorithm module* $A(p_i)$, denoted $H[i]$, is a finite or an infinite sequence of alternating states and events of type send, receive, queryFD, or internal. We assume that there is a function *time* that assigns every event to a certain point in time and define $H[i]/_t$ to be the maximal prefix of $H[i]$ where all events have occurred before time t. A *history* H of $A(\Pi)$ is a vector of local histories $\langle H[1], H[2], \ldots, H[n] \rangle$.

Reliable Links. A reliable link does not create, duplicate, or lose messages. Specifically, if there is no permanent omission between two processes and the recipient executes infinitely many receive actions, then it will eventually receive every message. We specify, that our underlying communication channels ensure reliable links.

Problem Specifications. Let Π be a set of processes and A be an algorithm. We define $\mathcal{H}(A(\Pi), \mathcal{E})$ to be the set of all tuples $(H, \mathcal{F})$ such that H is a history of $A(\Pi)$, $\mathcal{F} \in \mathcal{E}$, and H and $\mathcal{F}$ are compatible, that is crashed processes do not take any steps after the time of their crash, there are no receive-events after a permanent omission, etc. A *system* $\mathcal{S}(A(\Pi), \mathcal{E})$ of $A(\Pi)$ is a subset of $\mathcal{H}(A(\Pi), \mathcal{E})$. A *problem specification* Σ is a set of tuples of histories and failure patterns, because (permanent) omission failures are not necessarily reflected in a history (e.g., if a process sends no messages). A system $\mathcal{S}$ satisfies a problem specification Σ, if $\mathcal{S} \subseteq \Sigma$. We say that an algorithm A satisfies a problem specification Σ in environment $\mathcal{E}$, if $\mathcal{H}(A(\Pi), \mathcal{E}) \subseteq \Sigma$.

Take consensus as an example (see Table 1): It is specified by making statements about some variables *propose* and *decide* in the states of a history (e.g. the value of *decide* has eventually to be equal at all (crash-)correct processes). This can be expressed as the set of all tuples $(H, \mathcal{F})$ where there exists a time t and a value v, such that for all $p_i \in cr.\text{-}correct(\mathcal{F})$, there exists an event e in $H[i]$ with $time(e) \leq t$ and for all states s after event e, the value of the variable *decide* in s is v.

3   From Crash-Stop to Permanent Omission

We will give here two transformations: one general transformation for all environments, where we provide only restricted guarantees for disconnected processes, and one for environments where less than half of the processes may not be connected, where we are able to provide for all processes the same guarantees as for the crash-stop case.

To improve the fault-tolerance of algorithms, we simulate a single state of the original algorithm with several states of the simulation algorithm. For these additional states, we *augment* the original states with additional variables. Since an event of the simulation algorithm may lead to a state where only the augmentation variables change, the sequence of the original variables may *stutter*. We call a local history $H'[i]$ a stuttered and augmented extension of a history $H[i]$ ($H[i] \leq_{sa} H'[i]$), if $H[i]$ and $H'[i]$ differ only in the value of the augmentation variables and some additional states caused by differences in these variables (in particular, $H[i] \leq_{sa} H[i]$ for all $H[i]$). If $H[i] \leq_{sa} H'[i]$ for all $p_i \in \Pi$, we write $H \leq_{sa} H'$. We say that a problem specification Σ is closed under stuttering and augmentation, if $(H, \mathcal{F}) \in \Sigma$ and $H \leq_{sa} H'$ implies that $(H', \mathcal{F})$ is also in Σ. Most problems satisfy this natural closure property (e.g. consensus).

3.1   The General Transformation

Transformation of Problem Specifications. To transform a problem specification, we first show a transformation of a tuple of a trace and a failure pattern. Based on this transformation, we transform a whole problem specification. The intuition behind this transformation is that we demand only something from processes as long as they are connected. After their disconnection, processes may behave arbitrary. More formally, let $t_{c.s.}(i)$ be the time at which process p_i crashes in $\mathcal{F}$ ($t_{c.s.}(i) = \infty$, if p_i never crashes). Analogously, let $t'_{p.o.}(i)$ be the time at which process p_i becomes disconnected in $\mathcal{F}'$ ($t'_{p.o.}(i) = \infty$, if p_i never becomes disconnected). Then:

$$(H', \mathcal{F}') \in trans((H, \mathcal{F})) \quad :\Leftrightarrow \quad \forall p_i \in \Pi : \; H[i]/_{t_{c.s.}(i)} \leq_{sa} H'[i]/_{t'_{p.o.}(i)}$$

and for a whole problem specification:

$$trans(\Sigma) := \{(H', \mathcal{F}') \mid (H', \mathcal{F}') \in trans((H, \mathcal{F})) \wedge (H, \mathcal{F}) \in \Sigma\}$$

A transformation of non-uniform consensus, where properties of certain propose- and decision-variables of (crash-)correct processes are specified would lead to a specification where the same properties are ensured for the states of connected processes, because only histories with the same states (disregarding the augmentation variables) are allowed in the transformation at this processes (see Table 1). We also take the states of processes *before* they become disconnected into account, because they (e.g. their initial states for the propose variables) may also have an influence on the fulfillment of a problem specification, although they are after their disconnection not allowed to have this influence anymore. Since we impose no restriction on the behavior of processes after their disconnection, the transformed problem specification allows them to decide a value that was never proposed (although our transformation algorithms guarantee that this will not happen).

A transformation of uniform consensus leads to a problem specification where the uniform agreement is only demanded for processes before their time of disconnection. This means that it is allowed that after a partitioning of the network, the processes in the different network partitions come to different decision values. Another transformation, in which uniform consensus remains truly uniform is given in Section 3.2.

Transformation of Failure Detector Specifications. We allow all failure detector histories for a failure pattern $\mathcal{F}$ in $trans(\mathcal{D})$ that are allowed in the crash-stop version $\mathcal{F}'$ of $\mathcal{F}$ in $\mathcal{D}$:

$$trans(\mathcal{D})(\mathcal{F}) := \bigcup_{\mathcal{F}'} \{\mathcal{D}(\mathcal{F}') \mid \mathcal{F}' \leq_{om} \mathcal{F}\}$$

Consider failure detector Ω [1]. Ω outputs only failure detector histories that eventually provide the same crash-correct leader at all crash-correct processes. Then, $trans(\Omega)$ outputs these failure detector histories if and only if they provide a *connected* common leader at all *connected* processes.

Transformation of Algorithms. In our algorithm transformation, we add new communication layers such that some of the omission failures in the system become transparent to the algorithm (see Figure 1). We transform a given algorithm A into another algorithm $A' = trans(A)$ in two steps:

- In the first step, we remove the send and receive actions from A and simulate them with a *three-way-handshake (3wh) algorithm*. The algorithm is described in Figure 2. The idea of the 3wh-algorithm is to substitute every send-action with an exchange of three messages. This means that to send a message to a certain process, it is necessary for a process to be able to send *and* to receive messages from it. Moreover, while the communication between connected processes is still possible, processes that are only in-connected or only out-connected (and not both) become totally disconnected. Hence, we eliminate influences of disconnected processes not existing in the crash-stop case.
- Then, in the second step, we remove the send and receive actions from the three way handshake algorithm and simulate them with a *relaying algorithm*.

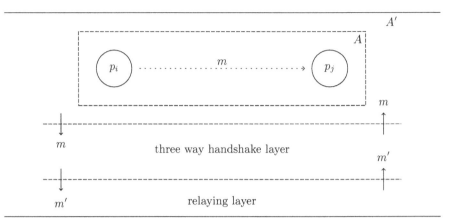

Fig. 1. Additional Communication Layers

The idea of the relay algorithm is to relay every message to all other processes, such that they relay it again and all connected processes can communicate with each other, despite the fact that they are not directly-reachable. It is similar to other algorithms in the literature [19]. Its detailed description can be found in Figure 3.

To execute the simulation algorithms in parallel with the actions from A, we add some new (augmentation) variables to the set of variables in the states of A. Whenever a step of the simulation algorithms is executed, the state of the original variables in A remains untouched and only the new variables change their values. Whenever a process queries a local failure detector module $\mathcal{D}(p_i)$, we translate it to a query on $trans(\mathcal{D})(p_i)$. The relaying layer overlays the network with the best possible communication graph and the 3wh-layer on top of it cuts the unidirectional edges from this graph.

Algorithm *3wh*
1:   **procedure** *3wh-send*(m, p_j)
2:       *relay-send*$([1, m], p_j)$;
3:
4:   **procedure** *3wh-receive*(m)
5:       *relay-receive*$([l, m'])$;
6:       **if** $(l = 1)$ **then**   *relay-send*$([2, m'], sender([l, m']))$; $m := \perp$;
7:       **elseif** $(l = 2)$ **then**   *relay-send*$([3, m'], sender([l, m']))$; $m := \perp$;
8:       **elseif** $(l = 3)$ **then** $m := m'$;
9:       **elseif** $[l, m'] = \perp$ **then** $m := \perp$;

Fig. 2. The Three Way Handshake Algorithm for Process p_i

Algorithm *Relay*

1:   **procedure** *init*
2:       $relayed_i := \emptyset;\ delivered_i := \emptyset;$
3:
4:   **procedure** *relay-send*(m, p_j)
5:       **for** $k := 1$ **to** n **do**
6:           $send([m, p_j], p_k);$
7:       $relayed_i := relayed_i \cup \{[m, p_j]\};$
8:
9:   **procedure** *relay-receive*(m)
10:      $receive([m', p_k]);$
11:      **if** $([m', p_k] = \bot)$ **then** $m := \bot;$
12:      **elseif** $(k = i)$ **and** $(m' \notin delivered_i)$ **then**
13:          $m := m';\ delivered_i := delivered_i \cup \{m'\};$
14:      **elseif** $(k \neq i)$ **and** $([m', p_k] \notin relayed_i)$ **then**
15:          **for** $l := 1$ **to** n **do**
16:              $send([m', p_k], p_l);$
17:          $relayed_i := relayed_i \cup \{[m', p_k]\};\ m := \bot;$

Fig. 3. The Relaying Algorithm for Process p_i

3.2   The Transformation for $n > 2f$

If only less than a majority of the processes are disconnected $(n > 2f)$, then we only need to adapt the problem specification to the failure patterns of the new environment. We indicate this adaptation of a problem specification with the index *p.o.* and specify it in the following way:

$$\Sigma_{p.o.} := \{(H, \mathcal{F}) \mid \exists (H, \mathcal{F}') \in \Sigma \wedge \mathcal{F}' \leq_{om} \mathcal{F}\}$$

If we adapt consensus to omission failures, then we get Consensus$_{p.o.}$ as in Table 1. The failure detector specifications can be transformed as in Section 3.1. The algorithm transformation *trans*$_2$ works similar as in the previous section, but we add an additional *two-way-handshake (2wh) layer* between the relaying layer and the 3wh layer. The algorithm is described in Figure 4 and is similar to an algorithm in the literature [13]. The idea of the algorithm is to broadcast every message to all other processes and to block until $f + 1$ processes have acknowledged the message. In this way, disconnected processes block forever (since they receive less than $f + 1$ acknowledgements) and connected processes can continue. Thus, we emulate a crash-stop environment.

Table 1. Transformations of the Consensus Problem

	Consensus	$trans$(Consensus)	Consensus$_{p.o.}$
Validity:	The decided value of every process must have been proposed.	The decided value of every *connected* process must have been proposed.	The decided value of every process must have been proposed.
Non-Uniform Agreement:	No two *cr.-correct* processes decide differently.	No two *connected* processes decide differently.	No two *connected* processes decide differently.
Uniform Agreement:	No two processes decide differently.	No two processes decide differently *before their disconnection.*	No two processes decide differently.
Termination:	Every *cr.-correct* process eventually decides.	Every *connected* process eventually decides.	Every *connected* process eventually decides.

Algorithm *2wh*

1: **procedure** *init*
2:      $received_i := \emptyset$; $Ack_i := 0$;
3:
4: **procedure** *2wh-send*(m, p_j)
5:      *relay-send*$([m, p_j, ONE], p_k)$ to all other p_k; $Ack_i := 1$;
6:      **while** $(Ack_i \leq f)$ **do**
7:          *relay-receive*$([m', p_k, num]))$;
8:              **if** $(num = TWO)$ **and** $(m' = m)$ **and** $(k = j)$ **then**   inc(Ack_i);
9:              **elseif** $(num = ONE)$ **then**   add $[m', p_k, num]$ to $received_i$;
10:
11: **procedure** *2wh-receive*$(m))$
12:      $m := \bot$; *relay-receive*(m');
13:      **if** $(m' \neq \bot)$ **then**   add m' to $received_i$;
14:      **if** $([m'', p_k, ONE] \in received_i)$ for any m'', p_k **then**
15:          *relay-send*$([m'', p_k, TWO], sender([m', p_k, ONE]))$;
16:          **if** $(k = i)$ **then** $m := m''$;

Fig. 4. The Two Way Handshake Algorithm for Process p_i

4   Results

In our first theorem, we show that for any algorithm A, for any failure detector $\mathcal{D}$, and for any problem specification Σ, $trans(A)$ using $trans(\mathcal{D})$ solves $trans(\Sigma)$ in a permanent omission environment if and only if A using $\mathcal{D}$ solves Σ in a crash-stop environment. This theorem does not only show that our transformation works, it furthermore ensures that we do not transform to a trivial problem specification, but to an equivalent one, since we prove both directions.

Theorem 1. *Let Σ be a problem specification closed under stuttering and augmentation. Then, if A is an algorithm using a failure detector $\mathcal{D}$ and $A' = trans(A)$ is the transformation of A using $trans(\mathcal{D})$, it holds that:*

$$\forall f \text{ with } 0 \leq f \leq n : \ (\mathcal{H}(A(\Pi), \mathcal{E}^f_{c.s.}) \subseteq \Sigma \ \Leftrightarrow \ (\mathcal{H}(A'(\Pi), \mathcal{E}^f_{p.o.}) \subseteq trans(\Sigma)$$

Proof. (Sketch) Due to lack of space, we only sketch the proof of the theorem here. The detailed proof can be found elsewhere [18]. The proof is divided up into two parts. Let $\mathcal{S}_{c.s.} := (\mathcal{H}(A(\Pi), \mathcal{E}^f_{c.s.})$ and $\mathcal{S}_{p.o.} := (\mathcal{H}(A'(\Pi), \mathcal{E}^f_{p.o.})$ and assume that $A' = trans(A)$.

"$\Rightarrow$": *Assume that $\mathcal{S}_{c.s.} \subseteq \Sigma$. By constructing for a given $(H, \mathcal{F})$ in $\mathcal{S}_{p.o.}$ a tuple $(H', \mathcal{F}')$ in $\mathcal{S}_{c.s.}$ with $(H, \mathcal{F}) \in trans((H', \mathcal{F}'))$, we can show that $\mathcal{S}_{p.o.} \subseteq trans(\mathcal{S}_{c.s.})$. In this construction, we remove the added communication layers from H and use the properties of our two send-primitives to prove the reliability of the links in H'. We ensure "No Loss" with the relaying algorithm and "No Creation" with the three way handshake algorithm. As we know from the definition of trans, that $trans(\mathcal{S}_{c.s.}) \subseteq trans(\Sigma)$, we can conclude that $\mathcal{S}_{p.o.} \subseteq trans(\Sigma)$.*

"$\Leftarrow$": *Assume that $\mathcal{S}_{p.o.} \subseteq trans(\Sigma)$ and $(H, \mathcal{F}) \in \mathcal{S}_{c.s.}$. We then build a new history H' from H and simulate all links according to the specification of the three-way-handshake and the relay algorithm such that $(H', \mathcal{F}) \in trans((H, \mathcal{F}))$ and $(H', \mathcal{F}) \in \mathcal{S}_{p.o.} \subseteq trans(\Sigma)$ ($\mathcal{F} \in \mathcal{E}^f_{c.s.}$ implies that $\mathcal{F}$ is in $\mathcal{E}^f_{p.o.}$). This means that there exists a $(H'', \mathcal{F}'') \in \Sigma$, with $(H', \mathcal{F}) \in trans((H'', \mathcal{F}''))$.*
Since in both, $\mathcal{F}''$ and $\mathcal{F}$ occur only crash failures, $\mathcal{F}'' = \mathcal{F}$ and therefore for all p_i, $H''[i] \leq_{sa} H'[i]$. Together with the fact that Σ is closed under stuttering and augmentation, we can conclude that $(H', \mathcal{F}) \in \Sigma$. H' and H differ only in the augmentation variables that are not relevant for the fulfillment of $trans(\Sigma)$ and therefore: $(H, \mathcal{F}) \in \Sigma$.

Our second theorem shows, that with a majority of connected processes ($n > 2f$), $trans_2$ can be used to solve the adaptation of a problem to the general omission model.

Theorem 2. *If A is an algorithm using a failure detector $\mathcal{D}$ and $A' = trans_2(A)$ is the transformation of A using $trans_2(\mathcal{D})$ and Σ is closed under stuttering and augmentation, then it holds that:*

$$\forall f \text{ with } f < n/2 : \ (\mathcal{H}(A(\Pi), \mathcal{E}^f_{c.s.}) \subseteq \Sigma \ \Rightarrow \ (\mathcal{H}(A'(\Pi), \mathcal{E}^f_{p.o.}) \subseteq \Sigma_{p.o.}$$

Proof. (Sketch) Due to lack of space, we only sketch the proof of the theorem here. The detailed proof can be found elsewhere [18]. Let $\mathcal{S}_{c.s.} := (\mathcal{H}(A(\Pi), \mathcal{E}^f_{c.s.})$ and $\mathcal{S}_{p.o.} := (\mathcal{H}(A'(\Pi), \mathcal{E}^f_{p.o.})$ and assume that $A' = trans(A)$. It is sufficient to show, that

$$\forall (H, \mathcal{F}) \in \mathcal{S}_{p.o.}, \exists (H', \mathcal{F}') \in \mathcal{S}_{c.s.} : \ (H' \leq_{sa} H) \wedge (\mathcal{F}' \leq_{om} \mathcal{F}) \tag{1}$$

To show this, we construct $(H', \mathcal{F}') \in \mathcal{S}_{c.s.}$ for a given $(H, \mathcal{F}) \in \mathcal{S}_{p.o.}$ in the following way: We first remove the variables, events, and states of the relay-algorithm, then remove the same for the 2wh-algorithm, and then remove the 3wh-algorithm to get H'. $\mathcal{F}'$ is a failure pattern, such that $\mathcal{F}' \leq_{om} \mathcal{F}$. We need to show, that $(H', \mathcal{F}')$ fulfills the properties of equation 1. From the construction it is clear, that $H' \leq_{sa} H$ and $\mathcal{F}' \leq_{om} \mathcal{F}$. It remains to show, that $(H', \mathcal{F}') \in \mathcal{S}_{c.s.}$. This means, that at most f processes crash in $\mathcal{F}'$, H' is a history of $A(\Pi)$ using $\mathcal{D}$, all links are reliable in $(H', \mathcal{F}')$, and H' and $\mathcal{F}'$ are compatible. Here we can use the properties of the 2wh-algorithm to ensure that a process that is crashed in $\mathcal{F}'$ takes no steps in H' after the time of its crash.

Weakest Failure Detectors. A failure detector [1] is a weakest failure detector for a problem specification Σ in environment $\mathcal{E}$, if it is necessary and sufficient. Sufficient means, that there exists an algorithm using this failure detector that satisfies Σ in $\mathcal{E}$, whereas necessary means, that every other sufficient failure detector is reducible to it. A failure detector $\mathcal{D}$ is reducible to another failure detector $\mathcal{D}'$, if there exists a transformation algorithm $T_{\mathcal{D} \to \mathcal{D}'}$, such that for every tuple $(H, \mathcal{F}) \in \mathcal{H}(T_{\mathcal{D} \to \mathcal{D}'}(\Pi), \mathcal{E})$, H is equivalent to a failure detector history FDH in $\mathcal{D}'(\mathcal{F})$. We call the problem specification that arises in emulating $\mathcal{D}'$, $Probl(\mathcal{D}')$. In the following theorem, we show that *trans* preserves the weakest failure detector property for non-uniform[1] failure detectors.

Theorem 3. *For all f with $1 \leq f \leq n$: If a non-uniform failure detector $\mathcal{D}$ is a weakest failure detector for Σ in $\mathcal{E}_{c.s.}^{f}$ and Σ is closed under stuttering and augmentation, then $trans(\mathcal{D})$ is a weakest failure detector for $trans(\Sigma)$ in $\mathcal{E}_{p.o.}^{f}$.*

Proof. If $\mathcal{D}$ is a weakest failure detector for Σ in $\mathcal{E}_{c.s.}^{f}$, then $trans(\mathcal{D})$ is sufficient for $trans(\Sigma)$ in $\mathcal{E}_{p.o.}^{f}$ (Theorem 1). It remains to show that $trans(\mathcal{D})$ is also necessary.

Assume a failure detector $\mathcal{D}'$ is sufficient for $trans(\Sigma)$ in $\mathcal{E}_{p.o.}^{f}$. Clearly, $\Sigma \subseteq trans(\Sigma)$ (since $H \leq_{sa} H$ for all H). Therefore, $\mathcal{D}'$ is sufficient for Σ in $\mathcal{E}_{c.s.}^{f}$, and moreover, $\mathcal{D}'$ is reducible to $\mathcal{D}$ in $\mathcal{E}_{c.s.}^{f}$ (since $\mathcal{D}$ is a weakest failure detector for Σ in $\mathcal{E}_{c.s.}^{f}$). This means that it is possible to emulate $\mathcal{D}$ using $\mathcal{D}'$ (i.e. a problem specification $Probl(\mathcal{D})$ that is equivalent to $\mathcal{D}$). If the reduction algorithm is $T_{\mathcal{D}' \to \mathcal{D}}$, then $trans(T_{\mathcal{D}' \to \mathcal{D}})$ using $trans(\mathcal{D}')$ emulates $trans(Probl(\mathcal{D}))$ in $\mathcal{E}_{p.o.}^{f}$ (Theorem 1) and since $\mathcal{D}$ is non-uniform, the transformation of the problem specification, $trans(Probl(\mathcal{D}))$ is equivalent to the transformation of the failure detector $trans(\mathcal{D})$ (trans does not change the meaning of $Probl(\mathcal{D})$ since only the states of connected processes matter). Therefore, $\mathcal{D}'$ is reducible to $trans(\mathcal{D})$ in $\mathcal{E}_{p.o.}^{f}$.

With Theorem 1, 2, and 3 we are able to show, the following:

Theorem 4. *$trans(\Omega)$ is a weakest failure detector for uniform $Consensus_{p.o.}$ with a majority of correct processes.*

---

[1] A non-uniform failure detector $\mathcal{D}$ outputs always the same set of histories for two failure patterns $\mathcal{F}$ and $\mathcal{F}'$ in which $correct(\mathcal{F}) = correct(\mathcal{F}')$ (i.e. $\mathcal{D}(\mathcal{F}) = \mathcal{D}(\mathcal{F}')$).

Proof. Since we know, that Ω is a weakest failure detector for non-uniform Consensus [1] and Ω is clearly non-uniform, together with Theorem 3, trans(Ω) is a weakest failure detector for non-uniform trans(Consensus). Since non-uniform trans(Consensus) is strictly weaker than uniform Consensus$_{p.o.}$, trans(Ω) is especially necessary for uniform Consensus$_{p.o.}$. To show that trans(Ω) is sufficient for uniform Consensus$_{p.o.}$, we can simply use Theorem 2, since we know that Ω is sufficient for uniform Consensus with a majority of correct processes.

5 Conclusion

We have given transformations for algorithms, failure detectors, and problem specifications, so crash-stop resilient algorithms can be automatically enhanced to tolerate the more severe general omission failures, highly applicable in practical settings running security problems. Furthermore we have shown that $trans(\Omega)$ is the weakest failure detector for consensus in an environment with permanent omission failures where less than half of the processes may crash. Additionally, we have proven that our transformation preserves the weakest failure detector property for all non-uniform failure detectors. As an open problem, we think that it would be interesting to replace the requirement of a correct majority in our second transformation with a failure detector Σ [20] that will also be sufficient. Apart from that, it may be possible to give more specific transformations that are less general, but also less communication expensive than our transformation.

References

1. Chandra, T.D., Hadzilacos, V., Toueg, S.: The weakest failure detector for solving consensus. In: Herlihy, M. (ed.) PODC'92. Proceedings of the 11th Annual ACM Symposium on Principles of Distributed Computing, Vancouver, BC, Canada, pp. 147–158. ACM Press, New York (1992)
2. Fort, M., Freiling, F., Penso, L.D., Benenson, Z., Kesdogan, D.: Trustedpals: Secure multiparty computation implemented with smartcards. In: Gollmann, D., Meier, J., Sabelfeld, A. (eds.) ESORICS 2006. LNCS, vol. 4189, pp. 34–48. Springer, Heidelberg (2006)
3. Freiling, F., Herlihy, M., Penso, L.D.: Optimal randomized omission-tolerant uniform consensus in message passing systems. In: Anderson, J.H., Prencipe, G., Wattenhofer, R. (eds.) OPODIS 2005. LNCS, vol. 3974. Springer, Heidelberg (2006)
4. Avoine, G., Gärtner, F.C., Guerraoui, R., Vukolic, M.: Gracefully degrading fair exchange with security modules. In: Dal Cin, M., Kaâniche, M., Pataricza, A. (eds.) EDCC 2005. LNCS, vol. 3463, pp. 55–71. Springer, Heidelberg (2005)
5. Hadzilacos, V.: Issues of fault tolerance in concurrent computations (databases, reliability, transactions, agreement protocols, distributed computing). PhD thesis, Harvard University (1985)
6. Perry, K.J., Toueg, S.: Distributed agreement in the presence of processor and communication faults. IEEE Trans. Softw. Eng. 12(3), 477–482 (1986)
7. Lamport, L., Shostak, R., Pease, M.: The byzantine generals problem. ACM Trans. Program. Lang. Syst. 4(3), 382–401 (1982)

8. Chaudhuri, S.: Agreement is harder than consensus: set consensus problems in totally asynchronous systems. In: Proceedings of Principles of Distributed Computing 1990 (1990)
9. Fischer, M.J., Lynch, N.A., Paterson, M.S.: Impossibility of distributed consensus with one faulty process. J. ACM 32(2), 374–382 (1985)
10. Chandra, T.D., Toueg, S.: Unreliable failure detectors for reliable distributed systems. Journal of the ACM 43(2), 225–267 (1996)
11. Doudou, A., Garbinato, B., Guerraoui, R., é Schiper, A.: Muteness failure detectors: Specification and implementation. In: Hlavicka, J., Maehle, E., Pataricza, A. (eds.) Dependable Computing - EDDC-3. LNCS, vol. 1667, pp. 71–87. Springer, Heidelberg (1999)
12. Delporte-Gallet, C., Fauconnier, H., Freiling, F.C.: Revisiting failure detection and consensus in omission failure environments. In: Van Hung, D., Wirsing, M. (eds.) ICTAC 2005. LNCS, vol. 3722, pp. 394–408. Springer, Heidelberg (2005)
13. Basu, A., Charron-Bost, B., Toueg, S.: Simulating reliable links with unreliable links in the presence of process crashes. In: Babaoğlu, Ö., Marzullo, K. (eds.) WDAG 1996. LNCS, vol. 1151, pp. 105–122. Springer, Heidelberg (1996)
14. Neiger, G., Toueg, S.: Automatically increasing the fault-tolerance of distributed algorithms. Journal of Algorithms 11(3), 374–419 (1990)
15. Delporte-Gallet, C., Fauconnier, H., Guerraoui, R., Pochon, B.: The perfectly-synchronised round-based model of distributed computing. Information & Computation (to appear, 2007)
16. Bazzi, R.A., Neiger, G.: Simulating crash failures with many faulty processors (extended abstract). In: Segall, A., Zaks, S. (eds.) WDAG 1992. LNCS, vol. 647, pp. 166–184. Springer, Heidelberg (1992)
17. Dolev, D., Friedman, R., Keidar, I., Malkhi, D.: Brief announcement: Failure detectors in omission failure environments. In: Symposium on Principles of Distributed Computing, p. 286 (1997)
18. Delporte-Gallet, C., Fauconnier, H., Freiling, F., Penso, L.D., Tielmann, A.: Automatic transformations from crash-stop to permanent omission. HAL archives ouvertes, hal-00160626 (2007)
19. Srikanth, T.K., Toueg, S.: Simulating authenticated broadcasts to derive simple fault-tolerant algorithms. Distributed Computing 2(2), 80–94 (1987)
20. Delporte-Gallet, C., Fauconnier, H., Guerraoui, R., Hadzilacos, V., Kouznetsov, P., Toueg, S.: The weakest failure detectors to solve certain fundamental problems in distributed computing. In: PODC '04. Proceedings of the twenty-third annual ACM symposium on Principles of distributed computing, pp. 338–346. ACM Press, New York (2004)

Deterministic Distributed Construction of Linear Stretch Spanners in Polylogarithmic Time

Bilel Derbel[1], Cyril Gavoille[2,*], and David Peleg[3,**]

[1] Laboratoire d'Informatique Fondamentale (LIF),
Université de Provence Aix-Marseille 1, France
derbel@cmi.univ-mrs.fr
[2] Laboratoire Bordelais de Recherche en Informatique (LaBRI),
Université de Bordeaux, France
gavoille@labri.fr
[3] Department of Computer Science and Applied Mathematics,
The Weizmann Institute, Rehovot, Israel
david.peleg@weizmann.ac.il

Abstract. The paper presents a deterministic distributed algorithm that given an n node unweighted graph constructs an $O(n^{3/2})$ edge 3-spanner for it in $O(\log n)$ time. This algorithm is then extended into a deterministic algorithm for computing an $O(k\, n^{1+1/k})$ edge $O(k)$-spanner in $2^{O(k)} \log^{k-1} n$ time for every integer parameter $k \geqslant 1$. This establishes that the problem of the deterministic construction of a linear (in k) stretch spanner with few edges can be solved in the distributed setting in polylogarithmic time.

The paper also investigates the distributed construction of sparse spanners with almost pure additive stretch $(1 + \epsilon, \beta)$, i.e., such that the distance in the spanner is at most $1 + \epsilon$ times the original distance plus β. It is shown, for every $\epsilon > 0$, that in $O(\epsilon^{-1} \log n)$ time one can deterministically construct a spanner with $O(n^{3/2})$ edges that is both a 3-spanner and a $(1 + \epsilon, 8 \log n)$-spanner. Furthermore, it is shown that in $n^{O(1/\sqrt{\log n})} + O(1/\epsilon)$ time one can deterministically construct a spanner with $O(n^{3/2})$ edges which is both a 3-spanner and a $(1 + \epsilon, 4)$-spanner. This algorithm can be transformed into a Las Vegas randomized algorithm with guarantees on the stretch and time, running in $O(\epsilon^{-1} + \log n)$ expected time.

Keywords: distributed algorithms, graph spanners, time complexity.

1 Introduction

Background: The purpose of this paper is to study the *locality properties* of *graph spanners*, and particularly, of efficient *deterministic distributed* construction methods for spanners. Graph spanners are a fundamental graph structure

---

* Supported by the ANR-project "GRAAL", and the équipe-projet INRIA "CÉPAGE".
** Supported in part by grants from the Israel Science Foundation and the Minerva Foundation.

A. Pelc (Ed.): DISC 2007, LNCS 4731, pp. 179–192, 2007.

which can be thought of intuitively as a generalization of the concept of spanning trees. We say that H is an (α, β)-*spanner* of a graph G if H is a spanning subgraph of G and $d_H(u, v) \leqslant \alpha \cdot d_G(u, v) + \beta$ for all nodes u, v of G, where $d_X(u, v)$ denotes the distance from u to v in the graph X. A pair (α, β) for which H is an (α, β)-spanner is called *stretch* of H, and the *size* of H is the number of its edges. An $(\alpha, 0)$-spanner is also referred to as an α-spanner. The quality of a spanner is measured by the trade-off between its stretch and size.

The locality level of constructing a graph spanner can be measured by the time needed to construct such a spanner. In the distributed setting, the best a node can do in t time units is to collect information from its t neighborhood. Hence the time complexity of a distributed algorithm for a given problem can be related to the amount of information needed to solve the problem. Many fundamental problems such as maximal independent set (MIS), coloring, and sparse covers and decompositions, have been studied from the locality point of view in the past. In general, such problems appear to have time efficient distributed algorithms in the randomized setting or for some restricted families of graphs. By "efficient" we mean algorithms breaking the polylogarithmic time barrier. However, no deterministic distributed algorithms having a polylogarithmic running time for every graph are known for any of these problems. The main difficulty in solving such problems is to break the symmetry in a distributed and efficient way when making decisions. While randomization helps to achieve the goal of symmetry breaking, trying to do it by a deterministic method leads to nontrivial combinatorial and algorithmic problems, essentially due to the local nature of distributed computations. Deterministic construction of graph spanners is also a typical problem where breaking the symmetry appears as the major problem for finding fast algorithms. In this paper we overcome this difficulty, showing that near-optimal high quality graph spanners can be constructed in polylogarithmic time. Our algorithm is based on breaking the symmetry using independent dominating sets and on a new sequential construction of spanners exploiting some particular stretch-size properties for bipartite graphs.

Constructing spanners efficiently is also of interest from a practical point of view, since such structures are often used in many applications. In fact, graph spanners are in the basis of various applications in distributed systems (cf. [23]). For instance, the relationship between the quality of spanners and the time and message complexity of network synchronizers is established in [24] (see also [1,21]). Spanners are also implicitly used for the design of low stretch routing schemes with compact tables [11,16,25,27,29], and appear in many parallel and distributed algorithms for computing approximate shortest paths and for the design of compact data-structures, a.k.a. distance oracles [8,20,28,30,10].

Related Work: We consider unweighted connected graphs with n nodes. Sparse and low stretch spanners can be constructed from the sparse partitions and covers of [6] or the (d, c)-decompositions of [5], which give a partition of the graph into clusters of diameter at most d such that the graph obtained by contracting each cluster can be properly c-colored. There are several deterministic algorithms for constructing (d, c)-decompositions [2,3,4,22]. The resulting distributed algorithms provide $O(k)$-spanners of size $O(n^{1+1/k})$, for any integral parameter $k \geqslant 1$. However, these algorithms run in $\Omega(n^{1/k+\epsilon})$ time, where $\epsilon = \Omega(1/\sqrt{\log n})$, and provide a stretch at least $4k-3$. Better stretch-size trade-offs exist but with an increasing time complexity. More recently, a deterministic distributed algorithm has been proposed for constructing a $(2k-1)$-spanner of size $O(n^{1+1/k})$ in $O(n^{1-1/k})$ time [13]. The latter stretch-size trade-off is optimal since, according to an Erdös Conjecture verified for $k = 1, 2, 3, 5$ [32], there are graphs with $\Omega(n^{1+1/k})$ edges and girth $2k + 2$ (the length of the smallest induced cycle), thus for which every (α, β)-spanner requires $\Omega(n^{1+1/k})$ edges if $\alpha + \beta < 2k + 1$.

More time efficient algorithms were given in [12] at the price of slightly increasing the stretch. The algorithm runs in $n^{O(1/\sqrt{\log n})}$ times and provides (α_k, β_k)-spanners with $O(\log k \cdot n^{1+1/k})$ edges where α_k and β_k depend on the positions of the two leading 1's in the binary representation of k and are essentially in order of $k^{\log_2 5}$. In particular, for $k = 2$, the stretch is $(3, 2)$.

Randomized distributed algorithms achieving better performances exist. There is a straightforward (Las Vegas[1]) randomized implementation of the algorithms of [12] that provides $O(k^{\log_2 5})$-spanners of $O(\log k \cdot n^{1+1/k})$ edges in $O(\log n)$ expected time. An algorithm for sparsifying a graph was used in [15] at the bottleneck of constructing small connected dominating sets. This (Monte-Carlo[2]) algorithm constructs, with high probability, a $O(\log n)$-spanner with $O(n)$ edges in $O(\log^3 n)$ time. A (Monte Carlo) algorithm that computes a $(2k-1)$-spanner with expected size $O(k\,n^{1+1/k})$ in $O(k^2)$ time was given in [9].

However, as mentioned in [3], a randomized solution (in particular those coming from Monte Carlo algorithms) might not be acceptable in some cases, especially for distributed computing applications. In the case of graph spanners, deterministic algorithms that *guarantee* a high quality spanner are of more than a theoretical interest. Indeed, one cannot just run a randomized distributed algorithm several times to guarantee a good decomposition, since checking the global quality of the spanner in the distributed model is time consuming.

Sequential and distributed algorithms for constructing $(1 + \epsilon, \beta)$-spanners were developed in [17,19,18]. The resulting spanner size is $O(\beta n^{1+\delta})$ and the construction time is $O(n^\delta)$, where $\beta = \beta(\delta, \epsilon)$ is independent of n but grows super-polynomially in δ^{-1} and ϵ^{-1}. Recently, a sequential algorithm based on a randomized sampling technique was given in [31], providing a spanner with $O(k\,n^{1+1/k})$ edges such that the distance d between any two nodes in the original graph is bounded by $d + o(d)$ in the spanner. Pure additive spanners, i.e., spanners whose stretch is on the form $(1, \beta)$, are known only for $k = 2$ and $k = 3$. Sequential algorithms that construct a $(1, 2)$-spanner with $O(n^{3/2})$ edges and a $(1, 6)$-spanner with $O(n^{4/3})$ edges were given respectively in [18] and in [7]. See [26] for further discussions.

Main results: In this paper, we construct in $O(\log n)$ time and for every graph a 3-spanner with $O(n^{3/2})$ edges. This result is generalized to construct in $2^{O(k)}$

---

[1] The bounds on the stretch and the size are always guaranteed.

[2] There are no deterministic guarantees for the size and the stretch.

$\log^{k-1} n$ time and for every graph a $(4k-3)$-spanner with $O(k\,n^{1+1/k})$ edges for every $k \geqslant 1$. Our construction improves all previous deterministic constructions of low stretch spanners with few edges.

Our algorithms are based on two main ideas. The first idea enables us to achieve the polylogarithmic time complexity. It is based on clustering the graph using any known time-efficient algorithm for constructing an *independent ρ-dominating set*, namely, a set X of pairwise non-adjacent nodes such that every node of the graph is at distance at most ρ from X. The second idea enables us achieve the linear stretch bound with the desired size. It is based on spanning independently in parallel *(i)* the intra-cluster edges using any known sequential algorithm, and *(ii)* the inter-cluster edges in the border of each cluster using a new size-constrained spanner for bipartite graphs. Known algorithms for constructing independent ρ-dominating sets are more time consuming when ρ is small (typically when ρ is a constant). The key point of our fast construction is to use our spanner algorithm for bipartite graphs in order to keep the stretch low and to choose ρ to be any parameter possibly depending on n. In particular, we show that the parameter ρ does not affect the stretch but only the time construction. The construction time of low stretch spanner is then dominated by the construction of an independent ρ-dominating set. Since the fastest known deterministic algorithm for constructing an independent ρ-dominating set is obtained for $\rho = O(\log n)$ and has running time $O(\log n)$, we are able to construct the desired low stretch spanner in polylogarithmic time.

A generic scheme called GENERIC_SPANNER that utilizes these ideas is first described and analyzed in Section 2. Our generic scheme assumes the existence of a sequential algorithm Z_SPANNER$_k$ for bipartite graphs that constructs a spanner with some desired constraints on the size and the stretch. For the case $k = 2$, such an algorithm is described and analyzed in detail in Section 3, yielding our first main result: the deterministic construction of an optimal 3-spanner with $O(n^{3/2})$ edges in $O(\log n)$ time (Theorem 1). This result is generalized for any k in Section 4, giving Algorithm Z_SPANNER$_k$ which yields our second main result: the deterministic construction of a $(4k-3)$-spanner with $O(k\,n^{1+1/k})$ edges in $2^{O(k)} \log^{k-1} n$ time (Theorem 2).

We also investigate the construction of almost pure additive spanners for $k = 2$. In Section 5, we construct an almost pure additive $(1 + \epsilon, \beta)$-spanner with $O(n^{3/2})$ edges for any $\epsilon > 0$. This is obtained by simply adding breadth-first searching (BFS) trees up to some fixed parameter around the dense clusters constructed by GENERIC_SPANNER for $k = 2$. This allows us to reduce the stretch while preserving the size bound and increasing the time complexity by only a small factor. Several bounds on the stretch and the time complexity are then obtained by using either an independent $O(\log n)$-dominating set algorithm or a MIS algorithm. More precisely, we refine our 3-spanner construction to obtain two fast distributed algorithms. The first one runs in $O(\epsilon^{-1} \log n)$ time and provides additive stretch $\beta = 8 \log n$. The second algorithm runs in $n^{O(1/\sqrt{\log n})} + O(\epsilon^{-1})$ time and provides additive stretch $\beta = 4$. The latter algorithm can also be implemented in $O(\epsilon^{-1} + \log n)$ expected time (using $O(\log n)$ expected time algorithm for MIS) with deterministic stretch and size.

Model and definitions: We assume the classical $\mathcal{LOCAL}$ distributed model of computation (cf. [23], Chapter 2). More precisely, the network is modeled by a connected graph G, whose nodes represent the autonomous computation entities of the network and whose edges represent direct communication links. For simplicity, we assume that communication is synchronous, i.e., there exists a common global clock that generates pulses. At each pulse, nodes can send and receive messages of unlimited size. We assume that a message which is sent at a given pulse arrives before the beginning of the next pulse. The local computations done by a node are assumed to take negligible time. Define the time complexity of a distributed algorithm to be the worst-case number of pulses from the beginning of the algorithm execution to its termination.

Given an integer $t \geqslant 1$, the t-th power of G, denoted by G^t, is the graph obtained from G by adding an edge between any two nodes at distance at most t in G. For a set of nodes H, $G[H]$ denotes the subgraph of G induced by H. For $X, Y \subseteq V$, let $d_G(X, Y) = \min \{d_G(x, y) : x \in X \text{ and } y \in Y\}$.

We associate with each $v \in V$ a *region*, denoted by $R(v)$, which is a set of nodes containing v and inducing a connected subgraph of G. We denote by $R^+(v) = \{u \in V : d_G(u, R(v)) \leqslant 1\}$. Given a set $U \subseteq V$, we denote by $\Gamma_G(U)$ the neighborhood of the set U, i.e., $\Gamma_G(U) = \{u \in V : d_G(u, U) = 1\}$. Note that $\Gamma_G(R(v)) = R^+(v) \setminus R(v)$.

Given a region $R(v)$, the *surrounding graph of* $R(v)$ is the graph B_v induced by the edges $\{x, y\} \in E(G)$ such that $x \in R(v)$ and $y \in \Gamma_G(R(v))$. Informally speaking, B_v is the collection of the outgoing edges of $R(v)$, namely, the edges having one of their end-points in $R(v)$ and the other one outside $R(v)$. One can easily see that B_v is a collection of connected bipartite subgraphs of G lying at the frontier of $R(v)$.

The *eccentricity* of a node v in G is defined as $\max_{u \in V} d_G(u, v)$. For a node $v \in X$, we denote by $\text{BFS}(v, X)$ a breadth-first search tree rooted at v and spanning X. We denote by $\text{IDS}(G, \rho)$ (respectively, $\text{MIS}(G)$) any independent ρ-dominating set (resp., maximal independent set) of G. One can check that a set is an $\text{MIS}(G)$ if and only if it is an $\text{IDS}(G, 1)$. We denote by $\text{IDS}(n, \rho)$ the time complexity needed to construct an independent ρ-dominating set on a graph of n nodes. We note that $\text{MIS}(n) = IDS(n, 1)$.

Due to lack of space, the proofs of our lemmas and theorems are omitted and will appear in the full version of the paper.

2   A General Scheme

In this section we give a high level description of Algorithm GENERIC_SPANNER (see Fig 1). It uses two sub-routines:

- SEQ_SPANNER$_k$: can be any algorithm that given an n-node graph and a parameter $k > 0$ constructs a $s(k)$-spanner with $O(k\, n^{1+1/k})$ edges.

- Z_SPANNER$_k$: can be any algorithm that given a bipartite graph $B = (W \cup V, E)$ and a parameter $k > 0$ constructs a $z(k)$-spanner with $O(|V \cup W| + |W| \cdot |V \cup W|^{1/k})$ edges.

These two algorithms are executed by only some nodes *locally* and in a *non-interfering manner*. Thus, we can use any two possibly sequential algorithm without affecting the distributed time complexity of the overall algorithm.

Many algorithms are known for the first of the latter tasks, namely, providing spanners with $O(k\, n^{1+1/k})$ edges and stretch $s(k) = 2k - 1$ for any graph. In contrast, no trivial constructions are known for the second task, of providing spanners with both a low stretch $z(k)$ and the constrained size $O(|V \cup W| + |W| \cdot |V \cup W|^{1/k})$ for bipartite graphs. Solving this latter task will be the aim of sections 3 and 4. In the rest of this section, we simply assume the existence of such a construction and focus on the properties of the general scheme defined by GENERIC_SPANNER.

2.1   Description of the Generic Scheme

Algorithm GENERIC_SPANNER (Fig. 1) is based on clustering the dense regions of the graph and spanning the edges of these regions efficiently. The algorithm works in at most k iterations, each of six steps. Step 1 computes the set L of light nodes, that is, the nodes whose corresponding regions have a sparse neighborhood. Step 2 considers (in parallel) each light region $R(v)$ and its surrounding graph B_v. Fig. 2 gives an idea of how a region $R(v)$ and the graph B_v may look like. Each connected component of B_v is a bipartite subgraph having one set of nodes on the border of $R(v)$ and the other set outside $R(v)$. The intra-region edges are

---

Input: a graph $G = (V, E)$ with $n = |V|$, and integers $\rho, k \geqslant 1$.
Output: a spanner S of G with stretch $\max\{z(k), s(k)\}$ and size $O(k\, n^{1+1/k})$.

Set $U := V$; $r = 0$; $S := \varnothing$; $\forall v \in V$, $R(v) := \{v\}$ and $c(v) := v$;
For $i := 1$ to k do:
    Span light regions
        1. $L := \{v \in U : |R^+(v)| \leqslant n^{i/k}\}$;
        2. For all $v \in L$ **do (in parallel):**
            (a) Let B_v be the surrounding graph $R(v)$;
            (b) $S := S \cup \text{SEQ\_SPANNER}_k(G[R(v)]) \cup \text{Z\_SPANNER}_k(B_v)$;
    Form new dense regions
        3. $X := \text{IDS}(G^{2(r+1)}[U \setminus L], \rho)$;
        4. $\forall z \in U$, if $d_G(z, X) \leqslant (2\rho+1)r + 2\rho$, then set $c(z)$ to be the closest
            node of X, breaking ties with identities;
        5. $\forall v \in X$, $R(v) := \{z \in V : c(z) = v\}$;
        6. $U := X$ and $r := (2\rho + 1)r + 2\rho$;

Fig. 1. Algorithm GENERIC_SPANNER

using Algorithm SEQ_SPANNER$_k$ whereas the inter-region edges (those, of the surrounding graph B_v) are spanned using Algorithm Z_SPANNER$_k$. This step can be performed efficiently by collecting a copy of $R^+(v)$ in v that computes the result and then broadcasts this information.

Algorithm Z_SPANNER$_k$ spans inter-region edges using paths zigzagging from the border to the outside of a region, thus avoiding to use long paths going from the border to the center v. The intra-region edges are spanned using any distributed or sequential algorithm in order to guarantee the best possible stretch-size trade-offs inside a region. The radius of constructed regions (which depends only on parameter ρ) will affect only the time complexity but not the stretch of the obtained spanner. This observation will enable us to use a fast IDS algorithm without constraining ρ to be too small (typically, by taking ρ order of $\log n$).

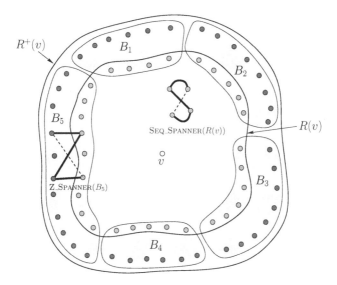

Fig. 2. A region $R(v)$ and its surrounding graph $B_v = \bigcup_{j \in [1,5]} B_j$.

After Step 2, only the neighborhood of sparse regions are spanned. In the other steps, the remaining dense regions are processed the in order to merge them together. The goal here is to grow the dense regions until they become sparse. Thus, we would be able to span them without adding too many edges.

In fact, in Steps 3, 4, and 5, we construct new dense regions centered around some well chosen dense nodes. First, we construct an independent ρ-dominating set X of the graph $G^{2(r+1)}[U \setminus L]$ where r is an upper bound of the radius of any region and U is the set of remaining dense nodes. Then, using a classical consistent coloring mechanism (cf. [23], Chapter 22, Lemma 22.1.2), all dense regions are merged into new regions having the nodes of the IDS as their centers (note that a light region might get merged with a dense one). The merging process guarantees that the new regions are disjoint and connected, and their radius grows up by at most a multiplicative factor $O(\rho)$. In addition, one should remark that by considering the $2(r + 1)$ power of G, it is guaranteed that the neighborhood of the regions induced by the set X are disjoint. Thus, each new formed region contains at least its neighborhood. This observation is essential to obtain the desired size for our spanner.

In Step 6, the set of dense regions is updated for the next iteration. On iteration k the sparsity condition of Step 1 is always true, hence all the regions are light, which guarantees that all nodes are spanned.

2.2   Analysis of the Algorithm

For every phase i, denote by L_i (resp. X_i) the set L (resp. X) computed during phase i, i.e., after Steps 1 and 3 of phase i. Similarly, denote by $c_i(z)$ the color of z assigned during phase i, i.e., after Step 4 of phase i. Denote by U_i the set U at the beginning of phase i, and let r_i denote the value of r at the beginning of phase i. Observe that $U_i = X_{i-1}$ for every $i > 1$. For a node $v \in U_i$, denote by $R_i(v)$ the region of v at the beginning of phase i. The following lemma is easily proved by induction relying on the description of the algorithm.

Lemma 1. *For every phase $i > 0$, and for every $v \in U_i$, $|R_i(v)| \geqslant n^{(i-1)/k}$, and if $v \in X_i$, then $R_i^+(v) \subseteq R_{i+1}(v)$.*

Inspired by the proofs of lemmas 1 to 4 in [12], one can prove the following:

Lemma 2. *in Algorithm GENERIC_SPANNER, the following holds:*

- *For every phase i and for every $v \in U_i$, r_i is the eccentricity of v in $G[R_i(v)]$.*
- *For every phase i and for all nodes $u \neq v \in U_i$, $R_i(u) \cap R_i(v) = \varnothing$.*
- *For every node $u \in V$, there exists a phase i and a node v such that $u \in R_i(v)$ and $v \in L_i \cap U_i$.*

The following two main lemmas are used in our construction.

Lemma 3. *The output S of Algorithm GENERIC_SPANNER is a $\max\{z(k), s(k)\}$-spanner of G with at most $O(k\, n^{1+1/k})$ edges.*

Lemma 4. *Algorithm GENERIC_SPANNER can be implemented in the distributed $\mathcal{LOCAL}$ model in $O((2\rho + 1)^{k-2} \cdot \mathrm{IDS}(n, \rho) + (2\rho + 1)^{k-1})$ time.*

3   3-Spanner Construction

In order to apply Lemma 3, it is necessary to provide an algorithm that given a surrounding graph B_v of some region $R(v)$ constructs a spanner with the desired constraints on the stretch and the size. Since any surrounding graph B_v is a collection of connected bipartite components, it is clear that the desired stretch and size spanner can be obtained by providing an algorithm with these properties for bipartite graphs and then applying that algorithm in parallel for each connected component.

In this section we describe in detail a Z_SPANNER algorithm providing the desired properties for a bipartite graph. More precisely, we prove the following more powerful result.

Lemma 5. *Every connected bipartite graph $B = (W \cup V, E)$ has a spanner S with at most $O(|V| + |W| \cdot \sqrt{|V|})$ edges satisfying the following stretch properties:*

$$\forall v, w \in V \cup W, \quad d_S(v, w) \leqslant \begin{cases} 2 \cdot d_B(v, w) + 1 & \textit{if } d_B(v, w) \textit{ is odd} \\ 2 \cdot d_B(v, w) + 2 & \textit{otherwise.} \end{cases}$$

Let us remark that for $k = 2$ in GENERIC_SPANNER, Lemma 5 leads to the construction of a 3-spanner. In [23], it is shown how to construct a $(2 \log n, 3)$-ruling set in $O(\log n)$ deterministic time. A (ρ, s)-ruling set with $s > 1$ is in particular an independent ρ-dominating set. Thus, one can construct an independent $2 \log n$-dominating set deterministically in $O(\log n)$ time. Hence, for $k = 2$ and $\rho = 2 \log n$ in GENERIC_SPANNER, we obtain:

Theorem 1. *There exists a distributed algorithm that given an n-node graph constructs a 3-spanner with $O(n^{3/2})$ edges in $O(\log n)$ deterministic time.*

In the rest of this section, we give a Z_SPANNER$_2$ algorithm providing the properties claimed in Lemma 5.

3.1   Description of Z_Spanner$_2$

Algorithm Z_SPANNER$_2$ with input a bipartite graph B is based on a sequential greedy technique (see Fig. 3):

Input: a connected bipartite graph $B = (W \cup V, E)$.
Output: a 3-spanner S of B with $O(|V| + |W| \cdot \sqrt{|V|})$ edges.

Set $V_1 := V$; $W_1 := W$; $B_1 := B$; $S := \varnothing$; $i := 1$;
While $W_i \neq \varnothing$ **do**:
  1. Let $w_i \in W_i$ with the highest degree in B_i, breaking ties arbitrary.
  2. $N_i := \Gamma_{B_i}(\{w_i\})$.
  3. $S := S \cup B_i[N_i]$.
  4. For every $j < i$ such that $w_i \in \Gamma_B(N_j)$ **do**:
      (a) Let e_{j, w_i} be an edge in E connecting N_j to w_i.
      (b) $S := S \cup \{e_{j, w_i}\}$.
  5. Construct the new graph B_{i+1}:
      (a) $V_{i+1} := V_i \setminus N_i$ and $W_{i+1} := W_i \setminus \{w_i\}$.
      (b) $B_{i+1} := B_i[V_{i+1} \cup W_{i+1}]$.
  6. $i := i + 1$;

Fig. 3. Algorithm Z_SPANNER$_2$

In each iteration $i \in \{1, \ldots, |W|\}$, a new graph $B_i = (W_i \cup V_i, E_i)$ is considered on the basis of the graph B_{i-1} corresponding to the previous iteration ($B_1 := B$). Some edges of B are added to the spanner S as follows: Select a node $w_i \in W_i$ with the highest degree in B_i, and add to S its neighborhood N_i in B_i (with its incident edges). Then, if w_i is connected in the original graph B to N_j with $j < i$, a set computed at some previous step, an edge e_{i,w_j} connecting w_i to N_j is added to S. (See Fig. 4).

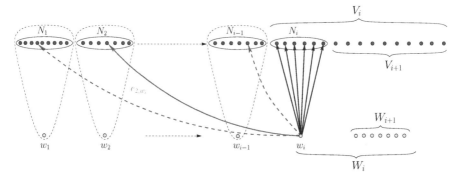

Fig. 4. The i-th iteration Algorithm Z_SPANNER$_2$

3.2   Analysis of Z_Spanner$_2$

Lemma 6. *Let u, v, w be three nodes of a bipartite graph $B = (W \cup V, E)$ such that $u \in V$, $\{u, v\} \in E$ and $\{u, w\} \in E$. The output spanner S of Algorithm Z_SPANNER$_2(B)$ satisfies $d_S(u, v) \leqslant 3$ and $d_S(v, w) \leqslant 4$.*

Lemma 7. *For any bipartite graph $B = (W \cup V, E)$, the output spanner of Z_SPANNER$_2(B)$ has $O(|V| + |W| \cdot \sqrt{|V|})$ edges.*

Using the previous lemmas, we are able to prove the stretch and size bounds as stated in Lemma 5.

4 $O(k)$-Spanner Construction

Algorithm Z_SPANNER$_2$ can be extended for $k > 2$. The extended algorithm, Z_SPANNER$_k$, is given in Fig. 5. Given a bipartite graph $B = (W \cup V, E)$, we carefully construct a partial partition of B containing clusters of small radius. More precisely, at each iteration, a cluster is grown in a layered fashion around some node $w \in W$ until the cluster becomes sparse. Once a cluster is constructed, the neighborhood of the cluster is spanned by a BFS tree and the cluster is removed from the graph B. The algorithm terminates when all the nodes of W are clustered. We remark that at the end of our algorithm, some nodes in V may remain uncovered by the clustering, however each node in W belongs to a cluster.

The originality of our algorithm comparing with classical sparse partition (or covers) algorithms is to compute the sparsity of a layer depending on the range of the layer. Let C be a cluster being constructed in the while loop of Z_SPANNER$_k$. Suppose that C contains i successive layers $\mathcal{L}_0, \ldots, \mathcal{L}_{i-1}$. Then, consider the new layer $\mathcal{L}_i$ to be processed. Since B is bipartite, then either $\mathcal{L}_i \subseteq V$ (if i is odd) or $\mathcal{L}_i \subseteq W$ (if i is even). In the first case, we add $\mathcal{L}_i$ to the cluster C if it is dense enough comparing with layer $\mathcal{L}_{i-1}$. In the second case, we add $\mathcal{L}_i$ to the cluster C if it is dense enough comparing with layer $\mathcal{L}_{i-2}$. The main observation that will guarantee the desired size is that in the two cases layers $\mathcal{L}_{i-1}$ or $\mathcal{L}_{i-2}$ belong to W.

Input: a connected bipartite graph $B = (W \cup V, E)$ and an integer $k > 0$.
Output: a $(4k - 3)$-spanner S of B with $O(|V \cup W| + |W| \cdot |V \cup W|^{1/k})$ edges.

$S := \varnothing$;
while $W \neq \varnothing$ **do**
    pick a node $v \in W$;
    $C := \{v\}$, $\mathcal{L}_0 := \{v\}$ and $i := 1$;
    dense := TRUE;
    while dense **do**
        $\mathcal{L}_i := \Gamma_B(C)$;
        $j := i - 2 + (i \bmod 2)$;
        if $|\mathcal{L}_i| > |V \cup W|^{1/k} \cdot |\mathcal{L}_j|$ **then**
            $C := C \cup \mathcal{L}_i$;
            $i := i + 1$;
        else
            dense := FALSE;
    $S := S \cup \mathrm{BFS}(v, C \cup \mathcal{L}_i)$;
    $W := W \setminus C$ and $V := V \setminus C$;

Fig. 5. Algorithm Z_SPANNER$_k$

By analyzing Algorithm Z_SPANNER$_k$, we can show that:

Lemma 8. *Let $k \geqslant 1$. Every connected bipartite graph $B = (V \cup W, E)$, has a $(4k - 3)$-spanner with $O(|V \cup W| + |W| \cdot |V \cup W|^{1/k})$ edges.*

Combining Lemma 3 and 4 for $\rho = 2 \log n$, we obtain:

Theorem 2. *There exists a distributed algorithm that given an n-node graph and an integer $k \geqslant 1$, constructs a $(4k - 3)$-spanner for it with $O(k\, n^{1+1/k})$ edges in $2^{O(k)} \log^{k-1} n$ deterministic time.*

5   Improving the Stretch for $k = 2$

It is shown in [14,18] that every graph has a $(1, 2)$-spanner with $O(n^{3/2})$ edges. Nevertheless, no fast distributed construction of such a spanner is known. In this section, we give fast distributed constructions that enable us to obtain 3-spanners of size $O(n^{3/2})$ which are also almost pure additive spanners. More precisely, the multiplicative component on the stretch is $(1+\epsilon)$ and the additive component is independent of ϵ but depends on the time complexity.

Our construction works in two stages. In the first stage, we run Algorithm GENERIC_SPANNER with parameter $k = 2$ and we obtain a spanner S_1 and a set of dense nodes X. The set X here denotes the set of nodes computed by the first iteration of GENERIC_SPANNER, i.e., $X = X_1$. In the second stage, we add to S_1 a BFS tree up to a depth $2\rho + \beta$ rooted at each node $v \in X$ (β is a given parameter).

By setting $\rho = 2\log n$ and $\beta = \Theta(\epsilon^{-1}\log n)$ with $\epsilon > 0$, and using the $O(\log n)$ time deterministic algorithm for independent $(2\log n)$-dominating sets, one can prove:

Lemma 9. *There exists a distributed algorithm that given an n-node graph G and a parameter $\epsilon > 0$, constructs in $O(\epsilon^{-1}\log n)$ deterministic time a 3-spanner S with $O(n^{3/2})$ edges and satisfying the following stretch properties:*

$$\forall u, v \in V, \quad d_S(u,v) \leqslant \begin{cases} d_G(u,v) + 8\log n & \text{if } d_G(u,v) \leqslant 8\epsilon^{-1}\log n \\ (1+\epsilon)\, d_G(u,v) + 8\log n & \text{otherwise.} \end{cases}$$

Note that if the distance to be approximated is $d = \omega(\log n)$, then the distance in the spanner is at most $(1+\epsilon) \cdot d + o(d)$. Also, by choosing $\epsilon = o(1)$, Lemma 9 implies the construction in $\log^{1+o(1)} n$ time of a 3-spanner with $O(n^{3/2})$ edges which is also a $(1 + o(1), 8\log n)$-spanner.

In order to obtain a better additive stretch, we use an MIS algorithm at the price of increasing the time complexity. In fact, it is also well-known that a MIS can be constructed by a deterministic (resp. randomized) algorithm in $n^{O(1/\sqrt{\log n})}$ (resp. $O(\log n)$ expected) time. Thus by taking $\rho = 1$ and $\beta = \Theta(\text{MIS}(n))$, one can prove:

Lemma 10. *There exists a distributed algorithm that given an n-node graph G, constructs in $n^{O(1/\sqrt{\log n})}$ deterministic time a spanner S with $O(n^{3/2})$ edges and stretch (α, β) as given by Table 1.*

Table 1. Stretches (α, β) for distances d

$d_G(u,v)$	$d_S(u,v)$	(α, β)
1	3	$(2,1)$
2	6	$(2,2)$
3	7	$(2,1)$
4	8	$(2,0)$
5	9	$(1.8,0)$
$d > n^{O(1/\sqrt{\log n})}$	$(1 + o(1))\, d$	$(1+o(1), 0)$
$d \leqslant n^{O(1/\sqrt{\log n})}$	$d + 4$	$(1,4)$

We observe that the spanner constructed in Lemma 10 has stretch at most $(2, 1)$ except for nodes at distance 2.

Combining previous lemmas we obtain:

Theorem 3. *There exists a distributed algorithm that given an n-node graph G and a parameter $\epsilon > 0$ constructs in $n^{O(1/\sqrt{\log n})} + O(\epsilon^{-1})$ (resp. $O(\epsilon^{-1} \log n)$) deterministic time a 3-spanner with $O(n^{3/2})$ edges which is also a $(1 + \epsilon, 4)$-spanner (resp. a $(1 + \epsilon, 8 \log n)$-spanner).*

6   Open Problems

While it is well-known that every graph has a $(1, 2)$-spanner with $O(n^{3/2})$ edges, we leave open the problem to find (distributively or not), for each $k > 2$, a $(1, f(k))$-spanner of size $O(n^{1+1/k})$ where f is a polynomial (or even an exponential) function.

References

1. Awerbuch, B.: Complexity of network synchronization. J. ACM 32, 804–823 (1985)
2. Awerbuch, B., Berger, B., Cowen, L.J., Peleg, D.: Near-linear cost sequential and distributed constructions of sparse neighborhood coverss. In: 34th IEEE Symp. on Foundations of Computer Science, pp. 638–647. IEEE Computer Society Press, Los Alamitos (1993)
3. Awerbuch, B., Berger, B., Cowen, L.J., Peleg, D.: Fast distributed network decompositions and covers. J. Parallel and Distributed Computing 39, 105–114 (1996)
4. Awerbuch, B., Berger, B., Cowen, L.J., Peleg, D.: Near-linear time construction of sparse neighbourhood covers. SIAM J. on Computing 28, 263–277 (1998)
5. Awerbuch, B., Goldberg, A., Luby, M., Plotkin, S.: Network decomposition and locality in distributed computation. In: Proc. 30th IEEE Symp. on Foundations of Computer Science, pp. 364–369. IEEE Computer Society Press, Los Alamitos (1989)
6. Awerbuch, B., Peleg, D.: Sparse partitions. In: 31th IEEE Symp. on Foundations of Computer Science, pp. 503–513. IEEE Computer Society Press, Los Alamitos (1990)
7. Baswana, S., Kavitha, T., Mehlhorn, K., Pettie, S.: New constructions of (α, β)-spanners and purely additive spanners. In: 16th ACM-SIAM Symp. on Discrete Algorithms, pp. 672–681. ACM Press, New York (2005)
8. Baswana, S., Sen, S.: Approximate distance oracles for unweighted graphs in $\tilde{O}(n^2)$ time. In: 15th ACM-SIAM Symp. on Discrete Algorithms, pp. 271–280. ACM Press, New York (2004)
9. Baswana, S., Sen, S.: A simple and linear time randomized algorithm for computing sparse spanners in weighted graphs. Random Structures and Algorithms 30, 532–563 (2007)
10. Cohen, E.: Fast algorithms for constructing t-spanners and paths with stretch t. SIAM J. on Computing 28, 210–236 (1998)
11. Cowen, L.J.: Compact routing with minimum stretch. J. Algorithms 38, 170–183 (2001)

12. Derbel, B., Gavoille, C.: Fast deterministic distributed algorithms for sparse span-
    ners. In: Flocchini, P., Gąsieniec, L. (eds.) SIROCCO 2006. LNCS, vol. 4056, pp.
    100–114. Springer, Heidelberg (2006)
13. Derbel, B., Mosbah, M., Zemmari, A.: Fast distributed graph partition and ap-
    plication. In: 20th IEEE Int. Parallel and Distributed Processing Symp., IEEE
    Computer Society Press, Los Alamitos (2006)
14. Dor, D., Halperin, S., Zwick, U.: All pairs almost shortest paths. SIAM J. Com-
    puting 29, 1740–1759 (2000)
15. Dubhashi, D., Mai, A., Panconesi, A., Radhakrishnan, J., Srinivasan, A.: Fast dis-
    tributed algorithms for (weakly) connected dominating sets and linear-size skele-
    tons. J. of Computer and System Sciences 71, 467–479 (2005)
16. Eilam, T., Gavoille, C., Peleg, D.: Compact routing schemes with low stretch factor.
    J. Algorithms 46, 97–114 (2003)
17. Elkin, M.: Computing almost shortest paths. In: 20th ACM Symp. on Principles
    of Distributed Computing, pp. 53–62. ACM Press, New York (2001)
18. Elkin, M., Peleg, D.: $(1 + \epsilon, \beta)$-spanner constructions for general graphs. SIAM J.
    on Computing 33, 608–631 (2004)
19. Elkin, M., Zhang, J.: Efficient algorithms for constructing $(1 + \epsilon, \beta)$-spanners in
    the distributed and streaming models. In: 23rd ACM Symp. on Principles of Dis-
    tributed Computing, pp. 160–168. ACM Press, New York (2004)
20. Gavoille, C., Peleg, D., Pérennès, S., Raz, R.: Distance labeling in graphs. J. Al-
    gorithms 53, 85–112 (2004)
21. Moran, S., Snir, S.: Simple and efficient network decomposition and synchroniza-
    tion. Theoretical Computer Science 243, 217–241 (2000)
22. Panconesi, A., Srinivasan, A.: On the complexity of distributed network decompo-
    sition. J. Algorithms 20, 356–374 (1996)
23. Peleg, D.: Distributed Computing: A Locality-Sensitive Approach. SIAM Mono-
    graphs on Discrete Mathematics and Applications (2000)
24. Peleg, D., Ullman, J.D.: An optimal synchornizer for the hypercube. SIAM J.
    Computing 18, 740–747 (1989)
25. Peleg, D., Upfal, E.: A trade-off between space and efficiency for routing tables. J.
    ACM 36, 510–530 (1989)
26. Pettie, S.: Low distortion spanners. In: 34th International Colloquium on Au-
    tomata, Languages and Programming. LNCS, vol. 4596. Springer, Heidelberg
    (2007)
27. Roditty, L., Thorup, M., Zwick, U.: Roundtrip spanners and roundtrip routing in
    directed graphs. In: 13th ACM-SIAM Symp. on Discrete Algorithms, pp. 844–851.
    ACM Press, New York (2002)
28. Roditty, L., Thorup, M., Zwick, U.: Deterministic constructions of approximate dis-
    tance oracles and spanners. In: Caires, L., Italiano, G.F., Monteiro, L., Palamidessi,
    C., Yung, M. (eds.) ICALP 2005. LNCS, vol. 3580, pp. 261–272. Springer, Heidel-
    berg (2005)
29. Thorup, M., Zwick, U.: Compact routing schemes. In: 13th ACM Symp. on Parallel
    Algorithms and Architectures, pp. 1–10. ACM Press, New York (2001)
30. Thorup, M., Zwick, U.: Approximate distance oracles. J. ACM 52, 1–24 (2005)
31. Thorup, M., Zwick, U.: Spanners and emulators with sublinear distance errors. In:
    17th ACM-SIAM Symp. on Discrete Algorithm, pp. 802–809. ACM Press, New
    York (2006)
32. Wenger, R.: Extremal graphs with no C^4's, C^6's, or C^{10}'s. J. Combinatorial Theory,
    Series B 52, 113–116 (1991)

On Self-stabilizing Synchronous Actions Despite Byzantine Attacks

Danny Dolev* and Ezra N. Hoch

School of Engineering and Computer Science,
The Hebrew University of Jerusalem, Israel,
{dolev,ezraho}@cs.huji.ac.il

Abstract. Consider a distributed network of n nodes that is connected to a global source of "beats". All nodes receive the "beats" simultaneously, and operate in lock-step. A scheme that produces a "pulse" every $Cycle$ beats is shown. That is, the nodes agree on "special beats", which are spaced $Cycle$ beats apart. Given such a scheme, a clock synchronization algorithm is built. The "pulsing" scheme is self-stabilized despite any transient faults and the continuous presence of up to $f < \frac{n}{3}$ *Byzantine* nodes. Therefore, the clock synchronization built on top of the "pulse" is highly fault tolerant. In addition, a highly fault tolerant general stabilizer algorithm is constructed on top of the "pulse" mechanism.

Previous clock synchronization solutions, operating in the exact same model as this one, either support $f < \frac{n}{4}$ and converge in linear time, or support $f < \frac{n}{3}$ and have **exponential convergence time** that also depends on the value of $max\text{-}clock$ (the clock wrap around value). The proposed scheme combines the best of both worlds: it converges in **linear time** that is independent of $max\text{-}clock$ and is tolerant to up to $f < \frac{n}{3}$ *Byzantine* nodes. Moreover, considering problems in a self-stabilizing, *Byzantine* tolerant environment that require nodes to know the global state (clock synchronization, token circulation, agreement, etc.), the work presented here is the first protocol to operate in a network that is not fully connected.

1 Introduction

Most distributed tasks require some sort of synchronization. Clock synchronization is a very basic and intuitive tool for supplying this. PULSE synchronization can be used as an underlying building block to achieve clock synchronization, as well as solving other synchronization problems; in a sense, PULSE synchronization is a more fundamental synchronization problem.

It thus makes sense to require an underlying PULSE synchronization mechanism to be highly fault-tolerant. This paper presents a PULSE synchronization algorithm that is self-stabilizing and is tolerant to permanent presence of

---

* Part of the work was done while the author visited Cornell university. The work was funded in part by ISF, ISOC, NSF, CCR, and AFOSR.

Byzantine faults. That is, it attains synchronization, once lost, while containing the influence of the permanent presence of faulty nodes.

Consider a system in which the nodes execute in lock-step by regularly receiving a common "pulse" or "tick" or "beat". The objective is to agree on some "special beats" that are *Cycle* beats apart. We will use the "beat" notation for the "global" signal received, and "pulse" for the "special beats" agreed upon.

The PULSE synchronization problem is to ensure that eventually all correct nodes PULSE together, and as long as enough nodes remain correct, they continue to PULSE together, *Cycle* beats apart. For example, given *Cycle* = 7 we would like all correct nodes, that may start at arbitrary initial states, to eventually PULSE together every 7 beats, and continue so as long as there are enough correct nodes.

The global beat system provides some measure of synchronization. For example, given a global beat system with beat interval at least as long as the worst-case execution-time for terminating *Byzantine* agreement, the PULSE synchronization problem is solved by initiating a *Byzantine* agreement on the next time when the nodes should PULSE, each time a beat is received. The crux of the problem is to achieve synchronization when it is not given by the global beat system; that is, when the beat interval length is in the order of the communication's end-to-end delay. Since in that scenario the global beat system does not provide - by itself - enough synchronization, and a more complex algorithm is required to exert the required synchronization. The main contribution of the current paper is achieving exactly that.

Related Work: PULSEing has been used as an underlying fault tolerant mechanism in clock synchronization, token circulation and to create a general stabilizer (see [4] for an overview). All of these algorithms are self-stabilizing and *Byzantine* tolerant, due to the fault tolerant nature of the underlying PULSE mechanism. This gives the motivation for producing robust and efficient PULSEing algorithms, as they can be used to improve the robustness of a variety of applications.

Clock synchronization is one of the first problems that was solved in a self-stabilizing and *Byzantine* tolerant fashion. In [9] and [12] it was solved directly, and in [4] it was solved using an underlying PULSEing algorithm. [9] was the first work to discuss the exact same model as presented here, as opposed to [4], which operates without a global beat system.

Synchronization of clocks of integer values was previously termed digital clock synchronization ([2,7,8,16]) or "synchronization of phase-clocks" ([11]). However, in this paper we concentrate on the PULSEing mechanism, as it yields clock synchronization as well as other fault tolerant protocols.

Several fault tolerant stabilizers exist (see [1], [10] and [13]) with varying requirement and features (such as local containment of faults). In [3], it was shown that PULSE synchronization can be used to create a generalized stabilizer. However, in [3] the stabilizer is complex, and can stabilize a narrow class of algorithms. In Section 9 we show a simpler stabilizer, which can stabilize a wider range of algorithms.

Some of the previous results combining *Byzantine* faults and self-stabilization consider a class of problems in which the state of each correct node is determined locally. Usually such solutions can operate in a general graph (see [17], [15] and [14]) without the need to aggregate or accumulate information across the network. In the class of problems in which the state of each correct node is correlated with the state of the other correct nodes, the current paper is the first paper to present a solution that operates in a network that is not fully connected.

Contributions: We construct a self stabilizing PULSEing algorithm, that is tolerant to up to $f < \frac{n}{3}$ *Byzantine* nodes, and converges in linear time, for any target interval of pulsing.

As will be shown in Section 8, clock synchronization and PULSE synchronization are equivalent. Hence, this work is compared to the state of the art of previous clock synchronization results that operate in the exact same model.

Previous results have either linear convergence time with $f < \frac{n}{4}$ (see [12]) or exponential convergence time with $f < \frac{n}{3}$ (see [9]). In this paper we obtain a linear convergence time with $f < \frac{n}{3}$. Moreover, our convergence time is independent of the *max-clock* value (the clock wrap around value) of the digital clock, in contrast to [9].

In addition, our algorithm is the first one in this model and for this type of problems that does not require each node to be connected to every other node, it only requires that there are $2 \cdot f + 1$ distinct routes between any two correct nodes, matching the lower bound of [5].

2 Model and Definitions

Consider a fully connected network of n nodes (we later generalize the results to a more general network). All the nodes are assumed to have access to a "global beat system" that provides "beats" with regular intervals. The communication network and all the nodes may be subject to severe transient failures, which might leave the system in an arbitrary state.

We say that a node is *Byzantine* if it does not follow the instructed algorithm and *non-Byzantine* otherwise. Thus, any node whose failure does not allow it to exactly follow the algorithm as instructed is considered *Byzantine*, even if it does not behave fully maliciously. A non-*Byzantine* node will be called *non-faulty*. In the following discussion f will denote the upper bound on the number of *Byzantine* nodes.[1] The presented solution supports $f < \frac{n}{3}$.

Definition 1. *The system is* coherent *if there are at most f Byzantine nodes, and each message sent at a beat to a non-faulty destination arrives and is processed at its destination before the next beat.*

Nodes are instructed to send their messages immediately after the occurrence of a beat from the global beat system. Therefore, when the system is coherent

---

[1] In the literature the term "permanent" *Byzantine* node is sometimes used.

message delivery and the processing involved can be completed between two consecutive global beats, by any node that is non-faulty. More specifically, the time required for message delivery and message processing is called a *round*, and we assume that the time interval between global beats is greater than and in the order of such a round. Due to transient faults, different nodes might not agree on the current beat/round number. We will use the notion of an external beat number r, which the nodes are not aware of, but will simplify the proofs' presentation and discussion.

At times of transient failures there can be any number of concurrent *Byzantine* faulty nodes; the turnover rate between faulty and non-faulty behavior of nodes can be arbitrarily large and the communication network may also behave arbitrarily. Eventually the system behaves coherently again. At such case a non-faulty node may still find itself in an arbitrary state. Since a non-faulty node may find itself in an arbitrary state, there should be some time of continues non-faulty operation before it can be considered correct.

Definition 2. *A non-faulty node is considered* correct *only if it remains non-faulty for Δ_{node} rounds during which the system is coherent.[2]*

The algorithm parameters n, f, as well as the node's id are fixed constants and thus are considered part of the incorruptible correct code at the node. Thus, it is assumed that non-faulty nodes do not hold arbitrary values of these constants.

2.1 The PULSEing Problem

We say that a system is $[\phi, \psi]$-PULSING if all correct nodes PULSE together in the following pattern: ϕ consecutive beats of PULSEs followed by ψ consecutive beats of non-PULSE. That is, the system has a *Cycle* of length $\phi + \psi$ beats, out of which only the first ϕ beats are PULSEs. More formally, denote by $pulsed_p(r) = True$ if p PULSEd on beat r and $pulsed_p(r) = False$, otherwise.

Definition 3. *A system is $[\phi, \psi]$-PULSING in the beat interval $[r_1, r_2]$ if there exists some $0 \le k < \phi + \psi$, such that for every correct node p, and for every beat $r \in [r_1, r_2]$, it holds that:*

1. *$pulsed_p(r) = True$, in case $0 \le r - k \pmod{\phi + \psi} < \phi$; and*
2. *$pulsed_p(r) = False$ in case $\phi \le r - k \pmod{\phi + \psi} < \phi + \psi$.*

(k denotes the offset, from r_1, of the first PULSE in the pattern.)

For example, consider "1" to represent a beat in which all correct nodes PULSE, and "0" a beat in which all correct nodes do not PULSE. Using this notation, the following is a PULSEing pattern of a $[\phi, \psi]$-PULSING system.

$$[\dots, \overbrace{1, 1, \dots, 1}^{\phi \text{ beats}}, \overbrace{0, 0, \dots, 0}^{\psi \text{ beats}}, \overbrace{1, 1, \dots, 1}^{\phi \text{ beats}}, \overbrace{0, 0, \dots, 0}^{\psi \text{ beats}}, \dots]$$

$$\underbrace{\hspace{3cm}}_{Cycle \text{ beats}} \quad \underbrace{\hspace{3cm}}_{Cycle \text{ beats}}$$

---

[2] The assumed bound on the value of Δ_{node} is defined in Remark 3.

Definition 4. The PULSEing problem:
Convergence: *Starting from an arbitrary state, the system becomes*
$[\phi, \psi]$-PULSING *after a finite number of beats.*
Closure: *If the system is $[\phi, \psi]$-PULSING in the beat interval $[r_1, r_2]$ it is also*
$[\phi, \psi]$-PULSING *in the interval $[r_1, r_2 + 1]$.*

Definition 5. *a $[\phi, \psi]$-PULSER is an algorithm $\mathcal{A}$, such that once the system is*
coherent (and stays so), it solves the PULSEing problem.

The objective is to develop an algorithm that PULSEs only once every *Cycle*.

Notation: We denote a $[1, \psi]$-PULSER as $[\psi + 1]$-PULSER.

Using the previously used notation of "1" for PULSEing and "0" for non-
PULSEing, a $[Cycle]$-PULSER looks as follows:

$$[\ldots, \underbrace{1, 0, 0, \ldots, 0,}_{Cycle \text{ beats}} \underbrace{1, 0, 0, \ldots, 0,}_{Cycle \text{ beats}} \ldots]$$

The goal is to build a $[Cycle]$-PULSER for any $Cycle > 0$. That is, a self-
stabilizing, *Byzantine* tolerant algorithm that eventually PULSEs every *Cycle*
beats. The following section outlines the solution.

3   Constructing a $[Cycle]$-PULSER

In contrast to previous solutions that were very involved, the new solution presented below is more modular. Addressing the problem in a modular way enabled us to unwrap the difficulties in solving the problem, and to come up with
a tight solution. Its modularity also enables to simplify the proof of correctness and to better present the intuition behind it. The core of the protocol is
the Large-Cycle-Pulser algorithm that produces a $[\Delta, \Delta + Cycle']$-PULSER. This
module uses another module called $\mathcal{BBB}$ to limit the ability of the *Byzantine*
nodes to disrupt the protocol. To obtain the complete solution the core protocol
is wrapped with two additional modules, as detailed below.
    We first show how to construct a $[\Delta, \Delta + Cycle']$-PULSER $\mathcal{A}$ for any $Cycle' >$
Δ, where Δ is a bound on running a given distributed agreement protocol. We
continue by showing how to construct a $[\phi + \psi]$-PULSER from any $[\phi, \psi]$-PULSER.
Using this, we construct a $[2 \cdot \Delta + Cycle']$-PULSER $\mathcal{A}'$ for any $Cycle' > \Delta$. Lastly,
using $\mathcal{A}'$, we construct a $[Cycle]$-PULSER for any $Cycle \geq 1$.

Remark 1. Note that $[\phi + \psi]$-PULSER is actually $[1, \phi + \psi - 1]$-PULSER, and hence
a $[\phi, \psi]$-PULSER (pulses for ϕ beats then it is quiet for ψ beats) is transformed
into a $[1, \phi + \psi - 1]$-PULSER (PULSEs once, then it is quiet for $\phi + \psi - 1$ beats).

The construction of $\mathcal{A}$ uses a building block that is essentially a *Byzantine* consensus. We denote this building block by $\mathcal{BBB}$ (*Byzantine* Black Box).

3.1   The *Byzantine* Black Box Construction

$\mathcal{BBB}$ is defined to be a round based distributed protocol, such that each node p has a binary input value v_p and a binary output value $\mathcal{V}_p$. $\mathcal{BBB}$ has the following properties:

1. *Termination*: The algorithm terminates within Δ rounds.
2. *Agreement*: All *non-faulty*[3] nodes agree on the same output value $\mathcal{V}$. That is, for any two *non-faulty* nodes p, p' it holds that $\mathcal{V}_p = \mathcal{V}_{p'} = \mathcal{V}$.
3. *Validity*: If $n - f$ *non-faulty* nodes have the same input value ν then that is the output value, $\mathcal{V} = \nu$.

$\mathcal{BBB}$ is required to be *Byzantine* tolerant, but is not required to be self-stabilizing. The self-stabilization of the $[\phi + \psi]$-PULSER $\mathcal{A}$ (presented later) will not be hampered by this.[4] In addition, $\mathcal{A}$ will rely only on the properties of $\mathcal{BBB}$ (when it is executed by enough correct nodes) for its operation. In $\mathcal{A}$ all messages exchanged among the nodes will use $\mathcal{BBB}$. Since the presented $\mathcal{BBB}$ can tolerate $f < \frac{n}{3}$ faulty nodes, $\mathcal{A}$ can tolerate the same failure ratio.

Remark 2. $\mathcal{BBB}$ can be implemented via any algorithm that solves the *Byzantine* consensus problem; the only difference lies in the "validity" condition, where instead of limiting the validity to the case that "all correct nodes" start with the same initial value, $\mathcal{BBB}$ limits the validity condition to having only $n - f$ non-faulty nodes with the same initial value, even if there happen to be more non-faulty nodes at that instance.

Remark 3. A non-faulty node that has recently recovered from a transient failure cannot immediately be considered correct. In the context of this paper, a non-faulty node is considered *correct* once it remains non-faulty for at least $\Delta_{node} = \Delta + 1$, and as long as it continues to be non-faulty.

3.2   A $[\Delta, \Delta + Cycle']$-PULSER

Figure 1 presents an algorithm that produces a $[\Delta, \Delta + Cycle']$-PULSER, for $Cycle' > \Delta$. This algorithm executes Δ simultaneous $\mathcal{BBB}$ protocols. Consider $\mathcal{BBB}_i$ as a "pointer" to a $\mathcal{BBB}$ instance, hence the statement

$$\mathcal{BBB}_2 := \mathcal{BBB}_1; \mathcal{BBB}_1 := new\ \mathcal{BBB}(\text{"1"});$$

means that $\mathcal{BBB}_2$ will contain the previous instance of $\mathcal{BBB}_1$, and $\mathcal{BBB}_1$ will contain a new instance of $\mathcal{BBB}$ initialized with the input value 1. The output value of $\mathcal{BBB}_i$ is $\mathcal{V}(\mathcal{BBB}_i)$.

---

[3] In the context of $\mathcal{BBB}$, a node is considered non-faulty only if it is non-faulty throughout the whole execution of $\mathcal{BBB}$.

[4] $\mathcal{BBB}$ is initiated, executed and terminated repeatedly; each instance starts with a "clean slate", thus not harming the self-stability of the algorithm that uses it.

Algorithm **Large-Cycle-Pulser**   /* *executed repeatedly at each beat* */

1. for each $i \in \{1, .., \Delta\}$ do
   execute the ith round of the $\mathcal{BBB}_i$ protocol;
2. (a) if $Counter > 0$ then
       $Counter := \min\{Counter - 1, Cycle'\}$;
       $WantToPulse := 0$;
   (b) else
       $WantToPulse := 1$;
3. if $\mathcal{V}(\mathcal{BBB}_\Delta) = 1$ then
   (a) do PULSE;
   (b) $Counter := Cycle'$;
4. for each $i \in \{2, ..., \Delta\}$ do
   $\mathcal{BBB}_i := \mathcal{BBB}_{i-1}$;
5. initialize a new instance of $\mathcal{BBB}$, $\mathcal{BBB}_1 = \mathcal{BBB}(WantToPulse)$.

Fig. 1. A $[\Delta, \Delta + Cycle']$-PULSER algorithm for $Cycle' > \Delta$

4 Proof of Large-Cycle-Pulser's Correctness

All the lemmata, theorems, corollaries and definitions hold only as long as the system is coherent. We assume that nodes may start in an arbitrary state, and nodes may fail and recover, but from some time on, at any round there are at least $n - f$ correct nodes.

Let $\mathcal{G}$ denote a group of non-*Byzantine* nodes that behave according to the algorithm, and that are not subject to (for some pre-specified number of rounds) any new transient failures. We will prove that if $|\mathcal{G}| \geq n - f$ and all of these nodes remain non-faulty for a long enough period of time ($\Omega(\Delta)$ global beats), then the system will converge.

For simplifying the notations, the proofs refer to some "external" beat number. The nodes do not maintain it and have no access to it; it is only used for the proofs' clarity.

Definition 6. *A group $\mathcal{G}$ is* CORRECT(α, β) *if* $|\mathcal{G}| \geq n - f$, *and every node* $p \in \mathcal{G}$ *is correct during the beat interval* $[\alpha, \beta]$. *Let* δ *mark the length of the interval, that is* $\delta = \beta - \alpha + 1$.

Note that each node $p \in \mathcal{G}$, when $\mathcal{G}$ is CORRECT(α, β), has not been subject to a transient failure in the beat interval $[\alpha - \Delta_{node}, \beta]$; and is non-faulty during that interval.

Definition 7. *We say that a system is* CORRECT(α, β) *if there exists a set* $\mathcal{G}$ *such that* $\mathcal{G}$ *is* CORRECT(α, β).

In the following lemmata, $\mathcal{G}$ refers to any set implied by CORRECT(α, β), without stating so specifically. The proofs hold for any such set $\mathcal{G}$.

Note that if the system is coherent, and there has not been a transient failure for at least $\Delta + 1$ beats, then, by definition, $\mathcal{G}$ contains all nodes that were non-faulty during that period.

Lemma 1. $\forall \beta \geq \alpha$: *If the system is* CORRECT(α, β) *then at any beat* $r \in [\alpha, \beta]$, *either all nodes in* $\mathcal{G}$ PULSE *or they all do not* PULSE.

Proof. A node PULSEs only in Line 3.a, which is executed only when the value of $\mathcal{V}(\mathcal{BBB}_\Delta) = 1$. All nodes in $\mathcal{G}$ have not been subject to transient failures in the $\Delta_{node} = \Delta + 1$ beats preceding r. Therefore, $\mathcal{BBB}_\Delta$ has been initialized properly Δ beats ago, and during the Δ rounds of $\mathcal{BBB}_\Delta$'s execution, it has been executed properly by at least $n - f$ nodes. Hence, according to *Agreement* of $\mathcal{BBB}$, all nodes in $\mathcal{G}$ have the same value of $\mathcal{V}(\mathcal{BBB}_\Delta)$. Therefore, all nodes in $\mathcal{G}$ "act the same" when considering Line 3.a: either all of them execute Line 3.a or they all do not execute it. This holds for any beat after α (as long as $\mathcal{G}$ continues to contain $n - f$ correct nodes). Therefore, at any such beat $r \in [\alpha, \beta]$, either all nodes in $\mathcal{G}$ PULSE or they all do not PULSE. $\square$

Lemma 2. $\forall \beta \geq \alpha + \Delta + Cycle'$: *If the system is* CORRECT(α, β), *then at some beat* $r \in [\alpha, \beta]$ *all nodes in* $\mathcal{G}$ PULSE.

Proof. According to the previous lemma, all nodes in $\mathcal{G}$ PULSE together during the interval $[\alpha, \beta]$. Hence, if one of them PULSEd in the interval $[\alpha, \alpha + Cycle']$, all of them PULSEd, proving the claim.

Otherwise, consider the case where no node in $\mathcal{G}$ has PULSEd in the interval $[\alpha, \alpha + Cycle']$. Hence, at beat $\alpha + Cycle'$, for all the nodes in $\mathcal{G}$, the *Counter* variable has decreased to 0 or is negative. This is because *Counter* is bounded from above by $Cycle'$ (which is a fixed parameter of the protocol and is identical at all nodes); and as long as it holds a positive value, it decreases by 1 during each beat of the interval $[\alpha, \alpha + Cycle']$ (since no node PULSEs in that interval, *Counter* never increases). Since the interval is at least $Cycle'$ beats long, the value of *Counter* is less than (or equal to) 0.

Therefore, at beat $\alpha + Cycle'$ there are $|\mathcal{G}| \geq n - f$ correct nodes with *WantToPulse* = 1. Therefore, according to *Validity* of $\mathcal{BBB}$, Δ beats afterwards $\mathcal{V}(\mathcal{BBB}_\Delta)$ will output 1, and all nodes in $\mathcal{G}$ will PULSE. Thus, in the interval $[\alpha, \alpha + \Delta + Cycle']$ all nodes in $\mathcal{G}$ PULSE. Therefore, the claim holds for any beat interval $[\alpha, \beta]$, where $\beta \geq \alpha + \Delta + Cycle'$. $\square$

Remark 4. The above lemma proves progress. That is, starting from any state, eventually there will be a PULSE.

Consider a system that is CORRECT(α, β) (for $\beta \geq \alpha + \Delta + Cycle'$), from Lemma 1, starting from beat α all nodes in $\mathcal{G}$ PULSE together. From Lemma 2, by beat $\alpha + \Delta + Cycle'$ all nodes in $\mathcal{G}$ have PULSEd. Therefore, by that round they have all reset their *Counter* values at the same beat. Since *WantToPulse* depends solely on the value of *Counter*, and since all nodes in $\mathcal{G}$ agree on the output value of the $\mathcal{BBB}$ protocols, all nodes in $\mathcal{G}$ perform exactly the same lines of code following each beat in the beat interval $[\alpha + \Delta + Cycle', \beta]$.

Lemma 3. $\forall \beta \geq \alpha + 3 \cdot \Delta + 2 \cdot Cycle'$: *If the system is* CORRECT(α, β), *then the system is* $[\Delta, \Delta + Cycle']$-PULSING *in the beat interval* $[\alpha + 3 \cdot \Delta + 2 \cdot Cycle', \beta]$.

Proof. According to previous lemmas, all correct nodes PULSE at some beat γ, no later than beat $\alpha + \Delta + Cycle'$; and from then on they all PULSE together. At beat γ they all reset their counters and will have positive $Counter$ values for at least $Cycle'$ rounds. Since $Cycle' > \Delta$, in the following Δ beats, the value of $WantToPulse$ will be 0, and hence $\mathcal{BBB}_1$ is initialized during these beats with the value 0. Therefore, once these values will emerge from $\mathcal{BBB}$, there will be a period of $Cycle' > \Delta$ with no pulses. That "quiet" period will start at beat $\gamma + \Delta$. This quiet period might be longer than $Cycle'$, if there were other PULSEs during the beat interval $[\gamma, \gamma + \Delta]$. In any case, a quiet period will commence at beat $\gamma + \Delta$ and will be at least $Cycle'$ beats long, and no more than $Cycle' + \Delta$ beats long.

Now consider what happens after this quiet period. Eventually, the value of $WantToPulse$ will be set to 1 (after no more than $Cycle' + \Delta$ beats), and will stay so until the next PULSE. Mark the beat at which all nodes in $\mathcal{G}$ set $WantToPulse$ to 1 as γ'. Notice that because the quiet period is greater than Δ, then once its values start emerging of $\mathcal{BBB}_\Delta$ there will be a quiet period for at least Δ beats. Hence, once $WantToPulse$ is set to 1, it will stay that way for Δ beats, until 1 comes out of $\mathcal{BBB}_\Delta$. This will happen at beat $\gamma' + \Delta$. Once this happens, there are Δ 1's "on the way" in the coming $\mathcal{BBB}$s. Therefore, there will be a PULSE for Δ beats. Due to the first PULSE, $WantToPulse$ will be 0 for all the Δ PULSE beats. After the last PULSE beat, $WantToPulse$ will be 0 for an additional $Cycle'$ beats. Afterwards, $WantToPulse$ will turn to 1, and will stay so for Δ beats. Thus there is a pattern of $WantToPulse$ being 0 for $\Delta + Cycle'$ beats then being 1 for Δ beats, and so on. Therefore, the PULSEing pattern will satisfy the requirement.

Note that the PULSEing pattern starts on beat $\gamma' + \Delta$, and the pattern continues (at least) until beat β. Hence, the system is $[\Delta, \Delta + Cycle']$-PULSING in the beat interval $[\gamma' + \Delta, \beta]$. Because $\gamma' \leq \gamma + Cycle' + \Delta$ and since $\gamma \leq \alpha + \Delta + Cycle'$, we conclude that $\gamma' + \Delta \leq \alpha + 3 \cdot \Delta + 2 \cdot Cycle'$, as required.   □

Remark 5. The above lemma shows that the convergence time of the PULSEing algorithm depends on the value of $Cycle$. However, since for clock synchronization the value of $Cycle$ is in the order of Δ, the convergence of the clock synchronization will depend on Δ and not on the value of *max-clock* (the wrap around value of the digital clock).

The following theorem states that we have constructed a $[\Delta, \Delta + Cycle']$-PULSER.

Theorem 1. *The Large-Cycle-Pulser algorithm is a $[\Delta, \Delta + Cycle']$-PULSER.*

Proof. By Lemma 3, once there are enough nodes that have not been subject to transient failures for $3 \cdot \Delta + 2 \cdot Cycle'$ beats, the system becomes $[\Delta, \Delta + Cycle']$-PULSING for the beat interval $[\gamma' + \Delta, \beta]$. This is true for any $\beta \geq \alpha + 3 \cdot \Delta + 2 \cdot Cycle'$. Hence, as long as the system is coherent, once the system is $[\Delta, \Delta + Cycle']$-PULSING in the beat interval $[\gamma' + \Delta, \beta]$, it is also $[\Delta, \Delta + Cycle']$-PULSING in the beat interval $[\gamma' + \Delta, \beta + 1]$; and therefore Large-Cycle-Pulser algorithm is a $[\Delta, \Delta + Cycle']$-PULSER.   □

5   A $[Cycle]$-PULSER for $Cycle > 0$

In the previous section a $[\Delta, \Delta + Cycle']$-PULSER was presented, for any value of $Cycle' > \Delta$. Now a general way to transform a $[\phi, \psi]$-PULSER into a $[\phi + \psi]$-PULSER is given. Combining this with the previous result produces a $[2 \cdot \Delta + Cycle']$-PULSER. Since $Cycle' > \Delta$, this technique constructs a $[Cycle]$-PULSER, for any $Cycle > 3 \cdot \Delta$. In Subsection 5.2 this requirement is eliminated, and the objective of building $[Cycle]$-PULSER is achieved for any $Cycle > 0$.

5.1 $[\phi, \psi]$-PULSER to $[\phi + \psi]$-PULSER

Given a $[\phi, \psi]$-PULSER $\mathcal{A}$, the algorithm $\mathcal{B}$ in Figure 2 uses $\mathcal{A}$ as a black-box:

Note that the above algorithm $\mathcal{B}$ does not rely on anything other than the output of $\mathcal{A}$ in the current and previous beats. Hence, if $\mathcal{A}$ is self-stabilizing, so is $\mathcal{B}$.

Algorithm $[\phi + \psi]$-PULSER   /* executed repeatedly at each beat */

1. execute a single round of $\mathcal{A}$;
2. if $\mathcal{A}$ PULSEd at the current beat and $\mathcal{A}$ did not PULSE at the previous beat, then $\mathcal{B}$ PULSEs at the current beat.

Fig. 2. An algorithm that transforms a $[\phi, \psi]$-PULSER into a $[\phi + \psi]$-PULSER

Theorem 2. *The algorithm $\mathcal{B}$ is a $[\phi + \psi]$-PULSER.*

Proof. $\mathcal{A}$ is a $[\phi, \psi]$-PULSER, hence, it PULSEs in a pattern of ϕ pulses, then ψ quiet rounds. Therefore, once every $\phi + \psi$ beats, there is a transition from not PULSEing to PULSEing. Thus, the PULSEing output of $\mathcal{A}$, implies that exactly once every $\phi + \psi$ beats it holds that $\mathcal{A}$ PULSEd at the current beat, and did not PULSE at the previous beat. This is continuously true (as long as $\mathcal{A}$ continues to PULSE), which implies that the proposed algorithm $\mathcal{B}$ will PULSE exactly once every $\phi + \psi$ beats, in a pattern of a single PULSE, and then $\phi + \psi - 1$ beats of quiet rounds.

Since $\mathcal{A}$ is a $[\phi, \psi]$-PULSER, starting from an arbitrary state, it eventually starts PULSEing in the required pattern, and continues so as long as the system is coherent. Hence, the above algorithm $\mathcal{B}$ will eventually start PULSEing in the expected pattern, and will continue so as long as the system is coherent. Hence it is a $[\phi + \psi]$-PULSER.   □

5.2   Case $Cycle \leq 3 \cdot \Delta$

Building upon the $[2 \cdot \Delta + Cycle']$-PULSER, $\mathcal{B}$, from the previous subsection, a $[Cycle]$-PULSER, $\mathcal{C}$, for any $Cycle \leq 3 \cdot \Delta$ is presented in Figure 3.

Theorem 3. *The algorithm $\mathcal{C}$ is a $[Cycle]$-PULSER for any $1 \leq Cycle \leq 3 \cdot \Delta$.*

Algorithm $[Cycle \leq 3 \cdot \Delta]$-PULSER   /* executed repeatedly at each beat */

/* set $Cycle' > \Delta$ to be such that $Cycle' + 2 \cdot \Delta$ is divisible by $Cycle$ */

1. execute $\mathcal{B}$;
2. if $\mathcal{B}$ PULSEd at the current beat then
   $Counter := Cycle' + 2 \cdot \Delta$;
3. if $Counter$ is divisible by $Cycle$ then
   $\mathcal{C}$ PULSEs at the current beat;
4. $Counter := Counter - 1$.

Fig. 3. A $[Cycle]$-PULSER algorithm for $1 \leq Cycle \leq 3 \cdot \Delta$

Proof. Since $\mathcal{B}$ is a $[Cycle' + 2 \cdot \Delta]$-PULSER, starting from an arbitrary state, eventually it starts PULSEing in a pattern of a single PULSE, and then $Cycle' + 2 \cdot \Delta - 1$ beats of quiet rounds (and continues so as long as the system is coherent). Therefore, eventually, all correct nodes will see the same PULSEing output from $\mathcal{B}$. Hence, each time $\mathcal{B}$ pulses, all correct nodes set $Counter$ to $Cycle' + 2 \cdot \Delta$, and have the same value of $Counter$ at each beat (because they all set it together, and decrease it together). Thus, each time a correct node enters Line 3, all correct nodes do the same. Therefore, all correct nodes have $\mathcal{C}$ PULSE together. Lastly, since each $Cycle$ beats $Counter$ will be divisible by $Cycle$, $\mathcal{C}$ PULSEs once every $Cycle$ beats.

Therefore, for each PULSE of $\mathcal{B}$ we have $\frac{2 \cdot \Delta + Cycle'}{Cycle}$ PULSEs of $\mathcal{C}$. Due to the choice of $Cycle'$ such that $2 \cdot \Delta + Cycle'$ is divisible by $Cycle$, the PULSEs are nicely aligned with the PULSEs of $\mathcal{B}$; and therefore, the above algorithm $\mathcal{C}$ is a $[Cycle]$-PULSER. $\square$

Theorem 4. *For any $Cycle > 0$, a $[Cycle]$-PULSER can be constructed.*

Proof. If $Cycle > 3 \cdot \Delta$, then set $Cycle' := Cycle - 2 \cdot \Delta$. By Theorem 1, construct a $[\Delta, \Delta + Cycle']$-PULSER and by Theorem 2 construct a $[2 \cdot \Delta + Cycle']$-PULSER. According to the choice of $Cycle'$ the required $[Cycle]$-PULSER is constructed.

If $Cycle \leq 3 \cdot \Delta$, calculate $Cycle'$ such that $Cycle' > \Delta$ and $\frac{2 \cdot \Delta + Cycle'}{Cycle}$ is an integer number. Now, by Theorem 1 build a $[\Delta, \Delta + Cycle']$-PULSER. From Theorem 2 construct a $[2 \cdot \Delta + Cycle']$-PULSER. Finally, from the above algorithm construct an algorithm that is a $[Cycle]$-PULSER, as required. $\square$

6 Network Connectivity

The above discussion did not assume anything about the network connectivity. More precisely, the only connectivity assumption was about the behavior of the $\mathcal{BBB}$ protocol. That is, whatever connectivity $\mathcal{BBB}$ requires to operate properly, is the required connectivity in order for the $[Cycle]$-PULSER construction to work properly.

In [5] it is shown that *Byzantine* agreement is achievable if and only if:

1. f is less than one-third of the total number of nodes in the system.
2. f is less than one-half of the connectivity of the system (that is, between any two nodes there are at least $2 \cdot f + 1$ distinct paths).

These lower bounds clearly hold for *Byzantine* consensus. Therefore, since $\mathcal{BBB}$ is implemented by executing *Byzantine* Consensus for each node's input value, $\mathcal{BBB}$ can be tolerant to up to $\frac{n-1}{3}$ *Byzantine* faults. In addition $\mathcal{BBB}$ can work properly even if the connectivity graph is not fully connected, but rather there are at least $2 \cdot f + 1$ distinct paths between any two non-faulty nodes.

Remark 6. As noted in [5], the nodes are required to know the connectivity graph while executing the algorithm. This implies, due to self-stabilization, that each node has the network connectivity as incorruptible data.[5]

Since the PULSEing algorithm presented in this paper depends solely on $\mathcal{BBB}$ for communication with other nodes, it is tolerant up to $\frac{n-1}{3}$ *Byzantine* faults and can operate in a network where there are at least $2 \cdot f + 1$ distinct paths between any two nodes, and it is optimal with respect to these two parameters.

Previous synchronization algorithms do not easily extend to operate in a network that is not fully connected. This is a result of the dependency of their "current state" on messages received in the "current round"; in a network that is not fully connected, such messages are received $\mathcal{D}$ rounds later, where $\mathcal{D}$ is the diameter of the network.

For example, in [12], the $DigiClock$ value depends on the values sent in the current round. Therefore, if the network is not fully connected, node p does not receive messages from node p' that is not his neighbor, in the same round. Hence, p cannot change its current state according to the algorithm's definition. This does not mean that previous algorithms cannot be transformed to operate in such a setting, just that it is not straightforward.

7   Complexity Analysis

Using PULSEing for clock synchronization leads using a *Cycle* that is in the order of Δ. Hence, the PULSEing algorithm presented in the previous sections converges in $O(\Delta)$ beats. If the system is fully connected, then $\Delta = 2f + 3$, because efficient implementations of *Byzantine* consensus require about $2f + 3$ rounds. Therefore, convergence is reached in $O(f)$ beats.

If the system is not fully connected, as discussed in the previous section, and the diameter is $\mathcal{D}$, then $\Delta = \mathcal{D} \cdot 2 \cdot (f + 1)$. Therefore, convergence is reached in $O(\mathcal{D} \cdot f)$ beats.

---

[5] One can somewhat relax this assumption, but then either a flooding algorithm needs to be used, or one needs to come up with an algorithm that finds enough independent paths on the fly - despite the *Byzantine* behavior; we are not aware of any self-stabilizing algorithm to do that.

Considering message complexity, at each beat Δ $\mathcal{BBB}$s are executed simultaneously. Since $\mathcal{BBB}$ can be implemented via *Byzantine* consensus (see Remark 2), it requires n^2 messages at each beat. Hence we have that the message complexity at each beat is $O(f \cdot n^2)$. Note that one can use early stopping agreements. Such agreements will use less messages, if the number of faults is small, but will still take the same worse case time.

8   The Digital Clock Synchronization Problem

In the digital clock synchronization problem, each node has a variable $DigiClock$, and the objective is to have all correct nodes agree on the value of $DigiClock$ and increase it by one at each beat. A more detailed discussion of this problem (along with a solution) is given in [12].

The digital clock synchronization problem is equivalent to the PULSEing problem. Given an algorithm that solves the digital clock synchronization problem, simply PULSE every time the $DigiClock$ variable is divisible by $Cycle$. This produces a $[Cycle]$-PULSER algorithm.

The other direction is a bit more complicated. Given a $[f + 2]$-PULSER algorithm, every PULSE execute a *Byzantine* agreement on what the $DigiClock$ value will be in the next PULSE. In addition, each beat $DigiClock$ is increased by 1, and when the *Byzantine* agreement terminates, the $DigiClock$ is set to the agreement value (similar to [6]). This way, all nodes agree on the value of $DigiClock$ and increase it by one at each beat.

Note that the digital clock synchronization problem has been solved directly in [12] for $f < \frac{n}{4}$ and assuming a fully connected graph. Due to the equivalence to the PULSEing problem, a digital clock synchronization algorithm can be built with an underlying PULSEing algorithm presented in this paper, which supports $f < \frac{n}{3}$ and assumes only that there are $2 \cdot f + 1$ distinct paths between any two nodes. That produces a digital clock synchronization algorithm that is optimal in these two aspects.

9   *Byzantine* Tolerant Stabilizer

We now present briefly how a stabilizer can be built using the PULSEing algorithm provided in the above sections. The stabilizer will *stabilize* a *Byzantine* tolerant algorithm $\mathcal{A}_0$. That is, given a *Byzantine* tolerant algorithm $\mathcal{A}_0$ that is not self-stabilizing, the stabilizer will transform it into a self stabilizing version of $\mathcal{A}_0$ (preserving the *Byzantine* tolerance).

Clearly, not all algorithms can be viewed as self-stabilizing. E.g. an algorithm that is allowed to do some action ACT only once, cannot be a self-stabilizing algorithm. We do not discuss here the requirements of an algorithm $\mathcal{A}_0$ so that it can be stabilized. For a more in depth discussion of such requirements, refer to [10] and [13]. In the following, it is assumed that the *Byzantine* tolerant algorithm $\mathcal{A}_0$ has a meaning as a self-stabilizing algorithm.

Intuitively, every so often, all nodes will collect a global snapshot $\mathcal{S}$ of the local states of all nodes. Then, all nodes inspect $\mathcal{S}$ for any inconsistencies. If any are found, all nodes reset their local state to some consistent state.

Given a general *Byzantine* tolerant algorithm $\mathcal{A}_0$, we construct an algorithm Byz-State-Check. Byz-State-Check gathers a global snapshot of the local states at each node and ensures that the local states are consistent. In addition if the states were consistent to start with, then Byz-State-Check does not alter them. That is, Byz-State-Check alters the local states to a consistent state, only if required. Figure 4 presents the algorithm Byz-State-Check.

Algorithm **Byz-State-Check**   /* *executed at node p*/

1. execute a *Byzantine* agreement on local state of $\mathcal{A}_0$;
2. Δ_{agree} beats after the the beginning of the execution of line 1:
   (a) if $\mathcal{S}$ represents a legal state
       repair local state if it is inconsistent with $\mathcal{S}$;
   (b) otherwise
       reset local state.

Fig. 4. A *Byzantine* tolerant state validation and reset

Remark 7. Δ_{agree} is an upper bound on the number of rounds it takes to execute *Byzantine* agreement ($2f+3$ for a typical efficient implementation). Since all correct nodes wait Δ_{agree} beats from entering line 1 until entering line 2, it is ensured that all correct nodes enter line 2 after they see the same global snapshot $\mathcal{S}$.

Given a general *Byzantine* tolerant algorithm $\mathcal{A}_0$, a $[\Delta_{agree} + 1]$-PULSER $\mathcal{P}$ and a Byz-State-Check algorithm $\mathcal{C}$, the algorithm SS-Byz-Stabilizer is constructed, as in Figure 5.

Algorithm **SS-Byz-Stabilizer**   /* *executed at each beat* */
                              /* $\mathcal{A}_0$ *is the algorithm to be stabilized* */
                              /* $\mathcal{C}$ *is an instance of Byz-State-Check*/
                              /* $\mathcal{P}$ *is a* $[\Delta_{agree} + 1]$-PULSER */

1. execute a single round of $\mathcal{A}_0$;
2. execute a single round of $\mathcal{C}$;
3. execute a single beat of $\mathcal{P}$;
4. if $\mathcal{P}$ PULSEd this beat re-initialize $\mathcal{C}$.

Fig. 5. A Self-stabilizing *Byzantine* tolerant Stabilizer

Theorem 5. *SS-Byz-Stabilizer transforms a* Byzantine *tolerant algorithm* $\mathcal{A}_0$ *into Self-stabilizing* Byzantine *tolerant algorithm.*

Proof. $\mathcal{P}$ is a $[\Delta_{agree}+1]$-PULSER. Hence, eventually it starts PULSEing $\Delta_{agree}+1$ beats apart. When this happens, $\mathcal{C}$ is re-executed periodically, and terminates between such 2 executions . Hence, $\mathcal{C}$ performs correctly. This means that the local states of $\mathcal{A}_0$ will be consistent. And we have that starting from any initial state of $\mathcal{A}_0$'s local states, eventually $\mathcal{A}_0$'s local states are consistent.   □

Acknowledgments

We would like to thank Ariel Daliot for helpful discussions and insightful comments.

References

1. Afek, Y., Dolev, S.: Local stabilizer. In: Proc. of the 5th Israeli Symposium on Theory of Computing Systems (ISTCS97), Bar-Ilan, Israel (June 1997)
2. Arora, A., Dolev, S., Gouda, M.G.: Maintaining digital clocks in step. Parallel Processing Letters 1, 11–18 (1991)
3. Daliot, A., Dolev, D.: Self-stabilization of byzantine protocols. In: Tixeuil, S., Herman, T. (eds.) SSS 2005. LNCS, vol. 3764. Springer, Heidelberg (2005)
4. Daliot, A., Dolev, D., Parnas, H.: Linear time byzantine self-stabilizing clock synchronization. In: Papatriantafilou, M., Hunel, P. (eds.) OPODIS 2003. LNCS, vol. 3144, Springer, Heidelberg (2004), http://arxiv.org/abs/cs.DC/0608096
5. Dolev, D.: The byzantine generals strike again. Journal of Algorithms 3, 14–30 (1982)
6. Dolev, D., Halpern, J.Y., Simons, B., Strong, R.: Dynamic fault-tolerant clock synchronization. J. Assoc. Computing Machinery 42(1), 143–185 (1995)
7. Dolev, S.: Possible and impossible self-stabilizing digital clock synchronization in general graphs. Journal of Real-Time Systems 12(1), 95–107 (1997)
8. Dolev, S., Welch, J.L.: Wait-free clock synchronization. Algorithmica 18(4), 486–511 (1997)
9. Dolev, S., Welch, J.L.: Self-stabilizing clock synchronization in the presence of byzantine faults. Journal of the ACM 51(5), 780–799 (2004)
10. Gopal, A.S., Perry, K.J.: Unifying self-stabilization and fault-tolerance. In: IEEE Proceedings of the 12th annual ACM symposium on Principles of distributed computing, Ithaca, New York (1993)
11. Herman, T.: Phase clocks for transient fault repair. IEEE Transactions on Parallel and Distributed Systems 11(10), 1048–1057 (2000)
12. Hoch, E.N., Dolev, D., Daliot, A.: Self-stabilizing byzantine digital clock synchronization. In: Datta, A.K., Gradinariu, M. (eds.) SSS 2006. LNCS, vol. 4280, Springer, Heidelberg (2006)
13. Katz, S., Perry, K.J.: Self-stabilizing extensions for message-passing systems. Distributed Computing 7(1), 17–26 (1993)
14. Nesterenko, M., Arora, A.: Dining philosophers that tolerate malicious crashes. In: 22nd Int. Conference on Distributed Computing Systems (2002)
15. Nesterenko, M., Arora, A.: Tolerance to unbounded byzantine faults. In: SRDS, p. 22 (2002)
16. Papatriantafilou, M., Tsigas, P.: On self-stabilizing wait-free clock synchronization. Parallel Processing Letters 7(3), 321–328 (1997)
17. Sakurai, Y., Ooshita, F., Masuzawa, T.: A self-stabilizing link-coloring protocol resilient to byzantine faults in tree networks. In: OPODIS, pp. 283–298 (2004)

Gossiping in a Multi-channel Radio Network

An Oblivious Approach to Coping with Malicious Interference
(Extended Abstract)

Shlomi Dolev[1], Seth Gilbert[2], Rachid Guerraoui[3], and Calvin Newport[4]

[1] Ben-Gurion University
dolev@cs.bgu.ac.il
[2] MIT CSAIL, EPFL IC
seth.gilbert@epfl.ch
[3] EPFL IC
rachid.guerraoui@epfl.ch
[4] MIT CSAIL
cnewport@mit.edu

Abstract. We study oblivious deterministic gossip algorithms for multi-channel radio networks with a malicious adversary. In a multi-channel network, each of the n processes in the system must choose, in each round, one of the c channels of the system on which to participate. Assuming the adversary can disrupt one channel per round, preventing communication on that channel, we establish a tight bound of $\max\left(\Theta\left(\frac{(1-\epsilon)n}{c-1} + \log_c n\right), \Theta\left(\frac{n(1-\epsilon)}{\epsilon c^2}\right)\right)$ on the number of rounds needed to solve the ϵ-gossip problem, a parameterized generalization of the all-to-all gossip problem that requires $(1-\epsilon)n$ of the "rumors" to be successfully disseminated. Underlying our lower bound proof lies an interesting connection between ϵ-gossip and extremal graph theory. Specifically, we make use of Turán's theorem, a seminal result in extremal combinatorics, to reason about an adversary's optimal strategy for disrupting an algorithm of a given duration. We then show how to generalize our upper bound to cope with an adversary that can simultaneously disrupt $t < c$ channels. Our generalization makes use of selectors: a combinatorial tool that guarantees that any subset of processes will be "selected" by some set in the selector. We prove this generalized algorithm optimal if a maximum number of values is to be gossiped. We conclude by extending our algorithm to tolerate traditional Byzantine corruption faults.

1 Introduction

Malicious adversaries pose a particular threat to radio networks. Due to the shared nature of the communication medium, an adversary can prevent *any* information exchange between honest processes by jamming the channel with noise. The first attempts to tackle this problem assumed that the malicious adversary could only corrupt honest processes, but not interfere with communication [1, 2, 3]. Another approach assumed that the adversary interferes only in a probabilistic manner, causing either random transient message corruption [4], or random permanent process corruptions [5]. More recent work allows malicious interference—but bounds the number of times that the adversary can disrupt communication [6, 7].

A. Pelc (Ed.): DISC 2007, LNCS 4731, pp. 208–222, 2007.

In this paper, we place no such restrictions on the adversary. Instead, we shift our focus to multi-channel radio networks in which each process can make use of any one of c available channels in each round. The adversary can disrupt communication by broadcasting concurrently on a channel with an honest process, causing a collision. This setting is appealing because of its practicality. Almost every major commercial/industrial/military radio device—including sensor motes, laptops running 802.11, and bluetooth-enabled devices—has the capability to switch between multiple communication channels. These multi-channel networks have been studied previously in the context of communication capacity and throughput (e.g., [8, 9]). They have also been studied in the field of Cognitive Radio Networks [10, 11, 12], where algorithms attempt to adaptively compensate for (semi-permanently) disrupted communication channels.

The Gossip Problem. We study the fundamental problem of *gossip* in which processes attempt to exchange *rumors*. Variants of this problem have been well-studied in (synchronous) single-channel radio networks: for broadcast in a fault-free network, see, for example, [13, 14, 15, 16]; for omissions and crash failures, see, for example, [17, 18]. We introduce a parameterized version of the gossip problem, called ϵ-gossip, in which $(1 - \epsilon)n$ rumors must be disseminated to at least $n - 1$ processes. (As we later show, it is impossible to disseminate even a single value to all n receivers in this setting). The ϵ-gossip problem is a generalization of classical *all-to-all gossip* (0-gossip) that allows for flexibility in the number of rumors that need to be spread—a desirable feature for many applications (e.g., when only a majority vote is needed).

Basic Setting. We assume that honest processes maintain no shared secrets (e.g., information unknown to the adversary). The honest processes could use such information to derive a transmission pattern that appears random to an outside observer. (Military communication systems, like those used by the MILSTAR satellite system, use such a scheme to evade eavesdroppers). We omit this possibility for three reasons. First, we are interested in deterministic solutions that guarantee correctness even in the worst case. Second, for low-resource devices—such as RFID tags or tiny sensor motes—cryptographic calculations (particularly of the public-key variety) and secure key dissemination may be prohibitively expensive. Third, shared secrets are hard to maintain when the adversary can corrupt and hijack honest devices (addressed in Section 9).

With such devices in mind, we focus on oblivious algorithms—those in which a process's decision to transmit or listen in a given round on a given channel is a function only of its unique identifier, the round number, and the number of processes and channels in the network. Oblivious algorithms are appealing because they are considered easy to construct and deploy. (In Section 10, we briefly discuss randomized and adaptive solutions.)

Results. We prove that $\max\left(\Theta\left(\frac{(1-\epsilon)n}{c-1} + \log_c n\right), \Theta\left(\frac{n(1-\epsilon)}{\epsilon c^2}\right)\right)$ rounds are necessary and sufficient to solve ϵ-gossip in a setting where the adversary can disrupt one channel per round, and n is the total number of processes. We demonstrate necessity by first reducing ϵ-gossip to a graph-theoretic game—(n, ϵ)-*clique destruction*—in which a player tries to remove enough edges from an n-clique to destroy any clique of size greater than ϵn, and then proving a lower bound on this game by appealing to Turán's Theorem [19], a seminal result in extremal combinatorics.

To demonstrate sufficiency, we describe a matching deterministic oblivious algorithm that proceeds in two phases. During the first phase, a sufficient number of values are disseminated to a distinguished group of *listeners* distributed among the channels. The resulting construction, when considered in the context of extremal graph theory, produces a Turán Graph. During the second phase, these values are disseminated to increasingly larger sets of processes until $n-1$ have learned the total requisite knowledge.

We then generalize our algorithm for the multi-channel adversary that can simultaneously disrupt up to $t < c$ channels. This models a network with t adversarial processes, each potentially disrupting a different channel. Our algorithm presented for $t = 1$ extends naturally to this scenario: the generalized first phase, in fact, relates to a conjectured hypergraph-generalization of Turán's Theorem; the second phase uses *selectors*, a combinatorial device introduced by [20], to generalize the dissemination schedule. We show this solution to be optimal for the natural case of $\epsilon = t/n$ (i.e., trying to gossip the maximum possible number of values). We conclude by describing how to modify our algorithm to tolerate traditional Byzantine corruption faults.

2   Model

We consider a system of n honest processes, each assigned a unique identifier in the range $[1..n]$. The processes inhabit a single-hop radio network comprised of c communication channels: $1 < c \leq n$. We first assume the presence of a malicious adversary that can corrupt one channel per round. We then consider the general case where it can simultaneously disrupt $t < c$ channels in each round.

Synchronous Rounds. Executions proceed in synchronous rounds. In each round, each process chooses a single channel on which to participate: it can either transmit or receive on that channel. In each round the adversary chooses up to t channels to disrupt. If exactly one process transmits a message m on channel k in a round, and the adversary does not disrupt channel k, then every process receiving on channel k receives message m. When two processes broadcast in the same round on the same channel, the message is lost. (We do not assume that the processes have the capacity to detect collisions.)

Deterministic and Oblivious. We consider deterministic, oblivious gossip algorithms. An oblivious algorithm is one in which the broadcast schedule is determined in advance. Formally, a *deterministic oblivious algorithm* is a sequence $\mathcal{A} = \langle A_1, \ldots, A_r \rangle$ where each $A_r : [1..n] \to \{\text{trans}, \text{recv}, \bot\} \times [1..c]$ is a function describing the behavior of the processes in round i. For example, when $A_r(i) = \langle \text{trans}, k \rangle$, it indicates that in round r, process i transmits on channel k; when $A_r(i) = \langle \text{recv}, k \rangle$, then process i receives on channel k. Without loss of generality, for the lower bound we consider *full information protocols* in which processes always transmit their entire state. Also without loss of generality, we assume each initial value is unique.

3   The Gossip Problem

Each process begins with an initial value (or "rumor") which it attempts to disseminate to the other processes. In this paper we consider the (ϵ, δ)-gossip problem in which all but δn processes must receive a common set of all but ϵn of the initial values. This definition is a generalization of commonly considered communication primitives: for example, all-to-all gossip is $(0,0)$-gossip and one-to-all broadcast is $(1 - \frac{1}{n}, 0)$-gossip. Formally, algorithm $\mathcal{A}$ *solves* the (ϵ, δ)-gossip problem if and only if, for all possible adversarial choices, at least $(1 - \delta)n$ honest processes successfully receive a common set of at least $(1 - \epsilon)n$ initial values.

In this setting, it is clearly impossible to ensure that *all* n honest processes successfully receive even one common initial value. Assume there existed such an $(\epsilon, 0)$-gossip algorithm $\mathcal{A}$, and consider the adversarial strategy $\mathcal{C}$ in which the adversary always disrupts the channel on which process 1 either transmits or receives. Under these conditions, process 1 can never successfully transmit or receive any value: it neither learns the initial value of any other process, nor does any other process learn its initial value, implying that $\mathcal{A}$ does not solve $(\epsilon, 0)$-gossip. By the same argument, it is impossible to solve $(0, \delta)$-gossip.

Hence, we focus on solving the $(\epsilon, t/n)$-gossip problem where $t/n \leq \epsilon \leq 1$, that is, the problem in which all but ϵn initial values are disseminated to all but t processes. (Considering larger values of δ does not allow for significantly faster termination for most values of ϵ.) For the remainder of the paper, we refer to the $(\epsilon, \frac{t}{n})$-gossip problem where $t/n \leq \epsilon \leq 1$ simply as: ϵ-gossip.

Roadmap. In Sections 4, 5 and 6, we address the case where $t = 1$. In Section 4 we present a lower bound, in Section 5 we present a matching algorithm, and in Section 6 we outline the proof. In Section 7, we extend our algorithm to tolerate a multi-channel adversary that can block an arbitrary $t < c$ channels. In Section 9, we consider a more general model in which the adversary can corrupt honest players (rather than simply disrupting communication). We conclude with a discussion of open questions in Section 10.

4   A Lower Bound for ϵ-Gossip Where $t = 1$

Let $\mathcal{A}$ be an arbitrary deterministic oblivious algorithm for ϵ-gossip where $t = 1$. We show that $\mathcal{A}$ requires

$$\max\left(\Theta\left(\frac{(1 - \epsilon)n}{c - 1} + \log_c n \right), \ \Theta\left(\frac{n(1 - \epsilon)}{\epsilon c^2} \right) \right)$$

rounds to terminate. The first term dominates when $\epsilon \geq 1/c$ (i.e., only a small number of values need to be disseminated), and it follows from the observation that at most $c - 1$ values can be broadcast in each round. In this section, we focus predominantly on the (more interesting) case where $\epsilon < 1/c$. For every execution α of algorithm $\mathcal{A}$, let round $R^{\text{trans}}(\alpha)$ be the minimum round such that the following is true: at least $(1-\epsilon)n$ of the honest processes have broadcast without being disrupted by the adversary in the prefix of α through round $R^{\text{trans}}(\alpha)$. We show that for some execution α of $\mathcal{A}$, $R^{\text{trans}}(\alpha) \geq \Omega(\frac{n(1-\epsilon)}{\epsilon c^2})$. It follows that the protocol cannot terminate in α prior to round $R^{\text{trans}}(\alpha)$—implying the second term of our bound.

We prove this result by exploiting an interesting connection between oblivious ϵ-gossip and graph theory. An oblivious algorithm can be imagined as a sequence of edge removals from an n-clique, and the adversary's optimal strategy can be described by the largest clique that remains after these removals. Accordingly, we turn to the field of extremal combinatorics and apply Turán's Theorem [19] to argue precisely about the size of the cliques that remain in a graph, which in turn tells us the adversary's best strategy.

Definition 1 (The (n, ϵ)-Clique Destruction Game). *Let $G = (V, E)$ be a graph describing a clique on n nodes. We say that a subset of edges $S \subseteq E$ is a solution to the (n, ϵ)-clique destruction game if and only if the graph $G' = (V, E - S)$ contains no clique of size greater than ϵn.*

Turán's theorem relates the largest clique in a graph and the number of edges in a graph:

Theorem 1 (Turán's Theorem [19]). *If graph $G = (V, E)$ has no subgraph that is a clique of size $k + 1$, then $|E| \leq (1 - 1/k) \left(n^2/2 \right)$.*

From this we derive an immediate corollary:

Corollary 1. *Fix $S \subseteq E$ a solution to the (n, ϵ)-clique destruction game. Then $|S| \geq n(1 - \epsilon)/(2\epsilon)$.*

Proof. By Theorem 1 where $k = \epsilon n$: subtract from the $\binom{n}{2}$ edges in an n-clique the maximum number of edges in a graph with no cliques of size $\epsilon n + 1$, as per Theorem 1, to get the minimum size of S.

We next connect the (n, ϵ)-clique destruction game to the ϵ-gossip problem:

Lemma 1. *If for every execution α of algorithm $\mathcal{A}$, $R^{\text{trans}}(\alpha) \leq r$, then there exists a solution S to the (n, ϵ)-clique destruction game such that $|S| \leq c^2 r$.*

Proof. Without loss of generality, assume that $\mathcal{A}$ assigns exactly one process to transmit on each channel in each round. Construct S as follows: add edge (a, b) to S if, for some round $r' \leq r$, processes a and b both broadcast in round r'. Since for each $r' \leq r$ there are at most $\binom{c}{2}$ such pairs, we conclude that $|S| \leq c^2 r$.

Suppose, for contradiction, that nodes $V' \subseteq V$ form a clique of size $> \epsilon n$ in the residual graph. We construct the following strategy to thwart $\mathcal{A}$: whenever a process in V' attempts to broadcast on channel k, the adversary disrupts channel k. This is always possible as no two processes in V' broadcast in the same round (by the construction of S). This violates the correctness of $\mathcal{A}$, implying a contradiction.

We combines these two lemmas to obtain our final bound:

Theorem 2. *For any deterministic oblivious algorithm, $\mathcal{A}$, that solves ϵ-gossip,*

$$|\mathcal{A}| \geq \max\left(\Theta\left(\frac{(1 - \epsilon)n}{c - 1} + \log_c n \right), \Theta\left(\frac{n(1 - \epsilon)}{\epsilon c^2} \right) \right).$$

Proof. If $\mathcal{A}$ solves ϵ-gossip, then for every execution α of algorithm $\mathcal{A}$, there exists a round r such that $R^{\mathsf{trans}}(\alpha) \leq r$. We begin by establishing the first term of the bound. Since at most $c - 1$ values can be transmitted without disruption in each round, it is clear that $r \geq (1 - \epsilon)n/(c - 1)$. Let r' be the round in which the last of these $(1 - \epsilon)n$ values is transmitted. For each of the $n - 1$ processes that ultimately learn all $(1 - \epsilon)n$ values, there must be some round $\geq r'$ in which it listens on a non-disrupted channel. Let r'' be the latest of these rounds. We know $r'' \geq r' + \log_c n - 1$, as over the first $\log_c n - 1$ rounds there are only $c^{\log_c n - 1} < n - 1$ different channel-listening patterns a process can follow; by the pigeonhole principle this results in two processes listening on the same channels for these first $\log_c n - 1$ rounds, allowing the adversary to block both processes. Together these two pieces form the first term of the lower bound.

For the second term of the lower bound we turn to our Turán-derived results. From Lemma 1 we know there exists a set of edges S that solves the (n, ϵ)-clique destruction game, such that $c^2 r \geq |S|$. By Corollary 1 we know: $|S| \geq n(1 - \epsilon)/(2\epsilon)$. This implies $r \geq \Theta\left(\frac{n(1-\epsilon)}{\epsilon c^2}\right)$.

5   An Upper Bound for ϵ-Gossip Where $t = 1$

In this section we describe a deterministic oblivious algorithm for solving the ϵ-gossip problem when $\epsilon < 1/c$. In Section 8, we discuss the (simpler) case where $\epsilon \geq 1/c$. For the sake of concision, we make a few simplifying assumptions. First, we assume that $n > 6c$. For smaller values of n, the algorithm can simply restrict itself to a subset of the channels. Second, we assume that the number of channels c is even. For odd c, the algorithm can restrict itself to $c - 1$ channels. Finally, we assume that $\epsilon \geq \frac{2c+1}{n}$ (slightly larger than the trivial $\epsilon \geq 1/n$ lower bound for ϵ). In Section 5.3 we describe how to remove this last assumption.

5.1   The *Gossip* Protocol

The gossip protocol (see Figure 1) constructs an oblivious algorithm that solves the ϵ-gossip problem for $\epsilon < 1/c$. Recall, an oblivious algorithm is a sequence $\mathcal{A} = A_1, A_2, \ldots$ where each A_i is a function from processes $[1 \ldots n]$ to actions $\{\mathsf{trans}, \mathsf{recv}\}$ and channels $[1 \ldots c]$. Throughout the description, we use the notation divide(S, k) to refer to a partition of the set S into $\lceil |S|/k \rceil$ sets of size k, one of which may have fewer than k elements if $|S|$ does not divide evenly by k. Also, $i[b]$ refers to the bth bit of the binary representation of i. Our protocol proceeds in two parts.

Part I: Initially, the processes are divided into two sets: a set of $2c$ *listeners*, consisting of processes $P_\ell = \{1, \ldots, 2c\}$, and a set of (at least $4c$) *transmitters* P_{tran}, consisting of the remaining processes. Each channel is assigned a pair of two listeners. Next, the InfoTransfer(ϵ') routine is used to transfer all but $\epsilon'n + 2c$ of the initial values to some pair of listeners. (The additive $2c$ represents the listeners' values that are not transmitted.) By choosing $\epsilon' = \epsilon - 2c/n$, this ensures that all but ϵn initial values are known to some pair of listeners (in Section 5.3 we discuss how to allow the listeners to participate).

Part II: The goal of the second part is to disseminate the information acquired by each pair of listeners to all but one process. We say that a set is *knowledgeable* with respect to

---

1 **Gossip**(ϵ)
2   ; *Part I: Transfer info from transmitters to listeners.*
3    $P_\ell \leftarrow \{i \mid 1 \leq i \leq 2c\}$
4    $P_{tran} \leftarrow \{i \mid 2c < i \leq n\}$
5   *channel-assignment* $\leftarrow$ divide$(P_\ell, 2)$
6   InfoTransfer$(\epsilon - \frac{2c}{n}, P_{tran}, P_\ell, channel\text{-}assignement, \langle A_1, \dots \rangle)$
7
8   ; *Part II, Step 1: Create c knowledgable sets in two steps.*
9   *Psets* $\leftarrow$ divide$(P_{tran}, \lceil P_{tran}/c \rceil)$
10   **for** $(chan = 1$ **to** $c/2)$ **do**
11   disseminate2$(channel\text{-}assignment[chan], Psets[chan], chan, chan+c/2, \langle B_1, \dots \rangle)$
12   **for** $(chan = c/2+1$ **to** $c)$ **do**
13      $L \leftarrow channel\text{-}assignment[chan]$
14   disseminate2$(channel\text{-}assignment[chan], Psets[chan], chan-c/2, chan, \langle C_1, \dots \rangle)$
15
16   ; *Part II, Step 2: Combine channels.*
17    $r \leftarrow 1$
18   **while** $(|Psets| > 1)$ **do**
19   *newPsets* $\leftarrow \emptyset$
20      $s \leftarrow \lfloor |Psets|/2 \rfloor$
21   **for** $(i = 1$ **to** $s)$ **do**
22        $P \leftarrow$ combine$(Psets[i], Psets[i+s], i, i + c/2, \langle D_r, \dots \rangle)$
23   *newPsets* $\leftarrow$ *newPsets* $\cup P$
24   ; *If the size of Psets is odd, we let the last set pass through uncombined.*
25   **if** $(2s+1 = |Psets|)$ **then**
26   *newPsets* $\leftarrow$ *newPsets* $\cup Psets[2s+1]$
27   *Psets* $\leftarrow$ *newPsets*
28      $r \leftarrow r + 6\lceil \log n \rceil + 36$
29   **return** $\mathcal{A}.\mathcal{B}.\mathcal{C}.\mathcal{D}$

Fig. 1. An algorithm for solving the ϵ-gossip problem $(\epsilon < 1/c)$

some set of initial values if all but one process in the set has received the initial values. The second part of the gossip protocol proceeds in two steps. First, the transmitter processes are divided into c sets, one per channel. (The variable *Psets* stores these c sets). The two listeners associated with each channel disseminate the information acquired in Part I to the set of transmitters assigned to that channel. This dissemination step uses two channels, and thus we can run $c/2$ instances in parallel: in the first $\lceil \log n \rceil$ rounds, we perform the dissemination for channels $1, \dots, c/2$; in the next $\lceil \log n \rceil$ rounds, we perform the dissemination for channels $c/2 + 1, \dots, c$. In each case, this dissemination is accomplished using the disseminate2 routine. At the end of this step, each set of processes in *Psets* is knowledgeable with respect to the set of values known to the listeners on their channel.

In the second step, we repeatedly combine pairs of knowledgeable sets (via the combine routine) into larger knowledgeable sets in which the processes know values from both of the original sets. We continue combining sets until we are left with a single set in which the processes know the required $(1 - \epsilon)n$ values.

```
1  InfoTransfer(ε', P_{tran}, P_ℓ, channel-assignment, ⟨A_1, . . .⟩)
2     ; Assign listeners to channels.
3     for every round r, for every channel k do
4        {a, b} ← channel-assignment[k]
5        A_r(a) ← ⟨recv, k⟩
6        A_r(b) ← ⟨recv, k⟩
7     ; Assign transmitters to channels.
8     r ← 0
9     for every B ∈ divide(P_{tran} ∪ P_ℓ, 1/ ε') do
10       B_{subs} ← divide(B, c/2)
11       for every (S_1, S_2) ∈ B_{subs} × B_{subs} do
12          chan ← 1
13          for every i ∈ S_1 ∪ S_2
14             A_r(i) ← ⟨trans, chan⟩
15             chan ← chan+1
16          r ← r+1
```

Fig. 2. Routines to transfer information from transmitters to listeners

```
1  disseminate2(L, P, c_1, c_2, ⟨A_1, . . .⟩)
2     {a_1,a_2} ← L
3     for b = 1 to ⌈lg n⌉
4        A_b(a_1) ← ⟨trans, c_1⟩
5        A_b(a_2) ← ⟨trans, c_2⟩
6     for b = 1 to ⌈lg n⌉
7        for each i ∈ P
8           if i[b] = 0 then
9              A_b(i) ← ⟨recv, c_1⟩
10          else if i[b] = 1 then
11             A_b(i) ← ⟨recv, c_2⟩
```

Fig. 3. A routine that disseminates data from listeners to arbitrary sets

The Information Transfer Routine. The goal of the InfoTransfer routine (Figure 2) is to ensure that all but $\epsilon'n + 2c$ of the initial values are received by some pair of listeners. Each channel is assigned two listeners, and we assign transmitters to each channel in each round such that the resulting induced graph, as formulated in terms of Lemma 1 and the clique destruction game, forms a Turán Graph.[1]

We divide all processes into sets $\{B_1, B_2, \ldots, B_{\epsilon'n}\}$ of size $1/\epsilon'$; there are $\epsilon'n$ such sets. Our goal is to ensure that all but (at most) one transmitter in each set B_i succeeds in transmitting its value to a pair of listeners. We proceed as follows: For each set B_i, we sub-divide B_i into subsets of size $c/2$, and schedule each of the $\binom{2/\epsilon'c}{2}$ pairs of subsets to broadcast in a round (omitting listeners, which are already occupied).

---

[1] A Turán Graph for value k (say, $k = \epsilon n + 1$), is the unique graph, as proved by Turán, to contain no cliques of size k and to contain the maximum number of edges for which this condition can be true, as established by the theorem of the same name.

```
 1 combine(S₁, S₂, c₁, c₂, ⟨A₁, ...⟩)
 2    r ← 0
 3    for (i = 1 to 2) do
 4       ; Use i and i+2 as witnesses for S₁ :
 5       L ← S₁[i] ∪ S₁[i+2]
 6       P ← S₁ ∪ S₂ − L
 7       disseminate2(L, P, c₁, c₂, ⟨B₁, ...⟩)
 8       A ← A . B
 9    for (i = 1 to 3) do
10       ; Use i and i+3 as witnesses for S₂ :
11       L ← S₂[i] ∪ S₂[i+2]
12       P ← S₁ ∪ S₂ − L
13       disseminate2(L, P, c₁, c₂, ⟨B₁, ...⟩)
14       A ← A . B
15    return S₁ ∪ S₂
```

Fig. 4. A routine to combine knowledgeable sets

Since every pair of non-listeners in B_i broadcast together in some round, the adversary can block at most one non-listener in each set B_i from communicating its value to a listener.   **Running Time:** $\lceil \epsilon' n \binom{2/\epsilon'c}{2} \rceil$.

The Disseminate Routines. The disseminate2$(L, P, c_1, c_2, \ldots)$ routine (Figure 3) disseminates all values known by *both* processes in the set L to all but (at most) one process in the set P, using channels c_1 and c_2. (We assume $|L| = 2$). First, we assign the two processes in L to transmit on channels c_1 and c_2 for $\lceil \log n \rceil$ rounds. In each round b, each process in P chooses a channel on which to receive based on its identifier i: if $i[b] = 0$, it chooses channel c_1; if $i[b] = 1$, it chooses channel c_2. Thus, for any pair of processes in P, there is some round in which they receive on different channels.   **Running Time:** $\lceil \log n \rceil$.

The Combine Routine. The combine$(S_1, S_2, c_1, c_2, \ldots)$ routine (Figure 4) begins with two knowledgeable sets. (We assume that S_1 and S_2 each contain at least 6 processes.) Using two channels, the combine function creates a new knowledgeable set $S_1 \cup S_2$ such that all but (at most) one process in the combined set knows the shared information from *both* S_1 and S_2. The routine accomplishes this goal by running disseminate2 five times. The first two times, it uses pairs of witnesses from set S_1 to disseminate information to set S_2. Since at most one node in S_1 is not knowledgeable, we can conclude that one of these pairs of witnesses is knowledgeable. Hence after the first two calls to the disseminate2 routine, all but one node in $S_1 \cup S_2$ are knowledgeable with respect to the values from S_1. The next three times, it uses pairs of witnesses from set S_2 to disseminate information to set S_1. Notice that there may be two nodes in S_2 that are not fully knowledgeable: one node may not be knowledgeable about S_2's values, and one node may not be knowledgeable about S_1's values. Thus for one of the three pairs of witnesses, both are knowledgeable, and the dissemination succeeds in informing all but one node in $S_1 \cup S_2$.   **Running Time:** $5\lceil \log n \rceil$.

5.2 Running Time of the *Gossip* Protocol

The running time for Gossip is calculated as:

$$[InfoTransfer] + 2[disseminate2] + \lceil \log c \rceil [combine] .$$

This equals: $\lceil \epsilon' n \binom{2/\epsilon' c}{2} \rceil + 2\lceil \log n \rceil + \lceil \log c \rceil (5\lceil \log n \rceil])$. We can simplify this to $\Theta(\frac{n}{\epsilon' c^2})$. Because $\epsilon < 1/c \leq 1/2$, this is equivalent to $\Theta(\frac{n(1-\epsilon)}{\epsilon' c^2})$. The modified algorithm, presented in the next section, improves the running time (marginally) to $\Theta(\frac{n(1-\epsilon)}{\epsilon c^2})$, exactly matching our lower bound for the case where $\epsilon < 1/c$. As mentioned, in Section 8 we provide an algorithm (matching within an additive factor of $\log^2 c$) for the less involved case of $\epsilon \geq 1/c$.

5.3 Achieving ϵ-Gossip for Small ϵ

The algorithm presented in the previous section assumes that $\epsilon \geq (2c + 1)/n$. We now discuss modifying the algorithm to require only $\epsilon \geq 1/n$, the minimum value of ϵ for which the problem can be solved. The difficulty occurs in the InfoTransfer routine, where the listeners do not participate in transmitting their values. Unlike the transmitters, their initial values are known only to themselves, not to a pair of processes. The first step in our modification is to schedule the listeners, P_ℓ, as well as the transmitters, P_{tran}, to transmit their values during the InfoTransfer. If only one of the two listeners assigned to channel k is scheduled to transmit in a round, then it broadcasts on channel k, resulting in no difficulties.

Consider the problematic case where both listeners for channel k are scheduled to transmit in the same round. Since the division into sub-blocks of size $c/2$ is arbitrary, we can ensure that each of the listeners for channel k is in a different sub-block. Thus, there is only one round for which both listeners for a channel might be forced to broadcast. In this case, two "backup listeners" are recruited to monitor channel k during that round. Since there are only c processes scheduled to broadcast in that round, and only $2c$ listeners, there remain at least $2c$ processes to play the role of backup listener. Every channel may be forced to recruit one pair of backup listeners, resulting in $4c$ listeners and backup listeners whose values need to be propagated in the second part of the protocol; the described algorithm extends immediately to this case.

6 Analysis

We now outline an argument that the algorithm from Section 5 solves ϵ-gossip (when $\epsilon < 1/c$). We focus on some of the key invariants satisfied by the different components of the construction. First, we observe that the InfoTransfer routine guarantees that a sufficient number of values are transmitted without adversarial disruption:

Lemma 2. *During the first* $r = \lceil \epsilon n \binom{2/\epsilon c}{2} \rceil$ *rounds, all but* ϵn *of the processes transmit their values in some round* $\leq r$ *without disruption.*

This claim follows from the construction of the schedule: for each of the ϵn sets, all pairs of processes broadcast together in some round. We therefore conclude that the listeners receive a sufficient set of values:

Corollary 2. *At the end of the* InfoTransfer *routine, there exists some set of values* V *of size at least* $(1 - \epsilon)n$ *such that each value* $v \in V$ *is known to some set of* 2 *listeners or backup listeners.*

We next observe that after the first step of Part II (i.e., after the disseminate2 routines) each set in *Psets* is knowledgeable with respect to some subset of the values V:

Lemma 3. *There exists a partition* $V_1, \ldots V_c$ *of the values in* V *such that after the* disseminate2 *routines (i.e., by line 15), each set* $Psets[i]$ *is knowledgeable with respect to* V_i, $1 \le i \le c$.

The proof for this claim follows from the fact that the disseminate2 routine successfully transmits the values from the listeners (or backup listeners) to the remaining nodes in the set; since every node's identifier is unique, there will be some round during the disseminate2 routine in which each pair of nodes is listening on a different channel, and hence will receive the appropriate set of values. Finally, we observe that the combine routine successfully merges knowledgeable sets, which concludes the proof:

Lemma 4. *If* P_i *and* P_j *are knowledgeable sets with respect to some sets of values* V_i *and* V_j, *then set* $P \leftarrow$ combine$(P_i, P_j, \ldots)$ *is knowledgeable with respect to* $V_i \cup V_j$.

This fact follows from the correctness of the disseminate2 routine. We thus conclude:

Theorem 3. *Let* $\mathcal{A}$ *be the deterministic oblivious algorithm constructed by* Gossip. *If* $\epsilon < 1/c$, *then* $\mathcal{A}$ *solves the* ϵ-*gossip problem in time* $O(n(1 - \epsilon)/\epsilon c^2)$.

7   The Multi-channel Adversary $(t < c)$

The algorithm described in Section 5 tolerates an adversary that can disrupt one channel in each round. The algorithm naturally extends to an adversary that can disrupt $t < c$ channels. (Again, for the purpose of brevity, we focus on the case where $\epsilon < t/c$, as this is the more interesting case. The case of $\epsilon \ge t/c$ is described in Section 8.) The overall algorithm maintains the same structure as that presented in Section 5: in the first part, the nodes transmit their values to a set of listeners; in the second part, the listeners become transmitters and create ever-expanding knowledgeable sets.

Part I.   First, we assign $t + 1$ listeners to each channel, instead of 2 listeners. The InfoTransfer routine is modified as follows: The processes are divided into $\epsilon n/t$ sets of size t/ϵ (instead of ϵn sets of size $1/\epsilon$). Each of these sets is subdivided into subsets of size $c/(t+1)$ (instead of size 2). All $\binom{t(t+1)/c\epsilon}{t+1}$ combinations of subsets are scheduled. This ensures that any combination of $t + 1$ nodes in a set broadcast in the same round, and thus that there are at most $t \cdot \epsilon n/t$ nodes that fail to transmit their value. The resulting running time is $O\left(\frac{ne^{t+1}}{c\epsilon^t}\right)$ (approximating the binomial and the fact that $t < c$). Notice that the resulting schedule can be reduced to a $(t + 1)$-hypergraph, in the same manner that the schedules for $t = 1$ could be reduced to a graph. If this construction is optimal, then it corresponds to a hypergraph-generalization of a Turán Graph. Finding such an entity (and proving it optimal) remains an open problem in extremal graph theory.

Part II. In the second part, the listeners disseminate the information to groups of nodes. The basic routine here is a disseminate$[t + 1]$ routine that uses $t + 1$ channels to distribute data from $t + 1$ listeners to a set that becomes knowledgeable. Each of $t + 1$ listeners transmits on one channel throughout the dissemination phase; the rest of the nodes in the set are scheduled to listen on different channels in different rounds such that any set of $t + 1$ nodes is scheduled in some round to listen on different channels.

To accomplish this, we need to introduce an additional tool: selectors, as introduced by Komlos and Greenberg [20] (the term "selector" was coined later by [21]). Let $\mathcal{S}$ be a family of sets, where each $S \in \mathcal{S}$ is a subset of $[1, \ldots, n]$. For integer $k \le n$, we say that $\mathcal{S}$ is a $(n, k, 1)$-**selector** if for every set $A \subseteq [1, \ldots, n]$ where $|A| = k$, there exists a set $S \in \mathcal{S}$ such that $|S \cap A| = 1$. In [20], it was shown that there exist $(n, k, 1)$-selectors of size at most $O(k \log n/k)$, and [22] shows how to explicitly construct selectors of size $O(k\mathrm{polylog}(n))$. For this section, we use the existential bounds from [20], and assume that for all $k \le n$, $\mathcal{S}_k$ is a family of selectors of size $O(k \log n/k)$.

The schedule is constructed recursively. We define $T(c')$ recursively to be the number of rounds needed to construct the schedule for c' channels. In the beginning, we are constructing a schedule for all $c' = t + 1$ channels. If $c' = 2$, then the recursion terminates: schedule the remaining nodes to listen on those two channels as per the disseminate2 routine, i.e., each node chooses a channel based on its identifier. This takes $T(2) = O(\log n)$ rounds. If $c' > 2$, then we use the family of selectors $\mathcal{S}_{c'}$: for each set $S \in \mathcal{S}_{c'}$, schedule the nodes in S to listen on one channel for $T(c' - 1)$ rounds, and recursively schedule the remaining nodes on the remaining $c' - 1$ channels. For each set in $\mathcal{S}_k$ this takes $T(c' - 1)$ rounds, and thus $T(c') = |\mathcal{S}_{c'}|T(c' - 1)$. Since selector $\mathcal{S}_{c'}$ is of size at most $O(c' \log n/c')$, we conclude that the entire schedule for $T(t + 1)$ is (roughly) $O((t + 1)^t \log^t n)$. To see that it satisfies the desired property, consider any subset of $t + 1$ nodes: by definition, exactly one node is selected by one of the sets in $\mathcal{S}_{t+1}$; at the next step of the recursion, one node is selected by a set in $\mathcal{S}_t$, one by a set in $\mathcal{S}_{t-1}$, and so on, until the recursion bottoms out at the simple two-channel case. Thus there exists some round in which all $t + 1$ nodes listen in the same round.

The remaining generalizations of the algorithm from Section 5 are straightforward: the combine routine merges sets S_1 and S_2 as follows: first, it chooses $(t + 1)(t + 1)$ witnesses from set S_1 and runs $t + 1$ iterations of disseminate$[t + 1]$ to set S_2; it then chooses $(2t+1)(t+1)$ witnesses from set S_2 and runs $2t+1$ iterations of disseminate$[t+1]$ to set S_1. (By contrast, in the $t = 1$ case, there were two pairs of witnesses chosen for the first dissemination and three pairs of witness chosen for the second.) It should be noted that using selectors here too would result in improved performance. Thus each combine costs $O((t + 1)^{t+1} \log^t n)$. Since each combine uses $t + 1$ channels, it requires $\frac{c}{t+1} \log c$ iterations of the main loop to combine all c knowledgeable sets.

Noting that $t < c < n$, we thus conclude that the total running time of the gossip protocol is:

$$O\left(\frac{ne^{t+1}}{ce^t} + c(t + 1)^t \log^{t+1} n\right)$$

Lower Bound. Proving a matching lower bound for the general case remains an open question. We can prove that the result is optimal for the natural case of $\epsilon = t/n$, that is, trying to disseminate the maximum possible number of values. Specifically, we claim

$\binom{n}{t+1}/\binom{c}{t+1}$ rounds to be necessary for all but t nodes to transmit even once without being disrupted. The numerator follows from the observation that in order to transmit all but t values without interference, there must exist, for each combination of $t + 1$ processes, a round in which all $t + 1$ processes transmit concurrently (otherwise, the t adversaries can always interference when any of these processes transmit). The denominator follows from the observation that at most $\binom{c}{t+1}$ unique sets of $t + 1$ processes can transmit concurrently on c channels during a single round. This fraction simplifies directly to $\Theta(\frac{n^{t+1}}{c^{t+1}})$, matching our above bound for InfoTransfer (within a factor of $O(e^t)$). Again, notice that proving a hypergraph-generalization of Turán's Theorem would result in an immediate lower bound. (See [23, 24] for more on hypergraph generalizations of Turán's Theorem.)

8   Achieving ϵ-Gossip for Large ϵ

In this section, we describe an algorithm to solve ϵ-gossip when $\epsilon > t/c$.

In the case where $t = 1$, we again divide the protocol into a transmission phase and a dissemination phase. In the transmission phase, we attempt to ensure that $(1 - \epsilon)n$ values are known to a set of $6c$ processes. This is accomplished by assigning six listeners to each channel, and dividing the nodes into groups of size c; each group is assigned one round to broadcast for $(1 - \epsilon)n/(c - 1) \leq n/c$ rounds, ensuring that in each round $c - 1$ nodes succeed. The listeners then exchange their values amongst themselves using the combine routine described in Section 5. The total running time of the transmission phase is $O((1 - \epsilon)n/(c - 1) + \log^2 c)$.

In the dissemination phase, we repeat the following twice, each time with a disjoint set of c "listeners" from the previous phase: each of the "listeners" broadcasts on one of the c channels, and each of the remaining nodes chooses a channel to listen on in each round using the "base-c" representation of its identifier. Since each identifier is unique, we can be sure that for any pair of nodes, in one of these rounds the two nodes choose different channels to listen on, and hence at least one receives the appropriate set of values. The total running time for the dissemination phase is $O(\log_c n)$. Thus the final overall running time of both phases is $O((1 - \epsilon)n/(c - 1) + \log_c n + \log^2 c)$.

When $t > 1$, this strategy generalizes in the natural way: we assign $(2t + 1)(t + 1)$ listeners in the transmission phase, and c nodes broadcast in each round; at least $c - t$ of them succeed, resulting in at least $(1 - \epsilon)n$ values being received by listeners since $(1 - \epsilon)n/(c - t) \leq n/c$; as before, the combine routine, generalized for the multichannel adversary, is then used to combine the data. The total running time in this case is $(1 - \epsilon)n/(c - t) + O(c(t + 1)^t \log^{t+1} n)$.

9   Byzantine Adversary

The algorithms described in Sections 5 and 7 tolerate an adversary that can disrupt communication, but not an adversary that can directly corrupt an "honest" player. It is easy, however, to extend our algorithm to tolerate a Byzantine adversary that corrupts up to t honest players. Each corrupt player can either disrupt a channel or send a message in each round. (Thus, up to t channels can be disrupted, as in the previous case.)

The main modification involves the transmission phase: more listeners are needed on each channel, as some may be Byzantine. Instead of $t+1$ listeners on each channel, we assign $(2t+1)(t+1)$. We then run the disseminate and combine routines $2t+1$ times, each time with a different set of $t+1$ listeners representing each channel. An honest process accepts a value as authentic only if it was received in at least $t+1$ of the $(2t+1)$ runs of disseminate and combine. The running time is increased by a factor of $\Theta(t)$. With further care, the number of listeners can be reduced. However, we conjecture that the problem is solvable only if $n = \Omega(tc)$, for example, in the case where $t = c-1$.

10   Open Questions

The problems discussed introduce several new directions for future research. First, it remains to close the gap between the upper and lower bounds in the case of a multi-channel adversary. Such a result would have interesting connections to a hypergraph generalization of Turán's Theorem, an open problem in extremal graph theory.

Second, adaptive algorithms can likely achieve better performance than oblivious algorithms. It remains an interesting open question to determine how much efficiency adaptiveness provides. Similarly, it is possible to achieve better performance using a randomized algorithm, at the cost of some probability of failure. A trivial randomized algorithm can solve $1/n$-gossip in $O(n \log n)$ time (w.h.p.). Is it possible to do better?

Third, we believe the techniques developed here for single-hop networks extend to multi-hop networks. Fourth, prior research on the problem of malicious interference has assumed that the adversary can cause only a bounded number of collisions. It may be interesting to consider the possibility of bounded collisions in a multi-channel network.

Finally, this paper considers an adversary who wants to prevent communication. Other research (e.g., [25]) has considered an eavesdropper who wants to compromise the secrecy of the information (but who may not disrupt communication). This leaves open the question of whether it is possible to achieve reliable *and secret* communication in a multi-channel network in the presence of a malicious and disruptive adversary.

References

1. Koo, C.Y.: Broadcast in radio networks tolerating byzantine adversarial behaviour. In: Proceedings of the 23rd Symposium on Principles of Distributed Computing (PODC), pp. 275–282 (2004)
2. Bhandari, V., Vaidya, N.H.: On reliable broadcast in a radio network. In: Proceedings of the 24th Symposium on Principles of Distributed Computing (PODC), pp. 138–147 (2005)
3. Bhandari, V., Vaidya, N.H.: On reliable broadcast in a radio network: A simplified characterization. Technical report, University of Illinois at Urbana-Champaign (May 2005)
4. Pelc, A., Peleg, D.: Feasibility and complexity of broadcasting with random transmission failures. In: Proceedings of the 24th Symposium on Principles of Distributed Computing (PODC), pp. 334–341 (2005)
5. Bhandari, V., Vaidya, N.H.: Reliable broadcast in wireless networks with probabilistic failures. In: Proceedings of the 26th Conference on Computer Communications (Infocom), pp. 715–723 (2007)

6. Gilbert, S., Guerraoui, R., Newport, C.: Of malicious motes and suspicious sensors: On the efficiency of malicious interference in wireless networks. In: Shvartsman, A.A. (ed.) OPODIS 2006. LNCS, vol. 4305, pp. 215–229. Springer, Heidelberg (2006)
7. Koo, C.Y., Bhandari, V., Katz, J., Vaidya, N.H.: Reliable broadcast in radio networks: The bounded collision case. In: Proceedings of the 25th Symposium on Principles of Distributed Computing (PODC), pp. 258–264 (2006)
8. Kyasanur, P., Vaidya, N.H.: Capacity of multi-channel wireless networks: Impact of number of channels and interfaces. In: Proceedings of the 11th Annual International Conference on Mobile Computing and Networking (Mobicom), pp. 43–57 (2005)
9. Bhandari, V., Vaidya, N.H.: Connectivity and capacity of multi-channel wireless networks with channel switching constraints. Technical report, University of Illinois at Urbana-Champaign (January 2007)
10. Mitola, J.: Cognitive Radio: An Integrated Agent Architecture for Software Defined Radio. PhD thesis, Royal Institute of Technology, Sweden (2000)
11. Krishnamurthy, S., Chandrasekaran, R., Mittal, N., Venkatesan, S.: Brief announcement: Synchronous distributed algorithms for node discovery and configuration in multi-channel cognitive radio networks. In: Dolev, S. (ed.) DISC 2006. LNCS, vol. 4167, pp. 572–574. Springer, Heidelberg (2006)
12. Krishnamurthy, S., Thoppian, M., Kuppa, S., Chanrasekaran, R., Venkatesan, S., Mittal, N., Prakash, R.: Time-efficient layer-2 auto-configuration for cognitive radios. In: Procedings of the International Conference on Parallel and Distributed Systems (PDCS), pp. 459–464 (2005)
13. Alon, N., Bar-Noy, A., Linial, N., Peleg, D.: A lower bound for radio broadcast. Journal of Computer and System Sciences 43(2), 290–298 (1992)
14. Bar-Yehuda, R., Goldreich, O., Itai, A.: On the time-complexity of broadcast in multi-hop radio networks: an exponential gap between determinism and randomization. Journal of Computer and System Sciences 45(1), 104–126 (1992)
15. Czumaj, A., Rytter, W.: Broadcasting algorithms in radio networks with unknown topology. In: Proceedings of the 44th Symposium on Foundations of Computer Science (FOCS), pp. 492–501 (2003)
16. Kowalski, D.R., Pelc, A.: Time of deterministic broadcasting in radio networks with local knowledge. SIAM Journal on Computing 33(4), 870–891 (2004)
17. Diks, K., Pelc, A.: Almost safe gossiping in bounded degree networks. SIAM Journal on Discrete Mathematics 5(3), 338–344 (1992)
18. Kranakis, E., Krizanc, D., Pelc, A.: Fault-tolerant broadcasting in radio networks. Journal of Algorithms 39(1), 47–67 (2001)
19. Turán, P.: On an extremal problem in graph theory. Matematicko Fizicki Lapok 48 (1941)
20. Komlos, J., Greenberg, A.: An asymptotically fast non-adaptive algorithm for conflict resolution in multiple access channels. Transactions on Information Theory 31(2), 302–306 (1985)
21. Bonis, A.D., Gasieniec, L., Vaccaro, U.: Optimal two-stage algorithms for group testing problems. SIAM Journal on Computing 34(5), 1253–1270 (2005)
22. Indyk, P.: Explicit constructions of selectors and related combinatorial structures, with applications. In: Proceedings of the 13th Symposium on Discrete Algorithms (SODA), pp. 697–704 (2002)
23. de Caen, D.: Extension of a theorem of Moon and Moser on complete subgraphs. Ars Combinatoria 16, 5–10 (1983)
24. Sidorenko, A.F.: What we know and what we do not know about Turán numbers. Graphs and Combinatorics 11(2), 179–199 (1995)
25. Miller, M.J., Vaidya, N.H.: Leveraging channel diversity for key establishment in wireless sensor networks. Technical report, U. of Illinois at Urbana-Champaign (December 2005)

The Space Complexity of Unbounded Timestamps

Faith Ellen[1], Panagiota Fatourou[2], and Eric Ruppert[3]

[1] University of Toronto, Canada
[2] University of Ioannina, Greece
[3] York University, Canada

Abstract. The timestamp problem captures a fundamental aspect of asynchronous distributed computing. It allows processes to label events throughout the system with timestamps that provide information about the real-time ordering of those events. We consider the space complexity of wait-free implementations of timestamps from shared read-write registers in a system of n processes.
We prove an $\Omega(\sqrt{n})$ lower bound on the number of registers required. If the timestamps are elements of a nowhere dense set, for example the integers, we prove a stronger, and tight, lower bound of n. However, if timestamps are not from a nowhere dense set, this bound can be beaten; we give an algorithm that uses $n - 1$ (single-writer) registers.
We also consider the special case of anonymous algorithms, where processes do not have unique identifiers. We prove anonymous timestamp algorithms require n registers. We give an algorithm to prove that this lower bound is tight. This is the first anonymous algorithm that uses a finite number of registers. Although this algorithm is wait-free, its step complexity is not bounded. We also present an algorithm that uses $O(n^2)$ registers and has bounded step complexity.

Keywords: timestamps, shared memory, anonymous, lower bounds.

1 Introduction

In asynchronous systems, it is the unpredictability of the scheduler that gives rise to the principle challenges of designing distributed algorithms. One approach to overcoming these challenges is for processes to determine the temporal ordering of certain events that take place at different locations within the system. Examples of tasks where such temporal information is essential include implementing first-come first-served processing of jobs that arrive at different locations in the system and knowing whether a locally cached copy of data is up-to-date. Temporal information about the scheduling of events can also be used to break symmetry, *e.g.*, the first process to perform some step can be elected as a leader.

If processes communicate via messages or shared read-write registers, it is impossible for them to determine the exact temporal ordering of all events. However, timestamps provide partial information about this ordering in such systems. A timestamp algorithm allows processes to ask for labels, or *timestamps*,

A. Pelc (Ed.): DISC 2007, LNCS 4731, pp. 223–237, 2007.

which can then be compared with other timestamps. Timestamps have been used to solve several of the most fundamental problems in distributed computing. Examples include mutual exclusion [17] (and the more general k-exclusion problem [2]), randomized consensus [1], and constructing multi-writer registers from single-writer registers [13, 19, 22]. Timestamps have also been employed in anonymous systems as building blocks for implementations of wait-free atomic snapshots and other data structures [12].

Despite the central importance of the timestamp problem, its complexity is not well-understood. In this paper, we present the first study on the number of registers required for wait-free implementations of timestamps.

The history of timestamps begins with Lamport [18], who defined a partial ordering on events in a message-passing system; one event "happens before" another if the first could influence the second (because they are by the same process or because of messages sent between processes). He defined a logical clock, which assigns integer timestamps to events such that, if one event happens before another, it is assigned a smaller timestamp. There is no constraint on the relationship between timestamps assigned to other pairs of events.

Fidge and Mattern [11, 20] introduced the notion of vector clocks, where timestamps are vectors of integers rather than integers. Two vectors are compared component-wise: one vector is smaller than or equal to another when each component of the first is smaller than or equal to the corresponding component of the second. Their vector clock algorithms satisfy the property that one event gets a smaller vector than another if *and only if* it happens before the other event. This property is not possible to ensure using integer timestamps, because concurrent events may need to be assigned incomparable vectors. Charron-Bost [5] proved that the number of components required by a vector clock is at least the number of processes, n.

In message-passing algorithms, the timestamps reflect the partial order representing (potential) causal relationships. In shared-memory systems, we are concerned, instead, with the real-time ordering of events.

The simplest shared-memory timestamp algorithm uses single-writer registers [17]. To get a new timestamp, a process collects the values in all the single-writer registers and writes one plus the maximum value it read into its single-writer register. This value is its new timestamp.

Dwork and Waarts [8] described a vector timestamp algorithm that uses n single-writer registers. To obtain a new timestamp, a process increments its register and collects the values in the registers of all other processes. It returns the vector of these n values as its timestamp. These timestamps can be compared either lexicographically or in the same way as in the vector clock algorithm.

Attiya and Fouren [3] gave a vector timestamp algorithm that is considerably more complicated. It uses an unbounded number of registers but has the advantage that the number of components in the timestamp (and the time required to obtain it) is a function of the number of processes running concurrently.

Guerraoui and Ruppert [12] described an anonymous wait-free timestamp algorithm, but the number of registers used and the time-complexity of getting a timestamp increases without bound as the number of labelled events increases. Thus, their algorithm is not bounded wait-free.

In all the above algorithms, the size of timestamps grows without bound as the number of labelled events increases. This is necessary to describe the ordering among an unbounded number of non-concurrent events. For some applications, one can restrict the events about which order queries can be made, for example, only the most recent event by each process. This restriction allows timestamps to be reused, so they can be of bounded size. This restricted version of timestamps is called the *bounded timestamp* problem. In contrast, the general version of the problem is sometimes called the *unbounded timestamp* problem. Israeli and Li [14] gave a bounded timestamp algorithm, assuming timestamps are only generated by one process at a time. Dolev and Shavit defined and solved the problem allowing multiple processes to obtain timestamps concurrently [6]. This and other known implementations of bounded concurrent timestamps [7, 8, 13, 15] are quite complex, as compared to unbounded timestamps.

It is known that bounded timestamp algorithms must use $\Omega(n)$ bits per timestamp [14]. In contrast, unbounded timestamp algorithms can use timestamps whose bit lengths are logarithmic in the number of events that must be labelled. Thus, if the number of events requiring timestamps is reasonable (for example, less than 2^{64}), timestamps will easily fit into one word of memory. The work on the bounded timestamp problem is of great interest and technical depth. However, since bounded timestamp algorithms are complicated and require long timestamps, the unbounded version is often considered more practical. This paper focusses exclusively on the unbounded timestamp problem.

1.1 Our Contributions

In this paper, we study the number of read-write registers needed to implement timestamps. We present both upper and lower bounds. For our upper bounds, we give wait-free algorithms. The lower bounds apply even if algorithms must only satisfy the weaker progress property of obstruction-freedom. Our most general lower bound shows that any timestamp algorithm must use $\Omega(\sqrt{n})$ registers. Previously known wait-free algorithms use n registers. We show how to modify one of these algorithms to use $n-1$ registers.

Some existing timestamp implementations use timestamps drawn from a nowhere dense set. Intuitively, this means that between any two possible timestamps, there are a finite number of other timestamps. For this restricted case, we show that any such implementation must use at least n registers, exactly matching known implementations. Interestingly, our lower bound can be beaten by using timestamps from a domain that is not nowhere dense, namely, pairs of integers, ordered lexicographically.

We also prove matching upper and lower bounds for anonymous systems, where processes do not have unique identifiers and are programmed identically. We give a wait-free algorithm using n registers, whereas previous algorithms used an unbounded number. We also provide another, faster anonymous algorithm. It uses $O(n^2)$ registers and a process takes $O(n^3)$ steps to obtain a timestamp.

We prove a tight lower bound of n for the number of registers required for an anonymous timestamp implementation. This establishes a small but interesting space complexity separation between the anonymous and general versions of the timestamp problem, since $n - 1$ registers suffice for our algorithm, which uses identifiers. Lower bounds for anonymous systems are interesting, in part, because they provide insight for lower bounds in more general systems [9, 10].

Guerraoui and Ruppert [12] used timestamps as a subroutine for their anonymous implementation of a snapshot object. Plugging in our space-optimal anonymous timestamp algorithm yields an anonymous wait-free implementation of an m-component snapshot from $m + n$ registers. This is the first such algorithm to use a bounded number of registers. Similarly, if our second anonymous timestamp algorithm is used, we obtain an anonymous wait-free snapshot implementation from $O(m + n^2)$ registers where each SCAN and UPDATE takes $O(n^2(m + n))$ steps. This is the first bounded wait-free anonymous snapshot implementation.

2   The Model of Computation

We use a standard model for asynchronous shared-memory systems, in which a collection of n processes communicate using atomic read-write registers. We consider only *deterministic* algorithms. If processes have identical programmes and do not have unique identifiers, the algorithm is called *anonymous*; otherwise, it is called *eponymous* [21]. An *execution* of an algorithm is a possibly infinite sequence of steps, where each step is an access to a shared register by some process, followed by local computation of that process. The subsequence of steps taken by each process must conform to the algorithm of that process. Each read of a register returns the value that was most recently written there (or the initial value of the register if no write to it has occurred). If $\mathcal{P}$ is a set of processes, a $\mathcal{P}$-*only* execution is an execution in which only processes in $\mathcal{P}$ take steps. A *solo execution* by a process p is a $\{p\}$-only execution. We use $\alpha \cdot \beta$ to denote the concatenation of the finite execution α and the (finite or infinite) execution β. A *configuration* is a complete description of the system at some time. It is comprised of the internal state of each process and the value stored in each shared register. A configuration C is *reachable* if there is an execution from an initial configuration that ends in C. In an execution, two operation instances are called *concurrent* if neither one ends before the other begins.

We consider processes that may fail by halting. An algorithm is *wait-free* if every non-faulty process completes its tasks within a finite number of its own steps, no matter how processes are scheduled or which other processes fail. A stronger version of the wait-freedom property, called *bounded wait-freedom*, requires that the number of steps be bounded. A much weaker progress property is *obstruction-freedom*, which requires that each process must complete its task if it is given sufficiently many consecutive steps.

In our algorithms, each register need only be large enough to store one timestamp. For our lower bounds, we assume that each register can hold arbitrarily large amounts of information. In our algorithms, we use the convention that shared registers have names that begin with upper-case letters and local variables begin with lower-case letters. If $\mathcal{R}$ is a set or array of registers, we use COLLECT($\mathcal{R}$) to denote a read of each register in $\mathcal{R}$, in some unspecified order.

Our lower bounds use covering arguments, introduced by Burns and Lynch [4]. We say a process p *covers* a register R in a configuration C if p will write to R when it next takes a step. A set of processes $\mathcal{P}$ *covers* a set of registers $\mathcal{R}$ in C if $|\mathcal{P}| = |\mathcal{R}|$ and each register in $\mathcal{R}$ is covered by exactly one process in $\mathcal{P}$. If $\mathcal{P}$ covers $\mathcal{R}$, a *block write* by $\mathcal{P}$ is an execution in which each process in $\mathcal{P}$ takes exactly one step writing its value.

3   The Timestamp Problem

A *timestamp implementation* provides two algorithms for each process: GETTS and COMPARE. GETTS takes no arguments and outputs a value from a universe U. Elements of U are called *timestamps*. COMPARE takes two arguments from U and outputs a Boolean value. If an instance of GETTS, which outputs t_1, finishes before another instance, which outputs t_2, begins, then any subsequent instances of COMPARE(t_1, t_2) and COMPARE(t_2, t_1) must output true and false, respectively. Thus, two non-concurrent GETTS operations cannot return the same timestamp. Unlike the bounded timestamp problem, COMPARE can compare any previously granted timestamps, so U must be infinite.

This definition of the timestamp problem is weak, which makes our lower bounds stronger. It is sufficient for some applications [12], but it is too weak for other applications. For example, consider the implementation of atomic multi-writer registers from single-writer registers [13, 19, 22]. Suppose readers determine which value to return by comparing timestamps attached to each written value to find the most recently written value. If two writers write different values concurrently, and two readers later read the register, the readers should agree on which of the two values to return. To handle this kind of application, we can define a stronger version of the timestamp problem which requires that, for each pair t and t', all COMPARE(t, t') operations in the same execution must return the same value. A *static* timestamp algorithm is one that satisfies a still stronger property: for each pair, t and t', the COMPARE(t, t') always returns the same result in *all* executions. Static timestamp algorithms have the nice property that COMPARE queries need not access shared memory. The algorithms we present in this paper are all static. The lower bounds in Sections 4.1 and 7 apply even for non-static implementations.

A natural way to design a static timestamp algorithm is to use timestamps drawn from a partially ordered universe U, and answer COMPARE queries using that order; COMPARE(t_1, t_2) returns true if and only if $t_1 < t_2$. A partially ordered set U is called *nowhere dense* if, for every $x, y \in U$, there are only a finite number of elements $z \in U$ such that $x < z < y$. The integers, in their natural order, and the set of all finite sets of integers, ordered by set inclusion, are nowhere dense. Any set of fixed-length vectors of integers, where $x \leq y$ if and only if each component of x is less than or equal to the corresponding component of y is too. However, for $k \geq 2$, the set of all length-k vectors of integers, ordered lexicographically, is not nowhere dense.

Another desirable property is that all timestamps produced are distinct, even for concurrent GETTS operations. In eponymous systems, this property is easy to satisfy by incorporating the process's identifier into the timestamp generated [17]. In anonymous systems, it is impossible, because symmetry cannot be broken using registers.

4   Eponymous Lower Bounds

We prove lower bounds on the number of registers needed to implement timestamps eponymously. First, we give the most general result of the paper, proving that $\Omega(\sqrt{n})$ registers are needed. Then, we prove a tight lower bound of n if the timestamps are chosen from a partially ordered set that is nowhere dense.

4.1   A General Space Lower Bound

We use a covering argument, showing that, starting from a configuration where some registers are covered, we can reach another configuration where more registers are covered. The following lemma allows us to do this, provided the original registers are covered by *three* processes each. The complement of a set of processes $\mathcal{S}$ is denoted by $\overline{\mathcal{S}}$.

Lemma 1. *Consider any timestamp algorithm. Suppose that, in a reachable configuration C, there are three disjoint sets of processes, $\mathcal{P}_1$, $\mathcal{P}_2$, and $\mathcal{Q}$ that each cover the set of registers $\mathcal{R}$. Let C_i be the configuration obtained from C by having the processes in $\mathcal{P}_i$ do a block write, β_i, for $i = 1, 2$. Then for all disjoint sets $\mathcal{S}_1 \subseteq \overline{\mathcal{P}_2 \cup \mathcal{Q}}$ and $\mathcal{S}_2 \subseteq \overline{\mathcal{P}_1 \cup \mathcal{Q}}$, with some process not in $\mathcal{S}_1 \cup \mathcal{S}_2$, there is an $i \in \{1, 2\}$ such that every $\mathcal{S}_i$-only execution starting from C_i that contains a complete GETTS writes to a register not in $\mathcal{R}$.*

Proof. Suppose there exist disjoint sets $\mathcal{S}_1 \subseteq \overline{\mathcal{P}_2 \cup \mathcal{Q}}$ and $\mathcal{S}_2 \subseteq \overline{\mathcal{P}_1 \cup \mathcal{Q}}$, an $\mathcal{S}_1$-only execution α_1 from C_1 and an $\mathcal{S}_2$-only execution α_2 from C_2 that both write only to registers in $\mathcal{R}$, and $q \notin \mathcal{S}_1 \cup \mathcal{S}_2$. Also suppose α_1 and α_2 contain complete instances of GETTS, I_1 and I_2, that return t_1 and t_2, respectively. Let γ be an execution starting from C that begins with a block write to $\mathcal{R}$ by $\mathcal{Q}$, followed by a solo execution in which q performs a complete instance of COMPARE(t_1, t_2). Then, $\beta_1 \cdot \alpha_1 \cdot \beta_2 \cdot \alpha_2 \cdot \gamma$ and $\beta_2 \cdot \alpha_2 \cdot \beta_1 \cdot \alpha_1 \cdot \gamma$ are valid executions starting from C that are indistinguishable to q. Hence, in both, q returns the same result for COMPARE(t_1, t_2). This is incorrect, since I_1 precedes I_2 in $\beta_1 \cdot \alpha_1 \cdot \beta_2 \cdot \alpha_2 \cdot \gamma$, but I_2 precedes I_1 in $\beta_2 \cdot \alpha_2 \cdot \beta_1 \cdot \alpha_1 \cdot \gamma$. $\square$

Theorem 2. *Every obstruction-free timestamp algorithm for n processes uses more than $\frac{1}{2}\sqrt{n-1}$ registers.*

Proof. First, we show that at least one register is required. To derive a contradiction, suppose there is an implementation that uses no shared registers. Let

α and β be solo executions of GETTS by different processes, p and q, starting from the initial configuration. Suppose they return timestamps t and t'. Let γ be a solo execution of COMPARE(t, t') by p immediately following α. Since $\alpha \cdot \beta \cdot \gamma$ is indistinguishable from $\beta \cdot \alpha \cdot \gamma$ to p, it must return the same result for COMPARE(t, t') in both. However, it must return true in $\alpha \cdot \beta \cdot \gamma$ and false in $\beta \cdot \alpha \cdot \gamma$. This is a contradiction. This suffices to prove the claim for $n \leq 4$.

For the remainder of the proof, we assume that $n \geq 5$. Consider any timestamp algorithm that uses $r > 0$ registers. To derive a contradiction, assume $r \leq \frac{1}{2}\sqrt{n-1}$. We show, by repeated applications of Lemma 1 that it is possible to reach a configuration where all r registers are covered by three processes each. One further application of Lemma 1 will then show that some process must write to some other register, to produce the desired contradiction. We prove the following claim by induction on k.

Claim: For $k = 1, \ldots, r$, there is a reachable configuration with k registers each covered by $r - k + 3$ processes.

Base case ($k = 1$): Let p_1, p_2 and q be any three processes. Applying Lemma 1 with initial configuration C, $\mathcal{R} = \emptyset$, $\mathcal{P}_1 = \mathcal{P}_2 = \mathcal{Q} = \emptyset$, $\mathcal{S}_1 = \{p_1\}$, and $\mathcal{S}_2 = \{p_2\}$ proves that the solo execution of GETTS by either p_1 or p_2 must write to some register. Thus, all except possibly one process must write to a register during a solo execution of GETTS starting from C. Consider an execution consisting of the concatenation of the longest write-free prefixes of $n - 1$ of these solo executions. In the resulting configuration, there are $n - 1$ processes covering registers. Since there are r registers and $n - 1 \geq (2r)^2 > r(r+1)$, there is some register that is covered by at least $r + 2 = r - k + 3$ processes.

Induction Step: Let $1 \leq k \leq r - 1$ and suppose the claim is true for k. Let C be a reachable configuration in which there is a set $\mathcal{R}$ of k registers that are each covered by $r - k + 3 \geq 3$ processes. Let $\mathcal{P}_1, \ldots, \mathcal{P}_{r-k+3}$ be disjoint sets that each cover $\mathcal{R}$ with $|\mathcal{P}_i| = k$ for all i.

Divide the $n - (r - k + 3)k$ processes not in $\mathcal{P}_1 \cup \cdots \cup \mathcal{P}_{r-k+3}$ into two sets, $\mathcal{U}_1$ and $\mathcal{U}_2$, each containing at least $\lfloor (n - (r - k + 3)k)/2 \rfloor$ processes. Let $\mathcal{S}_1 = \mathcal{P}_1 \cup \mathcal{U}_1$ and $\mathcal{S}_2 = \mathcal{P}_2 \cup \mathcal{U}_2$. Then $\mathcal{S}_1 \subseteq \overline{\mathcal{P}_2 \cup \mathcal{P}_3}$ and $\mathcal{S}_2 \subseteq \overline{\mathcal{P}_1 \cup \mathcal{P}_3}$ are disjoint. Since $|\mathcal{P}_3| = k \geq 1$, there is a process $q \in \mathcal{P}_3 - (\mathcal{S}_1 \cup \mathcal{S}_2)$. For $i = 1, 2$, let C_i be the configuration obtained from C by having the processes in $\mathcal{P}_i$ do a block write. By Lemma 1, there exists $i \in \{1, 2\}$ such that every $\mathcal{S}_i$-only execution starting from C_i that contains a complete GETTS writes to a register not in $\mathcal{R}$.

Let $m = |\mathcal{S}_i|$. We inductively define a sequence of solo executions $\alpha_1, \alpha_2, \ldots, \alpha_m$ by each of the processes of $\mathcal{S}_i$ such that $\alpha_1 \cdot \alpha_2 \cdots \alpha_m$ is a legal execution from C_i that does not write to any registers outside $\mathcal{R}$ and each process covers a register not in $\mathcal{R}$. Let $1 \leq j \leq m$. Assume that $\alpha_1, \ldots, \alpha_{j-1}$ have already been defined and satisfy the claim. Consider the $\mathcal{S}_i$-only execution $\delta = \alpha_1 \cdot \alpha_2 \cdots \alpha_{j-1} \cdot \alpha$ from C_i, where α is a solo execution by another process $p_j \in \mathcal{S}_i$ that contains a complete GETTS operation. Then δ must include a write by p_j to a register outside $\mathcal{R}$ during α. Let α_j be the prefix of α up to, but not including, p_j's first write outside of $\mathcal{R}$. This has the desired properties.

Let C' be the configuration reached from C_i by performing the execution $\alpha_1 \cdot \alpha_2 \cdots \alpha_m$. Then at C', each process in $\mathcal{S}_i$ covers one of the $r-k$ registers not in $\mathcal{R}$ and $|S_i| \geq k + \lfloor (n-(r-k+3)k)/2 \rfloor \geq ((2r)^2 - (r-k+1)k)/2 > (r-k)(r-k+1)$, since $2r > 2r - k, r - k + 1 > 0$. Thus, by the pigeonhole principle, some register R not in $\mathcal{R}$ is covered by at least $r - k + 2$ processes. Let $\mathcal{R}' = \mathcal{R} \cup \{R\}$. Each register in $\mathcal{R}$ is covered by one process from each of $\mathcal{P}_3, \ldots, \mathcal{P}_{r-k+3}$ and $\mathcal{P}_{3-i}$. Thus, each of the $k+1$ registers in $\mathcal{R}'$ is covered by $r - k + 2$ processes in the configuration C', proving the claim for $k + 1$.

By induction, there is a reachable configuration in which all r registers are covered by three processes each. By Lemma 1, there is an execution in which a process writes to some other register. This is impossible.   □

The first paragraph of the proof also shows that, if a timestamp algorithm uses only single-writer registers, then at most one process never writes and, hence, at least $n - 1$ single-writer registers are necessary.

4.2   A Tight Space Lower Bound for Static Algorithms Using Nowhere Dense Universes

We now turn to the special case where timestamps come from a nowhere dense partial order, and COMPARE operations can be resolved using that order, without accessing shared memory. The following theorem provides a tight lower bound, since it matches a standard timestamp algorithm [17].

Theorem 3. *Any static obstruction-free timestamp algorithm that uses a nowhere dense partially ordered universe of timestamps requires at least n registers.*

Proof. We prove by induction that, for $0 \leq i \leq n$, there is a reachable configuration C_i in which a set $\mathcal{P}_i$ of i processes covers a set $\mathcal{R}_i$ of i different registers. Then, in configuration C_n, there are processes poised at n different registers.
Base Case $(i = 0)$: Let C_0 be the initial configuration and let $\mathcal{P}_0 = \mathcal{R}_0 = \emptyset$.
Inductive Step: Let $1 \leq i \leq n$. Assume $C_{i-1}, \mathcal{R}_{i-1}$ and $\mathcal{P}_{i-1}$ satisfy the claim.

If $i = 1$, let p be any process. Otherwise, let $p \in \mathcal{P}_{i-1}$. Consider an execution α that starts from C_{i-1} with a block write by the processes in $\mathcal{P}_{i-1}$ to the registers of $\mathcal{R}_{i-1}$, followed by a solo execution by p in which p completes its pending operation, if any, and then performs GETTS, returning some timestamp t. Let q be a process not in $\mathcal{P}_{i-1} \cup \{p\}$. We show that a solo execution by q, starting from C_{i-1}, in which it performs an infinite sequence of GETTS operations must eventually write to a register not in $\mathcal{R}_{i-1}$. Let t_j be the timestamp returned by the j'th instance of GETTS by q in this solo execution. Then $t_j < t_{j+1}$ for all $j \geq 1$. Since $\{j \in \mathbf{N} \mid t_1 < t_j < t\}$ is finite, there exists $j \in \mathbf{N}$ such that $t_j \not< t$.

Suppose that q does not write to any register outside $\mathcal{R}_{i-1}$ during the solo execution, β, of j instances of GETTS, starting from C_{i-1}. Then $\beta \cdot \alpha$ is indistinguishable from α to p, so p returns t as the result of its last GETTS in $\beta \cdot \alpha$. Therefore, $t_j < t$. This contradicts the definition of j, so q must write outside $\mathcal{R}_{i-1}$. Consider the solo execution of q starting from C_{i-1} until it first

Code for process p_i (for $1 \leq i \leq n-1$):
GETTS
    $t \leftarrow \max(\text{COLLECT}(R)) + 1$
    $R[i] \leftarrow t$
    return $(t, 0)$

Code for process p_n:
GETTS
    $t \leftarrow \max(\text{COLLECT}(R))$
    if $t > oldt$ then $c \leftarrow 0$
    $c \leftarrow c + 1$
    $oldt \leftarrow t$
    return (t, c)

Fig. 1. An eponymous algorithm using $n - 1$ registers

covers some register R outside $\mathcal{R}_{i-1}$. Let C_i be the resulting configuration. Then $\mathcal{P}_i = \mathcal{P}_{i-1} \cup \{q\}$ and $\mathcal{R}_i = \mathcal{R}_{i-1} \cup \{R\}$ satisfy the claim for i. □

Jayanti, Tan and Toueg proved that linearizable implementations of perturbable objects require at least $n - 1$ registers [16]. Roughly speaking, an object is perturbable if some sequence of operations on the object by one process must be visible to another process that starts executing later. General timestamps do not have this property. However, the proof technique of [16] can be applied to the special case considered in Theorem 3 (even though timestamps are not linearizable). The proof technique used in Theorem 3 is similar to theirs, but is considerably simpler, and gives a slightly stronger lower bound. Although our improvement to the bound is small, it is important, since it proves a complexity separation, showing that using nowhere dense sets of timestamps requires more registers than used by the algorithm of the next section.

5   An Eponymous Algorithm

In this section, we show that there is a simple wait-free eponymous algorithm that uses only $n - 1$ single-writer registers, which is optimal. The timestamps generated will be ordered pairs of non-negative integers, ordered lexicographically. This shows that the lower bound in Sect. 4.2 is not true for all domains.

The algorithm uses an array $R[1..n-1]$ of single-writer registers, each initially 0. Processes $p_1, \ldots, p_{n-1}$ use this array to collaboratively create the first component of the timestamps by the simple method [17] discussed in Sect. 1. The second component of any timestamp they generate is 0. The last process, p_n, reads the registers of the other processes to determine the first component of its timestamp, and produces the values for the second component of its timestamp on its own. Process p_n does not write into shared memory.

The implementation of GETTS is presented in Figure 1. In the code for p_n, $oldt$ and c are persistent variables, initially 0. COMPARE$((t_1, c_1), (t_2, c_2))$ returns true if and only if either $t_1 = t_2$ and $c_1 < c_2$ or $t_1 < t_2$. The value stored in each component of R does not decrease over time. So, if two non-concurrent COLLECTS are performed on R, the maximum value seen by the later COLLECT will be at least as big as the maximum value seen by the earlier COLLECT.

Theorem 4. *Figure 1 gives a timestamp algorithm using $n - 1$ registers with step complexity $O(n)$.*

Proof. Suppose an instance, I_1, of GETTS returns (t_1, c_1) before the invocation of another instance I_2 of GETTS, returns (t_2, c_2). We show that COMPARE((t_1, c_1), (t_2, c_2)) returns true. We consider several cases.

Case 1: I_1 and I_2 are both performed by p_n. It follows from the code that p_n generates an increasing sequence of timestamps (in lexicographic order): each time p_n produces a new timestamp, it either increases the first component or leaves the first component unchanged and increases the second component.

Case 2: p_n performs I_2 but some process $p_i \neq p_n$ performs I_1. During I_2, the value p_n sees when it reads $R[i]$ is at least t_1, so $t_2 \geq t_1$. Furthermore, $c_2 \geq 1 > 0 = c_1$.

Case 3: I_2 is not performed by p_n. Then t_1 was the value of some component of R some time before the end of I_1 (because it was either read by p_n while performing I_1, or was written by another process while performing I_1). The value of this component of R is at least t_1 when I_2 reads it, so $t_2 \geq t_1 + 1$.

In all three cases, a COMPARE($(t_1, c_1), (t_2, c_2)$) will return true, as required. Since R has $n - 1$ components, the step complexity of GETTS is $O(n)$.   □

6   Anonymous Algorithms

We present two new anonymous timestamp algorithms. The first uses n registers and, as we shall see in Sect. 7, it is space-optimal. However, this algorithm, like Guerraoui and Ruppert's algorithm [12], is not bounded wait-free. The second algorithm uses $O(n^2)$ registers, but it is bounded wait-free. It is an open question whether there is a bounded wait-free algorithm that uses $O(n)$ registers.

6.1   A Wait-Free Algorithm Using n Registers

The first algorithm uses an array $A[1..n]$ of registers, each initially 0. The timestamps are non-negative integers. Before a process returns a timestamp, it records it in A so that subsequent GETTS operations will see the value and return a larger one. We ensure this by having a process choose its timestamp by reading all timestamps in A and choosing a larger one. The anonymity of the algorithm presents a challenge, however. In a system with only registers, two processes running in lockstep, performing the same sequence of steps, have the same effect as a single process: there is no way to tell these two executions apart. Even the two processes themselves cannot detect the presence of the other. Consider an execution where some process p takes no steps. We can construct another execution where p runs as a *clone* of any other process q, and p stops taking steps at any time, covering any register that q wrote to. Thus, at any time, a clone can overwrite any value written in a register (except the first such value) with an older value. In the timestamp algorithm, if the value t chosen by one process and recorded in A is overwritten by values smaller than t, another process that begins performing GETTS after the value t has been chosen could again choose t as a timestamp, which would be incorrect.

To avoid this problem, we ensure that the evidence of a timestamp cannot be entirely overwritten after GETTS returns it. We say that a value v is *established*

GETTS
    $t \leftarrow \max(\text{COLLECT}(A)) + 1$
    for $i \leftarrow 1..M(t)$
        for $j \leftarrow 1..n$
            if $A[j] < t$ then $A[j] \leftarrow t$
        end for
    end for
    return(t)

Fig. 2. A wait-free anonymous timestamp algorithm using n registers

in configuration C if there exists a shared register that, in every configuration reachable from C, contains a value larger than or equal to v. (Note that, if a value larger than v is established, then v is also established.) Once a value v is established, any subsequent GETTS can perform a COLLECT of the registers and see that it should return a value greater than v. Thus, our goal is to ensure that values are established before they are returned by GETTS operations.

The algorithm, shown in Fig. 2, uses several measures to do this. The first is having processes read a location before writing it and never knowingly overwrite a value with a smaller value. This implies a value in a register is established whenever there are no processes covering it, poised to write smaller values. This measure alone is insufficient: if p writes to a register between q's read and write of that register, q may overwrite a larger value with a smaller one. However, it limits the damage that a process can do. Another measure is for GETTS to record its output in many locations before terminating. It also writes to each of those locations repeatedly, using a larger number of repetitions as the value of the timestamp gets larger. The number of repetitions, $M(t)$, that GETTS uses to record the timestamp t, is defined recursively by $M(1) = 1$ and $M(t) = n(n-1)\sum_{i=1}^{t-1} M(i)$ for $t > 1$. Solving this recurrence yields $M(t) = n(n-1)(n^2-n+1)^{t-2}$ for $t > 1$. The COMPARE(t_1, t_2) algorithm simply checks whether $t_1 < t_2$. Correctness follows easily from the following lemma.

Lemma 5. *Whenever GETTS returns a value t, the value t is established.*

Theorem 6. *Figure 2 gives a wait-free anonymous timestamp algorithm using n registers.*

When GETTS returns t, it performs $\Theta(n^{2t-1})$ steps. Thus, the algorithm is wait-free, but not bounded wait-free. In an execution with k GETTS operations, all timestamps are at most k, since GETTS can choose timestamp t only if another (possibly incomplete) GETTS has chosen $t - 1$ and written it into A. Each of the n registers must contain enough bits to represent one timestamp.

6.2 A Bounded Wait-Free Algorithm Using $O(n^2)$ Registers

The preceding algorithm is impractical because of its time complexity. Here, we give an algorithm that runs in polynomial time and space. As in the preceding algorithm, timestamps are non-negative integers and a process chooses

GETTS
    $t \leftarrow \max(\max(\text{COLLECT}(A), t) + 1$
    $row \leftarrow t \bmod (2n - 1)$
    for $i \leftarrow 1..n$
        $A[row, i] \leftarrow t$
        if $\max(\text{COLLECT}(A)) \geq t + n - 1$ then return(t)
    end for
    return(t)

Fig. 3. A bounded wait-free anonymous timestamp algorithm using $O(n^2)$ registers

a timestamp that is larger than any value recorded in the array A. However, now, $A[0..2n - 2, 1..n]$ is a two-dimensional array of registers and the method for recording a chosen value in A is quite different. Before a process p returns a timestamp t, it writes t into the entries of one row of the array, chosen as a function of t. A careful balance must be maintained: p should not write too many copies of t, because doing so could overwrite information written by other, more advanced processes, but p must write enough copies to ensure that t is not expunged by other, less advanced processes.

Process p attempts to write t into all entries of one row, but stops writing if it sees value $t + n - 1$ or larger anywhere in the array. We show that, if this occurs, then another process q has already returned a timestamp larger than t. (In that case, q will have already ensured that no future GETTS will ever return a value smaller than its own timestamp, so p can safely terminate and return t.) This avoids the problem of p writing too many copies of t.

To avoid the problem of p writing too few copies of t, the rows are chosen in a way that ensures that one value cannot be overwritten by another value unless those two values are sufficiently far apart. This ensures that other processes will terminate before obliterating all evidence of the largest timestamp written in A.

The algorithm is presented in Fig. 3. In addition to the shared array A, each process has a persistent local variable t, initialized to 0. Again, COMPARE(t_1, t_2) is performed by simply checking whether $t_1 < t_2$.

We remark that, if a value $v > 0$ is written into A, then $v - 1$ appeared in A earlier. The correctness of the algorithm follows easily from the lemma below.

Lemma 7. *Whenever GETTS returns a value t, the value t is established.*

Proof. We prove the lemma by induction on the number of return events.
Base case: If no return events have occurred, the lemma is vacuously satisfied.
Induction step: Let $k > 0$. Assume that, at each of the first $k - 1$ return events, the returned value is established.

Consider the configuration C just after the kth return event, in which process p returns t. We show t is established in C by considering two cases, depending on the termination condition that p satisfies.

Case 1: Suppose p returns t because it saw some value $m \geq t + n - 1$ in A.
Some process wrote m before p read it. It follows that each of the values $t, t+1, t+2, \ldots, t+n-1, \ldots, m$ appeared in A at some time during the execution

before C. For $1 \leq i \leq n - 1$, let p_i be the process that first wrote the value $t + i$ into A. These processes do not include p, since p returns t at configuration C. If all of these $n - 1$ processes are distinct, then no process will ever write a value smaller than t after C, so t is established. Otherwise, by the pigeonhole principle, $p_i = p_j$ for some $i < j$. Process p_i must have completed the instance of GetTS that first wrote $t + i$ before it began the instance of GetTS that first wrote $t + j$. The former instance returns $t + i$, so the value $t + i$ is established when it is returned, by the induction hypothesis. Thus, in C, the value $t + i$ is established and, hence, so is the value t.

Case 2: Suppose p terminates after it has completed all n iterations of the loop.

If $t < 2n - 1$, in the first loop iteration of the GetTS that returns t, p writes t into $A[t, 1]$. No value smaller than t can ever be written there, so t is established.

Now assume $t \geq 2n - 1$. The values $t - 1, t - 2, \ldots, t - n$ were written into A prior to the completion of p's first COLLECT. For $0 \leq i < n$, let p_i be the process that first wrote the value $t - n + i$ into A. If $p_i = p$ for some i, then p returned $t - n + i$ before starting the instance of GetTS that returned t, and the value $t - n + i$ is established, by the induction hypothesis. Otherwise, by the pigeonhole principle, we must have $p_i = p_j$ for some $0 \leq i < j < n$. When process p_i first wrote $t - n + i$, it returns $t - n + i$, that value is established, by the induction hypothesis. In either case, some value greater than or equal to $t - n$ is established by the time that p completes its first COLLECT. Hence, $t - n$ is also established.

We show no process writes values smaller than t in row $t \bmod (2n - 1)$ more than once after p's first write of t. Suppose not. Let q be the process that first does a second such write. Suppose the first such write by q writes the value $t_1 < t$ and the second writes the value $t_2 < t$. Then $t_1 \leq t - (2n - 1)$, since $t_1 \bmod (2n - 1) = t \bmod (2n - 1)$ and $t_1 < t$. Similarly, $t_2 \leq t - (2n - 1)$. When q performs COLLECT just after it writes t_1, it sees a value $t - n$ or larger in A, since $t - n$ is established. Furthermore, $t - n \geq (t_1 + 2n - 1) - n = t_1 + n - 1$ and the loop terminates. So, when q writes t_2, that write is part of a different instance of GetTS. Again, when q performs COLLECT in the first line of that instance of GetTS, it must see a value $t - n$ or larger, since $t - n$ is established. Thus, $t_2 \geq t - n + 1$, contradicting the fact that $t_2 \leq t - 2n$.

Thus, when p returns t, it has written the value t into all n entries of row $t \bmod (2n-1)$ of A and at most $n-1$ of those copies are subsequently overwritten by smaller values. So, t is established. $\square$

The worst-case running time of GetTS is $O(n^3)$, since each COLLECT takes $\Theta(n^2)$ steps. Timestamps are bounded by the number of GetTS operations invoked, and each register must be large enough to contain one timestamp.

Theorem 8. *Figure 3 gives a wait-free anonymous timestamp algorithm using $O(n^2)$ registers with step complexity $O(n^3)$.*

7 A Tight Space Lower Bound for Anonymous Algorithms

The anonymous timestamp algorithm given in Sect. 6.1 uses n registers. In it, a process may write its timestamp value to each of the n registers. Intuitively, this is done to ensure that other processes, which could potentially cover $n - 1$ of the registers, cannot overwrite all evidence of the timestamp. Here, we sharpen this intuition into a proof that at least n registers are required for anonymous timestamp algorithms. This applies to obstruction-free implementations of timestamps (and therefore to wait-free implementations).

Lemma 9. *Let $n \geq 2$. In any anonymous obstruction-free timestamp implementation for n processes, a solo execution of $k \leq n$ instances of* GETTS, *starting from an initial configuration, writes to at least k different registers.*

Proof. Suppose not. Consider the smallest k such that there is a solo execution of $k \leq n$ instances of GETTS by a process p, starting from an initial configuration, which writes to a set $\mathcal{R}$ of fewer than k different registers. Let α be the prefix of this execution consisting of the first $k - 1$ instances of GETTS. By definition of k, it writes to at least $k - 1$ different registers. Thus, $|\mathcal{R}| = k - 1$ and $\mathcal{R}$ is the set of registers written to during α. Let C be the configuration immediately after the last write in α (or the initial configuration, if there are no writes in α).

We define another execution β. First, add clones of p to execution α, such that one clone continues until just before p last writes to each register in $\mathcal{R}$. Let q be the last of these clones to take a step. (If $\mathcal{R}$ is empty, then let q be any process other than p.) Then p performs one more instance of GETTS after those it performed in α. Let t be the value returned by this operation. Note that p only writes to registers in $\mathcal{R}$. Next, let the clones do a block write to $\mathcal{R}$. Let C' be the configuration immediately after the block write. Finally, q runs solo to complete its operation, if necessary, and then does one more GETTS.

Each register has the same value in configurations C and C' and p's state in C is the same as q's state in C'. Thus, q's steps after C' will be identical to p's steps after C, and q's last GETTS will also return t. This is a contradiction, since that operation begins after p's last GETTS, which also returned t, ended. $\blacksquare$

Theorem 10. *Any n-process anonymous obstruction-free timestamp algorithm uses at least n registers.*

Acknowledgements. We thank Rachid Guerraoui for helpful discussions. Funding was provided by the Natural Sciences and Engineering Research Council of Canada and by the Scalable Synchronization Group at Sun Microsystems.

References

[1] Abrahamson, K.: On achieving consensus using a shared memory. In: Proc. 7th ACM Symposium on Principles of Distributed Computing, pp. 291–302 (1988)

[2] Afek, Y., Dolev, D., Gafni, E., Merritt, M., Shavit, N.: A bounded first-in, first-enabled solution to the l-exclusion problem. ACM Transactions on Programming Languages and Systems 16(3), 939–953 (1994)

[3] Attiya, H., Fouren, A.: Algorithms adapting to point contention. Journal of the ACM 50(4), 444–468 (2003)

[4] Burns, J., Lynch, N.: Bounds on shared memory for mutual exclusion. Information and Computation 107(2), 171–184 (1993)

[5] Charron-Bost, B.: Concerning the size of logical clocks in distributed systems. Information Processing Letters 39(1), 11–16 (1991)

[6] Dolev, D., Shavit, N.: Bounded concurrent time-stamping. SIAM Journal on Computing 26(2), 418–455 (1997)

[7] Dwork, C., Herlihy, M., Plotkin, S., Waarts, O.: Time-lapse snapshots. SIAM Journal on Computing 28(5), 1848–1874 (1999)

[8] Dwork, C., Waarts, O.: Simple and efficient bounded concurrent timestamping and the traceable use abstraction. Journal of the ACM 46(5), 633–666 (1999)

[9] Fatourou, P., Fich, F.E., Ruppert, E.: Time-space tradeoffs for implementations of snapshots. In: Proc. 38th ACM Symposium on Theory of Computing, pp. 169–178 (2006)

[10] Fich, F., Herlihy, M., Shavit, N.: On the space complexity of randomized synchronization. Journal of the ACM 45(5), 843–862 (1998)

[11] Fidge, C.: Logical time in distributed computing systems. Computer 24(8), 28–33 (1991)

[12] Guerraoui, R., Ruppert, E.: Anonymous and fault-tolerant shared-memory computing. Distributed Computing. A preliminary version appeared in Distributed Computing. In: 19th International Conference, pp. 244–259, 2006 (to appear)

[13] Haldar, S., Vitányi, P.: Bounded concurrent timestamp systems using vector clocks. Journal of the ACM 49(1), 101–126 (2002)

[14] Israeli, A., Li, M.: Bounded time-stamps. Distributed Computing 6(4), 205–209 (1993)

[15] Israeli, A., Pinhasov, M.: A concurrent time-stamp scheme which is linear in time and space. In: Proc. 6th Int. Workshop on Distributed Algorithms, pp. 95–109 (1992)

[16] Jayanti, P., Tan, K., Toueg, S.: Time and space lower bounds for nonblocking implementations. SIAM Journal on Computing 30(2), 438–456 (2000)

[17] Lamport, L.: A new solution of Dijkstra's concurrent programming problem. Communications of the ACM 17(8), 453–455 (1974)

[18] Lamport, L.: Time, clocks and the ordering of events in a distributed system. Communications of the ACM 21(7), 558–565 (1978)

[19] Li, M., Tromp, J., Vitányi, P.M.B.: How to share concurrent wait-free variables. Journal of the ACM 43(4), 723–746 (1996)

[20] Mattern, F.: Virtual time and global states of distributed systems. In: Proc. Workshop on Parallel and Distributed Algorithms, pp. 215–226 (1989)

[21] Mavronicolas, M., Michael, L., Spirakis, P.: Computing on a partially eponymous ring. In: Proc. 10th International Conference on Principles of Distributed Systems, pp. 380–394 (2006)

[22] Vitányi, P.M.B., Awerbuch, B.: Atomic shared register access by asynchronous hardware. In: Proc. 27th IEEE Symposium on Foundations of Computer Science, pp. 233–243. IEEE Computer Society Press, Los Alamitos (1986)

Approximating Wardrop Equilibria with Finitely Many Agents

Simon Fischer*, Lars Olbrich**, and Berthold Vöcking***

Dept. of Computer Science, RWTH Aachen, Germany
{fischer,lars,voecking}@cs.rwth-aachen.de

Abstract. We study adaptive routing algorithms in a round-based model. Suppose we are given a network equipped with load-dependent latency functions on the edges and a set of commodities each of which is defined by a collection of paths (represented by a DAG) and a flow rate. Each commodity is controlled by an agent which aims at balancing its traffic among its paths such that all used paths have the same latency. Such an allocation is called a Wardrop equilibrium.

In recent work, it was shown that an infinite population of users each of which carries an infinitesimal amount of traffic can attain approximate equilibria in a distributed and concurrent fashion quickly. Interestingly, the convergence time is independent of the underlying graph and depends only mildly on the latency functions. Unfortunately, a direct simulation of this process requires to maintain an exponential number of variables, one for each path.

The focus of this work lies on the distributed and efficient computation of the adaptation rules by a finite number of agents. In order to guarantee a polynomial running time, every agent computes a randomised path decomposition in every communication round. Based on this decomposition, agents remove flow from paths with high latency and reassign it proportionally to all paths. This way, our algorithm can handle exponentially large path collections in polynomial time.

1 Introduction

We consider routing problems in the Wardrop model. We are given a network equipped with non-decreasing latency functions mapping flow on the edges to latency. For each of several commodities a fixed flow rate has to be routed from a source to a sink via a collection of paths. A flow vector is said to be at Wardrop equilibrium if for all commodities the latencies of all used paths are minimal with respect to this commodity. Whereas such equilibria can be formulated as

---

  * Supported by DFG grant Vo889/1-3 and by DFG through German excellence cluster UMIC at RWTH Aachen.
 ** Supported by the DFG GK/1298 "AlgoSyn"
*** Supported in part by the the EU within the 6th Framework Programme under contract 001907 (DELIS) and by DFG through German excellence cluster UMIC at RWTH Aachen.

A. Pelc (Ed.): DISC 2007, LNCS 4731, pp. 238–252, 2007.

convex programs (under some mild assumptions on the latency functions) and can thus be solved by centralised algorithms in polynomial time, in this work, we study *distributed* algorithms to compute Wardrop equilibria.

A common interpretation of the Wardrop model is that flow is controlled by an infinite number of selfish agents each of which carries an infinitesimal amount of flow. In [12] it was shown that in this setting such a population approaches Wardrop equilibria quickly by following a simple round-based load-adaptive rerouting policy. This policy, called the *replication policy*, is executed by all agents in parallel and proceeds in the following way. Each agent samples another agent at random and, if this improves the latency, migrates to this agent's path with a probability that increases with the latency gain. In this setting, a natural goal is to reach approximate equilibria in the following bicriterial sense. We say that a flow is at δ-ϵ-equilibrium if at most an ϵ-fraction of the flow utilises paths whose latency exceeds the average latency of their commodity by more than a δ-fraction of the overall average latency. Remarkably, the number of rounds to reach an approximate equilibrium in this sense is independent of the size and the topology of the underlying graph and chiefly depends on the approximation parameters and the elasticity of the latency functions.

In this work, we consider a different setting, in which the flow is controlled by a finite number of agents only, each of which is responsible for the entire flow of one commodity. Each agent has a set of admissible paths among which it may distribute its flow. To be able to represent exponentially large collections of paths we assume that these are represented by an arbitrary DAG connecting the source and the sink of the agent. Each agent aims at balancing its own flow such that the jointly computed allocation will be at Wardrop equilibrium. Let us remark that agents do not aim at minimising the overall latency of their flow, but seek to minimise the maximum latency of their commodity. Unfortunately, the replication policy does not yield a feasible distributed algorithm in this setting directly. Simulating an infinite number of agents each of which chooses one out of the given collection of paths would require maintaining one variable for each path and computing a quadratic number of migration rates between pairs of paths. As the number of paths may be exponential in the size of the network this approach is rendered computationally infeasible.

We present two approaches to circumvent this problem. Our first approach exploits the fact that, for a simplified variant of the replication policy, the updates of the edge flows can be expressed in a way that merely uses the edge flow variables themselves (rather than the path flow variables). Thus, the updates can be computed in polynomial time. Unfortunately, the convergence time of this variant is only pseudopolynomial in the latency functions since it depends on the maximum slope of the latency functions.

Since the original replication policy cannot be expressed in this compact way, we consider a second approach to achieve convergence in a polynomial number of communication rounds. Consider a collection of paths for one of the commodities. In a first step, our algorithm samples a polynomial number of paths with probability proportional to their flow. We thus obtain a randomised path decomposition. We consider paths in this decomposition with above-average latency. From such paths, a fraction of the flow is removed and reallocated proportionally among all admissible paths. If this is done carefully, oscillations can be avoided, and a potential function argument ensures convergence towards Wardrop equilibria. Thus, we achieve essentially the same convergence rates as in the setting with an infinite number of agents and keep the computation time of one communication round polynomial. Altogether, we can compute approximate Wardrop equilibria in polynomial time.

1.1 Related Work

The game theoretic traffic model considered in this paper was introduced by Wardrop [19]. Many aspects of Wardrop equilibria have been studied, the most prominent being the degradation of performance due to the selfish behaviour, called the price of anarchy [18] as well as the inverse, the increase of the maximum latency incurred to an agent due to optimal routing [17]. It has also been shown that the price of anarchy can be decreased by imposing taxes on the edges [9,14]. Cominetti *etal.* consider the price of anarchy in a model with finitely many agents aiming at minimising their average latency [10].

For solving the corresponding classical goal of finding a minimum cost multicommodity flow, several algorithms are known. For an overview see, e. g., [1] and [7]. An efficient distributed steepest-descent algorithm for solving multicommodity flow problems with linear latency functions has been presented recently in [3]. In [2], a stateless algorithm for this problem is presented.

It is also known that the problems of finding an optimal allocation and finding a Wardrop equilibrium are essentially equivalent. Under mild conditions on the latency functions, a flow at Wardrop equilibrium with respect to so-called *marginal-cost* latency functions is optimal with respect to the original latency functions, see e. g. [5] and [18].

Several authors (e. g. [4,8]) consider dynamic routing from an online-learning perspective. Awerbuch and Kleinberg [4] present an algorithm for the online shortest path problem in an end-to-end feedback model. Blum *etal.* [8] show that approximate Wardrop equilibria defined in a similar way can be attained if the agents follow no-regret algorithms. Their bounds on the convergence time depend polynomially on the regret bounds and network size and depend pseudopolynomially on the maximum slope of the latency functions.

The problem of load-balancing has also been studied in various discrete settings for networks of parallel links. For the case of identical links, both sequential [15] and concurrent distributed algorithms were considered [6]. Even-Dar et al. [11] consider distributed algorithms for load balancing on links with speeds using sampling rules which depend pseudopolynomially on the speed of the links.

The rerouting policy upon which our algorithms are based was introduced in [13] and [12]. It was shown that an infinite number of agents executing this policy can attain a Wardrop equilibrium quickly in a concurrent setting.

2 Model and Problem Statement

2.1 Wardrop's Traffic Model

We consider Wardrop's traffic model originally introduced in [19]. We are given a graph $G = (V, E)$ with non-decreasing differentiable latency functions $\ell_e : \mathbb{R}_{\geq 0} \to \mathbb{R}_{\geq 0}$. Furthermore, we are given a set of commodities $[k] = \{1, \dots, k\}$ specified by source-sink-pairs $(s_i, t_i) \in V \times V$, a directed acyclic subgraph G_i of G connecting s_i and t_i and flow demands $r_i \in \mathbb{R}_{\geq 0}$. The total demand is $r = \sum_{i \in [k]} r_i$, and we normalise $r = 1$ for simplicity. Let $\mathcal{P}_i$ denote the admissible paths of commodity i, i.e., all paths connecting s_i and t_i in G_i, and let $\mathcal{P} = \bigcup_{i \in [k]} \mathcal{P}_i$. We may assume that the sets $\mathcal{P}_i$ are disjoint and define i_P to be the unique commodity to which path P belongs.

A non-negative path flow vector $(f_P)_{P \in \mathcal{P}}$ is *feasible* if it satisfies the flow demands $\sum_{P \in \mathcal{P}_i} f_P = r_i$ for all $i \in [k]$. We denote the set of all feasible flow vectors by $\mathcal{F}$. A path flow vector $(f_P)_{P \in \mathcal{P}}$ induces an edge flow vector $f = (f_{e,i})_{e \in E, i \in [k]}$ with $f_{e,i} = \sum_{P \in \mathcal{P}_i : e \in P} f_P$. The total flow on edge e is $f_e = \sum_{i \in [k]} f_{e,i}$. Furthermore, for $v \in V$ and $i \in [k]$, the total flow of commodity i through node v is $f_{v,i} = \sum_{(u,v) \in E} f_{(u,v),i} = \sum_{(v,w) \in E} f_{(v,w),i}$ for $v \notin \{s_i, t_i\}$ and $f_{s_i,i} = f_{t_i,i} = r_i$. The latency of an edge $e \in E$ is given by $\ell_e(f_e)$ and the latency of a path P is given by the sum of the edge latencies $\ell_P(f) = \sum_{e \in P} \ell_e(f_e)$. Finally, the weighted average latency of commodity $i \in [k]$ is given by $L_i(f) = \sum_{e \in E} \ell_e(f) \cdot (f_{e,i}/r_i)$ and the overall average latency is $L(f) = \sum_{e \in E} \ell_e(f) \cdot f_e/r$. We drop the argument f of $\ell(\cdot)$ and $L(\cdot)$ whenever it is clear from the context.

A flow vector in this model is considered stable when no fraction of the flow can improve its sustained latency by moving unilaterally to another path. This implies that all used paths must have the same minimal latency. Unused paths may have larger latency.

Definition 1 (Wardrop equilibrium). *A feasible flow vector f is at* Wardrop equilibrium *if for every commodity $i \in [k]$ and paths $P_1, P_2 \in \mathcal{P}_i$ with $f_{P_1} > 0$ it holds that $\ell_{P_1}(f) \leq \ell_{P_2}(f)$.*

It is well-known that Wardrop equilibria are exactly those allocations that minimise the following potential function introduced in [5]:

$$\Phi(f) = \sum_{e \in E} \int_0^{f_e} \ell_e(u) \, du \ .$$

This potential precisely absorbs progress: If an infinitesimal amount of flow dx is shifted from path ℓ_P to ℓ_Q, thus improving its latency by $(\ell_P - \ell_Q)$, the potential decreases by $(\ell_P - \ell_Q) \, dx$. We will make use of this fact frequently. The minimum potential is denoted by $\Phi^* = \min_{f \in \mathcal{F}} \Phi(f)$. Every flow vector f with $\Phi(f) = \Phi^*$ is then at Wardrop equilibrium. We assume that Φ^* is positive. The case that $\Phi^* = 0$ can be treated by adding virtual offsets to the latency functions. For a detailed treatment see [12].

Let us remark, that the problems of computing a Wardrop equilibrium and computing a flow minimising L are equivalent. It is sufficient to replace the latency functions ℓ_e by so-called *marginal-cost* latency functions $h_e(x) = (x \cdot \ell_e(x))' = \ell_e(x) + x \cdot \ell'_e(x)$. If for all $e \in E$, $x \cdot \ell_e(x)$ is convex, then Wardrop equilibria with respect to $(h_e)_{e \in E}$ minimise L [5,18].

The algorithms presented in this paper will compute approximate equilibria in the following bicriterial sense.

Definition 2 (δ-ϵ-equilibrium). *Consider a flow vector f and let $\mathcal{P}_i^\delta = \{P \in \mathcal{P}_i \mid \ell_P(f) > L_i(f) + \delta\, L(f)\}$ denote the set of δ-expensive paths. A flow vector is at a δ-ϵ-equilibrium if $\sum_{i \in [k]} \sum_{P \in \mathcal{P}_i^\delta} f_P \le \epsilon$.*

This definition of approximate Wardrop equilibria requires that almost all flow utilises paths with a latency that is close to the average of their own commodity. A similar definition of approximate Nash equilibria is used, e.g., in [8].

2.2   Elasticity of Latency Functions

Our algorithms take the steepness of the latency functions into account when deciding how much flow to shift from one path to another. In [12] it was shown that the critical parameter in this setting is not the slope but the elasticity.

Definition 3. *For any positive differentiable function $\ell : \mathbb{R}_{\ge 0} \to \mathbb{R}_{\ge 0}$, the elasticity of ℓ at x is $d(x) = \frac{x \cdot \ell'(x)}{\ell(x)}$.*

In other words, the elasticity of a function is bounded from above by d if the (absolute) slope at any point is at most by a factor of d larger than the slope of the line connecting the origin and the point $(x, \ell(x))$. Note that a polynomial with positive coefficients and degree d has elasticity at most d, hence, elasticity can be considered as a generalisation of the degree of such a polynomial. The function $a \cdot \exp(\lambda x)$, $x \in [0, 1]$ has maximum elasticity λ.

2.3   Implicit Path Decomposition

Wardrop equilibria are defined with respect to path flows. Our algorithms, however, will make use only of the edge flow vectors, which do not determine a vector of path flows uniquely. However, in a DAG, an edge flow vector $(f_e)_{e \in E}$ induces a natural vector of path flows by starting with the flow injected at the source, and splitting the flow at each node v such that the set of paths containing the outgoing edge e receives a flow proportional to f_e. Since the decomposition for one commodity $i \in [k]$ is independent of the flow of other commodities, we can omit the index i for simplicity.

Definition 4. *Consider any edge flow vector $(f_e)_{e \in E}$ (for some commodity i). For any path $P = (v_1, \ldots, v_l)$ let*

$$\tilde{f}_P = f_{v_1} \cdot \prod_{j=1}^{l-1} \frac{f_{(v_j, v_{j+1})}}{f_{v_j}} \quad .$$

It is easily verified by induction on the distance from the source that this is actually a valid flow decomposition of $(f_e)_{e \in E}$, i.e., $f_e = \sum_{P \ni e} \tilde{f}_P$.

2.4 Distributed Computation Model

Our algorithms operate in the following setting. Agents operate in a synchronous, round-based fashion. We assume that there is a billboard via which the agents are able to share information. On this billboard, each agent can observe the edge flows of its own commodity and the latency values of the paths it uses. Agents know an upper bound d on the elasticity of the latency functions, but they do not know the latency functions themselves. However, it is easily possible to extend our algorithm such that it does not rely on the knowledge of a bound on the elasticity.

In every round an agent can update the edge flows of its own commodity on the billboard. These updates become visible to all agents only in the next round. All agents execute the same algorithm in parallel. Therefore, in the descriptions of our algorithms, we may omit the index for the commodity, i.e., f_e refers to the flow $f_{e,i}$ of commodity i on edge e.

3   A Pseudopolynomial Algorithm

Our first approach works by simulating the replication policy presented in [12]. We will see that this can be done in polynomial time although this policy operates on an exponential number of paths.

3.1 The Replication Policy

Let us start by introducing the replication policy formally. We consider an infinite population of agents each of which controls an infinitesimal amount of flow which it assigns to a path. In each round agents may migrate their flow from the current path to another one. Consider an agent in commodity $i \in [k]$ currently using path $P \in \mathcal{P}_i$. Whenever activated, it performs two steps.

1. *Sampling.* Sample another path Q where the probability to sample any path Q' equals $f_{Q'}/r_i$.
2. *Migration.* There are two cases:
   (a) $\ell_Q \geq \ell_P$. In this case, the agent stays with its old path.
   (b) $\ell_Q < \ell_P$. The agent migrates to the sampled path Q with probability $\lambda \cdot (\ell_P - \ell_Q)$ for some constant $\lambda > 0$ to be determined later.

Altogether, we can characterise our policy by specifying the rate of agents migrating from one path $P \in \mathcal{P}_i$ to another path $Q \in \mathcal{P}_i$ with $\ell_Q(f) < \ell_P(f)$ within one round. This rate can be obtained by multiplying the probabilities speciefied in steps (1) and (2) with the volume of agents using path P. For this rate we obtain

$$\rho_{PQ} = \lambda \cdot f_P \cdot \frac{f_Q}{r_i} \cdot (\ell_P - \ell_Q)$$

if $\ell_Q < \ell_P$ and $\rho_{PQ} = 0$ otherwise. Thus, we can compute a sequence of flow vectors $(f_P(t))_{P \in \mathcal{P}}$ generated by this policy by summing over all paths Q:

$$
\begin{aligned}
f_P(t+1) &= f_P(t) + \sum_{Q \in \mathcal{P}_i} \rho_{QP} - \sum_{Q \in \mathcal{P}_i} \rho_{PQ} \\
&= f_P(t) + \lambda f_P \sum_{Q \in \mathcal{P}_i} \frac{f_Q}{r_i}(\ell_Q - \ell_P) \\
&= f_P(t) + \lambda f_P (L_i - \ell_P) \ .
\end{aligned}
\tag{1}
$$

3.2 Convergence Towards Equilibria

For the time being assume that agents are migrating in a continuous fashion as described by the above rules. Then, an infinitesimal amount of flow dx migrating from a path P to another path Q improving its latency from ℓ_P to ℓ_Q causes the potential Φ to reduce by $(\ell_P - \ell_Q) \, dx$. Since we only accept migrations that improve the latency, this implies that the potential always decreases which in turn implies convergence towards a Wardrop equilibrium by Lyapunov's direct method if all paths are used in the initial flow. However, in our concurrent round-based model, flow is not shifted continuously, but in finite chunks. Thus, if these chunks are chosen too large, overshooting and oscillation effects may occur. This issue can be resolved by choosing the migration rate in step 2b of the replication policy carefully. In [13] it was shown that if we choose $\lambda = \Theta(1/\ell'_{\max})$ small enough with

$$
\ell'_{\max} = \max_{P \in \mathcal{P}} \max_{f \in \mathcal{F}} \sum_{e \in P} \ell'_e(f) \ ,
$$

convergence towards Wardrop equilibria can be guaranteed. We may assume that $\ell'_{\max} > 0$ since otherwise all latency functions are constant and our problem can be solved trivially by assigning the entire flow to the path with lowest latency.

Theorem 1 ([13,12]). *If $\lambda = \Theta(1/\ell'_{\max})$ sufficiently small, the replication policy given by Equation (1) with initial flow $f(0) = f^0$ converges towards a Wardrop equilibrium if $f_P^0 > 0$ for all $P \in \mathcal{P}$. Furthermore, the number of rounds in which the flow is not at a δ-ϵ-equilibrium is*

$$
\mathcal{O}\left(\frac{1}{\epsilon^2 \delta^2} \cdot \frac{\ell'_{\max}}{\ell_{\min}} \cdot \ln\left(\frac{\Phi(f^0)}{\Phi^*} \right) \right) \ .
$$

One may observe that the ratio between maximum slope and minimum latency used in this theorem depends on the scale by which we measure flow. This scale, however, is fixed since we have normalised the total flow demand to be $r = 1$.

3.3 Simulating the Replication Policy

By a naive application of Theorem 1 we can compute a sequence of flow vectors $(f(t))_{t \geq 0}$ according to Equation (1) to obtain approximate Wardrop equilibria.

However, this approach is rendered computationally intractable by the fact that there may be an exponential number of variables f_P.

In the following, we describe an algorithm that computes the iterative change rates of the edge flows according to the implicit flow decomposition $\tilde{f}$ described in the preceding section. To that end, we show that the change rates of the edge flows f_e can be expressed solely in terms of edge flows and edge latencies (i.e., without explicit reference to the f_P variables). It suffices to know the weighted average latencies of all paths containing e defined as

$$L_e = \sum_{P \ni e} \frac{f_P}{f_e} \cdot \ell_P$$

Recall that we have fixed a commodity here, so we may drop the index i.

Lemma 1. *Consider an edge flow vector $(f_e(t))_{e \in E}$ and its path decomposition $\tilde{f}(t)$, and let $\tilde{f}(t+1)$ denote the flow generated by the replication policy in Equation (1) from $\tilde{f}(t)$. Finally, let $f_e(t+1) = \sum_{P \ni e} \tilde{f}_P(t+1)$. Then,*

$$f_e(t+1) = f_e(t) + \lambda \cdot f_e \cdot (L - L_e) \ .$$

Proof. Let $f = f(t)$ and $f' = f(t+1)$. By definition of f_e,

$$f'_e - f_e = \sum_{P \ni e} f'_P - f_P = \lambda \cdot \sum_{P \ni e} f_P \cdot (L - \ell_P) = \lambda \cdot f_e \cdot \left(L - \frac{\sum_{P \ni e} f_P \ell_P}{f_e} \right) \ ,$$

where the last term equals L_e.   □

In order to obtain the value of L_e, we implicitly compute the path decomposition $\tilde{f}$, i.e., for every edge e' we compute the flow caused by paths containing e on edge e'. This is done by Algorithm SIMULATEDREPLICATION (Algorithm 1) in time $\mathcal{O}(m)$ for every edge $e \in E$. Since there are m edges, each iteration can be performed in time $\mathcal{O}(m^2)$.

Algorithm 1. SIMULATEDREPLICATION() (executed by all commodities in parallel; $(f_e)_{e \in E}$ denotes the edge flows vector of commodity i)

1: **for** all edges $e \in E$ **do**
2:     sort all edges (v, w) in the subgraph reachable from e topologically
3:     compute total flow of all paths containing e and (v, w) $\tilde{f}_e^{(v,w)} = \sum_{(u,v) \in E} \tilde{f}_e^{(u,v)} \cdot \frac{f_{(v,w)}}{f_v}$
4:     reverse all edges and repeat steps 2 and 3 for edges between e and s
5:     compute $L_e = \sum_{e'} \frac{f_e^{e'}}{f_e} \ell_{e'}$
6:     $f'_e \leftarrow f_e + \lambda \cdot f_e \cdot (L - L_e)$ with $\lambda = 1/\ell'_{max}$
7: **end for**
8: replace $(f_e)_{e \in E}$ on the billboard with $(f'_e)_{e \in E}$

Corollary 1. *The sequence of flow vectors computed by Algorithm* SIMULAT-EDREPLICATION *converges towards the set of Wardrop equilibria. Furthermore, the number of rounds in which the flow is not at a* δ-ϵ-*equilibrium with respect to* $\tilde{f}$, *is bounded by*

$$\mathcal{O}\left(\frac{1}{\epsilon^2\,\delta^2}\cdot\frac{\ell'_{\max}}{\ell_{\min}}\cdot\ln\left(\frac{\Phi(f^0)}{\Phi^*}\right)\,,\right)$$

where f^0 *is the initial flow vector. Each iteration takes time* $\mathcal{O}\left(m^2\right)$.

Proof. Lemma 1 implies that the edge flow vector computed by the algorithm equals the edge flow vector obtained by applying the replication policy given by Equation (1) to the path decomposition $(\tilde{f})_{P\in\mathcal{P}}$. Combining this with the upper bounds on the convergence time given in [12], the claim follows.   □

4   The Polynomial Time Algorithm

The migration probability specified for step 2b of the replication policy can get very small since the latency difference $\ell_P - \ell_Q$ may become small in relation to λ if λ is chosen constant. This causes the algorithm to obtain only a pseudopolynomial convergence time depending on the maximum slope of the latency functions. In this section we present an approach that gets rid of this dependence.

To this end, we choose the amount of flow removed from a path proportional to its *relative* deviation $(\ell_P - L_{i_P})/\ell_P$ from the average and the reciprocal of the elasticity d to obtain a polynomial number of communication rounds. Whereas in the preceding section the amount of flow removed or added to a path within one round could be expressed in a nice closed form as $\lambda \cdot f_P \cdot (L - \ell_P)$ (Equation (1)), this is now no longer possible.

To compute flow updates in polynomial time we use a randomised flow decomposition. First we sample a path at random according to the implicit path decomposition $\tilde{f}$, i.e., the probability to sample path P is $\tilde{f}_P/r_{i_P}$. Since the length of a path is bounded by n this is possible in time $n \log n$ by representing adjacent nodes and their flows in a binary tree. Now, the path is assigned a certain flow volume f_P. For the time being, assume that we assign the entire bottleneck flow to P. Then, if P has latency above L_{i_P}, we remove a portion of

$$x = \Theta\left(f_P \cdot \frac{\ell_P - L_{i_P}}{d\,\ell_P}\right)$$

of its flow and distribute it proportionally among all admissible paths, i.e., after removing a flow of x from path P, the flow on every edge $e \in E$ is increased by $(f_{e,i}/r_i) \cdot x$.

Why does this process decrease the potential quickly? As long as we are not at a δ-ϵ-equilibrium, the probability of sampling a δ-expensive path is at least ϵ. In this case, the latency gain and thus the potential gain *per flow unit* will be large and proportional to $\tilde{f}_P$. If we sample only a single path, we may in fact assign the entire bottleneck flow to it. We can lower bound the probability that this bottleneck flow is not too small (Lemma 2). To increase the potential gain we repeat this process several times. Doing this, we can no longer assign the entire bottleneck to a path since it may happen that an edge is sampled several times. Hence, we assign at most a $\Theta(1/\log m)$ fraction of the bottleneck while at the same time sampling $T = m \log m$ paths rather than only a single one. It thus becomes unlikely that an edge becomes empty along the way if its flow is $\mathcal{O}(1/m)$. In order to achieve the same result for edges with larger flow, we limit the amount of flow consumed in one step to $\mathcal{O}(1/(m \log m))$. More precisely, let

$$\Delta_e = \min\left\{\frac{1}{7\,m\,\log m}, \frac{f_e}{7\,\log m}\right\} \ .$$

We start with an empty decomposition. In a round in which path P is sampled we increase f_P by Δ_{e^*} where e^* is a bottleneck edge in P. We say that an edge is *alive* if the overall flow assigned to paths containing e is at most $f_e - \Delta_e$ (i. e. it can be sampled one more time without having our decomposition exceeding the flow of e). Our algorithm terminates as soon as there are any edges that are not alive. The final algorithm RANDOMISEDBALANCING(d) is described in Algorithm 2.

Under the assumption that the latency functions are constant, we can thus show that the potential decreases in every round by a factor that only depends on ϵ and δ, and the elasticity d (Lemma 5). We furthermore show that due to our careful migration rate the potential gain with respect to the true latency functions is still at least half of the potential gain with respect to constant latencies (Lemma 4). Finally, we show that the expected potential gain implies a bound on the time to reach a minimum potential (Lemma 6). Altogether, this yields the following upper bound for our algorithm.

Theorem 2. *The sequence of flow vectors computed by Algorithm* RANDOM-ISEDBALANCING *converges towards the set of Wardrop equilibria. Furthermore, the expected number of rounds in which the flow is not at a δ-ϵ-equilibrium with respect to $\tilde{f}$, is bounded by*

$$\mathcal{O}\left(\frac{d}{\epsilon^3\,\delta^2}\log\left(\frac{\Phi(f_0)}{\Phi^*}\right)\right) \ ,$$

if d is an upper bound on the elasticity of the latency functions. The computation time of each round is bounded by $\mathcal{O}\left(n\log n \cdot m\log m\right)$.

We present the proof after establishing the necessary lemmas.

Note that our algorithm can be easily modified for the case that the elasticity of the latency functions is not known to the algorithm in advance.

4.1 Randomised Decomposition

Our algorithm generates a randomised flow decomposition using a sampling process based on $\tilde{f}$. In this section, we lower bound the probability that the bottleneck flows of the sampled paths are not too small. Furthermore, we show that the flow removed from every edge is at most f_e with high probability.

Algorithm 2. RANDOMISEDBALANCING(d) (executed by all commodities in parallel; $(f_e)_{e \in E}$ denotes the edge flows vector of commodity i)

1: **for** $T = m \log m$ times **do**
2:     sample a path P where $\mathbb{P}[P] = \frac{\tilde{f}_P}{r_i}$
3:     let e^* denote the bottleneck edge of P; let $f_P = \Delta_{e^*}$
4:     **if** $\ell_P > L_i$ **then**
5:         reduce the flow on all edges $e \in P$ by $\Delta f_P = f_P \cdot \frac{\ell_P - L_i}{4 \, d \, \ell_P}$
6:         **if** for any $e \in P$, e is not alive **then**
7:             abort loop and continue in line 11
8:         **end if**
9:     **end if**
10: **end for**
11: increase the flow on all edges $e \in E$ proportionally by $\frac{f_e}{r_i} \cdot \sum_{P \in \mathcal{P}_i} \Delta f_P$

Lemma 2. *Consider a flow vector f of volume 1 and a set of paths $\mathcal{P}_\epsilon$ with $\sum_{P \in \mathcal{P}_\epsilon} \tilde{f}_P = \epsilon$. Then, $\mathbb{P}_{P \sim \tilde{f}} \left[P \in \mathcal{P}_\epsilon \wedge \min_{e \in P} f_e \geq \frac{\epsilon}{2m} \right] \geq \frac{\epsilon}{2}$.*

Proof. We consider a scaled flow vector which supports only paths in $\mathcal{P}_\epsilon$.

$$f'_P = \begin{cases} \frac{\tilde{f}_P}{\epsilon} & P \in \mathcal{P}_\epsilon \\ 0 & P \notin \mathcal{P}_\epsilon \end{cases}.$$

Observe that the total volume of f' is 1 again, hence $\mathbb{P}_{P \sim f'}[P = Q] = \mathbb{P}_{P \sim \tilde{f}}[P = Q \mid P \in \mathcal{P}_\epsilon]$. Now,

$$\mathbb{P}_{P \sim \tilde{f}} \left[P \in \mathcal{P}_\epsilon \wedge \min_{e \in P} f_e \geq \frac{\epsilon}{2m} \right] = \mathbb{P}_{P \sim \tilde{f}}[P \in \mathcal{P}_\epsilon] \cdot \mathbb{P}_{P \sim \tilde{f}} \left[\min_{e \in P} f'_e \geq \frac{1}{2m} \mid P \in \mathcal{P}_\epsilon \right]$$

$$= \epsilon \cdot \mathbb{P}_{P \sim f'} \left[\min_{e \in P} f'_e \geq \frac{1}{2m} \right] \geq \frac{\epsilon}{2} \,, \tag{2}$$

where the first equality uses the definition of f' and the second one uses the above observation.

Now, let $d(x, y)$ denote the number of edges of a shortest path connecting x and y. We can show that $\mathbb{P}[e = (v, w) \in P] = f_e$ by induction on $d(s, v)$. This holds for $d(s, v) = 0$ by definition of $\tilde{f}$. Now, assume that the statement holds for all edges (u, v) with $d(s, u) = k$ and consider an edge $e = (v, w)$ with $d(s, v) = k + 1$.

$$\mathbb{P}[e \in P] = \mathbb{P}[v \in P] \cdot \mathbb{P}[e \in P \mid v \in P] = \sum_{(u,v)} \mathbb{P}[(u, v) \in P] \cdot \frac{f_e}{f_v}$$

$$= \sum_{(u,v)} f_{(u,v)} \cdot \frac{f_e}{f_v} = f_e \,.$$

With $E' = \{e \in E \mid f_e \leq 1/(2\,m)\}$,

$$\mathbb{P}[P \ni e : e \in E'] \leq \sum_{e \in E'} \mathbb{P}[e \in P] \leq \sum_{e \in E'} f_e \leq \frac{|E'|}{2\,m} \leq \frac{1}{2} \,.$$

Substituting this into Equation (2) yields our desired bound. $\square$

We now consider a sequence of $T = m \log m$ rounds. Observe that Δ_e is an upper bound on the flow removed from a path containing e by our algorithm, since for the bottleneck edge e^*, $\Delta_{e^*} = \min_{e \in P}\{\Delta_e\}$. The flow on e may decrease to below zero only if it is contained in the sampled path at least f_e/Δ_e times. In the following we show that this is unlikely.

Lemma 3. *With probability* $1-o(1)$, *after a sequence of* $T = m \log m$ *iterations, all edges are still alive.*

Proof. In the proof of Lemma 2 we have seen that the probability to hit edge e in one round equals f_e. Let the random variable X denote the number of hits in T rounds. We have $\mathbb{E}[X] = T f_e$. An edge is alive if $X \le f_e/\Delta_e - 1$. There are two cases:

1. $f_e < \frac{1}{m}$ implying $\Delta_e = f_e/(7 \log m)$. Then,

$$\mathbb{P}\left[X > \frac{f_e}{\Delta_e} - 1\right] = \mathbb{P}\left[X > \mathbb{E}[X] \cdot \left(\frac{7}{f_e\, m} - \frac{1}{T f_e}\right)\right]$$
$$\le \mathbb{P}\left[X > \mathbb{E}[X] \cdot \left(\frac{6}{f_e\, m}\right)\right]$$
$$\le 2^{-\mathbb{E}[X] \cdot \frac{6}{f_e\, m}} = m^{-6} .$$

   The first inequality is the definition of T and Δ_e and uses our assumption that $f_e \cdot m < 1$, and the second inequality is Chernoff's inequality (which asserts that $\mathbb{P}[X \ge r \cdot \mathbb{E}[X]] \le 2^{-r \cdot \mathbb{E}[X]}$ for $r \ge 6$ for a random variable X that is the sum of 0-1 random variables, see [16]).

2. $f_e \ge \frac{1}{m}$ implying $\Delta_e = 1/(7\,T)$. This case can be treated similarly.

In both cases, the probability that edge e is not alive at the end of a sequence of T iterations is bounded by m^{-6}. Using a union bound, the probability that at least one edge does not survive is at most m^{-5} and consequently the probability that all edges survive the sequence is at least $1 - m^{-5}$.   □

4.2   Lower Bounding the Potential Gain

We use a potential function argument to prove convergence. In order to show that our algorithm avoids oscillations, we consider the potential gain achieved within one round. We show that this potential gain is at least half of the potential gain that would occur if latencies values were fixed at the beginning of a round. A second lemma shows that, in expectation, the potential decreases by a factor in every round, as long as we are not yet at an approximate equilibrium.

Lemma 4. *Let d denote an upper bound on the elasticity of the latency functions. For a flow vector f consider a flow vector f' generated by Algorithm* RAN- DOMISEDBALANCING(d) *(Algorithm 2) with positive probability. For any $P \in \mathcal{P}$ let Δf_P denote the amount of flow removed from path P. Then,* $\Phi(f) - \Phi(f') \ge \frac{1}{2} \cdot \sum_{P \in \mathcal{P}}(\ell_P(f) - L_{i_P}) \cdot \Delta f_P$.

Due to space limitations, we defer the proof to the full version.

Lemma 5. *Assume that f is a flow that is not at δ-ϵ-equilibrium and let the random variable f' denote a flow generated by our algorithm. Then, $\mathbb{E}\left[\Phi(f')\right] \leq \Phi(f) \cdot \left(1 - \Omega\left(\frac{\epsilon^3 \delta^2}{d}\right)\right).$*

Proof. For the time being, assume that the latency functions are constant. By Markov's inequality, the total volume of flow in commodities with $L_i > 2 \cdot L/\epsilon$ is at most $\epsilon/2$. We consider only commodities with $L_i \leq 2 \cdot L/\epsilon$. In total, at least a flow volume of ϵ utilises δ-expensive paths and there is still at least a volume of $\epsilon/2$ left in the commodities we consider. Consider such a commodity $i \in [k]$ and denote the flow volume using δ-expensive paths in this commodity by ϵ_i.

Consider any iteration satisfying the precondition that all edges are alive. Let P denote the path sampled by the algorithm. By Lemma 2, the probability that $\ell_P \geq L_i + \delta L$ and the minimum edge flow along P is at least $\epsilon_i/(2\,m)$ is at least $\epsilon_i/(2\,r_i)$ (we have to scale the flow of this commodity by a factor $1/r_i$ to make it a unit flow). The amount of flow removed from this path by our algorithm is

$$\frac{\epsilon_i}{2\,m} \cdot \frac{1}{7 \log m} \cdot \frac{\ell_P - L_i}{4\,d\,\ell_P} \geq \frac{\epsilon_i\,\epsilon\,\delta}{113\,d\,m\,\log m}$$

where we have used that $\ell_P \geq L_i + \delta L$ and $L_i \leq 2\,L/\epsilon$. The latency gain of this path is then at least δL and since this event happens with probability $\epsilon_i/(2\,r_i)$ the expected virtual potential gain of such a path is then at least

$$\frac{\epsilon_i^2\,\epsilon\,\delta^2}{226\,d\,r_i\,m\,\log m}\,L \ .$$

By Lemma 3 the probability that in this iteration all edges are alive is $1 - o(1)$ and the expected potential gain computed above is independent of this event. Summing up over all $T = m \log m$ iterations and all commodities, the total expected virtual potential gain of one round is at least

$$(1 - o(1)) \cdot \sum_{i \in [k]} \frac{\epsilon_i^2\,\epsilon\,\delta^2}{226\,d\,r_i}\,L \geq (1 - o(1)) \cdot \frac{\epsilon^3 \delta^2}{226\,d}\,L \ .$$

For the last inequality we have used the Cauchy-Schwarz Inequality which asserts that for two vectors (a_i) and (b_i), $\sum_i a_i^2 \geq \left(\sum_i a_i\,b_i\right)^2/\sum_i b_i^2$. Using $a_i = \epsilon_i/\sqrt{r_i}$ and $b_i = \sqrt{r_i}$ yields the result. This implies the claim since L is an upper bound on Φ and Lemma 4 ensures that the true potential gain with respect to the real latency functions is at least half of the potential gain with respect to the constant latency functions. $\qquad\square$

4.3   From Expected Potential Gain to Expected Stopping Time

The preceding section has shown that in every round the potential decreases by a factor in expectation. Intuitively, this implies an expected running time that is logarithmic in this factor and the initial values. This intuition is made precise by the following lemma.

Lemma 6. *Let $X_0, X_1, \ldots$ denote a sequence of non-negative random variables and assume that for all $i \geq 0$ $\mathbb{E}[X_i \mid X_{i-1} = x_{i-1}] \leq x_{i-1} \cdot \alpha$ for some constant $\alpha \in (0, 1)$. Furthermore, fix some constant $x^* \in (0, x_0]$ and let τ be the random variable that describes the smallest t such that $X_t \leq x^*$. Then, $\mathbb{E}[\tau \mid X_0 = x_0] \leq \frac{2}{\log(1/\alpha)} \cdot \log\left(\frac{x_0}{x^*}\right)$.*

We defer the proof to the full version. Finally, we can proof our main result.

Proof (Proof of Theorem 2). Let $f_0, f_1, \ldots$ denote a sequence of flow vectors generated by Algorithm 2. Lemma 5 implies that

$$\mathbb{E}[\Phi(f_{t+1}) \mid \Phi(f_t) = \phi] \leq \phi \cdot \left(1 - \Omega\left(\frac{\epsilon^3 \delta^2}{d}\right)\right) .$$

Thus, the sequence $(\Phi(f_t))_{t \geq 0}$ satisfies the conditions of Lemma 6 and the expected time until $\Phi(f_t)$ reaches its minimum Φ^* implying that f_t is a δ-ϵ-equilibrium is

$$\frac{2}{\log\left(\left(1 - \Omega\left(\frac{\epsilon^3 \delta^2}{d}\right)\right)^{-1}\right)} \log\left(\frac{\Phi(f_0)}{\Phi^*}\right) = \mathcal{O}\left(\frac{d}{\epsilon^3 \delta^2} \log\left(\frac{\Phi(f_0)}{\Phi^*}\right)\right) ,$$

our desired bound.

One path can be sampled in time $\mathcal{O}(n \log n)$, the bottleneck edge can be found in time $\mathcal{O}(n)$, and the flow update can be computed in time $\mathcal{O}(n)$. Altogether, at most $T = m \log m$ iterations have to be computed. Finally, the removed flow can be reinserted in time $\mathcal{O}(n)$. □

5   Open Problems

Our algorithm works by redistributing flow of overloaded paths. To identify such paths we face the subproblem of finding a flow decomposition that assigns much flow to paths with high latency. In our algorithm we have used a randomised path decomposition to achieve this goal. It is not obvious whether this randomisation can be avoided, and, in fact, naive deterministic approaches like longest path first decompositions fail.

In the long run, our algorithm converges towards the set of Wardrop equilibria. A weakness of our notion of approximate equilibria, however, is the fact that the average latency may be arbitrarily far away from the minimum latency. As an alternative, one could also consider deviations from the minimum latency rather than from the average latency. It is unclear whether convergence towards approximate equilibria in this sense can be guaranteed in polynomial time. Furthermore, it would be desirable to design specialised (not necessarily distributed) algorithms to compute (exact) Wardrop equilibria that improve upon the standard solution via convex programming.

References

1. Ahuja, R.K., Magnanti, T.L., Orlin, J.B.: Network flows: Theory, algorithms and applications. Prentince-Hall, Englewood Cliffs (1993)
2. Awerbuch, B., Khandekar, R.: Greedy distributed optimization of multi-commodity flows. In: Proc. 26th Ann. Symp. on Principles of Distributed Computing (PODC) (2007)
3. Awerbuch, B., Khandekar, R., Rao, S.: Distributed algorithms for multicommodity flow problems via approximate steepest descent framework. In: Proc. 18th Ann. Symp. on Discrete Algorithms (SODA) (2007)
4. Awerbuch, B., Kleinberg, R.D.: Adaptive routing with end-to-end feedback: Distributed learning and geometric approaches. In: Proc. 36th Ann. Symp. on Theory of Comput. (STOC), pp. 45–53 (2004)
5. Beckmann, M., McGuire, C.B., Winsten, C.B.: Studies in the Economics of Transportation. Yale University Press, New Haven and London (1956)
6. Berenbrink, P., Friedetzky, T., Goldberg, L.A., Goldberg, P., Hu, Z., Martin, R.: Distributed selfish load balancing. In: Proc. 17th Ann. Symp. on Discrete Algorithms (SODA) (2006)
7. Bertsekas, D.P.: Network Optimization: Continuous and Discrete Models. Athena Scientific (1998)
8. Blum, A., Even-Dar, E., Ligett, K.: Routing without regret: On convergence to Nash equilibria of regret-minimizing algorithms in routing games. In: Proc. 25th Ann. Symp. on Principles of Distributed Computing (PODC), pp. 45–52. ACM, New York (2006)
9. Cole, R., Dodis, Y., Roughgarden, T.: How much can taxes help selfish routing? In: Proc. 4th Conf. on Electronic Commerce, pp. 98–107 (2003)
10. Cominetti, R., Correa, J.R., Moses, N.E.S.: Network games with atomic players. In: Bugliesi, M., Preneel, B., Sassone, V., Wegener, I. (eds.) ICALP 2006. LNCS, vol. 4052, pp. 525–536. Springer, Heidelberg (2006)
11. Even-Dar, E., Mansour, Y.: Fast convergence of selfish rerouting. In: Proc. 16th Ann. Symp. on Discrete Algorithms (SODA), pp. 772–781 (2005)
12. Fischer, S., Räcke, H., Vöcking, B.: Fast convergence to Wardrop equilibria by adaptive sampling methods. In: Proc. 38th Symposium on Theory of Computing (STOC), pp. 653–662. ACM, New York (2006)
13. Fischer, S., Vöcking, B.: Adaptive routing with stale information. In: Aguilera, M.K., Aspnes, J. (eds.) Proc. 24th Symp. on Principles of Distributed Computing (PODC), pp. 276–283. ACM, New York (2005)
14. Fleischer, L.: Linear tolls suffice: New bounds and algorithms for tolls in single source networks. In: Díaz, J., Karhumäki, J., Lepistö, A., Sannella, D. (eds.) ICALP 2004. LNCS, vol. 3142, pp. 544–554. Springer, Heidelberg (2004)
15. Goldberg, P.W.: Bounds for the convergence rate of randomized local search in a multiplayer, load-balancing game. In: Proc. 23rd Symp. on Principles of Distributed Computing (PODC), pp. 131–140. ACM, New York (2004)
16. Hagerup, T., Rüb, C.: A guided tour of Chernoff bounds. Information Processing Letters 33, 305–308 (1990)
17. Roughgarden, T.: How unfair is optimal routing? In: Proc. 13th Ann. Symp. on Discrete Algorithms (SODA), pp. 203–204 (2002)
18. Roughgarden, T., Tardos, É.: How bad is selfish routing? J. ACM 49(2), 236–259 (2002)
19. Wardrop, J.G.: Some theoretical aspects of road traffic research. In: Proc. of the Institute of Civil Engineers, Pt. II, vol. 1, pp. 325–378 (1952)

Energy and Time Efficient Broadcasting in Known Topology Radio Networks

Leszek Gąsieniec[1,*], Erez Kantor[2,**], Dariusz R. Kowalski[1,*],
David Peleg[2,**], and Chang Su[1]

[1] Department of Computer Science,
The University of Liverpool, Liverpool L69 3BX, UK
{leszek,darek,suc}@csc.liv.ac.uk
[2] Department of Computer Science and Applied Mathematics,
The Weizmann Institute of Science, Rehovot, 76100 Israel
{erez.kantor,david.peleg}@weizmann.ac.il

Abstract. The paper considers broadcasting protocols in radio networks with known topology that are efficient in both time and energy. The radio network is modelled as an undirected graph $G = (V, E)$ where $|V| = n$. It is assumed that during execution of the communication task every node in V is allowed to transmit at most once. Under this assumption it is shown that any radio broadcast protocol requires $D + \Omega(\sqrt{n - D})$ transmission rounds, where D is the diameter of G. This lower bound is complemented with an efficient construction of a deterministic protocol that accomplishes broadcasting in $D + O(\sqrt{n} \log n)$ rounds. Moreover, if we allow each node to transmit at most k times, the lower bound $D + \Omega((n - D)^{1/(2k)})$ on the number of transmission rounds holds. We also provide a randomised protocol that accomplishes broadcasting in $D + O(kn^{1/(k-2)} \log^2 n)$ rounds. The paper concludes with a discussion of several other strategies for energy efficient radio broadcasting and a number of open problems in the area.

1   Introduction

1.1   Background

This paper concerns the study of simultaneously energy and time efficient communication protocols under an abstract model of radio networks, where uniform transmitting and receiving devices form a set of nodes V in an undirected graph $G = (V, E)$ of size $|V| = n$. Two nodes $v, w \in V$ are *neighbours* in G, i.e., there is an edge (v, w) in E, whenever v and w can communicate (i.e., send and receive messages) directly with each other. Nodes that are not connected by edges must communicate via intermediate nodes. We consider synchronous networks, where the processing and transmission speeds of nodes are uniform across the entire

---

* Supported in part by the Royal Society grant *Algorithmic and Combinatorial Aspects of Radio Communication*, IJP - 2006/R2.
** Supported in part by grants from the Minerva Foundation and the Israel Ministry of Science.

A. Pelc (Ed.): DISC 2007, LNCS 4731, pp. 253–267, 2007.

network. Communication is performed in *rounds*. During any round, each node can be either in a *transmitting mode* or in a *receiving mode*, meaning that a node cannot both transmit and receive messages during the same round. Moreover, if a node v transmits in a given round, the message is delivered to all its neighbours. However, a node w in a receiving mode in a given round will receive the message from its transmitting neighbour v if and only if v is the *only* transmitting neighbour of w in this round. The efficiency of communication protocols in synchronous networks is often expressed as the time (the number of rounds) required to accomplish the task. In this paper, apart from the time complexity we are also interested in another important efficiency measure, namely the *energy efficiency*. We consider strategies for efficient radio communication in the context of the broadcasting task.

In the broadcasting problem, a distinguished node s in the network, referred to as the *source node*, has a *message* that has to be distributed to all other nodes in the network. Energy efficient radio broadcasting was mostly studied in the context of geometric networks, where the network nodes are embedded into 2-dimensional plane. In particular, the goal in the *energy efficient broadcast tree* problem is to find a transmission graph that minimizes the total power consumption and contains a directed spanning tree rooted at the source node s. The problem is known to be NP-hard [8] and if the distance function is arbitrary, it has no logarithmic factor approximation unless $P = NP$ [16]. For the Euclidean distance model, Wan *et al.* [22] and with improved reasoning Klasing *et al.* [17] argued that the algorithm that computes a minimal spanning tree for the set of nodes yields the approximation ratio 12.15. The approximation ratio was further reduced to 7.6 by Flammini *et al.* [10] and later to 6.33 by Navarra [21]. Recently Ambühl [1] showed that the minimum spanning tree yields an approximation ratio 6, which is as far as one can go with this approach, in view of the lower bound presented in [22].

In our model of radio communication spatial information is not available, thus there is a need for an alternative definition of energy consumption. Since the network nodes are uniform, it is natural to assume that transmissions performed by every node cost exactly the same. Moreover, we are interested in *balancing* the energy consumption at the nodes. This would serve to avoid energy consumption bottlenecks at some wireless nodes, especially if they operate on limited power sources, e.g., batteries, and may thus help to prolong the operational lifetime of the entire system. With this goal in mind, we consider energy efficient strategies in which every node is allowed to transmit *at most once* during the execution of any communication task, in our case the broadcasting procedure. We refer to such energy efficient strategies as *1-shot protocols*. Such a strategy for energy efficient radio communication was very recently studied in the context of broadcasting and gossiping in radio networks of random topology, see [5].

Research on time efficient broadcasting in known topology radio networks, where an entire schedule of node transmissions can be precomputed in advance, was initiated in [6]. In this paper Chlamtac and Weinstein provided a broadcast schedule with the running time $O(D \log^2 n)$, where D is diameter of the network.

Later an $\Omega(\log^2 n)$ time lower bound was proved for the family of radius 2 graphs [3]. While it was known for quite a while [4] that for every n-vertex radio network of diameter D there exists a deterministic broadcasting schedule of length $O(D \log n + \log^2 n)$, an appropriate efficient construction for such a schedule was proposed only very recently in [18]. Another type of a broadcast schedule requiring $D + O(\log^5 n)$ rounds is due to Gaber and Mansour, see [11]. Elkin and Kortsarz in [9] presented deterministic constructions of broadcasting schedules of length $D + O(\log^4 n)$ for arbitrary graphs and $D + O(\log^3 n)$ for planar graphs. The existential proof that the optimal $D + O(\log^2 n)$ broadcast schedule is feasible was given by Gasieniec *et al.* in [12]. Explicit constructions of broadcasting schedules operating in $O(D + \log^2 n)$ and $D + O(\frac{\log^3 n}{\log \log n})$ rounds can be found in [19] and [7] respectively.

1.2   Our Results

In this paper we focus on simultaneously time and energy efficient broadcasting protocols in radio networks with known topology. In Section 2 we show that any 1-shot radio broadcast protocol requires $D + \Omega(\sqrt{n - D})$ rounds of transmission, where D is the diameter of G. In Section 3 we provide an efficient construction of a deterministic protocol that accomplishes broadcasting in $D + O(\sqrt{n} \log n)$ rounds. Section 4 contains results in the model where each node is allowed to transmit at most k times. We prove a lower bound $D + \Omega((n - D)^{1/(2k)})$ and we design a randomised protocol that accomplishes broadcasting in $D + O(kn^{1/(k-2)} \log^2 n)$ rounds. Finally in Section 5 we discuss several other strategies for energy efficient radio broadcasting and state a number of open problems in the area. All algorithms presented in the paper are deterministic and constructible in polynomial time.

2   A $D + \Omega(\sqrt{n - D})$ Lower Bound for 1-Shot Broadcasting

In this section we show that there exist radio networks in which every 1-shot broadcasting strategy requires at least $D + \Omega(\sqrt{n - D})$ rounds of transmissions. Specifically, we show that for any positive integer n there exists an n-node bipartite graph on which any 1-shot broadcasting protocol requires $\Omega(\sqrt{n})$ communication rounds. Consider the *binomial graph* $B(x) = (\{r\} \cup U \cup L, E)$, where $\{r\}$, U and L are disjoint, $|U| = x$, $|L| = y$, and $y = \binom{x}{2}$. The singleton set $\{r\}$ is intended as the source while the set U (respectively, L) forms the *upper* (resp., *lower*) layer of $B(x)$. The nodes in U are labelled by the integers 1 to x and the nodes in L by unordered pairs $\{a, b\}$ such that $1 \le a < b \le x$. The node r is connected to all the nodes in U, and a node in L labelled by $\{a, b\}$ is connected to exactly two nodes a and b in U. For example, see structures of $B(3)$ and $B(4)$ in Figures 1(a) and 1(b) respectively. In the first step, the message is transmitted by r to reach all the nodes in U. Our analysis concerns the process by which the message is disseminated from the nodes of U to the nodes of L.

The proof is based on the observation that in any 1-shot broadcasting protocol, exactly one node from the upper layer U is permitted to transmit in each round. Consider the first round of any broadcasting procedure. Assume first that two nodes a and b in U decide to transmit simultaneously. Their shared neighbour $\{a, b\}$ in the lower layer L gets neither of the messages due to collision. Moreover, this node will not receive any other messages in the future since its only neighbours already transmitted and they are allowed to do this only once. This proves that multiple transmissions in the first round are not allowed. Now assume that during the first round a single node a from U transmits and all neighbours of a in L receive the broadcast message. Removing a from U and all its neighbours from L, we obtain a smaller binomial graph $B(x-1)$. Thus the next round of the broadcasting protocol must again consist of a transmission from a single node in U. This argument is repeated until a binomial graph $B(1)$ with no edges between the layers U and L is obtained. This leads to the conclusion that any 1-shot broadcasting protocol in a binomial graph $B(x)$ requires $x-1$ consecutive transmission rounds. Since $n = x + y + 1$ for $y = \binom{x}{2}$, the number of communication rounds required by any 1-shot broadcasting procedure is $\Omega(\sqrt{n})$.

Theorem 1. *There exists a radio network of size n and diameter D in which any 1-shot broadcasting protocol requires $D + \Omega(\sqrt{n - D})$ transmission rounds.*

Proof. The lower bound of $D + \Omega(\sqrt{n - D})$ can be derived directly from the lower bound for 1-shot broadcasting strategies in binomial bipartite graphs. Consider a graph formed by attaching a path P of length $D - 2$ to the node r of the binomial bipartite graph $B(x)$, where x is the largest integer satisfying $D - 2 + x(x + 1)/2 \leq n$, and placing the broadcasting source at the far (from $B(x)$) end of the path P. The time required by any 1-shot broadcasting procedure includes $D - 2$ rounds to move the broadcast message along P and $\Omega(\sqrt{n - (D - 2)})$ additional rounds to inform every node in the lower layer of $B(x)$. The lower bound $D - 2 + \Omega(\sqrt{n - (D - 2)}) = D + \Omega(\sqrt{n - D})$ follows.

3   1-Shot Broadcasting in $D + O(\sqrt{n} \log n)$ Rounds

For ease of presentation, we first provide a 1-shot radio broadcasting strategy for all n-node bipartite graphs (with the message already available at all nodes of the upper layer), consisting of $O(\sqrt{n})$ transmission rounds. This result is then combined with the new ranking scheme given in Section 3.2, and admits 1-shot radio broadcasting in $D + O(\sqrt{n} \log n)$ rounds for arbitrary undirected graphs.

3.1   Broadcasting in Bipartite Graphs

Consider a bipartite graph $B = (U \cup L, E)$ with the upper layer U and the lower layer L. In what follows we assume that U forms a *minimal covering set (MCS)* of L, see [13], i.e., that the removal of any node from U, along with all edges incident to it, isolates some nodes in L. Define another graph $G' = (U, E')$ on the basis of B as follows. For every node $v \in L$ of degree at least two, pick two

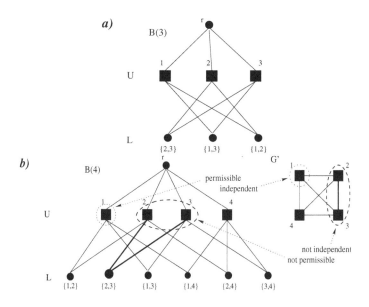

Fig. 1. (a) the structure of $B(3)$;(b) the graph G' based on $B(4)$

arbitrary neighbours of v in U, and add to E' an edge between them. Note that by this construction, $|E'| \leq |L|$. For example, a graph G' defined on the basis of the layers U and L in the binomial graph $B(4)$ is presented in Figure 1(b).

A set of nodes in an undirected graph is *independent* if no two nodes in it are directly connected by an edge. For a subset $Q \subseteq U$, let $I(Q) \subseteq L$ denote the set containing all nodes in L having exactly one neighbour in Q. We say that a subset $Q \subseteq U$ in the bipartite graph B is *permissible* if simultaneous transmissions from Q inform a subset $I(Q) \subseteq L$ and the removal of all nodes in Q from U, along with their incident edges, does not isolate nodes in $L \setminus I(Q)$.

Lemma 1. *An independent set of nodes Q in the graph G' forms a permissible set in B.*

Proof. By the definition of $I(Q)$, it suffices to show that removing all nodes in Q from the upper layer U, along with their incident edges, does not isolate any nodes in $L \setminus I(Q)$. Indeed, consider an arbitrary node $v \in L$ with neighbour set A in B. If v has no neighbour in Q, then after the removal, v is still connected to some node in $U \setminus Q$. If v has exactly one neighbour in Q, then $v \in I(Q)$, hence $v \notin L \setminus I(Q)$. Finally, suppose v is connected to at least two nodes in Q. In this case, v must also have another neighbour outside of Q. To see this, note that by construction, the graph G' includes an edge between some two nodes of A. Hence if $A \subseteq Q$, then Q fails to be independent in G', leading to contradiction.

The following fact, related to the efficient construction of large independent sets, was proved in the context of parallel computing in [14].

Lemma 2. *In a graph $G' = (U, E')$, where $|U| = x$ and $|E'| = y$, one can construct in time polynomial in $x + y$ an independent set $Q \subseteq U$ such that $|Q| \geq \frac{x^2}{2y+x}$.*

Combining Lemmas 1 and 2 we conclude:

Lemma 3. *In a bipartite graph $B(U \cup L, E)$, where $|U| = x$, $|L| = y$ and $x \geq \sqrt{y}$, there exists a permissible transmission set of size at least $\lceil \frac{x^2}{2y+x} \rceil$.*

We are ready to state the main theorem for 1-shot radio broadcasting strategies in bipartite graphs.

Theorem 2. *In any n-node bipartite graph, the broadcast message can be distributed from the upper layer to the lower layer in $O(\sqrt{n})$ rounds using a 1-shot broadcasting strategy.*

Proof. Assume that $U' \subseteq U$ is a subset of nodes in the upper layer that forms a minimal covering set of the lower layer L, where $|U'| = x$ and $|L| = y$. Note that if $x^2 \leq 2y + x$ then nodes from U' can transmit sequentially in time $x = O(\sqrt{n})$ since $x^2 \leq 2y + x < 2(y + x) = 2n$. Otherwise, assume that $x^2 > 2y + x$. We first show how to reduce the size of the upper layer to $\sqrt{y} \log y$ in $O(\sqrt{n})$ rounds, and later how to perform further reductions to obtain a set of size $\sqrt{y}$ in $O(\sqrt{y})$ additional rounds. After the reduction process is accomplished, the nodes still present in the upper layer transmit sequentially in at most $\sqrt{y} = O(\sqrt{n})$ rounds.

Assume first that after some number of rounds of the reduction process the size of the upper layer x' is still larger than $\sqrt{y} \log y$, where the size of the lower layer is $y' \leq y$. By Lemma 3, the current set U' (after the removal of nodes and edges in the construction process) contains a permissible transmission set of size at least $\frac{(x')^2}{2y'+x'}$. We can assume that $x' \leq y'$ (the upper layer constitutes a minimal covering set) and consequently that there exists a permissible transmission set of size at least $\frac{(x')^2}{3y'}$. In this case, after one round of transmissions the size of the upper layer is reduced to $x'' = x' - \frac{(x')^2}{3y'} = x'(1 - \frac{x'}{3y'})$. Since we assumed $x' > \sqrt{y} \log y$ and also $y' \leq y$, it follows that $x'' \leq x'(1 - \frac{\sqrt{y} \log y}{3y}) = x'(1 - \frac{\log y}{3\sqrt{y}})$. This means that the size of the upper layer can be reduced in one round by a fraction of $1 - \frac{\log y}{3\sqrt{y}}$ and consequently in at most $\frac{3\sqrt{y}}{\log y}$ rounds by a constant fraction, for as long as $x' > \sqrt{y} \log y$. Thus repeating this reduction process for $O(\log y)$ times, the size of the upper layer becomes smaller than $\sqrt{y} \log y$. The total number of rounds in the entire reduction process is $O(\sqrt{y})$, where $\sqrt{y} = O(\sqrt{n})$.

After the size of the upper layer is reduced to $\sqrt{y} \log y$, the remaining reduction process is split into $0 \leq i \leq \log \log y$ stages, where during stage i, the size x' of the upper layer U' is reduced from at most $\frac{\sqrt{y} \log y}{2^i}$ to at most $\frac{\sqrt{y} \log y}{2^{i+1}}$. Consider an arbitrary stage i, where $y' \geq x'$ is the size of the lower layer. By Lemma 3, U' contains a permissible transmission set of size at least $\frac{x'^2}{2y'+x'}$. Since $x' \leq y' \leq y$ and $x' \geq \frac{\sqrt{y} \log y}{2^{i+1}}$ we conclude that there exists a permissible transmission set of size $\frac{x'^2}{3y} \geq (\frac{\sqrt{y}\log y}{2^{i+1}})^2/3y \geq \frac{\log^2 y}{2^{2(i+2)}}$. To move from stage i to stage $i+1$ one has to remove from the upper layer U' at most $\frac{\sqrt{y}\log y}{2^{i+1}}$ nodes. Since during each round we know how to remove at least $\frac{\log^2 y}{2^{2(i+2)}}$ nodes, the number of rounds required to move to stage $i+1$ is bounded by $\frac{\sqrt{y}\log y}{2^{i+1}} / \frac{\log^2 y}{2^{2(i+2)}} = \frac{2^{i+3}\sqrt{y}}{\log y}$. Thus the total number of rounds of all $\log\log y$ stages is bounded by $\sum_{i=0}^{\log\log y} \frac{2^{i+3}\sqrt{y}}{\log y} = \frac{8\sqrt{y}}{\log y} \cdot \sum_{i=0}^{\log\log y} 2^i = O(\sqrt{y})$, and $\sqrt{y} = O(\sqrt{n})$.

Finally, when the size of the upper layer U' becomes smaller than $\sqrt{n}$, the remaining nodes accomplish broadcasting via sequential transmissions.

3.2 Broadcasting in Arbitrary Graphs

In this section we introduce a new tree ranking scheme that enables 1-shot broadcasting protocols in an arbitrary n-node graph $G = (V, E)$ of diameter D, in $D + O(\sqrt{n}\log n)$ rounds.

The most time-efficient radio broadcasting algorithms in known graphs use the concept of tree ranking, see e.g., [12,19], where the ranks are computed for especially designed BFS spanning tree rooted in the source node s. The algorithms use two types of transmissions. *Fast transmissions* are performed along paths in the tree containing nodes with the same rank. *Slow transmissions* are designed to move instances of the broadcast message between nodes with different ranks at neighbouring BFS levels. In this type of radio broadcasting algorithms, most nodes are involved in transmissions of both types. Note, however, that in the setting used in this paper, each node is allowed to transmit at most once, which means that the concepts of fast and slow transmissions have to be unified. We therefore propose a new ranking scheme in which the rank of a node corresponds to the unique number of a round when the node transmits. The new rank is a combination of two types of ranks, *external* and *internal*.

External ranks. The external rank of every node in the network is computed on the basis of the ranking mechanism proposed in the context of gathering-broadcasting BFS spanning trees [12]. The nodes in the spanning tree get ranks according to a simple principle. All leaves are assigned the rank 1 and each internal node calculates its rank by looking at the maximum rank among its children. If the maximum rank m occurs in only one child, then the rank of the parent is also set to m; otherwise, the parent gets the rank $m + 1$. It is known that the rank of the root s in a gathering-broadcasting spanning tree of size n is at most $\log n$. The spanning tree constructed in [12] has also an important property that at any BFS level d, if two nodes v and w as well as their respective (disjoint) parents $p(v)$ and $p(w)$ share the same rank, then there are no edges in the network G between nodes $p(v)$ and w as well as between $p(w)$ and v. This property allows simultaneous (collision free) transmissions from the two parents towards their children. Note that nodes having the same rank in the spanning tree form a collection of disjoined paths leading towards the root of the tree. We refer to these paths as *chains*. The bottom end (from the root) of each path is called a *tail* of the chain. Note that some chains can contain only singleton nodes.

For example, all leaves are tails in their chains. Now, if the rank (as defined in [12]) of a node is l, then the node is assigned the external rank $l_{ex} = 2l - 1$ if it is the tail of some chain; otherwise, it gets the external rank $2l$. Thus the external rank of the root s in the spanning tree is at most $2 \log n$. We refer to new shorter paths based on external ranks as *channels*.

Internal ranks. The system of internal ranks is computed on the basis of external ranks and the broadcasting scheme for bipartite graphs provided in Section 3.1. Let $d(v)$ be the distance between a node v and the root s. Network nodes with the same distance $d(\cdot)$ form *BFS layers* in G. Assume that all nodes in the network obtained the external rank from the range $1, \ldots, 2 \log n$. The set of network nodes V is partitioned into channels, where $P_{i,j}$ denotes j^{th} channel containing nodes with rank i. Each channel $P_{i,j}$ constitutes a *supernode* in the upper layer of the *internal rank bipartite graph* $B_{IR}(i)$, for $i = 1, \ldots, 2 \log n$. The bottom layer of each $B_{IR}(i)$ is formed of all nodes in the network. A supernode $P_{i,j}$ is connected to a node w in the lower layer of $B_{IR}(i)$ if there exists a node $v \in P_{i,j}$ such that $(v, w) \in E$, $d(w) - d(v) = 1$, and $l_{ex}(v) > l_{ex}(w)$. Note that each graph $B_{IR}(i)$, for $i = 1, \ldots, 2 \log n$, has at most $2n$ vertices, since there are at most n supernodes (they are disjoint subsets of nodes from graph G) and at most n nodes in the lower layer of graph $B_{IR}(i)$. In each $B_{IR}(i)$ we apply the broadcasting scheme from Section 3.1, which allocates to each supernode $P_{i,j}$ in the upper layer a unique number k (of a transmission round) from the range $1, \ldots, f(n) = O(\sqrt{2n}) = O(\sqrt{n})$. In fact, the number k defines the internal rank $l_{in}(v)$ for any node v present in the supernode $P_{i,j}$. The examples of internal and external ranking can be found in Figure 2.

Combined ranking scheme. The new ranking scheme provides a rank to each node $v \in V$ based on its BFS layer $d(v)$, as well as its internal and external ranks, $l_{in}(v)$ and $l_{ex}(v)$. More precisely, for any node $v \in V$, where $0 \le d(v) \le D, 1 \le l_{ex}(v) \le 2 \log n$ and $0 \le l_{in}(v) < f(n) = O(\sqrt{n})$, define the *delay factor* of v as $\delta(v) = 2 \log n - l_{ex}(v)$. The new rank of the node v is then

$$l(v) = d(v) + 3[\delta(v)f(n) + l_{in}(v)] . \tag{1}$$

Essentially, the new combined rank $l(v)$ corresponds to the transmission time of the node v. In other words, in the new broadcasting scheme the node v transmits only once, in round $l(v)$. This means, e.g., that the running time of the new broadcasting scheme is trivially bounded by $D + O(\sqrt{n} \log n)$. What is left to be shown is that the broadcasting scheme works correctly, i.e., that each network node receives the broadcast message on time (before its transmission round).

The intuition behind the definition of $l(v)$ is as follows. The summand $d(v)$ is necessary since in any case, node v cannot receive the source message faster than its distance from the source. Then, node v may need to wait for some number of rounds in order to avoid collisions, which is expressed by the second summand. The reason for the factor 3 is that in order to avoid collisions between the transmissions of v and those of nodes at distance 2 from it, we allow only nodes of distances $3, 6, 9 \ldots$ from node v to transmit simultaneously with it. To avoid collisions with nodes on the same BFS layer but with a different external

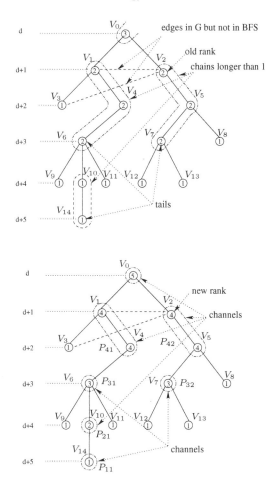

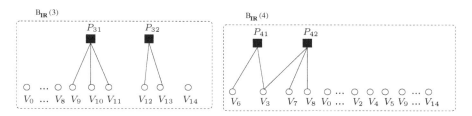

Fig. 2. The old ranks, new external ranks and bipartite graphs $B_{IR}(3)$ and $B_{IR}(4)$

ranking, node v waits for $\delta(v)$ "time windows" of $f(n)$ rounds each. Having done this, only nodes with the same external rank as v may interrupt its transmissions, which is dealt with by waiting an additional $l_{in}(v)$ rounds. The formal analysis of correctness of the algorithm follows.

The proof of the following lemma is deferred to the full version of the paper.

Lemma 4. *Each network node v with $0 \leq d(v) \leq D, 1 \leq l_{ex}(v) \leq 2 \log n$ and $0 \leq l_{in}(v) < f(n) = O(\sqrt{n})$ receives the broadcast message prior to the round $l(v) = d(v) + 3[\delta(v)f(n) + l_{in}(v)]$.*

The following theorem holds.

Theorem 3. *In every radio network of size n and a diameter D there exists a 1-shot broadcasting protocol that runs in $D + O(\sqrt{n} \log n)$ rounds*

Proof. Recall that each node v is scheduled to transmit only once during time $l(v) = d(v) + 3[\delta(v)f(n) + l_{in}(v)]$, where $0 \leq d(v) \leq D, \delta(v) = 2 \log n - l_{ex}(v), 1 \leq l_{ex}(v) \leq 2 \log n$ and $0 \leq l_{in}(v) < f(n) = O(\sqrt{n})$. Lemma 4 ensures that each node receives the broadcast message before its transmission time. The time complexity follows directly from the new ranking scheme, where the running time is bounded by the ranking of nodes at the BFS level farthest from the source node s, thus it is not more than $D + O(\sqrt{n} \log n)$.

4 k-Shot Protocols

A natural extension of 1-shot strategies is a model in which each node in the network can transmit at most k times. We show here that under this assumption, both deterministic and randomised radio broadcasting requires $\Omega(n^{1/(2k)})$ transmission rounds in bipartite graphs, and that this lower bound can be nearly matched by a randomised algorithm. These results could also be generalised for networks with a diameter D, in the same fashion as in Sections 2 and 3.2, resulting in the lower bound $D + \Omega(n^{1/(2k)})$ and the upper bound $D + O(kn^{1/(k-2)} \log n)$. Please note that due to the space limit almost all proofs in this section are deferred to the full version of the paper.

4.1   Lower Bound

The lower bound argument mimics the proof for 1-shot protocols.

Theorem 4. *There exist bipartite graphs of size n in which any k-shot broadcasting scheme requires $\Omega(n^{1/(2k)})$ transmission rounds.*

Using the same argument as in the proof of Theorem 1 we come to the following conclusion.

Corollary 1. *There exist bipartite graphs of size n and diameter D in which any k-shot broadcasting scheme requires $D + \Omega((n - D)^{1/(2k)})$ rounds.*

Moreover, it follows that in order to guarantee fast broadcast in bipartite graphs, namely, in $O(\text{polylog } n)$ rounds (or in general graphs in $D + O(\text{polylog } n)$ rounds), an $\Omega(\frac{\log n}{\log \log n})$-shot protocol must be used, since $n^{\frac{\log \log n}{2 \log n}} = \sqrt{\log n}$. The same bounds hold also for randomised protocols.

4.2   Randomised k-Shot Protocol

Consider a graph $G = (U, L, E)$. Assume that $n \geq 8$ (otherwise there exists a direct constant length schedule) and $5 \leq k < \frac{\log n}{5 + \log \log n} + 2$. Note that for $k \leq 4$ one can use efficient deterministic 1-shot protocol described in section 3. And for $k \geq \frac{\log n}{5 + \log \log n} + 2$ the broadcast protocol proposed in this section runs in at most $O(\log^3 n / \log \log n)$ rounds, i.e., almost matches the lower bound $\Omega(\log^2 n)$ for unbounded energy broadcast, see [3]. We say that an event holds *with high probability* if the probability is at least $1 - n^{-c/k}$, for some constant $c \geq 1$.

We compute first an MCS for $|U| \leq n/2 \leq |L|$ and then we define a k-shot protocol RANDBROADCAST(k) as follows. Let $a = k - 2$. Note that $3 \leq a < \frac{\log n}{5 + \log \log n}$. The protocol proceeds in a epochs, where each epoch (apart from the first one) is formed of $\mathcal{T} = 64 n^{1/a} \log n$ consecutive rounds. The first epoch is different and it is executed in $(a + 1) \cdot \mathcal{T}$ rounds. We define also a sequence of numbers $\langle p_i \rangle$, for $2 \leq i \leq a$, where

$$p_i = \frac{16 \log n}{n^{(i-1)/a}} \qquad \text{and} \qquad p'_i = \begin{cases} p_2, & i = 2, \\ \frac{p_i}{\prod_{j=2}^{i-1}(1 - p_j)}, & \text{otherwise.} \end{cases}$$

Applying the inequality $a < \frac{\log n}{5 + \log \log n}$ we get $p_i < 1/2$, for every $2 \leq i \leq a$, and consequently $p_i < (p_2)^{i-1} < (1/2)^{i-1} < \prod_{j=1}^{i}(1 - p_j)$. Therefore the following fact holds.

Fact 5. $0 < p_i \leq p'_i \leq 1$ *for every* $2 \leq i \leq a$.

A pseudocode of the k-shot protocol for a node $v \in U$ is presented below.

Algorithm RANDBROADCAST(k):

1. Epoch 1:
   - Select, one by one, uniformly at random (with repetitions allowed) $a + 1$ integers from the set $\{1, 2, \ldots, (a + 1) \cdot \mathcal{T}\}$; Let $\alpha_1(v)$ be the first selected integer.
   - During the period $\{1, 2, \ldots, (a + 1) \cdot \mathcal{T}\}$ transmit in rounds with the index corresponding to selected integers.

2. A random bit selection:
   - Select a random bit $\beta_2(v)$, set to 1 with probability p'_2 and to 0 otherwise.
   - For $i = 3$ to a do:
     (i) If $\beta_j(v) = 0$ for every $2 \leq j \leq i - 1$, then select a random bit $\beta_i(v)$, set to 1 with probability p'_i and to 0 otherwise.

3. For $i = 2$ to a do: *// iterating epochs $i = 2, \ldots, a$*
   If $\beta_i(v) = 1$ then
   - select uniformly at random an integer $1 \leq \alpha_i(v) \leq \mathcal{T}$, and
   - transmit in round $(a + i - 1)\mathcal{T} + \alpha_i(v)$.

Lemma 5. *For every $v \in U$,*

1. *$\beta_i(v) = 1$ with probability p_i, for every $2 \le i \le a$; and*
2. *$\sum_{j=2}^{a} \beta_j(v) \le 1$ with probability 1.*

Note that every node v transmits at most once throughout epochs $i = 2, ..., a$, and in epoch 1 it performs at most $a + 1$ additional transmissions. Hence obtain the following corollary.

Corollary 2. RANDBROADCAST(k) *is a k-shot protocol with probability 1.*

The algorithm runs in time $O(k)$ at each node. Thus the total number of transmission rounds is bounded by $(a + 1) \cdot \mathcal{T} + (a - 1) \cdot \mathcal{T} = O(kn^{1/(k-2)} \log n)$.

We prove here that the k-shot protocol performs radio broadcasting with high probability. We start with two technical observations referring to placing balls in bins. Given x balls and y bins, consider a process in which each ball is placed uniformly and independently in a random bin. This process is used to model random selection of transmitting rounds, where nodes (balls) choose their transmission rounds (bins) randomly. We say that an event is *good* when more than $x/2$ bins are occupied, i.e., which where more than $x/2$ different rounds are selected by a node. Let $\mathcal{P}$ be the probability of a good event. Note that a good event admits existence of a round selected by exactly one node among all considered subset of nodes. (This is due to the fact that at least one bin is occupied by exactly one ball).

Lemma 6. $\mathcal{P} \ge 1 - \sum_{j=1}^{\lfloor x/2 \rfloor} \left(\frac{e \cdot (x/2)}{y} \right)^{x-j}$.

Proof. Let j be the number of occupied bins. We have

$$\mathcal{P} = 1 - \sum_{j=1}^{\lfloor x/2 \rfloor} \binom{y}{j} \left(\frac{j}{y} \right)^x \ge 1 - \sum_{j=1}^{\lfloor x/2 \rfloor} \left(\frac{e \cdot y}{j} \right)^j \cdot \left(\frac{j}{y} \right)^x = 1 - \sum_{j=1}^{\lfloor x/2 \rfloor} e^j \cdot \left(\frac{j}{y} \right)^{x-j}$$

$$\ge 1 - \sum_{j=1}^{\lfloor x/2 \rfloor} \left(\frac{e \cdot (x/2)}{y} \right)^{x-j}.$$

Lemma 7. *If $8 \log n \le x \le 3\mathcal{T}/8$ and $y \ge \mathcal{T}$, then with probability at least $1 - 3/n^3$ there exists a bin with exactly one ball.*

Proof. It is sufficient to prove that $\mathcal{P} \ge 1 - 1/n^3$, since if the number of occupied bins is larger than $x/2$ then there is a bin containing exactly one ball. Using Lemma 6 for x balls and $y = \mathcal{T}$ bins,

$$\mathcal{P} \ge 1 - \sum_{j=1}^{\lfloor x/2 \rfloor} \left(\frac{e \cdot (x/2)}{y} \right)^{x-j} \ge 1 - \sum_{\ell=\lceil x/2 \rceil}^{x-1} \left(\frac{3e\mathcal{T}/16}{\mathcal{T}} \right)^\ell$$

$$\ge 1 - \left(\frac{3e}{16} \right)^{x/2} \cdot \frac{1}{1 - \frac{3e}{16}} \ge 1 - 3 \cdot \left(\frac{3e}{16} \right)^{(8 \log n)/2} \ge 1 - 3/n^3.$$

Lemma 8. *Every node $w \in L$ gets the source message with high probability.*

Therefore the following theorem holds.

Theorem 6. *Algorithm* RANDBROADCAST(k) *is a k-shot protocol and it accomplishes radio broadcasting in $O(kn^{1/(k-2)} \log n)$ rounds with high probability.*

Note that the ranking scheme proposed in Section 3.2 can be used in conjunction with k-shot protocols. I.e., any $O(f(n))$-time k-shot broadcasting scheme for bipartite graphs admits $D + O(f(n) \log n)$ broadcast in arbitrary graphs with the diameter D. In particular, the k-shot randomised protocol RANDBROADCAST(k) for bipartite graphs can be extended in polynomial time into a protocol for completing broadcast on an arbitrary D-hop radio network in $D + O(kn^{1/(k-2)} \log^2 n)$ rounds, with high probability. More precisely, given a arbitrary graph $G(V, E)$ with diameter D, we construct bipartite graphs $B_{IR}(i)$ as in section 3.2, and for each node v we compute k internal ranks $l_{in}(1, v), l_{in}(2, v), \ldots, l_{in}(k, v)$, instead of one internal rank $l_{in}(v)$, using RandBroadcast(k) algorithm in place of 1-shot deterministic algorithm. Note that $l_{in}(j, v)$, for $1 \leq j \leq k$, are now from the range $1, \ldots, f(k, n)$, where $f(n, k) = O(kn^{1/(k-2)} \log n)$ due to theorem 6. Thus combining the concept of external ranks with newly obtained k different internal ranks (there are at most k different rounds in which node v transmits) in the same fashion as in formula (1) in section 3.2 we get the following corollary.

Corollary 3. *There exists a polynomial time constructable k-shot randomised broadcasting protocol that runs in $D + O(kn^{1/(k-2)} \log^2 n)$ rounds in every radio network of size n and a diameter D, with high probability.*

5 Further Discussion

This paper presents a new broadcasting scheme that performs the communication task under assumption that each node can transmit at most once. It turns out that there is a clear distinction between the model with bounded and unbounded number of transmissions. In the unbounded model the lower bound and the upper bound is known to be $D + \Theta(\log^2 n)$ in view of [3] and [12] while in the model with unique transmissions the lower bound is $D + \Omega(\sqrt{n - D})$. Note also that our new 1-shot broadcasting scheme requires $D + O(\sqrt{n} \log n)$ rounds of communication. This leaves an interesting open problem on the exact complexity of 1-shot broadcasting strategies in radio networks with known topology.

Broadcasting with bounded number of transmissions at each node. In the more general case where each node can transmit up to k times during a broadcasting process, it is shown that radio broadcasting requires $\Omega(n^{1/(2k)})$ transmission rounds in bipartite graphs, and $D + \Omega((n - D)^{1/(2k)})$ in graphs of diameter D. These complexities can be nearly matched by randomised algorithms, however the *exact* complexity of k-shot broadcasting in bipartite and arbitrary radio networks with known topology remains open (the gap is nearly $n^{1/k}$). In particular, a randomised k-shot broadcasting algorithm needs $D + O(kn^{1/(k-2)} \log^2 n)$

rounds to succeed in any D-hop network, with high probability. Constructing, in polynomial time, an efficient k-shot deterministic protocol is another problem that remains open.

Broadcasting with the minimum number of transmissions. Another possible strategy for energy efficient radio broadcasting is to minimise the total number of transmissions, without targeting the best possible running time of a broadcasting procedure. In this model one can provide almost immediately an approximate solution based on the efficient computation of *minimal connected dominating sets* with logarithmic approximation ratio in general graphs [15] and constant approximation ratio in unit disk graphs, see e.g. [2]. An interesting related open problem is to look for trade-offs between the total number of transmissions and the broadcasting time.

Acknowledgments

We would like to thank Andrzej Lingas for valuable discussions on algorithmic issues related to the main themes of this paper.

References

1. Ambühl, C.: An optimal bound for the MST algorithm to compute energy efficient broadcast trees in wireless networks. In: Caires, L., Italiano, G.F., Monteiro, L., Palamidessi, C., Yung, M. (eds.) ICALP 2005. LNCS, vol. 3580, pp. 1139–1150. Springer, Heidelberg (2005)
2. Ambühl, C., Erlebach, T., Mihalak, M., Nunkesser, M.: Constant-factor approximation for minimum-weight (connected) dominating sets in unit disk graphs. In: Díaz, J., Jansen, K., Rolim, J.D.P., Zwick, U. (eds.) APPROX 2006 and RANDOM 2006. LNCS, vol. 4110, pp. 3–14. Springer, Heidelberg (2006)
3. Alon, N., Bar-Noy, A., Linial, N., Peleg, D.: A lower bound for radio broadcast. J. Computer and System Sciences 43, 290–298 (1991)
4. Bar-Yehuda, R., Goldreich, O., Itai, A.: On the time complexity of broadcasting in radio networks: an exponential gap between determinism and randomization. In: Proc. 5th Symposium on Principles of Distributed Computing(PODC), pp. 98–107 (1986)
5. Berenbrink, P., Cooper, C., Hu, Z.: Energy efficient randomised communication in unknown adhoc networks. In: Proc. 19th ACM Symposium on Parallelism in Algorithms and Architectures (SPAA), pp. 250–259 (2007)
6. Chlamtac, I., Weinstein, O.: The wave expansion approach to broadcasting in multihop radio networks. IEEE Trans. on Communications 39, 426–433 (1991)
7. Cicalese, F., Manne, F., Xin, Q.: Faster centralised communication in radio networks. In: Asano, T. (ed.) ISAAC 2006. LNCS, vol. 4288, pp. 339–348. Springer, Heidelberg (2006)
8. Clementi, A.E.F., Crescenzi, P., Penna, P., Rossi, G., Vocca, P.: On the complexity of computing minimum energy consumption broadcast subgraphs. In: Ferreira, A., Reichel, H. (eds.) STACS 2001. LNCS, vol. 2010, pp. 121–131. Springer, Heidelberg (2001)

9. Elkin, M., Kortsarz, G.: Improved broadcast schedule for radio networks. In: Proc. 16th ACM-SIAM Symposium on Discrete Algorithms (SODA), pp. 222–231 (2005)
10. Flammini, M., Navarra, A., Klasing, R., Perennes, S.: Improved approximation results for the minimum energy broadcasting problem. In: Proc. DIALM-POMC Workshop on Foundations of Mobile Computing, pp. 85–91 (2004)
11. Gaber, I., Mansour, Y.: Centralised broadcast in multihop radio networks. J. Algorithms 46(1), 1–20 (2003)
12. Gasieniec, L., Peleg, D., Xin, Q.: Faster communication in known topology radio networks. In: Proc. 24th Annual ACM Symposium on Principles of Distributed Computing (PODC), pp. 129–137 (2005)
13. Gasieniec, L., Potapov, I., Xin, Q.: Efficient gossiping in known radio networks. In: Kralovic, R., Sýkora, O. (eds.) SIROCCO 2004. LNCS, vol. 3104, pp. 173–184. Springer, Heidelberg (2004)
14. Goldberg, M., Spencer, T.: An efficient parallel algorithm that finds independent sets of guaranteed size. SIAM J. of Discrete Mathematics 6(3), 443–459 (1993)
15. Guha, S., Khuller, S.: Approximation algorithms for connected dominating sets. Algorithmica 20(4), 374–387 (1998)
16. Guha, S., Khuller, S.: Improved methods for approximating node-weighted Steiner trees and connected dominating sets. Information and Computation 150, 57–74 (1999)
17. Klasing, R., Navarra, A., Papadopoulos, A., Perennes, S.: Adaptive broadcast consumption (abc), a new heuristic and new bounds for the minimum energy broadcast routing problem. Networking, 866–877 (2004)
18. Kowalski, D.R., Pelc, A.: Centralised deterministic broadcasting in undirected multi-hop radio networks. In: Jansen, K., Khanna, S., Rolim, J.D.P., Ron, D. (eds.) RANDOM 2004 and APPROX 2004. LNCS, vol. 3122, pp. 171–182. Springer, Heidelberg (2004)
19. Kowalski, D.R., Pelc, A.: Optimal deterministic broadcasting in known topology radio networks. Distributed Computing 19(3), 185–195 (2007)
20. Mitzenmacher, M., Upfal, E.: Probability and Computing. Cambridge University Press, Cambridge (2005)
21. Navarra, A.: Tighter bounds for the minimum energy broadcasting problem. In: Proc. 3rd International Symposium on Modeling and Optimisation in Mobile, Ad-Hoc and Wireless Networks, pp. 313–322 (2005)
22. Wan, P.J., Calinescu, G., Li, X.Y., Frieder, O.: Minimum-energy broadcast routing in static ad hoc wireless networks. In: Proc. 20th Annual Joint Conference of the IEEE Computer and Communications Societies (INFOCOM), pp. 1162–1171 (2001)

A Distributed Algorithm
for Finding All Best Swap Edges
of a Minimum Diameter Spanning Tree*

Beat Gfeller[1], Nicola Santoro[2], and Peter Widmayer[1]

[1] Institute of Theoretical Computer Science, ETH Zurich, Switzerland
{gfeller,widmayer}@inf.ethz.ch
[2] School of Computer Science, Carleton University, Ottawa, Canada
santoro@scs.carleton.ca

Abstract. Communication in networks suffers if a link fails. When the links are edges of a tree that has been chosen from an underlying graph of all possible links, a broken link even disconnects the network. Most often, the link is restored rapidly. A good policy to deal with this sort of *transient* link failures is *swap rerouting*, where the temporarily broken link is replaced by a single *swap* link from the underlying graph. A rapid replacement of a broken link by a swap link is only possible if all swap links have been precomputed. The selection of high quality swap links is essential; it must follow the same objective as the originally chosen communication subnetwork. We are interested in a minimum diameter tree in a graph with edge weights (so as to minimize the maximum travel time of messages). Hence, each swap link must minimize (among all possible swaps) the diameter of the tree that results from swapping. We propose a distributed algorithm that efficiently computes all of these swap links, and we explain how to route messages across swap edges with a compact routing scheme.

1 Introduction

For communication in computer networks, often only a subset of the available connections is used to communicate at any given time. If all nodes are connected using the smallest number of links, the subset forms a spanning tree of the network. Depending on the purpose of the network, there is a variety of desirable properties of a spanning tree. We are interested in a *Minimum Diameter Spanning Tree* (MDST), i.e., a tree that minimizes the largest distance between any pair of nodes, thus minimizing the worst case length of any transmission path. The importance of minimizing the diameter of a spanning tree has been widely recognized (see e.g. [2]); essentially, the diameter of a network provides a lower bound on the computation time of most algorithms in which all nodes participate.

* We gratefully acknowledge the support of the Swiss SBF under contract no. C05.0047 within COST-295 (DYNAMO) of the European Union and the support of the Natural Sciences and Engineering Research Council of Canada.

A. Pelc (Ed.): DISC 2007, LNCS 4731, pp. 268–282, 2007.
© Springer-Verlag Berlin Heidelberg 2007

One downside of using a spanning tree is that a single link failure disconnects the network. Whenever the link failure is transient, i.e., the failed link soon becomes operational again, the best possible way of reconnecting the network is to replace the failed link by a single other link, called a *swap* link. Among all possible swap links, one should choose a *best swap* w.r.t. the original objective [5,6,7,8], that is in our case, a swap that minimizes the diameter of the resulting *swap tree*. Note that the swap tree is different from a minimum diameter spanning tree of the underlying graph that does not use the failed link. The reason for preferring the swap tree to the latter lies in the effort that a change of the current communication tree requires: If we were to replace the original MDST by a tree whose edge set can be very different, we would need to put many edges out of service, many new edges into service, and adjust many routing tables substantially — and all of this for a transient situation. For a swap tree, instead, only one new edge goes into service, and routing can be adjusted with little effort (as we will show). Interestingly, this choice of swapping against adjusting an entire tree even comes at a moderate loss in diameter: The swap tree diameter is at most a factor of 2.5 larger than the diameter of an entirely adjusted tree [6].

In order to keep the required time for swapping small, for each edge of the tree, a best swap edge is precomputed. We show in the following that this distributed computation of *all best swaps* has the further advantage of gaining efficiency (against computing swap edges individually), because dependencies between the computations for different failing edges can be exploited.

Related Work. Nardelli et al. [6] describe a centralized (i.e., non-distributed) algorithm for computing all best swaps of a MDST in $O(n\sqrt{m})$ time and $O(m)$ space, where the given underlying communication network $G = (V, E)$ has $n = |V|$ vertices and $m = |E|$ edges. For shortest paths trees, an earlier centralized algorithm has been complemented by a distributed algorithm [7] using totally different techniques for finding all best swap edges for several objectives [3,4], with either $O(n)$ messages of size $O(n)$ (i.e., a message contains $O(n)$ node labels, edge weights, etc.) each, or $O(n^*)$ short messages with size $O(1)$ each, where n^* denotes the size of the transitive closure of the tree, where edges are directed away from the root. In a so-called preprocessing phase of this algorithm, some information is computed along with the spanning tree construction using $O(m)$ messages. A distributed algorithm for computing a MDST in a graph $G(V, E)$ in an asynchronous setting has $O(n)$ time complexity (in the standard sense, as explained in Section 3) and uses $O(nm)$ messages [2]. However, no efficient distributed algorithm to compute the best swaps of a MDST had been found to date.

Our Contribution. In this paper, we propose a distributed algorithm for computing all best swaps of a MDST using no more than $O(\max\{n^*, m\})$ messages of size $O(1)$ each. The *size of a message* denotes the number of atomic values that it contains, such as node labels, edge weights, path lengths etc., and n^* is the size of the transitive closure of the MDST with edges directed away from a center of the tree. Both n^* and m are very natural bounds: When each subtree triggers as many messages as there are nodes in the subtree, the size of the transitive closure describes the total number of messages. Furthermore, it seems inevitable that each node receives some information from each of its neighbours in G, across each potential swap edge. Our algorithm runs in $O(\|\mathcal{D}\|)$ time (in the standard sense, as explained in Section 3), where $\|\mathcal{D}\|$ is the hop-length of the diameter path of G; note that this is asymptotically optimal. The message and time costs of our algorithm are easily subsumed by the costs of constructing a MDST distributively using the algorithm from [2]. Thus, it is cheap to precompute all the best swaps in addition to constructing a MDST initially.

Just like the best swaps algorithms for shortest paths trees [3,4], our algorithm (like many fundamental distributed algorithms) exploits the structure of the tree. This tree, however, is substantially different in that it requires a significantly more complex invariant to be maintained during the computation: We need to have just the right collection of pieces of paths available so that on the one hand, these pieces can be maintained efficiently, and on the other hand, they can be composed to reveal the diameter at the corresponding steps in the computation.

Furthermore, we propose a compact routing scheme for trees which can quickly and inexpensively adapt routing when a failing edge is replaced by a best swap edge. Notably, our scheme does not require an additional full backup table, but assigns a label of $c \log n$ bits to each node (for some small constant c); a node of degree δ stores the labels of all its neighbours (and itself), which amounts to $\delta c \log n$ bits per node, or $mc \log n$ bits in total. Given this labelling, knowledge of the labels of both adjacent nodes of a failing edge and the labels of both adjacent nodes of its swap edge is sufficient to adjust routing.

In Section 2, we formally define the *distributed all best swaps* problem. Section 3 states our assumptions about the distributed setting and explains the basic idea of our algorithm. In Section 4, we study the structure of diameter paths after swapping, and we propose an algorithm for finding best swaps. The algorithm uses information that is computed in a preprocessing phase, described in Section 5. Our routing scheme is presented in Section 6. Section 7 concludes the paper.

2   Problem Statement and Terminology

A communication network is a 2-connected, undirected, edge weighted graph $G = (V, E)$, with $n = |V|$ vertices and $m = |E|$ edges. Each edge $e \in E$ has a non-negative real *length* $w(e)$. The length $|\mathcal{P}|$ of a path $\mathcal{P}$ is the sum of the lengths of its edges, and the *distance* $d(x, y)$ between two vertices x, y is the length of a shortest path between x and y. The *hop-length* $\|\mathcal{P}\|$ of a path $\mathcal{P}$ is the number of edges that $\mathcal{P}$ contains. Throughout the paper, we are only dealing with *simple* paths. Given a spanning tree $T = (V, E(T))$ of G, let $\mathcal{D}(T) := \langle d_1, d_2, \ldots, d_k \rangle$ denote a *diameter* of T, that is, a longest path in T (see Fig. 1). Where no confusion arises, we abbreviate $\mathcal{D}(T)$ with $\mathcal{D}$. Furthermore, define the *center* d_c of $\mathcal{D}$ as a node such that the lengths of $\mathcal{D}_L := \langle d_1, d_2, \ldots, d_c \rangle$ and $\mathcal{D}_R := \langle d_c, d_{c+1}, \ldots, d_k \rangle$ satisfy $|\mathcal{D}_L| \geq |\mathcal{D}_R|$ and have the smallest possible difference $|\mathcal{D}_L| - |\mathcal{D}_R|$. The set of neighbours of a node z (excluding z itself) in G and in T is written as $N_G(z)$ and $N_T(z) \subseteq N_G(z)$, respectively.

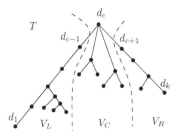

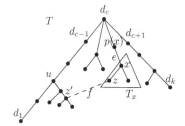

Fig. 1. A minimum diameter spanning tree T

Fig. 2. A swap edge $f = (z, z')$ for $e = (x, p(x))$

Let T be rooted at d_c, and let, for each node $x \neq d_c$, node $p(x)$ be the *parent* of x and $C(x)$ the set of its *children*. Furthermore, let $T_x = (V(T_x), E(T_x))$ be the subtree of T rooted at x, including x. Let V_L (L stands for "left") be the set of nodes in the subtree rooted at d_{c-1}, V_R the set of nodes in the subtree rooted at d_{c+1}, and V_C all other nodes.

Now, the removal of any edge $e = (x, p(x))$ of T partitions the spanning tree into two trees T_x and $T \backslash T_x$ (see Fig. 2). Note that $T \backslash T_x$ does not contain the node x. A *swap edge* f for e is any edge in $E \backslash E(T)$ that (re-)connects T_x and $T \backslash T_x$, i.e., for which $T \backslash \{e\} \cup \{f\} =: T_{e/f}$ is a spanning tree of $G \backslash \{e\}$. Let $S(e)$ be the set of swap edges for e. A *best swap edge* for e is any edge $f \in S(e)$ for which $|\mathcal{D}(T_{e/f})|$ is minimum. A *local* swap edge of node z for some failing edge e is an edge in $S(e)$ adjacent to z. The *distributed all best swaps* problem for a MDST is the problem of finding for every edge $e \in E(T)$ a best swap edge (with respect to the diameter). Throughout the paper, let $e = (x, p(x))$ denote a failing edge and $f = (z, z')$ a swap edge, where z is a node inside T_x, and z' a node in $T \backslash T_x$.

3   Algorithmic Setting and Basic Idea

In our setting, nodes have unique identifiers that possess a linear order. Further, let each node know its own neighbours in T and in G, and for each neighbour the length of the corresponding edge. We assume port-to-port communication between neighbouring nodes. The distributed system of nodes is totally asynchronous. Each message sent from some node to one of its neighbours eventually arrives (there is no message loss). As usual, we define the asynchronous time complexity of an algorithm as the longest possible execution time assuming that sending a message requires at most one time unit. Furthermore, nodes do not need to know the total number of nodes in the system (although it is easy to count the nodes in T using a convergecast).

3.1   The Basic Idea

Our goal is to compute, for each edge of T, a best swap edge. A swap edge for a given failing edge $e = (x, p(x))$ must connect the subtree of T rooted at x to the part of the tree containing $p(x)$. Thus, a swap edge must be adjacent to some node inside T_x. If each node in T_x considers its own local swap edges for e, then in total all swap edges for e are considered. Therefore, each node inside T_x finds a best *local* swap edge, and then participates in a *minimum finding process* that computes a (globally) best swap edge for e. The computation of the best local swap edges is composed of three main phases: In a first preprocessing phase, a root of the MDST is chosen, and various pieces of information (explained later) are computed for each node. Then, in a top-down phase each node computes and forwards some "enabling information" (explained later) for each node in its own subtree. This information is collected and merged in a third bottom-up phase, during which each node obtains its best local swap edge for each (potentially failing) edge on its path to the root. The efficiency of our algorithm will be due to our careful choice of the various pieces of information that we collect and use in these phases.

To give an overview, we now briefly sketch how each node computes a best local swap edge. First observe that after replacing edge e by f, the resulting diameter is longer than the previous diameter only if there is a path through f which is longer than the previous diameter, in which case the path through f is the new diameter. In this case, the length of the diameter equals the length of a longest path through f in the new tree. For a local swap edge $f = (z, z')$ connecting node $z \in V(T_x)$ and $z' \in V \backslash V(T_x)$, such a path consists of

(i) a longest path inside $T \backslash T_x$ starting in z',
(ii) edge f, and
(iii) a longest path inside T_x starting in z.

Part (i) is computed in a preprocessing phase, as described in Section 5. Part (ii) is by assumption known to z, because f is adjacent to z. Part (iii) is inductively computed by a process starting from the root x of T_x, and stopping in the leaves, as follows. A path starting in z and staying inside T_x either descends to a child of z (if any), or goes up to $p(z)$ (if $p(z)$ is still in T_x) and continues within $T_x \backslash T_z$. For the special case where $z = x$, node x needs to consider only the heights of the subtrees rooted at its children. All other nodes z in T_x additionally need to know the length of a longest path starting at $p(z)$ and staying inside $T_x \backslash T_z$. This additional *enabling information* will be computed by $p(z)$ and then be sent to z.

Once the best local swap edges are known, a best (global) swap edge is identified by a single minimum finding process that starts at the leaves of T_x and ends in node x. To compute all best swap edges of T, this procedure is executed separately for each edge of T. This approach will turn out to work with the desired efficiency:

Main Theorem. *All best swap edges of a MDST can be computed in an asynchronous distributed setting with $O(\max\{n^*, m\})$ messages of constant size, and in $O(\|\mathcal{D}\|)$ time.*

We will prove this theorem in the next sections, by proving that the preprocessing phase can be realized with $O(m)$ messages, and after that the computation of all best swap edges requires at most $O(n^*)$ additional messages.

This algorithm requires that each node knows which of its neighbours are children and which neighbour is its parent in T. Although this information is not known a priori, it can be easily computed in a preprocessing phase, during which a particular diameter and a root of T are chosen.

4   How to Pick a Best Swap Edge

In our distributed algorithm, we compute for each (potentially) failing edge the resulting new diameter for each possible swap edge candidate. This approach can be made efficient by exploiting the structure of diameter path changes, as described in the following.

4.1   The Structure of Diameter Path Changes

For a given failing edge e, let $\mathcal{P}_f$ be a longest path in $T_{e/f}$ that goes through swap edge f for e. Then, we have the following:

Lemma 1. *The length of the diameter of $T_{e/f}$ is $|\mathcal{D}(T_{e/f})| = \max\{|\mathcal{D}(T)|, |\mathcal{P}_f|\}$.*

Proof. Let T_1 and T_2 be the parts into which T is split if e is removed. It is easy to see that

$$|\mathcal{D}(T_{e/f})| = \max\{|\mathcal{D}(T_1)|, |\mathcal{D}(T_2)|, |\mathcal{P}_f|\}. \tag{1}$$

Since T is a MDST, we have

$$|\mathcal{D}(T_{e/f})| \geq |\mathcal{D}(T)|. \tag{2}$$

Because T_1 and T_2 are contained in T,

$$|\mathcal{D}(T_1)| \leq |\mathcal{D}(T)| \quad \text{and} \quad |\mathcal{D}(T_2)| \leq |\mathcal{D}(T)|. \tag{3}$$

If $|\mathcal{P}_f| \geq |\mathcal{D}(T)|$, it is clear that $|\mathcal{P}_f|$ is a largest term in (1), so the claim holds. On the other hand, if $|\mathcal{P}_f| < |\mathcal{D}(T)|$, then either T_1 or T_2 must contain a diameter of length exactly $|\mathcal{D}(T)|$ (otherwise, either (2) or (3) would be violated). Thus, the claim holds also in this case. □

That is, for computing the resulting diameter length for a given swap edge $f = (z, z')$ for e, we only need to compute the length of a longest path in $T_{e/f}$ that goes through f. For node z in the subtree T_x of T rooted in x, and z' outside this subtree, such a path $\mathcal{P}_f$ consists of three parts. To describe these parts, let $\mathcal{L}(H, r)$ denote a longest path starting in node r and staying inside the graph H. The first part is a longest path $\mathcal{L}(T\backslash T_x, z')$ in $T\backslash T_x$ that starts in z'. The second part is the edge f itself. The third part is a longest path $\mathcal{L}(T_x, z)$ starting in z and staying inside T_x. This determines the length of a longest path through f as $|\mathcal{P}_f| = |\mathcal{L}(T_x, z)| + w(f) + |\mathcal{L}(T\backslash T_x, z')|$.

4.2 Distributed Computation of $|\mathcal{L}(T_x, z)|$

For a given failing edge $e = (x, p(x))$, each node z in T_x needs its $|\mathcal{L}(T_x, z)|$ value to check for the new diameter when using a swap edge. This is achieved by a distributed computation, starting in x. As x knows the heights of the subtrees of all its children (from the preprocessing), it can locally compute the height of its own subtree T_x as $|\mathcal{L}(T_x, x)| = \max_{q \in C(x)}\{w(x, q) + height(T_q)\}$, where $C(x)$ is the set of children of x. For a node z in the subtree rooted at x, a longest simple path either goes from z to its parent and hence has length $|\mathcal{L}(T_x \backslash T_z \cup \{z\}, z)|$, or goes into the subtree of one of its children and hence has length $|\mathcal{L}(T_z, z)|$ (see Fig. 3). The latter term has just been described, and the former can be computed by induction by the parent r of z and can be sent to z. This inductive step is identical to the step just described, except that z itself is no candidate subtree for a path starting at r in the induction. In total, each node r computes, for each of its children $q \in C(r)$, the value of

$$|\mathcal{L}(T_x \backslash T_q \cup \{q\}, q)| =$$
$$w(q, r) + \max\left\{ |\mathcal{L}(T_x \backslash T_r \cup \{r\}, r)|, \max_{s \in C(r), s \neq q}\{w(r, s) + height(T_s)\} \right\},$$

and sends it to q, where we assume that the value $|\mathcal{L}(T_x \backslash T_r \cup \{r\}, r)|$ was previously sent to r by $p(r)$.

A bird's eye view of the process shows that each node z first computes $|\mathcal{L}(T_x, z)|$, and then computes and sends $|\mathcal{L}(T_x \backslash T_q \cup \{q\}, q)|$ for each of its children $q \in C(z)$. Computation of the $|\mathcal{L}(T_x, z)|$ values finishes in T_x's leaves. Note that a second value will be added to the enabling information if $(x, p(x)) \in \mathcal{D}$, for reasons explained in the next section.

4.3 Distributed Computation of $|\mathcal{L}(T \backslash T_x, z')|$

In the following, we explain how z can compute $|\mathcal{L}(T \backslash T_x, z')|$ for a given swap edge $f = (z, z')$. In case the failing edge $e = (x, p(x)) \notin \mathcal{D}$, we show below that the information obtained in the preprocessing phase is sufficient.

For the sake of clarity, we analyze two cases separately, starting with the simpler case.

Case 1: The removed edge e is not on the diameter. For this case, we know from [6] that at least one of the longest paths in $T \backslash T_x$ starting from z' contains d_c. If $z' \in V_L$, we get a longest path from z' through d_c by continuing on the diameter up to d_k, and hence we have $|\mathcal{L}(T \backslash T_x, z')| = d(z', d_c) + |\mathcal{D}_R|$. If z' is in V_C or V_R, some longest path from z' through d_c continues on the diameter up to d_1, yielding $|\mathcal{L}(T \backslash T_x, z')| = d(z', d_c) + |\mathcal{D}_L|$. Remarkably, in this case $|\mathcal{L}(T \backslash T_x, z')|$ does not depend on the concrete failing edge $e = (x, p(x))$, apart from the fact that (z, z') must be a swap edge for e.

Case 2: The removed edge e is on the diameter. We analyze the case $e \in \mathcal{D}_L$, and omit the symmetric case $e \in \mathcal{D}_R$. If $z' \in V_L$ or $z' \in V_C$, we know from [6] that again, one of the longest paths in $T \backslash T_x$ starting at z' contains d_c.

Thus, for $z' \in V_L$ we are in the same situation as for the failing edge not on the diameter, leading to $|\mathcal{L}(T \backslash T_x, z')| = d(z', d_c) + |\mathcal{D}_R|$. For $z' \in V_C$, after d_c a longest path may continue either on $\mathcal{D}_R$, or continue to nodes in V_L. In the latter case, the path now cannot continue on $\mathcal{D}_L$ until it reaches d_1, because edge e lies on $\mathcal{D}_L$. Instead, we are interested in the length of a longest path that starts at d_c, proceeds into V_L, but does not go below the parent $p(x)$ of x on $\mathcal{D}_L$; let us call this length $\lambda(p(x))$. As announced before, we include the $\lambda(p(x))$ value as a second value into the *enabling information* received by $p(x)$; then, we get $|\mathcal{L}(T \backslash T_x, z')| = d(z', d_c) + \max\{|\mathcal{D}_R|, \lambda(p(x))\}$. It remains to consider $z' \in V_R$. For this case (see Fig. 4), we know (from [6]) that at least one of the longest paths in $T \backslash T_x$ starting at z' passes through the node u' closest to z' on $\mathcal{D}(T)$. After u', this path may either continue on $\mathcal{D}_R$ up to d_k, or continue through d_c going inside V_C or V_L (without crossing $e = (x, p(x))$), or continue towards d_c only up to some node d_i on $\mathcal{D}_r$, going further on non-diameter edges inside V_R. It remains to show how the length of a longest path of this last type can be found efficiently. We propose to combine three lengths, in addition to the length of the path from z' to u'. The first is the length of a longest path inside V_R that starts at d_k; let us call this length μ_R. In general, this path goes up the diameter path $\mathcal{D}_R$ for a while, and then turns down into a subtree of V_R, away from the diameter, at a diameter node that we call ρ_R (see Fig. 4). Given μ_R, the distance from u' to ρ_R, and the distance from ρ_R to d_k, the desired path length of an upwards turning path inside V_R is $d(z', u') + d(u', \rho_R) + \mu_R - d(d_k, \rho_R)$. Note that while it may seem that ρ_R needs to lie above u' on $\mathcal{D}_R$, this is not really needed in our computation, because the term above will not be largest (among all path choices) if ρ_R happens to be below or at u'. In total, we get $|\mathcal{L}(T \backslash T_x, z')| = \max\{d(z', d_k), d(z', d_c) + \lambda(p(x)), \ d(z', u') + d(u', \rho_R) + \mu_R - d(d_k, \rho_R)\}$.[1]

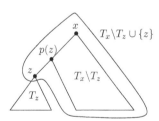

Fig. 3. Illustration of the tree $T_x \backslash T_z \cup \{z\}$

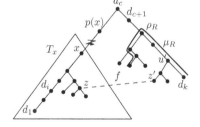

Fig. 4. Computing $|\mathcal{L}(T \backslash T_x, z')|$ if $e \in \mathcal{D}_L$, $z \in V_L$ and $z' \in V_R$

All of these path length computations can be carried out locally with no message exchanges, if the constituents of these sums are available locally at a node. We will show in the next section how to achieve this in an efficient preprocessing phase.

---

[1] Recall that in the definition of $\lambda(p(x))$, paths inside V_C starting from d_c are also considered.

4.4   The BESTDIAMSWAP Algorithm

For a given edge $e = (x, p(x))$ that may fail, each node z in the subtree T_x rooted at x executes the following steps:

(i)   Wait for the enabling information from the parent (unless $x = z$), and then compute $|\mathcal{L}(T_x, z)|$. Compute the enabling information for all children and send it.

(ii) For each local swap edge $f = (z, z')$, compute $|\mathcal{L}(T \backslash T_x, z')|$ as described in Section 4.3.

(iii) For each local swap edge $f = (z, z')$, locally compute

$$|\mathcal{D}(T_{e/f})| = \max\{|\mathcal{D}(T)|, |\mathcal{L}(T_x, z)| + w(f) + |\mathcal{L}(T \backslash T_x, z')|\}.$$

Among these, choose a best swap edge f^*_{local} and store the resulting new diameter as $|\mathcal{D}(T_{e/f^*_{local}})|$.

(iv) From each child $q \in C(z)$, receive the node label of a best swap edge candidate f^*_q and its resulting diameter $|\mathcal{D}(T_{e/f^*_q})|$. Pick a best swap edge candidate f^*_b among these, i.e., choose $b := \arg\min_{q \in C(z)} |\mathcal{D}(T_{e/f^*_q})|$. Compare the resulting diameter of f^*_b and f^*_{local}, and define f_{best} as the edge achieving the smaller diameter (or any of them if their length is equal), and its diameter as $|\mathcal{D}(T_{e/f_{best}})|$.

(v)   Send the information f_{best}, $|\mathcal{D}(T_{e/f_{best}})|$ to the parent.

The above algorithm computes the best swap edge for one (potentially) failing edge e, based on the information available after the preprocessing phase. In order to compute all best swap edges of T, we execute this algorithm for each edge of T independently.

Analysis of the Algorithm. We now show that the proposed algorithm indeed meets our efficiency requirements:

Theorem 1. *After preprocessing, executing the BESTDIAMSWAP algorithm independently for each and every edge $e \in E(T)$ costs at most $O(n^*)$ messages of size $O(1)$ each, and $O(\|\mathcal{D}\|)$ time, using a "Farthest-to-Go" queuing policy [1].*

Proof. Correctness follows from the preceding discussion. Preprocessing ensures that all precomputed values (such as $|\mathcal{L}(T \backslash T_x, z')|$) defined for the other end z' of a candidate swap edge are available locally at z'. As to the message complexity, consider the execution of the BESTDIAMSWAP algorithm for one particular edge $e = (x, p(x))$. Starting in node $x \in V \backslash \{d_c\}$, each node in T_x sends a message containing the "enabling information" (i.e., $\mathcal{L}(T_x \backslash T_q, q)$ and possibly $\lambda(p(x))$) containing $O(1)$ items to each of its children. Furthermore, each node in T_x (including finally x) sends another message with size $O(1)$ up to its parent in the minimum finding process. Hence, two messages of size $O(1)$ are sent across each edge of T_x, and one message is sent across e. Thus, the computation of a best swap for e requires $2 \cdot |E(T_x)| + 1 = 2 \cdot |V(T_x)| - 1$ messages. The number of messages exchanged for computing a best swap edge for *each and every* edge $(x, p(x))$ where $x \in V \backslash \{d_c\}$ is $\sum_x (2 \cdot |V(T_x)| - 1) = 2n^* - (n - 1)$.

As to the time complexity, note that the best swap computation of a *single* edge according to the BESTDIAMSWAP algorithm requires at most $O(\|\mathcal{D}\|)$ time. Now note that this algorithm can be executed independently (and thus concurrently) for each potential failing edge: In this fashion, each node x in T sends exactly one message to each node in T_x during the top-down phase. Symmetrically, in the bottom-up phase, each node u in T sends exactly one message to each node on its path to the root. The crucial point here is to avoid that some of these messages block others for some time (as only one message can traverse a link at a time). Indeed, one can ensure that each message reaches its destination in $O(\|\mathcal{D}\|)$ time as follows. A node z receiving a message with destination at distance d from z forwards it only after all messages of the protocol with a destination of distance more than d from z have been received and forwarded. By induction over the distance of a message from its destination, it is easily proven that this "Farthest-to-Go" queuing policy allows each message to traverse one link towards its destination after at most one time unit of waiting. Thus, the $O(\|\mathcal{D}\|)$ time complexity also holds for the entire algorithm.   □

Instead of sending many small messages individually, we can choose to sequence the process of message sending so that messages for different failing edges are bundled before sending (see also [3,4] for applications of this idea). This leads to an alternative with fewer but longer messages:

Corollary 1. *After preprocessing, the* distributed all best swaps *problem can be solved using $O(n)$ messages of size $O(n)$ each, and $O(\|\mathcal{D}\|)$ time.*

5   The Preprocessing Phase

The preprocessing phase serves the purpose of making the needed terms in the sums described in the previous section available at the nodes of the tree.

In the preprocessing phase, a diameter $\mathcal{D}$ of T is chosen, and its two ends d_1 and d_k as well as its center d_c are identified. This can be done essentially by a convergecast, followed by a broadcast to distribute the result (see e.g. [9]); we omit the details. Hence, after preprocessing exchanges $O(n)$ messages, each node knows the information that is requested in (A) and (C) below. It is crucial that during preprocessing, each node obtains enough information to later carry out all computational steps to determine path components (i), (ii) and (iii). More precisely, each node gets the following global information (the same for all nodes):

(A) The endpoints d_1 and d_k of the diameter, the length $|\mathcal{D}|$ of the diameter, and the lengths $|\mathcal{D}_L|$ and $|\mathcal{D}_R|$.

(B) The length μ_R of a longest path starting in d_k that is fully inside $T_{d_{c+1}}$, together with the node ρ_R on $\mathcal{D}$ where such a path leaves the diameter. Figure 5 illustrates such a longest path μ_R. Moreover, the distance $d(\rho_R, d_c)$ must be known. Symmetrically, the length μ_L of a longest path starting in d_1 that is fully inside $T_{d_{c-1}}$, with the corresponding node ρ_L and distance $d(\rho_L, d_c)$ are required.

In addition, each node z obtains the following information that is specific for z:

(C) For each child $q \in C(z)$ of its children, the height T_q of q's subtree.
(D) Is z on the diameter $\mathcal{D}$, yes or no.
(E) The distance $d(z, d_c)$ of z to d_c.
(F) The identification of the parent $p(z)$ of z in T.
(G) To which of V_L, V_C and V_R does z belong.
(H) If $z \notin \mathcal{D}$, the closest predecessor u of z on the diameter; the distance $d(u, d_c)$ from u to d_c.
(I) If z is on the left (right) diameter $\mathcal{D}_L$ ($\mathcal{D}_R$), with $z = d_i$, the length $\lambda(d_i)$ of a longest path in T starting at d_c and neither containing the node d_{c+1} (d_{c-1}) nor the node d_{i-1} (d_{i+1}) (see Fig. 5).
(J) For each of the neighbours z' of z in G, which of V_L, V_C and V_R contains z'; the distance $d(z', d_c)$ from z' to d_c; the nearest predecessor u' of z' on $\mathcal{D}$, the distance $d(u', d_c)$.

Computing the Additional Information. Recall that the first preprocessing part ends with a broadcast that informs all nodes about the information described in (A) and (C). The second part of the preprocessing phase follows now.

A node z receiving the message about $\mathcal{D}$ can infer from the previous convergecast whether it belongs to $\mathcal{D}$ itself by just checking whether the paths from z to d_1 and d_k go through the same neighbour of z.

Information (E) is obtained by having the center node send a "distance from d_c" $d(d_c, d_*)$ message to both neighbours d_{c+1} and d_{c-1} on $\mathcal{D}$, which is forwarded and updated on the diameter. This information is used by the diameter nodes for computing $\lambda(d_i)$, required in (I). The center initiates the inductive computation of $\lambda(d_i)$:

- $\lambda(d_c)$ is the depth of a deepest node in V_C.
- For each d_j, $1 \le j < c$, $\lambda(d_j) = \max\{\lambda(d_{j+1}), d(d_c, d_j) + h_2(d_j)\}$, h_2 being the height of a highest subtree of d_j apart from the diameter subtree.
- For each d_j, $c < j \le k$, $\lambda(d_j) = \max\{\lambda(d_{j-1}), d(d_c, d_j) + h_2(d_j)\}$.

In order to compute μ_L and μ_R as required in (B), we define $\mu(d_i)$ for each node d_i on $\mathcal{D}_L$ as the length of a longest path starting in d_1 that is fully inside T_{d_i}, together with the node $\rho(d_i)$ on $\mathcal{D}_L$ where such a path leaves the diameter. For d_i on $\mathcal{D}_R$, the definition is symmetric. We then have $\mu_L = \mu(d_{c-1})$ and $\mu_R = \mu(d_{c+1})$. The inductive computation of $\mu(d_i)$ is started by d_1 and d_k, and then propagated along the diameter:

- $\mu(d_1) = \mu(d_k) = 0$;
- for each d_j, $1 < j < c$, $\mu(d_j) = \max\{\mu(d_{j-1}), d(d_1, d_j) + h_2(d_j)\}$;
- for each d_j, $c < j < k$, $\mu(d_j) = \max\{\mu(d_{j+1}), d(d_k, d_j) + h_2(d_j)\}$.

Along with $\mu(d_j)$, $\rho(d_j)$ and $d(\rho(d_j), d_c)$ can be computed as well. The computation stops in d_c, which receives the messages $(\mu(d_{c-1}), \rho(d_{c-1}), d(\rho(d_{c-1}), d_c)) = (\mu_L, \rho_L, d(\rho_L, d_c))$ and $(\mu(d_{c+1}), \rho(d_{c+1}), d(\rho(d_{c+1}), d_c)) = (\mu_R, \rho_R, d(\rho_R, d_c))$. Altogether, this second preprocessing part operates along the diameter and takes $O(\|\mathcal{D}(T)\|) = O(n)$ messages.

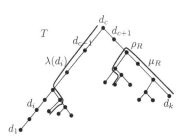

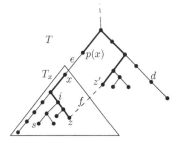

Fig. 5. Definition of $\lambda(d_i)$, μ_R and ρ_R

Fig. 6. Only some nodes need to know about failure of edge $e = (x, p(x))$

Distributing the Information. When the computation of $(\mu_L, \rho_L, d(\rho_L, d_c))$ and $(\mu_R, \rho_R, d(\rho_R, d_c))$ completes in d_c, the center packs these values plus the values $|\mathcal{D}_L|$ and $|\mathcal{D}_R|$ into one message M_*. It adds the appropriate one of the labels "V_L", "V_R" and "V_C" to M_*, before forwarding M_* to d_{c-1}, d_{c+1} and any other neighbour of d_c in T and then flooding the tree. Additionally, M_* contains the "distance from d_c" information which is updated on forwarding, such that all nodes know their distance to the center[2]. When M_* is forwarded from a node $u \in \mathcal{D}$ to a node not on $\mathcal{D}$, it is extended by the "distance from u" information, which is also updated on forwarding. In addition, $d(u, d_c)$ is appended to M_*. Finally, if node z receives M_* from node v, then z learns that v is its parent.

At the end of this second part of the preprocessing phase, each node z' sends a message M' to each of its neighbours z in $G \backslash T$. Note that this is the only point in our solution where messages need to be sent over edges in $G \backslash T$. M' contains $d(z', d_c)$ and exactly one of { "$z' \in V_L$", "$z' \in V_C$" , "$z' \in V_R$" }, whichever applies. Furthermore, let u' be the nearest ancestor of z' on $\mathcal{D}$; the distance $d(u', d_c)$ is also appended to M'.

As a consequence, after each node has received its version of the message M_*, the information stated in (B), (E), (F), (G), (H) is known to each node. Furthermore, each node that has received M' from all its neighbours in G knows the information stated in (J). The distribution of this information requires $O(\|\mathcal{D}(T)\|)$ time and $O(m)$ messages. Let us summarize.

Lemma 2. *After the end of the two parts of the preprocessing phase, which requires $O(\|\mathcal{D}\|)$ time, all nodes know all information $(A) - (J)$, and $O(m)$ messages have been exchanged.*

Recognizing Swap Edges Using Labels. A node $v \in T_x$ must be able to tell whether an incident edge $f = (v, w)$ is a swap edge for $e = (x, p(x))$ or not. We achieve this by the folklore method of numbering nodes in two ways, a preorder traversal and a reverse preorder traversal. After this, a node can decide in constant time whether an edge is a swap edge. For details, see [3,4].

---

[2] The nodes on $\mathcal{D}$ already have that information at this point, but all other nodes still require it.

6   Routing Issues

A natural question arises concerning routing in the presence of a failure: After replacing the failing edge e by a best swap edge f, how do we adjust our routing mechanism in order to guide messages to their destination in the new tree $T_{e/f}$? And how is routing changed back again after the failing edge has been repaired? Clearly, it is desirable that the adaptation of the routing mechanism is as fast and inexpensive as possible.

Existing Approaches. The simplest routing scheme uses a routing table of n entries at each node, which contains, for each possible destination node, the link that should be chosen for forwarding. This approach can be modified to allow swaps by storing additional n entries for the swap links at each node [3]. In [5] a scheme is proposed that stores only one swap entry, at the cost of choosing suboptimal swap edges. All these approaches require $O(n^2)$ routing entries in total.

In the following, we propose to use a *compact* routing scheme for arbitrary trees (shortest paths, minimum diameter, or any other) which requires only δ entries, i.e. $\delta c \log n$ bits, at a node of degree δ, thus n entries or $mc \log n$ bits in total, which is the same amount of space that the *interval routing* scheme of [10] requires. The header of a message requires $c \log n$ bits to describe its destination.

Our Routing Scheme. Our routing scheme for trees is based on the labelling $\gamma : V \to \{1, \dots, n\}^2$ described in the end of Section 5. Note that γ allows to decide in constant time whether a is in the subtree of b (i.e., $a \in T_b$) for any two given nodes a and b.

Basic Routing Algorithm:
A node s routes message M with destination d as follows: (i) If $d = s$, M has arrived at its destination. (ii) If $d \notin T_s$, s sends M to $p(s)$. (iii) Otherwise, s sends M to the child $q \in C(s)$ for which $d \in T_q$.

This algorithm clearly routes each message directly on its (unique) path in T from s to d. Before describing the adaptation in the presence of a swap, observe that a node s which receives a message M with destination d can locally decide whether M traverses a given edge $e = (x, p(x))$: edge e is used by M if and only if exactly one of s and d is in the subtree T_x of x, i.e., if $(s \in T_x) \neq (d \in T_x)$. Thus, it is enough to adapt routing if all nodes are informed about a failing edge (and later the repair) by two broadcasts starting at its two incident nodes (the points of failure). However, the following lemma shows that optimal rerouting is guaranteed even if only those nodes which lie on the two paths between the points of failure and the swap edge's endpoints are informed about failures, which allows "piggybacking" all information for routing adjustment on the first message arriving at the point of failure after the failure occurred.

Lemma 3. *Let $e = (x, p(x))$ be the failing edge, and $f = (z, z')$ the best swap of e, where z is in T_x and z' in $T \setminus T_x$, as shown in Figure 6. If all nodes on the path from x to z know that e is unavailable and that $f = (z, z')$ is a best swap* *edge, then any message originating in $s \in T_x$ will be routed on the direct path from s to its destination d. Symmetrically, if all nodes on the path from $p(x)$ to z' know about e and f, then any message originating in $s \in T \backslash T_x$ will be routed on the direct path from s to its destination d.*

Proof. Let M be any message with source $s \in T_x$. If $d \in T_x$, then trivially M will be routed on its direct path, because it does not require edge e. If $d \in T \backslash T_x$, consider the path $\mathcal{P}_T$ from s to d in T, and the path $\mathcal{P}_{T_{e/f}}$ from s to d in $T_{e/f}$. Consider the last common node i of $\mathcal{P}_T$ and $\mathcal{P}_{T_{e/f}}$ in T_x. The path composed of the paths $\langle x, \ldots, i \rangle$, $\langle i, \ldots, z \rangle$ is exactly the unique path in T from x to z, so node i lies on that path.

Obviously, M will be routed on the direct path towards d up to i. As i lies on the path from x to z, it knows about the failure and the swap, and will route M towards z. The lemma assumes that any node on the path from i to z also knows about the swap. Thus, such nodes will route M on the direct path to z. At z, M will be routed over the swap edge f, and from z' on M is forwarded on the direct path from z' to d.   □

Given Lemma 3, we propose the following "lazy update" procedure for informing nodes about an edge failure:

Algorithm SWAP:
If an edge fails, no action is taken as long as no message needs to cross it. As soon as a message M which should be routed over the failing edge arrives at the point of failure, information about the failure and its best swap is attached to message M, and M is routed towards the swap edge. On its way, all nodes which receive M route it further towards the swap edge, and remember for themselves the information about the swap.

Observation (Adaptivity). *After one message M has been rerouted from the point of failure to the swap edge, all messages originating in the same side of T as M (with respect to the failing edge) will be routed to their destination on the direct path in the tree (i.e., without any detour via the point of failure).*

If a failing edge has been replaced by a swap edge, then all nodes which know about that swap must be informed when the failure has been repaired. Therefore, a message is sent from the point of failure to the swap edge (on both sides if necessary), to inform these nodes, and to deactivate the swap edge.

7   Discussion

We have presented a distributed algorithm for computing all best swap edges for a minimum diameter spanning tree. Our solution is asynchronous, requires unique identifiers from a linearly ordered universe (but only for tiebreaking to determine a center node), and uses $O(\|\mathcal{D}\|)$ time and $O(\max\{n^*, m\})$ small messages, or $O(n)$ messages of size $O(n)$. It remains an open problem to extend our approach to subgraphs with other objectives; for instance, can we efficiently compute swap edges for failing edges in a spanner?

References

1. Andrews, M., Awerbuch, B., Fernández, A., Leighton, T., Liu, Z., Kleinberg, J.: Universal-stability results and performance bounds for greedy contention-resolution protocols. J. ACM 48(1), 39–69 (2001)
2. Bui, M., Butelle, F., Lavault, C.: A Distributed Algorithm for Constructing a Minimum Diameter Spanning Tree. Journal of Parallel and Distributed Computing 64, 571–577 (2004)
3. Flocchini, P., Enriques, A.M., Pagli, L., Prencipe, G., Santoro, N.: Point-of-failure Shortest-path Rerouting: Computing the Optimal Swap Edges Distributively. IEICE Transactions on Information and Systems E89-D(2), 700–708 (2006)
4. Flocchini, P., Pagli, L., Prencipe, G., Santoro, N., Widmayer, P.: Computing All the Best Swap Edges Distributively. In: Higashino, T. (ed.) OPODIS 2004. LNCS, vol. 3544. pp. 154–168. Springer, Heidelberg (2005)
5. Ito, H., Iwama, K., Okabe, Y., Yoshihiro, T.: Single Backup Table Schemes for Shortest-path Routing. Theoretical Computer Science 333(3), 347–353 (2005)
6. Nardelli, E., Proietti, G., Widmayer, P.: Finding All the Best Swaps of a Minimum Diameter Spanning Tree Under Transient Edge Failures. Journal of Graph Algorithms and Applications 5(5), 39–57 (2001)
7. Nardelli, E., Proietti, G., Widmayer, P.: Swapping a Failing Edge of a Single Source Shortest Paths Tree Is Good and Fast. Algorithmica 35(1), 56–74 (2003)
8. Di Salvo, A., Proietti, G.: Swapping a Failing Edge of a Shortest Paths Tree by Minimizing the Average Stretch Factor. In: Kralovic, R., Sýkora, O. (eds.) SIROCCO 2004. LNCS, vol. 3104. Springer, Heidelberg (2004)
9. Santoro, N.: Design and Analysis of Distributed Algorithms. Wiley Series on Parallel and Distributed Computing. Wiley, Chichester (2007)
10. Santoro, N., Khatib, R.: Labelling and Implicit Routing in Networks. The Computer Journal 28(1), 5–8 (1985)

On the Message Complexity of Indulgent Consensus

Seth Gilbert[1], Rachid Guerraoui[1], and Dariusz R. Kowalski[2]

[1] I&C School Of Computer & Communication Sciences
EPFL, 1015 Lausanne, Switzerland
seth.gilbert@epfl.ch, rachid.guerraoui@epfl.ch
[2] Department of Computer Science, University of Liverpool
Liverpool L69 3BX, UK
d.r.kowalski@csc.liv.ac.uk

Abstract. Many recommend planning for the worst and hoping for the best. In this paper we devise *efficient* indulgent consensus algorithms that can tolerate crash failures and arbitrarily long periods of asynchrony, and yet perform (asymptotically) optimally in well-behaved, synchronous executions with few failures. We present two such algorithms: In synchronous executions, the first has *optimal message complexity*, using only $O(n)$ messages, but runs in superlinear time of $O(n^{1+\varepsilon})$. The second has a message complexity of $O(n\,\text{polylog}(n))$, but has an optimal running time, completing in $O(f)$ rounds in synchronous executions with at most f failures. Both of these results improve significantly over the most message-efficient of previous indulgent consensus algorithms which have a message complexity of at least $\Omega(n^2)$ in well-behaved executions.

1 Introduction

As in many other fields, it is considered good computing practice to plan for the worst and hope for the best. In the context of distributed computing, this typically translates into devising algorithms that, on the one hand tolerate process failures and arbitrarily long periods of asynchrony, whilst on the other hand, are particularly effective under best-case conditions, namely, few failures and synchrony. Such best-case conditions are usually considered frequent in practice and it makes sense to optimize algorithms with these conditions in mind.

In this paper, we explore this idea in the context of *consensus* [1, 2] in a system of n processes of which a minority can fail by crashing. Given a set of n crash-prone processes, each with initial value v_i; each process needs to *decide* an output satisfying: (1) (agreement) every process decides the same value; (2) (validity) if a process decides value v, then v is the initial value for some process; (3) (termination) every correct process eventually decides.

The question we ask is how "efficient" can a consensus algorithm be when the system is synchronous and $f \leq \lceil n/2 \rceil - 1$ failures actually occur, if the algorithm needs to tolerate arbitrarily long periods of asynchrony. Consensus algorithms that tolerate arbitrarily long periods of asynchrony include [3, 4, 5, 6, 7, 8]: they have been called *indulgent* [9]; indulgent consensus is impossible when there are more than a minority of crash failures [3].

A. Pelc (Ed.): DISC 2007, LNCS 4731, pp. 283–297, 2007.

	Message Complexity	Round Complexity
Alg. 1 (Section 4):	$O(n)$	$O(n^{1+\varepsilon})$
Alg. 2 (Section 5):	$O(n \log^6 n)$	$O(f)$

Fig. 1. Message and round complexity of the two algorithms presented in this paper. Both refer to synchronous executions in which there are no more than $f \leq t$ failures.

Addressing this question requires defining what it means for a consensus algorithm to be "efficient." Usually, this is measured in terms of rounds of communication needed for processes to reach a decision (see, e.g., [10]). There indeed exists an indulgent consensus protocol that reaches a decision in $O(f)$ (in fact, $f + 2$) rounds when the system is synchronous and f processes fail [11]. This algorithm, and in fact all indulgent consensus algorithms that are optimized for synchronous periods (e.g., [12,4,8]), exchange $\Omega(n^2)$ messages: all processes send messages to all processes in every round. (In fact, most use at least $\Theta(n^2 f)$ messages.) This pattern of full message exchange is a key subprotocol underlying those algorithms, and is used to detect synchrony and adapt the decision time to the actual number of failures. It is natural to ask whether such a pattern is necessary and whether $\Theta(n^2)$ messages really need to be exchanged.

In other words, is it possible to devise an indulgent consensus protocol that reaches a decision in $O(f)$ rounds when the system is synchronous and no more than f processes fail, while exchanging fewer than $\Theta(n^2)$ messages? If the algorithm does not need to tolerate asynchrony, then the answer is yes [11]: [13] presented a protocol that uses $O((f + 1)n)$ messages and [14] later demonstrated that $O(n + fn^\varepsilon)$ messages are sufficient. However, it is not immediately obvious whether similar results can be achieved if the algorithm must tolerate periods of asynchrony. Clearly, during such a period processes could have divergent views: some may believe the system to be synchronous whereas others may not; some may observe only a small number of failures and hence believe it safe to decide, while others may not. In algorithms with a pattern of full message exchange, these inconsistencies are easy to resolve. The key difficulty in constructing an efficient algorithm that tolerates asynchrony is devising message-efficient techniques for producing a consistent view of the (a)synchrony of the world.

Results

We present in this paper two indulgent consensus algorithms (see Table 1). Both tolerate a minority of the processes failing, and output a decision when the system becomes stable. When the system is synchronous, both algorithms guarantee good performance, both in terms of message-efficiency and round complexity. Each is (asymptotically) optimal in a different sense. The first guarantees optimal message complexity—$O(n)$ messages—in synchronous executions, and terminates in $O(n^{1+\varepsilon})$ rounds. The second is adaptive: it guarantees optimal round complexity—$O(f)$ rounds—in a synchronous execution with no more than $f \leq t$ failures, and has a message complexity of $O(n \log^6 n)$.

The key idea in both algorithms is to simulate an efficient synchronous consensus algorithm, while at the same time detecting asynchrony. If the execution is synchronous, then efficient performance is achieved. If the execution is not synchronous, however, the processes synchronize their view of the world via message-efficient gossip, and eventually fall-back to a less efficient consensus protocol that can better tolerate the uncertain synchrony.

In the case of the second algorithm, which is adaptive, the simulation of the efficient synchronous protocol is more involved: different processes may complete the simulation at different times and (again) with different views of the world. In message-expensive algorithms, this is easy to resolve, as typically all processes decide within one round of each other due to nodes flooding their decision prior to termination. In our case, the combination of adaptivity and possible asynchrony complicated the matters. Throughout the simulation, processes must efficiently determine whether any processes have already produced a decision which is clearly difficult because a process cannot distinguish a failed process from one whose messages are delayed. The solution, again, is through careful use of efficient gossip protocols to synchronize the status of the processes prior to deciding.

Interestingly, both our algorithms can be viewed as generic transformations from synchronous consensus (and gossip) protocols to partially synchronous consensus protocols. Thus future improvements in synchronous algorithms will result immediately in improved indulgent consensus algorithms.

Previous and Related Work

The problem of consensus was first introduced by Pease, Shostak and Lamport [1]. Fisher, Lynch and Paterson [2] showed that consensus is unsolvable in an asynchronous system in which even one process can crash. Thus research on consensus has often focused on synchronous and partially synchronous models of computation. In a seminal paper [3], Dwork, Lynch, and Stockmeyer introduced a model of *eventual synchrony* in which clock skew and message delivery eventually stabilize at some unknown point in the execution. This is the model we adopt in this paper. They showed in [3] that consensus can be solved in the eventually synchronous model if and only if $n \geq 2t + 1$, where t is the tolerable number of crash failures. In [9], Guerraoui coins the term "indulgent" to describe algorithms that can tolerate arbitrarily long periods of asynchrony.

Fisher and Lynch [15] showed that a synchronous solution to consensus requires $t+1$ rounds, where t is the tolerable number of failures. Dolev and Strong [16] introduce the idea of *early stopping*, or adaptive, consensus protocols, and Lamport and Fischer [17] show that it is possible to terminate in only $f + 2$ rounds in executions with $f < t$ failures. Dolev, Reischuk and Strong [18] show that at least $\min(f + 2, t + 1)$ rounds are necessary. In the context of indulgent consensus, Dutta and Guerraoui [11] show that at least $t + 2$ rounds are required, even in a synchronous execution. There has been a significant amount of recent work on optimizing the running time of consensus in failure-free executions; see, for example [12, 19, 8].

In a synchronous setting, it is relatively straightforward to observe that there is an $\Omega(n)$ lower bound on the message complexity of fault-tolerant synchronous consensus. Dwork, Halpern and Waarts [20] found a solution with $O(n \log n)$ messages but exponential time. Finally, Galil, Mayer and Yung [14] developed an algorithm with $O(n)$ messages, thus showing that this is the optimal message-complexity. The drawback of their solution is that it runs in superlinear time $O(n^{1+\varepsilon})$, for any fixed $0 < \varepsilon < 1$. Galil, Mayer and Yung [14] also found an adaptive solution with $O(n + fn^\varepsilon)$ communication complexity, for any $0 < \varepsilon < 1$. Chlebus and Kowalski reduced the number of messages to $O(n \log^2 n)$ for consensus in case $n - t = \Omega(n)$ [21], and recently they developed an adaptive algorithm that tolerates up to $n - 1$ crashes and achieves $O(n \log^5 n)$ message complexity [22]. The message complexity of consensus when no failures actually occur, was studied by Amdur, Weber and Hadzilacos [23] and by Hadzilacos and Halpern [24], and results in the following fact which implies that $O(n)$ message complexity is optimal, regardless of the actual number of failures:

Fact 1 (Amdur, Weber and Hadzilacos [23]). *The message complexity of every (eventually)-synchronous consensus protocol is at least $\Omega(n)$, even in failure-free executions.*

Roadmap

In Section 2 we describe the eventually synchronous model, and in Section 3 we define a series of building blocks, synchronous protocols that will be used in the construction of our algorithms. In Section 4, we describe our first algorithm which guarantees optimal message complexity (in synchronous executions). In Section 5, we describe our second algorithm which is adaptive and guarantees optimal round complexity (in synchronous executions). We outline the proof of correctness in Section 6. In Section 7, we describe instantiations of the building blocks from Section 3, which allows us to analyze the performance of our algorithms in Section 8. We conclude in Section 9.

2   System Model

In this section we describe a basic system model for a *partially synchronous* (or *eventually synchronous*) system, as in [3]. The model is defined by three parameters that are known *a priori*: n, the number of processes, δ, an eventual bound on clock skew, and d, an eventual bound on message delay. There is also a stabilization time, referred to as GST, that is *unknown*. We say that an execution is *synchronous* if GST$= 0$.

In more detail, we consider a system consisting of n message-passing processes, each of which has a unique identifier from the set $[n] = \{1, 2, \ldots, n\}$. Each process is capable of communicating directly with all other processes: prior to GST, messages may be arbitrarily delayed; after GST, every message is delivered within d time. Each process has a local clock, and after GST the clock skew of every process is bounded by δ, i.e., eventually the ratio of the rates of two processes' clocks is at most δ.

We assume that up to $t < \lceil n/2 \rceil$ processes may *crash*, and that processes do not restart or recover. We say that a process is *correct* if it does not crash. We *do not* assume reliable multicast: if a process crashes while sending a message to multiple recipients, then an arbitrary subset of the recipients may receive the message.

We are specifically interested in the performance of algorithms in synchronous executions. We say that an algorithm $\mathcal{A}$ solves consensus *by time τ* in the presence of f failures if for every synchronous execution with no more than f failures, every node has decided by time τ. We say that algorithm $\mathcal{A}$ has message complexity μ if for every synchronous execution, the total number of messages sent is no more than μ.

3   Building Blocks Protocols

We construct our protocol out of three synchronous building blocks: synchronous consensus, synchronous gossip, and synchronous wake-up. We also use one eventually-synchronous building block, a consensus protocol. In this section, we describe each of these building blocks, and enumerate their properties. In Section 7 we describe how each building block can be implemented from existing protocols.

Synchronous Consensus Protocol. The first basic building block, SynchConsensus, is a protocol that solves consensus in synchronous executions. The protocol guarantees the following properties: (1) *Agreement*: In every synchronous execution, all decision values are the same. (2) *Unconditional validity*: In every execution (synchronous or otherwise), every decision is the initial value of some process. (3) *Termination*: In every synchronous execution, every process eventually decides and terminates.

The second property, unconditional validity, is the only guarantee in an execution that is not synchronous. For every $0 \leq f \leq t$, define $\tau^{\mathrm{cons}}(f)$ to be the earliest round in which every execution of SynchConsensus with no more than f failures terminates. (This is of particular relevance when the consensus protocol is adaptive.)

Synchronous Conditional Gossip. The second building block is a protocol Gossip(k) that solves the conditional gossip problem in synchronous executions with no more than k failures. It is called "conditional" since its guarantees only hold when there are $\leq k$ failures. Each process begins the gossip protocol with a *rumor* v_i. The protocol satisfies the following: (1) *Completion:* In every synchronous execution with at most $k \leq f < n$ failures, every non-failed process eventually receives a rumor from every non-failed process; and (2) *Unconditional validity:* In every execution (synchronous or otherwise), every rumor received is the initial value of some process. For every $0 \leq f \leq t$, define $\tau^{\mathrm{gossip}}(f)$ to be the earliest round in which every execution of Gossip(f) with no more than f failures terminates.

Synchronous Conditional Wake-Up. The third building block is a protocol WakeUp(k) that solves the conditional wake-up problem. In conditional wake-up, initially, some subset S of the processes are designated awake, while the rest are designated asleep. The goal of conditional wake-up is that if every process is initially asleep, i.e., $S = \emptyset$, then every process remains asleep and no messages are sent by any process. Conversely, if $S \neq \emptyset$, then every non-failed process wakes up. Again, it is referred to as "conditional" since its guarantees only hold when there are $\leq k$ failures. In more detail, the protocol guarantees the following: (1) *Completion:* In every synchronous execution with at most $k \leq f < n$ failures, if $S \neq \emptyset$, then eventually the protocol terminates and every process concludes that it is awake. (2) *Validity:* In every synchronous execution, if $S = \emptyset$, then every process remains asleep and no messages are sent. For every $0 \leq f \leq t$, define $\tau^{\mathrm{wakeup}}(f)$ to be the earliest round in which every execution of WakeUp(f) with no more than f failures terminates.

Partially-Synchronous Consensus Protocol. The final building block is an arbitrary eventually-synchronous consensus protocol PartSynchConsensus; it guarantees the usual properties of consensus: agreement, validity, and termination. There are a variety of protocols that satisfy these requirements, including, for example, [5, 3].

4 Indulgent Consensus

In this section we present our first indulgent consensus protocol. When instantiated using the appropriate building-block protocols, the result is an (asymptotically) message-optimal algorithm. (See Theorem 3.) The main idea is to first simulate an efficient *synchronous* consensus protocol SynchConsensus (see Section 7.1), and then determine whether it has completed successfully. If so, then each process can decide that value and terminate; otherwise processes run a fall-back partially synchronous consensus protocol that is not as message efficient. The main difficulty, then, is correctly detecting when an execution is synchronous without sending too many messages.

4.1 Simulating Synchronous Rounds

Each process simulates synchronous rounds in the standard manner based on message delay d and clock skew δ. Recall that in a synchronous execution, at time τ the clock at every process i is in the range $[(1 - \delta)\tau, (1 + \delta)\tau]$. Let $\rho = (1 + \delta)/(1 - \delta)$. The first simulated round r_1 ends at time $d/(1 - \delta)$ according to the local clock at each process. Simulated round r ends for each process at time: $\tau^{\mathtt{sim}}(r) = \frac{d}{1-\delta} \sum_{j=0}^{r-1} \rho^j$ according to the local clock of that process. In a synchronous execution, every message sent at the beginning of round r according to the local clock of the sending process is received by the end of round r according to the local clock of the receiving process.

4.2 Protocol Description

The protocol proceeds in four phases: (1) Agreement Phase, (2) Locking Phase, (3) Decision Phase, (4) Fall-back Phase. When the protocol begins, the proposal for process i is stored in e_i, its estimate. Process i also maintains a variable $status_i$ that indicates its current status. Initially $status_i = \mathsf{proposal}$, indicating that the estimate is the initial value. As the status advances during the protocol to higher levels, it never returns to a lower level.

1. Agreement Phase. In the first phase, the processes together simulate the consensus protocol SynchConsensus for $\tau^{\mathtt{cons}}(t)$ rounds. If the execution is, in fact, synchronous, then for each correct process the consensus simulation will output a decision; all such decisions will agree. If the execution is not synchronous, then the consensus protocol may not terminate, or may output different decisions at different processes. If a process discovers that its simulation reaches a decision, then this decision is stored as its estimate e_i, and its status is advanced to candidate. Notice that processes do not decide on the value output by SynchConsensus at this time.

The agreement phase continues until $\tau^{\mathtt{cons}}(t)$ rounds have been simulated (where $t < \lceil n/2 \rceil$ is the maximum tolerated number of failures). If the simulated consensus protocol SynchConsensus has not terminated, then the simulation is halted. In this case, any process that has not decided will (eventually) enter the fall-back phase.

2. Locking Phase. In the second phase, the processes together simulate the synchronous conditional gossip protocol Gossip(t) for $\tau^{\mathtt{gossip}}(t)$ rounds. Each process i uses e_i and $status_i$ as its initial rumor. Thus, in a synchronous execution, every non-failed process receives the rumors of all other non-failed processes. At the end of the phase, process i advances its status under the following conditions: (1) it has received a rumor from at least $\lfloor n/2 \rfloor + 1$ processes that have a status of candidate, locked, or decided for some value v; (2) estimate $e_i = v$; and (3) $status_i =$ proposal or candidate. In this case, process i updates its status to locked. We will argue (Lemma 1) that at most one value is locked in an execution.

3. Decision Phase. In the third phase, the processes repeat the (synchronous) conditional gossip protocol $\texttt{Gossip}(t)$ for $\tau^{\texttt{gossip}}(t)$ further (synchronous) rounds. Each process i again uses e_i and $status_i$ as its initial rumor. At the end of the third phase, process i advances its status under the following conditions: (1) it receives a rumor from at least $\lfloor n/2 \rfloor + 1$ processes that have a status of locked or decided for same value v; and (2) estimate $e_i = v$; and $status_i =$ locked. In this case, process i updates $status_i =$ decided, and decides e_i. If all the processes have decided, then from this point on no further messages are broadcast, and the protocol is considered to be terminated.

4. Fall-back Phase. In the final phase, if any process has not yet decided, then the processes all resort to the fall-back consensus protocol $\texttt{PartSynchConsensus}$. This phase occurs only in executions that are not synchronous. The synchronous round simulation is abandoned at this point.

The first step in the fall-back phase is to collect the final status of all the other processes. This proceeds as follows: (1) Each process i that has not yet decided in the previous phase sends a fall-back message to every other process: $\langle \text{fallback}, e_i, status_i \rangle$. (2) Any process that receives a fall-back message enters the fall-back phase and, if it has not already done so, immediately sends a fall-back message $\langle \text{fallback}, e_j, status_j \rangle$ to every process, even if it has previuosly decided. (3) When a process i receives $\lfloor n/2 \rfloor + 1$ fall-back messages, it determines if there are any locked values. That is, if any fall-back message contains status locked, then process i sets its estimate e_i to the value of that message.

Since every message is eventually delivered, and since a majority of processes are correct, it is easy to see that if any correct process begins the fall-back phase, then eventually every process receives $\lfloor n/2 \rfloor + 1$ fall-back messages. Thus, if any value has been locked by a majority of the processes during the initial three phases, then each process executing the fall-back phase will adopt that value as its estimate. Every process that has received a fall-back message then executes $\texttt{PartSynchConsensus}$, where process i uses estimate e_i as its proposal. Eventually $\texttt{PartSynchConsensus}$ produces a decision, and each process decides this value and terminates.

5   Adaptive Indulgent Consensus

In this section we show how to modify the protocol presented in Section 4 to develop an *adaptive* indulgent consensus protocol. Recall that the protocol in Section 4 begins by simulating the consensus protocol $\texttt{SynchConsensus}$ in the agreement phase. If $\texttt{SynchConsensus}$ is adaptive, it terminates early in synchronous executions with few failures. The goal of this section is to detect when the $\texttt{SynchConsensus}$ simulation has terminated. This detection is accomplished by pausing the consensus simulation every so often and executing a variant of the locking and decision phases, using conditional gossip primitives designed for $f \leq t$ failures. Before resuming the consensus protocol simulation, we execute a conditional wake-up protocol: if some processes have decided and other have not yet decided, this protocol wakes the processes that have already decided so that they can continue with the (simulated) consensus protocol.

We divide the agreement phase into $\log n$ epochs numbered from 0 to $\log n - 1$. Epoch x has length $O(2^x)$, and simulates $O(2^x)$ rounds of SynchConsensus. The epochs are structured such that by the end of epoch x, the system has finished executing round $\tau^{\text{cons}}(2^x)$ of SynchConsensus; thus in a synchronous execution with $\leq 2^x$ failures, SynchConsensus completes by the end of epoch x. (Notice that there are $< 2^{\log n - 1} = n/2$ failures.)

In more detail, each epoch consists of four phases: (1) *Wake-up:* waking the processes that have already decided; (2) *Agreement:* simulating some rounds of the consensus protocol; (3) *Locking:* execute conditional gossip and determine if any of the values can be locked, and (4) *Deciding:* execute conditional gossip and determine if any of the values can be decided. If, at the end of $\log n$ epochs a process has not yet decided, then it enters the fall-back phase.

1. Waking the Processes. At the beginning of epoch x, there are three possibilities: all the processes have decided, none have decided, or some have decided and some have not. In this last case, a problem might occur if some processes have decided, and thus stopped participating voluntarily in future epochs, while others have not yet decided and need to continue the protocol. The first step in epoch x, then, is to execute WakeUp(2^x): each process that has decided is initially asleep and each process that is undecided is initially awake. This step takes $\tau^{\text{wakeup}}(2^x)$ rounds, and guarantees that if the execution is synchronous and there are no more than 2^x failures, then every process is awake.

2. Agreement. The second step in epoch x is to simulate some rounds of the consensus protocol SynchConsensus, continuing from the last round simulated in the previous epoch. In epoch 0, the processes simulate the first $\tau^{\text{cons}}(1)$ rounds of the protocol. In epoch $x > 0$, the process simulate rounds $\tau^{\text{cons}}(2^{x-1}) + 1, \ldots, \tau^{\text{cons}}(2^x)$ of the consensus protocol. If a process has decided in an earlier epoch, then it continues to execute the simulation of SynchConsensus only if it was awoken in the wake-up step, and if there are further rounds to simulate.

As in Section 4, each process i maintains two variables: e_i, its estimate, and $status_i$, its status. Initially, e_i is process i's proposal, and $status_i = $ proposal. If process i discovers that its simulated consensus protocol has decided value v, and if process i has status equal to proposal, then process i sets $e_i = v$ and advances $status_i = $ candidate. If an execution is synchronous and has fewer than 2^x failures, then the simulated consensus protocol will terminate for all non-failed processes by the end of epoch x.

3. Locking. The third step in epoch x is to simulate the conditional gossip protocol Gossip(2^x) for $\tau^{\text{gossip}}(2^x)$ (simulated) rounds, with e_i and $status_i$ as the rumor for process i. This step is equivalent to the locking phase described in Section 4, except that Gossip(2^x) is executed, instead of Gossip(t). If at the end of the locking phase, process i has received rumors from at least $\lfloor n/2 \rfloor + 1$ processes that all have value e_i as a candidate, locked, or decided, and if $status_i = $ proposal or candidate, then process i

locks value e_i. If a process has decided in an earlier epoch, then it executes the gossip only if it was awoken in the wake-up step; otherwise, it remains silent.

4. *Deciding.* The fourth step in epoch x is to again together simulate $\texttt{Gossip}(2^x)$ for $\tau^{\texttt{gossip}}(2^x)$ (simulated) rounds, again with e_i and $status_i$ as the rumor for process i. This step is equivalent to the deciding phase described in Section 4, except that $\texttt{Gossip}(2^x)$ is executed, instead of $\texttt{Gossip}(t)$. If at the end of the deciding phase, process i has received rumors from at least $\lfloor n/2 \rfloor + 1$ processes that have all locked or decided value e_i, and if $status_i \neq$ decided, then process i decides value v. As in the previous step, if a process has decided in an earlier epoch, then it executes the gossip protocol only if was awoken in the wake-up step; otherwise, it remains silent.

Fall Back. If, at the end of all $\log n$ epochs, any process has not yet decided, then it enters the fall-back phase, as described in Section 4, sending and collecting fall-back messages, and running $\texttt{PartSynchConsensus}$.

6 Analysis

In this section we provide an outline of the proof that the protocol presented in Section 5 guarantees agreement, validity, and termination. Performance results are given in Section 8. We begin by showing that in every execution, there is at most one value that is decided. The key lemma, in this case, is that at most one value is locked during a locking phase. Notice that this does not depend in any way on the agreement property of $\texttt{SynchConsensus}$ which only holds in synchronous executions.

Lemma 1. *In every execution, there is at most one value v such that $e_i = v$ and $status_i = $ locked for any i.*

Proof. Assume for the sake of contradiction that i and j have locked two distinct values v and v' (possibly in two different epochs). This implies that each received rumors during a locking phase from a majority of processes indicating that v and v', respectively, were candidate, locked, or decided values. Thus, some process k (in the intersection of the two majorities) must have at one point had value v as a candidate, locked, or decided value and at another point value v' as a candidate, locked, or decided value. But a process never changes its estimate after it has become a candidate, implying a contradiction.

Lemma 2. *In every execution, there is at most one value v that is decided.*

Proof. Suppose for contradiction that processes i and j decide two different values v and v'. There are three cases: (Case 1) Both decide prior to the fall-back phase: This contradicts Lemma 1, as prior to the fall-back phase, a process only decides a value that has been previously locked. (Case 2) Both decide during the fall-back phase: This contradicts the agreement property of $\texttt{PartSynchConsensus}$, which guarantees that at most one value is decided. (Case 3) One (say, i) decides v prior to the fall-back phase and one (say, j) decides v' during the fall-back phase: We argue that every process k begins the fall-back phase with initial value v. Process i decides prior to the fall-back phase only if it receives gossip messages indicating that a majority of processes have locked value v. In the first step of the fall-back phase, process k receives fall-back messages from a majority of the processes. Since a process never changes its estimate once it is locked (prior to the fall-back phase), we can conclude that process k receives a message indicating that value v has been locked. Since there is at most one locked value, by Lemma 1, we conclude that process k adopts value v as its proposal in the fall-back phase. Since every process proposes value v in the fall-back phase, the validity of PartSynchConsensus implies that every non-failed process decides v, resulting in a contradiction.

Next, it follows immediately from the unconditional validity of SynchConsensus and Gossip(t), and from the validity of PartSynchConsensus, that the decision is valid:

Lemma 3. *If v is decided in some execution, then for some process i, initially $e_i = v$.*

Finally, it is easy to see that, due to the fall-back protocol, the protocol eventually terminates in all executions:

Lemma 4. *In all executions, every process eventually decides and stops sending messages.*

7   Implementing the Three Synchronous Building Blocks

In this section we describe efficient implementations of the building-block protocols described in Section 3.

7.1   Implementing SynchConsensus

This section describes two synchronous consensus protocols, both derived from prior work. The first is adaptive and uses $O(n \log^6 n)$ messages; the second uses a superlinear number of rounds but has optimal $O(n)$ message complexity.

Adaptive Synchronous Consensus. In this section, we outline the construction of an adaptive synchronous consensus protocol that is message efficient. We proceed in three steps: we start with a synchronous binary consensus developed in [22]; then we construct a multivalue consensus protocol; finally we transform the resulting protocol into an *adaptive* protocol. In each step, the challenge is to not increase the asymptotic running time and message complexity too much.

Efficient binary synchronous consensus. In [22], Chlebus and Kowalski introduce a binary, message-efficient consensus protocol that tolerates up to $n - 1$ failures, decides in time $O(n)$ and sends $O(n \log^5 n)$ point-to-point messages.

From binary to multivalue consensus. While the protocol presented in [22] is for binary consensus, it can be readily modified to efficiently support multivalue consensus. Typically, binary consensus protocols are translated into multivalue consensus protocols by agreeing on each bit one at a time. In order to achieve unconditional validity and to avoid increasing time complexity above $\Theta(n)$, a slightly different approach is needed.

We construct a binary tournament tree and use binary consensus to navigate the tree. This results in a synchronous multivalue consensus protocol that runs in $O(n)$ times and $O(n \log^6 n)$ message complexity.

Adaptive synchronous consensus Chlebus and Kowalski show in [22] how to transform a message-efficient, synchronous consensus protocol into an *adaptive* message-efficient synchronous consensus protocol, with an (additive) additional $O(n \log^4 n)$ message complexity. The end result is a synchronous, adaptive, message-efficient, that is having $O(n \log^6 n)$ message complexity, consensus protocol SynchConsensus that guarantees unconditional validity:

Proposition 1. *There exists a synchronous multivalue consensus protocol with message complexity $O(n \log^6 n)$ and round complexity $O(f)$ in executions with $\leq f$ failures.*

Message-Optimal Synchronous Consensus. In this section we outline the construction of a message-optimal synchronous consensus protocol that uses only $O(n)$ messages and runs in times $O(n^{1+\varepsilon})$ for every $0 < \varepsilon < 1$. We begin by describing a protocol that solves the Interactive Consistency problem, a stronger variant of consensus in which processes agree not simply on a single value, but rather on a vector of decision values, including one for each correct process[1]. Formally, the IC problem is defined as follows: each process i begins with an initial value v_i, and outputs a decision vector D_i such that the following properties are satisfied: (1) *Agreement*: In every synchronous execution, the decision vector D_i of all processes is the same. (2) *Unconditional validity*: In every execution (synchronous or otherwise), if D_i is the decision vector of process i, then $D[j]_i$ is either the initial value of process j or $\perp$. (3) *Conditional validity*: If the execution is synchronous and j is correct, then $D[j]_i \neq \perp$. (4) *Termination*: Eventually every process outputs a decision vector D_i and terminates.

In [14], there is a synchronous protocol that efficiently solves the *checkpoint* problem, a variant of IC. In particular, the checkpoint problem requires each process i to output a set of processes P_i (rather than a set of values) where every correct process is in the set P_i, and every process in P_i is non-failed at the beginning of the execution. We claim that every synchronous checkpoint protocol can be transformed into a synchronous algorithm for IC:

Lemma 5. *If A solves synchronous checkpoint in τ rounds with message complexity μ, then there exists a synchronous protocol $\mathcal{A}'$ that solves IC in τ rounds with message complexity μ.*

We conclude from Lemma 5, along with the checkpoint protocol from [14]:

Proposition 2. *There exists a synchronous multivalue consensus protocol with message complexity $O(n)$ and round complexity $O(n^{1+\varepsilon})$, for any $0 < \varepsilon < 1$.*

7.2 Implementing Gossip(k)

In this section, we describe two synchronous (conditional) gossip protocols. The first terminates in $O(k)$ rounds and uses $O(n \log^4 n)$ messages, while the second uses a superlinear number of rounds but has $O(n)$ message complexity.

---

[1] It is interesting to notice that IC cannot be solved in a partially synchronous model [9]. We depend on the IC protocol only in synchronous executions, and hence there is no contradiction.

Adaptive Conditional Gossip. In [22], Chlebus and Kowalski present a gossip protocol tolerating up to $n - 1$ failures that has message complexity $O(n \log^4 n)$ and completes in $O(\log^3 n)$ rounds. When $k \geq \log^3 n$, the running time is $O(k)$, as desired.
When $k \leq \log^3 n$, we resort to a simpler two-round protocol in order to guarantee
termination time $O(k)$: in the first round, each process sends its rumor to processes
$[1, \ldots, k + 1]$; in the second round, processes $[1, \ldots, k + 1]$ send all the received rumors to all the other processes. Notice that this satisfies the conditional completion
property, as there are at most k failures, and is message efficient, as it requires at most
$2(k + 1)n = O(n \log^3 n)$ messages when $k < \log^3 n$.

Proposition 3. *For all $f < n$, there exists a synchronous conditional gossip protocol
with message complexity $O(n \log^4 n)$ and round complexity $O(f)$ in executions with at
most f failures.*

Message-Efficient Conditional Gossip. Recall from Section 7.1, there exists a protocol solving Interactive Consistency in $O(n^{1+\varepsilon})$ rounds with $O(n)$ messages. Notice
that any solution to Interactive Consistency is also a solution to gossip, as each process
outputs a set of initial values from every correct process. We thus conclude:

Proposition 4. *There exists a synchronous conditional gossip protocol with message
complexity $O(n)$ and round complexity $O(n^{1+\varepsilon})$ in executions, for any $0 < \varepsilon < 1$.*

7.3   Implementing `WakeUp`(k)

The conditional wake-up problem is quite close to the conditional gossip problem; the
primary difference is that processes initially designated to be asleep must not send any
messages at least until they have received a message from a process that was initially
awake. Thus, from the point of view of the gossip algorithm, a sleeping process can be
treated as faulty until it is awoken. Thus the wake-up problem can be solved using any
synchronous gossip protocol that satisfies the following additional *Polling Property*:
in every execution, for every faulty process i there is some process j that, prior to
failing, sends a message to i. Nearly every "reasonable" gossip protocol, including the
one described in Section Section 7.2, has this property. The simple two-round protocol
(when $k \leq \log^3 n$)) also clearly has this property. We conclude:

Proposition 5. *For all $f \leq t$, there exists a synchronous conditional wake-up protocol
that has message complexity $O(n \log^4 n)$ and round complexity $O(f)$ in executions with
at most f failures.*

8   Performance Analysis

In this section, we analyze the efficiency of the two algorithms. We begin with the
adaptive protocol from Section 5 where `SynchConsensus` is instantiated by the consensus protocol posited by Proposition 1, `Gossip`(k) is instantiated by the gossip protocol posited by Proposition 3, and `WakeUp`(k) is instantiated by the wake-up protocol
posited by Proposition 5.

Lemma 6. *For every synchronous execution with no more than $f \leq t$ failures, every process decides by time $O(f)$, terminating prior to the beginning of the fall-back phase.*

Proof. If $f = 1$, consider epoch $x = 0$; otherwise, consider epoch x such that $2^{x-1} < f \leq 2^x$. There are two possibilities at the beginning of epoch x: either some process has already decided in an earlier epoch, or no process has decided in an earlier epoch. By the conditional guarantee of the wake-up protocol, however, in either case every non-failed process awakes to participate in epoch x.

Next, by the adaptivity property of SynchConsensus, we can conclude that the simulated consensus protocol has output a decision at each non-failed process by the end of the agreement step of epoch x. Thus every non-failed process has status either a candidate, locked, or decided. Since the simulated consensus protocol guarantees agreement, every process with status candidate has the same value. Since every value that is locked or decided was previously a candidate, we can conclude that every process in fact has the same value.

In the locking step of epoch x, since there are no more than 2^x failures, the conditional gossip ensures that each non-failed process receives rumors from a majority of processes, all of which have value v as candidate, locked, or decided. We can thus conclude that at the end of the locking step, every non-failed process has either locked or decided value v. Similarly, in the decision step of epoch x, since there are no more than 2^x failures, the conditional gossip ensures that each non-failed process receives rumors from a majority of processes. We can thus conclude that at the end of the decision phase, every process has decided value v. From this point on, no process sends any further messages. Thus we conclude that by the end of epoch x, every non-failed process has terminated.

Finally, we calculate the total running time through the end of epoch x. First, simulating SynchConsensus through the end of epoch x requires $O(\tau^{\mathrm{cons}}(2^x))$ rounds, which by the choice of SynchConsensus is $O(2^x)$ rounds. Next, notice that for every epoch $y \leq x$, each process executes two instances of Gossip(2^y) and one instance of WakeUp(2^y); these instances take time $O(\tau^{\mathrm{gossip}}(2^y))$ and $O(\tau^{\mathrm{wakeup}}(2^y))$, respectively, which are both, by assumption, $O(2^y)$. Thus, for each epoch y, the wake-up, locking, and decision phases cost $O(2^y)$ rounds, and hence when summed from epoch 0 to epoch x result in a running time of $O(2^x)$ rounds. Thus the total running time to the end of epoch x, in terms of synchronous rounds, is $O(2^x) = O(f)$, implying a termination time of $\tau^{\mathrm{sim}}(O(f)) = O(f)$.

We next argue that the resulting protocol is message efficient:

Lemma 7. *In every synchronous execution, the processes send $O(n \log^6 n)$ messages.*

Proof. During the entire simulation of SynchConsensus, the processes collectively send $O(n \log^6 n)$ messages. In each epoch x, each (non-failed) process executes two instances of Gossip(x) and one instance of WakeUp(x); each such instance uses $O(n \log^4 n)$ messages, resulting in $O(n \log^6 n)$ messages total. By Lemma 6, we conclude that each process decides no later than the final epoch, as desired.

Thus we conclude:

Theorem 2. *There exists an adaptive indulgent consensus protocol with message complexity $\Theta(n \log^6 n)$ and running time $O(f)$ in synchronous executions with no more than f failures.*

We next briefly examine the performance of the protocol presented in Section 4, where SynchConsensus is instantiated by the protocol posited by Proposition 2 and Gossip(k) is instantiated by the gossip protocol posited by Proposition 4. Since the structure of the protocol is identical to that of one epoch of the adaptive protocol, we conclude (much as in Section 6, and omitted to avoid redundancy and save space) that the protocol solves the gossip problem and eventually terminates:

Theorem 3. *There exists an indulgent consensus protocol with message complexity $\Theta(n)$ and a running time $O(n^{1+\varepsilon})$ in synchronous executions.*

9   Discussion and Open Questions

We have shown how to implement efficient indulgent consensus algorithms in an eventually-synchronous network. In fact, the algorithms described, with minor modifications, tolerate an even less well-behaved environment. First, even if messages are lost prior to GST, both algorithms continue to behave correctly, as long as each process that has entered the fall-back phase repeats its fall-back message until a decision is reached. Second, even if the bounds d and δ are incorrect, both algorithms continue to solve consensus as long as the network eventually stabilizes for some (unknown) $\hat{d}$ and $\hat{\delta}$; only the message-efficiency is sacrificed. Third, in synchronous executions both algorithms can tolerate more failures, in fact, up to $n - 1$ failures, as long as no more than a minority fail in executions that are not synchronous.

One major open question raised by this paper is whether there exists a protocol that is both optimal in message complexity and linear in round complexity. The answer is unknown even for synchronous networks. Another question is whether it is possible to achieve better message complexity in an adaptive algorithm. For some values of f (when f is much smaller than n), it is possible to use an alternative instantiation of the building blocks derived from [14] to achieve a somewhat better message complexity, while terminating in $O(f)$ time.

References

1. Pease, M., Shostak, R., Lamport, L.: Reaching agreement in the presence of faults. Journal of the ACM 27(2), 228–234 (1980)
2. Fisher, M., Lynch, N., Paterson, M.: Impossibility of distributed consensus with one faulty process. Journal of the ACM 32(2), 374–382 (1985)
3. Dwork, C., Lynch, N., Stockmeyer, L.: Consensus in the presence of partial synchrony. Journal of the ACM 35(2), 288–323 (1988)
4. Chandra, T., Toueg, S.: Unreliable failure detectors for reliable distributed systems. Journal of the ACM 43(2), 225–267 (1996)
5. Lamport, L.: The part-time parliament. ACM Transactions on Computer Systems 16(2), 133–169 (1998)

6. Mostefaoui, A., Raynal, M.: Solving consensus using chandra-toueg's unreliable failure detectors: A general quorum-based approach. In: Jayanti, P. (ed.) DISC 1999. LNCS, vol. 1693, pp. 49–63. Springer, Heidelberg (1999)
7. Guerraoui, R., Raynal, M.: The information structure of indulgent consensus. IEEE Transactions on Computers 53(4), 453–466 (2004)
8. Schiper, A.: Early consensus in an asynchronous system with a weak failure detector. Distributed Computing 10(3), 149–157 (1997)
9. Guerraoui, R.: Indulgent algorithms (preliminary version). In: Proceedings of the 19th Symposium on Principles of Distributed Computing (PODC), pp. 289–297 (2000)
10. Lynch, N.: Distributed Algorithms. Morgan Kaufman, San Francisco (1996)
11. Dutta, P., Guerraoui, R.: The inherent price of indulgence. In: Proceedings of the 21st Symposium on Principles of Distributed Computing (PODC), pp. 88–97 (2002)
12. Lamport, L.: Fast paxos. Technical Report MSR-TR-2005-12, Microsoft (2005)
13. Chandra, T., Toueg, S.: Time and message efficient reliable broadcasts. In: van Leeuwen, J., Santoro, N. (eds.) Distributed Algorithms. LNCS, vol. 486, pp. 289–303. Springer, Heidelberg (1991)
14. Galil, Z., Mayer, A., Yung, M.: Resolving message complexity of byzantine agreement and beyond. In: Proceedings of the 36th Symposium on Foundations of Computer Science (FOCS), pp. 724–733 (1995)
15. Fisher, M., Lynch, N.: A lower bound for the time to assure interactive consistency. Information Processing Letters (IPL) 14(4), 183–186 (1982)
16. Dolev, D., Strong, H.: Requirements for agreement in a distributed system. Technical Report RJ 3418, IBM Research, San Jose, CA (March 1982)
17. Lamport, L., Fisher, M.: Byzantine generals and transaction commit protocols. Unpublished (April 1982)
18. Dolev, D., Reischuk, R., Strong, H.R.: Early stopping in byzantine agreement. Journal of the ACM 37(4), 720–741 (1990)
19. Charron-Bost, B., Schiper, A.: Improving Fast Paxos: being optimistic with no overhead. In: Proceedings of the 12th Pacific Rim International Symposium on Dependable Computing (PRDC), pp. 287–295 (2006)
20. Dwork, C., Halpern, J., Waarts, O.: Performing work efficiently in the presence of faults. SIAM Journal on Computing 27(5), 1457–1491 (1998)
21. Chlebus, B., Kowalski, D.: Gossiping to reach consensus. In: Proceedings of 14th Symposium on Parallel Algorithms and Architectures (SPAA), pp. 220–229 (2002)
22. Chlebus, B., Kowalski, D.: Robust gossiping with an application to consensus. Journal of Computer and System Science 72(8), 1262–1281 (2006)
23. Amdur, S., Weber, S., Hadzilacos, V.: On the message complexity of binary agreement under crash failures. Distributed Computing 5(4), 175–186 (1992)
24. Hadzilacos, V., Halpern, J.: Message-optimal protocols for byzantine agreement. Mathematical Systems Theory 26(1), 41–102 (1993)

Gathering Autonomous Mobile Robots with Dynamic Compasses: An Optimal Result

Taisuke Izumi, Yoshiaki Katayama, Nobuhiro Inuzuka, and Koichi Wada

Nagoya Institute of Technology
Gokiso-cho, Showa-ku, Nagoya, Aichi 466-8555, Japan
{t-izumi,katayama,inuzuka,wada}@nitech.ac.jp

Abstract. Let consider n autonomous mobile robots that can move in a two dimensional plane. The gathering problem is one of the most fundamental tasks of autonomous mobile robots. In short, given a set of robots with arbitrary initial locations, gathering must make all robots meet in finite time at a point that is not predefined. In this paper, we study about the feasibility of gathering by mobile robots that have ϕ-*absolute error dynamic compasses*. While the direction of each local coordinate system is fixed in usual systems, the dynamic compass model allows the angle difference between a local coordinate system and the global coordinate system to vary with time in the range of $[0, \phi]$. This paper proposes a semi-synchronous gathering algorithm for n robots with $(\pi/2 - \epsilon)$-absolute error dynamic compasses, where ϵ is an arbitrary small constant larger than zero. To the best of our knowledge, the proposed algorithm is the first one that considers both inaccurate compass models and more than two robots. We also show the optimality of our algorithm. It is proved that for any $\phi \geq \pi/2$, there is no algorithm to gather two robots with ϕ-absolute error dynamic compasses.

1 Introduction

In recent years, cooperations of a large number of autonomous mobile robots have received much attention. Because of its interesting features, such as inexpensiveness, fault tolerance, and high-level parallelism, many researchers study about them from several kinds of aspects. In particular, the algorithmic issues of autonomous mobile robots are actively studied in the literature of the distributed computing.

In most of algorithmic studies about autonomous mobile robots, a robot is modeled as a point in a plane, and its capability is quite weak. It is usually assumed that robots are *oblivious* (no memory to record past situations), *anonymous* and *uniform* (no IDs to distinguish two robots, and all robots run an identical algorithm). In addition, it is also assumed that each robot has no explicit direct means of communication. Typically, the communication between two robots is done in the implicit way that each robot observes the environment, which includes the position of other robots. From practical aspects, such weak capabilities of robots are favorable in the point of cost and implementability. However, too-weak robot systems are hard to accomplish the task to be

A. Pelc (Ed.): DISC 2007, LNCS 4731, pp. 298–312, 2007.

completed. Thus, revealing "the weakest" capability of robot systems to accomplish a given task is one of worthwhile challenges in the theoretical studies of autonomous mobile robots.

This paper is also an exploration of such weakest capabilities. The problem considered in this paper is *gathering*, which is one of the most fundamental tasks of autonomous mobile robots. In short, given a set of robots with arbitrary initial locations, gathering must make all robots meet in finite time at a point that is not predefined. Because of its simplicity, the gathering problem is actively studied before now: Many researchers tackle this problem, and show a number of possibility/impossibility results under the different assumptions [1,2,4,5,7,10,11,12,13,14]. In particular, we focus on the disagreement of local coordinate systems. As we mentioned, robots implicitly communicate with each other by observing environments. Then, the observation of each robot is done in terms of its local coordinate system, and thus it differentiates the capability of robots how local coordinate systems agree with each other. The seminal paper by Suzuki and Yamashita [13] shows that even two oblivious robots cannot achieve gathering if there is no agreement about their local coordinate systems. On the other hand, it also shows that it is possible to gather any number of robots if all of their local coordinate systems are consistent. These two results yield an interesting question, "how much agreement is necessary to accomplish gathering task?"

The study to answer this question is independently and concurrently originated by two papers [6,11]. Both of two papers quantify the agreement level of local coordinate systems by the angle difference for the global coordinate system (Figure 1), and show that, in asynchronous systems, two-robot gathering is possible if the differences of two robots' coordinate systems are bounded by a certain degree. The upper bounds proposed by the above two papers are $\pi/4$, and it is improved to $\pi/3$ by Katayama et al. [7]. More recently, this upper bound is drastically improved to $\pi - \epsilon$, where ϵ is an arbitrary small constant larger than zero [14]. While these results assume that the differences of local coordinate systems are fixed constants, the paper by Katayama et al. [7] also considers the *dynamic compass model*, which allows the difference of a local coordinate system to vary with time. It also shows that it is possible to gather two robots with dynamic compasses in asynchronous systems if the maximum angle difference of each local coordinate systems is at most $\pi/4$.

This paper has also the same research direction as the above papers. The contribution of this paper is as follows: This paper assumes the Suzuki-Yamashita model (SYM), which is also known as the *semi-synchronous* systems [13]. In typical algorithmic robot models, an execution of a robot consists of consecutive *cycles*. One cycle includes the observation of environments, local computation, and movement. While fully-asynchronous systems assume no bound on the time length of one cycle, semi-synchronous ones assume that each robot works under synchronized rounds. Each robot can execute one cycle in one round. However, different from fully-synchronous systems, every robot does not necessarily execute one cycle in every round. Only a subset of all robots, which is determined

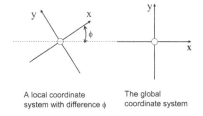

A local coordinate
system with difference ϕ

The global
coordinate system

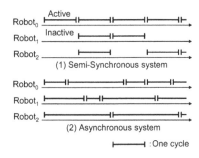

(1) Semi-Synchronous system

(2) Asynchronous system

$\longmapsto$:One cycle

Fig. 1. A local coordinate system with difference

Fig. 2. Two timing models

by the scheduler, executes one cycle in each round (Figure 2). We present an algorithm that gathers n robots having the dynamic compasses whose maximum difference is at most $\pi/2 - \epsilon$, where ϵ is an arbitrary small constant. The most important contribution of our result is to consider n robots. To the best of our knowledge, our gathering algorithm is the first one considering both the disagreement of local coordinate systems and more than two robots. We present a comparison between existing algorithms and ours in Figure 3. The n-robot algorithm is designed in a constructive way: We first design the algorithm for gathering two robots having dynamic compasses whose maximum difference is $\pi/2 - \epsilon$. Then, slightly modifying the two-robot algorithm, we obtain a conditional n-robot algorithm, where "conditional" implies that the algorithm correctly works only when the initial configuration satisfies a certain condition. To remove the condition, we further design an algorithm that reduces any configuration to one satisfying the condition. The general n-robot algorithm is obtained by combining these two algorithms. We also show that there is no algorithm that gathers two robots having the dynamic compasses whose maximum difference is larger than or equal to $\pi/2$ in SYM. This impossibility results implies that our algorithm is optimal in the sense of the angle difference of local coordination systems.

The rest of this paper is organized as follows. In Section 2, we introduce the robot model, dynamic compass model, and several necessary definitions and notations. In Section 3, we present a two-robot gathering algorithm, which is the basis of the n-robot one. In Section 4, we explain the construction of the n-robot gathering algorithm which is obtained from the two-robot algorithm in Section 3. The impossibility result is shown in Section 5. Section 6 addresses the relation between our model and another inaccurate compass models.

2   The System Model

2.1   Robots with Dynamic Compasses

The robot system considered in this paper is the Suzuki-Yamashita model (SYM), which is also known as the semi-synchronous robot model [13]. The system consists of a set of autonomous mobile robots $\mathcal{R} = \{R_1, R_2, \cdots, R_n\}$. One robot is

	Timing Assumption	Compass Model	Angle Difference	#Robots
Souissi et al. [11]	Async.	Fixed	$\pi/4$	2
Imazu et al. [6]	Async.	Fixed	$\pi/4$	2
Katayama et al. [7]	Async.	Fixed	$\pi/3$	2
Katayama et al. [7]	Async.	Dynamic	$\pi/4$	2
Yamashita et al. [14]	Async.	Fixed	$\pi - \epsilon$ *	2
This paper	SemiSync.	Dynamic	$\pi/2 - \epsilon$ *	n

* : Optimal Upper Bound
Async. : Asynchronous Systems
SemiSync. : Semi-Synchronous Systems

Fig. 3. The comparison of this paper's algorithm

modeled as a point located on a two-dimensional space. To specify the location of each robot consistently, we introduce the global Cartesian coordinate system. In addition, we also introduce the discrete global time $0, 1, 2, \ldots$. Notice that these global entities are introduced only for ease of explanations, and thus each robot cannot be aware of them. Each interval $[t, t+1]$ is called a *round*. The global coordinate where a robot R_i stays at time t is denoted by $\mathbf{R}_i(t)$. Throughout this paper, any coordinate is represented by a vector. To denote vectors, we use bold-faced characters. For a vector $\mathbf{V}$, $|\mathbf{V}|$ and $\theta(\mathbf{V})$ denote the length and the polar angle of $\mathbf{V}$ (i.e., the value d and θ ($0 \leq \theta < 2\pi$) satisfying $\mathbf{V} = d(\cos\theta, \sin\theta)^T$).

The robots are *anonymous* and *oblivious*. That is, each robot has no identifier distinguishing itself and others, and cannot explicitly remember the history of its execution. In addition, no device for direct communication is equipped. Cooperations of robots are done in an implicit manner: Each robot has a sensor device to observe the environment (i.e., the positions of all robots). The observation of an environment is represented as the set of points on the *local coordinate system* that the observer has. The local coordinate system of a robot is the Cartesian coordinate system whose origin is the current position of the robot. Local coordinate systems have only weak (or no) agreement on their unit lengths and the directions of x-axis and y-axis. A *compass model* defines the agreement level of local coordinate systems. In this paper, we consider the ϕ-*absolute error dynamic compass model*, which is first introduced by Katayama et al. [7].[1] The ϕ-absolute error model allows each robot to have a local coordinate system that is counterclockwisely tilted from the global coordinate system by a degree less than or equal to ϕ.[2] The dynamism of compasses implies that the tilt angle of

---

[1] While the original paper defines two kinds of dynamic compass models, called *semi-dynamic compass* and *full-dynamic compass*, we do not distinguish them and simply use the term "dynamic compass" because the original two compass models are defined on the fully-asynchronous model (CORDA) [8,9] and they are equivalent in SYM.

[2] The original paper defines the range of tilt angle in ϕ-absolute error model as $[-\phi/2, \phi/2]$. However, this paper defines it as $[0, \phi]$ for ease of presentations. Both of two definitions are equivalent.

each local coordinate system can vary with time. The tilt angle of R_i's local coordinate system in round t is called the *compass difference* of R_i at t, and is denoted by $\phi_i(t)$ $(0 \leq \phi_i(t) \leq \phi)$. The *compass configuration* $\Phi(t)$ in round t is the n-tuple whose i-th entry is $\phi_i(t)$. The compass model considered in this paper also allows each robot has a different unit length. For any robot R_i, the ratio of the unit length in R_i's coordinate system to that in the global coordinate system is called the *scaling ratio* of R_i, and is denoted by sc_i. For each robot R_i, we define the *observation function* $Z_{(i,t)}(\mathbf{p})$ that transforms a global coordinate $\mathbf{p}$ to the coordinate in terms of R_i's local coordination system at t. Formally, the observation function $Z_{(i,t)}(\mathbf{p})$ of R_i at time t is defined as follows:

$$Z_{(i,t)}(\mathbf{p}) = \frac{1}{sc_i} \begin{pmatrix} \cos\phi_i(t) & \sin\phi_i(t) \\ -\sin\phi_i(t) & \cos\phi_i(t) \end{pmatrix} (\mathbf{p} - \mathbf{R}_i(t))$$

The inverse function of $Z_{(i,t)}$ is denoted by $Z_{(i,t)}^{-1}$. The *configuration* $C(t)$ at time t is defined as the n-tuple of global coordinates $(\mathbf{R}_1(t), \mathbf{R}_2(t), \ldots, \mathbf{R}_n(t))$. We also define the *point set* $P(t)$ as a set of global coordinates $\{\mathbf{R}_i(t) | i \in [1, \cdots, n]\}$ without multiplicity. In this paper, we assume that each robot cannot detect the *multiplicity* of robots. That is, robots cannot distinguish the configuration where two or more robots are located at a point and one where only one robot is located at the same point. It implies that if a robot observes the environment it cannot obtain the current configuration, but the current point set. We also define the observation function $Z_{(i,t)}$ over all point sets, i.e., $Z_{(i,t)}(P(t)) = \{Z_{(i,t)}(p) | p \in P(t)\}$.

2.2 Algorithms, Executions, and the Gathering Problem

At any round $t(t = 0, 1, 2, \cdots)$, each robot is either *active* or *inactive*. If a robot is active at t, it observes the environment, and computes the destination point of the movement performed in round t. Therefore, an algorithm is defined as a function ψ that maps any point set to a vector that represents the destination. Since each robot observes an environment in terms of its local coordinate systems, the current point set $P(t)$ does not directly passed to ψ as an input. Actually, in activation of robot R_i at time t, the conversion of $P(t)$ by the observation function $Z_{(i,t)}$ is passed to the algorithm. By the same reason, the output of the algorithm is also converted by the inverse function $Z_{(i,t)}^{-1}$. Therefore, if a robot R_i is active at t, the global coordinate where R_i stays at $t + 1$ is $Z_{(i,t)}^{-1}(\psi(Z_{(i,t)}(P(t))))$.

Since this paper considers only deterministic algorithms, the configuration $C(t + 1)$ is determined by the previous configuration $C(t)$, the set of active robots in round t, and the compass configuration in round t. Thus, we can describe an *execution* of the system as an alternating sequence $C(0), (\Gamma(0), \Phi(0)), C(1), (\Gamma(0), \Phi(0)), C(2), \cdots$, where $\Gamma(t)$ is the set of active robots in round t. In this paper, we only consider *fair executions*, i.e., infinite executions where every robot becomes active infinitely many times. The *gathering problem* must ensure that all robots eventually meet at a point that is not

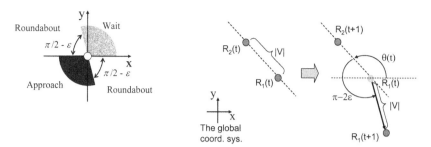

Fig. 4. The illustration of the algo- **Fig. 5.** The illustration of the roundabout move
rithm

predefined, beginning from any configuration. Formally, we say that an algorithm $\mathcal{A}$ solves the gathering problem if for any fair execution of $\mathcal{A}$, there exists a time t_e such that $|P(t)| = 1$ holds for any $t > t_e$.

3   The Two-Robot Algorithm

3.1   Algorithm GatherTwoRobots

In this section, we first show a gathering algorithm GatherTwoRobots for two robots with $(\pi/2 - \epsilon)$-absolute error dynamic compasses, where ϵ is an arbitrary small constant satisfying $0 < \epsilon < \pi/2$. The algorithm GatherTwoRobots consists of three types of moves, *Approach*, *Wait*, and *Roundabout*. The approach is a movement that the robot moves to the point of the other robot. The wait is a movement that the robot has no movement actually. Letting a robot R observe the other at the coordinate $\mathbf{V}$ in its local coordinate system, it performs approach move if $\pi < \theta(\mathbf{V}) \leq 3\pi/2 + \epsilon$, and performs wait move if $0 < \theta(\mathbf{V}) \leq \pi/2 + \epsilon$. Otherwise, the robot R performs roundabout move: The destination of R's roundabout move is the coordinate $|\mathbf{V}|(\cos(\theta(\mathbf{V}) + \pi - 2\epsilon), \sin(\theta(\mathbf{V}) + \pi - 2\epsilon))$ (i.e., the robot R moves to the direction at angle $\theta(\mathbf{V}) + \pi - 2\epsilon$ by length $\mathbf{V}$). We illustrate the behavior of our algorithm in Figure 4 and 5.

The correctness of our algorithm derives from two key properties: The first one is that any movement decreases the angle formed by the global Y-axis and the line passing through the positions of two robots unless gathering is achieved. Then, it is guaranteed that two robots eventually observe each other in the directions near the global north and south respectively [3] if they does not gather. The second key idea is that if two robots observe each other in the direction near the global north or south, they necessarily performs approach-move and wait-move respectively, regardless of their difference. Then, gathering is achieved.

We show the correctness of the algorithm GatherTwoRobots. We define a vector $\mathbf{AB}(t_1, t_2)$ as $\mathbf{B}(t_2) - \mathbf{A}(t_2)$, where $A, B \in \{R_1, R_2\}$ and t_1 and t_2 are global times. In particular, let $\mathbf{R_1 R_2}(t, t) = \mathbf{R}(t)$ for short. Without loss of generality,

---

[3]   The global north/south imply the positive/negative direction of the global Y-axis.

we assume $\pi/2 - \epsilon < \theta(\mathbf{R_1R_2}(0)) \leq 3\pi/2 - \epsilon$ (i.e., the names R_1 and R_2 are assigned in the manner satisfying this assumption).

Lemma 1. *If $\pi/2 - \epsilon < \theta(\mathbf{R}(t)) \leq \pi/2 + \epsilon$ holds, no roundabout move occurs at t or later.*

Proof. *The robots R_1 and R_2 observe each other in the direction $\theta(\mathbf{R}(t)) - \phi_1(t)$ and $\theta(\mathbf{R}(t)) + \pi - \phi_2(t)$ in terms of their local coordinate systems respectively. Then, we obtain $0 < \theta(\mathbf{R}(t)) - \phi_1(t) \leq \pi/2 - \epsilon$ and $\pi < \theta(\mathbf{R}(t)) + \pi - \phi_2(t) \leq -\epsilon + 3\pi/2$. These imply that R_1 and R_2 can perform only wait and approach move respectively.* □

This lemma yields the following corollary because simultaneous wait of two robots never occurs.

Corollary 1. *If $\pi/2 - \epsilon < \theta(\mathbf{R}(t)) \leq \pi/2 + \epsilon$ holds, two robots eventually gather.*

Lemma 2. *For any t, $2\epsilon \geq \theta(\mathbf{R}(t)) - \theta(\mathbf{R}(t+1)) \geq \epsilon$ holds unless gathering is achieved at $t + 1$.*

Proof(sketch). *If two robots respectively perform approach and wait, the gathering clearly achieved. Since simultaneous wait of two robots never occurs, we need to consider only the cases a robot R_1 performs roundabout. Figure 6 shows all of such cases. The illustrations (a), (b), and (c) respectively indicate the cases where the other robot R_2 performs wait, approach, roundabout. In any case, we can see $\theta(\mathbf{R}(t))$ decreases by ϵ' such that $\epsilon \leq \epsilon' \leq 2\epsilon$ holds. This implies that the lemma holds.* □

Theorem 1. *The algorithm* GatherTwoRobots *achieves gathering of two robots with $(\pi/2 - \epsilon)$-absolute error dynamic compasses.*

Proof. *By Lemma 2, the value $\theta(\mathbf{R}(t))$ gradually decreases with the progress of time t, and eventually $\theta(\mathbf{R}(t)) \in (\pi/2 - \epsilon, \pi/2 + \epsilon]$ holds at a certain time t. Then, by Corollary 1, gathering is achieved.* □

4   The n-Robot Algorithm

This section provides a gathering algorithm for n robots with $(\pi/2 - \epsilon)$-absolute error dynamic compasses. The n-robot algorithm consists of two sub-algorithms. The first one, called GatherNRobots, is obtained from the algorithm GatherTwo-Robots. It achieves gathering of n robots under the assumption that the point set of the initial configuration has a unique *longest-distance segment*(LDS): The LDS at t is the maximum-length segment of all defined by any pair of points in $P(t)$. Notice that two or more segments become LDSs because of the equality of their lengths. If the initial configuration has two or more LDSs, the algorithm GatherNRobots does not work correctly. To handle such initial configuration, we use the second algorithm ElectOneLDS, which works as a preprocessor of

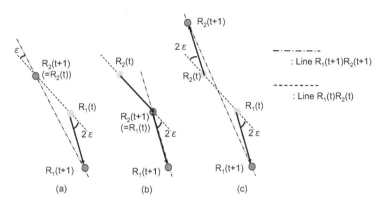

Fig. 6. The proof of Lemma 2

GatherNRobots. The objective of ElectOneLDS is to make the system reach a configuration where (1) a unique LDS is elected, or (2) gathering is achieved. Consequently, the combination of GatherNRobots and ElectOneLDS becomes an n-robot gathering algorithm that works correctly from any arbitrary initial configuration.

4.1 Gathering Under a Unique Longest-Distance Segment

In this subsection, we first introduce the algorithm GatherNRobots that achieves gathering under the assumption of a unique LDS. The LDS at time t is denoted by $l(t)$ if it is uniquely determined. Let $p_{la}(t)$ and $p_{lb}(t)$ be two endpoints of $l(t)$. The vector $p_{lb}(t) - p_{la}(t)$ is denoted by $l(t)$. Then, without loss of generality, we assume $\pi/2 - \epsilon < \theta(l(t)) \leq 3\pi/2 - \epsilon$. For a time t when the LDS is uniquely determined, we define $Rl(t) = \{R_i \in \mathcal{R} | R_i(t) = p_{la}(t)$ or $R_i(t) = p_{lb}(t)\}$. Intuitively $Rl(t)$ is the set of robots that stay at one of the end points of the LDS. If $Rl(t) = \mathcal{R}$, we say that the configuration $C(t)$ (or the point set $P(t)$) is *2-gathered*.

The algorithm GatherNRobots has the algorithm GatherTwoRobots as its subroutine, and its key idea is almost same as that of GatherTwoRobots: The algorithm GatherNRobots first gathers all robots at the endpoints of the unique LDS. Then, by the same scheme as GatherTwoRobots, it gradually reduces the angle $\theta(l(t))$ to $\pi/2$. If $\theta(l(t))$ is near $\pi/2$ and all robots are gathered at two endpoints of $l(t)$, all robots perform approach move or wait move. Thus, gathering is achieved.

In the followings, we briefly explain the behavior of GatherNRobots: If the current configuration is not 2-gathered, the algorithm first makes the configuration 2-gathered. More precisely, if a robot $R_i \notin Rl(t)$ observes and recognizes that the current configuration is not 2-gathered, it moves to either $p_{la}(t)$ or $p_{lb}(t)$. All robots in $Rl(t)$ wait until the current configuration becomes 2-gathered. If the current configuration becomes 2-gathered, the behavior of each robot follows the algorithm GatherTwoRobots. The robots decrease the angle $\theta(l(t))$ by counterclockwisely rotating the LDS. Then, even if all robots are gathered at the

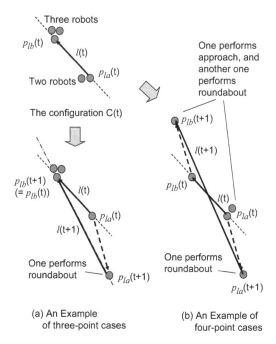

Fig. 7. The proof of Lemma 4

endpoints of the LDS before the rotation, robots may stay at three or more points at the configuration after the rotation (notice that two robots at a same point can behave differently because their compass difference is not same). However, even in the case where the robots stay at three or more points, it is guaranteed that a LDS $l(t + 1)$ satisfying $\epsilon \leq \theta(l(t)) - \theta(\mathbf{l}(\mathbf{t} + \mathbf{1})) \leq 2\epsilon$ is uniquely determined.

We present a proof outline for the correctness of GatherNRobots. A number of proofs are omitted because of lack of space. The following lemma clearly holds.

Lemma 3. *Let $C(t)$ be a configuration that has a unique LDS, but that is not 2-gathered. Then, the system reaches to a 2-gathered configuration having the same LDS as $C(t)$.*

Lemma 4. *Let $C(t)$ be a 2-gathered configuration. Then, the system eventually reaches to the configuration $C(t')$ such that gathering is achieved in $C(t')$ or $\epsilon \leq \theta(\mathbf{l}(t)) - \theta(\mathbf{l}(t')) \leq 2\epsilon$ holds.*

Proof(sketch). *If no roundabout move occurs, the system eventually achieves gathering because any approach movement is performed (1) only by ones at $\mathbf{p_{la}}(t)$ and the destination is $\mathbf{p_{lb}}(t)$, or (2) only by ones at $\mathbf{p_{lb}}(t)$ and the destination is $\mathbf{p_{la}}(t)$. Thus we only have to consider the case where a roundabout move eventually occurs. Assume that a roundabout move occurs in round $t'-1$ ($t' > t$). Then, the point set $P(t')$ consists of two, three or four points (Figure 7). In the case of two points we can show the lemma by the same way as Lemma 2. In the* *case of three points or four points, the configuration is not 2-gathered. However, in both cases, the point set $P(t')$ has a unique LDS $l(t+1)$. In addition, by the same argument as the proof of Lemma 2, we can show $2\epsilon \geq \theta(\mathbf{l}(t)) - \theta(\mathbf{l}(t')) \geq \epsilon$ holds. Thus, the lemma holds.* $\qquad\qquad\qquad\qquad\qquad\qquad\qquad\qquad\qquad\qquad\qquad\quad\square.$

The following lemma is a simple extension of Lemma 1 for n-robot systems, and can be proved by the same way as the proof of Lemma 1.

Lemma 5. *If $\pi/2 - \epsilon \leq \theta(\mathbf{l}(t)) \leq \pi/2 + \epsilon$ holds, no roundabout move occurs at t or later.*

By combining Lemmas 3, 4, and 5, we can obtain the following theorem. The proof is almost same as that for Theorem 1.

Theorem 2. *If the point set of the initial configuration $C(0)$ has a unique LDS, the algorithm GatherNRobots achieves gathering of n robots with $(\pi/2 - \epsilon)$-absolute error dynamic compasses.*

In addition to the above main theorem, we also show the following subtheorem, which guarantees that the behavior of GatherNRobots and one of ElectOneLDS do not conflict (the proof is omitted).

Theorem 3. *Let $C(t)$ be the configuration having a unique LDS. Then, any configuration following $C(t)$ has a unique LDS unless it achieves gathering.*

4.2   Election of a Unique LDS

This section provides the algorithm ElectOneLDS that reduces any configuration to one where a unique LDS is elected or gathering is achieved. To explain the behavior of ElectOneLDS, we first introduce the several notations and definitions. For a point set $P(t)$, we define $H(t)$ as its convex hull. The number of edges constituting $H(t)$ is denoted by $\#H(t)$. A convex hull $H(t)$ is *symmetric* if all edges constituting the convex hull $H(t)$ have a same length.[4] The convex hull that is not symmetric is *asymmetric*. We say that the configuration $C(t)$ is *contractable* if (1) its convex hull $H(t)$ is symmetric and any point in $P(t)$ is a vertex of $H(t)$ or the center of gravity of $H(t)$, or (2) $H(t)$ is asymmetric and any point in $P(t)$ is a vertex of $H(t)$. Let R_i be the robot such that its coordinate $\mathbf{R}_i(t)$ is a vertex of $H(t)$. Then, we define the *left neighbor* of R_i at t as the next vertex of $\mathbf{R}_i(t)$ in the counterclockwise traversal on $H(t)$'s border. We also define the *right neighbor* in the same fashion. Then the segments between R_i and its right/left neighbors are called the *left/right arm* of R_i at t respectively.

The algorithm ElectOneLDS works only when the current point set has two or more LDS. By Theorem 3, once the system reaches to the configuration having a unique LDS, it is guaranteed that ElectOneLDS never works again. In addition, the algorithm GatherNRobots works only when a unique LDS is elected. These imply that the algorithms ElectOneLDS and GatherNRobots do not disturb each other, and thus their composition is possible.

---

[4] Notice that, while it is not essential, a symmetric convex hull is not necessarily a regular polygon. For example, a rhomboid is symmetric.

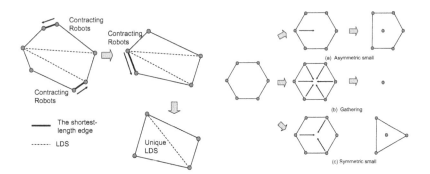

Fig. 8. Edge contractions   **Fig. 9.**   Symmetry-breaking move-ments

Roughly speaking, the behavior of ElectOneLDS is that (1) if the current con-figuration is not contractable, the algorithm reduces it to a contractable one, and (2) if the current configuration is contractable, the algorithm carries forward the election of a unique LDS. More precisely, in the first case, each robot that does not stay at a vertex of $H(t)$ (or stay at neither a vertex of $H(t)$ nor $H(t)$'s center of gravity when $H(t)$ is symmetric) moves to a certain vertex of $H(t)$. Then, the convex hull eventually becomes contractable. In the second case, the algorithm decreases the number of edges $\#H(t)$ until the point set has a unique LDS. Notice that this scheme necessarily elects a unique LDS because the convex hull $H(t)$ eventually becomes a segment when $\#H(t) = 2$. The number of edges $\#H(t)$ is decreased by contracting a shortest-length edge in $H(t)$: A *contracting robot* are defined as one whose left arm is a shortest-length edge in $H(t)$ and the right arm is not the shortest.If a contracting robot observes and recognizes that the current configuration is contractable, it moves the coordinate of its left neighbor. The contracting robots move to their left neighborhood points, and consequently their left arms are contracted (Figure 8). Then, during the con-traction, all non-contracting robots do not move. The shortest-edge contraction correctly works if the current convex hull $H(t)$ is asymmetric. However, if $H(t)$ is symmetric, all edges in $H(t)$ is shortest, and thus no edge contraction occurs. To handle this case, we introduce another contraction scheme (symmetry-breaking movement): If a robot recognizes that the current configuration is contractable but the corresponding convex hull is symmetric, it moves to $H(t)$'s center of gravity. Then, if all robots simultaneously moves to the center of gravity, gath-ering is clearly achieved. Otherwise, the number of edges constituting the convex hull eventually decreases (Figure 9).

We can show that the following theorem (The proof is omitted for lack of space). This theorem implies that the composition of ElectOneLDS and Gather-NRobots becomes a gathering algorithm for n robots with $(\pi/2 - \epsilon)$-absolute error dynamic compasses.

Theorem 4. *The algorithm* ElectOneLDS *correctly elects a unique LDS unless gathering is achieved.*

5   Impossibility Result

In this section, we show that there is no gathering algorithm for two robots with ϕ-absolute error dynamic compass when $\phi \geq \pi/2$.

Throughout the following proofs, we suppose for contradiction that there exists a gathering algorithm for two robots with ϕ-absolute error dynamic compasses ($\phi \geq \pi/2$), which is denoted by $\mathcal{A}$. We first give the definition of *termination vector*, which is an important notion to prove the impossibility.

Definition 1 (Termination vector). *The vector* $\mathbf{V} = Z_{(1,t)}(\mathbf{R_1R_2}(t))$ *is a termination vector of* $\mathcal{A}$ *if* $\mathbf{R_1}(t) = \mathbf{R_1}(t + 1)$ *holds in the execution* $C(t), (\{R_1\}, (0, 0)), C(t + 1)$.

Intuitively, a termination vector $\mathbf{V}$ is one such that even if an active robot observing the other at the coordinate $\mathbf{V}$ in terms of its local coordinate system, it does not change the position. The following lemma is a fundamental lemma about gathering algorithms for robots with erroneous compasses.

Lemma 6. *Letting* $\mathbf{V_1}$ *and* $\mathbf{V_2}$ *be any two termination vectors of the algorithm* $\mathcal{A}$, $|\theta(\mathbf{V_1}) - \theta(\mathbf{V_2})| < \pi - \phi$ *holds.*

Proof. *Suppose* $|\theta(\mathbf{V_1}) - \theta(\mathbf{V_2})| \geq \pi - \phi$ *for contradiction. Without loss of generality, we assume* $\theta(\mathbf{V_1}) > \theta(\mathbf{V_2})$. *Let* $\tau = \theta(\mathbf{V_1}) - \theta(\mathbf{V_2})$. *Then, we consider the initial configuration* $C(0)$ *as follows:*

- *The robot* R_1 *is located at the origin of the global coordinate system. The local coordinate system of* R_1 *is identical to the global one.*
- *The robot* R_2 *is located at the point represented by* $\mathbf{V_1}$. *The scaling ratio* sc_2 *is* $|\mathbf{V_1}|/|\mathbf{V_2}|$.

Now we consider the execution E *beginning from* $C(0)$ *such that* $\phi_2(t) = \pi - \tau$ ($\leq \phi$) *and* $\phi_1(t) = 0$ *holds for any* t. *Then, since* $Z_{(1,t)}(\mathbf{R_1R_2}(t,t)) = \mathbf{V_1}$ *and* $Z_{(2,t)}(\mathbf{R_2R_1}(t,t)) = \mathbf{V_2}$ *hold for any* t, *both* R_1 *and* R_2 *do not move at all, and thus gathering is not achieved. It is a contradiction.* □

Let $C(t)$ be a configuration. We say that $C(t)$ is *2-movement* if there exist two tilt angles $\rho_1, \rho_2 \in \{0, \pi/2\}$ such that two robots changes their position in the one-round execution $E = C(t), (\{R_1, R_2\}, (\rho_1, \rho_2)), C(t + 1)$.

Lemma 7. *Any configuration* $C(t)$ *is 2-movement.*

Proof. *Let* $\mathbf{V} = \mathbf{R_1R_2}(t, t)$ *for short. We first consider the execution* $E = C(t), (\{R_1, R_2\}, (0, 0)), C(t + 1)$. *If both* R_1 *and* R_2 *moves in* E, *the* $C(t)$ *is 2-movement. Thus, we only consider the case where at least one robot does not change its position in* E. *From Lemma 6, either* $\mathbf{V}$ *or* $-\mathbf{V}$ *is not termination vector. Thus, one robot changes the position in* E. *Without loss of generality, we assume that* R_2 *is such one. Then, we consider the execution* $E' = C(t), (\{R_1, R_2\}, (\pi/2, 0)), C(t+1)$. *From Lemma 6, the vector* $Z_{(1,t)}(\mathbf{V})$ *in* E' *is not termination vector because* $|\theta(Z_{(1,t)}(\mathbf{V})) - \theta(\mathbf{V})| = \pi/2$ *holds in* E'. *It follows that two robots change their positions in the execution* E'. *That is,* $C(t)$ *is 2-movement.* □

Lemma 8. *There exists an infinite execution of $\mathcal{A}$ where gathering is not achieved and both R_1 and R_2 become active infinitely-many times.*

Proof. *Let $C(t)$ be a configuration. From lemma 7, there exists an execution $E = C(t), (\{R_1, R_2\}, (\rho_1, \rho_2)), C(t+1)$, where R_1 and R_2 change their positions. Then, we consider two executions $E_1 = C(t), (\{R_1\}, (\rho_1, \rho_2)), C_1(t+1)$ and $E_2 = C(t), (\{R_2\}, (\rho_1, \rho_2)), C_2(t+1)$. If $C(t+1)$ achieves gathering, both $C_1(t+1)$ and $C_2(t+2)$ do not achieve gathering. In contrast, if either E_1 or E_2 achieves gathering, E does not achieve gathering. This implies that for any configuration C, there exists one-round execution beginning from C where (1) gathering is not achieved, and (2) arbitrary one of R_1 and R_2 is active. It follows that there exists infinite fair execution where gathering is not achieved.* □

This lemma implies the main theorem.

Theorem 5. *There is no gathering algorithm for two robots with ϕ-absolute error dynamic compasses when $\phi \geq \pi/2$.*

6 Discussion

More recently, Cohen and Peleg introduced another model of erroneous compasses [3], where each robot may observe another robot at a position slightly different from the actual one. In this section, we explain the relation between the above model and our model.

The model by Cohen and Peleg introduces two accuracy measurements θ_0 and ϵ_0 for angle and distance respectively. In this model, each robot R_1 at the coordinate $d(\cos\theta, \sin\theta)$ can be observed by other robots as it stays a coordinate $d'(\cos\theta', \sin\theta')$ such that $d' \in [d - \epsilon_0, d + \epsilon_0]$ and $\theta' \in [\theta - \theta_0, \theta + \theta_0]$ holds. The model restricting by $\epsilon_0 = 0$ (say MRR$_-$) may seem to be equivalent to our model with θ_0-absolute error dynamic compasses. However, those two models inherently different and incomparable. In our model, while the coordinate system within each robot is agreed (i.e., in each cycle of a robot, the observation phase and move phase uses a same coordinate system), the coordinate systems between two or more robots are not agreed. On the other hand, the model MRR$_-$ has no agreement between observation phases and move phases in each cycle, however, the tilt angle of each local coordinate system is the same as the global one (and thus all local coordinate systems are agreed with each other). A typical example that differentiates the ability of these compass models is as follows: Let us consider the system of two robots. In our model, it is possible that a robot moves to the position of another robot, which is impossible in MRR$_-$ because the robot cannot detect the exact location of another one. In contrast, in the model MRR$_-$, it is possible that two robot moves to a same direction (e.g., the global north). However, such movement is impossible in our model because tilt angles of local coordinate systems can be different.

It should be noted that the original paper of dynamic compass models [7] introduces two different classes of dynamic compass models, *semi-dynamic compass model* and *full-dynamic compass model*. The semi-dynamic compass is one considered in this paper. The full-dynamic compass is more weaker model of semi-dynamic one, which allows compass differences to vary during a cycle, i.e., the compass difference can be disagreed between the observation phase and the move phase within a cycle. This implies that the full-dynamic compass model is also weaker than MRR_-.

Acknowledgment

This work is supported in part by the Japan Society for the Promotion of Science: Grant-in-Aid for Scientific Research on Priority Area 'New Horizons in Computing(C08)' and Grant-in-Aid for Young Scientists(B) (19700058).

References

1. Agmon, N., Peleg, D.: Fault-tolerant gathering algorithms for autonomous mobile robots. SIAM Journal of Computing 36(1), 56–82 (2006)
2. Cieliebak, M., Flocchini, P., Prencipe, G., Santoro, N.: Solving the robots gathering problem. In: Baeten, J.C.M., Lenstra, J.K., Parrow, J., Woeginger, G.J. (eds.) ICALP 2003. LNCS, vol. 2719, pp. 1181–1196. Springer, Heidelberg (2003)
3. Cohen, R., Peleg, D.: Convergence of autonomous mobile robots with inaccurate sensors and movements. In: Durand, B., Thomas, W. (eds.) STACS 2006. LNCS, vol. 3884, pp. 549–560. Springer, Heidelberg (2006)
4. Défago, X., Gradinariu, M., Messika, S., Parvédy, P.R.: Fault-tolerant and self-stabilizing mobile robots gathering. In: Dolev, S. (ed.) DISC 2006. LNCS, vol. 4167, pp. 46–60. Springer, Heidelberg (2006)
5. Flocchini, P., Prencipe, G., Santoro, N., Widmayer, P.: Gathering of asynchronous robots with limited visibility. Theoreical Computer Science 337(1-3), 147–168 (2005)
6. Imazu, H., Itoh, N., Inuzuka, K.Y.N., Wada, K.: A gathering problem for autonomous mobile robots with disagreement in compasses. In: Proc. of First Workshop on Theoretical Computer Science in Izumo, pp. 43–44, 2005 (in Japanese)
7. Katayama, Y., Tomida, Y., Imazu, H., Inuzuka, N., Wada, K.: Dynamic compass models and gathering algorithm for autonomous mobile robots. In: Proc. of 14th International Colloquium on Structural Information and Communication Complexity (SIROCCO). LNCS, vol. 4474, pp. 274–288 (2007)
8. Prencipe, G.: CORDA: distributed coordination of a set of autonomous mobile robots. In: Proc. of Fourth European Research Seminar on Advances in Distributed Systems(ESRADS) (2001)
9. Prencipe, G.: Distributed Coordination of a Set of Autonomous Mobile Robots. PhD thesis, University of Pisa (2002)
10. Prencipe, G.: On the feasibility of gathering by autonomous mobile robots. In: Pelc, A., Raynal, M. (eds.) SIROCCO 2005. LNCS, vol. 3499, pp. 246–261. Springer, Heidelberg (2005)
11. Souissi, S., Défago, X., Yamashita, M.: Gathering asynchronous mobile robots with inaccurate compasses. In: Shvartsman, A.A. (ed.) OPODIS 2006. LNCS, vol. 4305, pp. 333–349. Springer, Heidelberg (2006)

12. Souissi, S., Défago, X., Yamashita, M.: Using eventually consistent compasses to gather oblivious mobile robots with limited visibility. In: Datta, A.K., Gradinariu, M. (eds.) SSS 2006. LNCS, vol. 4280, pp. 471–487. Springer, Heidelberg (2006)
13. Suzuki, I., Yamashita, M.: Distributed anonymous mobile robots: Formation of geometric patterns. SIAM Journal of Computing 28(4), 1347–1363 (1999)
14. Yamashita, M., Souissi, S., Défago, X.: Tight bound on the gathering of oblivious-mobile robots with inconsistent compasses. Unpublished (2007)

Compact Separator Decompositions in Dynamic Trees and Applications to Labeling Schemes

Amos Korman[1,*] and David Peleg[2,**]

[1] Information Systems Group, Faculty of IE&M, The Technion, Haifa 32000, Israel
pandit@tx.technion.ac.il
[2] Department of Computer Science and Applied Mathematics,
The Weizmann Institute of Science, Rehovot 76100, Israel
david.peleg@weizmann.ac.il

Abstract. This paper presents an efficient scheme maintaining a *separator decomposition representation* in dynamic trees using asymptotically optimal labels. In order to maintain the short labels, the scheme uses relatively low message complexity. In particular, if the initial dynamic tree contains just the root, then the scheme incurs an $O(\log^3 n)$ amortized message complexity per topology change, where n is the current number of nodes in the tree. As a separator decomposition is a fundamental decomposition of trees used extensively as a component in many static graph algorithms, our dynamic scheme for separator decomposition may be used for constructing dynamic versions to these algorithms.

The paper then shows how to use our dynamic separator decomposition to construct rather efficient labeling schemes on dynamic trees, using the same message complexity as our dynamic separator scheme. Specifically, we construct efficient routing schemes on dynamic trees, for both the designer and the adversary port models, which maintain optimal labels, up to a multiplicative factor of $O(\log \log n)$. In addition, it is shown how to use our dynamic separator decomposition scheme to construct dynamic labeling schemes supporting the ancestry and NCA relations using asymptotically optimal labels, as well as to extend a known result on dynamic distance labeling schemes.

Keywords: Distributed algorithms, dynamic networks, routing schemes, graph decompositions, informative labeling schemes.

1 Introduction

Background: A distributed representation scheme is a scheme maintaining global information using local data structures (or *labels*). Such schemes play an extensive and sometimes crucial role in the fields of distributed computing and communication networks. Their goal is to locally store useful information about

* Supported in part at the Technion by an Aly Kaufman fellowship.
** Supported in part by grants from the Israel Science Foundation and the Israel Ministry of Science and Art.

the network and make it readily and conveniently accessible. As a notable example, the basic function of a communication network, namely, message delivery, is performed by its *routing scheme*, which in turn requires maintaining certain topological knowledge. Often, the performance of the network as a whole may be dominated by the quality of the routing scheme and the accuracy of the topological information. Representation schemes in the *static* (fixed topology) setting were the subject of extensive research (e.g., [1,5,6,9,13,15]). The common measure for evaluating a static representation scheme is the *label size*, i.e., the maximum number of bits used in a label. In this paper, a representation scheme with asymptotically optimal label size is termed *compact*.

The more realistic (and more involved) distributed *dynamic* setting, where processors may join or leave the network or new connections may be established or removed, has received much less attention. Clearly, changes in the network topology may necessitate corresponding changes in the representation. Consequently, in the distributed dynamic setting, an *update protocol* is activated where the topology change occurs, and its goal is to update the vertices, by transmitting messages over the links of the underlying network. Ideally, the update protocol maintains short labels using only a limited number of messages.

In this paper we consider representation schemes in dynamic trees, operating under the *leaf-dynamic* tree model, in which at each step, a leaf may either join or leave the tree. We consider the controlled dynamic model, which was also considered in [3,16], in which the topological changes do not occur spontaneously. Instead, when an entity wishes to cause a topology change at some node u, it enters a *request* at u, and performs the change only after the request is granted a permit from the update protocol. The controlled model may be found useful in Peer to Peer applications and in other popular overlay networks. See [16] for more details and motivations regarding the controlled model.

In this paper, we present several dynamic representation schemes, which are efficient in both their label size and their communication complexity. Specifically, if the initial tree contains only the root, then all our dynamic schemes incur $O(\log^3 n)$ amortized message complexity, per topological change. We first present a compact representation scheme of a separator decomposition in dynamic trees, and then use this basic scheme to derive compact labeling schemes supporting the ancestry and NCA relations on dynamic trees. In addition, we present dynamic routing schemes which have optimal label size up to $O(\log \log n)$ multiplicative factor, for both the adversary and the designer port models. Finally, we show how to use our dynamic separator decomposition to extend a known result on dynamic distance labeling schemes.

Related work: An elegant and simple compact labeling scheme was presented in [13], for supporting the ancestry relation on static n-node trees using labels of size $2 \log n$. Applications to XML search engines motivated various attempts to improve the constant multiplicative factor in the label size, see [1,2].

Static compact labeling schemes were presented for two types of NCA relations on trees. For the id-based NCA relation (which is the type of NCA relation we consider in this paper), a static labeling scheme was developed in [19] using labels of $\Theta(\log^2 n)$ bits on n-node trees. A static labeling scheme supporting the label-based NCA relation using labels of $\Theta(\log n)$ bits on n-node trees was presented in [5]. In addition, [5] gave a survey on applications and previous results concerning NCA queries on trees, in both the distributed and centralized settings.

Labeling schemes for routing on static trees were investigated in a number of papers until finally optimized in [9,10,24]. For the *designer port* model, in which the designer of the scheme can freely enumerate the port numbers of the nodes, [9] shows how to construct a routing scheme using labels of size $O(\log n)$ on n-node trees. In the *adversary port* model, where the port numbers are fixed by an adversary, it is shown how to construct a routing scheme using labels of size $O(\log^2 n/\log \log n)$ on n-node trees. In [10] it is shown that both label sizes are asymptotically optimal. Independently, a routing scheme for trees of label size $(1 + o(1)) \log n$ was given in [24] for the designer port model.

Dynamic data structures for trees have been studied extensively in the centralized model, cf. [7,22,21]. For comprehensive surveys on centralized dynamic graph algorithms see [11,20].

A survey on popular link state dynamic routing protocols (e.g. OSPF) can be found in [23]. Compared to our dynamic routing schemes, these routing schemes are more robust on weaker dynamic models, such as ones which allow spontaneous faults, however, their message complexity is higher.

The controlled model is presented in [3], which also establishes an efficient dynamic controller that can operate in the *leaf-increasing* tree model, where the only topology change allowed is that a leaf joins the tree. This controller can, in particular, be used to maintain a constant approximation of the number of nodes in the (leaf-increasing) tree, using $O(n \log^2 n)$ messages. In [16] an extended controller was derived for the controlled model, which can operate under both insertions and deletions of both leaves and internal nodes. In particular, that controller can be used to efficiently maintain a constant approximation of the number of nodes in the dynamic tree, undergoing both deletions and additions of nodes, using low message complexity. Specifically, the approximation scheme incurs $O(n_0 \log^2 n_0) + O(\sum_j \log^2 n_j)$ messages, where n_0 is the initial tree size, and n_j is the size of the tree immediately after the j'th topology change. (Note, that if the initial tree contains just the root, then this complexity can be considered as $O(\log^2 n)$ amortized message complexity, per topology change).

A dynamic routing scheme in the leaf-increasing tree model was given in [4] using identities of size $O(\log^2 n)$, database size $O(\Delta \log^3 n)$ (where Δ is the maximum degree in the tree) and amortized message complexity $O(\log n)$.

Dynamic distance labeling schemes on trees were presented in [17,18] for the *serialized model*, in which it is assumed that the topology changes are spaced enough so that the update protocol can complete its operation before the next topology change occurs. Two dynamic β-approximate distance labeling schemes (in which given two labels, one can infer a β-approximation to the distance between the corresponding nodes) were presented in [17]. The first scheme applies to a model in which the tree topology is fixed but the edge weights may change, and the second applies to a model in which the only topological event that may occur is that an edge increases its weight by one. The amortized message complexity of the first scheme depends on the local density parameter of the underlying graph and the amortized message complexity of the second scheme is polylogarithmic. Both schemes have label size $O(\log^2 n + \log n \log W)$ where W denotes the largest edge weight in the tree.

Two general translation methods for extending static labeling schemes on trees to the dynamic setting were considered in [18] and [14], for the serialized model. Both approaches fit a number of natural functions on trees, such as ancestry relation, routing, NCA relation etc. The translation methods incur overheads (over the static scheme) in both the label size and the message complexity. Specifically, the method of [14] yields dynamic compact labeling schemes, although the amortized message complexity is high, namely, $O(n^\epsilon)$. On the other hand, the label sizes of the dynamic labeling schemes in [14], which use polylogarithmic amortized message complexity, have a multiplicative overhead factor of $O(\log n / \log \log n)$ over the optimal size.

Our contributions: In this paper we consider a dynamic tree T operating under the leaf-dynamic tree model and the controlled model, and present several efficient dynamic schemes for T. All our schemes incur $O(n_0 \log^3 n_0) + O(\sum_j \log^3 n_j)$ messages, where n_0 is the initial number of nodes and n_j is the number of nodes immediately after the j'th topology change. Note, that if the initial tree contains just the root, then the amortized message complexity is $O(\log^3 n)$, per topological change, where n is the current number of nodes in T.

We first present an efficient protocol maintaining a compact (i.e., with optimal label size) separator decomposition representation in T. Let us note that, the general translation method of [14] may also yield such a dynamic compact scheme, however, their resulted scheme uses high amortized message complexity, namely, $O(n^\epsilon)$.

Our basic dynamic separator scheme is then used in order to construct several other dynamic labeling schemes for the dynamic tree T, which improve known results. Specifically, we present dynamic compact labeling schemes supporting the ancestry and the NCA relations, and we establish routing schemes for both the designer and the adversary port models, which use optimal label size up to a multiplicative $O(\log \log n)$ factor. For any of the above mentioned functions f, the best known label size for dynamic labeling schemes supporting f, that use polylogarithmic amortized message complexity, has a multiplicative overhead of $O(\log n / \log \log n)$ over the optimal label size. In addition, the best known amortized message complexity for dynamic compact labeling schemes supporting f is $O(n^\epsilon)$.

Finally, we show that our dynamic separator decomposition can also be used to allow the dynamic distance labeling schemes of [17] to operate under a more general dynamic model. In addition to allowing the edges of the underlying tree to change their weight, the extended dynamic model allows also leaves to be added to or removed from the tree. The extended scheme incurs an extra $O(n_0 \log^3 n_0) + O(\sum_j \log^3 n_j)$ additive factor to the message complexity.

Paper outline: For clarity of presentation, in the extended abstract we consider only the serialized model, and defer the modifications required for operating under the controlled model. We first assume the leaf-increasing tree model. The adaptation to the leaf-dynamic model is done according to the method described in [16] (the idea is to ignore deletions, maintain an estimate to the number of topological changes and initialize the tree every $\Theta(n)$ topological changes). Also, due to lack of space, this extended abstract contains mainly intuition regarding the construction of the dynamic separator decomposition and its applications to dynamic ancestry and routing labeling schemes, in the leaf-increasing model. The formal description and analysis of the separator decomposition construction, as well as the description and analysis of the other applications and the adaptation to the leaf-dynamic model, will appear in the full paper.

Our separator scheme for the leaf-increasing tree model is based on an adaptation of our static scheme (described in Section 3). The adaptation requires a number of components whose tasks are maintaining estimates on the sizes of the various subtrees managed in the decomposition, manipulating and reorganizing these subtrees, and maintaining the corresponding labels and topological data. These components are Protocol SHUFFLE, Protocol MAINTAIN_W and Protocol DYN_SEP. Generally speaking, Protocol MAINTAIN_W is used to allow each separator v to maintain a constant approximation to the number of nodes in the the subtree $T^*(v)$ for which v was chosen as a separator. Whenever the size of $T^*(v)$ grows by some constant factor, the main protocol DYN_SEP invoke Protocol SHUFFLE on $T^*(v)$ which calculates a new separator decomposition on $T^*(v)$ which is consistent with the global separator decomposition. The correct operation of each of these protocols relies on the assumption that certain properties hold at the beginning of their execution, and in turn, each of these components guarantees that certain properties hold upon their termination. Hence the correctness proof of the entire algorithm depends on establishing an intricate set of invariants and showing that these invariants hold throughout the execution.

2   Preliminaries

Our communication network model is restricted to tree topologies. Let T be a tree rooted at vertex r and let $T(v)$ denote the subtree of T rooted at v. For every vertex $v \in T$, let $D(v)$ denote the *depth* of v, i.e., the unweighted distance between v and the root r. For a non-root vertex v, denote by $p(v)$ its parent in the tree. The *ancestry* relation is defined as the transitive closure of the parenthood relation. Define the *weight* of v, denoted $\omega(v)$, as the number of vertices in $T(v)$, i.e., $\omega(v) = |T(v)|$. Let n denote the number of vertices in the tree, i.e., $n = \omega(r)$. The ports at each node (leading to its different neighbors) are assigned unique *port-numbers*. The enumeration of the ports at a node v is known only to v.

For every two numbers $a < b$, let $[a, b)$ denote the set of integers $a \leq i < b$. For every integer $q \geq -1$ let $I_q = [3 \cdot 2^{q+2}, 3 \cdot 2^{q+3})$ and for every $m \leq n$ and $-1 \leq q \leq \log m$, let $J_q(m) = [\frac{m}{2^{q+1}}, \frac{m}{2^q})$ and let $\widehat{J}_q(m) = [\frac{m}{2^{q+1}}, \frac{m}{2^{q-1}})$. In other words, $\widehat{J}_q(m) = J_q(m) \cup J_{q-1}(m)$.

Separator decomposition: We first define a *separator decomposition* of a tree T recursively as follows. At the first stage we choose some vertex v in T to be the *level-1* separator of T. By removing v, T breaks into disconnected subtrees which are referred to as the subtrees *formed* by v. Each such subtree is decomposed recursively by choosing some vertex to be a level-2 separator, etc.

Let $T^{subtrees}$ be the collection of all subtrees obtained by the resulting partitioning, on all levels of the recursion. Note that the trees on each level are disjoint but the entire collection contains overlapping trees. Moreover, in this partitioning, each vertex v in T belongs to a unique subtree $T_l(v) \in T^{subtrees}$ on each level l of the recursion, up to the level $l(v)$ in which v itself is selected as the separator. The subtrees $T = T_1(v), T_2(v), \cdots, T_{l(v)}(v)$ are referred to as the *ancestor subtrees* of v. Define the *separator tree* T^{sep} to be the tree rooted at the level-1 separator of T, with the level-2 separators as its children, and generally, with each level $j + 1$ separator as the child of the level j separator above it in the decomposition. For a vertex v in T, let $s_j(v)$ denote the *level-j separator of* v, i.e., the ancestor of v in T^{sep} at depth j. We associate each vertex v with the subtree $T^*(v) = T_{l(v)}(v)$ for which v is chosen as its separator. If v is a level j separator, then $T^*(v)$ is referred to as a *level j subtree*. (See Figure 1.)

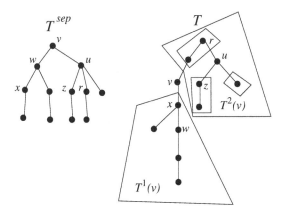

Fig. 1. In the depicted tree T, rooted at r, the node v is the level-1 separator of T. By deleting v, T breaks into $T^1(v)$ and $T^2(v)$. Similarly, w is the separator of $T^1(v)$ and u is the separator of $T^2(v)$, therefore w and u are the children of v in T^{sep}. By deleting u, $T^2(v)$ breaks into three subtrees, one of which contains z as its separator. We have $T^*(v) = T$, $T^*(w) = T^1(v)$ and $T^*(u) = T^2(v)$.

For $1/2 \leq \delta < 1$, a δ-*separator* of T is a vertex v whose removal breaks T into disconnected subtrees of at most $\delta|T|$ vertices each. It is a well known fact that every tree has a δ-separator (even for $\delta = 1/2$), and that one can recursively partition the tree by δ-separators. Such a decomposition is termed δ-*separator decomposition*. It is easy to see that the depth of the corresponding separator tree T^{sep} is $O(\log|T|)$. In the special case where $\delta = 1/2$, the separator node is called a *perfect separator*, and the decomposition is called a *perfect separator decomposition*.

Representations for separator decompositions: One may define a distributed representation for separator decompositions in trees in various ways. For our purposes, we define a *separator decomposition representation* as follows. Each vertex v in a tree T is given a label $L(v)$ so that the following hold.

1. Each vertex has a unique label, i.e., $L(u) \neq L(v)$ for every two vertices $u, v \in T$.
2. Given the label $L(v)$ of some vertex v and an integer $1 \leq i \leq l(v)$, one can extract the label $L(u)$ where u is the level-i separator of v.

Note that by the first requirement, the maximum number of bits in a label in any n-node tree is $\Omega(\log n)$ for any separator decomposition representation.

The functions: We consider the following functions F on pairs of vertices u, v of a rooted tree.

(a) Routing: $F(u, v)$ is the port number at u leading to the next vertex on the (shortest) path from u to v.

(b) Ancestry relation: if u is an ancestor of v in the tree then $F(u, v) = 1$, otherwise, $F(u, v) = 0$.

(c) NCA relation: assuming each vertex z has a unique identifier $id(z)$ (encoded using $O(\log n)$ bits), $F(u, v)$ is the identifier $id(z)$ of the nearest common ancestor (NCA) z of u and v, i.e., the common ancestor of both u and v of maximum depth.

Labeling schemes: An *F-labeling scheme* $\pi = \langle \mathcal{M}_\pi, \mathcal{D}_\pi \rangle$ is composed of the following components:

1. A *marker* algorithm $\mathcal{M}_\pi$ that given a tree, assigns a label $L(v)$ to each vertex v in the tree.
2. A polynomial time *decoder* algorithm $\mathcal{D}_\pi$ that given the labels $L(u)$ and $L(v)$ of two vertices u and v in the tree, outputs $F(u, v)$.

We note that in our schemes, the labels given to the vertices may contain several fields. In order to distinguish between the different fields of some label one can use an additional label $L'(v)$ for v, which has the same number of bits as $L(v)$ and whose 1's mark the locations where the fields of $L(v)$ begin. Clearly, adding $L'(v)$ does not increase the asymptotic label size.

The dynamic models: The following types of topology changes are considered.
Add-leaf: A new vertex u is *added* as a child of an existing vertex v.
Remove-leaf: A leaf u of a tree is *deleted*.

Subsequent to a topology change, both relevant nodes u and v are informed of it. When a new edge is attached to a node v, the corresponding port at v is assigned (either by an adversary or by v) a unique port-number (i.e., at any time, the port numbers at v are distinct), encoded using $O(\log n)$ bits.

In this paper, all our results, except for our results on routing, concern the *weak adversary model* in which an adversary can freely select and change the port numbers at any node (as long as they remain disjoint at that node). Our dynamic routing schemes consider the following two port models. In the *designer port model*, each node v is allowed at any time, to freely select and change the port numbers on its incident ports (as long as they remain disjoint) and in the *adversary port model*, the port numbers at each node are fixed by an adversary (once the adversary assigns a port number, the number remains unchanged).

Various dynamic models are considered in the literature. In the *leaf-increasing* tree model, cf. [4,14,18], the only topology change allowed is that a leaf joins the tree, and in the more general *leaf-dynamic* tree model, cf. [3,14,18], leaves can either be added to or removed from the tree. All the results in this paper apply for the leaf-dynamic tree model.

After every topological change, an update protocol $\mathcal{U}$ is activated in order to maintain the labels $L(v)$ of the vertices v to fit the requirements of the corresponding problem. As mentioned before, in the context of distributed networks, the messages are sent over the edges of the underlying graph.

For simplicity of presentation, in this extended abstract, we analyze our protocols assuming the *serialized model* (e.g., [18,17,14]) in which the topological changes occur in a serialized manner and are sufficiently spaced so that the update protocol has enough time to complete its operation in response to a given topological change, before the occurrence of the next change. This model allows us to concentrate on the combinatorial aspects of the problem without considering asynchrony issues. Let us remark, however, that our schemes can operate under the weaker *controlled model* (considered also in [16,3], see [16] for more details and motivations). In this model, when a topological change τ wishes to occur at vertex v, a *request* R_τ to perform τ arrives at v. Vertex v performs the topological change τ only when the request R_τ is granted a *permit* from the update protocol. It is guaranteed that every request to perform a topological change is eventually granted a permit. Moreover, in the leaf-increasing model, our dynamic schemes can operate under the weak *uncontrolled* model in which the topological changes may occur in rapid succession or even concurrently. Correctness, however, is required only at quiet times, i.e., times for which all updates concerning the previous topological changes have occurred. (It can easily be shown that no dynamic compact separator decomposition scheme, can be expected to operate correctly also in non-quiet times). Due to lack of space, the analysis of our schemes under the weaker models is deferred to the full paper.

For a static scheme π on n-node trees, model, we are interested in the following complexity measures.

The *label size*, $\mathcal{LS}(\pi, n)$, is the maximum number of bits in $L(v)$ taken over any vertex v.

The *message complexity*, $\mathcal{MC}(\pi, n)$, is the maximum number of messages (of size $O(\log n)$) sent by a distribute algorithm assigning the labels of π.

For a dynamic scheme π, operating in the leaf-increasing model, the above definitions are taken over all scenarios where n is the final (and maximum) number of nodes in the tree. In the leaf-dynamic tree model, instead of measuring the message complexity in terms of the maximal number of nodes in the scenario, we use more explicit time references employing the notation $(n_1, n_2, \ldots, n_t)$ where n_j is the size of the tree immediately after the j'th topological event takes place.

3   The Static Separator Representation Scheme π_{Stat_Sep}

Let us first note that a static compact separator representation scheme is implicitly described in [12]. However, we were not able to extend that scheme to the dynamic scenario. Instead, in this section we present a new static compact separator decomposition representation scheme π_{Stat_Sep} (which is in some sense a relaxation of the scheme in [12]), which we find easier to extend to the dynamic scenario. Scheme π_{Stat_Sep} enjoys label size $\Theta(\log n)$ and message complexity $O(n \log n)$.

Recall that in a δ-separator decomposition of the tree T, each node v is a separator of some level. Given a δ-separator decomposition, a simple way of constructing a representation for it is to assign each vertex a disjoint identity and then to label each vertex by the list of identities of v's ancestors in T^{sep}. However, this simple scheme has label size $O(\log^2 n)$. In order to reduce the label size to $O(\log n)$ we exploit the liberty of choosing the labels of the separators. As in the simple scheme described above, our marker algorithm assigns each vertex v a different label $L^{sep}(v)$ containing $l(v)$ fields. However, in contrast to the simple scheme mentioned above, for any $1 < l \leq l(v)$, the l'th field $L_l^{sep}(v)$ of $L^{sep}(v)$ does not contain the identity of the level-l separator of v. Instead, it contains the binary representation of a number proportional to $|T_{l-1}(v)|/|T_l(v)|$. Moreover, the label of the level-k separator of v is the prefix of $L^{sep}(v)$ containing the first k fields in $L^{sep}(v)$. Informally, these properties are achieved in the following manner. Define the labels $L^{sep}(v)$ of the separators v by induction on their level. The label of the level-1 separator is set to be $\langle 0 \rangle$. Assume that we have defined the labels of all the level-$(l-1)$ separators. For each level-$(l-1)$ separator v, we now define the labels of its children $v_1, v_2, \cdots$ in T^{sep} as follows. For each k, v_k is first assigned a unique number $\rho(v_k)$ (in the sense that if $k \neq g$ then $\rho(v_k) \neq \rho(v_g)$) such that $\rho(v_k) \in [3 \cdot 2^{q+2}, 3 \cdot 2^{q+3})$ iff $|T^*(v)|/2^{q+1} < |T^*(v_k)| \leq |T^*(v)|/2^q$, or in other words, $\rho(v_k) \in I_q$ iff $|T^*(v_k)| \in J_q(|T^*(v)|)$.

Note that for each q, there could be at most 2^{q+1} children v_k of v in T^{sep} such that $|T^*(v)|/2^{q+1} < |T^*(v_k)| \leq |T^*(v)|/2^q$. Therefore, the interval $I_q = [3 \cdot 2^{q+2}, 3 \cdot 2^{q+3})$ contains sufficiently many integers so that every separator v_k satisfying $|T^*(v_k)| \in J_q(|T^*(v)|)$ can be issued a distinct integer in I_q.

For every k, after assigning each vertex v_k a number $\rho(v_k)$ as described above, the label of v_k is set to be the concatenation $L^{sep}(v_k) = L^{sep}(v) \circ \rho(v_k)$. The fact that for each k, $\rho(v_k)$ is unique is used to show that the labels are disjoint. Note that the label of a level-l separator u can be considered as a sequence of l fields $L^{sep}(u) = L_1^{sep}(u) \circ \cdots \circ L_l^{sep}(u)$. Moreover, for each $1 \leq j < l$, the label of the level-j separator of u is simply $L_1^{sep}(u) \circ \cdots \circ L_j^{sep}(u)$. In addition, for $1 \leq j \leq l$, the $j+1$'st field $L_{j+1}^{sep}(u)$ is proportionate to $|T_j(u)|/|T_{j+1}(u)|$. This property is used to show that the label size is $O(\log n)$.

In order to implement π_{Stat_Sep} by a distributed protocol, when the separator v wishes to assign a unique value $\rho(v_k) \in I_q$ to one of its children (in T^{sep}), it somehow needs know which values it had already assigned in the range I_q. For this purpose, for every $-1 \leq q \leq \lceil \log n \rceil$, v maintains a counter $c_q(v)$ counting the number of values $\rho(v_k) \in I_q$ that were already assigned by it. Whenever v

wishes to assign a new value $\rho(v_k) \in I_q$, it simply selects $3 \cdot 2^{q+2} + c_q(v)$ and then raises $c_q(v)$ by 1. The fact that $\rho(v_k)$ indeed belongs to I_q follows from the following invariant, which holds throughout the execution at every vertex v.

Counters invariant at v: For every $-1 \le q \le \lceil \log n \rceil$, the set of currently assigned values in I_q is a prefix of I_q, namely, $[3 \cdot 2^{q+2}, 3 \cdot 2^{q+2} + c_q(v) - 1]$.

The formal description and analysis of the distributed Protocol STAT_SEP(T), which is initiated at the root of a given tree T and assigns each vertex v the label $L^{sep}(v)$, are deferred to the full paper.

Lemma 1. *Protocol* STAT_SEP(T) *constructs a compact separator decomposition on a static n-node tree T using $O(n \log n)$ messages.*

4   Protocol SHUFFLE

Protocol SHUFFLE is invoked in the dynamic scenario on subtrees $T' \in T^{subtrees}$ that are suspected to violate some balance properties required in order to maintain the compact separator decomposition on the whole tree T. The goal of Protocol SHUFFLE(T') is to recompute a separator decomposition representation on T' while keeping it consistent with the global separator decomposition representation on T. Specifically, we assume that each separator v keeps $\omega_0^*(v)$, the number of vertices in $T^*(v)$ after the last application of Protocol SHUFFLE on a subtree containing $T^*(v)$. Let v be a level-l separator and let $T^1(v), T^2(v), \cdots$ be the subtrees formed by v. Let T' be one of those subtrees, w.l.o.g. $T' = T^1(v)$.

The correct operation of Protocol SHUFFLE relies on the fact that throughout the dynamic scenario, the following invariants are maintained for every level-l separator v.

The balance invariants:
B1: For every vertex $u \in T^*(v)$, if $L^{sep}_{l+1}(u) \in I_q$ for some q then $|T_{l+1}(u)| \in \widehat{J}_q(\omega_0^*(v))$.
B2: $|T^*(v)| \in [\omega_0^*(v), \frac{5}{4} \cdot \omega_0^*(v)]$.

The growth property:
Just before Protocol SHUFFLE is invoked on $T^*(v)$, we have $|T^*(v)| \ge \gamma \cdot \omega_0^*(v)$ where $\gamma = \sqrt{5/4}$.

Protocol SHUFFLE(T') is conceptually composed of three stages. In the first stage, all the labels in T' are initialized to be $L^{sep}(v)$ (which contains l fields). At the second stage, the $l+1$'st field of the labels in T', $\rho(T')$, is initialized so that it is proportionate to $\omega_0^*(v)/|T'|$ and disjoint from $\rho(T^i)$ for every $i > 1$. At the third stage, Protocol STAT_SEP is invoked on T' to initialize the following (i.e., the $l+2$'nd, $l+3$'rd, etc) fields of the labels in T' according to a perfect separator decomposition of T'. It is relatively easy to implement the first and third stages of Protocol SHUFFLE(T').

Let us now describe informally how Protocol SHUFFLE implements the second stage. In order for the new assigned value $\rho_{new}(T')$ to be proportionate to $\omega_0^*(v)/|T'|$, it may need to be in some different interval I_q than before. We use the counters $c_q(v)$ (described in the previous section) to count the number of values in I_q that were already assigned. When v wishes to assign T' a new value $\rho_{new}(T') \in I_q$, it selects the value $3 \cdot 2^{q+2} + c_q(v)$ and then raises $c_q(v)$ by 1. However, in contrast to Protocol STAT_SEP, the counters invariant is not necessarily maintained. Instead, the fact that $3 \cdot 2^{q+2} + c_q(v) \in I_q$ results from the following more involved argument. After applying $\mathcal{S}$, the last Protocol SHUFFLE to be applied on a subtree containing v, $c_q(v)$ was relatively small. Let T'' be one of the subtrees $T^i(v)$ that received a new value in I_q after $\mathcal{S}$ was invoked and let $\mathcal{S}''$ be the SHUFFLE protocol applied on T'' after which T'' received this value. By combining the balance invariant B2 (for the separator of T'') with the growth property (for T''), we obtain that the number of vertices that have joined T'' from the time $\mathcal{S}$ was invoked until the time $\mathcal{S}''$ was invoked is proportionate to $\omega_0^*(v)/2^q$. On the other hand, by B2, the total number of nodes joining $T^*(v)$ from the time $\mathcal{S}$ was invoked is at most $\omega_0^*(v)/4$. Combining these two observations, we obtain that the number of subtrees that received a new value in I_q after $\mathcal{S}$ was invoked is small enough to guarantee that $3 \cdot 2^{q+2} + c_q(v) \in I_q$.

The formal description of Protocol SHUFFLE as well as its analysis are deferred to the full paper, where we show the following Lemma.

Lemma 2. $\mathcal{MC}(\text{SHUFFLE}(T')) = O(|T'| \log |T'|)$.

5 Protocol MAINTAIN_W

The goal of Protocol MAINTAIN_W is to allow each separator v in the dynamically growing tree to maintain a constant approximation to the number of nodes in $T^*(v)$. In [3] and [16], they show how to allow the root to maintain a constant approximation to the number of nodes in a growing tree, using $O(n \log^2 n)$ messages, where n is the final (and maximum) number of nodes in the growing tree. Let us denote such a protocol by Protocol WEIGHT_WATCH. In this section, for each separator v, we consider $T^*(v)$ as rooted at v. Protocol MAINTAIN_W simply invokes Protocol WEIGHT_WATCH on $T^*(v)$, for each separator v. Therefore, each vertex u participates in $l(u)$ applications of Protocol WEIGHT_WATCH, one for each subtree $T_i(u)$. This can be implemented easily assuming each node u knows, for each $1 \leq i < l(u)$, the port number leading to its parent in $T_i(u)$ and the port numbers leading to its children in $T_i(u)$. This assumption can be removed by slightly modifying protocol SHUFFLE.

Note that if a δ-separator decomposition is maintained then every vertex u participates in $l(u) = O(\log n)$ concurrent executions of Protocol WEIGHT_WATCH. We therefore obtain the following lemma.

Lemma 3. *Assuming the leaf-increasing tree model, Protocol* MAINTAIN_W *allows each vertex v in the dynamic tree to maintain a constant approximation to the number of nodes in $T^*(v)$. Moreover, if a δ-separator decomposition is maintained at all times then* $\mathcal{MC}(\text{MAINTAIN\_W}, n) = O(n \log^3 n)$.

6 Dynamic Separator Decomposition

We now briefly sketch Protocol DYN_SEP, whose goal is to maintain a compact separator decomposition representation in the leaf-increasing model. Protocol DYN_SEP uses Protocol MAINTAIN_W as a subroutine and from time to time invokes Protocol SHUFFLE on different subtrees. Therefore, the correctness of Protocol DYN_SEP depends on the correctness of Protocol MAINTAIN_W and on the fact that the SHUFFLE properties are maintained whenever a SHUFFLE protocol is invoked. However, these are only guaranteed assuming that the balance invariants and the growth property are maintained when the SHUFFLE protocols take place and assuming that a δ-separator decomposition is maintained at all times. Protocol DYN_SEP guarantees these assumptions by invoking Protocol SHUFFLE$(T^*(v))$ whenever the number of vertices in some $T^*(v)$ grows by some constant factor. This is implemented as follows. Every vertex v keeps the value $\omega_0^*(v)$ which is the number of vertices in $T^*(v)$ after the last SHUFFLE protocol on a subtree containing v. Whenever the counter $\tilde{\omega}^*(v)$ (which is used by v in order to estimate $|T^*(v)|$) satisfies $\tilde{\omega}^*(v) \geq \sqrt{5/4} \cdot \omega_0^*(v)$, vertex v invokes Protocol SHUFFLE$(T^*(v))$. The formal description of Protocol DYN_SEP and the proof of the following theorem are deferred to the full paper.

Theorem 1. *Assuming the leaf-increasing tree model, Protocol* DYN_SEP *maintains a compact separator decomposition using* $O(n \log^3 n)$ *messages.*

7 Applications: Dynamic Labeling Schemes for Trees

In this section we describe the ideas behind our dynamic labeling schemes, all of which use $O(\log^3 n)$ amortized message complexity. In this extended abstract we sketch the improved dynamic ancestry and routing schemes. The formal description and analysis of these applications as well as the formal description and analysis of the NCA labeling schemes and the extended distance labeling are deferred to the full paper. We begin with sketching the ideas behind our dynamic compact ancestry labeling schemes.

Improved ancestry labeling schemes on dynamic trees: We first introduce a new static compact labeling scheme, $\pi_{Stat\_Anc} = \langle \mathcal{M}_{SA}, \mathcal{D}_{SA} \rangle$, supporting the ancestry relation, and then show how to extend it to the dynamic setting. Scheme π_{Stat_Anc} uses the separator decomposition representation obtained by Scheme π_{Stat_Sep}. For every two vertices v and u, let $s(v, u)$ denote the NCA of v and u in T^{sep}. Scheme π_{Stat_Anc} is based on the fact that a vertex v is an ancestor of a vertex u iff v is an ancestor of $s(v, u)$ and u is a descendant of $s(v, u)$. The label $L(v)$ given by the marker algorithm $\mathcal{M}_{SA}$ to a vertex v is composed of two sublabels, namely, the *separation sublabel*, $L^{sep}(v)$, and the *relative sublabel*, $L^{rel}(v)$. The separation sublabel $L^{sep}(v)$ is the label given to v by the scheme π_{Stat_Sep}. The relative sublabel $L^{rel}(v)$ is composed of $l(v)$ fields. The j'th field of $L^{rel}(v)$ contains two bits indicating whether $s_j(v)$, the level-j separator of v, is an ancestor of v in T, descendant of v in T or neither.

Given two labels $L(v)$ and $L(u)$, of two vertices v and u, one can extract the level i of $s(v,u)$ using the corresponding separation sublabels and then find whether in T, v is an ancestor of $s(v,u)$ and u is a descendant of $s(v,u)$, using the i'th field of the corresponding relative sublabels.

In the dynamic scenario, the separation sublabels are maintained using the dynamic scheme π_{Dyn_Sep}. Throughout the dynamic scenario, whenever a vertex v is assigned a new level j separator, the j'th field in its relative sublabel is updated appropriately, according to whether v is an ancestor (or a descendant) of this separator. By Theorem 1 we therefore obtain the following theorem.

Theorem 2. *Assuming the leaf-increasing model, Scheme π_{Dyn_Anc} maintains a compact ancestry labeling scheme using $O(n\log^3 n)$ messages.*

Dynamic routing labeling schemes: We now sketch our dynamic routing schemes π_{rout} which have optimal label size up to a multiplicative factor of $O(\log\log n)$. I.e., the label size of π_{rout} is $O(\log n \cdot \log\log n)$ for the designer port model, and $O(\log^2 n)$ for the adversary port model.

Let v be some vertex, and let $l(v)$ be level for which v was chosen as a separator. For each $1 \le i \le l(v)$, let $s_i(v)$ be the i'th separator of v. The label of v given by π_{rout} is composed of three sublabels. The first is the *separator sublabel* $L^{sep}(v)$ which is the label given to v by π_{Dyn_Sep} (recall that $L^{sep}(v)$ contains $l(v)$ fields). The second and third sublabels are the *port-to-separator sublabel* $L^{to-sep}(v)$ and the *port-from-separator sublabel* $L^{from-sep}(v)$. Each of these sublabels also contains $l(v)$ fields. The i'th field in $L^{to-sep}(v)$, namely $L_i^{to-sep}(v)$, is the port number leading from v to the next vertex on the shortest path connecting v and $s_i(v)$. The i'th field in $L^{from-sep}(v)$, namely $L_i^{from-sep}(v)$, is the port number leading from $s_i(v)$ to the next vertex on the shortest path connecting $s_i(v)$ and v. By slightly modifying Protocol SHUFFLE, we can ensure that whenever Protocol Dyn_Sep updates the i'th field in $L^{sep}(v)$, the i'th fields in the sublabels $L^{to-sep}(v)$ and $L^{from-sep}(v)$ are also updated appropriately.

Given the labels $L(u)$ and $L(v)$ of two vertices u and v, the port number leading from u to the next vertex on the shortest path connecting u and v is determined as follows. If $L^{sep}(u)$ is a prefix of $L^{sep}(v)$ and $L^{sep}(u)$ contains i fields, then $u = s_i(v)$ and therefore the desired port number is $L_i^{from-sep}(v)$. If, on the other hand, $L^{sep}(u)$ is not a prefix of $L^{sep}(v)$ then let i be the last index such that $L_i^{sep}(u) = L_i^{sep}(v)$. In this case, the i'th separator of u, $s_i(u)$, must be on the path connecting u and v and must be different than u. Therefore, the desired port number is $L_i^{to-sep}(u)$.

Scheme π_{rout} is clearly a correct dynamic routing schemes. Let us now analyze its label size. First, for each vertex v, the separator sublabel $L^{sep}(v)$ contains $O(\log n)$ bits. Both the port-to-separator sublabel $L^{to-sep}(v)$ and the port-from-separator sublabel $L^{from-sep}(v)$ contain $O(\log n)$ fields, where each such field contains a port number. Recall that it is assumed that each port number is encoded using $O(\log n)$ bits. It follows that in the adversary port model, the label size of Scheme π_{rout} is $O(\log^2 n)$. Let us now consider the designer port model and describe the method by which each vertex u chooses its port numbers, so that the label size of Scheme π_{rout} is $O(\log n \cdot \log\log n)$. Let $E^{sep}(u)$ be the set of edges leading from u to the next vertex on the shortest path connecting u and one of its ancestors in T^{sep}. Since u has $l(u) = O(\log n)$ such ancestors, $E^{sep}(u)$ contains $O(\log n)$ edges. For each edge $e \in E^{sep}(u)$, vertex u chooses a unique port number in the range $\{1, 2, \cdots, l(u)\}$. Therefore, each such port number can be encoded using $O(\log \log n)$ bits. We therefore immediately get that for every vertex v, the port-to-separator sublabel $L^{to-sep}(v)$ can be encoded using $O(\log n \cdot \log \log n)$ bits. We now describe the method by which each vertex u chooses its remaining port numbers, i.e., the port numbers of the edges not in $E^{sep}(u)$. For each such edge e, let $T^i(u)$ be the corresponding subtree formed by u. The corresponding port number at u is set to be the number $l(u) + \rho(T^i(u))$, where $\rho(T^i(u))$ is the number given to $T^i(u)$ by Protocol Dyn_Sep. We therefore obtain that the port numbers incident to u are disjoint. For a fixed vertex v and $i \leq l(v)$, the port number $L_i^{from-sep}(v)$ is leading from $s_i(v)$ to x, the next vertex on the shortest path connecting $s_i(v)$ and v. If the edge $(s_i(v), x)$ belongs to $E^{sep}(s_i(v))$ then $L_i^{from-sep}(v)$ is encoded using $O(\log \log n)$ bits. Otherwise, the number of bits in $L_i^{from-sep}(v)$ is $O(\log \log n)$ plus the number of bits used to encode the $i+1$'st subfield in $L^{sep}(v)$. Therefore, the number of bits used to encode $L^{from-sep}(v)$ is at most $O(\log n \cdot \log \log n) + O(\log n) = O(\log n \cdot \log \log n)$. We therefore obtain the following theorem.

Theorem 3. *Assuming the leaf-increasing model, Scheme π_{rout} is a correct dynamic routing scheme that uses $O(n \log^3 n)$ messages. Moreover, the labels it produces are of optimal length, up to a multiplicative factor of $O(\log \log n)$. I.e., the label size of π_{rout} is $O(\log^2 n)$ for the adversary port model, and $O(\log n \cdot \log \log n)$ for the designer port model.*

References

1. Abiteboul, S., Alstrup, S., Kaplan, H., Milo, T., Rauhe, T.: Compact Labeling Scheme for Ancestor Queries. SIAM J. Computing 35(6), 1295–1309 (2006)
2. Abiteboul, S., Kaplan, H., Milo, T.: Compact Labeling Schemes for Ancestor Queries. In: Proc. 12th ACM-SIAM Symp. on Discrete Algorithms. ACM Press, New York (2001)
3. Afek, Y., Awerbuch, B., Plotkin, S.A., Saks, M.: Local Management of a Global Resource in a Communication. J. ACM 43, 1–19 (1996)
4. Afek, Y., Gafni, E., Ricklin, M.: Upper and Lower Bounds for Routing Schemes in Dynamic Networks. In: Proc. 30th Symp. on Foundations of Computer Science, pp. 370–375 (1989)
5. Alstrup, S., Gavoille, C., Kaplan, H., Rauhe, T.: Nearest Common Ancestors: A Survey and a new Distributed Algorithm. Theory of Computing Systems 37, 441–456 (2004)
6. Alstrup, S., Rauhe, T.: Small induced-universal graphs and compact implicit graph representations. In: Proc. 43'rd IEEE Symp. on Foundations of Computer Science. IEEE Computer Society Press, Los Alamitos (2002)
7. Cole, R., Hariharan, R.: Dynamic LCA Queries on Trees. SIAM J. Computing 34(4), 894–923 (2005)

8. Eppstein, D., Galil, Z., Italiano, G.F.: Dynamic Graph Algorithms. In: Atallah, M.J. (ed.) Algorithms and Theoretical Computing Handbook, ch. 8. CRC Press, Boca Raton, USA (1999)
9. Fraigniaud, P., Gavoille, C.: Routing in Trees. In: Orejas, F., Spirakis, P.G., van Leeuwen, J. (eds.) ICALP 2001. LNCS, vol. 2076, pp. 757–772. Springer, Heidelberg (2001)
10. Fraigniaud, P., Gavoille, C.: A space lower bound for routing in trees. In: Proc. 19th Int. Symp. on Theoretical Aspects of Computer Science, pp. 65–75 (March 2002)
11. Feigenbaum, J., Kannan, S.: Dynamic Graph Algorithms. In: Handbook of Discrete and Combinatorial Mathematics. CRC Press, Boca Raton, USA (2000)
12. Gavoille, C., Katz, M., Katz, N.A., Paul, C., Peleg, D.: Approximate Distance Labeling Schemes. In: 9th European Symp. on Algorithms, pp. 476–488 (August 2001)
13. Kannan, S., Naor, M., Rudich, S.: Implicit Representation of Graphs. SIAM J. on Discrete Math. 5, 596–603 (1992)
14. Korman, A.: General Compact Labeling Schemes for Dynamic Trees. In: Proc. 19th Symp. on Distributed Computing (September 2005)
15. Korman, A.: Labeling Schemes for Vertex Connectivity. In: Proc. 34th Int. Colloq. on Automata, Languages and Prog (ICALP) (July 2007)
16. Korman, A., Kutten, S.: Controller and Estimator for Dynamic Networks. In: Proc. 26th ACM Symp. on Principles of Distributed Computing. ACM Press, New York (2007)
17. Korman, A., Peleg, D.: Labeling Schemes for Weighted Dynamic Trees. In: Proc. 30th Int. Colloq. on Automata, Languages & Prog. (July 2003)
18. Korman, A., Peleg, D., Rodeh, Y.: Labeling Schemes for Dynamic Tree Networks. STACS 2002 37(1), 49–75 (2004) Special Issue of STACS'02 papers.
19. Peleg, D.: Informative Labeling Schemes for Graphs. Theoretical Computer Science 340, 577–593 (2005) Special Issue of MFCS'00 papers
20. Peterson, L.L., Davie, B.S.: Computer Networks: A Systems Approach. Morgan Kaufmann, San Francisco (2007)
21. Schieber, B., Vishkin, U.: On finding Lowest Common Ancestors: Simplification and Parallelization. SIAM J. Computing 17(6), 1253–1262 (1988)
22. Sleator, D.D., Tarjan, R.E.: A Data Structure for Dynamic Trees. J. Computer & System Sciences 26(1), 362–391 (1983)
23. Tanenbaum, A.S.: Computer Networks. Prentice-Hall, Englewood Cliffs (2003)
24. Thorup, M., Zwick, U.: Compact Routing Schemes. In: Proc. 13th ACM Symp. on Parallel Algorithms and Architecture, pp. 1–10. ACM Press, New York (2001)

On the Communication Surplus
Incurred by Faulty Processors

Dariusz R. Kowalski[1] and Michał Strojnowski[2,*]

[1] Department of Computer Science, The University of Liverpool, UK
darek@csc.liv.ac.uk
[2] Instytut Informatyki, Uniwersytet Warszawski, Poland
stromy@mimuw.edu.pl

Abstract. We study the impact of faulty processors on the communication cost of distributed algorithms in a message-passing model. The system is synchronous but prone to various kinds of processor failures: crashes, message omissions, (authenticated) Byzantine faults. One of the basic communication tasks, called *fault-tolerant gossip*, or *gossip* for short, is to exchange the initial values among all non-faulty processors. In this paper we address the question if there is a gossip algorithm which is both fault-tolerant, fast and communication-efficient? We answer this question in affirmative in the model allowing only crash failures, and in some sense negatively when the other kinds of failures may occur. More precisely, in an execution by n processors when f of them are faulty, each non-faulty processor contributes a constant to the message complexity, each crashed processor contributes $\Theta(f^\varepsilon)$ ($\varepsilon > 0$ could be an arbitrarily small constant independent from n, f but dependent on the algorithm), each omission (or authenticated Byzantine) processor contributes $\Theta(t)$, and each—even potential—Byzantine failure results in additional $\Theta(n)$ messages sent.

1 Introduction

Communication tasks, like broadcast, multicast or gossip, are among fundamental algorithmic problems in distributed computing. All of them have fast and fault-tolerant solutions in a synchronous message-passing system. However still not much is known about the communication complexity incurred by faulty processors while performing a communication task. In this paper we address this issue for a gossip problem. A *fault-tolerant gossip* requires that all non-faulty processors learn initial values (called rumors) of all other non-faulty processors. We study deterministic solutions terminating in *constant time*, which is asymptotically the best time complexity we can achieve for this problem, and tolerating different kinds of failures: crashes, message omissions, authenticated Byzantine and Byzantine faults.

Gossip algorithms are important tools for solving decision problems (e.g., consensus [3,4,11]) and cooperation problems (e.g., performing tasks [12]). The additional motivation for studying constant-time message-efficient algorithms comes

---

* Supported in part by KBN Grant N206 001 32/00924 and COST Action 295.

A. Pelc (Ed.): DISC 2007, LNCS 4731, pp. 328–342, 2007.

from the crucial property that reducing the number of messages increases the stability of many underlying networking systems (see e.g., [5]). More precisely, substantially reducing the number of messages in the system is more important for efficient queuing and processing of messages than decreasing latency by a constant number of rounds.

We denote the number of processors in the system by n, the upper bound on the number of failures (in other words, the number of *potential failures*) by $t < n$, and the real number of failures that occur during the execution of the algorithm by $f \leq t$. Parameters n, t are known to all processors. Algorithm is called *t-resilient* if it solves the problem correctly unless the number of failures exceeds t.

The naive fault-tolerant gossip solution, in which each processor sends its rumor to all other processors in the first round, suffers from the fact that *every* processor, even non-faulty one, sends $n - 1 = \Omega(n)$ messages. Another popular algorithm, based on the set of leaders (see e.g., [10,13]), requires that firstly each processor sends its rumor to all the leaders, and then every leader sends back the combined message to all other processors. This approach however is inefficient if the number of leaders, and hence the number of tolerated failures, is big. For example, an algorithm tolerating up to t failures should choose at least $t + 1$ leaders, which yields $\Omega(t)$ messages per *each*, again even non-faulty, processor. Our goal is to improve the message complexity of deterministic fault-tolerant time-efficient gossip algorithms, wherever it is possible, and show the actual impact of faulty processors to the message complexity of the gossip problem.

1.1   Our Contribution

A straightforward lower bound for the message complexity of a gossip problem is $\Omega(n)$, since each processor must send its value at least once. In the model without failures, this lower bound is matched by the algorithm with one leader, described above. If crashes or even more malicious failures are allowed, this algorithm no longer works since the leader may crash and every other processor receives no message.

We show that indeed every crash failure induces additional cost of $\Omega(t^\varepsilon)$ messages for any constant-time t-reliable gossip algorithm, where $\varepsilon > 0$ could be an arbitrarily small constant which depends on the algorithm. This distinguishes between the models with crash failures and without failures, for $f > n^{1-\varepsilon}$. On the other hand, we design a deterministic gossip algorithm where each crash failure contributes $O(f^\varepsilon)$ to the message complexity, for any constant $\varepsilon > 0$. This can not be achieved against omission failures, since each such failure contributes $\Theta(t)$ to the message complexity (we show both a lower bound and a deterministic algorithm that matches it). The same holds for authenticated omission failures.

Finally, we show that Byzantine failures are the most costly ones, since each even *potentially* Byzantine fault results in additional $\Theta(n)$ message complexity. Similarly as above, we show a lower bound and refer to the algorithm described in [8] that matches this bound. Table 1 summarizes the results.

Table 1. Message complexity incurred by different kinds of failures. $\varepsilon > 0$ is a constant that depends on the algorithm. The results without a reference are obtained in this paper.

Kind of failures	Lower bound	Upper bound
additional cost per crash	$\Omega(f^{\varepsilon})$	$O(f^{\varepsilon})$
additional cost per omission/auth.-Byzantine	$\Omega(t)$	$O(t)$
additional cost per *potential* Byzantine failure	$\Omega(n)$	$O(n)$ [8]

Another important contribution of this paper is a general framework for fault-tolerant gossip algorithms, which is used to obtain efficient gossip algorithms in every considered model of failures. It is based on two classes of generic subroutines: (adaptive) mix and request. Using specific combinations of these subroutines allows to handle efficiently different kinds of failures.

1.2   Previous and Related Work

There is a vast body of literature concerning fault-tolerant gossip in different settings, here we present only the most relevant results. Dolev and Reischuk [8] introduced a simple constant-time t-resilient gossip algorithm with $O(n)$ messages per each potentially Byzantine failure. Chlebus and Kowalski [3] developed a t-resilient gossip algorithm against crash failures, where $t < cn$ for a positive constant $c < 1$, working in $O(\log^2 n)$ rounds with message complexity $O(\text{polylog } n)$ per each crash during the execution. That result was extended over all values $t < n$ by Georgiou et al. [12] who presented a gossip algorithm working in time $O(\log^2 n)$ and with $O(n^{\varepsilon})$ communication cost per each crash, for any constant $0 < \varepsilon < 1$. Recently, Chlebus and Kowalski [4] developed a solution tolerating up to $n - 1$ crashes in time $O(\log^3 n)$ and with $O(n \log^4 n)$ message complexity. Note that apart from Dolev and Reischuk's [8], those results are not in constant number of rounds, therefore they can not be directly compared with or transformed into *constant-time* gossip solutions. In the more restricted model of static crashes, Diks and Pelc [7] solved a gossip problem with cn faults (for any constant $0 < c < 1$) in time $O(\log n)$ and with $O(n)$ messages.

Book [13] presents some aspects of fault-tolerant solutions of the gossip problem in general networks. Related problems of gathering and spreading information in shared-memory system were also broadly studied, but from slightly different perspective, see e.g., [6]. For the purpose of our algorithms we define graphs with specific fault-tolerant properties. Different kinds of graphs with expansion properties were studied before in the context of fault-tolerant communication in a message-passing system [3,4,7,12], networks in general (for references see e.g., [2]) and shared memory [6]. Graphs defined in this paper have not been studied before.

We compare the results obtained for the gossip problem with another fundamental problem in fault-tolerant distributed computing, which is a consensus problem. Fisher and Lynch [9] showed that a synchronous solution requires $f + 1$ rounds. This proves that consensus—as a decision problem— is more complex than the gossip problem from the perspective of time complexity. For crash failures, Galil, Mayer and Yung [11] designed a consensus algorithm working in time $O(f)$ and with communication complexity overhead $O(t^\varepsilon)$ per each crash, for any constant $\varepsilon > 0$. Their solution was based on a diffusion tree. This result has been recently improved by Chlebus and Kowalski [4] who decreased the communication complexity overhead to $O(\text{polylog } n)$ per each crash. That result compared with the result from this paper emphasizes another difference between gossip and consensus problems: for time-optimal algorithms, the communication impact of a crash is much smaller for consensus than for gossip. Regarding the other types of faults, the additional message complexity incurred in a consensus algorithm by an omission or an authenticated Byzantine failure is $\Theta(t)$, and $\Theta(n)$ by a Byzantine failure, as shown by Dolev and Reischuk [8]. Surprisingly, for these kinds of failures the results for gossip and consensus problems are the same.

1.3 Organization of the Paper

Basic definitions and notations are given in Section 2. Section 3 provides the main framework for efficient gossip algorithms against all considered types of failures. The following three sections present the results for the gossip problem in considered models of failures: Section 4 for crash failures, Section 5 for omission and authenticated Byzantine failures, and Section 6 for Byzantine failures. A discussion in Section 7 concludes the paper. The missing proofs, due to the lack of space, are deferred to the full version of the paper.

2 Technical Preliminaries

In this paper we consider a synchronous message-passing model with failures, as described in [1,15].

Processors and communication. A distributed system considered in this paper is synchronous, with all processors having access to a global clock. There are n processors, each with a unique integer name (identifier) in set $\mathcal{P} = \{1, \ldots, n\}$. Parameter n is known to all processors, in the sense that it is a part of code of an algorithm. Processors communicate by sending messages. Clock cycles are partitioned into *rounds* during which every processor can receive all the messages delivered at the beginning of this round, perform any finite computation (with exception of breaking cryptographic protocols used in the authenticated Byzantine case), and send point-to-point messages to *any* subset of processors. A message sent in a round is delivered to its destination at the beginning of the next round, unless the sender or the receiver is faulty; in that case a message could be lost (see the next paragraph for description of the models of failures).

Processor failures. We consider the classic model of processor failures (see i.e., [1,15] for detailed description). To avoid much formalism, we use the notion of an adversary who incurs failures into the system. The adversary is *adaptive* in the sense that it knows the algorithm and may cause failures during the execution of the algorithm. A processor failure is *permanent*, that is once a processor becomes faulty it remains faulty till the end of the computation. The total number of processor failures in any execution is bounded by $t < n$. The real number of failures occurring during an execution is denoted by $f \leq t$. We consider the following types of failures.

Crash failures: after crashing a processor stops its activity, in particular it stops sending and receiving any messages till the end of the computation. When a processor crashes while sending a message to a subset of processors, the message can be delivered only to some of them, depending on the choice of the adversary.

General omission failures: a faulty processor may omit to send or receive any message. More precisely, the adversary has a choice for every message sent by or to a faulty processor if it is received or not. Although the number of faulty processors is bounded by t, there is no limit on the number of omitted messages during the execution. Note that this model is more severe than one with crashes since here no processor can infer a failure of any other by lack of messages from it (since it might be faulty itself). This model also differs from one in which particular faulty links can drop off messages (see [14] for details and further references).

Byzantine failures: a faulty processor may behave in any malicious way desired by the adversary. In particular, it may avoid sending messages or send messages with malicious content. In authenticated Byzantine model there is a restriction that each processor may *sign* any part of a message with its identifier, and such messages may not be forged (only relied unchanged to other processors or be omitted by a faulty processor). From the point of view of performing a communication task, an authenticated Byzantine processor is similar to an omission-prone processor [15].

Fault-tolerant gossip problem. We are given a set of n processors. Initially each of them has a distinct piece of information, called a *rumor*. A *t-resilient gossip solution* must satisfy the following requirements in the presence of any pattern of at most t failures, and under the assumption that all processors start in the same round:

Correctness: Each non-faulty processor learns the rumors of all non-faulty processors;

Termination: Each non-faulty processor terminates its protocol.

We assume that an algorithm (code) executed by each processor is the same, and that each processor knows at the beginning values n and t, as well as its own unique identifier $i \in \{1, 2, \ldots, n\}$ and its own unique data $rumor_i$.

Complexity measures. In this paper we consider *constant-time* algorithms, i.e., terminating in a constant number of rounds. We measure their *message complexity*, that is, the total number of point-to-point messages sent by processors before termination. We compute this complexity as a function of parameters n, t and f. Note that message complexity is also an upper bound on the number of received messages.

3   Algorithmic Framework

In this section we define a basic framework for our gossip algorithms. This includes a specification of local data structures, content of messages and update procedures based on received messages, communication patterns and subroutines. An adaptation of this framework to particular model of failures may require additional data structures; this will be addressed while describing specific algorithms.

3.1   Local Memory, Messages and Updates

Local memory. A processor $\mathbf{p}$ stores the following structures:

$Rumors_\mathbf{p}[1 \ldots n]$: array of known processor's rumors. A field $Rumors_\mathbf{p}[\mathbf{q}]$ contains a rumor of processor q, or one of the special values *faulty* or *unknown*. Initially $Rumors_\mathbf{p}[\mathbf{p}] = rumor_\mathbf{p}$, and all remaining fields contain value *unknown*.

$Active_\mathbf{p}[1 \ldots n]$: array of processors' activities. A field $Active_\mathbf{p}[\mathbf{q}]$ contains value *unknown* (initial) or *active* (the meaning of this value depends on particular algorithm and will be made clear later).

$Informed_\mathbf{p}[1 \ldots n]$: array of known processors' statuses in the gossip task. A field $Informed_\mathbf{p}[\mathbf{q}]$ contains value *unknown* (initial) or *informed* (which means that processor $\mathbf{q}$ has collected all required rumors).

All the arrays are gradually filled in during the execution. In particular, array $Rumors_\mathbf{p}$ is filled in with rumors or values *faulty* for processors that are known to be faulty. When processor $\mathbf{p}$ has no value *unknown* in the array $Rumors_\mathbf{p}$, is sets $Informed_\mathbf{p}[\mathbf{p}] = informed$, and is called *informed*. If all non-faulty processors are informed, the gossip is solved (however some of them may not terminate yet).

Messages and memory update. For simplicity, we use only one format of messages. It contains the local data structures of the sender. At the beginning of each round, every processor receives messages and updates its local data structures by overwriting values *unknown* with newly received values.

3.2   Communication Graphs

Before describing subroutines used in our algorithms, we need to define three classes of graphs which will be used in subroutines to determine the communication pattern. In each subroutine we identify the processors with nodes of the used graph, and we assume that processors send messages only to their neighbors in this graph.

All graphs presented below are undirected, and nodes/processors usually communicate both ways along the adjacent edges (unless stated otherwise). For a graph $G = (V, E)$ and a subset of nodes $B \subseteq V$, we denote the set of all neighbors of B in graph G by $N_G(B)$.

Constructions and probabilistic proofs of existence of the following graphs are deferred to the full version of the paper.

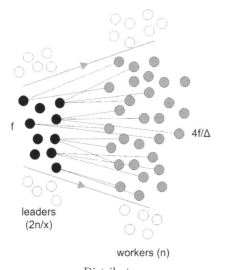
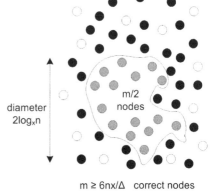

Distributor	Communicator
Each sufficiently big set of workers (grey) has a big set of neighboring leaders (black) *(only some edges displayed)*	After removing any set of nodes (black) there remains a big set with small diameter (grey) *(edges not displayed)*

Distributors. A distributor is a bipartite unbalanced expander graph with degree Δ and expansion rate $\frac{\Delta}{4}$ (for small subsets) on the bigger side. Formally, we say that a bipartite graph $G = (W, L, E)$, where W, L are disjoint sets of nodes, is a (n, x, Δ)-*distributor* iff it satisfies the following properties:

(a) $|W| = n$, $|L| = \frac{2n}{x}$;

(b) maximum degree of a node in set W is at most Δ;

(c) for every $f < \frac{2n}{x^2}$, every set $Y \subseteq W$ of size $\frac{4f}{\Delta}$ has more than f neighbors.

Set W is called a set of *workers* and set L is called a set of *leaders*.

Theorem 1. *There exists a (n, x, Δ)-distributor, for any n, $\Delta \geq 4$ and $x \geq 8$.*

Communicators. A communicator is a graph in which every large subset of nodes contains a large subgraph with small diameter. We say that graph $G = (L, E)$ with n nodes and of degree Δ is a (n, x, Δ)-*communicator*, iff

For each set $B \subseteq L$ of size $m \geq \frac{6nx}{\Delta}$ there exists set $C \subseteq B$ of size bigger than $\frac{m}{2}$, such that the subgraph of G induced by set C has diameter at most $2 \log_x n$.

Theorem 2. *There exists a (n, x, Δ)-communicator, for any n, Δ and $x \geq 2 \log n$.*

Adaptive communicators. An adaptive communicator is a graph in which removal of a small set of nodes never detaches a bigger set from the main connected part. Formally, graph $G = (L, E)$ of n nodes and degree Δ is called a (n, x, Δ)-*adaptive-communicator* iff

For each $f \leq \frac{n}{x}$ and set $B \subseteq L$ of size $n - f$ there exists set $C \subseteq B$ of size at least $n - 2f$, such that the subgraph of G induced by C has diameter at most $2 \log_\Delta n$.

Theorem 3. *There exists a (n, x, Δ)-adaptive-communicator, for any n, $x \geq 6$ and $\Delta \geq 36$.*

Note that a complete graph with n nodes is a $(n, x, n - 1)$-(adaptive)-communicator, for any $1 \leq x \leq n$.

3.3   Subroutines

Using the classes of graphs defined above, we design three simple subroutines that are used in our algorithms. Each subroutine gets the following input parameters: a set of leaders L, parameters x and Δ. For a given subroutine and its input parameters L, x, Δ, there is a fixed corresponding graph, which is, a $(|L|, x, \Delta)$-distributor for subroutine $DistributedRequest(L, x, \Delta)$, a $(|L|, x, \Delta)$-communicator for subroutine $Mixing(L, x, \Delta)$, and a $(|L|, x, \Delta)$-adaptive communicator for subroutine $AdaptiveMixing(L, x, \Delta)$. In particular, it means that for a given subroutine and parameters L, x, Δ, each processor knows its neighboring processors in the corresponding graph. Based on the input and the properties of the corresponding graph, the exact running time of a subroutine can be computed, as it will be described later for each kind of subroutine. Therefore if processors start the same subroutine all in the same round, they will also finish it simultaneously, which is important for the coordination of processors' actions in the course of the algorithm.

DistributedRequest(L, x, Δ), where $\Delta \geq 4$. The aim of this subroutine is to gather a large number of processors' rumors in the leaders. Recall that all processors running this subroutine know the same fixed (n, x, Δ)-distributor graph $G = (L, W, E)$, where L is a pre-defined set of leaders and W is the set of all processors. In the first round of the subroutine every processor from set L requests its neighbors in G. During the second round every requested processor replies for all the requests (by sending a message to each processor from which it has received a request), and in the third round the answers are received and processed by the leaders.

We will use three variants of this subroutine, depending on if a leader $\mathbf{p} \in L$ wants to request *all* its neighbors in graph G, or only those neighbors whose rumors are unknown (those $\mathbf{q}$ for which $Rumors_\mathbf{p}[\mathbf{q}] = unknown$), or only *uninformed* neighbors (those $\mathbf{q}$ for which $Informed_\mathbf{p}[\mathbf{q}] = unknown$).

Summarizing the complexity, the subroutine works in 3 rounds, with $O(n\Delta)$ message complexity.

Mixing(L, x, Δ). The purpose of this subroutine is to exchange knowledge among the leaders. Recall again that all processors running this subroutine know the same $(|L|, x, \Delta)$-communicator graph $G = (L, E)$, where L is a pre-defined set of leaders given as a part of the input. Every processor in L keeps sending a message to all its neighbors in G during $2 \log_x n$ subsequent rounds.

This subroutine works in $2 \log_x n$ rounds, and processors send $O(|L|\Delta \log_x n)$ point-to-point messages in total. We will use this subroutine only for x being a polynomial in n, and in that case the subroutine takes a (fixed) constant number of rounds and has $O(|L|\Delta)$ message complexity.

AdaptiveMixing(L, x, Δ), where $\Delta \geq 36$. This procedure is identical to sub-routine $Mixing(L, x, \Delta)$, with the only difference that instead of a communicator graph, a fixed $(|L|, x, \Delta)$-adaptive-communicator is used.

This subroutine works in $2 \log_\Delta n$ rounds and generates $O(|L|\Delta \log_\Delta n)$ point-to-point messages. It will be applied only for Δ being a polynomial in n, and in that case the subroutine lasts a (fixed) constant number of rounds and has $O(|L|\Delta)$ message complexity.

4   Crash Failures

Theorem 4. *Every t-crash-resilient gossip algorithm terminating in constant time sends $\Omega(n + f^{1+\varepsilon})$ messages when $f \leq t$ crashes occur during the execution, for some constant $\varepsilon > 0$. I.e., each faulty processor contributes $\Omega(f^\varepsilon)$.*

Proof. Consider a t-resilient gossip algorithm $\mathcal{A}$. The lower bound $\Omega(n)$ is obvious from the fact that in the execution without failures each processor must send at least one message. We show the lower bound $\Omega(f^{1+\varepsilon})$. Let c be a constant upper bound on the time complexity of algorithm $\mathcal{A}$. We prove the existence of an admissible execution with f crashes, for any $1 \leq f \leq t$, in which algorithm $\mathcal{A}$ sends more than $\frac{f^{1+\varepsilon}}{2}$ messages, where $\varepsilon = \frac{1}{c+1}$. We consider only a nontrivial case when $f^\varepsilon > 2$.

Assume the contrary, that the message complexity $\mathcal{M}$ of algorithm $\mathcal{A}$ is smaller than $\frac{f^{1+\varepsilon}}{2}$. We show a strategy of the adversary in which it crashes f processors in a way that algorithm $\mathcal{A}$ turns out to be incorrect. The strategy is as follows: in each round the adversary crashes each processor that receives at least f^ε messages in this round. By the assumption, the number ℓ of such processors in the whole execution is at most $\frac{\mathcal{M}}{f^\varepsilon} < \frac{f}{2}$, thus only $\ell < \frac{f}{2}$ processors are crashed in that way. In order to be consistent with the assumption that the adversary fails f processors during the execution, at the end of the last round c the adversary additionally crashes some of the remaining processors in order to have the total number of crashes equal to f; we call them *last-minute crashes* and define later. We denote the whole execution by $\mathcal{E}$ and the part of the execution before last-minute crashes by $\mathcal{E}^*$. Note that $\mathcal{E}$ is an admissible execution and, by the fact that time complexity is at most c, all messages received in $\mathcal{E}$ are also received during $\mathcal{E}^*$.

It remains to prove that execution $\mathcal{E}$ violates correctness of gossip algorithm $\mathcal{A}$, which means that there is a non-crashed processor that has *not* got all the rumors of non-crashed processors by the end of round c. Consider the partial execution $\mathcal{E}^*$. A straightforward inductive argument shows that since each non-crashed processor receives at most $f^\varepsilon - 1$ messages in any round i, it knows at most $\prod_{i=1}^{j} f^{\varepsilon}$ rumors by the end of round $j \leq c$. Consequently, it knows at most $\prod_{i=1}^{c} f^{\varepsilon} = f^{c\varepsilon} = f^{c/(c+1)} = f^{1-\varepsilon} < \frac{f}{2} < f - \ell$ rumors at the end of the partial execution $\mathcal{E}^*$. Still there are $f - \ell$ last-minute crashes to be done by the adversary at the very end of the execution $\mathcal{E}$. Therefore, if the adversary chooses a processor **p** that is non-faulty in $\mathcal{E}^*$ and in the last-minute it crashes all processors which rumors have been collected by **p** (there are less than $f - \ell$ of them), **p** knows no rumor of non-faulty processor at the end of the whole execution. Additionally the adversary does some other last-minute crashes (arbitrarily selected), still keeping processor **p** alive, to assure that the total number of crashes during execution $\mathcal{E}$ is exactly f. Thus $\mathcal{E}$ violates correctness of the gossip algorithm.   □

Observe that the lower bound does not depend on parameter t. Moreover, a large number of crashes, e.g., $n/3$, increases the message complexity by polynomial factor, comparing to the executions without failures.

We now show how to solve the gossip task in the presence of crash failures, in constant number of rounds and with $O(n + f^{1+\varepsilon})$ message complexity, for any given $\varepsilon > 0$. Our algorithm GOSCRASH(ε) is composed of two parts. Part I (see Figure 1) attempts to solve the gossip using a small number $2n^{1-\varepsilon/6}$ of leaders. It uses $O(n)$ messages, independently of the number of failures. If most of the leaders are non-crashed, precisely $f < n^{1-\varepsilon/3}$, after this part the gossip is completed and all processors are informed. Otherwise, all processors that are uninformed after Part I perform Part II (see Figure 2), which costs additional $O(1)$ rounds and $O(f^{1+\varepsilon})$ messages in total.

Algorithm initialization and control. For a given constant parameter $0 < \varepsilon \leq 1$, let $k = \lceil \frac{6}{\varepsilon} \rceil$ and $s = \max\{2, \lceil n^{\varepsilon/6} \rceil\}$. We define L (the set of leaders) to be the set of the first $\lceil 2n/s \rceil$ processors. Recall that $\mathcal{P}$ stands for the set of all processors. Each processor first runs Part I of the algorithm. If, after Part I, it is still not informed then it executes Part II. Otherwise, it waits during the period corresponding to the execution of Part II, and it only replies to all messages received during this period (by sending back all its local data as described in Section 3).

Part I. In this part we first run $k + 1$ gathering *Phases*, parameterized by $i = 0, \ldots, k$, in order to gather the rumors by the leaders, and then we perform $k + 1$ informing *Phases*, parameterized by $i = 0, \ldots, k$, in order to spread gathered information from the leaders to all non-faulty processors. The processes of gathering and informing are symmetric to each other, in the sense that they both use the same communication pattern and the only difference is that in the gathering process the goal is to request and get the answer, while in the informing part the aim is to send the data and then get the confirmation. Therefore we give a pseudo-code for a *generic phase*, see Figure 1, pointing our clearly all the places where both processes differ, that is, where either *unknown* processors (in gathering phases) or *uninformed* processors (in informing phases) are considered. Parameter i is responsible for limiting the number of requests sent during *Phase(i)*; more precisely, s^i is the upper bound on the number of requests arriving at a single processor. Intuitively, we start with a

Generic *Phase(i)* **(code for processor p):**   *% a generic phase can be either*
                                                       gathering or informing

1. Run AdaptiveMixing($L, 6, s$)
2. If there are at most $8n/s^i$ values *unknown* in $Rumors_p$ (in gathering phase) or
   $Informed_p$ (in informing phase), set $Active_p[p] = active$ and reset the rest of the
   array $Active_p$. If not, reset the whole array $Active_p$
3. Run AdaptiveMixing($L, 6, s$)
4. If $Active_p[p] = active$ and there are more than $|L|/2$ values *active* in $Active_p$, set
   $Active_p[p] = active$ and reset the rest of the array $Active_p$. If not, reset the whole
   array $Active_p$
5. Run AdaptiveMixing($L, 6, s$)
6. If $Active_p[p] = active$ and there are more than $|L|/2$ values *active* in $Active_p$, run
   DistributedRequest(L, s, s^i), requesting *unknown* neighbors (in gathering phase)
   or *uninformed* neighbors (in informing phase)
7. After receiving any replies, set $Rumor_p[q] = faulty$ for every unknown processor
   q requested in the previous line

Algorithm GOSCRASH, **Part I:**

− For $i := 0$ to k run gathering *Phase(i)*
− For $i := 0$ to k run informing *Phase(i)*

Fig. 1. Algorithm GOSCRASH, Part I

small number of requests, and increase this number gradually with the consecutive phases in order to assure that each processor will be asked eventually by
some other processor.

We briefly describe a gathering *Phase(i)*; an informing phase—as we argued—
is analogous. In line (1) the leaders exchange their knowledge running Adaptive-
Mixing($L, 6, s$). Any leader that knows enough rumors, that is all but at most
$8n/s^i$, considers itself active in line (2). Only an active processor will have a
chance to send requests later in line (6). In lines (3) to (5), every active leader
perform two additional AdaptiveMixing($L, 6, s$), in order to check if it has sufficiently many leaders (at least $3n/s^{i-1}$) in distance $2k$, and to exchange its
knowledge with other leaders with this property. The reason why it performs
adaptive mixing twice is that the information exchange between two such leaders is in practice made via some intermediate leader, which is in distance $2k$ from
both of them. In line (6) only the leaders that in both predeceasing runs of adaptive mixing (lines (3) and (5)) had at least $3n/s^{i-1}$ leaders in distance at most
$2k$ perform DistributedRequest(L, s, s^i). This protocol guarantees that any two
requesting leaders exchanged their knowledge while executing lines (3) to (5).
As we will show in the analysis, this also gives a desired upper bound on the
number of requested processors, and therefore on the total number of requests
(contributing substantially to the message complexity). On the other hand, the
property of subroutine DistributedRequest(L, s, s^i) assures that at least $1/s$ fraction of rumors that are unknown to active leaders does not receive any request
from them, providing there are sufficiently many active leaders. Finally, every

---

Generic $Phase(i,j)$ **(code for processor p):**   % *a generic phase can be either*
gathering or informing

1. Run Mixing$(\mathcal{P}, s, s^i)$
2. If $(i = j)$ or there are at most $3n/s^{j-2}$ values *unknown* in $Rumors_\mathbf{p}$ (in gathering phase) or $Informed_\mathbf{p}$ (in informing phase), set $Active_\mathbf{p}[\mathbf{p}] = active$ and reset the rest of the array $Active_\mathbf{p}$. If not, reset the whole array $Active_\mathbf{p}$
3. Run Mixing$(\mathcal{P}, s, s^i)$
4. If $Active_\mathbf{p}[\mathbf{p}] = active$ and there are more than $3n/s^{i-1}$ values *active* in $Active_\mathbf{p}$, set $Active_\mathbf{p}[\mathbf{p}] = active$ and reset the rest of the array $Active_\mathbf{p}$. If not, reset the whole array $Active_\mathbf{p}$
5. Run Mixing$(\mathcal{P}, s, s^i)$
6. If $Active_\mathbf{p}[\mathbf{p}] = active$ and there are more than $3n/s^{i-1}$ values *active* in $Active_\mathbf{p}$, send requests to *unknown* neighbors (in gathering phase) or *uninformed* neighbors (in informing phase) in the (n, s, s^j)-communicator
7. After receiving any replies, process them and make updates; set $Rumor_\mathbf{p}[\mathbf{q}] = faulty$ for every unknown processor $\mathbf{q}$ requested in the previous line

$Epoch(i)$:

- For $j := i$ to k run gathering $Phase(i,j)$
- For $j := i$ to k run informing $Phase(i,j)$

Algorithm GOSCRASH, **Part II:**

- For $i := 1$ to k run $Epoch(i)$

Fig. 2. Algorithm GOSCRASH, Part II

processor that was requested in line (6) answers in line (7), and therefore the number of unknown rumors to the active leaders decreases by fraction $1/s$ (again, providing there are sufficiently many active leaders).

Part II. Part II contains k *Epochs*, each being a slightly modified version of Part I, handling a different range of the number of failures. The main difference from Part I is that different graphs for mixing and requests are used, due to the fact that subsequent epochs handle larger and larger number of crashes, trading them for the increasing communication cost. More precisely, we will show that for each i, $Epoch(i)$ costs $O(n^{1+\varepsilon/3})$ messages, and successfully solves gossip whenever the number of correct processors is at least $6n/s^{i-1}$. In each $Epoch$, consecutive *Phases* work analogously to *Phases* in Part I, with the similar role of corresponding lines in the pseudo-code; therefore we skip an informal description and refer directly to Figure 2 for details.

4.1   Analysis of Algorithm GOSCRASH

Correctness of the algorithm follows from the fact that in the first line of $Epoch(k)$ of Part II, uninformed processors send messages to all their neighbors in $(n, s, n-1)$-communicator (which is a complete graph), and receive the answers. After this line all processors are informed.

Time complexity is a constant, which can be seen directly from the construction: k is a constant, each used subroutine lasts $O(1)$ rounds, and each line of the code of Part I and Part II lasts a constant number of rounds. We now analyze the message complexity. The following lemmas describe the progress and the message complexity of the algorithm after Part I and Part II.

Lemma 1. *If $f \leq n^{1-\varepsilon/3}$ then after Part I all non-faulty processors are informed.*

Lemma 2. *The number of messages sent during Part I is $O(n)$.*

Lemma 3. *If there are at least $6n/s^{i-1}$ non-faulty processors at the end of $Epoch(i)$ of Part II, then all of them are informed by that time.*

Lemma 4. *Each epoch of Part II contributes $O(n^{1+\varepsilon/3})$ to the message complexity.*

Lemma 5. *The number of messages sent during Part II is $O(f^{1+\varepsilon})$.*

Combining Lemmas 2 and 5 we obtain the final result.

Theorem 5. *Each crash failure contributes $O(f^\varepsilon)$ to the message complexity of algorithm* GOSCRASH.

5   Omission and Authenticated Byzantine Failures

Since an omission-faulty processor may, for example, omit all messages starting from some given round, omission failures are at least as hard to handle as crashes. In this section we prove that from the point of view of the gossip they are *substantially* more severe. In particular, each omission-faulty processor contributes $\Theta(t)$ to the message complexity of the gossip problem. The following lower bound holds for *all* t-omission-reliable gossip algorithms.

Theorem 6. *Every t-omission-resilient gossip algorithm has message complexity $\Omega(n + ft)$, that is, each faulty processor contributes $\Omega(t)$.*

We present an algorithm, called GOSOMISSION, based on the generic framework described in Section 3. It uses subroutines DistributedRequest and AdaptiveMixing. The main difference between this algorithm and algorithm GOSCRASH is that in case of omission failures it might be not enough to send a request once to every processor. The lack of answer might as well indicate that the sender is faulty, not necessarily the receiver as it was for crashes. Thus in order to confirm that some processor is faulty, at least $t + 1$ messages must be sent to it, each by different processor. Let L be the set of the first $2n^{\frac{5}{6}}$ processors, T be the set of the first $\min\{3t + 1, n\}$ processors, and $\mathcal{P}$ be the set of all processors. Figure 3 presents the pseudo-code of the algorithm. A detailed description and the analysis are deferred to the full version of the paper.

Theorem 7. GOSOMISSION *is a constant-time omission-resilient gossip algorithm with message complexity $O(n + ft)$, that is, $O(t)$ per each faulty processor.*

Using the simulation from [15], our algorithm can be adapted to tolerate authenticated Byzantine faults with the same asymptotic time and message complexity.

1. Run DistributedRequest($L, n^{\frac{1}{6}}, 8$)
2. Run AdaptiveMixing($L, n^{\frac{1}{6}}, n^{\frac{1}{6}}$)
3. Run DistributedRequest($L, n^{\frac{1}{6}}, 8$)
4. Run AdaptiveMixing($\mathcal{P}, 6, n^{\frac{1}{3}}$); a processor that knows more than $n - 2n^{\frac{2}{3}}$ rumors only answers the requests
5. Each processor in T that knows at least $n - 4t$ rumors sends requests to all unknown processors; requested processors reply in the next round, and the answers are delivered in the second next round
6. Run DistributedRequest($L, n^{\frac{1}{6}}, 8$)
7. Run AdaptiveMixing($L, n^{\frac{1}{6}}, n^{\frac{1}{6}}$)
8. Run DistributedRequest($L, n^{\frac{1}{6}}, 8$)
9. Run AdaptiveMixing($\mathcal{P}, 6, n^{\frac{1}{3}}$); an informed processor only answers the requests
10. Finalizing phase: every uninformed processor sends requests to all processors in T; requested processors reply in the next round, and the answers are delivered in the second next round

Fig. 3. Algorithm GOSOMISSION

6   Byzantine Failures

From the message complexity point of view, the Byzantine failures are indeed the most severe failures among the considered ones.

Theorem 8. *Every potentially-Byzantine processor contributes $\Omega(n)$ to the message complexity of a t-Byzantine-resilient gossip algorithm.*

The proof of Theorem 8 is deferred to the full version of the paper. On the other hand, the matching upper bound was established in [8].

Theorem 9. [8]   *There is a constant-time t-Byzantine-resilient gossip algorithm for which each potential Byzantine failure results in additional $O(n)$ messages, for every $0 < t < n$.*

7   Conclusions and Applications

In this paper we analyzed the impact of different kinds of failures to the message complexity of a constant-time gossip problem. In particular we showed that crashes cost more messages than non-faulty processors, however still polynomially less than more severe types of failures like omissions and (authenticated) Byzantine. There are several additional properties of the gossip algorithms designed in this paper, apart that they are fast, fault-tolerant and generate minimum required number of messages. The algorithms designed to handle crashes and omissions also provide to each non-faulty processor some extra information about each faulty processor: its rumor or a special value *faulty*. The extra information provided by the algorithm for authenticated Byzantine failures is slightly weaker: a message sent by the faulty processor at some point of the execution or a special value *faulty*.

There are several open questions related to the efficient fault-tolerant gossip. A tradeoff between time and message complexity in the model with crash failures is one of the intriguing problems (compare this work with [3,4]). Another open direction is to analyze fast fault-tolerant gossip in general network topologies.

References

1. Attiya, H., Welch, J.: Distributed Computing. John Willey & Sons, West Sussex, England (2004)
2. Capalbo, M.R., Reingold, O., Vadhan, S.P., Wigderson, A.: Randomness conductors and constant-degree lossless expanders. In: Proc. of 34th ACM Symposium on Theory of Computing (STOC), pp. 659–668 (2002)
3. Chlebus, B.S., Kowalski, D.R.: Robust gossiping with an application to consensus. Journal of Computer and System Sciences 72, 1262–1281 (2006)
4. Chlebus, B.S., Kowalski, D.R.: Time and communication efficient consensus for crash failures. In: Dolev, S. (ed.) DISC 2006. LNCS, vol. 4167, pp. 314–328. Springer, Heidelberg (2006)
5. Chlebus, B.S., Kowalski, D.R., Rokicki, M.A.: Adversarial queuing on the multiple-access channel. In: Proc. of 25th ACM Symposium on Principles of Distributed Computing (PODC), pp. 92–101 (2006)
6. Chlebus, B.S., Kowalski, D.R., Shvartsman, A.A.: Collective asynchronous reading with polylogarithmic worst-case overhead. In: Proc. of 36th ACM Symposium on Theory of Computing (STOC), pp. 321–330 (2004)
7. Diks, K., Pelc, A.: Optimal adaptive broadcasting with a bounded fraction of faulty nodes. Algorithmica 28(1), 37–50 (2000)
8. Dolev, D., Reischuk, R.: Bounds on information exchange for Byzantine Agreement. Journal of ACM 32(1), 191–204 (1985)
9. Fischer, M., Lynch, N.: A lower bound for the time to assure interactive consistency. Information Processing Letters 14(4), 183–186 (1982)
10. Fujita, S., Yamashita, M.: Optimal group gossiping in hypercubes under circuit switching model. SIAM J. on Computing 25(5), 1045–1060 (1996)
11. Galil, Z., Mayer, A., Yung, M.: Resolving message complexity of Byzantine agreement and beyond. In: Proc. of 36th IEEE Symposium on Foundations of Computer Science (FOCS), pp. 724–733 (1995)
12. Georgiou, C., Kowalski, D.R., Shvartsman, A.A.: Efficient gossip and robust distributed computation. In: Fich, F.E. (ed.) DISC 2003. LNCS, vol. 2848, pp. 224–238. Springer, Heidelberg (2003)
13. Hromkovic, J., Klasing, R., Pelc, A., Ruzicka, P., Unger, W.: Dissemination of information in communication networks: broadcasting, gossiping, leader election, and fault-tolerance. In: Theoretical Computer Science. EATCS Series. Springer, Heidelberg (2005)
14. Lynch, N.: Distributed Algorithms. Morgan Kaufmann, San Francisco (1996)
15. Neiger, G., Toueg, S.: Automatically increasing the fault-tolerance of distributed systems. Journal of Algorithms 11, 374–419 (1990)

Output Stability Versus Time Till Output

(Extended Abstract)

Shay Kutten[1],[*] and Toshimitsu Masuzawa[2]

[1] Dept. of Industrial Engineering & Management, The Technion, Haifa 32000, Israel
[2] Graduate School of Information Science and Technology, Osaka University, Japan

Abstract. Consider a network whose inputs change rapidly, or are subject to frequent faults. This is expected often to be the case in the foreseen huge sensor networks. Suppose, that an algorithm is required to output the majority value of the inputs. To address such networks, it is desirable to be able to stabilize the output fast, and to give guarantees on the outputs even before stabilization, even if additional changes occur.

We bound the *instability* of the outputs (the number of times the output changes) of majority consensus algorithms even before the final stabilization. We show that the instability can be traded off with their *time adaptvity* (how fast they are required to stabilize the output if f faults occurred). First, for the extreme point of the trade-off, we achieve instability that is optimal for the class of algorithms that are optimal in their output time adaptivity. This is done for various known versions of majority consensus problem. The optimal instability for this case is $\Omega(\log f)$ and is shown to be $O(\log f)$ for most versions and $O(\log n)$ in some cases. Previous such algorithms did not have such a guarantee on the behaviour of the output before its final stabilization (and their instability was $\Omega(n)$). We also explain how to adapt the results for other points in the trade off.

The output stabilization in previous algorithms was adaptive only if the faults ceased for $O(\mathbf{Diam})$ time. An additional result in this paper uses adaptations of some previous tools, as well as the new tools developed here for bounding the instability, in order to remove this limitation that is undesirable when changes are frequent.

1 Introduction

Consider an action that is to be taken according to some value measured by sensors composing a network. The measurements at some of the sensors may be different (possibly, because of measurements inaccuracies, or because of faults). To overcome that, the network computes a majority consensus. An outside action may be taken according to this consensus. For example, travelers in the woods may consult the sensor near them to decide whether to unfold a tent, since a

---

[*] This research was supported in part by a grant for research on sensor networks from the Israeli Ministry of Science and Technology.

A. Pelc (Ed.): DISC 2007, LNCS 4731, pp. 343–357, 2007.

storm is coming, or whether to fold the tent and continue the walk in the case that the rain has gone.

A fast answer is sometimes crucial. However, if one insists that a warning always come as fast as possible, then some false warnings are unavoidable. For example, if all the near-by sensors predict a storm, then the initial answer must be that a storm is about to break. If those near by sensors are a small minority, then the answer changes eventually. The false alarm may have consumed some resources (e.g., the effort of unfolding and then re-folding). An external system using the output may even act incorrectly if the output changes too frequently. For example, various machines, if turned on and off too often, would break.

Note, that changes in the output may be unavoidable even if the travelers are willing to wait. The inputs of the sensors may change, for example, when a chance of a storm is indeed increasing. Moreover, the inputs change not all at the same time. Hence, at some point, the travelers should decide that they are willing to act upon the best answer the network can give them at present.

The stability (or instability) of the output for a distributed consensus was discussed in [1,2]. It is the number of times the output may change when the input changes. The output time complexity, or the output stabilization time, in self stabilizing systems[1], is the time it takes for the system to start outputting the correct and final output, following input changes (e.g. introduced by faults). These two measures of complexity seem, intuitively, related. (For example, the number of changes in the output of a node cannot be larger than the time complexity). Still, they were discussed only separately in the literature. The stability problem was studied also outside the setting of distributed systems, in the context of mechanical engineering, see e.g. [11].

Note, that instability cannot be avoided altogether. In every setting of the Consensus problem, some inputs dictate a certain output value, while some others dictate a different one. For any other set of inputs, the algorithm enjoys the freedom to decide the value to output. In [1], they explore how the stability is increased (the instability is decreased) as a function of this freedom.

In this paper, we explore the way the freedom along another dimension influences the stability. In the Majority Consensus problem, the output value must be that of the majority (as opposed to cases studied in [1]). However, (a different kind of) freedom exists in this system too: if there are changes in the inputs of some f nodes (or any other changes by f state faults), then the output is permitted to be incorrect (i.e., different than the majority of the inputs) for some finite time. We note that allowing such a freedom is unavoidable in distributed systems where inputs may change. This is because it takes some time for a changed input in one node to be communicated to the other nodes. Such a freedom is especially assumed in the context of self stabilization [18] (except for the case of a very limited set of tasks [8] that does not include the task of Consensus).

In optimal *time adaptive* systems [16,12], this unavoidable output freedom is restricted to the unavoidable duration, as a function of the number of faults. For

---

[1] Self stabilization and stability are two different notions. The use of both may be confusing, but we chose not to change terms that are common in the literature.

Majority Consensus, if f faults occur, the output is required to *stabilize* to the correct final value in $O(f)$ time.

Definition 1. *Assume, that the outputs of all the network nodes is stable (will not change unless the inputs are changed) at some time t_0. Assume further, that a set of faults and changes occur at some time $t_f > t_0$. The instability of an algorithm is the number of times the output will change in the worst case starting from t_f and until the output eventually stabilizes (if it ever does) or until further faults or input changes occur.*

Several time adaptive algorithms exist for the Persistent Value Problem [16,12] and the Majority Consensus with Persistence Problem [21]. For these algorithms, the instability for an optimal time adaptive algorithm was $\Omega(n)$. This means that the output of a node could change every time unit until the final stabilization. Some algorithms give (different kinds of) guarantees for outputs even before the final stabilization, but these guarantees apply only for non- faulty nodes, and the algorithms were not time adaptive. See, e.g. [15]. Self stabilizing algorithms in general have been criticized for not giving much guarantee for the value of the outputs before stabilization. This is especially problematic in networks that rarely stabilize. Hence, reducing the instability (especially of faulty nodes) below $O(n)$ can be viewed as a step in the right direction for such network. Another result the can be obtained using our methods for and with fast changing networks as a motivation, is time adaptivity even when additional faults occur before stabilization.

Main results: We address the problems of (One Time) Majority Consensus, Persistent Value (and the related "Majority Consensus with Persistence"), and Repeated Majority Consensus. On the negative side, it is easy to show that no algorithm for these problems that is asymptotically optimal in its time adaptivity can have instability that is better than $\Omega(\log f)$. This is the case even if the algorithm is not required to self stabilize. We then present algorithms that both have optimal time adaptivity and have $O(\log f)$ instability for non-faulty nodes, and $O(\log f)$ (for some cases) or $O(\log n)$ (for other cases) for faulty nodes. That is, our algorithms are asymptotically optimal in their output stability for the class of optimal time adaptive algorithms. We then show how to generalize the results, such that if the time complexity is allowed to grow beyond $O(f)$, the instability shrinks below $\Omega(\log f)$. The instability of our algorithms in most cases is adaptive too, that is, it does not depend on n, but only on f.

Additional results: The proofs of the following additional results are deferred because of space considerations, and do not appear in this extended abstract. While previous algorithms for the Persistent Value Problem self stabilized in any case (as do the algorithms in the current paper), they were time adaptive only when the faults occurred in one batch at a time, and no additional faults occurred until the eventual full state stabilization (not just until output stabilization). This happens in $\Omega(n)$ time. Our results can be proved for a more realistic model, where faults can occur at any time, and not just in batches.

As tools for the our algorithms, we had to design a building block broadcast module (Protocol ABC) that is both error confined ([15]) and time adaptive ([12]). In contrast, the error confined tool of [15] was not time adaptive, while the time adaptive tool of [12,19] was not error confined. We also had to add to the tool a snap stabilizing (see [8]) action we term `Cancel`.

2   Model, Definitions, and Some Very Related Work

The system is modeled as a fixed undirected connected graph $G = (V, E)$, where $|V| = n$. Nodes represent processors and edges represent bi-directional communication links. Every node has a unique identity ID that cannot be changed by faults. For the sake of this extended abstract, we assume that the network is synchronous, even though methods to translate protocols such as ours to asynchronous networks are known, such as in [19,21]. The distance between two nodes $u, v \in V$, denoted $\mathbf{dist}(u, v)$, is the minimum number of edges in a path connecting them. Given a node $v \in V$, let $\mathtt{Ball}_v(r) = \{u \in V \mid \mathbf{dist}(v, u) \leq r\}$ be the *ball* of radius r around v. The radius of the network around a node v, denoted $\mathbf{Radius}_v$, is the minimal r such that $\mathtt{Ball}_v(r) = V$. $\mathbf{RRadius}_v$ is the first power of 2 larger than or equal to $\mathbf{Radius}_v$. $\mathbf{Diam}$ (the diameter) is the maximum over all $v \in V$ of $\mathbf{Radius}_v$. For the purpose of saving in memory only, we assume that the diamter is bounded by $Max\mathbf{Diam}$. For simplicity of exposition, we assume often that $\mathbf{RRadius}_v = \mathbf{Radius}_v$. In the extended abstract, we assume that the topology of the network is known (this assumption is lifted in the full paper, see a short discussion in Section 6 below).

Definition 2. *A* state corrupting fault *is an action that alters the state arbitrarily in some subset of nodes. We terms these node* faulty.

For simplicity, we assume that after a fault, each node is in a legal *local* state (otherwise, the node can detect the fault). Our approach in modeling faults is similar to the one in [9,22]. The model of state-corrupting faults is implicit in the work of Dijkstra about *self stabilization* [18]: put in our terminology, a system is called *self-stabilizing* if after some arbitrary state-corrupting faults occur (possibly, hitting all nodes) the system starts behaving correctly eventually. (Issues arising from different definitions of self stabilization are discussed in [10]). See the full paper for more detailed definitions.

We find it convenient to define two sets $\Pi_{state}, \Pi_{output}$ of correct behaviors. For defining Π_{output}, we assume that every node has a part of its state called the *output*. Moreover, only assignment to this variable are external actions of the protocol. Hence, only such actions show in *behaviors* in this case. The specific legal behavior Π_{output} is given in the definition of every problem to be solved. We say that Π_{output} determines *output stabilization*.

A protocol is *time adaptive* for the output stabilization if the system starts behaving correctly after a time which depends only on f, the number of faults (rather than on n). In other words, the output stabilization time is $O(g(f))$ for some function $g(f)$. The problems we solve is defined next.

Definition 3. *The* One Time Majority Consensus *problem: Every node has an* input *that can be changed only once and only by the environment and an* output *variable read by the environment. (In the extended abstract, we assume that b is binary). For every node, it is required that,*
Eventual Agreement- *the output stabilizes to the majority value of the inputs eventually.*

To unify the discussion, we consider the majority value as the correct one, and nodes with the minority input as faulty. A second problem- the Persistent Value Problem, is defined below.

Definition 4. *The* Persistent Value *problem [16,12] (somewhat rephrased): A value b was given* exactly once *by the environment to every node (the same b to all the nodes) before the faults started. (In the extended abstract, we assume that b is binary). This value was stored in each node in a storage variable. To be compatible with previous papers dealing with the persistent value problem, we name this storage variable the* input *variable. This (and every other) variable can be changed by faults, or by the node. Every node also has an* output *variable read by the environment. It is required that:*
Persistence: *it is required that both the output and the input of every node stabilize to b eventually.*

We note that persistence implies eventual agreement. The algorithm we present here solves only the requirements for the output, while the requirement for the *input* variable is solved by the Input Correction Module taken from [12] (the current algorithm and the above module are executed as co-routines). We note that we termed the storage variable the *input* since that storage variable is the input for the algorithm module designed in the current paper (though it may be changed by the other module, the one taken from [12]). The properties of the Input Correction Module are listed in Subsection 5.2.

Note, that designing the Output Stabilization Module for the Persistent Value problem is a harder task than designing the One Time Majority Consensus, since our algorithm must take into account the fact that its input may be changed not only by the environment (at some time t_f the faults occur), but also (later) by the Input Correction Module.

In *Repeated Majority Consensus*, changes may continue to occur. The time and the number of changes are counted from the last time the network was stable.

Additional very related work: The distinction between output stabilization and state stabilization is used and discussed in a number of papers [4,16,12,28,3,5]. Fast stabilization of output variables has been demonstrated in a number of algorithms [7,6,24,25,16,17,26,19,5] and some general methods to achieve time adaptivity [12,26]. In [20], the importance of output stability for practical Internet protocols was emphasized and obtained using time adaptivity methods.

3   Lower Bound

We establish a lower bound for the instability of a protocol given that the output of the protocol is required to stabilize (to the correct value) as fast as possible (asymptotically). The requirement about the fast output stabilization is used heavily in the proof. Furthermore, we see in this section that relaxing this requirement leads to weakening the lower bounds. This establishes the lower bound side of the trade off between output time and instability. We note that the lower bound holds even for synchronous networks, and even for algorithms that are not required to self stabilize.

Theorem 1. *The instability of any deterministic asymptotically optimal time adaptive protocol for the Persistent Value Problem, or for the Majority Consensus Problem, is $\Omega(\log f)$.*

The formal proof are deferred to the full paper. Informally, it considers a line network with v as the first node in the line. In the first, say, X time units, v receives only *votes* (broadcasts of input values) from the nearest X nodes. If all of them vote some value b_1, then v cannot distinguish between this case and the case that $f = 0$. To be time adaptive, v must start outputting b_1 within some constant time C. (We then choose $X = C$). Next, assume that out of the C^2 closest to v, the majority ($C^2 - C$) vote b_0. Now, v must change its output to b_0 to be time adaptive (since it may be the case that $f = C$). Next, we consider the C^3 nodes closest to v. This argument is carried forward to show $\Omega(\log f)$.

A problem with initial algorithmic ideas: At first glance, the proof of the lower bound seems to suggest an algorithm: (1) collect *votes* (broadcasted input values of the other nodes), (2) after changing the output, do not change the output again, before the number of votes received is grows by a factor of some C. This would have implied a logarithmic instability in the case that no vote may change or may be corrupted by a fault. Unfortunately, it is possible that votes arriving at v (by broadcasts) cease to arrive, or change their value. This can be caused by faults at the sources of such votes, or at nodes on the route from them to v, or by the action of the algorithm that corrects the faults.

4   A Building Block: Error-Confined and Adaptive Broadcast

As mentioned at the end of Section 3, changes in a vote received at v increase the instability. Some such changes cannot be avoided, since they represent real changes in the inputs. We use a tool that avoids *some* changes- informally, it allows a node s to broadcast its input such that if s and a recipient v are not faulty, no node on the way from s to v can change the value received at v (though the protocol may fail to deliver any value sometimes). This is termed an *error confined* broadcast in [15]. See the exact properties of this protocol,

ABC (*Adaptive Broadcast with Confinement*, in Theorem 2 (the definitions of the broadcast task and of error confinement appear in the appendix).

As compared in "Additional Results" above, these properties of ABC are a combination of those of the tools used in previous papers [16,12,21,8]. Still, if the algorithms of those papers are modified to use our tool, instead of their own tools, their instabilities would still be high. However, the ABC tool proved useful for our algorithms and may prove useful by itself in the future.

Definition 5. *The value of the broadcast of a node s received in a node v is authentic if it was indeed communicated by s (rather than a value resulting from a corruption in some channel or some intermediate node) $2\mathbf{dist}(v,s)$ time earlier. Operation* Cancel *performed by v on the ABC of s causes the value of s received at v to become undefined ($\bot$). Moreover, if v starts again receiving s's broadcast, then the value received is authentic, and was broadcast by s after the last* Cancel *of v (unless v itself suffered another fault meanwhile). (The motivation for this operation is similar to that of* snap stabilization. *[8]).*

The detailed description of protocol ABC and the proof of the following theorem are deferred to the full paper. They do not use cryptographic assumptions (but alternative implementations that do use cryptographic assumptions may save in communication complexity).

Theorem 2. *Consider any node v. Let t_f be the last time the faults occurred. Let t_b be the time that s started broadcasting a value b. Finally, let $t_{\mathtt{Cancel}}$ be either the last time v performed* Cancel *on the broadcast of s, or the last time that the value of the broadcast of s at v became $\bot$ (whichever came later). Below, if some of these times t_i is undefined, then $\max\{t_i, t_j, t_k\} = \max\{t_j, t_k\}$.*

1. Speed: *As long as the value b broadcast by the source node s does not change, Protocol ABC of s at v outputs b starting at time $\max\{t_f, t_b, t_{\mathtt{Cancel}}\} + 2\mathbf{dist}(s, v)$.*
2. Time adaptivity: *(even for faulty nodes): At any time t such that $t \geq \max\{t_f + f, t_{\mathtt{Cancel}}\}$, the output value (for s's broadcast) is either authentic or is undefined (equal to $\bot$).*
3. Error Confinement *(for non-faulty nodes): Let $t_{f(v)}$ be the last time that a fault hit node v. Assume, that the vote of some s changed in v **from** some $b \neq \bot$ after time $t_{f(v)}$. Then, it first changes to $\bot$. In addition, starting from that time, the output value (for s's broadcast in v) is either authentic or is $\bot$. Finally, if the value does become authentic (after changing first to $\bot$ then is stays authentic, unless additional faults occur.*

5   Instability Upper Bounds

Theorem 3. *There exists a self stabilizing protocol for Majority Consensus, such that if the local states of f of the nodes are changed arbitrarily, then*

- *Time Adaptivity: The output values are restored everywhere in $O(f)$ time;*
- *Instability: The instability in each process is $O(\log f)$.*

Theorem 4. *There exists a protocol for the Persistent Value Problem such that if the local states of $f < n/2$ of the nodes are changed arbitrarily, then Time Adaptivity is achieved, and, in addition,*

- *Instability: The instability is $O(\log f)$ for non- faulty nodes and $O(\log n)$, for faulty nodes .*
- *Complete state stabilization occurs in $O(\mathbf{Diam})$ time units.*
- *There is no change in the input of any correct process.*

Note, that the requirement that $f < n/2$ in the statement of Theorem 4 is required by the Input Correction Module of [12], to ensure persistence (not stability, nor stabilization). We note that these are the best possible output- and state-stabilization times even when the instability is allowed to be higher [12]. However, if the time is allowed to be higher then the instability can be smaller. The protocols claimed in the theorems are presented in two subsections below.

5.1 Stable Adaptive Majority Algorithm (Theorem 3)

The algorithm for this easier problem is given in figure 1. Its informal description is given in the full paper. In short, each node broadcasts (using ABC) its input and collects the values broadcasted by the others. The node outputs the majority of the votes it receives, but only from a ball of radius Scanned around

Broadcast (using algorithm ABC) input_v;
Receive every arriving broadcast of other nodes;   (* possibly, $\perp$ *)

Let NearestUndef $= \min\{\text{dist}(s, v) \mid \text{value}_v[s] = \perp\}$;
                              (* $\text{value}_v[s]$ is s's vote as received in v *)
If NearestUndef $\neq$ Undefined then   (* Received some $\perp$ *)
    Let Reduced $\leftarrow \max\{\text{integer } i | 2^i < \text{NearestUndef}\}$.   (* Reduce to exclude $\perp$ *)
    Set Majority to the majority value in $\text{Ball}_v(2^{\text{Scanned}})$;
    Suspects $\leftarrow \{w \in \text{Ball}_v(2^{\text{Scanned}}) \mid \perp \neq (\text{value}_v[w] \neq \text{Majority}$
    Wait $\leftarrow \min\{\text{Wait} - 1, |\text{Suspects}|\}$;   (* Delay reducing Scanned *)
    If Wait ≤ 0 and Reduced $<$ Scanned then   (* without violating adaptivity. *)
        Scanned $\leftarrow \min\{\text{Reduced, Scanned }\}$;
        Cancel the broadcast of every node outside $\text{Ball}_v(\text{Scanned})$;
        Wait $\leftarrow |\text{Ball}_v(2^{\text{Scanned}})|$.

If for every node u in $\text{Ball}_v(2^{\text{Scanned}+1})$ the arriving $\text{value}_v[s]$ is not $\perp$ then
    Scanned $\leftarrow \min\{\log \mathbf{RRadius}_v, \text{Scanned} + 1\}$;
    Wait $\leftarrow |\text{Ball}_v(2^{\text{Scanned}})|$;
    Cancel the broadcast of every node outside $\text{Ball}_v(2^{\text{Scanned}})$.

Set output to the majority value in $\text{Ball}_v(2^{\text{Scanned}})$.

Fig. 1. Stable Adaptive Majority Consensus Algorithm (with adaptive instability)

it. The algorithm decreases Scanned, carefully, to exclude votes it suspects their authenticity, and increases Scanned, carefully, when it guesses that votes in a larger ball are authentic. It is easy to demonstrate that changing the algorithm so that it would change Scanned more "drastically" (e.g. would restart from Scanned $= 0$ every time a vote changes) would either not be adaptive, or would have high instability, or both. For example, the event that some vote becomes $\perp$ can happen f times. Had the algorithms restarted to Scanned $= 0$ each time some vote became $\perp$, the instability could have grown to $\Omega(f)$.

Had there been only increases (the last "If" statement), it seems easy to prove the $O(\log n)$ upper bound (maybe also the $O(\log f)$). Bounding the number of decreases in the radius (the first "If" statement) is somewhat harder. Still harder, is bounding the number of decreases to be $O(\log f)$ rather than $O(\log n)$ even in a node v that is faulty. Intuitively, all the votes that a faulty node v "believes" it received, it may have not received actually (which means that they are not authentic in v), so the effect on the instability at v is as if there were n faults. The "wait" mechanism in the code is intended to allow non- authentic votes at v to disappear before decreasing Scanned. The node cannot wait too much, however, since this would have caused it not to be time adaptive. Hence, the node waits as much as possible given a lower bound (|Suspects|) it computes for the number of faults. This Wait method bounds the number of times Scanned is decreased, even in a faulty node.

Lemma 1. *The instability of the Stable Adaptive Majority Algorithm of Figure 1 is $O(\log f)$.*

The proof of the lemma is deferred to the full paper. We bring here only the most interesting case (that uses the Wait mechanism). This is the case that the value of Scanned is reduced at some time $\tau_0 < Cf$. The main reason this case is interesting, since this is the case that votes in v may not be authentic (they become either authentic or $\perp$ after $O(f)$ time). This can have an effect on v that is similar to a number of faults that is larger than f, which makes the proof of $O(\log f)$ instability harder.

Let v's output after the reduction be some b_1. By the selection of the size of Wait, the number of votes received at v for $\flat_1$ ($\neq b_1$) must be some $X_0 \leq Cf$.

Now, consider the next reduction at time τ_1, that flips the value of the output to $\flat_1$. The number of votes for $\flat_1$ may have increased by some X_1 nodes who were not counted among the X_0 above. (Some, or all of the old X_0 may have changed their vote too.) Note, that these X_1 nodes voted b_1 right after τ_0 (and not $\perp$, nor $\flat_1$). By Item 3 of Theorem 2, the votes of these X_1 nodes at τ_1 are authentic. Hence, their votes will not change, by the same theorem. If $X_1 > Cf$ then the next flipping reduction (to output b_1) is delayed Cf time, and there are no more changes in v's output, as shown above. Hence, $X_1 < Cf$.

Let us now consider the next flipping reduction (to output b_1) at τ_2. As in the previous argument, there may now be some new Y_2 nodes who did not support b_1 in the previous flipping reduction, but do support b_1 now, and $Y_2 < Cf$.

So far, we established that the number of supporters of b_1, as well as the number of supporters of $\flat_1$ are smaller than Cf. From the code, it is easy to see that the new value of Scanned is selected such that there are no $\perp$ voters in $\mathsf{Ball}_v(2^{\mathsf{Scanned}})$. Hence, at that point, Scanned $\leq 2Cf$. The number of additional reductions possible before the next increase is $O(\log f)$. The lemma then follows from the proof for the increases in the value of Scanned (which follows immediately from the fact that Cancel is performed when the value of Scanned changes, and from Theorem 2; details are deferred to the full paper). The following lemma that bounds the "damage" of the Wait mechanism.

Lemma 2. *The Stable Adaptive Majority Algorithm of Fig. 1 is time adaptive.*

The proof of Lemma 2 bears similarities to those of [12,13]. The differences result from the following three mechanisms used in the current algorithm: (a) the algorithms in the previous paper outputs the majority of all the arriving votes, while here the algorithm outputs just those in a certain ball; (b) the current algorithm outputs the majority (in a ball) only when there are non- $\perp$ votes from all the nodes (in the ball); (c) the Wait here may cause v to wait before changing the output to that of the majority. Correspondingly, the current proof needs to show the following: (a) the radius of the ball indeed reaches a size that is larger than $2f$ fast enough (so the majority of the votes in the radius are of correct nodes); (b) the radius of the ball is not too large (since otherwise, authentic votes from all the nodes it in may not be received fast enough; (c) the Wait mechanism does not delay the final output longer than $O(f)$. The proof is deferred to the full paper. Intuitively, within $O(f)$ time all the non-authentic votes disappear by Theorem 2 and authentic votes arrive from all the nodes in the ball of radius $O(f)$ around v. If Scanned starts "small" after the faults, then it can be increased to more than $O(2f+1)$, since the $\perp$ values disappear from that ball in $O(f)$ time. More than f authentic votes in that ball imply a correct output. If Scanned starts large, when the non- authentic votes disappear (in $O(f)$ time) the majority it receives is correct. If v receives "many" non- $\perp$ votes, then the output is correct. Otherwise, $\mathsf{Scanned}_v$ is reduced. Finally, when non- authentic votes disappear, $|\mathsf{Suspects}| \leq f$ and hence, Wait $\leq f$.

5.2   Stable Time Adaptive Self Stabilized Persistent Value

(The proof of Theorem 4): We now move to deal with problems where the input may change not just as a result of faults. In particular, solutions for the the Persistent Value Problem have two modules. One, the Input Correction module, maintains (and changes) the storage (*input*) value (see Definition 4). Here, we only replace the second module- the Output Stabilization Module. The latter uses the above storage value as its input. We assume the use of the Input Correction Module introduced in [12]. The following is assumed for that Module (and proven in [12], given a module that stabilizes the output in $O(f)$ time): If $f < n/2$ then the Input Correction Module never changes the value of a non-faulty node. It changes the value of an incorrect node at most twice: the last of these changes is from the incorrect value to the correct one.

The algorithm presented in this section is a modification of the algorithm of Figure 1. Recall, that each decrease in Scanned in that algorithm may cause the output to change. An additional down side to decreasing Scanned is that if $|\texttt{Ball}_v(2^{\mathsf{Scanned}})|$ becomes smaller than $2f$, then the output may be incorrect (since the majority in the ball may be the faulty nodes) late after the algorithm was supposed to stabilize. This is why the algorithm of Figure 1 would not have been adaptive had it been used for the Persistent Value Problem. (Recall, that here a vote arriving at v may become $\bot$, and then change value, after $\Omega(n)$ time; we do not want that to cause a reduction in Scanned).

The new algorithm does not cut the value of Scanned every time an arriving broadcast changes its value. Instead, Scanned is reduced only when a constant fraction of the nodes in the ball change their mind. In addition, the algorithm attempts to output in the new ball the same value it outputted the previous time (if any) it used for that ball. Only if a significant number of votes changed in the new ball (from that last time) the output is not the output used the last time that new ball was used. This reduces the instability. Additional informal explanations, as well of the proofs of the following claim, are deferred to the full paper. The pseudo code appears in Figure 2.

Claim. For any i, the second time (after the faults ended, and after the first increase in Scanned after the faults) that Scanned $= i + 1$, all the votes received at v are authentic.

Lemma 3. *If each input changes only a constant number of times (starting from some time t) in the Stable Persistent Value Algorithm, then the number of times Scanned $\neq i$ gets assigned the value i is bounded by a constant.*

Proof Sketch: First, we claim that the number of times Scanned can be reduced from some $i + 1$ to i is bounded by a constant. Let s be the node such that the change in its ABC broadcast vote caused v to cut Scanned from $i + 1$ to i. First consider the case that the changed vote had not been authentic. By Claim 5.2, this can happen at most twice per value of Scanned.

Now, assume that Scanned is reduced because the number of authentic votes for **OldOutput**$(i + 1)$ is below $\frac{1}{4}|\texttt{Ball}_v(2^{i+1})|$ (or below $\frac{1}{4}|\texttt{Ball}_v(\mathbf{RRadius})|$).

The first sub-case is when Scanned $< \log \mathbf{RRadius}_v$. The first time Scanned is reduced from $i + 1$ after the faults, the value of **OldOutput**$(i + 1)$ could be one that was set by the adversary (remember the setting of self stabilization). However, in later times this value is one that was set by the algorithm, since we are computing the instability at a period when there are no additional faults. Hence, and by Claim 5.2, every time (starting from the second time) Scanned $=$ is increased to $i + 1$, the real majority of the inputs in $\texttt{Ball}_v(2^{i+1})$ is the value assigned to **OldOutput**$(i + 1)$. This means that at the kth time Scanned is reduced from $i+1$ ($k \geq 3$), at least a quarter of the nodes in $\texttt{Ball}_v(2^{i+1})$ changed their input since the $(k - 1)th$ time. However, by the properties of the input correction module, a node can change its input at most twice after the faults (if it is a faulty node, otherwise, it cannot change its value at all). Hence, the number of times Scanned can be reduced from $i+1$ to i is a constant. The second sub-case is when Scanned is reduced from $\log \mathbf{RRadius}_v$ to $\log \mathbf{RRadius}_v - 1$. (The proof is similar to the proof of the previous sub-case.)

Now, consider the case that Scanned is set to i by an increase (and not by a reduction). To be increased again to i, the value of Scanned must first be reduced to $i - 1$, since a reduction is performed to a consecutive value. Thus, the proof follows from the proof for reductions.   ∎

Finally, notice that v may change its output only when it changes the value of Scanned. Since the number of different values for Scanned is $\log \mathbf{RRadius}$, this leads only to an instability of $O(\log \mathbf{RRadius})$ which is $O(\log n)$. By a somewhat more precise analysis we obtain the following improved result. In most of the cases, the proof of the following lemma resembles that of Lemma 3. The main difference is in the case that a decrease in Scanned is due to unauthentic votes that disappear. This can happen only at a faulty node v. A sketch of the proof of the next lemma, highlighting the differences between this proof and that of Lemma 3 is deferred to the full paper, together with the proof of Lemma 5 (which bears similarities to the proof of Lemma 2). Theorem 4 follows from the two lemmas bellow and from the assumptions on the Input Correction Module.

Lemma 4. *The instability of the algorithm of Figure 2 is $O(\log f)$ for a non-faulty node, and $O(\min\{\log n, f\})$ for a faulty nodes.*

Broadcast the **input** value and receive every arriving broadcast of other nodes
(*possibly, undefined $(\perp)$*).

Do while Scanned > 0 **and**

$\Big($ (Scanned $< \log \mathbf{RRadius}_v$

     and $NumVotes(\mathbf{OldOutput}(\text{Scanned}) < \frac{1}{4}|\mathbf{Ball}_v(2^{\text{Scanned}})|)$

  or

   (Scanned $= \log \mathbf{RRadius}_v$

     and $NumVotes(\mathbf{OldOutput}(\text{Scanned}) < \lfloor \frac{1}{2}|\mathbf{Ball}_v(2^{\text{Scanned}})|\rfloor + 1)$

  or

   $\mathbf{OldOutput}(\text{Scanned}) = \perp \Big)$

  $\mathbf{OldOutput}(\text{Scanned}) \leftarrow \perp$;

  Scanned $\leftarrow$ Scanned $- 1$;

  Cancel the broadcast of every node outside $\mathbf{Ball}_v(2^{\text{Scanned}})$.

If Scanned $= 0$ then $\mathbf{OldOutput}(\text{Scanned}) \leftarrow$ output $\leftarrow$ input;

else output $\leftarrow \mathbf{OldOutput}(\text{Scanned})$.

Let $i >$ Scanned be the smallest for which $\exists b \neq \perp |NumVotes(b) > \frac{1}{2}|\mathbf{Ball}_v(2^i)|$;

(* If i is not undefined then *) Scanned $\leftarrow i$;

Set output to the majority value in $\mathbf{Ball}_v(\text{Scanned})$;

$\mathbf{OldOutput}(\text{Scanned}) \leftarrow$ output;

Cancel the broadcast of every node outside $\mathbf{Ball}_v(2^{\text{Scanned}})$.

Fig. 2. Stable Persistent Value Algorithm: actions at node v. NumVotes(b) is the number of votes v is currently receiving by ABC from nodes in $\mathbf{Ball}_v(2^{\text{Scanned}})$ for the value b.

Lemma 5. *The Stable Persistent Value Algorithm Algorithm of Figure 2 is time adaptive.*

5.3 Repeated Faults, Majority Consensus with Persistence, and Repeated Majority Consensus

Previous algorithms for the Persistent Value problem assumed (for the sake of obtaining time adaptivity) that all the faults occurred in one batch, and another batch may occur only after full state stabilization. A useful property of the algorithm of Figure 2 is that this assumption is not necessary. Indeed, we did not use it in the proofs. Given that, it is not difficult to change that algorithm to solve the problem of Majority Consensus with Persistence, and using that solution to solve also the Repeated majority Consensus. We omit the changes required to solve these problems from the extended abstract.

6 Conclusion and Future Work

As claimed above, if the algorithms are allowed to be less adaptive, it is easy to change them to have a lower instability, to match the more generalized lower bound of Section 3.

In the extended abstract, we assumed that the topology of the network is known to every node in advance. To lift this assumption, a node needs to detect that some broadcasts it receives are claimed to be arriving from nodes that do not actually exist. We deffer this in the full paper.

We studied the instability for the case that the freedom was in the time till stabilization. It may be interesting to combine that with the freedom to decide what is correct, as studied in [1]. This may be especially interesting since it was demonstrated in [2] that multiple possible input values complicate their problem, while this does not seem the case here.

We studied instability in the context of Consensus (and in the context of Persistence). Instability is expensive in other contexts as well. For example, when a network changes, the routing changes. Instability in the routing tables causes routed messages to loop. It is hoped that the understanding gained here will prove useful for increasing the stability for other problems.

A common criticisms against self stabilizing algorithms is that they do not provide much guarantees on the output of nodes until the stabilization. The current paper provides some such guarantees. It would be interesting to find which additional such guarantees are possible.

References

1. Dolev, S., Rajsbaum, S.: Stability of long-lived consensus. In: JCSS (2003)
2. Davidovitch, L., Dolev, S., Rajsbaum, S.: Consensus continue? Stability of multi-valued continuous consensus! In: GETCO 2004, Amsterdam, pp. 21–24 (October 4, 2004)

3. Dolev, S., Gouda, M., Schneider, M.: Memory requirements for silent stabilization. In: PODC 1996, pp. 27–34 (1996)
4. Awerbuch, B., Kutten, S., Mansour, Y., Patt-Shamir, B., Varghese, G.: Time optimal self-stabilizing synchronization. In: STOC 1993, San Diego, CA, pp. 652–661 (1993)
5. Ghosh, S., Gupta, A., Herman, T., Pemamraju, S.V.: Fault-containing self-stabilizing algorithms. In: PODC 1996 (1996)
6. Ghosh, S., He, X.: Fault-containing self-stabilization using priority scheduling. IPL 73(3-4), 145–151 (2000)
7. Ghosh, S., Pemmaraju, S.V.: Tradeoffs in fault-containing self-stabilization. WSS, 157–169 (1997)
8. Bui, A., Datta, A.K., Petit, F., Villain, V.: State-optimal snap-stabilizing PIF in tree networks. WSS, 78–85 (1999)
9. Lynch, N.: Distributed Algorithms. Morgan Kaufmann, San Francisco (1996)
10. Burns, J.E., Gouda, M.G., Miller, R.E.: Stabilization and Pseudo-Stabilization. Distributed Computing 7(1), 35–42 (1993)
11. Dayan, J., Kobett, J.J., Kutten, M.: Control of Surge Drums by Different Types of D. D. C. Algorithms. IJT 10(4) (1972)
12. Kutten, S., Patt-Shamir, B.: Stabilizing Time Adaptive Protocols. TCS 220(1), 93–111 (1999)
13. Kutten, S., Patt-Shamir, B.: Adaptive Stabilization of Reactive Tasks. In: Lodaya, K., Mahajan, M. (eds.) FSTTCS 2004. LNCS, vol. 3328. Springer, Heidelberg (2004)
14. Afek, Y., Kutten, S., Yung, M.: The Local Detection Paradigm and its Applications to Self Stabilization. TCS 186(1–2), 199–230 (1997)
15. Azar, Y., Kutten, S., Patt-Shamir, B.: Distributed Error Confinement. In: PODC 2003, Boston (July 2003)
16. Kutten, S., Peleg, D.: Fault-local distributed mending. J. of Alg. 30, 144–165 (1999)
17. Kutten, S., Peleg, D.: Tight Fault Locality. SIAM J. on Comp. 30(1), 247–268 (2000)
18. Dijkstra, E.W.: Self-stabilizing systems in spite of distributed control. CACM 17(11), 643–644 (1974)
19. Afek, Y., Bremler, A.: Self-stabilizing unidirectional network algorithms by power-supply. In: SODA (1997)
20. Bremler-Barr, A., Afek, Y., Schwarz, S.: Improved BGP Convergence via Ghost Flushing. In: INFOCOM 2003 (2003)
21. Burman, J., Herman, T., Kutten, S., Patt-Shamir, B.: Time-Adaptive Majority Consensus. In: Anderson, J.H., Prencipe, G., Wattenhofer, R. (eds.) OPODIS 2005. LNCS, vol. 3974. Springer, Heidelberg (2006)
22. Breitling, M.: Modeling faults of distributed, reactive systems. In: Joseph, M. (ed.) FTRTFT 2000. LNCS, vol. 1926, pp. 58–69. Springer, Heidelberg (2000)
23. Fischer, M.j., Lynch, N.A., Paterson, M.S.: Impossibility of distributed consensus with one faulty process. J. ACM 32(2), 374–382 (1985)
24. Arora, A., Zhang, H.: LSRP: Local Stabilization in Shortest Path Routing. In: DSN 2003, pp. 139–148 (2003)
25. Zhang, H., Arora, A.: Guaranteed fault containment and local stabilization in routing. Computer Networks 50(18)
26. Afek, Y., Dolev, S.: Local Stabilizer. J. Par. & Dist. Comput. 62(5), 745–765 (2002)
27. Dolev, S., Herman, T.: SuperStabilizing Protocols for Dynamic Distributed Systems. C.J.TCS 1997 4 (1997)

28. Parlati, G., Yung, M.: Non-exploratory self-stabilization for constant-space symmetry-breaking. In: van Leeuwen, J. (ed.) ESA 1994. LNCS, vol. 855, pp. 26–28. Springer, Heidelberg (1994)

A   Appendix

Definitions for Broadcast with Error Confinement

Definition 6. *A protocol P is said to be an* error-confined *protocol for task Π if for any execution with behavior β (possibly, containing a fault) there exists a legal behavior β' of Π such that*

(1) For each non-faulty node v, $\beta_v = \beta'_v$.

(2) For each faulty node v, there exists a suffix $\overline{\beta_v}$ of β_v and a suffix $\overline{\beta'_v}$ of β'_v such that $\overline{\beta_v} = \overline{\beta'_v}$.

The main point in the definition above is that the behavior of non-faulty nodes must be exactly as in the specification: only faulty nodes may have some period (immediately following the fault) in which their behavior does not agree with the specification.

The broadcast task is defined as follows.

Broadcast (BCAST

Input actions: $\mathbf{inp}_s(b)$, done at node $s \in V$, for b in some set D. Node s is called the *source*.

Output actions: $\mathbf{outp}(b)$, required at every node $v \in V$, where $b \in D \cup \{\bot\}$.

Legal behaviors: There is at most one $\mathbf{inp}_s$ action. Each node v outputs $\mathbf{outp}(\bot)$ in each step up to some point, and then it outputs $\mathbf{outp}(b)$ in each step, where b is the value input by the $\mathbf{inp}$ action.

A Distributed Maximal Scheduler for Strong Fairness

Matthew Lang and Paolo A.G. Sivilotti

Department of Computer Science and Engineering
The Ohio State University, Columbus OH, USA, 43210-1277
{langma,paolo}@cse.ohio-state.edu

Abstract. Weak fairness guarantees that continuously enabled actions are executed infinitely often. Strong fairness, on the other hand, guarantees that actions that are enabled infinitely often (but not necessarily continuously) are executed infinitely often. In this paper, we present a distributed algorithm for scheduling actions for execution. Assuming weak fairness for the execution of this algorithm, the schedule it provides is strongly fair. Furthermore, this algorithm is maximal in that it is capable of generating *any* strongly fair schedule. This algorithm is the first strongly-fair scheduling algorithm that is both distributed and maximal.

1 Introduction

An action system models a distributed systems as a set of actions, each of which is either enabled or disabled. A fairness assumption controls the selection of actions from this set for execution. For example, weak fairness requires that an action that is enabled continuously be selected while enabled infinitely often. Strong fairness, on the other hand, requires that an action that is enabled infinitely often (but perhaps not continuously) be selected while enabled infinitely often.

Weak fairness is useful because of the minimal assumption it makes and the simple scheduling algorithm required to implement it: Select every action infinitely often. Strong fairness, on the other hand, is useful for simplifying the design of synchronization and communication protocols since it rules out the starvation of actions that are repeatedly enabled. While weak fairness reflects an asynchronous and independent scheduling of individual actions, strong fairness reflects some scheduling coordination to rule out certain pathological traces. The advantages of both models can be achieved by constructing a strongly-fair scheduler on top of an assumption of weak fairness.

A program is correct if it can exhibit *only* behaviors permitted by its specification. A correct program is maximal [4] if it can exhibit *all* behaviors permitted by its specification. Maximal programs are important for testing component-based systems because they prevent a component implementation from providing unnecessarily deterministic behavior and, in this way, masking errors in its clients. For example, if a scheduling algorithm is not maximal, it is incapable of generating some traces that are otherwise possible under the corresponding fairness

A. Pelc (Ed.): DISC 2007, LNCS 4731, pp. 358–372, 2007.

assumption. These traces are no longer observable behaviors for the system built on top of such a limited scheduler.

In this paper, we present a strongly-fair scheduler, layered on top of a weak fairness assumption. This algorithm is distributed: it does not maintain a global set of enabled actions and it permits concurrent selection of independent actions. Furthermore, this algorithm is maximal: any trace that satisfies strong fairness is a possible behavior of the scheduler. To our knowledge, this is the first strongly-fair scheduler that is both distributed and maximal.

2   Maximality and Fairness

2.1   Maximality

A program is maximal if it is capable of generating any behavior permitted by a specification [5,12]. This notion is similar to bisimulation [11,13]. However, bisimulation involves relating artifacts with similar mathematical representations, while maximality relates a program text to a formal specification.

Proving the maximality of a program P with respect to a specification S is carried out in three stages. Firstly, one defines a set of specification variables mentioned by S and derives properties of traces of these variables from S. Next, one shows that an arbitrary trace $\sigma \in |S|$ satisfying these properties is a possible execution of an instrumented version P' of P (*chronicle correspondence*). Finally, one proves that every fair execution of P' corresponds to a fair execution of P (*execution correspondence*). Since σ is a possible execution of P' and every execution of P' corresponds to a possible execution of P, σ is a possible execution of P. Hence, any trace in S is a possible execution of P.

Constructing P' is carried out by adding new variables, assignments to new variables within existing actions, guards to existing actions, and actions that assign to only new variables. These additions ensure that safety properties of P are safety properties of P'. The new variables typically include read-only *chronicle variables* that encode the trace σ and auxiliary variables (e.g., variables that encode the current point in the computation).

Proving *chronicle correspondence*, requires showing that the execution of P' follows a given trace σ. Proving *execution correspondence* requires showing that (i) each added guard in P' is infinitely often true and (ii) the truth of each added guard is preserved by the execution of every other action in P'. These properties ensure that each action is infinitely often executed in a state where the additional guard is true. Thus, every weakly-fair execution of P' corresponds to a weakly-fair execution of P.

2.2   Fairness

Consider the following UNITY [2] program:

Program *fairness*
var b : boolean
                x, y : int
initially b
assign
    A :   **true** $\longrightarrow$ $x := x + 1 \parallel b := \neg b$
    B : $b \longrightarrow y := x$

Action A is always enabled. It increments x and sets b to $\neg b$. Action B is enabled in states where b is true and assigns to y the value of x.

Weak fairness requires that every action be selected infinitely often. Under this assumption, the *fairness* program satisfies: the safety property (i) x increases by at most one in each step, and the progress properties (ii) x eventually increases and (iii) b eventually changes value. More formally: (i) $x = k$ **next** $|x-k| \leq 1$, (ii) $x = k \rightsquigarrow x \neq k$, and (iii) $b = k \rightsquigarrow b \neq k$. Progress properties (ii) and (iii) follow from the fact that action A is infinitely often executed in a state where it is enabled.

The only property involving y is one of safety: at each step of the computation, y either remains the same or changes to the value of x. Since action B may never be selected while enabled, no progress properties for y can be proven. For example, consider the sequence of actions: $\langle A, B, A, A, B, A, A, B, \ldots \rangle$. This schedule is weakly fair since all actions are selected infinitely often, but B never executes from an enabled state and so y never changes value.

Strong fairness, on the other hand, requires that any action that is infinitely often enabled be selected while enabled infinitely often. Under strong fairness, the *fairness* program satisfies the same properties as it did under weak fairness. In addition, the program also satisfies new properties, including the progress property y increases eventually

2.3   Maximality and Scheduling

Assertions should be as strong as possible and must hold in every possible program execution. A maximal scheduler ensures that the strongest properties we prove using the program text and a notion of fairness are the strongest properties of the actual system behavior. A non-maximal scheduler eliminates possible executions and therefore allows us to assert stronger properties that hold on only a subset of possible program executions.

To illustrate, consider a non-maximal strongly-fair scheduler that allows an action to be disabled at most twice before being scheduled for execution in a state in which it is enabled. This scheduler is correct—actions which are infinitely often enabled are infinitely often executed in a state in which they are enabled. However, the scheduler clearly generates a small subset of possible correct schedules.

If we schedule the program *fairness* using this scheduler, we see action A can execute at most four times before action B must execute in a state in which it is enabled. This allows us to prove much stronger properties about y, for example: $x - y \leq 4$ is a program invariant.

Although we can now assert a stronger program property, this is undesirable, for instance, in the case of testing. If one were to test the program *fairness* composed with such a non-maximal scheduler, one may be led to believe that $x - y \leq 4$ is indeed an invariant of the system. In fact, it would be impossible to design a test case to expose the fact that it is not.

3   Specification

3.1   Description of the System

The system is comprised of a set of processes, each comprised of two components—a *client* layer and a *scheduler* layer. Clients can be *enabled*, and an enabled client can be granted a *lock*. Holding a lock allows the client to access some resource, perform some action(s), or otherwise modify the system state, including enabling or disabling other clients. When a client modifies system state, it simultaneously increments its own *count* and releases the lock it holds.

The scheduler layer manages locks. If a process is infinitely often enabled, the scheduler ensures that it is infinitely often granted a lock. We say two processes u and v are neighbors if u or v's client can affect the other's enabledness. If the scheduler guarantees that no two neighboring processes simultaneously hold a lock, the client layer guarantees that held locks are eventually relinquished.

The composed system generates a strongly-fair schedule—if a process is infinitely often enabled, it infinitely often changes its count.

3.2   Formal Specification of the Strong Fairness Problem

The system is comprised of a set of processes, $\mathcal{P}$. All processes have access to a symmetric *neighbor relation* $N \subseteq \mathcal{P}^2$. We define $N(u, v)$ if u or v can affect the other's enabledness.[1] Each process $u \in \mathcal{P}$ has boolean variables *u.enabled* and *u.lock* representing that process being enabled and holding a lock, respectively. A third variable, *u.count*, is the number of times action u has executed. Since the execution of actions is atomic, there is no state in which an action is executing. Consequently, we require that when an action u executes, *u.count* is incremented.

3.3   Client Layer Specification

The client layer is responsible for execution of the action associated with a process. Intuitively, a client is "idle" until it is granted a lock. When granted a lock, the client eventually executes its action and increments its count, releasing the lock. The specification for client u is:

---

[1] This neighbor relation is irreflexive, it is never the case $N(u, u)$. This is not to say that a process cannot enable/disable itself by executing its action; this is captured in the specification. The irreflexitivity of N only simplifies presentation.

$$(\forall v : v \neq u : \textbf{constant } v.lock \;) \tag{C0}$$

$$(\forall v : v \neq u : \textbf{constant } v.count \;) \tag{C1}$$

$$(\forall v, b : \neg N(u,v) : \textbf{constant } v.enabled = b \;) \tag{C2}$$

$$(\forall v, b, a, k : N(u,v) : \textbf{stable } \neg u.lock \wedge u.count = k$$
$$\wedge \; v.enabled = b \wedge u.enabled = a \;) \tag{C3}$$

$$(\forall v, b, a, k : N(u,v) : u.lock \wedge u.count = k$$
$$\wedge \; v.enabled = b \wedge u.enabled = a$$
$$\textbf{unless } \neg u.lock \wedge u.count = k+1 \;) \tag{C4}$$

Hypothesis: **invariant** $(\forall v : N(u,v) : \neg(u.lock \wedge v.lock) \;)$,
$\qquad\qquad$ **invariant** $u.lock \Rightarrow u.enabled$

Conclusion: $u.lock \rightsquigarrow \neg u.lock$ $\hfill$ (C5)

Properties (C0)–(C2) ensure that clients can modify only the enabledness of neighbors. Property (C3) ensures that a lock is necessary for a client to act. Propery (C4) ensures that count is incremented and enabledness of neighbors affected only with the release of a lock. Property (C5) is a conditional property; if the scheduling layer maintains the properties that neighbors do not hold locks simultaneously and that only enabled clients hold locks, the client layer guarantees that a lock is eventually relinquished.

The mutual exclusion property and the invariant in the hypothesis of (C5) are important; neighboring processes are permitted to modify the enabledness of their neighbors. If two neighboring processes u and v simultaneously hold locks, a process, say u, may execute its action and disable the other. Then v is not guaranteed to become re-enabled and execute its action, releasing the lock.

3.4   Scheduler Layer Specification

This layer schedules actions for execution by granting client processes locks— when a client process holds a lock it is free to execute its associated action.

$$\textbf{constant } u.count \tag{S0}$$

$$\textbf{stable } u.lock \tag{S1}$$

$$\textbf{invariant } u.lock \Rightarrow u.enabled \tag{S2}$$

$$\textbf{invariant } (\forall v : N(u,v) : \neg(u.lock \wedge v.lock) \;) \tag{S3}$$

Hypothesis: **true** $\rightsquigarrow u.enabled$, C0, C2, C3, C4, C5,

Conclusion: **true** $\rightsquigarrow u.lock$ $\hfill$ (S4)

Properties (S0) and (S1) ensure that the scheduling layer does not modify the count, nor revoke a lock once granted. Property (S2) ensures that locks are granted only to enabled processes, while property (S3) ensures that neighbors do not hold locks simultaneously. Property (S4) is a conditional property that captures the notion of strong fairness. If a correct client process is infinitely often enabled, the scheduler infinitely often grants the process a lock.

3.5   Composed Specification

Given the *client* and *scheduler* specifications, the composed specification of the system satisfies the strong fairness property: if a process is infinitely often enabled, it infinitely often increases its execution count.

Formally, *client* ∥ *scheduler* satisfies:

Hypothesis: **true** $\rightsquigarrow u.enabled$

Conclusion: $u.count = k \rightsquigarrow u.count = k + 1$

4   Algorithm for Scheduling Layer

Solving the strong fairness scheduling problem entails providing an algorithm that satisfies the specification of the scheduling layer from the previous section. In addition, our goal is for this algorithm to be maximal with respect to the composed specification.

The challenge in designing a strongly fair scheduler lies in limiting concurrency—no correct scheduler can *always* allow processes sharing a mutual neighbor to concurrently hold locks. As an illustration, consider the system with $\mathcal{P} = \{x, y, z\}$ and $\{\langle x, y \rangle, \langle x, z \rangle\}$ representing N. Suppose y and z are enabled while x is disabled. A scheduler that always allows processes sharing a mutual neighbor to concurrently hold locks permits both y and z to acquire locks. Now suppose y executes its action, leaving x and y both enabled. Since z still holds its lock and $N(x, z)$, x may not acquire a lock. Now suppose z executes its action, disabling x but leaving z enabled. The system is now in back in the state where y and z are enabled while x is disabled. A scheduler that always allows processes with a mutual neighbor to concurrently hold locks allows this sequence of events to repeat continually, resulting in a schedule where x is infinitely often enabled but never executed.

We overcome this challenge by bounding the number of times a process allows its neighbors to hold locks concurrently. Although unintuitive, this will not affect the maximality of our solution: our scheduler will be capable of generating any schedule satisfying the strong fairness property. Furthermore, any correct algorithm satisfying the strong fairness scheduler specification can be viewed as a refinement of our algorithm.

4.1   Scheduler Design

In order to ensure the mutual exclusion property S3, we associate with each pair of neighboring processes u, v a shared *lock token*, $tok(u, v)$. A process may only be granted a lock if it holds all of its shared tokens. A process u also stores a read-only boolean array, $u.en$, storing the enabledness of its neighbors. A process v notifies a neighbor u of its enabledness by assigning to $u.en[v]$.

To ensure progress, each process u is has a height, $u.ht$, representing its priority. A process is higher-priority than another if it has greater height. We require a process's height to be unique among its neighbors. Ties in priority between non-neighbors are broken by a static order on processes, say by process id. We will call lock tokens shared with higher-priority neighbors *high tokens* and lock tokens share with lower-priority neighbors *low tokens*.

A process only changes its priority after it has executed its action and released a held lock, at which point it lowers its height by a nondeterministically chosen finite but unbounded amount. A process which has released a lock holds all of its tokens until it lowers its height, at which point it gives up all its high tokens.

Processes always release tokens to higher-priority neighbors (*high neighbors*). An enabled process does not relinquish tokens to lower priority neighbors (*low neighbors*) and, in order to limit concurrency while still ensuring progress, a disabled process releases at most one low token.

In order to ensure there are no wait-cycles, a disabled process u releases a low token only to its highest priority low neighbor, v. If $u.en[w]$ holds later for some higher-priority low neighbor w, u retrieves the shared token from v by assigning **true** to $v.en[u]$. It is guaranteed to eventually receive the token as processes always relinquish high tokens.

In addition, process u includes a boolean variable $u.gate$. If $u.gate$ is true, u is free to exchange tokens with its neighbors or grant itself a lock. When u grants itself a lock, it sets $u.gate$ to false. Upon releasing a lock, the process sets $u.gate$ to true, lowers its height, and releases its high tokens.

The following predicates are associated with a process u:

- $u.sendtok.v$ for all neighbors v of u. $u.sendtok.v$ is true if a process u should send its shared token to process v. $u.sendtok.v$ is true if v is a high neighbor of u and either $u.en[v]$ or $\neg u.enabled$. $u.sendtok.v$ is true when v is a low neighbor of u and v is the highest-priority among all low neighbors of u, $w \neq v$, for which $u.en[w] = \textbf{true}$.

$$
\begin{aligned}
u.sendtok.v \equiv\ & tok(u,v) = u \\
\wedge\ (\ (\ & u.ht < v.ht \wedge (\neg u.enabled \vee u.en[v])) \\
\vee\ (\ & u.ht > v.ht \wedge u.en[v] \\
& \wedge\ (\forall w\ :\ N(u,w) \wedge w.ht < u.ht\ :\ tok(u,w) = u\ ) \\
& \wedge\ v.ht = (\mathbf{Max}\, w\ :\ N(u,w) \wedge w.ht < u.ht \wedge u.en[w]\ :\ w.ht\ )))
\end{aligned}
$$

- $u.maylock$. $u.maylock$ is true if u is enabled and holds all its tokens.

$$
u.maylock \equiv u.enabled \wedge (\forall v\ :\ N(u,v)\ :\ tok(u,v) = u\ )
$$

- $u.retr.v$ for all neighbors v of u. $u.retr.v$ is true if u has granted a low token to v and now some higher low neighbor of u is enabled.

$$
\begin{aligned}
u.retr.v \equiv\ & tok(u,v) = v \\
& \wedge\ (\exists w\ :\ N(u,w) \wedge u.en[w]\ :\ v.ht < w.ht < u.ht\ )
\end{aligned}
$$

Figure 1 shows this implementation of u's *scheduler* layer. Actions $U_{u,v}$ and $T_{u,v}$ are understood to be quantified across all neighbors v of u.

Program SF_u
var $u.enabled, u.gate, u.lock$: bool
               $u.ht$: integer
               $u.en$: array of bool
initially $(\forall v : N(u,v) : u.ht \neq v.ht)$
               $\neg u.lock$
               $u.gate$
assign
   $U_{u,v}$ **true** $\longrightarrow$ $v.en[u] := u.enabled \lor u.retr.v$
   $T_{u,v}$ $u.sendtok.v \land u.gate \longrightarrow tok(u,v) := v$
   L_u $u.maylock \land u.gate \longrightarrow u.lock := \textbf{true};$
               $u.gate := \textbf{false}$
   D_u $\neg u.lock \land \neg u.gate \longrightarrow u.gate := \textbf{true};$
               $u.ht :=?$ **st** $u.ht < u.ht' \land (\forall v : N(u,v) : u.ht \neq v.ht);$
               $(\parallel v : N(u,v) \land u.ht < v.ht : tok(u,v) := v)$

Fig. 1. Maximal Strong Fairness Scheduling Algorithm

Action $U_{u,v}$ updates $v.en[u]$ by assigning true if $u.enabled$ or $u.retr.v$ and assigns false otherwise. Action $T_{u,v}$ sends a token to v if u is free to exchange tokens and $u.sendtok.v$ is true. Action L_u grants a lock to process u and stops further communication by setting $u.gate$ to false. Finally, action D_u frees u to exchange tokens with neighbors, lowers its height by a finite but unbounded amount, and releases u's high tokens. D_u is enabled only after a process has relinquished a lock and executed its action.

Note: In the algorithm SF, we assume that a process can read the height of its neighbors. In practice, this information can be encoded on shared tokens as differences in height, and by storing locally the height of the (unique) low neighbor holding a token.

5   Correctness of SF_u

Properties (S0), (S1), and (S2) follow directly from the program text. Property (S3) is satisfied since a process must hold all its shared tokens to grant itself a lock and a process does not relinquish its tokens while it holds a lock.

The progress property (S4) (that an infinitely often enabled process holds a lock infinitely often) requires a more thorough treatment. In the interest of space, however, we only sketch the key proof ideas here. The complete proof is available in [9].

In order to prove (S4), we show: (i) the system is free from deadlock, (ii) a process with no higher priority neighbors that becomes enabled eventually acquires a lock, (iii) a continually enabled process eventually is granted a lock, and finally (iv) an infinitely often enabled process eventually is granted a lock.

Part (i) follows from the acyclicity of the partial order of priorities. The remaining parts rely on the identification of a metric. We define $u.M$ to be the sum of the difference in height between u and all processes with higher priority than u that are reachable from u by following the neighbor relation through higher-priority processes. More formally, we define the set $u.ab = \bigcup u.ab_n$ where $u.ab_n$ is defined by recursion:

$$u.ab_0 = \{\, v \mid u.ht < v.ht \wedge N(u,v) \,\}$$
$$u.ab_{i+1} = \{\, v \mid (\,\exists w \,:\, w \in u.ab_i \,:\, N(v,w) \wedge u.ht < w.ht\,)\,\}$$

Then $u.M = (\,\sum v \,:\, v \in u.ab \,:\, v.ht - u.ht\,)$.

By definition, $u.M$ is bounded below by zero when $u.ab = \emptyset$ and u has no higher-priority neighbors. Furthermore, $u.M$ is non-increasing unless u acquires a lock and lowers its height. To show the progress property, we demonstrate that if $u.M = k$ and u is infinitely often enabled, eventually either $u.M < k$ or $u.lock$. Since $u.M$ is bounded below and non-increasing unless u acquires a lock, eventually u acquires a lock.

6   The Maximality of SF

Since maximality is noncompositional, we use the rely-guarantee style proof outlined in [10] as a template. This method for proving the maximality of composed systems involves stipulating that other processes in the system satisfy certain properties beyond their formal specification and proving the maximality of the composed system using these properties. These additional properties entail that the client process our system is composed with is maximal and can be constrained in a way to establish its maximality.

In the interest of space and clarity, we only present the intuition behind the proof of maximality in this section. The interested reader should refer to [9] for a thorough proof of maximality of SF.

In this section we reverse the priority relation described in Section 4 to clarify presentation and allow the reader to maintain an intuition about the behavior of the constrained system. In Section 4 a process was higher priority if it had a greater height and processes lowered their priority by lowering their height. In this section, we will reverse this—a process has higher priority if it has a *lesser* height, thus a process *lowers* its priority by *increasing* its height.

6.1   Proving the Maximality of SF

In order to prove SF is a maximal implementation of the strong-fairness specification, we need to show that any trace satisfying the strong-fairness specification is a possible trace of SF. In order to accomplish this, we create a constrained program SF' from SF that accepts as input any trace σ satisfying the strong-fairness specification. We then show that at each point i in the trace σ, the state of the system is exactly that of σ_i. This establishes σ as a possible execution of SF'.

Next we need to show that any fair execution of SF' corresponds to a fair execution of SF. Then, since any trace σ satisfying the specification of the strong fairness problem is a possible execution of SF', any trace satisfying the strong fairness problem is a possible execution of SF.

However, this simple view is not quite complete. Since we want to show that *any* schedule of action executions is a possible behavior of the composed system, we need to stipulate that the client process composed with SF satisfies some additional requirements. Namely, we require that this client process can be constrained to produce *client'* which, when composed with SF', can take the "steps" in the computation that σ dictates. *i.e.*, if at some point i in σ some process u is to execute and enable/disable itself or its neighbors, *client'* can compute this step. The additional requirements are that the client process is maximal, *client'* satisfies the safety properties of the *client* specification, and that *client'* is created in a way that ensures the correspondence between executions of *client'* and the client process.

In order to compute σ, we introduce a variable p shared by *client'* and SF' that marks the current point in the trace (i.e., σ_p). We then prove (i) it is invariant that the current state is σ_p and (ii) the point p eventually increases. It follows that σ is a possible execution of $SF' \parallel client'$.

6.2 A Strong Fairness Trace

Let σ be a stutter-free sequence of tuples $\sigma = \langle \sigma_0, \sigma_1 \ldots \rangle$ representing the state of processes in an execution satisfying the strong-fairness specification. $\sigma_i = \langle E, C \rangle_i$ is a tuple containing two arrays, E_i and C_i, representing the enabledness and *count* of processes in state σ_i. That is, $E_i^u = \textbf{true}$ if *u.enabled* in σ_i and $C_i^u = k$ if *u.count* $= k$ in σ_i. σ is stutter-free in that each tuple in the sequence differs from the previous by at least one element, *unless* the execution is in a state of quiescence (each processes is disabled forever).

Since σ is a correct trace of the strong fairness scheduling problem, it obeys certain properties. Namely, it satisfies the following: in subsequent states in σ, at most one process changes count (by incrementing it by one) and if a process changes enabledness, a process must change count. Also, if a process is infinitely often enabled in the trace, it infinitely often changes its count.

Given a trace σ, we create an isomorphic trace σ' by inserting a stuttering-state in between every σ_i and σ_{i+1}. That is, $\sigma'_0 = \sigma_0$ and σ'_{i+1} is σ'_i if i is even and is $\sigma_{(i+1)/2}$ if i is odd.

6.3 Requirements of $client'_u$

We require that a client process u can be constrained to produce $client'_u$. The requirements on $client'_u$ are as follows:

- $client'_u$ is produced from the client process by only adding new variables, assignments to new variables, and new guards referencing new and existing program variables. Furthermore, if random assignments in the client process are replaced with deterministic assignments, we require that the assigned value satisfy the predicate on the random assignment. These requirements ensure that $client'_u$ satisfies the safety properties of the client process.
- The additional guards of $client'_u$ are infinitely often true and the enabledness of each guard is preserved by the execution of any other action in the system.

- At each point p in the computation, it is invariant that $u.enabled = E_p^u$ and $u.count = C_p^u$.
- $client'_u$ does not assign to σ and only changes p by at most one.
- If SF'_u ensures u holds a lock at a point $p = k$ in the trace where $C_k^u \neq C_{k+1}^u$ (*i.e.,* u executes its action), $client'_u$ guarantees that p is incremented and the lock is released.

These requirements on the client process ensure that $client'$ will compute the transitions dictated by σ . It is then the obligation of SF' to ensure that processes hold locks when σ dictates u executes its action and increments its count.

6.4   The Constrained Program SF'_u

In the constrained program SF'_u we introduce the following objects not found in SF_u : the input trace σ and the point p , a function $u.next$ to compute the next point at which process u executes its action and increments its count, a predicate $u.done$ to indicate whether or not u increments its count again after the current point in the computation, and a predicate $u.quiet$ which indicates whether or not u is enabled after the current point in the computation.

Formally, $u.quiet$, $u.done$, and $u.next$ are defined as the following.

$$u.quiet \equiv (\forall i : i \geq p : \neg E_i^u)$$

$$u.done \equiv (\forall i : i \geq p : C_i^u = C_{i+1}^u)$$

$$u.next = (\mathbf{Min}\, i : i \geq p : C_i^u \neq C_{i+1}^u) \text{ if } \neg u.done$$
$$(\mathbf{Min}\, i : i \geq p : (\forall j : j \geq i : \neg E_j^u \wedge$$
$$(\forall v : v \neq u : v.ht \neq j))) \text{ otherwise}$$

Figure 2 shows the instrumented program.

The key property that follows from this instrumentation is that a process u's height corresponds to the next point in the computation when u increments its count. At that point, u is the highest priority enabled process among its neighbors (*i.e., lowest height*). Any process with a higher priority (lower height) than u at that point is in a state of quiescence.

If a process u has executed for the last time, we set its height to be after the last point in the trace that it is enabled. This ensures that any process that executes and enables/disables u will be higher priority than u until u is quiescent. Such a point is guaranteed to exist by the assumption that the process has executed for the last time; if no such point exists, the process must be infinitely often enabled (and therefore execute again).

The motivation for the introduction of stutter states in σ is to ensure that a process that never executes again can be assigned a unique height. If σ were stutter-free, it is not guaranteed that such a point exists.

Program SF'_u

var	$u.enabled, u.gate, u.lock$: bool
	$u.ht$: integer
	$u.en$: array of bool
initially	$p = 0$
	$u.enabled = E^u_p$
	$\neg u.done \;\Rightarrow\; u.ht = u.next$
	$u.done \;\Rightarrow\; u.ht \;\geq\; \mathbf{min}\, i\,(\,\forall j \;:\; i \leq j \;:\; \neg E^u_j\,)$
	$(\,\forall v \;:\; N(u,v) \;:\; u.ht \neq v.ht\,)$
	$\neg u.lock$
	$u.gate$

assign

$U'_{u,v}$ **true** $\longrightarrow$
    true $\longrightarrow$ $v.en[u] := u.enabled \;\vee\; u.retr.v$

$T'_{u,v}$ **true** $\longrightarrow$
    $u.sendtok.v \;\wedge\; u.gate \;\longrightarrow\; tok(u,v) := v$

L'_u $(u.ht = p \;\wedge\; \neg u.done) \;\vee\; u.quiet \;\longrightarrow$
    $u.maylock \;\wedge\; u.gate \;\longrightarrow\; u.lock := \mathbf{true};$
        $u.gate := \mathbf{false}$

D'_u **true** $\longrightarrow$
    $\neg u.lock \;\wedge\; \neg u.gate \;\longrightarrow\; u.gate := \mathbf{true};$
        $u.ht := u.next;$
        $(\;\|\; v \;:\; N(u,v) \;\wedge\; u.ht < v.ht \;:\; tok(u,v) := v\;)$

Q' $\sigma_i = \sigma_{i+1} \;\longrightarrow\; p := p + 1$

Fig. 2. Constrained Strong Fairness Scheduling Algorithm

A key invariant of SF'_u is that if $\neg u.done$ and $u.gate$ hold, $u.ht = u.next$. SF'_u inherits the safety properties of SF_u as guards are only strengthened and existing program variables are not assigned to, except for the replacement of the random assignment to $u.ht$ with a deterministic assignment. However, at the point of the assignment to $u.ht$, $u.next > u.ht$ and is unique by definition of $u.next$ and the properties of σ.

6.5   Proof Sketch of the Maximality of SF

There are two main obligations to dispatch: (i) $SF' \parallel client'$ computes σ and (ii) every fair execution of $SF' \parallel client'$ corresponds to a fair execution of the original system.

(i) is proved by showing $u.enabled = E^u_p \;\wedge\; u.count = C^u_p$ is an invariant of the system and $p = k \rightsquigarrow p = k+1$. (ii) requires showing that the truth of each additional guard in the system is preserved by the execution of any other action and that each additional guard is infinitely often true. Then each additional guard is executed infinitely often in a state where it is true, corresponding to a fair execution of the original program.

Proving the invariant: The invariant in (i) is initially true by the initially predicates in SF'_u. Also, each action of SF' maintains the invariant as no action assigns to the trace, $u.enabled$, or $u.count$ and the only action that assigns to

p only increments p in a stuttering state. Thus, since the invariant is also a property of $client'_u$, it is an invariant of the composed system.

Proving $p = k \leadsto p = k + 1$: There are two cases to consider — the case where the current point is a stuttering-state, in which action Q' increments p, and a non-stuttering state. In a non-stuttering state, there exists some process u such that $C^u_p = C^u_{p+1}$. It was a requirement on $client'_u$ that if u holds a lock in such a state, $client'_u$ eventually increments p. It is the responsibility of SF' to ensure that in such a state process u eventually acquires a lock.

At that point in the computation $u.next = p$ and $\neg u.done$ holds. Without loss of generality, assume $u.gate$ holds as well, so by the invariant of SF'_u, $u.ht = p$. Also, by the way height is assigned u is the highest priority process among all its neighbors that are enabled. So u eventually acquires all its tokens and acquires a lock.

Proving the stability of additional guards: Since $client'_u$ is required to satisfy this property, it suffices to show that the guard of L'_u is not falsified by any action of SF'_u. It is easy to see that the only actions which might affect the truth of the additional guard of L'_u are Q', which assigns to p, and D'_u, which assigns to $u.ht$.

Since $u.quiet$ is stable, neither Q' nor D'_u can falsify it. Now, if $u.ht = p \wedge \neg u.done$ hold, it is implied by the invariant that $\sigma_p \neq \sigma_{p+1}$, so Q' is disabled in such a state. If action D'_u is enabled, $\neg u.lock \wedge \neg u.gate$ holds. Then since $\neg u.lock \wedge \neg u.gate$ holds, $client'_u$ must have released a lock and incremented the point, which implies $u.ht < p$. So if L'_u is enabled, D'_u is not.

Proving additional guards are infinitely often true: Again, since this was a requirement of $client'_u$, we only need consider the guard of L'_u. Now, since $u.quiet$ is stable and if $u.done$ ever holds, eventually $u.quiet$ holds, it suffices to show that $u.ht = p \wedge \neg u.done$ is infinitely often true if $\neg u.quiet$ is an invariant of the trace. Assuming $\neg u.quiet$ is an invariant of the trace, $\neg u.done$ is an invariant of the trace as well.

Now, if $\neg u.gate$ holds at any point in the computation, it must be the case $\neg u.lock$ holds as well and both continue to hold until eventually D'_u is executed. The execution of D'_u in an enabled state ensures $u.gate$ holds. Then the invariant of SF'_u dictates that $u.ht = u.next$ and, since $u.next \geq p$ and $p = k \leadsto p = k + 1$, eventually $u.ht = p$. Thus, the additional guard of L'_u is infinitely often true.

The Maximality of SF: The preceding arguments establish that any trace σ satisfying the strong-fairness specification is a possible execution of SF composed with a client process meeting the requirements described. It follows that SF is a maximal strongly-fair scheduler.

7   Discussion

Fairness is a well-researched and developed notion in existing literature, both in terms of interaction fairness [1] and in terms of selection of actions in non-deterministic guarded command programs [8]. Although a large body of work surrounds fairness issues, our algorithm is unique in that it is the first solution for strongly-fair scheduling of atomic actions that is both maximal and distributed.

In [7], Karaata gives a distributed self-stabilizing algorithm for the strongly-fair scheduling of atomic actions under weak fairness. A key property of the algorithm is that an action u can disable another action v at most twice before action v must execute, and therefore this algorithm is not maximal. In addition, although there is no notion of a "lock," the algorithm precludes two processes with a shared neighbor from both having the "right" to execute their actions. Although this does not affect the possible schedules the algorithm can generate, it does limit the algorithm from being generalized to a situation where the mutual exclusion property of the strong-fairness specification can benefit processes (e.g., processes perform some computation before releasing the lock and affecting their neighbors). Then the concurrency of non-neighboring processes holding locks is a valuable property. Karaata's algorithm has the advantage of being self-stabilizing, whereas ours does not. Also, Karaata provides a brief message complexity analysis of the algorithm while we make no claims regarding the message complexity of our algorithm.

In [6], Joung develops a criterion for implementability of fairness notions for multiparty interactions. If a fairness notion fails to meet the criterion, then no deterministic scheduling algorithm can meet the fairness requirement in an asynchronous system. In the general case, both strong interaction fairness and strong process fairness fail to meet the criterion.

The dining philosophers problem proposed by Dijkstra [3] is superficially similar (as also pointed out in [7]) to the strong-fairness problem in that one can map the state $\neg u.enabled$ to *thinking*, $u.enabled \land \neg u.lock$ to *hungry*, and $u.enabled \land u.lock$ to *eating*. However, in the dining philosophers problem, a process becomes hungry autonomously, not as a result of the behavior of other processes in the system. Furthermore, processes remain hungry until the arbitration layer affects a change in state to eating.

The possibility for processes to affect the enabledness of neighboring processes adds complexity to the strong fairness scheduling problem. For example, a solution to the dining philosophers problem can maintain an invariant that if a process holds a request from a neighbor, that neighbor is hungry. No corresponding invariant can be shown for a solution to the strong-fairness problem without synchronization between a process and its neighbor's neighbors.

8   Conclusions

In this work we presented a formal specification of the distributed strong fairness scheduling problem and described a maximal solution SF to the problem.

The importance of a maximal scheduling algorithm was discussed in detail in Section 2, making the maximality of the SF algorithm a key contribution of the work. The maximality of SF also implies that any correct implementation of the strong-fairness specification is a refinement of the SF algorithm in that any correct algorithm's behavior is a subset of the behavior of SF.

References

1. Apt, K.R., Francez, N., Katz, S.: Appraising fairness in distributed languages. In: POPL '87: Proceedings of the 14th ACM SIGACT-SIGPLAN symposium on Principles of programming languages, pp. 189–198. ACM Press, New York (1987)
2. Chandy, K.M., Misra, J.: Parallel Program Design: A Foundation. Addison-Wesley, Reading, Massachusetts (1988)
3. Dijkstra, E.W.: Hierarchical ordering of sequential processes. Acta Informatica 1(2), 115–138 (1971)
4. Joshi, R., Misra, J.: Maximally concurrent programs. Formal Aspects of Computing 12(2), 100–119 (2000)
5. Joshi, R., Misra, J.: Toward a theory of maximally concurrent programs. In: Proceedings of PODC '00, pp. 319–328 (2000)
6. Joung, Y.-J.: On fairness notions in distributed systems, part I: A characterization of implementability. Information and Computation 166, 1–34 (2001)
7. Karaata, M.H.: Self-stabilizing strong fairness under weak fairness. IEEE Trans. Parallel Distrib. Syst. 12(4), 337–345 (2001)
8. Lamport, L.: Fairness and hyperfairness. Distrib. Comput. 13(4), 239–245 (2000)
9. Lang, M., Sivilotti, P.A.G.: A distributed maximal scheduler for strong fairness. Technical Report OSU-CISRC-7/07-TR61, The Ohio State University (July 2007)
10. Lang, M., Sivilotti, P.A.G.: The maximality of unhygienic dining philosophers. Technical Report OSU-CISRC-5/07-TR39, The Ohio State University (May 2007)
11. Milner, R.: Communication and concurrency. Prentice-Hall, Inc., Upper Saddle River, NJ, USA (1989)
12. Misra, J.: A Discipline of Multiprogramming: Programming Theory for Distributed Applications. Springer, New York (2001)
13. Park, D.: Concurrency and automata on infinite sequences. In: Proceedings of the 5th GI-Conference on Theoretical Computer Science, London, UK, pp. 167–183. Springer, Heidelberg (1981)

Cost-Aware Caching Algorithms for Distributed Storage Servers

Shuang Liang[1], Ke Chen[2], Song Jiang[3], and Xiaodong Zhang[1]

[1] The Ohio State University, Columbus, OH 43210, USA
[2] University of Illinois, Urbana, IL 61801, USA
[3] Wayne State University, Detroit, MI 48202, USA

Abstract. We study replacement algorithms for non-uniform access caches that are used in distributed storage systems. Considering access latencies as major costs of data management in such a system, we show that the total cost of any replacement algorithm is bounded by *the total costs of evicted blocks* plus the total cost of the optimal off-line algorithm (OPT). We propose two off-line heuristics: MIN-d and MIN-cod, as well as an on-line algorithm: HD-cod, which can be run efficiently and perform well at the same time.

Our simulation results with Storage Performance Council (SPC)'s storage server traces show that: (1) for off-line workloads, MIN-cod performs as well as OPT in some cases, all is at most three times worse in all test case; (2) for on-line workloads, HD-cod performs closely to the best algorithms in all cases, and is the single algorithm that performs well in all test cases, including the optimal on-line algorithm (Landlord). Our study suggests that the essential issue to be considered be the trade-off between the costs of victim blocks and the total number of evictions in order to effectively optimize both efficiency and performance of distributed storage cache replacement algorithms.

1 Introduction

Widely used distributed storage systems have two unique features: storage device heterogeneity and multi-level caching management. In a typical multi-level heterogeneous distributed storage system, I/O buffer caches are installed at hierarchical levels. Access latencies to data blocks are no longer a constant due to non-uniform access times caused by heterogeneous storage devices and hierarchical caching. This adds another dimension to the management of distributed storage caches, which is a significant impact factor to the system performance. However, most existing replacement algorithms in practice focus on minimizing miss rate as the single metric for performance optimization, treating access latency as a constant. For example, recent studies on replacement algorithms such as 2Q, ARC, LIRS, and MQ mainly aim to improve the traditional LRU heuristic[1], which consider only block recency or balance both recency and frequency

---

[1] A brief overview of these algorithms is available in [1].

A. Pelc (Ed.): DISC 2007, LNCS 4731, pp. 373 387, 2007.

to reduce miss rate. These algorithms may not be suitable to manage caches of variable access latencies in distributed storage systems.

The replacement problem for caches with non-uniform access latencies can be modeled by the *weighted caching* problem, which can be solved off-line in $O(kn^2)$ time by reduction to the *minimal cost flow* problem [2], where k is the cache size and n is the number of total requests. However, this optimal algorithm is resource intensive in terms of both space and time for real-world system workloads, particularly when k and n are large. As an example, for a sequence of only $16K$ requests and a buffer cache of as small as 1.5 MBytes, the best known implementation of the minimum-cost flow algorithm [3] takes more than 17 GBytes of memory and multiple days to run on a dual-core 2.8GHz SMP Xeon server. Therefore, as current workloads and cache capacity continue to scale up, it becomes too unrealistic to timely make optimal replacement schedules.

In face of this problem, we study replacement algorithms for non-uniform access latency caches. Similar to previous studies, we use variable *cost* to model the non-uniform access latency in order to improve the efficiency and performance of replacement algorithms. In general, our model can be used for a distributed storage system with other non-uniform features, such as non-uniform energy consumption per access by instantiating costs as energy access consumption for different blocks to minimize total the energy consumption.

We show that for any replacement algorithm, the total access cost is bounded by *the total cost of the evicted blocks* (see Section 3) of the replacement algorithm plus the total access cost of the optimal algorithm (OPT). Therefore, the key to design variable-cost cache replacement algorithms lies in the trade-off between the number of evictions and the cost of victim blocks. Based on this principle, we propose two off-line algorithms: MIN-d and MIN-cod. Specifically, we take the variable cost consideration into MIN – the optimal replacement algorithm for uniform caches [4]. We found that choosing replacement victims based on the ratio of cost and *forward distance* (see Section 3.1) is effective for minimizing the total costs. Using this heuristic, we also propose an on-line replacement algorithm HD-cod, which adaptively selects victims among blocks of largest recency from different cost groups.

We have evaluated the performance of the proposed algorithms with Storage Performance Council's storage server traces [5] by comparing our algorithms with OPT, Landlord [6] – a theoretically optimal on-line cost-aware algorithm , and other well-known cost-unaware replacement algorithms such as LRU, LFU, MRU, and Minimal Cost First (MCF). The results demonstrate that the proposed algorithms can be executed efficiently. Among all the algorithms, MIN-cod performs best in all cases, whose total cost is the same as OPT in some cases, and is at most four times of the lower bound of OPT in all cases. MIN-d performs similarly to MIN-cod when the cost distribution is small. In on-line scenarios, HD-cod performs close to the best algorithms in all cases and is the single algorithm that performs well in all test cases.

2 Preliminaries

The *weighted caching* problem [6] is defined as follows. Given a request sequence of data blocks:$r_1, ..., r_n$, each block has a cost (or weight) $\mathsf{cost}(r)$. For a cache of size k, upon each request r, if the requested block is not in cache(a miss), it is fetched in with $\mathsf{cost}(r)$. At the same time, one block in the cache is replaced to make space for r. If the requested block is already in cache, then no cost is involved. The goal is to minimize the total cost to serve the request sequence. An algorithm for the problem which assumes prior knowledge of the complete request sequence is an *off-line algorithm*. If an algorithm only knows the current and past requests in the sequence, then it is an *on-line algorithm*.

OPT: An Optimal Off-Line Algorithm. Chrobak *et al.* [7] gave an optimal off-line algorithm for the weighted caching problem by reducing it to the *minimal cost maximum flow* problem [2]. Since the minimum-cost maximum flow problem can be solved in $O(kn^2)$ time and the reduction step takes only $O(n^2 + k)$ time, the problem can be solved in $O(kn^2)$ in total. Therefore, this optimal offline algorithm is resource intensive, especially when k and n are large. For example, for a request sequence of one million blocks, the flow network has around one thousand billion arcs to process and needs several terabytes storage, which is well beyond the capability of current off-the-shelf servers.

2.1 MIN: An Off-Line Algorithm for Uniform Cost Cases

Belady's MIN algorithm [4] is based on the assumption of a uniform block access cost. It always replaces the block to be requested furthest in the future. Belady proved that MIN can minimize the total number of misses, thus minimizing the total cost when the access cost to each block is uniform. Compared with OPT, MIN is much more efficient – it can be implemented in $O(n \log k)$ time and $O(n)$ space.

In a variable-cost cache, MIN's replacement decision can be far from optimal, since the furthest blocks can carry high fetch costs and lead to subsequent high miss penalties. Next we analyze its performance in variable-cost cases.

Definition 1. *A* cache configuration *is the set of (distinct) blocks resident in a given cache C.*

Given a request sequence S and an initial cache configuration $\mathsf{cfg}(C)$, let $\mathsf{tc}(\textsc{Alg}, \mathsf{cfg}(C), S)$ denote the total fetch costs incurred by an algorithm $\textsc{Alg}$; and let $\mathsf{tf}(\textsc{Alg}, \mathsf{cfg}(C), S)$ denote the total number of fetches (misses).

Let S be a request sequence, and $\mathsf{cfg}(C)$ be an initial cache configuration. Let $\mathsf{cost}_{min} = \min_{r \in S} \mathsf{cost}(r)$ and $\mathsf{cost}_{max} = \max_{r \in S} \mathsf{cost}(r)$ be the minimal fetch cost and the maximum fetch cost among all requests, respectively. it is easy to verify the following relationship.

$$\mathsf{tf}(\mathrm{MIN}, \mathsf{cfg}(C), S) * \mathsf{cost}_{min} \leq \mathsf{tc}(\mathrm{OPT}, \mathsf{cfg}(C), S) \leq$$
$$\mathsf{tc}(\mathrm{MIN}, \mathsf{cfg}(C), S) \leq \mathsf{tf}(\mathrm{MIN}, \mathsf{cfg}(C), S) * \mathsf{cost}_{max}$$

When $\mathsf{cost}_{max}/\mathsf{cost}_{min}$ is sufficiently small, MIN works pretty well; indeed, $\mathsf{tc}(\text{MIN}, \mathsf{cfg}(\mathsf{C}), S)$ is bounded together with $\mathsf{tc}(\text{OPT}, \mathsf{cfg}(\mathsf{C}), S)$ – the optimal cost by a narrow range. Actually, if a cache-resident block with an access cost of cost_{min} is to be referenced furthest in the future, it is the optimal victim candidate for replacement. However, it is not easy to choose victims when the furthest-to-be-referenced block has a non-minimal cost. Therefore, a new heuristic is needed to choose victims efficiently and accurately.

3   Cost-Aware Cache Replacement

A storage cache is a fully associative cache. It has two kinds of misses: *cold miss* and *capacity miss* [8]. Therefore, any replacement algorithm's total fetch cost can be divided into cold-miss cost and capacity-miss cost. Since cold miss is compulsory, it is the same for any algorithm including OPT, which means the cold-miss cost is no greater than the total cost of OPT. Therefore, we have the following observation.

Definition 2. *Given a request sequence S, on each fetch of any replacement algorithm, a block is* evicted *if it is replaced and is to be requested later in the remaining request sequence.*

Observation 1. Let S be a request sequence, $\mathsf{cfg}(\mathsf{C})$ be an initial cache configuration, ALG be a replacement algorithm. Let $v_1, v_2, \ldots, v_m$ be the sequence of blocks evicted by ALG when it serves S. It holds that $\mathsf{tc}(\text{ALG}, \mathsf{cfg}(\mathsf{C}), S) \leq \mathsf{tc}(\text{OPT}, \mathsf{cfg}(\mathsf{C}), S) + \sum_1^m \mathsf{cost}(v_i)$.

Observation 1 shows that the key to design replacement algorithms for a weighted cache is the trade-off between the cost of eviction victims and the total number of evictions to minimize $\sum_1^m \mathsf{cost}(v_i)$. If a replacement algorithm is wise in choosing replacement victims such that no eviction is needed, then the total cost involved is the same as OPT. Otherwise, it performs at most $\sum_1^m \mathsf{cost}(v_i)$ worse than OPT.

In addition, unlike competitive analysis involving some unknown constant, observation 1 shows that a concrete upper bound of extra cost compared with OPT can be determined by simply adding the costs of all the evicted blocks, which can be implemented with negligible overhead in real systems. Such an upper bound is useful for evaluating the cache efficiency of a replacement algorithm. On the other hand, it can also be used to calculate the lower bound of OPT so as to estimate its total cost by deducting the eviction costs from the total costs of tested replacement algorithms.

Aimed at minimizing $\sum_1^m \mathsf{cost}(v_i)$, next we propose two off-line algorithms and one on-line algorithm.

3.1   MIN-d Algorithm

Our first algorithm, MIN-d, is an extension of MIN. It chooses the minimal-cost block from the $d+1$ furthest blocks ($d \geq 0$) as victim rather than choose the one

Input: request sequence S and initial cache configuration $\mathsf{cfg}(\mathsf{C})$.
for each request r in S **do**
    if $r \notin \mathsf{cfg}(\mathsf{C})$ **then**
        Let $Q \subseteq \mathsf{cfg}(\mathsf{C})$ be the set of $d+1$ resident cache blocks having the largest
        forward distances. Let $b \in Q$ be the block having the smallest cost among Q.
        Replace b and read block r.
    Update $\mathsf{cfg}(\mathsf{C})$ and the forward distances of resident cache blocks.

Fig. 1. MIN-d Algorithm

furthest block without consideration of costs. In particular, when $d = 0$, MIN-d is MIN. Before giving the details of MIN-d, depicted in Figure 1, we make the following definition.

Definition 3. *Given a block r resident in the cache, the forward distance of r, denoted by $\mathsf{fwd}(r)$, is the number of distinct accesses from the current position to the next access of r in the request sequence.*

For example, suppose that the current cache configuration is $\{r_1, r_2, r_3\}$, and the remaining request sequence (that has not be served) is $r_2, r_4, r_5, r_4, r_3, r_1$. Then we have $\mathsf{fwd}(r_1) = 4$, $\mathsf{fwd}(r_2) = 0$, and $\mathsf{fwd}(r_3) = 3$.

We claim that MIN-d's total number of misses is small, if d is relatively small compared to the cache size. Actually, the extra number of misses for MIN-d can be at most $n * \ln \frac{k-1}{k-d-1}$, where k is the cache size, n is the number of total requests.

Bound of Miss Count for MIN-d. In what follows, we fix a request sequence S of length n. For simplicity of exposition, we assume that the ith request of S occurs at time i. Let $S[i, j]$ be the subsequence of S consisting of the requests at time from i to j (inclusive).

Given a set H and two elements x, y, the notation $H - x + y$ refers to the set $(H \setminus \{x\}) \cup \{y\}$.

Definition 4. *Let $\mathsf{seq}(t, b)$ be the first occurrence of a block b in the sequence S after time t; if b is not requested in S after time t then let $\mathsf{seq}(t, b) = \infty$. For example, if $S = \{a, b, a, d, c, b\}$, then $\mathsf{seq}(4, b) = 6$ and $\mathsf{seq}(3, a) = \infty$.*

Definition 5. *When S is being served by a given cache C, the cache configuration of C changes only when a miss occurs. Let $\mathsf{cur}_i(C)$ be the time when the ith miss occurs (namely, if the rth request of S incurs the ith miss, then $\mathsf{cur}_i(C) = r$). Let $\mathsf{cfg}_i(C)$ be the cache configuration of C after i misses have occurred. For example, $\mathsf{cfg}_0(C)$ is the initial cache configuration of C.*

Let $\mathsf{HS}_i(C) = \{\mathsf{seq}(\mathsf{cur}_i(C), b) \neq \infty \mid b \notin \mathsf{cfg}_i(C)\}$. In words, if a block b is not in the cache configuration $\mathsf{cfg}_i(C)$ and if b is requested after $\mathsf{cur}_i(C)$, then the first occurrence of b after $\mathsf{cur}_i(C)$ is in $\mathsf{HS}_i(C)$. Note that the next cache miss after $\mathsf{cur}_i(C)$, namely $\mathsf{cur}_{i+1}(C)$, would occur at the earliest time in $\mathsf{HS}_i(C)$.

Let H_1 and H_2 be two sets of positive integers, we write $H_2 \prec H_1$ if $|H_2 \cap [1,x]| \geq |H_1 \cap [1,x]|$, for any $x \geq 1$. For example, $\{1,2,4,5,7\} \prec \{2,3,5,6\}$.

Claim 1. (i) Let H_1' and H_2' be the (nonempty) set after removing the smallest element from H_1 and H_2, respectively. If $H_2 \prec H_1$ then $H_2' \prec H_1'$.
(ii) Let $H_1' = H_1 + h_1$ and $H_2' = H_2 + h_2$. If $H_2 \prec H_1$ and $h_2 \leq h_1$, then $H_2' \prec H_1'$.

Lemma 1. *Given a request sequence S, let C_1 and C_2 be two caches such that $|C_1| = d + 1 + |C_2|$ and $\mathsf{cfg}_0(C_2) \subset \mathsf{cfg}_0(C_1)$. If MIN-$d$ is used for C_1 and MIN is used for C_2, then $\mathsf{cur}_r(C_2) \leq \mathsf{cur}_r(C_1)$ and $\mathsf{HS}_r(C_2) \prec \mathsf{HS}_r(C_1)$, for each $r \geq 0$ (satisfying $\mathsf{HS}_r(C_1) \neq \emptyset$).*

Proof. By induction on r. When $r = 0$, it is easy to verify that the claim holds. Assume the claim holds for $r = i$. Next we show that the claim holds for $r = i+1$.

Let $z_1 = \mathsf{cur}_{i+1}(C_1)$ and $z_2 = \mathsf{cur}_{i+1}(C_2)$. By definition, z_1 and z_2 are the earliest times in $\mathsf{HS}_i(C_1)$ and $\mathsf{HS}_i(C_1)$, respectively. This immediately implies $z_2 \leq z_1$, since $\mathsf{HS}_i(C_2) \prec \mathsf{HS}_i(C_1)$. It remains to prove $\mathsf{HS}_{i+1}(C_2) \prec \mathsf{HS}_{i+1}(C_1)$.

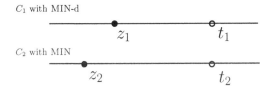

Fig. 2. Here, $z_1 = \mathsf{cur}_{i+1}(C_1)$ is the time when the $(i+1)$th miss occurs in C_1. At time z_1, the block h_1 is fetched into C_1 and v_1 is the victim block. The time t_1 is the first occurrence of v_1 (in S) after z_1. The numbers z_2 and t_2 are defined similarly on C_2. Note that $z_1 \geq z_2$, but t_1 may be smaller than t_2.

Let h_1 be the block being requested (in S) at time z_1, and v_1 be the victim block (in C_1) replaced by MIN-d at the same time. Let h_2 be the block being requested at time z_2, and v_2 be the victim block (in C_2) replaced by MIN at the same time. Let $t_1 = \mathsf{seq}(z_1, v_1)$ and $t_2 = \mathsf{seq}(z_2, v_2)$. See Figure 2.

For simplicity, we focus on the cases when $t_1 \neq \infty$ and $t_2 \neq \infty$, and omit the other cases (when $t_1 = \infty$ or $t_2 = \infty$) since they are similar. Consider the difference between $\mathsf{HS}_i(C_1)$ and $\mathsf{HS}_{i+1}(C_1)$. It is easy to see that z_1 is the earliest time in $\mathsf{HS}_i(C_1)$, and it is not in $\mathsf{HS}_{i+1}(C_1)$. Also note that t_1 is in $\mathsf{HS}_{i+1}(C_1)$ but not in $\mathsf{HS}_i(C_1)$. All other elements in $\mathsf{HS}_i(C_1)$ remains unchanged in $\mathsf{HS}_{i+1}(C_1)$. Therefore, it holds that

$$\mathsf{HS}_{i+1}(C_1) = \mathsf{HS}_i(C_1) - z_1 + t_1. \tag{1}$$

Similarly, we have

$$\mathsf{HS}_{i+1}(C_2) = \mathsf{HS}_i(C_1) - z_2 + t_2. \tag{2}$$

1. $t_1 \geq t_2$. By Claim 1 (i), we have $\mathsf{HS}_i(C_1) - z_1 \prec \mathsf{HS}_i(C_2) - z_2$, since z_1 and z_2 are the earliest times in $\mathsf{HS}_i(C_1)$ and $\mathsf{HS}_i(C_1)$, respectively. Now, by Claim 1 (ii), it is easy to verify $\mathsf{HS}_{i+1}(C_1) \prec \mathsf{HS}_{i+1}(C_2)$, since $t_2 \leq t_1$.

2. $t_1 < t_2$. We need to show that $|\mathsf{HS}_{i+1}(C_2) \cap [1, x]| \geq |\mathsf{HS}_{i+1}(C_1) \cap [1, x]|$, for any integer $x \geq 1$.

(i) $x \leq z_1$. We have $\mathsf{HS}_{i+1}(C_1) \cap [1, x] = \emptyset$ (recall that z_1 is the earliest time in $\mathsf{HS}_i(C_1)$, which implies that the earliest time in $\mathsf{HS}_{i+1}(C_1)$ is larger than z_1). The claim trivially follows.

(ii) $z_1 < x < t_1$. Note that $z_2 \leq z_1$ and $t_1 < t_2$. By Eq. (1) and Eq. (2), we have $|\mathsf{HS}_{i+1}(C_1) \cap [1, x]| = |\mathsf{HS}_i(C_1) \cap [1, x]| - 1$ and $|\mathsf{HS}_{i+1}(C_2) \cap [1, x]| = |\mathsf{HS}_i(C_2) \cap [1, x]| - 1$. The claim immediately follows, by the induction hypothesis $|\mathsf{HS}_i(C_1) \cap [1, x]| \leq |\mathsf{HS}_i(C_2) \cap [1, x]|$.

(iii) $x \geq t_1$. Note that $\mathsf{HS}_{i+1}(C_1) \cap [1, z_1] = \emptyset$ and $\mathsf{HS}_{i+1}(C_2) \cap [1, z_2] = \emptyset$, by similar arguments to (i). As such, it suffices to prove

$$|\mathsf{HS}_{i+1}(C_1) \cap [z_1 + 1, x]| \leq |\mathsf{HS}_{i+1}(C_2) \cap [z_2 + 1, x]|. \tag{3}$$

Let B_1 be the set of distinct blocks in $S[z_1 + 1, x]$, and $R_1 \subseteq B_1$ be the set of distinct blocks in $S[z_1 + 1, x]$ that are in $\mathsf{cfg}_{i+1}(C_1)$. Similarly, let B_2 be the set of distinct blocks in $S[z_2 + 1, x]$, and $R_2 \subseteq B_2$ be the set of distinct blocks in $S[z_2 + 1, x]$ that are in $\mathsf{cfg}_{i+1}(C_2)$. Now, notice that the LHS of Eq. (3) is the number of distinct blocks in $S[z_1 + 1, x]$ that are not in $\mathsf{cfg}_{i+1}(C_1)$, which is equal to $|B_1| - |R_1|$, and the RHS of Eq. (3) is the number of distinct blocks in $S[z_2 + 1, x]$ that are not in $\mathsf{cfg}_{i+1}(C_2)$, which is equal to $|B_2| - |R_2|$. Therefore, we need to prove that

$$|B_1| - |R_1| \leq |B_2| - |R_2|.$$

By the MIN-d algorithm, v_1 is one of the $d+1$ furthest block to be requested at time z_1. Therefore, $|R_1| \geq |C_1| - (d + 1) = |C_2|$. On the other hand, $|R_2| \leq |C_2|$. It follows that $|R_1| \geq |R_2|$. Furthermore, by the definition, $B_1 \subseteq B_2$, since $z_1 \geq z_2$. This implies that $|B_1| \leq |B_2|$. It thus follows that $|B_1| - |R_1| \leq |B_2| - |R_2|$, as required. $\qquad \square$

The following corollary is straightforward:

Corollary 1. *Let S be a request sequence, C_1 and C_2 be two caches such at $|C_1| = |C_2| + d + 1$ and $\mathsf{cfg}_0(C_1) \supseteq \mathsf{cfg}_0(C_2)$. It holds that $\mathsf{tf}(\text{MIN-}d, \mathsf{cfg}(C_1), S) <= \mathsf{tf}(\text{MIN}, \mathsf{cfg}(C_2), S)$.*

Due to the limit of space for presentation, we omit the proofs of the following lemma and theorem. Details can be found in [9].

Lemma 2. *Let S be a given request sequence and C_1 and C_2 be two caches such that $|C_1| = |C_2| + 1$ and $\mathsf{cfg}(C_1) \supseteq \mathsf{cfg}(C_2)$. The number of fetches by MIN on C_2 is at most $n/|C_2|$ larger than the number of fetches by MIN on C_1. That is, $\mathsf{tf}(\text{MIN}, \mathsf{cfg}(C_2), S) \leq \mathsf{tf}(\text{MIN}, \mathsf{cfg}(C_1), S) + n/|C_2|$.*

The following theorem follows from Corollary 1 and Lemma 2.

Input: request sequence S and initial cache configuration cfg(C).
for each request r in S **do**
   if $r \notin$ cfg(C) **then**
      Let $b \in$ cfg(C) be the resident block having the smallest Cod value $\frac{cost(b)}{fwd(b)}$
      in current cache configuration cfg(C). If there is a tie, choose b as the one
      with the largest forward distance. Replace b and read block r.
   Update cfg(C) and the forward distances of resident cache blocks.

Fig. 3. MIN-cod Algorithm

Theorem 1. *Let S be a request sequence of length n and C be a cache of size k. We have* $\mathsf{tf}(\text{MIN-}d, \mathsf{cfg}(C), S) \leq \mathsf{tf}(\text{MIN}, \mathsf{cfg}(C), S) + n \ln \frac{k-1}{k-d-1}$, *namely, the* MIN-$d$ *algorithm performs at most* $n \ln \frac{k-1}{k-d-1}$ *more fetches than* MIN.

3.2 MIN-cod Algorithm

The MIN-d algorithm takes block cost into consideration for replacement decisions without significantly increasing the number of misses. However, it is conservative in nature as the scope of the candidate victim blocks is small ($d + 1$ furthest blocks). In reality, it is possible that some blocks to be accessed recently are much cheaper than the $d + 1$ furthest blocks such that evicting those near blocks to keep those expensive blocks despite of more misses is still beneficial. Obviously, MIN-d cannot make efficient decisions in these cases, thus its performance is limited, especially when the cost differences among the blocks are large. Therefore, we propose an algorithm that more aggressively pursues an optimal trade-off between the number of evictions and block costs by considering every block as a potential replacement candidate.

As described in Figure 3, the algorithm MIN-cod makes replacement decisions based on the ratio of the cost over forward distance (Cod) among all the resident blocks in cache. If two blocks have the same ratio, the block with a larger forward distance is chosen. Clearly, if a block has the minimal cost among all resident blocks and is the furthest block, MIN-cod will replace it upon a miss, which is necessary for OPT too. However, if one block has a smaller cost and a shorter forward distance than another block, then it is unclear which one is a better victim block to reduce the total cost. Note that the number of evictions for keeping a block is closely related with its forward distance. Assuming keeping a block is beneficial, then it must not be evicted before its next request, otherwise the sooner it is evicted the better so as to save space for other blocks. Since the space for this block is occupied from the current request to the block's next request, keeping a block can be viewed as effectively reducing the cache size by one during this period. Based on the reasoning of Lemma 2, it is not difficult to know that the upper bound of extra misses caused for keeping this block in comparison to keeping a nearer block is roughly in proportion to its forward distance. Therefore, the $cost/fwd$ essentially represents the minimal average cost savings per extra miss. The Cod heuristic chooses to replace the furthest block that generates the smallest saving.

The Running Times of MIN-d and MIN-cod. A naive implementation of MIN-d and MIN-cod, on each request, scans the resident blocks in cache to find the victim and update fwd values. Therefore, the total execution times of both algorithms are $O(nk)$.

There are two observations that can lead to a faster implementation for MIN-d, which uses only $O(n \log k)$ time. First, MIN-d only requires to maintain the *relative* forward distances among the blocks to choose victims from. Second, after serving a new request, the cache configuration changes by only one element, and at most one resident cache block changes its relative forward distance. Therefore, if we use a priority queue to maintain the (relative) forward distances of resident blocks, we only need $\log k$ time for processing each request, resulting a total running time of $O(n \log k)$.

In real systems, the number of different fetch costs of blocks is relatively small, because only a limited number of different storage devices and levels exist in a system. Therefore, by keeping the resident blocks in binary trees of different costs, MIN-cod only needs to compare the blocks of the largest (relative) forward distance within each tree to find the right victim, whose total execution steps are in proportion to the number of different trees, thus can be considered as $O(1)$. Since the maintenance of each binary tree needs $O(\log k)$ time, the overall running time is bounded by $O(n \log k)$, which is much faster than OPT.

3.3   An On-Line Algorithm HD-cod

The off-line algorithms assume complete knowledge of future requests, which is not always realistic in practice. In this section, we present HD-cod, an on-line algorithm based on MIN-cod.

In on-line algorithms, we can only estimate the forward distance of a resident block. To this end, we use the *recency* of a resident cache block b as the estimated forward distance of b. (Recency is a concept borrowed from the well-known LRU replacement algorithm.) More specifically, the recency of b is the difference between its current request sequence number and the request sequence number of the last request of b.

It is widely recognized that the LRU replacement algorithm, which estimates the forward distance of a block by its recency, works well for most workloads with strong temporal locality. However, it performs poorly for workloads with weak locality such as those with looping or random access patterns, where a recent access of a block does not indicate its re-access is near. These observations suggest that different considerations of forward distance can be used when evaluating Cod value of each block for the choice of replacement victims.

In HD-cod, we use $\frac{cost}{fwd^\alpha}$ to evaluate each block, where α is a workload dependent parameter in $[0, 1]$. For workloads with LRU-like temporal locality, α approaches 1 because the forward distance estimation is accurate, so that the Cod heuristic is appropriate. For non-LRU-like workload, α approaches 0 because the estimation of forward distance is inaccurate and the forward distance becomes less relevant, so that the replacement decision can be more dependent on the cost.

To determine the workload type, HD-cod maintains an LRU queue (ordered by recency) for all the resident blocks. It divides the queue into multiple contiguous regions of a fixed size, which is a system run-time parameter and usually small. HD-cod traces the hit count in each recency region to generate the hit density curve of the workloads, so that α can be set dynamically based on the locality feature. Therefore the algorithm is called Hit Density(HD)-cod. On each replacement decision, HD-cod walks through the regions to calculate α. (More details can be found in [9]). Since HD-cod maintains each queue using LRU order whose overhead is very small, its time complexity is $O(n)$.

4   Evaluation

Methodology: We evaluate our proposed algorithms through trace-driven simulation. We compare the performance of our proposed algorithms with the optimal off-line algorithm OPT, representative non-cost-aware algorithms including MIN, Least Recently Used (LRU), Most Recently Used (MRU), Most Frequently Used (LFU) as well as cost-aware algorithms including Landlord and Minimal Cost First (MCF). Landlord is an optimal on-line cost-aware caching algorithm [10,6]. Upon each replacement, it chooses the block with the minimal residual cost as victim, and decreases each resident block's residual cost by this minimal value. Then upon each hit, the block's residual cost is updated by a value that is between current value and its original cost. It is proved in [6] that Landlord is a k-competitive algorithm, hence an optimal on-line replacement algorithm. It is also a generalization of the GreedyDual algorithm [11], which is studied in WWW-proxy cache management.

The traces used in our experiments are production storage I/O traces from Storage Performance Council (SPC) [5] – a vendor-neutral standards body. They include both OLTP application I/O and search engine I/O. The OLTP traces are with strong temporal locality, i.e. repeated accesses to the same block, if any, are usually separated by a small (compared with cache size in blocks) count of accesses to other blocks. And the OLTP traces also include a significant portions of concurrent sequential accesses due to both the nature of server workloads and OLTP itself. The search engine traces comprise mostly random accesses, which are mostly non-sequential accesses with weak temporal locality, i.e. repeated accesses to the same block, if any, are usually separated by a large (compared with cache size in blocks) count of accesses to other blocks. Due to the resource-intensive nature of the OPT algorithm, which makes replaying the complete trace computationally intractable on our system, we split an entire trace into smaller traces by the ASU (Application Specific Unit) field of each request, so that logically related requests are grouped in the same trace file. We randomly generate the cost for each block based on two cost distributions. One cost distribution spans a wide range with differences as large as 70,000 times, the other spans a small range with differences at most 3 times. Specific values used and their distributions can be found in [9].

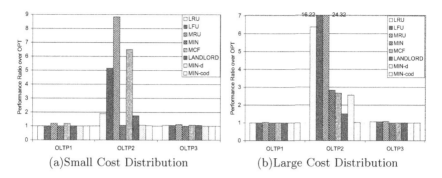

Fig. 4. Total cost comparison of three workloads between OPT and different algorithms

Impact of Cost-Aware Replacement: We compare OPT with both existing and our proposed replacement algorithms to evaluate the impact of weighted cache on replacement performance. In this experiment, we set one eighth of the working set size as the cache size.

Figure 4 shows the performance ratio of various algorithms over OPT for three small workloads using two different cost distributions. Overall, a significant performance degradation is observed using non-cost-aware replacement algorithms. For example, the optimal non-cost-aware algorithm MIN is 182% worse than OPT for OLTP2 using large cost distribution, so is LRU 537% worse. In contrast, the cost-aware algorithms including Landlord, MIN-d, and MIN-cod perform better almost in all these cases. The only exception is for the small cost distribution, MIN performs closer to OPT than Landlord, since in these scenarios, miss count is more important in the trade-off for overall performance.

The results also show that the extent of the performance degradation is related with the workload itself. As we can see, OLTP2 is much more sensitive to the cost-awareness of the algorithms than the other two, because the other two traces have very few reused blocks.

Miss Rate of MIN-d: We measure the miss rate of both OLTP and WebSearch workloads. The OLTP workload has a working set of around $300K$ blocks, while the WebSearch workload has a working set of around $480K$. The results show that the miss rate does not increase noticeably until d is larger than 6% of the cache size. Based on this empirically result, in the following experiments, we set d to be $1/16$ of the cache size.

Off-line Algorithm Results: Figure 5 shows the experiment results comparing off-line algorithms (MIN-d and MIN-cod) with existing off-line algorithm MIN. We also include the comparison with on-line algorithms: MCF and Landlord for two reasons: a) MIN and MCF represent two ends on the trade-off between miss count and cost. MIN considers only misses in replacement decisions, while MCF considers only cost; b)since Landlord is the state-of-the-art cost aware replacement algorithm, the inclusion of it gives us an idea on the benefit of complete request knowledge to variable-cost cache replacement.

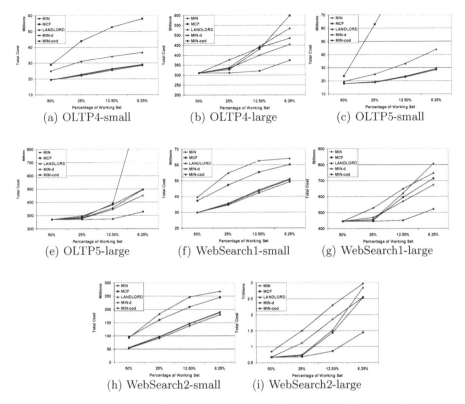

Fig. 5. Comparison of off-line cost aware algorithms using different cache sizes

Overall, MIN-cod consistently performs the best for all workloads. It reduces up to 62% of the total cost of MIN and up to 50% of Landlord. Other algorithms perform differently depending on the workloads. For example, as expected, MIN-d performs close to MIN-cod for the small cost distribution; however it is significantly worse than MIN-cod for the large distribution due to its scope limitation of victim candidates. Compared with Landlord, MCF performs poorly for the OLTP workloads, while it performs better for the Websearch workloads. Using the lower bound measured, it also shows that when the cache size is 50% of the workload, in seven out of the eight cases MIN-cod performs the same as OPT, while for one of the WebSearch workloads, MIN-cod has a total cost 20% larger than the lower bound of OPT. In all cases, using the bound reported, we can guarantee that MIN-cod's performance is at most four times of optimal.

The above results show that the Cod heuristic works well with all the workloads tested. Since MIN-cod balances the cost of evicted blocks and the number of misses the replacement decision can cause, it is effective for a cost-aware replacement algorithm.

On-line Algorithm Results: Figure 6 compares HD-cod with online algorithms: LRU, LFU, MRU, MCF, and Landlord. Overall, HD-cod performs very close to

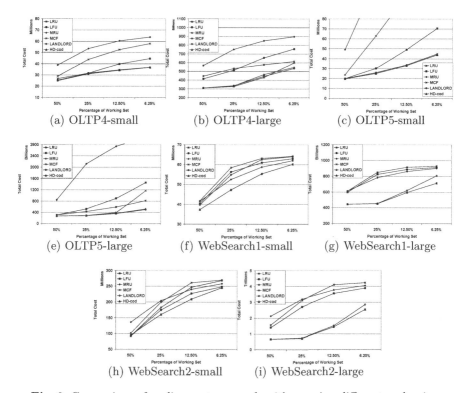

Fig. 6. Comparison of on-line cost aware algorithms using different cache sizes

the best algorithm in each test scenario. Specifically, for the OLTP workload, HD-cod performs comparably as Landlord, yet reduces up to 68% of the total cost of MCF; for the WebSearch workload, HD-cod performs similarly as MCF, yet reduces up to 15% of the total cost of Landlord.

The above results show that for on-line cost-aware replacement algorithms where the forward distance of a block is not known, the balance between the two metrics (cost and forward distance) needs to be conducted adaptively based on the workloads. Since the Landlord algorithm only considers future accesses as with LRU-like locality, it does not perform well for workloads with the non-LRU-like locality. Since HD-cod detects workload characteristics by tracing the hit density, it adapts itself to behave more like MCF when temporal locality is weak and to behave more like Landlord when temporal locality is strong. Therefore, HD-cod performs close to the best algorithm in all test cases.

5   Related Work

Previous work on cost-aware cache replacement includes both theoretical results and system studies. Young [12] studied the weighted caching problem and proposed an on-line algorithm – GreedyDual. Cao *et al.* [11] studied WWW-proxy caching and proposed GreedyDual-size to incorporate file size into replacement decision. Landlord [6] is a generalization of both GreedyDual and GreedyDual-size. Chrobak *et al.* [7] proposed on-line algorithms: Rotate and Balance. All these algorithms are proved to be k-competitive, thus theoretically optimal. GreedyDual-size has also been demonstrated to be effective experimentally using simulation experiments on Web proxy traces. Although competitive analysis provides a bound for approximation algorithms, the bound is usually too loose to be attractive. For example, k in the above results is the cache size in blocks, which is at the magnitude of millions with current technology; and it keeps increasing as the technology evolves. Although experimental results are provided to demonstrate the effective of GreedyDual-size [3], it focuses on the variance of document size rather than the access cost of uniform-sized block in storage system. Therefore, they compare with popular replacement algorithms such as LRU, LFU and other size-aware algorithms. Forney *et al.* [10] studied partition-based cache management scheme for heterogeneous storage devices and proposed to use equal device wait time as a metric for dynamic cache allocation, which is orthogonal to our studies.

Compared with previous work, our work demonstrates that the upper-bound of performance degradation of any replacement algorithm over OPT can be determined by keeping track of the costs of evicted blocks, which is more practical and meaningful than the k-competitive result. We also point out that the key design issue for efficient cost-aware replacement algorithms is to make an effective trade-off between victim blocks' cost and the total number of evictions. Our Cod heuristic which is based on the principle is demonstrated to outperform previous cost-aware and cost-unaware algorithms in real storage server traces simulations.

6   Conclusions

We have proposed both off-line and on-line algorithms that have performance comparable to the optimal replacement algorithm (OPT) measured by the total cost, yet are much faster to run in practice. The algorithms' design is guided by the following findings of ours. The performance of any replacement algorithm is deviated from OPT by at most the cost of evicted blocks, such that the key to design cost-aware replacement algorithm is to trade-off the number of evictions and the cost of victim blocks. Our work provides analytical bases for buffer cache management in distributed storage systems. We will further understand the implications of our study in our experimental system research.

References

1. Jiang, S., Zhang, X.: Making LRU friendly to weak locality workloads: A novel replacement algorithm to improve buffer cache performance. IEEE Trans. on Comp. 54(8), 939–952 (2005)
2. Cormen, T.H., Leiserson, C.E., Rivest, R.L., Stein, C.: Introduction to Algorithms. MIT Press, Cambridge (2001)

3. Goldberg, A.V.: An efficient implementation of a scaling minimum-cost flow algorithm. J. Algorithms 22(1), 1–29 (1997)
4. Belady, L.: A study of replacement algorithms for virtual storage computers. IBM Sys. J. 5, 78–101 (1966)
5. Storage Performance Council: SPC I/O Traces. Available at http://www.storageperformance.org
6. Young, N.E.: On-line file caching. In: Proc. 9th Annu. ACM-SIAM sympos. Discrete algorithms, pp. 82–86. ACM Press, New York (1998)
7. Chrobak, M., Karloff, H., Payne, T., Vishwanathan, S.: New results on server problems. SIAM J. Discret. Math. 4(2), 172–181 (1991)
8. Patterson, D.A., Hennessy, J.L.: Computer architecture: a quantitative approach. Morgan Kaufmann, San Francisco (1990)
9. Liang, S., Zhang, X., Jiang, S.: Cost-aware caching algorithms for distributed storage servers. Technical Report OSU-CISRC-3/07-TR23 (2007)
10. Forney, B., Arpaci-Dusseau, A.C., Arpaci-Dusseau, R.H.: Storage-aware caching: Revisiting caching for heterogeneous storage systems. In: Proc. 1st USENIX Sympos. File and Storage Tech., pp. 61–74 (2002)
11. Cao, P., Irani, S.: Cost-aware WWW proxy caching algorithms. In: Proc. 1997 Usenix Sympos. on Internet Tech. Sys. (1997)
12. Young, N.E.: The k-server dual and loose competitiveness for paging. Algorithmica 11(6), 525–541 (1994)

Push-to-Pull Peer-to-Peer Live Streaming

Thomas Locher, Remo Meier, Stefan Schmid, and Roger Wattenhofer

Computer Engineering and Networks Laboratory (TIK),
ETH Zurich, 8092 Zurich, Switzerland
{lochert,remmeier,schmiste,wattenhofer}@tik.ee.ethz.ch

Abstract. In contrast to peer-to-peer file sharing, live streaming based on peer-to-peer technology is still awaiting its breakthrough. This may be due to the additional challenges live streaming faces, e.g., the need to meet real-time playback deadlines, or the increased demands on robustness under churn. This paper presents and evaluates novel neighbor selection and data distribution schemes for peer-to-peer live streaming. Concretely, in order to distribute data efficiently and with minimal delay, our algorithms combine low-latency push operations along a structured overlay with the flexibility of pull operations. The protocols ensure that all peers are able to obtain the required data blocks of a live stream in time, and that due to the loop-free dissemination paths, the overhead is low.

1 Introduction

Currently, we are witnessing an explosion of online video content provided on websites such as *YouTube*[1]. It is likely that in the near future, the Internet will also revolutionize television. Due to its scalability, peer-to-peer (p2p) technology is an appealing paradigm for providing live TV broadcasts over the Internet. Live p2p streaming is not only an active field of research, but there are already commercial products emerging, e.g., *JumpTV*[2], *PPLive*[3], *SopCast*[4], among others, which provide television to thousands of viewers.

Live streaming faces several challenges that are not encountered in other p2p applications such as file sharing. The streaming content is required to be received with respect to hard *real-time constraints*, and data blocks that are not obtained in time are dropped, resulting in a reduced playback quality. Additionally, a live broadcast ought to be received by all users simultaneously and with *minimal delay*. Moreover, as video streams often already demand a high transmission rate themselves, it is of paramount importance that the overhead caused by redundant transmissions of the protocol itself be minimized. Yet another crucial property of any successful live streaming system is its robustness to peer dynamics: It is likely that peers join and leave the system continuously and concurrently, called *churn*.

---

[1] See http://www.youtube.com/
[2] See http://www.jumptv.com/
[3] See http://www.pplive.com/
[4] See http://www.sopcast.com/

A. Pelc (Ed.): DISC 2007, LNCS 4731, pp. 388–402, 2007.

While there already exist several solutions both in literature and in practice, many of these systems fail to take all the aforementioned criteria into account. This may partly be explained by the fact that some of the optimization goals are inherently antagonistic. For example, a low delay can be achieved by having each peer immediately forward all incoming data blocks to its neighboring peers (*pushing*). Unfortunately, such a naive solution results in a significant overhead, as a peer may receive the same block repeatedly from different neighbors. Alternatively, peers could request missing blocks *explicitly*. This scheme is referred to as *pulling* since all peers have to initiate the transmission of data blocks towards themselves. While a pull-based approach circumvents the problem of receiving duplicates, it comes at the cost of intolerable latencies, as notifications and requests have to be sent back and forth. Hence, there is a trade-off between overhead and efficiency.

This paper presents and evaluates novel data distribution mechanisms which combine the benefits of pull-based approaches with the advantages of push-based approaches. In our mechanism, a fresh data block is quickly pushed to a well-defined set of peers. Due to the structured, prefix-based neighbor selection policy, this can be achieved without any redundant transmissions. The remaining peers which have not received the blocks in this initial phase use the pull mechanism to distribute the new data block amongst themselves.

We have implemented the algorithms presented in this paper in our own peer-to-peer live streaming system *Pulsar*.[5] Apart from real-world tests such as the broadcast of the IPTPS 2007 conference, we have performed extensive simulations of our protocol. According to our emulations with up to 100,000 peers (using the real code base), the system scales well as the network topology has a low diameter and guarantees small round trip times due to the latency-aware choice of neighbors. The proposed push-to-pull data dissemination policy is efficient: The time required from the moment a fresh data block becomes available at the source until it has reached virtually all peers is around 1,500 ms in a overlay consisting of 10,000 peers, and having 100,000 peers instead of 10,000 incurs a moderate additional delay of less than 250 ms. Finally, the Pulsar system tolerates a large fraction of peers crashing simultaneously without entailing any *underflows* at the remaining peers, i.e., all packets arrive before their playback deadline. This indicates that our protocols also perform well in dynamic environments.

The remainder of this paper is organized as follows. After reviewing related work in Section 2, the design of our protocol is presented in Section 3, followed by its evaluation in Section 4. In Section 5, the paper concludes.

2 Related Work

Although it has been expected that one-to-many broadcast would be offered through *IP multicast* since the early 1990s, it is not used in practice at all due to its limited support by the Internet Service Providers (ISPs). An attractive

---

[5] See http://www.getpulsar.com/

alternative to native IP multicast is to use a peer-to-peer network overlay built on the application layer to distribute the content.

Existing peer-to-peer approaches are mainly categorized according to the topology maintained among the peers or, equivalently, the neighbor selection algorithms the peers employ. Simple multicast systems are based on overlay *trees* [2,4,13]. Trees have the advantage that the topology is simple, once it is constructed the overhead is small in a static setting, and there are no duplicates as every peer receives its data blocks from its sole parent. However, there are rather serious drawbacks which render such systems inefficient. For example, resources are wasted as all the leaves of such a tree do not contribute anything to the system. Moreover, inner nodes having two or more children need to upload at least at twice the bitrate of the stream. This means that high-quality video streams cannot be transmitted unless one can guarantee that all inner nodes have a lot of spare upload capacity. Finally, the fragile tree structure is not resilient to any kind of node failures or churn. In order to overcome these problems, systems have been proposed to split the content of the stream into several disjoint *stripes* and disseminate this information along multiple disjoint trees. SplitStream [1] is a prominent example which uses *multiple description coding* (MDC) [3] to split the stream into different stripes in order to distribute them on several trees. Multiple description coding allows for the reconstruction of the original stream using any subset of the stripes. As each peer is also required to be an inner node in one of the trees, this approach solves the single tree's problem of having a large fraction of free-riding leaf peers. The CoopNet [7] approach is similar in that it also uses MDC and multiple trees; however, its goal is merely to complement the traditional client-server model as opposed to completely replace it. In this protocol, the server handles all the join requests and centrally manages all trees which limits the system's scalability. MDC is still an active research effort and no implementations for practical use are available. In addition, the overhead of multiple description coding harms the system's efficiency which may raise concerns whether multiple description coding is currently suitable for this kind of application. While maintaining several trees improves the robustness of a system, each tree can break individually, and the overhead potentially increases as more trees have to be repaired continuously (and concurrently).

Various systems using other approaches to cope with the shortcomings of tree-based topologies have also been presented. The *Bullet* [6] system uses a *mesh* on top of an arbitrary tree overlay in order to increase robustness. The additional links introduced by the mesh increase robustness by reducing the dependency of peers on their parents. The stream is split into disjoint blocks and distributed within the tree. Only as many blocks are sent to children as bandwidth is available, and missing blocks are then localized and retrieved using the mesh. However, the encoding of blocks, the duplicates, the requests for missing blocks, and the tree maintenance entail a substantial overhead in Bullet. *ChunkySpread* [12] strives to redeem the shortcomings of tree-based topologies by providing more efficient protocols to build and repair trees. By adding a "weak" tit-for-tat model and locality awareness, additional important aspects of peer-to-peer live streaming are considered.

The overhead of any tree-based protocol is generally large as the trees have to be repaired and the topology maintained. This is particularly true if there is a lot of churn in the network. Another disadvantage of trees is its lack of control over selfish peers: It is difficult to enforce that peers actually forward the data blocks to their designated children. Due to these inherent problems, a lot of research has also focused on tree-less protocols.

Since a rigidly structured overlay requires permanent maintenance, care has to be taken not to burden the individual peers. Therefore, unstructured overlays have been favored over structured overlays, and various protocols based on unstructured overlays have been proposed, e.g., *CoolStreaming/DONet* [15], *Chainsaw* [8] and *GridMedia* [14], all published in 2005. CoolStreaming/DONet makes a strong case for a *data-centric* design of the overlay, which means that the availability of data at certain nodes must steer the content dissemination, in contrast to having the predefined overlay dictate the data flow. Chainsaw and Gridmedia also follow this paradigm and mainly differ in the number of stored links to other peers, block sizes, buffer lengths, etc.—generally, parameters which have an impact on the overlay's robustness and overhead.

Typically, in unstructured overlays, peers have to *notify* neighboring peers about available blocks of data, and peers that are interested in obtaining these blocks must explicitly *request* them before any data is exchanged, because there is no structure in the network that could be used to disseminate data. Note that this scheme has the disadvantage that notifying peers and subsequently requesting data blocks potentially results in long delays before any data is exchanged.

Our approach differs from all these protocols in that it uses a structured overlay, based on a *prefix-routing* neighbor selection policy [9,10]. This policy guarantees a logarithmic diameter, robustness to massive crash failures and churn, and it also ensures that the entire network remains connected. At the same time, the protocol uses the flexibility of this neighbor selection scheme to take latency and bandwidth considerations into account when building up and maintaining the routing tables. Our mechanism further uses novel push algorithms tailored specifically for prefix-routing-based topologies to quickly disseminate the content to a fraction of all peers, thereby significantly reducing the delay experienced in other pull-based protocols. The benefits of push-to-pull strategies are well-known in theory, e.g., in the context of efficient rumor spreading [5]. Hence, this push-to-pull-based technique possesses the advantages of the pull-based schemes and in addition has the efficiency of push-based algorithms.

3 Push-to-Pull Protocol

This section presents the design of our protocol for peer-to-peer live streaming. It is based on two concepts: First, the protocol defines the overlay structure, i.e., it specifies how peers are to select their neighboring peers. The overlay is inspired by the structured topologies of *distributed hash tables* (DHTs) which guarantee connectivity and a logarithmic diameter. The flexibility of the neighbor selection strategy is used to account for additional factors which influence performance, for instance, bandwidth requirements and latency constraints. The topology aims at being resilient to churn and massive correlated failures. Second, the protocol specifies how data is distributed in the overlay network. Concretely, the protocol advocates the data-driven streaming paradigm, and introduces a novel combination of fast pushing operations and robust pull operations.

3.1 Overlay and Neighbor Selection

The proposed overlay consists of an unstructured and a structured part. Initially, a peer is assigned a random set of neighbors by a *network entry point*. Over time, a refinement process takes place as peers learn about other peers from their neighbors and add them to their routing table depending on the following criteria: Since peers strive to maintain several connections to *close-by peers*, new neighbors are continuously accepted based on the latency measured to these peers.

While truly random networks are known to have desirable properties, constraining the choice of neighbors to peers that are close-by may lead to clusters and consequently threaten the efficiency or even the connectivity of the overlay. Therefore, our protocol uses d-bit peer identifiers in order to build a DHT-like topology (of course, without the data storage semantics). These identifiers can be used for prefix-routing, as links to neighbors are stored for different shared prefix lengths. Let β denote the number of bits that can be fixed at a peer to route any message to an arbitrary destination. For $i = \{0, \beta, 2\beta, 3\beta, \ldots\}$, a peer chooses, if possible, $2^\beta - 1$ neighbors whose identifiers are equal in the i most significant bits and differ in the subsequent β bits by one of $2^\beta - 1$ possibilities. For random bit strings, this ensures an expected logarithmic network diameter and peer degree. Similarly to DHTs based on prefix-routing, our solution has the advantage over more rigid DHT structures such as *Chord* [11] that there is a large choice of neighbors for short prefixes, which means that an optimizing secondary criterion can be used to pick neighbors. For example, as the identifiers of roughly half of all peers start with 0, any of those peers can be used as the routing table entry for this prefix, while about one fourth of all peers are suitable for the prefix 00 etc. This freedom is used in our protocol to choose peers according to their latency (locality awareness), but also in order to construct different push mechanisms as described in the following section.

3.2 Pushing and Pulling Data

The prime objective of the pushing component is to quickly distribute a data block to a certain number of peers, in order to fuel the subsequent pull-based exchanges. As we have argued before, such a mechanism is needed due to the long delays of purely pull-based approaches; the pushing phase brings the data block into the vicinity of virtually all peers.

In this section, various aspects of pushing data blocks to neighbors are discussed. In particular, we present two concrete algorithms where each of these algorithms has its own merits. The first algorithm, denoted by $\mathcal{ALG}_1$, is simple, robust, and has a low overhead; it needs fewer neighbors per peer and deals better with heterogenous bandwidths. However, it cannot guarantee that the push mechanism reaches a considerable share of all peers and specific care has to be taken to make sure that no duplicates can occur. The second algorithm, $\mathcal{ALG}_2$, is more sophisticated: All the peers can be reached without the use of the pulling mechanism, and there are provably no retransmissions. Note that a loop-free transmission implies that data is distributed on *induced spanning trees*, which are generally not comparable to structures where the overlay graph consists of one or more trees which must be used to disseminate data. Our graph is still hypercubic, and, in accordance with the data-driven streaming paradigm, each packet can theoretically induce a different tree on which it is broadcast.

Due to the simplicity and robustness of $\mathcal{ALG}_1$, it is better suited for dynamic environments and also in settings where peers may act selfishly. As we will show in Section 4, in order to boost the dissemination process it suffices to push fresh data blocks to a subset of all peers. This implies that the lack of guarantee that many peers can be reached using this push mechanism is not a severe limitation. Nevertheless, the ability of $\mathcal{ALG}_2$ to efficiently push new blocks to practically all peers may be preferable in various scenarios. For example, there may be situations where one wants to precisely control the fraction of peers reached by the pushing operation only. In a more stable network or a network where incentives are of no concern, more peers should be reached by pushing blocks for efficiency reasons, so that only a small number of pulls are necessary to distribute the new block among the remainder of the peers.

In the following, let, for two peers u and v with identifiers $b_0^u \ldots b_{d-1}^u$ and $b_0^v \ldots b_{d-1}^v$, where b_i^u and b_i^v, denote the ith bit of their respective identifiers, $\ell(u,v) = k$ if $b_j^u = b_j^v$ for all $j \in \{0, \ldots, k-1\}$ and $b_k^u \neq b_k^v$. Furthermore, let $\mathcal{N}_v$ be the set of all neighboring peers of v. We first present $\mathcal{ALG}_1$ and discuss its properties. Let β again denote the number of bits that the prefix routing algorithm fixes at each hop. The source selects 2^β peers from its routing table, if possible, such that the identifiers of any two peers differ in at least one bit of the first β bits. A new block is pushed to these peers along with the information that they must only forward the block to peers with which they share the first β bits of their identifiers. Recursively, upon receiving such a push message with the specified prefix length π that they must not modify, a recipient selects 2^β peers that share the prefix of length π with itself and that differ in at least one bit between the $(\pi + 1)^{st}$ and the $(\pi + \beta)^{th}$ bit and so on. This straightforward approach to pushing on prefix-based overlays has an obvious shortcoming: Assume that $\beta = 2$ and that the source peer has the identifier consisting of only zeros. It will push the block, among others, to a peer whose identifier starts with 00 which will in turn forward the block to a peer whose identifier starts with 0000. This peer might then forward the block back to the source again, as the identifier of the source also starts with 000000. Such loops can occur on all paths. If a peer v pushes the block solely to all the $2^\beta - 1$ peers that differ in at least one bit from the identifier of v itself, there are no duplicates; however, this reduction would cut off entire branches of peers which could never benefit from the push mechanism.

A viable solution to the duplicates problem is to include a list $\mathcal{L}$ of *critical* predecessors of the induced spanning tree. Only the peer identifiers having a prefix of length $\pi + \beta$ in common are sent along. The push message any peer v receives contains the parent p in the induced spanning tree, the fixed prefix length π, and the list of critical predecessors $\mathcal{L}$.[6] The parent is potentially a critical peer for one of the children, and therefore it is added to the list $\mathcal{L}$. Afterwards, using the local subroutine *getChildren*, the $l \leq 2^\beta$ children are selected from the routing table for which it holds that they all share a prefix of length at least π with peer v itself, the identifiers of any two of those children differ in at least one of the following β bits, and they do not occur in the list $\mathcal{L}$. In the next step, the lists $\mathcal{L}_j$ of critical predecessors are created for all children. Note that any critical predecessor p_i is added to at most one list $\mathcal{L}_j$, and only if it is still critical for this child v_j, i.e., $\ell(v_j, p_i) \geq \pi + \beta$. The source v_0 pushes data blocks containing the parameters $p := v_0$, $\pi := \beta$, and $\mathcal{L} := \emptyset$ to its children. This push strategy $\mathcal{ALG}_1$ is summarized in Algorithm 1.

Algorithm 1. $\mathcal{ALG}_1$: push$(p, \pi, \mathcal{L})$ at peer v.

1: $\mathcal{L} := \mathcal{L} \cup \{p\}$
2: $\{v_1, \ldots, v_l\} := \text{getChildren}(v, \pi, \mathcal{L})$
3: **for all** $p_i \in \mathcal{L}$ **do**
4:     $j := \arg\max_{j \in \{1, \ldots, l\}} \ell(v_j, p_i)$
5:     **if** $\ell(v_j, p_i) \geq \pi + \beta$ **then** $\mathcal{L}_j := \mathcal{L}_j \cup \{p_i\}$ **fi**
6: **od**
7: **for** $j = 1, \ldots l$ **do** send push$(v, \pi + \beta, \mathcal{L}_j)$ to v_j **od**

It is easy to see that $\mathcal{ALG}_1$ is indeed loop-free, and that the expected length of the list $\mathcal{L}$ is bounded by $\sum_{j=2}^\infty \frac{1}{(2^\beta)^j} = \frac{1}{2^\beta(2^\beta - 1)}$ which is less than one entry. However, the worst-case length of the list is $\log(n)/\beta$. Another shortcoming of this algorithm is that it is likely that not all peers can be reached, because once a peer is reached that only has connections to peers that are in the list $\mathcal{L}$ for a certain prefix, this branch of the tree is cut off.

$\mathcal{ALG}_2$ avoids these problems by modifying the topology and using a different routing scheme. For simplicity, we present the neighbor selection strategy and the push algorithm for the case $\beta = 1$. In order to use $\mathcal{ALG}_2$, the peers must store links to a totally different set of neighbors: A peer v with the identifier $b_0^v \ldots b_{d-1}^v$ stores links to peers whose identifiers start with $b_0^v b_1^v \ldots b_{i-1}^v \overline{b_i^v} b_{i+1}^v$ and $b_0^v b_1^v \ldots b_{i-1}^v \overline{b_i^v} \overline{b_{i+1}^v}$ for all $i \in \{0, \ldots, d-2\}$. For example, the peer with the identifier 0000 has to maintain connections to peers whose identifiers start with the prefixes 10, 11, 010, 011, 0010, and 0011. Pseudo-code for the algorithm is given in Algorithm 2.

---

[6] For simplicity, as the data contained in the push messages does not have any influence on the push procedures, it is omitted in our notation.

Algorithm 2. $\mathcal{ALG}_2$: push(π, v_c) at peer v.

1: $\mathcal{S} := \{v' \in \mathcal{N}_v \mid \ell(v', v) \geq \pi + 1\}$
2: choose $v_1 \in \mathcal{S}$: $\ell(v_1, v) \leq \ell(\tilde{v}, v) \; \forall \tilde{v} \in \mathcal{S}$
3: **if** $v_1 \neq \emptyset$ **then** send push$(\ell(v_1, v), v)$ to v_1 **fi**
4: **if** $v_c \neq \emptyset$ **then**
5:    choose $v_2 \in \mathcal{N}_v$: $\ell(v_2, v_c) = \pi + 1$
6:    **if** $v_2 = \emptyset$ **then** $v_2 := $ getNext(v) from v_c **fi**
7:    **if** $v_2 \neq \emptyset$ **then** send push$(\ell(v_2, v_c), v_c)$ to v_2 **fi**
8: **else**
9:    choose $v_2 \in \mathcal{N}_v$: $\ell(v_2, v) = \pi$
10:    **if** $v_2 \neq \emptyset$ **then** send push$(\pi + 1, v_c)$ to v_2 **fi**
11: **fi**

The parameters are again the length π of the prefix that is not to be modified, and at most one critical predecessor v_c. If $\beta = 1$, any node v tries to forward the push message to two peers v_1 and v_2. The procedure is called at the source v_0 with arguments $\pi := 0$ and $v_c := \emptyset$, resulting in the two push messages $push(1, v_0)$ to v_1 and $push(1, \emptyset)$ to v_2. The peer v_1 is chosen locally such that the prefix its identifier shares with the identifier of v is the shortest among all those whose shared prefix length is at least $\pi + 1$. This value $\ell(v_1, v)$ and v itself are the parameters included in the push message to peer v_1, if such a peer exists. The second peer is chosen similarly, but with respect to v_c and not v itself. If no suitable peer is found in the routing table, the peer v_c is inquired for a candidate using the subroutine *getNext* which is described in Algorithm 3.

Algorithm 3. getNext(v_s) at peer v

1: $\mathcal{S} := \{v' \in \mathcal{N}_v \mid \ell(v', v) > \ell(v_s, v)\}$
2: choose $v_r \in \mathcal{S}$: $\ell(v_r, v) \leq \ell(\tilde{v}, v) \; \forall \tilde{v} \in \mathcal{S}$
3: send v_r to v_s

This step is required because node v cannot deduce from its routing table whether a peer v_2 with the property $\ell(v_2, v_c) \geq \pi + 1$ exists. In the special case when $v_c = \emptyset$, v_2 is chosen locally, if possible, such that $\ell(v_2, v) = \pi$. In Figure 1, an example spanning tree resulting from the execution of $\mathcal{ALG}_2$ is depicted.

As mentioned earlier, $\mathcal{ALG}_2$ has the property that, at least in a static setting where peers neither join nor leave the network, all peers can be reached. Due to churn, any real overlay can never be considered static. However, this static property implies that this pushing procedure is expected to reach a large number of peers even if some peers appear and disappear during the push phase.

Theorem 3.1 *In a static overlay, the push algorithm $\mathcal{ALG}_2$ has the following properties:*

(a) It does not induce any duplicate messages (loop-free), and
(b) all peers are reached (complete).

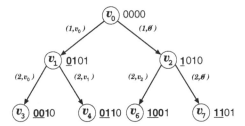

Fig. 1. The spanning tree induced by a push message initiated at peer v_0 is shown. The fixed prefix is underlined at each peer, whereas prefixes in bold print indicate that the parent peer has been constrained to push the packet to peers with these prefixes.

PROOF. Throughout the proof, we will use the fact that $\forall u, v, w : \ell(u, v) = \sigma$ and $\ell(v, w) = \tau$ implies that $\ell(u, w) = min(\sigma, \tau)$ which we will refer to as Fact (1).

(a) Loop-free: If a peer v receives a *push message* μ and forwards it to other peers which in turn forward the message and so on, let $\mathcal{C}_v(\mu)$ denote the set of peers that are reached recursively. We first show that if any peer v forwarding push messages μ' and μ'' to two peers v' and v'', these peers will subsequently forward the message to disjoint sets of peers, i.e., $\mathcal{C}_{v'}(\mu') \cap \mathcal{C}_{v''}(\mu'') = \emptyset$. Then, we will show that peers never send messages back to predecessors.

Let v be the peer receiving the push message and let π_v denote the prefix length that peer v can no longer modify. As in the description of the algorithm, the two peers the message is forwarded to are v_1 and v_2. Let further v_p denote the peer that sent the message to v. In order to prove that disjoint sets are constructed, it suffices to show that $\ell(v, v_1) \geq \pi_v + 1$ and $\ell(v, v_2) = \pi_v$ at any peer v.

The first inequality follows immediately from the algorithm. If $v_c = \emptyset$ then $\ell(v, v_2) = \pi_v$ also follows by definition. Therefore we can assume in the following that $v_c \neq \emptyset$. If $v_p = v_c$ we have that $\ell(v_p, v_2) \geq \pi_v + 1$, as v was chosen from $\mathcal{S}$ according to this criterion. It further holds that $\ell(v, v_p) = \pi_v$ because the parameter π_v that p sends to v in the message is precisely $\ell(v, v_p)$. According to Fact (1), we get that $\ell(v_2, v) = \pi_v$. Similarly, if $v_p \neq v_c$, it holds that $\ell(v_c, v_2) \geq \pi_v + 1$, due to the fact that either v_p found peer v in its routing table, implying that $\ell(v_c, v_2) = \pi_v + 1$, or the procedure *getNext* has been invoked which by definition means that $\ell(v_c, v_2) > \pi_v + 1$. As p sends the value $\ell(v, v_c)$ to v, it holds at peer v that $\pi_v = \ell(v, v_c)$, again leading us to the conclusion that $\ell(v, v_2) = \pi_v$.

This concludes the proof that the resulting peer sets are always disjoint. Since peers might forward push messages back to a predecessor, we cannot yet conclude that no duplicates are produced. Let $v^{(0)} \rightsquigarrow v^{(1)} \rightsquigarrow \ldots \rightsquigarrow v^{(k)}$, where $k \leq \pi_v$, denote the path from peer $v^{(0)} := v$ back to the source $v^{(k)}$. Note that the value π steadily increases downwards, implying that $\pi_{v^{(0)}} > \pi_{v^{(1)}} > \ldots > \pi_{v^{(k)}}$. Let us first assume that $v_c \neq \emptyset$ on the entire path. If $v_c = v^{(1)}$ then it holds that $\ell(v, v^{(1)}) = \pi_v$ according to the algorithm. In the case $v_c \neq v^{(1)}$, then by definition $\ell(v, v_c) = \pi_v$ and as $\ell(v^{(1)}, v_c) = \pi_{v^{(1)}} < \pi_v$, we get that in all cases $\ell(v, v^{(1)}) \le \pi_v$. Inductively, the same argument can be applied to the maximal prefix length between $v^{(1)}$ and $v^{(2)}$ which is bounded by $\pi_{v^{(1)}}$ etc. Using Fact (1), we have that $\ell(v, v^{(i)}) \le \pi_v$ for all $1 \le i \le k$. If for some $i^* \in \{0, \dots, k-1\}$ a peer is reached that received $v_c = \emptyset$ from $v^{(i^*+1)}$, it holds according to the definition of $\mathcal{ALG}_2$ that all other peers closer to the source on this path also received $v_c = \emptyset$. This entails that $\ell(v^{(k)}, v^{(k-1)}) = 0$, $\ell(v^{(k-1)}, v^{(k-2)}) = 1$ and so on, down to $\ell(v^{(i^*)}, v^{(i^*+1)}) = k - i^* \le \pi_v$. Applying the same inductive argument as before, we can conclude that $\ell(v, v^{(j)}) \le \pi_v$ also for all $j > i^*$ if such an i^* exists. Since the first π_v bits are not changed at peer v when forwarding the message to other peers, it is impossible for v to send the push message to a predecessor as all predecessors' identifiers differ in at least one bit among the first π_v bits, which concludes the proof that no duplicates can occur and the resulting structure is a spanning tree.

(b) *Complete:* It remains to be shown that all peers are reached using this procedure. Using $\ell(v, v_1) \ge \pi_v + 1$ and $\ell(v, v_2) = \pi_v$ at any peer v, it follows that, when forwarding push messages, the current prefix is extended with a 0 and a 1, and the value π is increased. Note that care has to be taken only if identifiers with certain prefixes do not exist. If no peer v_1 such that $\ell(v_1, v) = \pi + 1$ exists, the next bit can be tried by choosing v_1 such that $\ell(v_1, v) = \pi + 2$ and so on. Given that v_1 is chosen among all peers in $\mathcal{S}$ such that the $\ell(v_1, v)$ is minimal, it is guaranteed that no peer is left out. Similarly, if there is no peer v_2 such that $\ell(v_2, v_c) = \pi_v$, the next bit is tried by calling the function *getNext* at peer v_c which chooses v_2 the same way as peer v chooses v_1. This means that prefixes are only left out if no peer's identifier has this particular prefix and thus every peer can be reached.   □

Observe that at any time, at most one predecessor is critical and has to be included in a push packet. A disadvantage of $\mathcal{ALG}_2$, compared to $\mathcal{ALG}_1$, is that peers have to maintain twice as many connections to other peers. Since all peers ideally communicate regularly with all their neighbors, it is best to keep the set of neighboring peers small.

However, both algorithms are not sufficient to quickly disseminate data to all peers in dynamic environments such as the Internet. Due to the perpetual arrival and departure of peers, which results in inaccurate routing tables, only a certain fraction of all peers are effectively reached through pushing. Thus, a second mechanism has to be used where peers having received new data blocks *notify* their neighbors about the corresponding sequence numbers. A peer can then obtain data blocks it is interested in by explicitly requesting them from a neighbor (*pull operation*). Hence, a data block is never forwarded twice to the same peer, and there are no redundant transmissions. The initial distribution of new data blocks through pushing ensures that almost every peer has at least one other peer in its vicinity that offers the missing data block.

4 Evaluation

Our protocol has been evaluated in several respects. We have performed extensive *emulations* (simulations using the real code base of the *Pulsar* system in a simulated network) with up to 100,000 peers on a single Core2 Quad personal computer with 4GB of RAM. Our emulation results have also been confirmed in tests on PlanetLab. Finally, a real-world beta test has shown that the protocol manages to cope well with the peculiarities of the Internet and to distribute the content reliably. Due to space constraints, we only present results concerning the key concepts introduced in this paper, namely the neighbor selection and the push- and pull-based data dissemination policy.

4.1 Topology and Neighbor Selection

First, we have evaluated the properties of the streaming topology itself. We have streamed data over a network of 100 to 100,000 peers and counted the total number of hops taken by each data packet. Figure 2 shows that, as expected, the hypercubic structure induced by the neighbor selection results in a logarithmic network diameter.

As described in Section 3, the flexibility of our topology allows for locality awareness, i.e., for the choice of close peers as neighbors. This indeed helps to reduce the round trip times significantly compared to a random neighbor selection strategy, as Figure 3 clearly suggests. Figure 3 depicts the number of neighbors that the average peer maintains for any given round trip time. In this emulation, peers are distributed uniformly on a square with a minimum delay of 10 ms and maximum delay of 200 ms which corresponds to the square's diagonal.

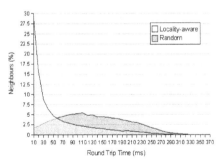

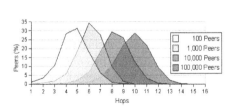

Fig. 2. Number of hops taken by each data packet to reach the destination peer. The network diameter scales logarithmically with the total number of peers.

Fig. 3. Effect of locality awareness with 10,000 peers: The average round trip times to all neighboring peers are significantly smaller in the network constructed using our protocol than in a network where neighbors are chosen at random

4.2   Push-to-Pull Data Distribution

Figure 4 compares the two push strategies $\mathcal{ALG}_1$ and $\mathcal{ALG}_2$ introduced in Section 3 with a pull-only strategy like the one adopted by Chainsaw.

The figure shows that, compared to pull-only protocols, pushing considerably speeds up the distribution of new data blocks and thereby reduces the playback delay. Once a sufficient number of peers have received a block, the remainder of the peers can retrieve the fresh data block using the pull mechanism with a moderate additional overhead. It is evident from Figure 4 that $\mathcal{ALG}_1$ is almost as fast as $\mathcal{ALG}_2$, although only about one third of all peers obtain the new data block through pushing, while almost all peers are reached using $\mathcal{ALG}_2$ in this test.

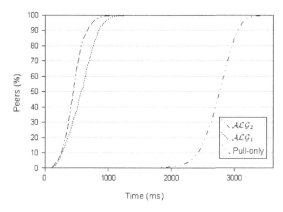

Fig. 4. Time required until the push strategies $\mathcal{ALG}_1$, $\mathcal{ALG}_2$, and a pull-only strategy reach a given fraction of all peers in a network of 10,000 peers

Figure 5 depicts the percentage of all data packets received through pushing for both algorithms $\mathcal{ALG}_1$ and $\mathcal{ALG}_2$ for increasing network sizes. Independent of the chosen algorithm, less packets are received through pushing as the network grows. This decline is due to the increased chance of branches of the distribution trees being cut off, because of inaccurate routing tables, before a substantial number of peers is reached. As expected, the fraction of pushed packets decreases much more rapidly when $\mathcal{ALG}_1$ is used. However, it is sufficient to reach only a fraction of all peers in the pushing phase, as the subsequent pull operations can be performed efficiently and with a small additional delay. Note that both pushing strategies greatly benefit from the locality awareness which not only decreases the chances of packet loss but also allows the use of short timeouts for acknowledgments.

A second test studies the scalability of the $\mathcal{ALG}_1$ pushing algorithm. Figure 6 indicates that the network scales well with the number peers, as exponentially more peers merely results in a linear increase of the delays. Moreover, all peers experience a delay of not more than 1.5 seconds.

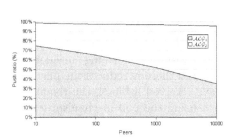
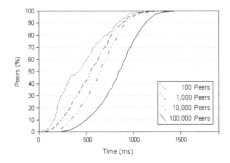

Fig. 5. As the network grows, less data is received in the pushing phase. The fraction of data obtained through pushing decreases considerably faster when algorithm $\mathcal{ALG}_1$ is used.

Fig. 6. Given an exponential increase of the number of peers, the delays increase only linearly

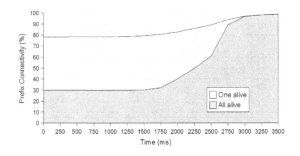

Fig. 7. Effect of 50% simultaneous random crashes in a network of 5,000 peers. "One alive" shows the percentage of prefixes for which at least one connection is present, while "All alive" depicts the percentage of prefixes for which all connections are still alive. In both cases, already after 3 seconds, the peers are again fully connected.

4.3   Robustness to Churn

The high connectivity of our hypercubic network topology and the flexible choice of neighbors allows to build up and fix routing tables quickly. Several scenarios have been considered in which a large fraction of peers leaves simultaneously. It turns out that it is easy to maintain the topology and to recover even from such massive concurrent network changes.

Figure 7 shows a network where a random set of 50% of the 5,000 peers leave simultaneously. A severe network failure is assumed where all the peers crash without notice (no "leave message"). For each prefix stored in the routing table, a peer maintains roughly 2 to 3 connections to other peers whose identifiers match the specific prefix. Immediately after the network failure, for approximately 80% of the stored prefixes, at least one connection to a peer that is still alive is retained. After roughly 3 seconds, the routing table is again almost completely repaired. The figure also depicts the percentage of prefixes for which all connections are still alive. This short loss of connectivity is only due to the lack of a proper leave message. In case disconnecting peers are able to send a leave message, which is certainly the normal case, the network is hardly affected if as many as 50% of the peers leave, and the prefix connectivity does not drop noticeably, as peers immediately search for suitable replacements.

Due to the fast repairing process, our system also copes well with membership changes occurring continuously over time.

5   Conclusions

Given the growing number of radio stations and TV channels available online, peer-to-peer live streaming is able to overcome the limitations of traditional, centralized approaches, and it enables content providers to both increase playback quality and to reduce costs. Thus, the p2p paradigm has the potential to democratize the streaming world in that it enables everyone to broadcast her own media content—similarly to how the world wide web revolutionized the distribution of information more than a decade ago: Nowadays, everyone can publish her thoughts on her own blog or website at virtually no cost.

By combining pull-based and push-based techniques, our push-to-pull protocol for live streaming achieves high efficiency and robustness, both essential features of a reliable p2p streaming service. As a second central ingredient, our protocol makes use of the lessons learnt from distributed hash tables by structuring the overlay topology while still maintaining a large degree of flexibility. The resulting system is locality-aware and has a guaranteed logarithmic diameter. Moreover, it enables the source to push new data blocks to speed up data dissemination. Having a push mechanism allows to reduce the notification frequency, which leads to a substantially smaller overhead.

References

1. Castro, M., Druschel, P., Kermarrec, A.-M., Nandi, A., Rowstron, A., Singh, A.: SplitStream: High-bandwidth Content Distribution in a Cooperative Environment. In: Kaashoek, M.F., Stoica, I. (eds.) IPTPS 2003. LNCS, vol. 2735, Springer, Heidelberg (2003)
2. Chu, Y., Rao, S., Zhang, H.: A Case For End System Multicast. In: Proc. Int. Conference on Measurement and Modeling of Computer Systems (SIGMETRICS), pp. 1–12 (2000)
3. Goyal, V.K.: Multiple Description Coding: Compression Meets the Network. IEEE Signal Processing Magazine 18(5), 74–93 (2001)
4. Jannotti, J., Gifford, D.K., Johnson, K.L., Kaashoek, M.F., O'Toole, J.W.: Overcast: Reliable Multicasting with an Overlay Network. In: Proc. 4th Symposium on Operating System Design and Implementation (OSDI) (2000)
5. Karp, R., Schindelhauer, C., Shenker, S., Vocking, B.: Randomized Rumor Spreading. In: Proc. 41st Annual Symposium on Foundations of Computer Science (FOCS). IEEE Computer Society Press, Los Alamitos (2000)

6. Kosti, D., Rodriguez, A., Albrecht, J., Vahdat, A.: Bullet: High Bandwidth Data Dissemination Using an Overlay Mesh. In: Proc. 19th ACM Symposium on Operating Systems Principles (SOSP), pp. 282–297. ACM Press, New York (2003)
7. Padmanabhan, V.N., Sripanidkulchai, K.: The Case for Cooperative Networking. In: Druschel, P., Kaashoek, M.F., Rowstron, A. (eds.) IPTPS 2002. LNCS, vol. 2429, pp. 178–190. Springer, Heidelberg (2002)
8. Pai, V., Tamilmani, K., Sambamurthy, V., Kumar, K., Mohr, A.: Chainsaw: Eliminating Trees from Overlay Multicast. In: Castro, M., van Renesse, R. (eds.) IPTPS 2005. LNCS, vol. 3640, Springer, Heidelberg (2005)
9. Plaxton, C.G., Rajaraman, R., Richa, A.W.: Accessing Nearby Copies of Replicated Objects in a Distributed Environment. In: Proc. 9th Annual ACM Symposium on Parallel Algorithms and Architectures (SPAA), pp. 311–320. ACM Press, New York (1997)
10. Rowstron, A., Druschel, P.: Pastry: Scalable, Decentralized Object Location, and Routing for Large-Scale Peer-to-Peer Systems. In: Proc. International Conference on Distributed Systems Platforms (Middleware), pp. 329–350 (2001)
11. Stoica, I., Morris, R., Karger, D., Kaashoek, F., Balakrishnan, H.: Chord: A Scalable Peer-To-Peer Lookup Service for Internet Applications. In: Proc. ACM SIGCOMM Conference, pp. 149–160. ACM Press, New York (2001)
12. Venkataraman, V., Francis, P., Calandrino, J.: Chunkyspread: Multi-tree Unstructured Peer-to-Peer. In: Proc. Int. Workshop on Peer-to-Peer Systems (IPTPS) (2006)
13. Wang, W., Helder, D.A., Jamin, S., Zhang, L.: Overlay Optimizations for End-host Multicast. In: Networked Group Communications (2002)
14. Zhang, M., Tang, Y., Zhao, L., Luo, J.-G., Yang, S.-Q.: Gridmedia: A Multi-Sender Based Peer-to-Peer Multicast System for Video Streaming. In: IEEE Int. Conference on Multimedia and Expo (ICME), pp. 614–617. IEEE Computer Society Press, Los Alamitos (2005)
15. Zhang, X., Liu, J., Li, B., Yum, Y.: CoolStreaming/DONet: A Data-Driven Overlay Network for Peer-to-Peer Live Media Streaming. In: Proc. Annual IEEE Conference on Computer Communications (INFOCOM), pp. 2102–2111. IEEE Computer Society Press, Los Alamitos (2005)

Probabilistic Opaque Quorum Systems

Michael G. Merideth[1] and Michael K. Reiter[2]

[1] Carnegie Mellon University, Pittsburgh, PA, USA
[2] University of North Carolina, Chapel Hill, NC, USA

Abstract. Byzantine-fault-tolerant service protocols like Q/U and FaB Paxos that optimistically order requests can provide increased efficiency and fault scalability. However, these protocols require $n \geq 5b + 1$ servers (where b is the maximum number of faults tolerated), owing to their use of *opaque Byzantine quorum systems*; this is $2b$ more servers than required by some non-optimistic protocols. In this paper, we present a family of *probabilistic* opaque Byzantine quorum systems that require substantially fewer servers. Our analysis is novel in that it assumes Byzantine clients, anticipating that a faulty client may seek quorums that maximize the probability of error. Using this as motivation, we present an optional, novel protocol that allows probabilistic quorum systems to tolerate Byzantine clients. The protocol requires only one additional round of interaction between the client and the servers, and this round may be amortized over multiple operations. We consider actual error probabilities introduced by the probabilistic approach for concrete configurations of opaque quorum systems, and prove that the probability of error vanishes with as few as $n > 3.15b$ servers as n and b grow.

1 Introduction

For distributed systems consisting of a large number of servers, a Byzantine-fault-tolerant replication algorithm that requires all servers to communicate with each other for every client request can be prohibitively expensive. Therefore, for large systems, it is critical that the protocol have good *fault scalability* [1]—the property that performance does not (substantially) degrade as the system size is increased—by avoiding this communication.

Byzantine-fault-tolerant service protocols must assign a total order to requests to provide replicated state machine semantics [2]. To minimize the amount of communication between servers, protocols like Q/U [1] and FaB Paxos [3] use opaque quorum systems [4] to order requests *optimistically*. That is, servers independently choose an ordering, without steps that would be required to reach agreement with other servers; the steps are performed only if servers choose different orderings. Under the assumption that servers independently typically choose the same ordering, the optimistic approach can provide better fault scalability in the common case than protocols like BFT [5], which require that servers perform steps to agree upon an ordering *before* choosing it [1]. However, optimistic protocols have the disadvantage of requiring at least $5b + 1$ servers to

A. Pelc (Ed.): DISC 2007, LNCS 4731, pp. 403–419, 2007.
© Springer-Verlag Berlin Heidelberg 2007

tolerate b server faults, instead of as few as $3b + 1$ servers, and so they cannot tolerate as many faults for a given number of servers.

In this paper, we present *probabilistic opaque quorum systems* (POQS), a new type of probabilistic quorum system [6], in order to increase the fraction of faults that can be tolerated by an optimistic approach from fewer than $n/5$ to as many as $n/3.15$. A POQS provides the same properties as the strict opaque quorum systems used by, e.g., Q/U and FaB Paxos, but is probabilistic in the sense that quorums are not guaranteed to overlap in the number of servers required to ensure safety. However, we prove that this error probability is negligible for large system sizes (for a given ratio of b to n). Application domains that could give rise to systems of such scale include sensor networks and edge services.

Byzantine clients are problematic for all probabilistic quorum systems because the combination of high fault tolerance and low probability of error that can be achieved is based on the assumption that clients choose quorums uniformly at random (and independently of other quorums and the state of the system, e.g., the values held by each server, and the identities of faulty servers). This can be seen in our results that show: (i) that probabilistic opaque quorum systems can tolerate up to $n/3.15$ faults (compared with less than $n/5$ faults for strict opaque quorum systems) assuming that all quorums are selected uniformly at random, but that the maximum fault tolerance drops to $n/4.56$ faults if Byzantine clients are allowed to choose quorums according to their own goals; and (ii) that to achieve a specified error probability for a given degree of fault tolerance, substantially more servers are required if quorums are not selected uniformly at random.

Therefore, we present a protocol with which we constrain clients to using pseudo-randomly selected access sets (sets of servers contacted in order to find quorums, c.f., [7]) of a prescribed size. In the limit, we can set the sizes of access sets to be the sizes of quorums, thereby dictating that all clients use pseudo-randomly selected quorums, and providing a mechanism that guarantees, in practice, the behavior of clients that is assumed by probabilistic quorum systems. However, as shown in Section 4.3, the notion of restricted access sets allows us a range of options in trading off the low error probability and high fault tolerance of completely random quorum selection, for the guaranteed single-round access provided when there is an available quorum (one in which all servers respond) in every access set.

Our contributions are as follows:

- We present the first family of probabilistic opaque quorum system constructions. For each construction, we: (i) show that we are able to reduce the number of servers below the $5b + 1$ required by protocols that use strict opaque quorums, (ii) prove that it works with vanishing error probability as the system size grows, and (iii) evaluate the characteristics of its error probability over a variety of specific system sizes and configurations.

- We present the first analysis of a probabilistic quorum system that accounts for the behavior of Byzantine clients. We anticipate that a faulty client may choose quorums with the goal of maximizing the error probability, and show the effects that this may have.

– We present an access-restriction protocol that allows probabilistic quorum systems to tolerate faulty clients with the same degree of fault tolerance as if all clients were non-faulty. One aspect of the protocol is that servers work to propagate the values of established writes to each other in the background. Therefore, we provide analysis, unique to opaque quorum systems, of the number of servers that must propagate a value for it to be accepted by another server.

2 Related Work

Strict Opaque Quorum Systems. Opaque Byzantine quorum systems were introduced by Malkhi and Reiter [4] in two variants: one in which the number of non-faulty servers in a quorum is at least half of the quorum, and the other in which the number of non-faulty servers represents a strict majority of the quorum. The first construction makes it unnecessary for the client to know the sets of servers of which the system can tolerate failure (hence the term 'opaque'), while the second construction additionally makes it possible to create a protocol that does not use timestamps. The paper also proves that $5b$ is the lower bound on the number of servers for the first version; simply changing the inequality to a strict inequality proves $5b+1$ is the lower bound for the second. In this paper, we are concerned with the second variant.

The constraints on strict opaque quorums have also been described in the context of consensus and state-machine-replication protocols, e.g., the Q/U [1] and FaB Paxos [3] protocols, though not explicitly as opaque quorums. Abd-El-Malek et al. [1] provide generic (not just threshold) opaque quorum system constraints that they prove sufficient for providing state-machine replication semantics where both writes and reads complete in a single (pipelined) phase when there is no write–write contention. Martin and Alvisi [3] use an opaque quorum system of acceptors in FaB Paxos, a two-phase consensus protocol (with a designated proposer) and three-phase state-machine-replication protocol requiring at least $5b+1$ servers.

Probabilistic Quorum Systems. A Probabilistic Quorum System (PQS), as presented by Malkhi et al. [6], can provide better availability and fault tolerance than provided by strict quorum systems; Table 1 compares probabilistic quorums with their strict quorum counterparts.[1] Malkhi et

Table 1. Minimum servers needed for probabilistic and strict quorum variants

	prob.	strict	presented
Opaque	$3.15b+1$	$5b+1$	Here
Masking	$2.62b+1$	$4b+1$	[6]
Dissemination	$b+1$	$3b+1$	[6]

al. provide constructions for dissemination and masking quorums, and prove properties of load and availability for these constructions. They do not address

---

[1] The $2.62b$ lower bound for masking quorums is not shown in [6], but can be quickly derived using our results from Section 4.

opaque quorum systems, or the effects of concurrent or Byzantine writers; we address each of these. In addition, in Section 4, we borrow analysis techniques from [6], but our analysis is more general in the sense that clients are not all assumed to communicate only with quorums of servers. We also use a McDiarmid inequality [8] in our technical report [9] for bounding the error probability; this provides a simpler bounding technique for our purposes than do the Chernoff bounds used there. The technique that we present in Section 5 for restricting access to limited numbers of servers should be applicable to the constructions of Malkhi et al. equally well.

Other Work. Signed Quorum Systems [10] and k-quorums [11,12] also weaken the requirements of strict quorum systems but use different techniques; our technical report [9] has a more detailed discussion. There has been work on strict quorum systems that can tolerate Byzantine clients (e.g., [13,14]) but this is fundamentally unconcerned with the way in which quorums are chosen because such choices cannot impact the correctness of strict quorum systems.

3   System Model and Definitions

We assume a system with a set U of servers, $|U| = n$, and an arbitrary but bounded number of clients. Clients and servers can fail arbitrarily (i.e., Byzantine [15] faults). We assume that up to b servers can fail, and denote the set of faulty servers by B, where $B \subseteq U$. Any number of clients can fail. Failures are permanent. Clients and servers that do not fail are said to be *non-faulty*. We allow that faulty clients and servers may collude, and so we assume that faulty clients and servers all know the membership of B (although non-faulty clients and servers do not). We make the standard assumption that nodes are computationally bound such that they cannot subvert the effectiveness of cryptographic primitives.

Throughout the paper, we use San Serif font to denote random variables, uppercase *ITALICS* for set-valued constants, and lowercase *italics* for integer-valued constants.

3.1   Behavior of Clients

We abstractly describe client operations as either *writes* that alter the state of the service or *reads* that do not. Informally, a non-faulty client performs a write to update the state of the service such that its value (or a later one) will be observed with high probability by any subsequent operation; a write thus successfully performed is called "established" (we define established more precisely below). A non-faulty client performs a read to obtain the value of the latest established write, where "latest" refers to the value of the most recent write preceding this read in a linearization [16] of the execution. Therefore, we define the *correct* value for the read to return to be the value of this latest established write; other values are called *incorrect*. We assume that the read and write operations by non-faulty clients take the following forms:

 - **Writes:** To perform a write, a non-faulty client selects a *write access set* $A_{wt} \subseteq U$ of size a_{wt} uniformly at random and attempts to inform all servers in A_{wt} of the write value. Formally, the write is *established* once all non-faulty servers in some set $Q_{wt} \subseteq A_{wt}$ of size $q_{wt} \leq a_{wt}$ servers have *accepted* this write. (Intuitively, an access set is a set of servers contacted in order to find a live quorum, c.f., [7].) We refer to q_{wt} as the *write quorum size*; to any $Q_{wt} \subseteq U$ of that size as a *write quorum*; and to $\mathcal{Q}_{wt} = \{Q_{wt} \subseteq U : |Q_{wt}| = q_{wt}\}$ as the *write quorum system*.
 - **Reads:** To perform a read, a non-faulty client selects a *read access set* A_{rd} of size a_{rd} uniformly at random and attempts to contact each server in A_{rd} to learn the value that the server last accepted. We denote the minimum number of servers from which a non-faulty client must receive a response to complete the read successfully by $q_{rd} \leq a_{rd}$. We refer to q_{rd} as the *read quorum size*; to any $Q_{rd} \subseteq U$ of that size as a *read quorum*; and to $\mathcal{Q}_{rd} = \{Q_{rd} \subseteq U : |Q_{rd}| = q_{rd}\}$ as the *read quorum system*.

In a read operation, we refer to each response received from a server in A_{rd} as a *vote* for a read value. We assume that votes for two read values that result from any two distinct write operations are distinguishable from each other, even if the corresponding write values are the same (this is discussed in Section 5). The read operation discerns the correct value from these votes in a protocol-specific way. It is possible in an optimistic protocol such as Q/U [1], for example, that the (at least q_{rd}) votes may reflect a write operation but not provide enough evidence to determine whether that write is established. In this case, the reader may itself establish, or *repair*, the write value before returning it, to ensure that a subsequent reader returns that value, as well (which is necessary to achieve linearizability). In such a protocol, the reader does so by copying its votes for that value to servers, in order to convince them to accept that write.

For this reason, the correctness requirements for POQS discussed in Section 4 treat not only the number of votes that a non-faulty reader observes for the correct value, but also the number of votes that a faulty client can gather for a *conflicting* value. A conflicting value is a specific type of incorrect value characterized by the property that a non-faulty server would accept either it or the correct value, but not both. Two values may conflict because, e.g., they both bear the same timestamp, or are "conditioned on" the same established write in the sense used in Q/U. We assume that this timestamp or similar information can be used to distinguish older (stale) values from newer values. Enabling a faulty client to obtain sufficiently many votes for a conflicting value would, e.g., enable it to convince other non-faulty servers to accept the conflicting value via the repair protocol, a possibility that must be avoided for correctness.

Consequently, an *error* is said to occur when a non-faulty client fails to return the correct value or a faulty client obtains sufficiently many votes for a conflicting value. This definition (or specifically "sufficiently many") will be made more precise in Section 4.4. The *error probability* then refers to the probability of an error when the client (non-faulty or faulty) reads from a read access set A_{rd} chosen uniformly at random. While we cannot force a faulty client to choose

A_{rd} uniformly at random, in Section 5 we demonstrate an access protocol that enables a faulty client to assemble votes for a value that can be verified by servers (and hence, e.g., to perform a repair in Q/U) only if A_{rd} was selected uniformly at random, which is good enough for our purposes. So, from here forward, we restrict our attention to read access sets chosen in this way.

3.2   Communication

The communication assumptions we adopt are common to prior works in probabilistic [6] and signed [10] quorum systems: we assume that each non-faulty client can successfully communicate with each non-faulty server with high probability, and hence with all non-faulty servers with roughly equal probability. This assumption is in place to ensure that the network does not significantly bias a non-faulty client's interactions with servers either toward faulty servers or toward different non-faulty servers than those with which another non-faulty client can interact. Put another way, we treat a server that can be reliably reached by none or only some non-faulty clients as a member of B.

This assumption enables us to refine the read protocol of Section 3.1 in a straightforward way so that non-faulty clients choose read quorums from an access set uniformly at random. (More precisely, a faulty server can bias quorum selection away from quorums containing it by not responding, but this decreases the error probability, and so we conservatively assume that non-faulty clients select read quorums at random from their access sets.) However, because a write is, by definition, established once all of the non-faulty servers in any write quorum within A_{wt} have accepted it, the write quorum at which a write is established contains all servers in $A_{\text{wt}} \cap B$; i.e., only the the non-faulty servers within the write quorum are selected uniformly at random by a non-faulty client.

The access-restriction protocol of Section 5 requires no communication assumptions beyond those of the probabilistic quorums it supports.

4   Probabilistic Opaque Quorum Systems

In this section, we present a family of probabilistic opaque quorum systems. We begin by reviewing the properties of strict opaque quorum systems [4]. Define the following functions (where Q_{rd} and Q_{wt} are as defined in Section 3.1):

$$\textbf{correct}(Q_{\text{rd}}, Q_{\text{wt}}) \quad : \quad |(Q_{\text{rd}} \cap Q_{\text{wt}}) \setminus B| \tag{1}$$

$$\textbf{conflicting}(Q_{\text{rd}}, Q_{\text{wt}}) \quad : \quad |(Q_{\text{rd}} \cap B) \cup (Q_{\text{rd}} \setminus Q_{\text{wt}})| \tag{2}$$

$\textbf{correct}(Q_{\text{rd}}, Q_{\text{wt}})$ returns the number of non-faulty servers in the intersection of a pair of read and write quorums, while $\textbf{conflicting}(Q_{\text{rd}}, Q_{\text{wt}})$ returns the other servers in the read quorum, all of which may return a conflicting value in some protocol execution. Let a read operation return a value that receives at least r votes. Then, the consistency property for strict opaque quorum systems is as follows:

O-Consistency : $\forall Q_{\mathrm{rd}} \in \mathcal{Q}_{\mathrm{rd}}, \forall Q_{\mathrm{wt}} \in \mathcal{Q}_{\mathrm{wt}}$:

$$\mathbf{correct}(Q_{\mathrm{rd}}, Q_{\mathrm{wt}}) \geq r > \mathbf{conflicting}(Q_{\mathrm{rd}}, Q_{\mathrm{wt}}). \tag{3}$$

The property states that the number of non-faulty servers in the intersection of any read quorum and write quorum must represent a majority of the read quorum. Because of this and the fact that newer values can be distinguished from older values, the correct value—which, by definition, is established by being written to all of the non-faulty servers in a write quorum—can be distinguished from other values, even if some non-faulty servers (and all faulty servers) present conflicting or stale values. At a high level, O-Consistency guarantees:

P1 No two conflicting writes are both established.
P2 Every read observes sufficiently many votes for the correct value to identify it as such.
P3 No (non-faulty or faulty) reader obtains votes for a conflicting value sufficient to repair it successfully.

Given that the stated assumptions of a strict opaque quorum system hold, the system behaves correctly. In contrast to this, probabilistic opaque quorum systems (POQS) allow for a (small) possibility of error. Informally, this can be thought of as relaxing O-Consistency so that a variant of it holds for most—but not all—quorums. To ensure that the probability of an error happening is small, POQS are designed so that P1, P2, and P3 hold with high probability.

In the remainder of this section, we model the worst-case behavior of faulty clients (Section 4.1); derive a constraint (PO-Consistency, Section 4.2) that determines the maximum fraction of faulty servers that can be tolerated (Section 4.3) by POQS; and prove that the error probability goes to zero as n (and b) is increased if this constraint is satisfied (Section 4.4).

4.1 Behavior of Faulty Clients

Because a faulty client can behave arbitrarily, we examine the way that a faulty client should choose quorums to maximize the chance of error. Throughout this section, let A_{wt} denote a write access set from which Q_{wt} (a quorum used for an established write) is selected by a faulty client, let A'_{wt} be a write access set used for a conflicting write by a faulty client, and let A_{rd} be a read access set from which Q_{rd}, a read quorum, is selected by a faulty client. Again, we assume that A_{wt}, A'_{wt}, and A_{rd} are selected uniformly at random, an assumption that can be enforced using the protocol of Section 5.

A faulty client can increase the error probability with a write in one of two ways: (i) by establishing a write at a write quorum that contains as many faulty servers as possible, or (ii) by performing the write of a conflicting value in a way that maximizes the number of non-faulty servers that accept it, i.e., by writing to all of $A'_{\mathrm{wt}} \setminus Q_{\mathrm{wt}}$. Since a faulty client may perform *both* such writes, we assume that this client has knowledge of A_{wt} and A'_{wt} simultaneously. However, it is important to note that a faulty client does not have knowledge of the read

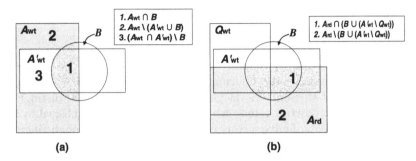

Fig. 1. The preference (1st, 2nd, 3rd) a faulty client gives to a server when choosing (a) Q_{wt}, or (b) Q_{rd}

access set A'_{rd} used by a non-faulty client—or specifically the non-faulty servers within it, i.e., $A'_{\mathrm{rd}} \setminus B$—and so Q_{wt} is chosen independently of $A'_{\mathrm{rd}} \setminus B$.[2]

Figure 1(a) shows the preferences that a faulty client gives to servers when choosing Q_{wt} to do both (i) and (ii). Goal (i) requires maximizing $|Q_{\mathrm{wt}} \cap B|$ to maximize the probability that P1 or P2 is violated; hence, first preference is given to the servers in $A_{\mathrm{wt}} \cap B$ in a write. Goal (ii) requires minimizing $|(Q_{\mathrm{wt}} \cap A'_{\mathrm{wt}}) \setminus B|$ to maximize the probability that P1 or P3 is violated; hence, the servers in $(A_{\mathrm{wt}} \cap A'_{\mathrm{wt}}) \setminus B$ are avoided to the extent possible.

A faulty client can increase the probability that P3 is violated by choosing a read quorum with the most faulty servers and non-faulty servers that share the same conflicting value. Figure 1(b) shows the preferences that a faulty client gives to servers to do so. Because a faulty client can collude with the servers in B, it can obtain replies from all servers in B that are also in A_{rd}, i.e., the servers in $A_{\mathrm{rd}} \cap B$. It can also wait for responses from all of the non-faulty servers in A_{rd} with the conflicting value, i.e., those in $A_{\mathrm{rd}} \cap (A'_{\mathrm{wt}} \setminus Q_{\mathrm{wt}})$. Only after receiving all such responses, and only if these responses number fewer than q_{rd}, must it choose responses from servers with other values.

4.2 Probabilistic Constraint

In this section, we present PO-Consistency, a constraint akin to O-Consistency specified in terms of expected values for POQS. As detailed below, let MinCorrect be a random variable for the minimum number of non-faulty servers that report the correct value in a randomly chosen read quorum taken by a non-faulty client. (Recall that an error is caused by MinCorrect being too small only for reads performed by a non-faulty client.) Also, let MaxConflicting be a random variable for the maximum number of servers that report a conflicting value in a read quorum taken from a randomly chosen read access set by a faulty client that seeks to maximize MaxConflicting. (Recall that an error is caused by MaxConflicting

---

[2] More precisely, with the access protocol in Section 5, A'_{rd} can be hidden unless, and until, that read access set is used for repair, at which point it is too late for faulty clients to choose Q_{wt} so as to induce an error in that read operation.

being too large even if the client is faulty.) Then the consistency property for POQS is:

$$\textbf{PO-Consistency} : \mathbb{E}\,[\mathsf{MinCorrect}] > \mathbb{E}\,[\mathsf{MaxConflicting}]\,. \tag{4}$$

As shown in Section 4.4, PO-Consistency allows us to choose a threshold, r, for the number of votes used to determine the result of a read operation, while ensuring that the error probability vanishes as we increase n (and b).

We now derive expressions for $\mathsf{MinCorrect}$ and $\mathsf{MaxConflicting}$. Recall that B is the set of up to b faulty servers. Let A_{wt} be a randomly chosen write access set, and let A_{rd} be a randomly chosen read access set. As stated in the system model, a write to A_{wt} is established once it has been accepted by all of the non-faulty servers in any Q_{wt}, a write quorum within A_{wt}. Therefore, we conservatively assume that the number of faulty servers in Q_{wt} is:

$$\mathsf{MalWrite} = |\mathsf{A}_{\mathrm{wt}} \cap B|. \tag{5}$$

Here, A_{wt} is a random variable taking on a write access set chosen uniformly at random from $\mathcal{A}_{\mathrm{wt}}$.

Q_{wt} also contains $q_{\mathrm{wt}} - \mathsf{MalWrite}$ non-faulty servers, not necessarily chosen at random, in addition to the $\mathsf{MalWrite}$ faulty servers. Let C_{wt} represent these non-faulty servers:

$$\mathsf{C}_{\mathrm{wt}} = \mathsf{Q}_{\mathrm{wt}} \setminus B, \tag{6}$$

$$|\mathsf{C}_{\mathrm{wt}}| = q_{\mathrm{wt}} - \mathsf{MalWrite}, \tag{7}$$

where Q_{wt} is a random variable taking on the write quorum at which the write is established, and C_{wt} is a random variable taking on the set of non-faulty servers within this write quorum. Then, the number of non-faulty servers that return the correct value in a read quorum selected by a non-faulty client is,

$$\mathsf{MinCorrect} = |\mathsf{Q}_{\mathrm{rd}} \cap \mathsf{C}_{\mathrm{wt}}|, \tag{8}$$

where Q_{rd} is a random variable taking on a read quorum chosen uniformly at random from A_{rd}, itself chosen uniformly at random from $\mathcal{A}_{\mathrm{rd}}$.

A faulty client may select its read quorum, Q_{rd}, to maximize the number of votes for a single conflicting value in an attempt to invalidate P3. Therefore, as described in Section 4.1, the client first chooses all faulty servers in A_{rd}. The number of such servers is,

$$\mathsf{Malevolent} = |\mathsf{A}_{\mathrm{rd}} \cap B|. \tag{9}$$

The faulty client also chooses the non-faulty servers that vote for the conflicting value that is most represented in A_{rd}; these servers are a subset of $(A_{\mathrm{rd}} \setminus (C_{\mathrm{wt}} \cup B))$. This conflicting value has an associated write access set A'_{wt} chosen uniformly at random from $\mathcal{A}_{\mathrm{wt}}$, and no vote from a non-faulty server not in A'_{wt} will be counted among those for this conflicting value (because votes for any two write operations are distinguishable from each other as discussed in

Section 3.1). Let A'_{wt} be a random variable taking on A'_{wt}. Then, the number of non-faulty servers in A_{rd} that vote for this conflicting value is,

$$\text{Conflicting} = |A_{rd} \cap (A'_{wt} \setminus (C_{wt} \cup B))|. \tag{10}$$

A faulty client can choose all of these servers for Q_{rd}. Therefore, since the sets of servers measured by Malevolent and Conflicting are disjoint (the former consists solely of faulty servers; the latter solely of non-faulty servers), the maximum number of instances of the same conflicting value that a faulty client will select for Q_{rd} is,

$$\text{MaxConflicting} = \text{Malevolent} + \text{Conflicting}. \tag{11}$$

4.3 Minimum System Sizes

In this section, we consider PO-Consistency under various assumptions concerning the sizes of access sets and quorums in order to derive the maximum fraction of faults that can be tolerated with decreasing error probability as a function of n (and b). Our primary result is Theorem 1 which provides an upper bound on b for which PO-Consistency holds. It is derived using the expectations of MinCorrect and MaxConflicting (derived in our technical report [9]) that are computed using the worst-case behavior of faulty clients presented in Section 4.1.

Theorem 1. *PO-Consistency holds iff*

$$b < \frac{(a_{rd}q_{wt}n - 2a_{rd}a_{wt}n + a_{wt}^2 a_{rd} + q_{rd}q_{wt}n)n}{n^2 a_{rd} - a_{rd}a_{wt}n + a_{wt}^2 a_{rd} + q_{rd}a_{wt}n}.$$

As shown in Section 4.4, a construction exhibits decreasing error probability in the limit with increasing n if PO-Consistency holds. Therefore, the remainder of this section is concerned with interpreting the inequality in Theorem 1. Our analysis of this inequality is given in Table 2 and shows that the best bounds are provided when: (i) both types of quorums are as large as possible (while still ensuring an available quorum), i.e., $q_{rd} = q_{wt} = n - b$; and (ii), given (i), that access sets as small as possible. Our

Table 2. Lower bounds on n for various configurations

n >	= n	= n − b	= n − 2b
3.15b	-	a_{rd} q_{rd} a_{wt} q_{wt}	-
3.83b	a_{rd}	q_{rd} a_{wt} q_{wt}	-
4.00b	a_{wt}	a_{rd} q_{rd} q_{wt}	-
4.08b	-	a_{rd} a_{wt} q_{wt}	q_{rd}
4.56b	a_{rd} a_{wt}	q_{rd} q_{wt}	-
4.73b	a_{wt}	a_{rd} q_{wt}	q_{rd}
5.49b	-	a_{rd} q_{rd} a_{wt}	q_{wt}
6.07b	a_{rd}	q_{rd} a_{wt}	q_{wt}
6.19b	-	a_{rd} a_{wt}	q_{rd} q_{wt}

technical report [9] provides a more detailed analysis including an inequality for systems with no Byzantine clients.

4.4 Bounding the Error Probability

Suppose a read operation always returns a value that receives more than r votes, where $\mathbb{E}[\text{MaxConflicting}] \leq r < \mathbb{E}[\text{MinCorrect}]$. Then, the error probability, ϵ, is

$$\epsilon = \Pr(\mathsf{MaxConflicting} > r \vee \mathsf{MinCorrect} \leq r). \tag{12}$$

Theorem 2 states that if r is chosen so that

$$\mathbb{E}\left[\mathsf{MinCorrect}\right] - r = \theta(n) \quad \text{and}$$
$$r - \mathbb{E}\left[\mathsf{MaxConflicting}\right] = \theta(n) \tag{13}$$

then ϵ decreases as a function of n, assuming that the ratio of each of b, a_{rd}, q_{rd}, a_{wt}, and q_{wt} to n remains constant. For example, r can be set equal to $(\mathbb{E}\left[\mathsf{MaxConflicting}\right] + \mathbb{E}\left[\mathsf{MinCorrect}\right])/2$.

Theorem 2. *Let* $\mathsf{MinCorrect}$, $\mathsf{MaxConflicting}$, *and* r *be defined as above (so PO-Consistency holds) and let the ratio of each of* b, a_{rd}, q_{rd}, a_{wt}, *and* q_{wt} *to* n *be fixed. Then,*

$$\epsilon = 2/e^{\Omega(n)} + 2/e^{\Omega(n)}.$$

5   Access-Restriction Protocol

Our analysis in the previous sections assumes that all access sets are chosen uniformly at random by all clients—even faulty clients. Therefore, here we present an access-restriction protocol that is used to enforce this. Recall from Section 3.1 that the need for read access sets to be selected uniformly at random is motivated by repair. As such, protocols that do not involve repair may not require this access-restriction protocol for read operations.

Our protocol must balance conflicting constraints. First, a client may be forced to discard a randomly chosen access set—and choose another—because a given access set (of size less than b servers more than a quorum) might not contain an available quorum. However, in order to support protocols like Q/U [1] that use opaque quorum systems for single-round writes, we cannot require additional rounds of communication for each operation. This precludes, for example, a protocol in which the servers collectively choose an access set at random and assign it to the client for every operation. As such, a client must be able to choose from multiple access sets without involving the servers for each. Yet, a faulty client should be prevented from discarding access sets in order to choose the one that has the highest probability of causing an error given the current system state. In addition, we should ensure that a faulty client does not benefit from waiting for the system state to change in order to use a previously chosen access set that becomes more advantageous as a result of the change.

In our protocol, the client obtains one or more random values, each called a Verifiable Random Value (VRV), with the participation of non-faulty servers. Each VRV determines a unique, verifiable, ordered sequence of random access sets that the client can use; the client has no control over the sequence. To deter a client from discarding earlier access sets in the sequence for potentially more favorable access sets later in the sequence, the protocol imposes an exponentially increasing cost (in terms of computation) for the ability to use later access sets.

The cost is implemented as a *client puzzle* [17]. We couple this with a facility for the propagation of the correct value in the background so that any advantages for a faulty client in the current system state are reduced if the client chooses to delay performing the operation while it explores later access sets. Finally, to deter a client from waiting for the system state to change, we tie the validity of a VRV (and its sequence of access sets) to the state of the system so that as execution proceeds, any unused access sets become invalid.

5.1 Obtaining a VRV

In order to get an access set, the client first must obtain a VRV from the servers. Servers implement a metering policy, in which each server responds to a request for a VRV only after a delay. The delay varies, such that it increases exponentially with the rate at which the client has requested VRVs during some recent interval of time—i.e., a client that has not requested a VRV recently will receive a VRV with little or no delay, whereas a client that has recently requested many VRVs will receive a VRV after a (potentially significant) delay. To offload work from servers to clients (e.g., for scalability), the servers can make it relatively more expensive (in terms of time) to ask for and receive a new VRV than to compute a given number of access sets (potentially for multiple operations) from a single VRV, using the mechanisms described below.

The VRV is characterized by the following properties:

- It can be created only with the consent of non-faulty servers;
- Its validity is tied to the state of the system, in the sense that as the system state evolves (possibly merely through the passage of time), eventually the VRV is invalidated;
- While it is valid, any non-faulty server can verify its validity and so will accept it.

The VRV must be created with the consent of non-faulty servers because otherwise faulty servers might collude to issue multiple VRVs to a faulty client with no delay. Therefore, l, the number of servers required for the issuance of a VRV, must be at least $b + 1$. However, of the non-faulty servers in the system, only those among the (at least $l - b$) used to issue a VRV will impose additional delay before issuing an additional VRV. Therefore, to minimize the time to get an additional VRV, a faulty client avoids involving servers that have issued VRVs recently. This strategy maximizes the number of VRVs to which the non-faulty server contributing to the fewest VRVs has contributed. Thus, once k VRVs have been issued, all $n - b$ non-faulty servers have contributed to the issuance of at least $\lfloor k(l - b)/(n - b) \rfloor$ of these k. Since all non-faulty servers have contributed to at least this many VRVs, and the delay is exponential in this number, the time $T(k)$ required for a client to obtain k VRVs is:

$$T(k) = \Omega \left(\exp \left\lfloor \frac{k(l - b)}{n - b} \right\rfloor \right)$$

In practice, $T(k)$ for a client decays during periods in which that client does not request additional VRVs, so that a client that does not request VRVs for a period can obtain one with small delay.

The validity of the VRV (and its sequence of access sets) is tied to the state of the system so that as execution proceeds, any unused access sets become invalid. To implement this, the replication protocol may provide some piece of data that varies with the state of the system—the *Object History Set* in Q/U [1] is an example of this—with which the servers can compute a VRV, but, in the absence of a suitable value from the protocol, the VRV can include a timestamp (assuming that the non-faulty servers have roughly synchronized clocks). The VRV consists of this value together with a digital signature created using a (l, n)-threshold signature scheme (e.g., [18]), i.e., so that any set of l servers can together create the signature, but smaller sets of servers cannot. The signature scheme must be *strongly unforgeable* [19], meaning that an adversary, given a VRV, is not able to find other valid VRVs. This is necessary because otherwise a faulty client would be able to generate variations of a valid VRV until finding one from which to select an access set that causes an error (see below).

5.2   Choosing an Access Set

As motivated above: (i) the VRV determines a sequence of valid access sets; and (ii) a client puzzle must make it exponentially harder to use later access sets in the sequence than earlier ones. In addition, it is desirable for our protocol to satisfy the following requirements:

- Each VRV must determine only a single valid sequence of access sets. This is to prevent a faulty client from choosing a preferred sequence.
- The puzzle solutions must be easy to verify, so that verification costs do not limit the scalability of the system in terms of the number of requests.
- There must be a solution to each puzzle. Otherwise a non-faulty client might be unable to use any access set.
- No server can know the solution to the puzzle beforehand due to the Byzantine fault model. Otherwise, a faulty client could avoid the exponential work by asking a faulty server for the solution.

In our protocol, the sequence of access sets is determined as follows. Let v be a VRV, let $\mathbf{g}$ be a hash function modeled as a random oracle [20], and let **access_set** be a deterministic operation that, given a seed value, selects an access set of the specified size from the set of all access sets of that size in a uniform fashion. Let the first seed, s_1, be $\mathbf{g}(v)$, and the i'th seed, s_i, be $\mathbf{g}(s_{i-1})$. Then the i'th access set is **access_set**(s_i). Our technical report [9] contains an example specification of **access_set**.

In order to use the i'th access set, the client must solve a puzzle of suitable difficulty. This puzzle must be non-interactive [21] to avoid additional rounds of communication. There are many suitable candidate puzzle functions [21].

5.3   Server Verification

Upon receiving a write request for the i'th access set, each non-faulty server in the chosen access set must verify that it is a member of the access set; for a repair request it must verify that the relevant votes are from servers in the access set of the read operation that gave rise to the repair. In addition, in either case, before accepting the value, each server must verify that the VRV is valid, that the access set corresponds to the i'th access set of the sequence, and that the client has provided a valid solution to a puzzle of the appropriate difficulty level to use the i'th access set.

While the client can obtain additional access sets from the VRV, each access set used is treated as a different operation by servers as stated in Section 3.1; e.g., a write operation using one access set, and then using another access set, is treated as two different writes,[3] so that a faulty client cannot "accumulate" more than a_{wt} servers for its operation through the use of multiple write access sets.

5.4   Background Propagation

As described above, servers work to propagate the values of established writes to each other in the background. Our main contribution in this area is our analysis of the threshold number of servers that must propagate a value for it to be accepted by another server. While related Byzantine diffusion protocols (e.g., [22]) use the number $b+1$, we require a larger number because opaque quorum systems allow that some non-faulty servers may accept conflicting values. We assume an appropriate propagation algorithm (e.g., a variant of an epidemic algorithm [23] such as [22]). At a high level, a non-faulty server has two responsibilities. First, having accepted a write value and returned a response to the client, it periodically informs other servers that it has accepted the value. Second, if it has not yet accepted a value upon learning that a threshold number, p, of servers have accepted the value, it accepts the value. Faulty servers are all assumed to have access to any conflicting value directly without propagation, so we assume no additional constraints on their behavior.

Lemma 1. *Let $n < 2q_{wt} - 2b$ and $p = n - q_{wt} + b + 1$. Then an established value will be accepted and propagated by at least p non-faulty servers, and no conflicting value can be propagated by p servers (faulty or non-faulty).*

For example, if $q_{wt} = n - b$ and $n > 4b$ we set $p = 2b + 1$. Since the established value will be accepted by at least p non-faulty servers, it will propagate. No conflicting value will propagate.

If the conditions of Lemma 1 do not hold, we must allow for some probability of error during propagation. We set p so that it is between the expectations of the minimum number of non-faulty servers that accept an established write (PCorrect), and the maximum number of servers that propagate a conflicting value (PConflicting).

---

[3] Typically, a Byzantine-fault-tolerant write protocol must already be resilient to partial writes, which is how these writes using different access sets might appear to the service.

Lemma 2. *PO-Consistency* $\Rightarrow \mathbb{E}\,[\mathsf{PCorrect}] > \mathbb{E}\,[\mathsf{PConflicting}].$

Lemma 2 shows that we can set p as described for any system in which PO-Consistency holds.

6   Evaluation

In this section, we analyze error probabilities for concrete system sizes. In addition to validating our results from Section 4, this shows that an access restriction protocol like that of Section 5 can provide significant advantages in terms of worst-case error probabilities.

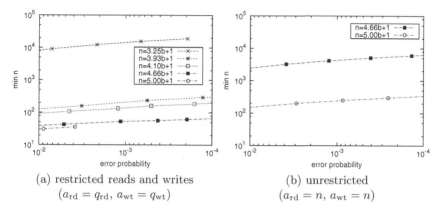

(a) restricted reads and writes
$(a_{\mathrm{rd}} = q_{\mathrm{rd}},\, a_{\mathrm{wt}} = q_{\mathrm{wt}})$

(b) unrestricted
$(a_{\mathrm{rd}} = n,\, a_{\mathrm{wt}} = n)$

Fig. 2. Number of servers required to achieve given calculated worst-case error probability

Figure 2 plots the total number of nodes required to achieve a given calculated error probability for two configurations that tolerate faulty clients where $q_{\mathrm{wt}} = q_{\mathrm{rd}} = n - b$: the *restricted* configuration $(a_{\mathrm{rd}} = q_{\mathrm{rd}},\, a_{\mathrm{wt}} = q_{\mathrm{wt}})$ and the *unrestricted* configuration $(a_{\mathrm{rd}} = n,\, a_{\mathrm{wt}} = n)$. Since the unrestricted configuration (Figure 2(b)) does not require the access-restriction protocol of Section 5, yet yields better maximum ratios of b to n than the other configurations listed in Table 2 in which $q_{\mathrm{wt}} = a_{\mathrm{wt}} - b$ or $q_{\mathrm{rd}} = a_{\mathrm{rd}} - b$ from Section 4.3, we do not evaluate the error probabilities for those configurations here. In all cases, the error probabilities are worst-case in that they reflect the situation in which all b nodes are in fact faulty. For each configuration, we provide plots for different ratios of n to b, ranging from the maximum b for a given configuration, to $n = 5b+1$, as a comparison with strict opaque quorum systems. Our technical report [9] provides details of our calculations, as well as calculations for additional configurations.

In the figure, we see that to decrease the worst-case error probability, we can either keep the same function of b in terms of n while increasing n, or hold n fixed while decreasing the number of faults the system can tolerate. In addition, we see that configurations that tolerate a larger b also provide better error probabilities for a given b. Overall, we find that our constructions can tolerate significantly more than $b = n/5$ faulty servers, while providing error probabilities in the range of 10^{-2} to 10^{-4} for systems with fewer than 50 servers to hundreds of servers. Coupled with the dissemination of correct values between servers (off the critical path), as described in Section 5.4, the error probability decreases between writes.

7 Conclusion

First, have presented probabilistic opaque quorum systems (POQS), a new type of opaque quorum system that we have shown can tolerate up to $n/3.15$ Byzantine servers (compared with $n/5$ Byzantine servers for strict opaque quorum systems) with high probability, while preserving the properties that make opaque quorums useful for optimistic Byzantine-fault-tolerant service protocols. Second, we have presented an optional, novel access-restriction protocol for POQS that provides the ability for servers to constrain clients so that they use randomly selected access sets for operations. With POQS, we expect to create probabilistic optimistic Byzantine fault-tolerant service protocols that tolerate substantially more faults than current optimistic protocols. While strict opaque quorums systems may be more appropriate for smaller systems that require no chance of error, a POQS can provide increased fault tolerance for a given number of nodes, with a worst-case error probability that is bounded and that decreases as the system scales.

Acknowledgments. This work was partially supported by NSF grant CCF-0424422.

References

1. Abd-El-Malek, M., Ganger, G.R., Goodson, G.R., Reiter, M.K., Wylie, J.J.: Fault-scalable Byzantine fault-tolerant services. In: Symposium on Operating Systems Principles (October 2005)
2. Schneider, F.B.: Implementing fault-tolerant services using the state machine approach: a tutorial. ACM Computing Surveys 22(4), 299–319 (1990)
3. Martin, J.P., Alvisi, L.: Fast Byzantine consensus. IEEE Transactions on Dependable and Secure Computing 3(3), 202–215 (2006)
4. Malkhi, D., Reiter, M.: Byzantine quorum systems. Distributed Computing 11(4), 203–213 (1998)
5. Castro, M., Liskov, B.: Practical Byzantine fault tolerance and proactive recovery. ACM Transactions on Computer Systems 20(4), 398–461 (2002)
6. Malkhi, D., Reiter, M.K., Wool, A., Wright, R.N.: Probabilistic quorum systems. Information and Computation 170(2), 184–206 (2001)
7. Bazzi, R.A.: Access cost for asynchronous Byzantine quorum systems. Distributed Computing 14(1), 41–48 (2001)
8. McDiarmid, C.: Concentration for independent permutations. Combinatorics, Probability and Computing 11(2), 163–178 (2002)
9. Merideth, M.G., Reiter, M.K.: Probabilistic opaque quorum systems. Technical Report CMU-CS-07-117, CMU School of Computer Science (March 2007)

10. Yu, H.: Signed quorum systems. Distributed Computing 18(4), 307–323 (2006)
11. Aiyer, A.S., Alvisi, L., Bazzi, R.A.: On the availability of non-strict quorum systems. In: Fraigniaud, P. (ed.) DISC 2005. LNCS, vol. 3724, pp. 48–62. Springer, Heidelberg (2005)
12. Aiyer, A.S., Alvisi, L., Bazzi, R.A.: Byzantine and multi-writer k-quorums. In: Dolev, S. (ed.) DISC 2006. LNCS, vol. 4167, pp. 443–458. Springer, Heidelberg (2006)
13. Liskov, B., Rodrigues, R.: Tolerating Byzantine faulty clients in a quorum system. In: International Conference on Distributed Computing Systems (2006)
14. Cachin, C., Tessaro, S.: Optimal resilience for erasure-coded Byzantine distributed storage. In: International Conference on Dependable Systems and Networks (2006)
15. Lamport, L., Shostak, R., Pease, M.: The Byzantine generals problem. ACM Transactions on Programming Languages and Systems 4(3), 382–401 (1982)
16. Herlihy, M., Wing, J.: Linearizability: A correctness condition for concurrent objects. ACM Transactions on Programming Languages and Systems 12(3), 463–492 (1990)
17. Juels, A., Brainard, J.: Client puzzles: A cryptographic countermeasure against connection depletion attacks. In: Network and Distributed Systems Security Symposium, pp. 151–165 (1999)
18. Shoup, V., Gennaro, R.: Securing threshold cryptosystems against chosen ciphertext attack. Journal of Cryptology 15(2), 75–96 (2002)
19. An, J.H., Dodis, Y., Rabin, T.: On the security of joint signature and encryption. In: Knudsen, L.R. (ed.) EUROCRYPT 2002. LNCS, vol. 2332, pp. 83–107. Springer, Heidelberg (2002)
20. Bellare, M., Rogaway, P.: Random oracles are practical: A paradigm for designing efficient protocols. In: Conference on Computer and Communications Security, pp. 62–73 (1993)
21. Jakobsson, M., Juels, A.: Proofs of work and bread pudding protocols. In: Communications and Multimedia Security, pp. 258–272 (1999)
22. Malkhi, D., Mansour, Y., Reiter, M.K.: Diffusion without false rumors: On propagating updates in a Byzantine environment. Theoretical Computer Science 299(1–3), 289–306 (2003)
23. Demers, A., Greene, D., Hauser, C., Irish, W., Larson, J., Shenker, S., Sturgis, H., Swinehart, D., Terry, D.: Epidemic algorithms for replicated database maintenance. In: Principles of Distributed Computing, pp. 1–12 (August 1987)

Detecting Temporal Logic Predicates on Distributed Computations

Vinit A. Ogale and Vijay K. Garg*

Parallel and Distributed Systems Laboratory,
Dept. of Electrical and Computer Engineering, University of Texas at Austin
{ogale,garg}@ece.utexas.edu

Abstract. We examine the problem of detecting nested temporal predicates given the execution trace of a distributed program. We present a technique that allows efficient detection of a reasonably large class of predicates which we call the Basic Temporal Logic or BTL. Examples of valid BTL predicates are nested temporal predicates based on local variables with arbitrary negations, disjunctions, conjunctions and the possibly (EF or ◊) and invariant(AG or □) temporal operators. We introduce the concept of a *basis*, a compact representation of all global cuts which satisfy the predicate. We present an algorithm to compute a basis of a computation given any BTL predicate and prove that its time complexity is polynomial with respect to the number of processes and events in the trace although it is not polynomial in the size of the formula. We do not know of any other technique which detects a similar class of predicates with a time complexity that is polynomial in the number of processes and events in the system. We have implemented a predicate detection toolkit based on our algorithm that accepts offline traces from any distributed program.

1 Introduction

In large distributed programs it is often desirable to have a formal guarantee that the program output is correct. One approach is to model check the entire program with respect to the given specification. This is impractical even for most moderately complex programs. For many applications, predicate detection offers a simple and efficient alternative over model checking the entire program. Predicate detection involves verifying the execution trace of a distributed program with respect to a given property (for example, violation of mutual exclusion). The correctness properties or the predicates, which enable us to formally define a correct execution, can have temporal implications.

In scientific computing, it may be vital to verify that the result of a computation was valid, and if it was invalid due to a rare 'chance' bug, the program can

---

* Supported in part by the NSF Grants CNS-0509024, Texas Education Board Grant 781, SRC Grant 2006-TJ-1426, and Cullen Trust for Higher Education Endowed Professorship.

A. Pelc (Ed.): DISC 2007, LNCS 4731, pp. 420–434, 2007.

be re-executed. Predicate detection provides a formal guarantee on the validity of the computation (assuming that the specifications are correct). If the specifications can be expressed in a supported logic then verification of the traces requires a comparatively insignificant overhead (polynomial in the number of processes and events) using the algorithm discussed in this paper. Note that this approach is obviously not useful for critical real time applications where it is essential that all runs be correct.

A distributed computation, i.e., the execution trace of a distributed program, can either be modeled as a total order, or as a partial order on the set of events in the computation. Representing the computation as a total order can mask some of the bugs in other possible consistent interleavings. A partial order, in contrast, captures all the possible causally consistent interleavings. In this paper we use a partial order representation based on Lamport's *happened before* relation [1].

The drawback of using a partial order model is that the number of global states of the computation is exponential in the number of processes. This makes predicate detection a hard problem in general [2,3]. A number of strategies like symbolic representation of states and partial order reduction have been explored to tackle the state explosion problem [4,5,6,7,8,9,10].

In this paper, we present a technique to efficiently detect all temporal predicates that can be expressed in, what we call, Basic Temporal Logic or BTL. An example of a valid BTL predicate would be a property based on local predicates and arbitrarily placed negations, disjunctions and conjunctions along with the possibly($\Diamond$) and invariant($\Box$) temporal operators (the EF and AG operators defined in [11]).

Our algorithm is based on computing a *basis* which is a compact representation of the subset of the computational lattice containing exactly those global states (or cuts) that satisfy the predicate. In general, it is hard to efficiently compute a basis for an arbitrary predicate. We utilize the fact that the set of global states of a computation forms a distributive lattice and restrict the predicates to BTL formulas. The basis introduced in this paper is a union of smaller sets of cuts called semiregular structures.

Note that, without any restrictions on the predicate formula, predicate detection is NP-complete with respect to the formula size, and for arbitrary predicates the time complexity could be exponential in the formula size. However, if the input formula is in a 'DNF like' form after pushing in negations, our technique detects it in polynomial time with respect to the formula size.

To summarize, this paper makes the following contributions:

– We introduce the concept of a basis and discuss representations of stable, regular and semiregular predicates.
– We present an algorithm to efficiently compute the basis for BTL predicates. This enables detection of BTL predicates in $O(2^k.|E|.n)$ time, where k is the number of operators in the predicate, E is the set of events in the computation and n is the number of processes. To the best of our knowledge, there is no other known technique that can detect nested temporal predicates

containing disjunctions or negations with a time complexity that is polynomial in n and $|E|$.

- We discuss the implementation of our algorithm and compare it with existing approaches like using SPIN [12] and POTA [13] to detect predicates in distributed programs. Our tool, *BTV* (Basis based Trace Verifier), can analyze traces in a compatible format generated by any distributed program.

Note that currently known approaches, like slicing [14] or model checking of traces, for detecting a similar class of predicates, are inefficient and require exponential time with respect to the number of processes.

The remainder of the paper is organized as follows: Section 2 discusses related work and section 3 explains in detail, the model and notation used in the paper. Section 4 introduces the concept of a basis of a computation with respect to a predicate and presents the main algorithm. In section 5, we present the complexity analysis of our algorithm. We follow that with an example and a short description of our implementation of a predicate detection toolkit based on the algorithm in this paper.

2   Related Work

A number of approaches for checking computations using temporal logic have been published. Temporal Rover [15], MaC [16] and JPaX [17] are some of the available tools. Many of the tools are based on total ordering of events and hence cannot be directly compared to our approach. These tools can miss potential bugs which would be detected by partial order representations. JMPaX [18] is based on a partial order model and supports temporal properties but its time complexity is exponential in the number of processes in the computation.

Another available option to verify computation traces is to use a model checking tool like SPIN [12,19]. The computation trace needs to be converted to the SPIN input computation and verification takes exponential time in the number of processes.

Computational slicing [14] based approaches can efficiently detect *regular* predicates. POTA [13] is such a partial order based tool which uses computational slicing to detect predicates. POTA guarantees polynomial time complexity only if the predicate can be expressed in a subset of CTL [11] called *Regular CTL* or RCTL [20]. Disjunctions and negations are not allowed in RCTL. If POTA is used with a logic that allows disjunctions or negations (like BTL), it uses a model checking algorithm to explore the reduced state space. Hence the asymptotic time complexity using POTA is exponential in the number of processes when the predicate contains disjunctions. Table 1 compares the time complexities of SPIN, POTA and our algorithms implemented in the BTV tool.

3   Model and Notation

This paper uses basic lattice theory constructs that are formally defined in the technical report [21]. We assume a loosely coupled, message-passing,

Table 1. Time complexities (n = number of processes)

	SPIN	POTA	BTV
RCTL	exponential in n	polynomial in n	polynomial in n
BTL	exponential in n	exponential in n	polynomial in n

asynchronous system model. A distributed program consists of n sequential programs $P_1, P_2, \ldots, P_n$. A computation is a single execution of such a program. A distributed computation $(\langle E, \rightarrow \rangle)$ is modeled as a partial order on the set of events E, based on the happened before relation ($\rightarrow$) [1]. The *size of the computation* is the total number of events, $|E|$, in the computation.

Definition 1. *(Consistent Cut) A consistent cut C is a set of events in the computation which satisfies the following property: if an event e is contained in the set C, then all events in the computation that happened before e are contained in C.*
$$\forall e_1, e_2 \in E : (e_2 \in C) \land (e_1 \rightarrow e_2) \Rightarrow e_1 \in C.$$

In figure 1(i) the set $\{e_1, f_1\}$ is a consistent cut, while $\{e_1, e_2\}$ is not. In the following discussion, we mean 'consistent cut' whenever we simply say 'cut'. For notational convenience, we simply mention the maximal elements on each process that are elements of the cut to represent that cut. For example, the cut $\{e_1, e_2, f_1, f_2, f_3\}$ is written as $\{e_2, f_3\}$. The set of all consistent cuts in a computation is denoted by $\mathcal{C}$. This set, $\mathcal{C}$, forms a distributive lattice [22] (also called the computational lattice) under the less than equal to relation defined as follows.

Definition 2. *Cut C_1 is less than or equal to cut C_2 if and only if, $C_1 \subseteq C_2$.*

A cut C, in a computation E, satisfies a predicate P if the predicate is true in the global state represented by the cut. This is denoted by $(C, E) \models P$ or simply $C \models P$ where the context is clear.

The *join* of two cuts is simply defined as their union, and the *meet* of two cuts corresponds to the intersection of those two cuts.

Figure 1 shows a computation and the distributive lattice formed by all the consistent cuts in the computation. Birkhoff's representation theorem [22] states that a distributive lattice can be completely characterized by the set of its join irreducible elements. Join irreducibles are elements of the lattice that cannot be expressed as the join of any two elements.[1] For example, in figure 1(ii), cuts $\{\}, \{f_1\}, \{f_2\}, \{f_3\}, \{e_1, f_1\}, \{e_2, f_1\}, \{e_3, f_1\}$ are join irreducible. The cut, $\{e_1, f_2\}$ is not join irreducible because it can be expressed as the join of cuts $\{f_2\}$ and $\{e_1, f_1\}$.

The *initial cut* is the least cut, i.e., the empty set $\{\}$ and the *final cut* is the greatest cut, i.e, the set of all events E, in the computational lattice.

---

[1] Commonly, the bottom element is not considered to be a join irreducible element. However, in this paper, for notational convenience, we include the bottom element (the initial cut $\{\}$) in the set of join irreducible elements.

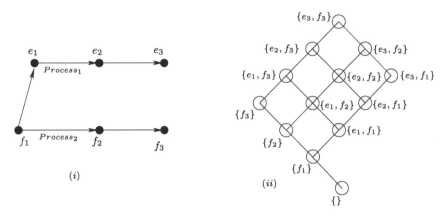

Fig. 1. A computation and the lattice of its consistent cuts

Detecting a predicate in a distributed computation is determining if the initial cut of the computation satisfies the predicate.

Definition 3. *(Join-closed, Meet-closed and Regular Predicates) A predicate P is join-closed if all cuts that satisfy the predicate are closed under union. i.e., $(C_1 \models P \wedge C_2 \models P) \Rightarrow (C_1 \cup C_2) \models P$.*

Similarly a predicate P is meet-closed if all the cuts that satisfy the predicate are closed under intersection. A predicate is regular if it is join-closed and meet-closed.

If cuts C_1 and C_2 satisfy a regular predicate, then by definition, $C_1 \cup C_2$ and $C_1 \cap C_2$ also satisfy that predicate. For example, the predicate "No process has the token and the token in not in transit" is regular. All conjunctions of local predicates are regular.

A predicate is stable if, once it becomes true, it remains true [23]. A stable predicate is always join-closed.

Definition 4. *A predicate P is stable, if $\forall C_1, C_2 \in \mathcal{C} : C_1 \models P \wedge C_1 \leq C_2 \Rightarrow C_2 \models P$.*

Some examples of stable predicates are loss of a token, deadlocks, and termination.

Figure 2 depicts examples of the cuts satisfied by meet-closed, join-closed, regular and stable predicates.

4   Basis of a Computation

We now introduce the concept of a *basis* of a computation. Informally, a basis is an exact compact representation of the set of cuts which satisfy the predicate.

Definition 5. *(Basis) Given a computational lattice $\mathcal{C}$, corresponding to a computation E, and a predicate P, a subset $S[P]$ of $\mathcal{C}$ is a basis of P if*

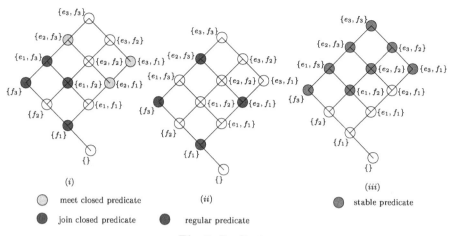

Fig. 2. Predicates

1. *(Compactness) The size of $S[P]$ is polynomial in the size of computation that generates C.*
2. *(Efficient Membership) Given any cut (global state) $C \in \mathcal{C}$, there exists a polynomial time algorithm that takes $S[P]$, E and C as inputs and determines if $(C, E) \models P$.*

We denote the basis with respect to a predicate P as $S[P]$. Given a predicate P, a cut C belongs to a basis $S[P]$, if C satisfies that predicate. i.e., $C \in S[P] \Leftrightarrow C \models P$.

Note that direct enumeration of all the states satisfied by a predicate is, in general, not a basis since determining if a cut is a member of that set could take exponential time.

For a simple example of an basis, consider a class of predicates, such that the cuts satisfying a predicate in that class form an ideal in the computational lattice. (An ideal is a sublattice that contains every cut that is less than the maximal cut in the sublattice.) A basis, for such a class of predicates, is just the maximal cut of the ideal. It can be efficiently determined if a cut $C \in \mathcal{C}_p$ by checking if the cut is less than or equal to the maximal cut.

Computational slicing, introduced in [14], is a technique to compute an efficient predicate structure for regular predicates.

Definition 6. *(Slice) The slice slice$[P]$ of a computation with respect to a predicate P is the poset of the join irreducible consistent cuts representing the smallest sublattice that contains all consistent cuts satisfying P.*

Though the number of consistent cuts satisfying the predicate may be large, the slice of a predicate can be efficiently represented by the set of the join irreducible cuts in the slice. *Slicing* is the operation of computing the slice for the given predicate.

When the predicate is regular, the computed slice represents exactly those cuts that satisfy the predicate. Given the slice with respect to a predicate, it is possible to efficiently detect if a cut satisfies that predicate. Therefore, a slice is an efficient basis for regular predicates. However, using slicing for predicate detection of non-regular predicates can take exponential time.

In the remainder of this paper, we explore a technique to compute a basis for a more general class of predicates, that we call BTL, which can have arbitrary negations, disjunctions, conjunctions and the temporal possibly($\Diamond$) operator. Since a BTL predicate can be non-regular, a slice of a BTL predicate is not a valid basis. One naive approach to compute a predicate structure is to maintain a set of slices instead of a single slice. Though this is polynomial in the number of processes n, it results in a large number of slices ($O(n^{2^k})$), where k is the size of the predicate. In this paper, we introduce a *semiregular structure* which can efficiently represent a more general class than regular predicates. A BTL predicate can be represented by using a set of semiregular structures.

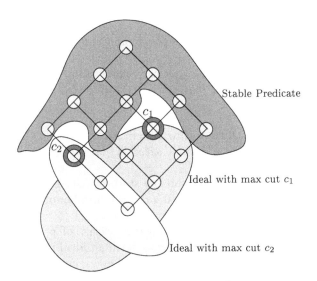

Fig. 3. Representing stable predicates

We start off by looking at the representation of a stable predicate. Figure 3 shows an example of a stable predicate. The set of states satisfying a stable predicate can be considered to be the union of a set of filters of the computational lattice. Thus, a stable predicate can be represented by the set of minimal cuts that satisfy the predicate.

Another representation is to identify a set of ideals, $\mathcal{I} = \{I_1, I_2, \ldots\}$ of the computational lattice such that all the cuts satisfying the stable predicate are contained in the complement of $\bigcup_{I \in \mathcal{I}} I$. The stable predicate in figure 3 can be represented by two ideals as seen in the figure. We use the set of ideals representation in this paper for computational efficiency while dealing with BTL predicates.

Definition 7. *(Stable Structure) Given a stable predicate P and the computational lattice $\mathcal{C}$, a stable structure is the set of ideals $\mathcal{I}$ such that a cut satisfies P iff it does not belong to any of the ideals in $\mathcal{I}$. Therefore, $C \models P \Leftrightarrow \neg(C \in \bigcup_{I \in \mathcal{I}} I)$.*

A cut C is said to belong to the stable structure if C does *not* belong to $\bigcup_{I \in \mathcal{I}} I$. Note that, any ideal is uniquely and efficiently represented by its maximal cut. In the remainder of this paper we use $\mathcal{I}$ to represent a set of ideals representing the stable predicate and simply $maxCuts$ to denote the set containing the maximal cut from each ideal in $\mathcal{I}$.

Note that, this representation is not a basis since, the set of ideals could be very large in general. However, we see later, that this leads to an efficient representation when the predicate is expressed in BTL.

4.1 Semiregular Predicates and Structures

The conjunction of a stable predicate and a regular predicate is called a semiregular predicate and is more expressive than either of them.

Definition 8. *P is a semiregular predicate if it can be expressed as a conjunction of a regular predicate with a stable predicate.*

We now list some properties of semiregular predicates.

1. All regular predicates and stable predicates are semiregular. This follows from the definition of semiregular predicates since *true* is a stable and regular predicate.
2. Since regular and stable predicates are join-closed, it follows that their conjunction, a semiregular predicate, is also join-closed. However not all join-closed predicates are semiregular. Figure 4 shows a join-closed predicate that is not semiregular.
3. Semiregular predicates are closed under conjunction, i.e., if P and Q are semiregular then $P \wedge Q$ is semiregular.
4. If P is a semiregular predicate then $\Diamond P$ and $\Box P$ are semiregular. If P is semiregular, P has a unique maximal cut, say C_{max} and $\Diamond P$ is an ideal of the lattice that contains all cuts less than or equal to C_{max}.

We now present an alternative characterization of a semiregular predicate that offers a different insight into the structure of the cuts satisfying such a predicate.

Lemma 1. *Predicate P is semiregular iff*

- *P is join-closed, i.e, $C_1 \models P \wedge C_2 \models B \Rightarrow (C_1 \cup C_2) \models P$ and*
- *The meet of two cuts that satisfy P is C, and C does not satisfy P, then any cut smaller than C does not satisfy P. i.e., $(C_1 \cap C_2) \models P \vee (\forall C' \leq (C_1 \cap C_2) : \neg(C' \models P))$.*

A few examples of semiregular predicates are listed below.

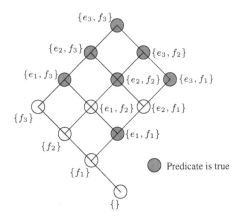

Fig. 4. A join-closed predicate may not be semiregular

- All processes are never *red* concurrently at any future state and process 0 has the token. That is $P = \neg\Diamond(\bigwedge red_i) \wedge token_0$.
- At least one process is beyond phase k (stable) and all the processes are red.

We now define a representation for semiregular predicates.

Definition 9. *(Semiregular Structure) A semiregular structure, g, is represented as a tuple $(\langle slice, \mathcal{I}\rangle)$ consisting of a slice and a stable structure, such that the predicate is true in exactly those cuts that belong to the intersection of the slice and the stable structure.*

$\qquad$ *Hence $C \in g \Leftrightarrow (C \in slice) \wedge \neg(C \in \bigcup_{I \in \mathcal{I}} I)$.*

Note that, a cut is contained in a semiregular structure if it belongs to the slice *and* the stable structure in the semiregular structure. The maximal cut in a semiregular structure is the maximal cut in the slice if the semiregular structure is nonempty.

$\qquad$ We see later that any BTL predicate can be expressed as a basis consisting of a union of semiregular structures. A semiregular structure enables us to easily handle predicates of the form $\neg\Diamond P$. Such a predicate can be represented by n slices or by a single stable structure or a semiregular structure. We use this in our algorithms and prove that it is possible to compute an efficient basis representation for any BTL predicate.

4.2   Logic Model (BTL)

In this section formally define Basic Temporal Logic (BTL), such that any predicate expressible in BTL can be efficiently detected using the algorithm presented later in this paper. The atomic propositions in BTL are local predicates, i.e., properties that depend on a single process in the computation. Local predicates and their negations are regular predicates. Let AP be the set of all atomic propositions. Given the set of all consistent cuts, $\mathcal{C}$, of a computation, a labeling function $\lambda : \mathcal{C} \rightarrow 2^{AP}$ assigns to each consistent cut, the set of predicates from AP that hold in it. The operators $\wedge$ and $\vee$ represent the boolean conjunction and disjunction operators as usual, $\neg$ represent the negation of a predicate and we define the *possibly* ($\Diamond$) temporal operator (called EF in [4]).

Definition 10. *If $\mathcal{C}$ is the set of all consistent cuts of the computation, then $\Diamond P$ holds at consistent cut C, if and only if, there exists $C' \in \mathcal{C}$ such that P is true at C' and $C \subseteq C'$.*

The formal BTL syntax is given below.

Definition 11. *A predicate in BTL is defined recursively as follows:*

1. *$\forall l \in AP$, l is a BTL predicate*
2. *If P and Q are BTL predicates then $P \vee Q$, $P \wedge Q$, $\Diamond P$ and $\neg P$ are BTL predicates*

We formally define the semantics of BTL.

- $(C, E, \lambda) \models l \Leftrightarrow l \in \lambda(C)$ for an atomic proposition l
- $(C, E, \lambda) \models P \wedge Q \Leftrightarrow C \models P$ and $C \models Q$
- $(C, E, \lambda) \models P \vee Q \Leftrightarrow C \models P$ or $C \models Q$
- $(C, E, \lambda) \models \Diamond P \Leftrightarrow \exists C' \in \mathcal{C} : (C \subseteq C'$ and $C' \models P)$
- $(C, E, \lambda) \models \neg P \Leftrightarrow \neg(C \models P)$

We use $(C, E) \models P$ or simply $C \models P$ in the rest of the discussion when E and λ are obvious from the context. Note that, the AG operator in CTL [4] can be written as $\neg\Diamond\neg$ in BTL.

4.3   Algorithm

We present an algorithm to compute a basis for any predicate expressed in BTL. The computed basis consists of a set of semiregular structures such that a cut belongs to the basis if it belongs to any semiregular structure in that set.

Definition 12. *Given a BTL predicate P, we define a representation S of the predicate that consists of a set of semiregular structures such that $C \models P \Leftrightarrow (\exists g \in S : C \in g)$.*

We assume that the input predicate has negations pushed in to the local predicates or the $\Diamond$ operators. In the following discussion, we often treat $\neg\Diamond$ as single operator. We see later that our algorithm returns an efficient predicate structure which allows polynomial time detection of the predicate.

Each semiregular structure, g, is represented as a tuple $\langle slice, maxCuts \rangle$ where $g.slice$ is the slice in g and $g.maxCuts$ is the set of cuts corresponding to the ideals representing the stable structure. The use of ideals instead of filters is very important and results in the 2^k bound (see theorem 2) on the size of the stable structure. (The stable structures calculated by the algorithm could require n^k filters to represent it.)

/*The input predicate P_{in} has all negations pushed
- inside to the $\Diamond$ operator or to the atomic propositions */
/* each semiregular structure is represented as a tuple $\langle slice, maxCuts \rangle$
- where $maxCuts$ is the set of maximal cuts
- of the ideals $\mathcal{I}$ representing the stable structure */

function getBasis(Predicate P_{in})
output: $S[P_{in}]$, a set of semiregular structures
    Case 1. (Base case: local predicates) : $P_{in} = l$ or $P_{in} = \neg l$
        $S[P_{in}] := \{\langle slice(P), \{\} \rangle\}$
    Case 2. $P_{in} = P \vee Q$
        $S[P] :=$ getBasis$(P); S[Q] =$ getBasis$(Q);$
        $S[P_{in}] := \{S[P] \cup S[Q]\};$
    Case 3. $P_{in} = P \wedge Q$
        $S[P] :=$ getBasis$(P); S[Q] =$ getBasis$(Q);$
        $S[P_{in}] := \bigcup_{g_p \in S[P], g_q \in S[Q]} \{(\langle g_p.slice \wedge g_q.slice, g_p.maxCuts \cup g_q.maxCuts \rangle)\};$
    Case 4. $P_{in} = \Diamond P$
        $S[P] :=$ getBasis$(P);$
        $S[P_{in}] := \bigcup_{g \in S[P]} \{\langle \Diamond(g.slice), \{\} \rangle\};$
    Case 5. $P_{in} = \neg \Diamond P$
        $S[P] :=$ getBasis$(P);$
        /* $slice_{orig}$ is the original computation */
        $S[P_{in}] := \{\langle slice_{orig}, \cup_{g \in S[P]} \{\text{maxCutIn}(g.slice)\} \rangle\};$

Remove all empty semiregular structures from $S[P_{in}]$;

return $S[P_{in}]$

Fig. 5. Computing a basis

Figure 5 outlines the main algorithm to compute a basis of the computation for any BTL predicate. For predicate detection, we simply check if the initial cut of the computation is contained in the computed basis. To determine if a cut is contained within the basis, we need to examine if it belongs to any semiregular structure in the basis. A basis is nonempty if the predicate is true in any consistent cut of the computation. Note that, in case we need to check whether a predicate P is true at any cut in the computation (and not just the initial cut), we can either apply our algorithm on the predicate $\Diamond P$ or alternatively apply the algorithm on P and check if the returned basis is nonempty.

The algorithm computes the basis by recursively processing the predicate inside out.

– The base case is a local predicate. Note that, the negation of a local predicate is also local. We know that for each atomic proposition l_i, $slice[l_i]$ can be computed in polynomial time. Efficient algorithms to compute $slice[l_i]$ (or $slice[\neg l_i]$) when the atomic propositions are local predicates, can be found in [14]. The basis of a local predicate has a single semiregular structure that consists of a slice and an empty set of ideals. (A local predicate and its negation are regular predicates and hence a slice is an efficient basis for such predicates).

- The second case handles disjunctions. If the input predicate P_{in} is of the form $P \vee Q$ the basis is the structure containing all the cuts in $S[P]$ and $S[Q]$ and is obtained by computing the union of the sets $S[P]$ and $S[Q]$.
- When the input predicate is of the form $P \wedge Q$, the resultant basis is the pairwise intersection of each semiregular structure in $S[P]$ and $S[Q]$. Each semiregular structure consists of a slice and a stable structure. The intersection of two semiregular structures, say g_p and g_q, is the tuple $\langle g_p.slice \cap g_q.slice, g_p.stable\_structure \cap g_q.stable\_structure \rangle$. The grafting algorithm described in [14] describes a technique to compute the intersection of two slices. Since we use ideals to represent stable structures, the intersection of the stable structures is represented by the *union* of the sets $g_p.maxCuts$ and $g_q.maxCuts$.
- The fourth case in the algorithm handles predicates of the form $P_{in} = \Diamond P$. $S[P]$ is the union of a set of semiregular structures. The resultant basis is obtained by computing $\Diamond g$ for each g in $S[P]$ and taking the union. Note that $\Diamond g$ is equivalent to $\Diamond(g.slice)$ and the algorithm for EF of a regular predicate in [20] can be used to determine $\Diamond(g.slice)$.
- Since $\neg \Diamond P$ is stable, the basis corresponding to $\neg \Diamond P$ contains a single semiregular structure g. The slice in this semiregular structure is the original computation while the ideals are represented by the maximal cuts of the slice in each of the semiregular structures that belong to $S[P]$. In this case, it becomes clear that using the 'set of ideals representation' for stable structures is more efficient. The number of ideals is guaranteed to be k if $S[P]$ had k semiregular structures. Using another representation like maintaining a set of filters would have resulted in expensive operations since the number of filters could be n^k in this case.

After each step, the algorithm checks if any of the semiregular structures are empty and discards the empty semiregular structures. A semiregular structure is empty, if the maximal element of the slice is less than or equal to each cut in $g.maxCuts$.

It can be seen that the structure returned by our algorithm contains exactly those cuts which satisfy the input predicate. We show in section 5 that the number of semiregular structures and the number of ideals required to represent the stable structures returned by our algorithm is polynomial in n. This enables us to check whether a cut belongs to the structure in polynomial time and hence the structure is efficient.

5   Complexity Analysis

The time taken by the algorithm in figure 5 depends on the number of ideals representing the stable structure in each semiregular structure and the total number of semiregular structures in the resultant basis (the size of the basis). The proofs for most the results in this section are presented in the technical report [21] due to space constraints. We first present a result on the bound on the size of computed basis.

Theorem 1. *The basis $S[P]$ computed by the algorithm in Figure 5 for a BTL predicate P with k operators has at most 2^k semiregular structures.*

This leads to the following theorem.

Theorem 2. *The total number of ideals $|I|$ in the basis computed by the algorithm in Figure 5 for a BTL predicate P is at most 2^k.*

The time required to compute the conjunction of two slices with respect to $\wedge$ is $O(|E|n)$ [14]. It takes $O(|E|n)$ time to compute the slice with respect to the $\Diamond$ operator.

Theorem 3. *The time complexity of the algorithm in figure 5 is polynomial in the number of events ($|E|$) and the number of processes (n) in the computation.*

The algorithm simplifies the predicate by computing the basis one operator at a time. Hence, if there are k operators in all, it requires k steps to compute the basis for the entire predicate.

Theorem 1 states that after the lth operator is processed at most 2^l new semiregular structures are generated. The generation of each semiregular structure takes less than or equal to $|E|n$ time. The time required to generate all the semiregular structures is $2^l.|E|n$.

The algorithm compares each ideal to the maximal cut of a slice to check if the semiregular structure is empty. There are at most 2^l semiregular structures (theorem 1) which implies that there are no more than 2^l slices (since each semiregular structure contains exactly one slice). The total number of ideals is less than or equal to 2^l (theorem 2). Since comparing two cuts requires $O(n)$ time, it takes $(2^l + 2^l)n$ time to check which semiregular structures are empty. Hence the time required to process the lth operator is $2^l.(|E|n) + n(2^{l+1})$, i.e, $2^{l+1}.n.(2|E| + 1))$

Therefore the total time required is $\Sigma_{l=1}^{k} 2^{l+1}.n.(2|E| + 1) = O(2^k|E|n)$.

If the input predicate is in a 'DNF-like' form then predicate detection is even more efficient (polynomial in k).

Theorem 4. *If the input predicate has conjunctions only over regular predicates, then the size of the predicate structure and the total number of ideals $|I|$, is at most k.*

Since conjunctions are allowed over regular predicates, the resulting predicate is regular and can be represented by exactly one semiregular predicate with no ideals.

6   Implementation

We have implemented a toolkit to verify computation traces generated by distributed programs. This toolkit accepts offline execution traces as its input.

We used a Java implementation of the distributed dining philosophers algorithm from [24] and checked for errors in the system. We injected faults in the traces and verified the traces using, both, our toolkit and POTA [13]. Note that, for predicates containing disjunctions, POTA reduces the computation size and uses SPIN [19] to check for predicate violations. The POTA-SPIN combination performs well in some runs (when the slice generated is lean or empty) but it runs out of memory when the number of processes is increased, especially when configured to list all predicate violations. BTV, as expected, scales well and we could use it to verify computations with large number of processes. Our implementation (including the Java source code) can be downloaded from our laboratory website. Note that the toolkit relies on offline traces and hence it is not necessary for the program that is being tested to be implemented in Java. It can be used with any arbitrary distributed program that outputs a compatible trace. The toolkit includes a utility to convert traces from the POTA trace format.

7   Conclusions

We conclude that it is possible to efficiently detect nested temporal predicates containing disjunctions and negations (along with conjunctions and $\Diamond$). We have introduced the notion of a semiregular structure and have presented techniques to efficiently compute an efficient basis given any BTL predicate. This has many practical applications which require verification of traces. Apart from ensuring the validity of runs, the technique discussed in this paper is also useful in distributed program debuggers. Since the computed basis contains exactly all states where the predicate holds, we can use it to pinpoint the faults in the program. One useful extension of this work would be an online version of the algorithm which could be used to control distributed programs by changing their behavior at runtime if faults are detected.

References

1. Lamport, L.: Time, clocks, and the ordering of events in a distributed system. Communications of the ACM 21(7), 558–565 (1978)
2. Stoller, S.D., Schneider, F.B.: Faster possibility detection by combining two approaches. In: Proc. of the 9th International Workshop on Distributed Algorithms, Le Mont-Saint-Michel, France, pp. 318–332. Springer, Heidelberg (1995)
3. Garg, V.K.: Elements of Distributed Computing. Wiley & Sons, Chichester (2002)
4. McMillan, K.L.: Symbolic Model Checking. Kluwer Academic Publishers, Dordrecht (1993)
5. Godefroid, P.: Partial-Order Methods for the Verification of Concurrent Systems. LNCS, vol. 1032. Springer, Heidelberg (1996)
6. Valmari, A.: A stubborn attack on state explosion. In: Clarke, E., Kurshan, R.P. (eds.) CAV 1990. LNCS, vol. 531, pp. 156–165. Springer, Heidelberg (1991)
7. Peled, D.: All from one, one for all: On model checking using representatives. In: Courcoubetis, C. (ed.) CAV 1993. LNCS, vol. 697, pp. 409–423. Springer, Heidelberg (1993)

8. Stoller, S.D., Unnikrishnan, L., Liu, Y.A.: Efficient Detection of Global Properties in Distributed Systems Using Partial-Order Methods. In: Emerson, E.A., Sistla, A.P. (eds.) CAV 2000. LNCS, vol. 1855, pp. 264–279. Springer, Heidelberg (2000)
9. Stoller, S.D., Liu, Y.: Efficient symbolic detection of global properties in distributed systems. In: Emerson, E.A., Sistla, A.P. (eds.) CAV 2000. LNCS, vol. 1855, pp. 264–279. Springer, Heidelberg (2000)
10. Esparza, J.: Model checking using net unfoldings. Science Of Computer Programming 23(2), 151–195 (1994)
11. Clarke, E.M., Emerson, E.A.: Design and synthesis of synchronization skeletons using branching-time temporal logic. In: Logic of Programs, Workshop, London, UK, pp. 52–71. Springer, Heidelberg (1982)
12. Holzmann, G.: The model checker SPIN. IEEE transactions on software engineering 23(5), 279–295 (1997)
13. Sen, A., Garg, V.K.: Partial order trace analyzer (POTA) for distributed programs. In: Proceedings of the Third International Workshop on Runtime Verification (RV) (2003)
14. Mittal, N., Garg, V.K.: Slicing a distributed computation: Techniques and theory. In: Welch, J.L. (ed.) DISC 2001. LNCS, vol. 2180, pp. 78–92. Springer, Heidelberg (2001)
15. Drusinsky, D.: The temporal rover and the ATG rover. In: Havelund, K., Penix, J., Visser, W. (eds.) SPIN Model Checking and Software Verification. LNCS, vol. 1885, pp. 323–330. Springer, Heidelberg (2000)
16. Kim, M., Kannan, S., Lee, I., Sokolsky, O., Viswanathan, M.: Java-MaC: A runtime assurance tool for Java programs. In: Runtime Verification 2001. ENTCS, vol. 55 (2001)
17. Havelund, K., Rosu, G.: Monitoring Java programs with Java PathExplorer. In: Runtime Verification 2001. ENTCS, vol. 55 (2001)
18. Sen, K., Rosu, G., Agha, G.: Detecting errors in multithreaded programs by generalized predictive analysis of executions. In: Steffen, M., Zavattaro, G. (eds.) FMOODS 2005. LNCS, vol. 3535, Springer, Heidelberg (2005)
19. Holzmann, G.: The Spin Model Checker. Addison-Wesley Professional, Reading (2003)
20. Sen, A., Garg, V.K.: Detecting temporal logic predicates in distributed programs using computation slicing. In: 7th International Conference on Principles of Distributed Systems (2003)
21. Ogale, V., Garg, V.K.: Predicate detection. In: Technical report TR-PDS-2007-001 (2007), available at
   http://maple.ece.utexas.edu/TechReports/2007/TR-PDS-2007-001.ps
22. Davey, B.A., Priestley, H.A.: Introduction to Lattices and Order. Cambridge University Press, Cambridge, UK (1990)
23. Chandy, K.M., Lamport, L.: Distributed snapshots: Determining global states of distributed systems. ACM Transactions on Computer Systems 3(1), 63–75 (1985)
24. Hartley, S.: Concurrent Programming: The Java Programming Language. Oxford University Press, Oxford (1998)

Optimal On-Line Colorings for Minimizing the Number of ADMs in Optical Networks

(Extended Abstract)

Mordechai Shalom[1,3], Prudence W.H. Wong[2], and Shmuel Zaks[1,⋆]

[1] Department of Computer Science, Technion, Haifa, Israel
{cmshalom,zaks}@cs.technion.ac.il
[2] Department of Computer Science, The University of Liverpool, Liverpool, UK
pwong@csc.liv.ac.uk
[3] Tel-Hai Academic College, Upper Galilee, 12210, Israel
cmshalom@telhai.ac.il

Abstract. We consider the problem of minimizing the number of ADMs in optical networks. All previous theoretical studies of this problem dealt with the off-line case, where all the lightpaths are given in advance. In a real-life situation, the requests (lightpaths) arrive at the network on-line, and we have to assign them wavelengths so as to minimize the switching cost. This study is thus of great importance in the theory of optical networks. We present an on-line algorithm for the problem, and show its competitive ratio to be $\frac{7}{4}$. We show that this result is best possible in general. Moreover, we show that even for the ring topology network there is no on-line algorithm with competitive ratio better than $\frac{7}{4}$. We show that on path topology the competitive ratio of the algorithm is $\frac{3}{2}$. This is optimal for this topology. The lower bound on ring topology does not hold when the ring is of bounded size. We analyze the triangle topology and show a tight bound of $\frac{5}{3}$ for it. The analyzes of the upper bounds, as well as those for the lower bounds, are all using a variety of proof techniques, which are of interest by their own, and which might prove helpful in future research on the topic.

1 Introduction

1.1 Background

Optical wavelength-division multiplexing (WDM) is today the most promising technology that enables us to deal with the enormous growth of traffic in communication networks, like the Internet. A communication between a pair of nodes is done via a *lightpath*, which is assigned a certain wavelength. In graph-theoretic terms, a lightpath is a simple path in the network, with a color assigned to it.

Given a WDM network $G = (V, E)$ comprising optical nodes and a set of full-duplex lightpaths $P = \{p_1, p_2, ..., p_N\}$ of G, the wavelength assignment (WLA)

⋆ This research was partly supported by the EU Project "Graphs and Algorithms in Communication Networks (GRAAL)" - COST Action TIST 293.

A. Pelc (Ed.): DISC 2007, LNCS 4731, pp. 435–449, 2007.

task is to assign a wavelength to each lightpath p_i. Most of the studies in optical networks dealt with the issue of assigning colors to lightpaths, so that every two lightpaths that share an edge get different colors.

When the various parameters comprising the switching mechanism in these networks became clearer, the focus of studies shifted, and today a large portion of the studies concentrates on the total hardware cost. The key point here is that each lightpath uses two Add-Drop Multiplexers (ADMs), one at each endpoint. If two adjacent lightpaths, i.e. lightpaths sharing a common endpoint, are assigned the same wavelength, then they can use the same ADM. Because ADMs are designed to be used mainly in ring and path networks in which the degree af a node is at most two, an ADM may be shared by at most two lightpaths. The total cost considered is the total number of ADMs. A more detailed technical explanation can be found in [GLS98].

Lightpaths sharing ADMs in a common endpoint can be thought as concatenated, so that they form longer paths or cycles. These paths/cycles do not use any edge $e \in E$ twice, for otherwise they cannot use the same wavelength which is a necessary condition to share ADMs.

1.2   Previous Work

Minimizing the number of ADMs in optical networks is a main research topic in recent studies. The problem was introduced in [GLS98] for the ring topology. An approximation algorithm for ring topology with approximation ratio of 3/2 was presented in [CW02], and was improved in [SZ04, EL04] to $10/7 + \epsilon$ and $10/7$, respectively. For general topology [EMZ02] describe an algorithm with approximation ratio of 8/5. The same problem was studied in [CFW02] and an algorithm with an approximation ratio of $\frac{3}{2} + \epsilon$ was presented. This algorithm is further analyzed in [FSZ06b].

The problem of on-line path coloring is studied in earlier works, such as [LV98]. The problem studied in these works has a different objective function, namely the number of colors.

All previous theoretical studies on the problem of minimizing the number of switches dealt with the off-line case, where all the lightpaths are given in advance. In a real-life situation, the requests (lightpaths) arrive at the network on-line, and we have to assign them wavelengths so as to minimize the switching cost. An on-line algorithm is said to be c-competitive if for any sequence of lightpaths, the number of ADMs used is at most c times that used by the optimal offline algorithm (see [BEY98]).

1.3   Our Contribution

We present an on-line algorithm with competitive ratio of $\frac{7}{4}$ for any network topology. We prove that no algorithm has a competitive ratio better than $\frac{7}{4}$ even if the topology is a ring.

We show that the same algorithm has a competitive ratio of $\frac{3}{2}$ in path topologies, and that this is also a lower bound for on-line algorithms in this topology.

The lower bound on ring topology does not hold when the ring is of a bounded size. We study the triangle topology, and show a tight bound of $\frac{5}{3}$ for the competitive ratio on this topology, using another algorithm.

The analyses of the upper bounds, as well as those for the lower bounds, use a variety of proof techniques, which are of interest on their own, and which might prove helpful in future research on the topic.

In Section 2 we describe the problem and some preliminary results. The algorithm and its competitive analysis are presented in Section 3. In Section 4 we present lower bounds for the competitive ratio of the problem on general topology, ring and path topologies. In Section 5 we present tight bounds for triangle networks. We conclude with discussion and open problems in Section 6. Some proofs are sketched in this Extended Abstract; for full details the reader is referred to [SWZ07].

2   Preliminaries

An instance α of the problem is a pair $\alpha = (G, P)$ where $G = (V, E)$ is an undirected graph and P is a set of simple paths in G. In an on-line instance, the graph G is known in advance and the set P of paths is given on-line. In this case we denote $P = \{p_1, p_2, ..., p_N\}$ where p_i is the i-th path of the input and $P_i = \{p_j \in P | j \leq i\}$ consists of the first i paths of the input.

In this work we need a number of notions introduced in [FSZ06a].

- The paths $p, p' \in P$ are *conflicting* or *overlapping* if they have an edge in common. This is denoted as $p \asymp p'$. The graph of the relation $\asymp$ is called the conflict graph of (G, P).
- A proper coloring (or wavelength assignment) of P is a function $w : P \mapsto \mathbb{N}$, such that $w(p) \neq w(p')$ whenever $p \asymp p'$.
- A valid chain (resp. cycle) of $\alpha = (G, P)$ is a path (resp.cycle) formed by the concatenation of distinct paths $p_{i_0}, p_{i_1}, ..., p_{i_{k-1}} \in P$ that do not go over the same edge twice. Note that the paths of a valid chain (resp. cycle) constitute an independent set of the conflict graph.
- A solution S of an instance $\alpha = (G, P)$ is a set of valid chains and valid cycles of P such that each $p \in P$ appears in exactly one of these sets.

Note that w is a proper coloring if and only if for any color $c \in \mathbb{N}$, $w^{-1}(c)$ is an independent set in the conflict graph.

In the sequel we introduce the shareability graph, which together with the conflict graph constitutes another (dual) representation of the instance α. In the sequel, except one exception, we will use the dual representation of the problem.

- The shareability graph of an instance $\alpha = (G, P)$, is the edge-labelled multi-graph $\mathcal{G}_\alpha = (P, E_\alpha)$ such that there is an edge $e = (p, q)$ labelled u in E_α if and only if $p \not\asymp q$, and u is a common endpoint of p and q in G.
- A valid chain (resp. cycle) of $\mathcal{G}_\alpha$ is a simple path $p_{i_0}, p_{i_1}, ..., p_{i_{k-1}}$ of $\mathcal{G}_\alpha$, such that any two consecutive edges in the path (resp. cycle) have distinct labels

and its node set is properly colorable with one color (in G), or in other words constitutes an independent set of the conflict graph.

- The sharing graph of a solution S of an instance $\alpha = (G, P)$, is the following subgraph $\mathcal{G}_{\alpha,S} = (P, E_S)$ of $\mathcal{G}_\alpha$. Two lightpaths $p, q \in P$ are connected with an edge labelled u in E_S if and only if they are consecutive in a chain or cycle in the solution S, and their common endpoint is $u \in V$. We will usually omit the index α and simply write $\mathcal{G}_S$. $d(p)$ is the degree of node p in $\mathcal{G}_S$.

Example: Let $\alpha = (G, P)$ be the instance in the left side of Figure 1. Its shareability graph $\mathcal{G}_\alpha$ is the graph at midle. In this instance $P = \{a, b, c, d\}$, and it constitutes the set of nodes of $\mathcal{G}_\alpha$. The edges together with their labels are $E_\alpha = \{(b, c, u), (a, c, w), (a, b, x), (a, d, x)\}$, because a and b can be joined in their common endpoint x, etc.. Note that, for instance $(b, d, x) \notin E_\alpha$, because although b and d share a common endpoint x, they can not be concatenated, because they have the edge (x, u) in common. The corresponding conflict graph is at the right side of the figure. It has the same node set and one edge, namely (b, d). The paths $b, d \in P$ are conflicting because they have a common edge, i.e. (u, x).

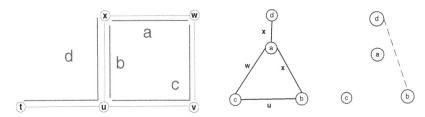

Fig. 1. A sample input

Note that the edges of the conflict graph are not in E_α. This immediately follows from the definitions. Note also that, for any node v of $\mathcal{G}_\alpha$, the set of labels of the edges adjacent to v is of size at most two.

Valid chains and cycles of $\mathcal{G}_\alpha$ correspond to valid chains and cycles of the instance α. In the above example the chain a, d which is the concatenation of the paths a and d in the graph G, corresponds to the simple path a, d in $\mathcal{G}_\alpha$ and the cycle a, b, c which is a cycle formed by the concatenation of three paths in G corresponds to the cycle a, b, c in $\mathcal{G}_\alpha$. Note that no two consecutive labels are equal in this cycle. On the other hand the paths b, a, d can not be concatenated to form a chain, because this would require the connection of a to both b and d at node x. The corresponding path b, a, d in $\mathcal{G}_\alpha$ is not a chain because the edges (b, a) and (a, d) have the same label, namely x.

$S = \{(d, a, c), (b)\}$ is a solution with two chains. The sharing graph of this solution has two edges (d, a) and (a, c). Note that for a chain of size at most two, the distinct labelling condition is satisfied vacuously, and the independent set condition is satisfied because no edge of $\mathcal{G}_\alpha$ can be an edge of the conflict graph.

We define $\forall i \in \{0, 1, 2\}, D_i(S) \stackrel{def}{=} \{p \in P | d(p) = i\}$ and $d_i(S) \stackrel{def}{=} |D_i(S)|$.

Note that $d_0(S) + d_1(S) + d_2(S) = |P| = N$.

An edge $(p, q) \in E_S$ with label u corresponds to a concatenation of two paths with the same color at their common endpoint u. Therefore these two endpoints can share an ADM operating at node u, thus saving one ADM. We conclude that every edge of E_S corresponds to a saving of one ADM. When no ADMs are shared, each path needs two ADM's, a total of $2N$ ADMs. Therefore the cost of a solution S is

$$cost(S) = 2\,|P| - |E_S| = 2N - |E_S|.$$

The objective is to find a solution S such that $cost(S)$ is minimum, in other words $|E_S|$ is maximum.

The following definitions and Lemma appeared in [FSZ06b], we repeat them here for completeness.

Given a solution S, $d(p) \leq 2$ for every node $p \in P$. Therefore, the connected components of $\mathcal{G}_S$ are either paths or cycles. Note that an isolated vertex is a special case of a path. Let $\mathcal{P}_S$ be the set of the connected components of $\mathcal{G}_S$ that are paths. Clearly, $|E_S| = N - |\mathcal{P}_S|$. Therefore $cost(S) = 2N - |E_S| = N + |\mathcal{P}_S|$.

Let S^* be a solution with minimum cost. For any solution S we define

$$\epsilon(S) \stackrel{def}{=} \frac{d_0(S) - d_2(S) - 2\,|\mathcal{P}_{S^*}|}{N}.$$

Lemma 2.1 *For any solution S, $cost(S) = cost(S^*) + \frac{1}{2}N(1 + \epsilon(S))$.*

Proof. Clearly $|E_{S^*}| = N - |\mathcal{P}_{S^*}|$. On the other hand $2\,|E_S|$ is the sum of the degrees of the nodes in $\mathcal{G}_S$, namely $2\,|E_S| = d_1(S) + 2d_2(S) = N - d_0(S) + d_2(S)$. We conclude:

$$cost(S) - cost(S^*) = |E_{S^*}| - |E_S| = N - |\mathcal{P}_{S^*}| - \frac{N - d_0(S) + d_2(S)}{2}$$

$$= \frac{N}{2} + \frac{d_0(S) - d_2(S) - 2\,|\mathcal{P}_{S^*}|}{2} = \frac{1}{2}N\left(1 + \frac{d_0(S) - d_2(S) - 2\,|\mathcal{P}_{S^*}|}{N}\right)$$

$\square$

3 Upper Bounds

In this section we first describe an on-line algorithm, show that it is 7/4-competitive on any network topology and 3/2-competitive on path topology.

3.1 Algorithm ONLINE-MINADM

In a general network, when the lightpaths are given one-by-one, we adopt a simple coloring procedure. Basically, a new lightpath with endpoints u and v looks for free ADM at its endpoints. If there are two of the same color, then it first tries to make a cycle with the existing lightpaths, and if this is impossible then it makes a path. If there are free ADMs (at one endpoint, or at both endpoints but of different colors), then it tries to connect to any of them. Otherwise - when there is no free ADM - it is assigned a new color.

When we attempt to color some lightpath p_i, a color λ is said to be *feasible* for p_i, if there is no other lightpath with the same color and overlapping with p_i. In other words λ is feasible for p_i, if we can assign $w(p_i) = \lambda$ and w is a proper coloring for P_i.

When a lightpath p_i with endpoints u_i and v_i arrives,

- If there exists a chain of lightpaths with the same color λ with endpoints u_i, v_i and λ is feasible for p_i then, assign $w(p_i) = \lambda$.
- Otherwise, If there exists a chain of lightpaths with the same color λ with one endpoint from $\{u_i, v_i\}$ and λ is feasible for p_i then, assign $w(p_i) = \lambda$.
- Otherwise, assign $w(p_i) = \lambda'$, where λ' is an unused color.

Note that, as in the last clause the algorithm resorts to an unused color, it will never construct two chains with the same color. Therefore in the first clause, the algorithm necessarily closes a cycle.

Algorithm ONLINE-MINADM is obviously correct: w is a proper coloring for P_i, because if p_i is colored by one the first two cases, then it is checked by the algorithm for feasibility, otherwise $w(p_i)$ is assigned an unused color, therefore no other path, in particular no path p_j conflicting with p_i may have $w(p_j) = w(p_i)$.

In this and the following section we prove the following theorem.

Theorem 3.1 *Algorithm ONLINE-MINADM is optimal for*

- *general topology, with competitive ratio of $\frac{7}{4}$,*
- *ring topology, with competitive ratio of $\frac{7}{4}$,*
- *path topology, with competitive ratio of $\frac{3}{2}$.*

3.2 Analysis for General Topology

Lemma 3.1 *The competitive ratio of ONLINE-MINADM is at least $\frac{7}{4}$.*

Proof. Let G be a cycle of three nodes $V = \{v_1, v_2, v_3\}$, $E = \{e_1, e_2, e_3\}$ where $e_1 = (v_1, v_2), e_2 = (v_2, v_3), e_3 = (v_3, v_1)$ and let $P = \{p_1, p_2, p_3, p_4\}$ where $p_1 = (e_3), p_2 = (e_1), p_3 = (e_2, e_3), p_4 = (e_1, e_2)$. The optimal solution assigns $w(p_1) = w(p_4) = \lambda_1$ and $w(p_2) = w(p_3) = \lambda_2$, and uses 4 ADMs. Recall that ONLINE-MINADM receives the paths of the input one at a time. It assigns $w(p_1) = \lambda_1$, then $w(p_2) = \lambda_1$ because λ_1 is feasible for p_2, then $w(p_3) = \lambda_2$ because λ_1 is not feasible for p_3 and finally $w(p_4) = \lambda_3$, because neither λ_1 nor λ_2 are feasible for p_4. It uses 7 ADM's in total.   □

In the sequel S is a solution returned by the ONLINE-MINADM and S^* is an optimal solution.

Lemma 3.2 *The competitive ratio of ONLINE-MINADM is at most $\frac{7}{4}$.*

Proof. We direct each edge of $\mathcal{G}_{S^*}$, such that each path becomes a directed path and each cycle becomes a directed cycle. The direction chosen for every path (resp. cycle) is arbitrary. Let $\overrightarrow{\mathcal{G}}_{S*}$ be the digraph obtained by this process.

Unless otherwise stated, $d_{in}(p)$ and $d_{out}(p)$ denote the in and out degrees of p in $\overrightarrow{\mathcal{G}}_{S^*}$, respectively. Clearly, $\forall p \in P$, $d_{in}(p) \leq 1$ and $d_{out}(p) \leq 1$. The following definitions refer to $\overrightarrow{\mathcal{G}}_{S*}$:

$LAST^*$ is the set of nodes that do not have successors in $\overrightarrow{\mathcal{G}}_{S*}$, namely

$$LAST^* \stackrel{def}{=} \{p \in P | d_{out}(p) = 0\}.$$

Note that $|LAST^*| = |\mathcal{P}_{S^*}|$.

The functions $Next^*$ and $Prev^*$ are defined as expected: $Next^*$ (resp. $Prev^*$) maps a node p to the next (resp. previous) node in $\overrightarrow{\mathcal{G}}_{S*}$ whenever such a node exists, namely:

$$Next^* : P \setminus LAST^* \mapsto P$$

and $Next^*(p)$ is the unique node u such that there is an edge from p to u in $\overrightarrow{\mathcal{G}}_{S*}$. $Prev^* = Next^{*-1}$.

With these definitions in hand, we partition $D_0(S)$ into the sets A, B, C and D using the following classification procedure : Given a path $p \in D_0(S)$, if $p \in LAST^*$ then p is in A and $f_A(p) = p$. Otherwise, there is a node $q = Next^*(p)$, we decide according to the degree of q in S: if it has degree 2, then p is in B and $f_B(p) = q$, if it has degree 1, then p is in C and $f_C(p) = \{p, q\}$, otherwise q has degree 0, then p is in D.

It is also immediate from the description that $f_A : A \mapsto LAST^*$, $f_B : B \mapsto D_2(S)$ and $f_C : C \mapsto 2^P$.

We first show that $D = \emptyset$. Assume, by contradiction that $p \in D$ for some $p \in D_0(S)$. Then there is $q \in D_0(S)$ such that $q = Next^*(p)$, therefore $(p, q) \in E_{S^*} \subseteq E_\alpha$. ONLINE-MINADM assigned unique colors to each of p and q. Assume without loss of generality that q comes later than p in the input sequence. p is assigned a unique color, therefore it is the only element in its chain. Then $w(p)$ is feasible for q. Then the algorithm should assign $w(q) = w(p)$, a contradiction.

$f_A(p) = p$, therefore it is a one-to-one function, i.e. $|A| \leq |LAST^*| = |\mathcal{P}_{S^*}|$.

$f_B(p) = Next^*(p)$. $Next^*$ is one-to-one, therefore f_B is one-to-one, i.e. $|B| \leq |D_2(S)| = d_2(S)$.

We will now show that the sets $f_C(p)$ are disjoint. Note that $f_C(p) = \{p, q\}$ where $p \in D_0(S)$ and $q \notin D_0(S)$. Assume that $f_C(p) \cap f_C(p') \neq \emptyset$. Let $f_C(p) = \{p, q\}$ and $f_C(p') = \{p', q'\}$. Then either $p = p'$ or $q = q'$. In the latter case $q = Next^*(p) = Next^*(p') = q'$, then $p = p'$. In both cases, we have $p = p'$. We conclude that if $p \neq p'$, $f_C(p) \cap f_C(p) = \emptyset$. As the sets $f_C(p)$, have exactly 2 elements, we conclude that $|C| \leq \frac{N}{2}$.

We have $d_0(S) = |D_0(S)| = |A| + |B| + |C| + |D| \leq |\mathcal{P}_{S^*}| + d_2(S) + \frac{N}{2}$. Then

$$\epsilon(S) \stackrel{def}{=} \frac{d_0(S) - d_2(S) - 2|\mathcal{P}_{S^*}|}{N} \leq \frac{1}{2}.$$

Substituting this in Lemma 2.1 and recalling that $cost(S^*) \geq N$ we get

$$Cost(S) \leq Cost(S^*) + \frac{1}{2}N(1 + \frac{1}{2}) = Cost(S^*) + \frac{3}{4}N \leq \frac{7}{4}Cost(S^*). \qquad \square$$

3.3 Analysis for Path Topology

Lemma 3.3 *ONLINE-MINADM is $\frac{3}{2}$-competitive in path topology.*

Proof. Let $V = \{v_1, v_2, ...\}$ be the nodes of the path from left to right, and σ_i (resp. τ_i) be the set of paths having v_i as their right (resp. left) endpoint. It is well known that the number of ADMs used by an optimal solution is $\Sigma_i \max \{|\sigma_i|, |\tau_i|\}$. In an optimal solution, at each node v_i, exactly $\min \{|\sigma_i|, |\tau_i|\}$ pairs of paths are assigned one color per pair. In fact these pairs constitute a maximum matching MM_i of the complete bipartite graph $(\sigma_i, \tau_i, \sigma_i \times \tau_i)$. The solution saves $|MM_i| = \min \{|\sigma_i|, |\tau_i|\}$ ADMs at node v_i, in other words $E_{S^*} = \uplus_i MM_i$. Note that every matching of a complete bipartite graph can be augmented to a maximum matching. Let S^* be an optimal solution, such that the matching in each node is obtained by augmenting the matching done by S to a maximum matching, i.e. $E_S \subseteq E_{S^*}$.

We will now define a function $f : (E_{S^*} \setminus E_S) \mapsto E_S$.

Let $e = (p_i, p_j) \in E_{S^*} \setminus E_S$. $e \in E_{S^*} = \uplus_i MM_i$. Let $e \in MM_k$. Assume without loss of generality that $i < j$, i.e. path p_i appears before p_j in the input. As $e \notin E_S$, none of p_i, p_j are paired with any path at node v_k. Therefore when p_j appears in the input $w(p_i)$ is feasible for p_j, if it is not assigned color $w(p_i)$, this can be only because it is assigned color $w(p_j) = w(p_{i'})$, for some $i' < j$. Let the common node of p_j and $p_{i'}$ be $v_{k'}$. Then $e' = (p_j, p_{i'}) \in E_{S^*}$. We define $f(e) = e'$. Note that e' is defined uniquely because there can not be a third path except p_j and $p_{i'}$ getting the same color and ending at node $v_{k'}$. Necessarily $k' \neq k$, because we know that p_j is not paired at node v_k.

We claim that f is one-to-one. Assume, by contradiction that there is some $e'' \neq e$, such that $f(e'') = e'$. Then $e'' \in E_{S^*}$, therefore $e'' \in MM_{k''}$ for some node $v_{k''}$. By the construction of f, k'' is the other endpoint of $p_{i'}$. Let $e'' = (p_{i'}, p_{i''})$. By the discussion in the previous paragraph, symmetrically it follows that $j < i'$, a contradiction. Therefore f is one-to-one, i.e. $|E_{S^*}| - |E_S| = |E_{S^*} \setminus E_S| \leq |E_S|$, thus $|E_S| \geq \frac{1}{2}|E_{S^*}|$.

We conclude as follows. $Cost(S) - Cost(S^*) = |E_{S^*}| - |E_S| \leq \frac{|E_{S^*}|}{2} \leq \frac{N}{2} \leq \frac{Cost(S^*)}{2}$, therefore:

$$Cost(S) \leq \frac{3}{2}Cost(S^*). \qquad \square$$

4 Lower Bounds

4.1 General Topology

Lemma 4.1 *There is no deterministic on-line algorithm with competitive ratio $< \frac{7}{4}$.*

Proof. Assume ALG is a deterministic on-line algorithm, with competitive ratio ρ. We show that $\rho \geq \frac{7}{4}$. For colors we use numbers $1, 2, ...$ The color assigned to a lightpath a by ALG is denoted by $w(a)$. We use the network depicted in

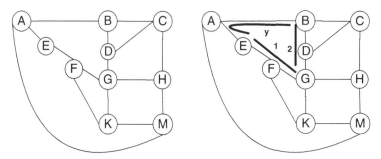

Fig. 2. Proof of Lemma 4.1

Figure 2. The first lightpath in the input is EFG. Without loss of generality, assume $w(EFG) = 1$.

The second lightpath in the input is. First assume $w(BDG) = 1$. In this case if lightpath EABDG arrives, we have $w(EABDG) = 2$, then when lightpath GFEAB arrives we have $w(GFEAB) = 3$. ALG thus uses 7 ADMs, while it is easy to see the an optimal solution can use only 4 ADMs, thus $\rho \geq \frac{7}{4}$, a contradiction. Hence, $w(BDG) = 2$.

When the third lightpath in the input y=BAE arrives The situation is as depicted in the right side of the figure. It is clear that $w(y) \neq 3$, since otherwise $\rho \geq \frac{6}{3} > \frac{7}{4}$, a contradiction. Thus $w(y) = 1$ or $w(y) = 2$.

- case a: $w(y) = 1$
  Let z=EFKMHG be the next lightpath in the input sequence. Clearly $w(z) \neq 1$. Hence $w(z) = 2$ or $w(z) = 3$. If $w(z) = 2$, when lightpaths GFEAB, EABDG, BDGFE and EABCDG arrive, we get $w(GFEAB) = 3, w(EABDG) = 4, w(BDGFE) = 5, w(EABCDG) = 6$, and $\rho = \frac{14}{8} = \frac{7}{4}$, a contradiction. In the case $w(z) = 3$ for u=EABDCHG we have $w(u) = 4$, and $\rho \geq \frac{9}{5} > \frac{7}{4}$, a contradiction.
- case b: $w(y) = 2$
  Let z=BDCHG. Clearly $w(z) \neq 2$. Hence $w(z) = 1$ or $w(z) = 3$. If $w(z) = 1$, when lightpaths EABDG, GFEAB, GKFEAB, and EFGDB arrive, we have $w(EABDG) = 3, w(GFEAB) = 4, w(GKFEAB) = 5, w(EFGDB) = 6$, and $\rho \geq \frac{14}{8} = \frac{7}{4}$, a contradiction. In the case $w(z) = 3$, for u=GHMKFEAB we have $w(u) = 4$. Then $\rho \geq \frac{9}{5} > \frac{7}{4}$, a contradiction.

□

4.2   Ring Topology

The result in the previous Lemma can be proven, though asymptotically even for ring topologies.

Lemma 4.2 *No deterministic on-line algorithm has a competitive ratio better than 7/4, even for the ring topology.*

Sketch of Proof. We first give the inutitive ideas behind the adversary. Suppose we divide the ring into four segments R_1, R_2, R_3 and R_4. The adversary first requests lightpaths R_1 and R_3.

- If the on-line algorithm assigns the same color to them, we then request two lightpaths (R_2, R_3, R_4) and (R_4, R_1, R_2). The on-line algorithm uses 8 ADMs while the offline algorithm can use 4 ADMs.
- If the on-line algorithm assigns different colors to them, we then request R_2. If the on-line algorithm assigns a third color to R_2, we further request R_4 making the on-line algorithm using at least 7 ADMs and the offline algorithm using 4 ADMs only.

The only problematic case for the adversary is that the on-line algorithm assigns R_1 and R_2 with the same color and R_3 using a different color. In this case, the adversary requests two lightpaths (R_2, R_3, R_4) and (R_3, R_4, R_1). Neither of these can share ADMs with existing lightpaths. The on-line algorithm uses 7 ADMs plus 2 ADMs for R_3 while the offline algorithm uses 4 ADMs plus 2 ADMs for R_3. The adversary then repeats the process for k times such that the on-line algorithm uses $7k + 2$ ADMs and the offline algorithm uses $4k + 2$ ADMs. This gives a competitive ratio at least $\frac{7}{4} - \epsilon$ for any $\epsilon > 0$. The crucial point in repeating the process is to ensure later arrival lightpaths cannot share ADMs with lightpaths in previous iterations. This can be done by careful division of the ring and shifting of the division in every iterations. The details can be found in [SWZ07].   □

4.3   Path Topology

Lemma 4.3 *For any $\epsilon > 0$, there is no $(\frac{3}{2} - \epsilon)$-competitive deterministic algorithm for path topology.*

Proof. We prove using the following adversary. Let G be a path with $2k$ nodes $u_1, v_1, u_2, v_2, ..., u_k, v_k$ (see Figure 3). Let ALG be any deterministic algorithm. The value of k will be determined later.

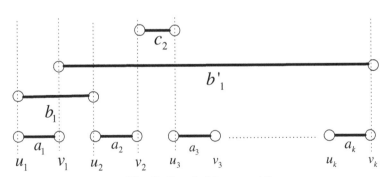

Fig. 3. Proof of Lemma 4.3

The adversary works in two phases. In the first phase the input is $a_1, a_2, ..., a_k$ where $\forall i, a_i = (u_i, v_i)$. In the second phase the input depends on the decisions made by ALG during the first phase. For every $1 \leq i < k$, if $w(a_i) = w(a_{i+1})$ then the input contains two paths $b_i = (u_1, u_{i+1})$ and $b'_i = (v_i, v_k)$, otherwise the input contains one path $c_i = (v_i, u_{i+1})$.

Let $0 \leq x \leq k-1$ be the number of times $w(a_i) = w(a_{i+1})$ is satisfied. Then $w(a_i) \neq w(a_{i+1})$ is satisfied $k-1-x$ times.

During the first phase the algorithm uses $2k$ ADMs, one for each node.

For the paths b_i and b_i', let $\lambda = w(a_i)(= w(a_{i+1}))$. λ is not feasible neither for b_i nor for b_i'. Then the algorithm assigns other colors to b_i and b_i', and it uses 4 ADMs, for a total of $4x$ ADMs.

For the path c_i, let $\lambda = w(a_i)$ and $\lambda' = w(a_{i+1})(\neq \lambda)$, coloring c_i with one of these colors ALG uses one ADM, otherwise it uses 2 ADMs. Therefore for the paths c_i, ALG uses at least $k-1-x$ ADMs.

Summing up, we get that ALG uses at least $2k+4x+(k-1-x) = 3(k+x)-1$ ADMs.

On the other hand the following solution is possible. For any consecutive paths $c_i, c_{i+1}, ..., c_{i+j}$ color such that $w(b_{i-1}) = w(a_i) = w(c_i) = w(a_{i+1}) = w(c_{i+1}) = ... = w(c_{i+j}) = w(a_{i+j+1}) = w(b_{i+j+1}')$. This solutions use $2k+2x$ ADM's, one ADM at each u_i, v_i, x additional ADMs at u_1, and x additional ADMs at v_k.

Therefore the competitive ratio of ALG is at least $\frac{3(k+x)-1}{2(k+x)} = \frac{3}{2} - \frac{1}{2(k+x)} \geq \frac{3}{2} - \frac{1}{2k}$. For any $\epsilon > 0$ we can choose $k > \frac{1}{2\epsilon}$, so that the competitive ratio of ALG is bigger then $\frac{3}{2} - \epsilon$.   □

5   Triangle Topology

In the previous sections we have shown that algorithm ONLINE-MINADM has an optimal competitive ratio, in general topologies, ring and path topologies. In this section we show an example of topology for which ONLINE-MINADM is not optimal. Note that the proof of Lemma 3.1 implies that ONLINE-MINADM is $\frac{7}{4}$-competitive in the triangle topology. We will show in this section a tight bound of $\frac{5}{3}$ for this topology. Note that the lower bound proof for ring networks requires the ring to be of unbounded size. The proof will not hold for rings of a bounded size. In this section we show that this lower bound does not hold for triangles, and give an optimal algorithm for this topology.

Lemma 5.1 *There is no on-line algorithm with competitive ratio $< \frac{5}{3}$ for tri-angle topology.*

Proof. Consider a triangle with edge set $\{e_1, e_2, e_3\}$. We will use the following adversary.

Release two lightpaths each of length 1, on edges e_1 and e_2. If $w(e_1) = w(e_2)$, then we continue as in Lemma 3.1, namely release two lightpaths of length 2 each $\{(e2-e3), (e_1, e_3)\}$, and we get a competitive ratio of $7/4 > 5/3$.

Otherwise $w(e_1) \neq w(e_2)$, w.l.o.g. assume $w(e_1) = 1, w(e_2) = 2$. Release a lightpath on edge e_3. If $w(e_3) \notin \{1, 2\}$ then the competitive ratio is $6/3 = 2 > 5/3$, otherwise w.l.o.g $w(e_3) = 1$. In this case we have $w(e_1) = w(e_3) = 1$ using 3 ADMs, $w(e_2) = 2$ using 2 ADMs, for a total of 5 ADMs. The competitive ratio is $5/3$.   □

For the triangle topology, let us name the three edges in the triangle network e_1, e_2, and e_3. There are only six types of lightpaths, namely, (e_1), (e_2), (e_3),

(e_1, e_2), (e_2, e_3) and (e_1, e_3). For any lightpath p, we say that p is *length-i* if it contains i edges. There are only length-1 and length-2 lightpaths in a triangle topology.

We now present another algorithm ONLINE-TRIANGLE and show that it is 5/3-competitive for triangle topology. Roughly speaking, the algorithm gives highest priority to a pair of length-2 and length-1 lightpaths to share the same color whenever possible. For length-1 lightpaths, we have seen in the lower bound of ONLINE-MINADM in Lemma 3.1 that, if an on-line algorithm always colors two adjacent length-1 lightpaths with the same color, the competitive ratio of the algorithm is at least $\frac{7}{4}$. To overcome this barrier, when a length-1 lightpath, say $p_i = (e_1)$, arrives, ONLINE-TRIANGLE does not always color p_i with an adjacent length-1 lightpath using the same color. However, if we color three length-1 lightpaths on a cycle each with a different color, this will result in a competitive ratio of 2. Therefore, if there are two lightpaths $p_j = (e_2)$ and $p_k = (e_3)$ with different colors, then ONLINE-TRIANGLE should color p_i with either of these colors if it is feasible. We formalize this concept by "marking" the three lightpaths to represent they are grouped together and should not be further considered when other length-1 lightpaths arrive.

Formally, the algorithm runs as follows. When a request of lightpath p_i with endpoints u_i and v_i arrives,

1. In case p_i is length-2,
   - If there exists a length-1 (marked or unmarked) lightpath with color λ with endpoints u_i, v_i, and λ is feasible for p_i, then assign $w(p_i) = \lambda$.
   - Otherwise, assign $w(p_i) = \lambda'$, where λ' is an unused color.
2. In case p_i is length-1,
   - If there exists a length-2 lightpath with color λ with endpoints u_i, v_i, and λ is feasible for p_i, then assign $w(p_i) = \lambda$.
   - Otherwise, if there exists a valid chain of two unmarked length-1 lightpaths with different colors λ_1 and λ_2 with endpoints u_i, v_i, and λ_1 or λ_2 is feasible for p_i (w.l.o.g. assume λ_1 is feasible), then assign $w(p_i) = \lambda_1$ and mark all three lightpaths involved.
   - Otherwise, assign $w(p_i) = \lambda'$, where λ' is an unused color.

For example, suppose $P = \{p_1, p_2, \cdots, p_7\}$ where p_i is, in order, (e_1), (e_2), (e_3), (e_2), (e_1), (e_3), (e_1, e_3). Then ONLINE-TRIANGLE will first assign $w(p_1) = \lambda_1$, $w(p_2) = \lambda_2$, $w(p_3) = \lambda_1$ and mark all three p_1, p_2 and p_3. Next, we assign $w(p_4) = \lambda_3$ because there is no unmarked lightpath available. We further assign $w(p_5) = \lambda_4$ and $w(p_6) = \lambda_3$. Finally, we assign $w(p_7) = \lambda_2$ because p_7 and p_2 form a cycle.

To analyze the performance of ONLINE-TRIANGLE, we first observe how lightpaths are colored in an optimal solution. The proof of the following lemma follows immediately from the definitions.

Lemma 5.2 *The optimal solution S^* always colors (e_1, e_2) and (e_3) with the same color if possible and similarly for the two other symmetric cases. Any* *remaining length-2 lightpath is colored a distinct color. If there are some length-1 lightpaths remained after this, cycles of three length-1 lightpaths are colored the same color; followed by chains of two length-1 lightpaths with same color and finally remaining length-1 lightpaths with distinct colors. It can be verified such coloring uses the minimum number of ADMs.*

We then compare S and S^* as follows. We first give a rough idea before formally prove it in Lemma 5.3. Roughly speaking, in S, a length-2 lightpath can always share ADM with a length-1 lightpath unless the length-1 lightpath has been marked with the same color with some other length-1 lightpath. In this case, S^* also has to use extra ADMs for these this length-1 lightpath, therefore, making S^* use a comparable number ADMs as S in total. As mentioned before, ONLINE-TRIANGLE does not always color adjacent length-1 lightpaths using same color to avoid the $\frac{7}{4}$ lower bound. Furthermore, there is no marked cycle of length-1 lightpaths all with different color; for any marked cycle, S^* uses at least 3 ADMs for such cycle while S uses at most 5, which is indeed the worst case leading to the $\frac{5}{3}$-competitive ratio. Also for the case S^* is able to color two length-1 lightpaths with the same color while S has to use two different colors, this only gives a ratio of $\frac{4}{3}$. Precisely, we prove the competitive ratio in the following lemma giving more details.

Lemma 5.3 *ONLINE-TRIANGLE is $\frac{5}{3}$-competitive in the triangle topology.*

Sketch of Proof. Consider the solution S, the lightpaths can be partitioned into five disjoint sets according to how they are colored. We start with defining the set A whose edges will not be included in later sets and similarly for other sets. Let A be the set of cycles containing a length-1 lightpath and a length-2 lightpath with the same color; B be the set of length-2 lightpaths with distinct color; C be the set of marked cycles containing two same colored length-1 lightpaths and a third different colored one (excluding those later share color with a length-2 lightpath and thus included in A); D be the set of marked chains containing two same colored length-1 lightpaths (excluding those in A or C); and E be the set of remaining length-1 lightpaths. In the example given above, A contains p_7 and p_2; C contains p_4, p_5 and p_6; D contains p_1 and p_3; B and E are empty.

We denote $|A|$, $|B|$, $|C|$, $|D|$, and $|E|$ by a, b, c, d and e, respectively. Note that $cost(S) = 2a + 2b + 5c + 3d + 2e$.

We consider four cases depending on the set B. *Case 1:* B is empty, in other words, every length-2 lightpath is colored the same color as a length-1 lightpath; this is actually the same as in S^*. For length-1 lightpaths, by Lemma 5.2, S^* colors all possible cycle of 3 lightpaths in the same color using 3 ADMs, then chains of 2 lightpaths with same color using 3 ADMs, and finally 1 lightpath with its own color using 2 ADMs. S needs at most 5, 4 and 2 ADMs for each of the cases, respectively. Therefore, $\frac{S}{S^*} \leq \frac{5}{3}$.

Case 2: B contains all three types of length-2 lightpaths . In this case, both C and E must be empty, otherwise, ONLINE-TRIANGLE would have colored some lightpath p in B with the same color as the corresponding lightpath in C or E, then p should be in A instead. In this case S^* outperform S by grouping lightpaths in B with lightpaths in D. Even if so, there are still $2d - b$ length-1 lightpaths left unpaired in D. So S^* uses at least $2a + 2b + 2d - b$ ADMs while S uses $2a + 2b + 3d$ ADMs. Then, $\frac{S}{S^*} \leq \frac{3}{2}$.

In *Case 3*, B contains two types of length-2 lightpaths only; w.l.o.g., assume they are (e_1, e_2) and (e_2, e_3). In *Case 4*, B contains one type of length-2 light-paths only; . For these two cases, we can employ a similar argument as in Cases 1 and 2 and show that $\frac{S}{S^*} \leq \frac{5}{3}$. The full details can be found in [SWZ07].   □

6   Conclusion and Possible Improvements

In this paper we presented an on-line algorithm with competitive ratio of $\frac{7}{4}$ for any network topology, and proved that no algorithm has a competitive ratio better than $\frac{7}{4}$, even if the topology is a ring. We showed that the same algorithm has a competitive ratio of $\frac{3}{2}$ in path topologies, and that this is also a lower bound for any on-line algorithm on this topology. The lower bound on ring topology does not hold when the ring is of a bounded size; we showed an optimal bound of $\frac{5}{3}$ for the competitive ratio for the triangle topology, using a different algorithm. The analyses of the upper bounds, as well as those for the lower bounds, are all using a variety of proof techniques, which are of interest by their own, and which might prove helpful in future research on the topic.

Our bounds pertain to deterministic on-line algorithms. It may be interesting to explore probabilistic algorithms and obtain similar bounds. Following our study, it might be interesting to determine the exact complexity of the on-line problem for tree topologies, as a function of some parameter of the tree, and of networks (e.g., rings or paths) of bounded size. An important extension is to consider the on-line version of the problem when grooming is allowed; in graph-theoretic terms, this amounts to coloring the paths so that at most g of them are crossing any edge, and where each ADM can serve up to g paths that come from at most two of its adjacent edges (see [GRS98, ZM03]). Another direction of extension is to the case where more involved switching functions are under consideration.

References

[BEY98] Borodin, A., El-Yaniv, R.: Online Computation and Competitive Analysis. Cambridge University Press, Cambridge (1998)

[CFW02] Călinescu, G., Frieder, O., Wan, P.-J.: Minimizing electronic line terminals for automatic ring protection in general wdm optical networks. IEEE Journal of Selected Area on Communications 20(1), 183–189 (2002)

[CW02]   Călinescu, G., Wan, P.-J.: Traffic partition in wdm/sonet rings to minimize sonet adms. Journal of Combinatorial Optimization 6(4), 425–453 (2002)

[EL04]   Epstein, L., Levin, A.: Better bounds for minimizing sonet adms. In: 2nd Workshop on Approximation and Online Algorithms (September 2004)

[EMZ02] Eilam, T., Moran, S., Zaks, S.: Lightpath arrangement in survivable rings to minimize the switching cost. IEEE Journal of Selected Area on Communications 20(1), 172–182 (2002)

[FSZ06a]   Flammini, M., Shalom, M., Zaks, S.: On minimizing the number of adms -
           tight bounds for an algorithm without preprocessing. In: Erlebach, T. (ed.)
           CAAN 2006. LNCS, vol. 4235, Springer, Heidelberg (2006)
[FSZ06b]   Flammini, M., Shalom, M., Zaks, S.: On minimizing the number of adms in
           a general topology optical network. In: Dolev, S. (ed.) DISC 2006. LNCS,
           vol. 4167, pp. 459–473. Springer, Heidelberg (2006)
[GLS98]   Gerstel, O., Lin, P., Sasaki, G.: Wavelength assignment in a wdm ring to
           minimize cost of embedded sonet rings. In: INFOCOM'98. 17th Annual
           Conference of the IEEE Computer and Communications Societies, pp. 69–
           77. IEEE Computer Society Press, Los Alamitos (1998)
[GRS98]   Gerstel, O., Ramaswami, R., Sasaki, G.: Cost effective traffic grooming in
           wdm rings. In: INFOCOM'98. 7th Annual Conference of the IEEE Com-
           puter and Communications Societies. IEEE Computer Society Press, Los
           Alamitos (1998)
[LV98]   Leonardi, S., Vitaletti, A.: Randomized lower bounds for online path color-
           ing. In: 2nd International Workshop on Randomization and Approximation
           Techniques in Computer Science, pp. 232–247 (1998)
[SWZ07]   Shalom, M., Wong, P.W., Zaks, S.: Optimal on-line colorings for minimizing
           the number of adms in optical networks. In: Technion, Faculty of Computer
           Science, Technical Report CS-2007-14 (July 2007)
[SZ04]   Shalom, M., Zaks, S.: A $10/7 + \epsilon$ approximation scheme for minimizing the
           number of adms in sonet rings. In: First Annual International Conference
           on Broadband Networks, pp. 254–262 (October 2004)
[ZM03]   Zhu, K., Mukherjee, B.: A review of traffic grooming in wdm optical net-
           works: Architecture and challenges. Optical Networks Magazine 4(2), 55–64
           (2003)

Efficient Transformations of Obstruction-Free Algorithms into Non-blocking Algorithms

Gadi Taubenfeld

The Interdisciplinary Center, P.O. Box 167, Herzliya 46150, Israel
tgadi@idc.ac.il
http://www.faculty.idc.ac.il/gadi/

Abstract. Three well studied progress conditions for implementing concurrent algorithms without locking are, obstruction-freedom, non-blocking and wait-freedom. Obstruction-freedom is weaker than non-blocking which, in turn, is weaker than wait-freedom. While obstruction-freedom and non-blocking have the potential to significantly improve the performance of concurrent applications, wait-freedom (although desirable) imposes too much overhead upon the implementation.

In [5], Fich, Luchangco, Moir, and Shavit have presented an interesting transformation that converts any obstruction-free algorithm into a wait-free algorithm when analyzed in the unknown-bound semi-synchronous model. The FLMS transformation uses n atomic single-writer registers, n atomic multi-writer registers and a single fetch-and-increment object, where n is the number of processes.

We define a time complexity measure for analyzing such transformations, and prove that the time complexity of the FLMS transformation is *exponential* in the number of processes n. This leads naturally to the question of whether the time and/or space complexity of the FLMS transformation can be improved by relaxing the wait-freedom progress condition. We present several efficient transformations that convert any obstruction-free algorithm into a non-blocking algorithm when analyzed in the unknown-bound semi-synchronous model. All our transformations have $O(1)$ time complexity. One transformation uses n atomic single-writer registers and a single compare-and-swap object; another transformation uses only a single compare-and-swap object which is assumed to support also a read operation.

1 Introduction

1.1 Motivation

Three well studied progress conditions for implementing concurrent algorithms without locking are, obstruction-freedom, non-blocking and wait-freedom. An algorithm is *wait-free* if it guarantees that *every* process will always be able to complete its pending operations in a finite number of its own steps. An algorithm is *non-blocking* if it guarantees that *some* process will always be able to complete its pending operation in a finite number of its own steps. An algorithm is *obstruction-free* if it guarantees that a process will be able to complete its pending operations in a finite number of its own steps, if all the other processes "hold still" long enough (that is, in the absence of interference from other processes).

A. Pelc (Ed.): DISC 2007, LNCS 4731, pp. 450–464, 2007.

Clearly, obstruction-freedom is weaker than non-blocking which, in turn, is weaker than wait-freedom. The term *lock-free* algorithms refers to algorithms that do not use locking in any way. Wait-free, non-blocking and obstruction-free algorithms are by definition lock-free algorithms.[1] Advantages of using lock-free algorithms are that they are not subject to deadlocks or priority inversion, they are resilient to process crash failures (no data corruption on process failure), and they do not suffer significant performance degradation from scheduling preemption, page faults or cache misses.

While non-blocking and obstruction-freedom have the potential to significantly improve the performance of concurrent applications, and can be used in place of using locks in various cases, wait-free synchronization (although desirable) imposes too much overhead upon the implementation. Wait-free algorithms are often very complex and memory consuming, and hence considered less practical than non-blocking algorithms. Furthermore, starvation can be sometimes efficiently handled by collision avoidance techniques such as exponential backoff.

Requiring implementations to satisfy only obstruction-freedom can significantly simplify the design of concurrent algorithms, as it eliminates the need to ensure progress under contention. However, since obstruction-free algorithms do not guarantee progress under contention, they may suffer from livelocks. Various contention management techniques have been proposed to efficiently improve progress of obstruction-free algorithms under contention. Existing lock-free contention managers, which allow processes to run without interference long enough until they can complete their operations, do not provide full guarantee to ensure progress in all cases.

While obstruction-free algorithms are easier to design and are efficient in various cases, it is most desirable that a lock-free implementation do satisfy the stronger non-blocking progress condition. Hence the importance of designing efficient transformations that automatically convert any obstruction-free algorithm into a non-blocking algorithm. Such transformations should not affect the behaviour of the original (obstruction-free) algorithm in uncontended cases, or in executions where the contention management technique used is effective.

The focus of this paper is on the design of such transformations in the unknown-bound semi-synchronous model, where it is assumed that there is an *unknown* upper bound on memory access time. All practical systems satisfy the unknown-bound assumption.

1.2 Results

In [5], Fich, Luchangco, Moir, and Shavit have presented an interesting transformation that converts any obstruction-free algorithm into a wait-free algorithm when analyzed in the unknown-bound semi-synchronous model. The FLMS transforma-

---

[1] In the literature, the terms lock-free and non-blocking are sometimes used as synonymous, or even with opposite meaning to the way they are defined here. As suggested in [16], it is useful to distinguish between algorithms that do not require locking (i.e., lock-free algorithms) and those that actually satisfy the non-blocking progress condition.

tion uses n atomic single-writer registers, n atomic multi-writer registers and a single fetch-and-increment object.

We start by defining a time complexity measure for analyzing such transformations, and prove that the time complexity of the FLMS transformation is *exponential* in the number of processes n. Then, we present several efficient transformations that convert any obstruction-free algorithm into a non-blocking algorithm when analyzed in the unknown-bound semi-synchronous model.

All our transformations have $O(1)$ time complexity. One of transformation uses n atomic single-writer registers and a single compare-and-swap object; another transformation uses only a single compare-and-swap object which is assumed to support also a read operation.

1.3   Related Work

Our work is based on the transformation presented in [5]. A comprehensive discussion of wait-free synchronization is given in [8]. In [11], the concept of a non-blocking data structure is introduced. The notion of obstruction-freedom is introduced in [9]. Contention management is discussed in [6,10,13].

The importance of the unknown-bound semi-synchronous model in the context of shared memory systems was first investigated in [1]. In [12,14], indulgent algorithm are investigated in semi-synchronous shared memory systems. The interested reader will find in [15] a pedagogical description of several families of semi-synchronous and timing-based algorithms. Message-passing algorithms for partially synchronous systems were presented in various papers [3,4].

In [7], the weakest failure detectors that allow boosting an obstruction-free implementation into a wait-free or a non-blocking implementation have recently been identified (eventual prefect failures detector [2] is the weakest to implement a wait-free contention manager, and Ω^* is the weakest to implement a non-blocking contention manager).

2   The Computational Model

The system is made up of n processes, denoted $p_1, \ldots, p_n$, which communicate via shared objects. It is assumed that any number of processes may crash. A process that crashes stops its execution in a definitive manner.

The possibility and complexity of synchronization in a distributed environment depends heavily on timing assumptions. We focus on a semi-synchronous shared-memory model of computation which provides a practical abstraction of the timing details of concurrent systems. In this model, it is assumed that there is an *unknown* upper bound on the time it takes a process to execute one step and, in particular, on the time it takes to execute a step which involves access the shared memory. This assumption is inherently different from the asynchronous model where no such bound exists.

In the semi-synchronous model a process can delay itself explicitly by executing a statement $delay(d)$, for some constant d. Executing the statement $delay(d)$ by a process p delays p for at least d time units before it can continue, and there is some (unknown) upper bound (as a function of d) on the time a correct process can be delayed (for example, this bound can be $2d$).

A key idea in designing algorithms for the semi-synchronous model is that a process can delay itself for increasingly longer periods, and by doing so it can ensure that eventually other processes will take "enough" steps during one of these waiting periods. The appeal of the semi-synchronous model lies in the fact that while it abstracts from implementation details, it is a better approximation of real concurrent systems compared to the asynchronous model, as all practical (shared memory) systems satisfy the unknown-bound assumption. Furthermore, it enables to obtain more efficient solutions.

We point out that the semi-synchronous model, as defined here, is similar (but not identical) to a model where it is assumed that there is an unknown bound on the ratio of the maximum time and minimum time between the steps of the processes. That is, some unknown bound exists on the relative execution rates of any two processes in the system. In such a model, the delay statement is simply implemented by counting steps. All our results and algorithms apply also to this variant of the unknown bound semi-synchronous model.

Lock-free algorithms usually require the use of powerful atomic operations such as compare-and-swap (CAS). A CAS operation takes three parameters: a shared register r, and two values: *old* and *new*. If the current value of the register r is equal to *old*, then the value of r is set to *new* and the value *true* is returned; otherwise r is left unchanged and the value *false* is returned.

We consider three types of shared objects: (1) Atomic register – a shared register that supports atomic read and write operations; (2) Compare-and-swap object – a shared object that supports an atomic CAS operation; (3) Compare-and-swap/read object – a shared object that supports both atomic CAS and atomic read operations.

The FLMS transformation, and our transformations are all *black box* transformations: A transformation does not change anything in the original obstruction-free algorithm, it only adds code to ensure that a stronger progress condition is satisfied. Thus, a transformed algorithm performs the original algorithm on the original shared objects and does not apply any other steps to these objects. Below we define a time complexity measure for analyzing such transformations. Let T be a transformation that converts an arbitrary obstruction-free algorithm, denoted ALG, into a non-blocking or a wait-free algorithm.

Enabled Process: *A process is enabled in a given finite run of transformation T if its next step is a step of the original obstruction-free algorithm ALG, or if its last step was a step of ALG.*

Being enabled corresponds to holding a lock (i.e., being in the critical section) in lock-based algorithms. We notice that being enabled is not exactly like being in a critical section since exclusiveness is not guaranteed.

Time Complexity: *The time complexity of transformation T, is the maximum number of steps which involve access to the shared memory that a process may* *need to take until it becomes enabled since the last time some process has been en-abled. Or, if no process has been enabled yet, since the beginning of the execution.*

This definition corresponds to the way time complexity is usually defined in lock-based (mutual exclusion) algorithms. In lock-based algorithms, time com-plexity is usually measured by counting the amount of "work" (time units) a winning process, a process that gets to enter its critical section, may need to do (wait) since the last time some process has released its critical section.

Since all our algorithms require very few accesses to shared memory locations, the definition does not distinguish between different types of shared memory accesses. In a different context, it would make sense to distinguish between rel-atively cheap operations like reads and writes to more expensive operations like compare-and-swap.

Remark: The new complexity measure is a special case of the following more general new complexity measure for synchronization algorithms, which might be interesting in its own right. Given an algorithm, denoted SYNC, let us divide its steps into three disjoint groups,

1. group A – the group of *synchronization* steps;
2. group B – the group of *real work* steps;
3. group C – the group of *inexpensive* steps.

In mutual exclusion algorithms, A may include the steps in the entry section, B the steps in the critical section, and C all other steps. For a transformation that converts an arbitrary obstruction-free algorithm, ALG, into a non-blocking or a wait-free algorithm, A may include all the step which involve access to the shared memory, B all the step of ALG, and C all other steps. A process is *enabled* in a given finite run of SYNC if its next step is a step from B or if its last step was a step from B. Next we define two possible complexity measures,

1. The maximum number of steps from group A that a process may need to take until it becomes enabled since the last time some process has been enabled. Or, if no process has been enabled yet, since the beginning of the execution.
2. The longest time interval where no process is enabled, assuming there is an upper bound of one time unit for step time and no lower bound.

The first measure generalizes the one used in this paper, the second measure is called *system response time* in the context of mutual exclusion algorithms. Other variants of these measures can be obtained by generalizing corresponding measures for lock-based algorithms (see [15], Section 1.4).

3   The Time Complexity of the FLMS Transformation

We prove that the time complexity of the FLMS transformation is at least *expo-nential* in the number of processes n. This exponential bound holds even when the transformation is executed in a fault-free environment. As already mentioned, the transformation converts any obstruction-free algorithm into a wait-free algorithm when analyzed in the unknown-bound semi-synchronous model, and uses n atomic single-writer registers, n atomic multi-writer registers and a single atomic fetch-and-increment object.

In the following, we describe only the part of the FLMS transformation that is needed for proving the time complexity bound. When a process p_i notices that there is contention, it begins to participate in a strategy to ensure progress, called the *panic* mode.

This strategy is as follows: using an atomic fetch-and-increment object, process p_i first acquires a timestamp, and initializes an atomic multi-writer register, denoted $T[i]$, with the value of its timestamp. Then p_i searches for the minimum timestamp by scanning the array $T[1..n]$. (Initially all entries of the T array are set to ∞.) During the search, all timestamps that are not ∞, but are larger than the minimum timestamp p_i has observed so far, are replaced by ∞. If process p_i determines that it has the minimum timestamp then p_i becomes enabled.

If process p_i determines that some other process, say p_k, has the minimum timestamp, p_i waits for some time (the amount of time waited is not relevant here), and then checks the status of p_k. If p_i does not notice (after checking some shared register) that p_k has taken steps while p_i was waiting, p_i overwrites p_k's timestamp by setting $T[k]$ to ∞. Then p_i restarts executing the strategy to ensure progress (i.e., go to the beginning of the *panic* mode) using its original timestamp (i.e., p_i uses the same timestamp from the previous round). Similarly, if after it waits, p_i notices that $T[k] = \infty$, then p_i also restarts executing the strategy to ensure progress using its original timestamp.

The above partial description of the FLMS transformation is sufficient for proving its exponential time complexity.

Theorem 1. *The time complexity of the FLMS transformation is exponential, in the number of processes n.*

Proof. Consider a finite run σ where: (1) all the n processes have just started to execute the strategy to ensure progress (i.e, the panic mode); (2) each process has chosen a timestamp such that process p_i has chosen timestamp i, for all $i \in \{1, ..., n\}$; and (3) all the entries of the T array are still set to their initial value ∞.

For every $i \in \{1, ..., n-1\}$, let R_i denotes the maximum number of times, that process p_n has to scan the array $T[1..n]$ starting from (the end of) run σ before p_n becomes the first enabled process, assuming that only the $i + 1$ processes $p_n, ..., p_{n-i}$ may take steps in an extension of σ. We prove by induction that $R_i \geq 2^i$ for every $i \in \{1, ..., n-1\}$, which would imply that the time complexity is of order $2^{n-1} \times n$. Actually, we prove by induction the following (stronger) claim:

For every $i \in \{1, ..., n-1\}$, there is an extension σ_i of σ where:
1. p_n has performed 2^i scans of T in σ_i.
2. Only the $i+1$ processes $p_n, ..., p_{n-i}$ have taken steps in the extension σ_i of σ.
3. p_n is enabled in σ_i, and no process is enabled in any strict prefix of σ_i which extends σ.
4. For every $j \in \{1, ..., n-1\}$, process p_j is (again) at the beginning of the (code of the) panic mode in σ_i, with timestamp j and $T[j] = \infty$.
5. In the last steps in σ_i process p_n has scanned the array $T[1..n]$. We denote by σ_i^* the prefix of σ_i which result from omitting this last single scan of T by p_n.
We notice that the existence of run σ_i implies that $R_i \geq 2^i$.

When $i = 1$, σ_1 is constructed as follows: we first let process p_{n-1} set $T[n-1]$ to $n-1$. Then, we run p_n *alone*. Process p_n searches for the minimum timestamp by scanning the array $T[1..n]$ once, and determines that process p_{n-1} has the minimum timestamp. Then, process p_n delays itself for some time and then checks the status of p_{n-1}. Since p_{n-1} has taken no steps while p_n was waiting, p_n overwrites p_{n-1}'s timestamp by setting $T[n-1]$ to ∞. Then p_n restarts executing the strategy to ensure progress (i.e., go to the beginning of the panic mode) using its original timestamp. Next, p_n sets $T[n]$ to n, searches again for the minimum timestamp by scanning T, determines that it has the minimum timestamp and becomes enabled. Since p_n has scanned T twice in σ_1, we get,

$$R_1 \geq 2^1. \tag{1}$$

When $i = 2$, σ_2 is constructed as follows: we first repeat the extension from the previous case and stop just *before* the last scan on T by p_n (i.e., the extension σ_1^*). Then we let process p_{n-2} set $T[n-2]$ to $n-2$, and let both p_{n-1} and p_n scan T (notice that so far the number of scans of p_n equals 2^1 as in σ_1). Both determine that process p_{n-2} has the minimum timestamp, each one delays itself for some time and then checks the status of p_{n-2}. Since p_{n-2} has taken no steps while p_{n-1} and p_n were waiting, they overwrite p_{n-2}'s timestamp by setting $T[n-2]$ to ∞. Then they restart executing the strategy to ensure progress. At this point, from process p_{n-1} and process p_n point of view, they are back at a situation similar to the one at run σ. So, we repeat the construction from the previous case of $i = 1$ (in which the number of scans of p_n equals 2^1). Since p_n has scanned T four times in σ_2, we get,

$$R_2 \geq 2^2. \tag{2}$$

Induction hypothesis: we assume that a run σ_{i-1} exists and prove that run σ_i exists.

We consider now the general case where $i+1$ processes participate. We first repeat the extension from the case when only i processes participate and stop just *before* the last scan on T by p_n (i.e., the extension σ_{i-1}^*). Then we let process p_{n-i} set $T[n-i]$ to $n-i$, and let the i processes p_{n-i+1} through p_n

scan T (notice that so far the number of scans by p_n equals 2^{i-1} as in σ_{i-1}). All the processes determine that process p_{n-2} has the minimum timestamp, they delay themselves for some time and then check the status of p_{n-i}. Since p_{n-i} has taken no more steps, they overwrite p_{n-i}'s timestamp by setting $T[n-i]$ to ∞. Then they restart executing the strategy to ensure progress. At this point, from processes p_{n-i+1} through p_n point of views, they are back at a situation similar to run σ. So, we repeat the construction from the $i-1$ case in which only i processes participate (in which the number of scans of p_n equals 2^{i-1}). Since p_n has scanned T $2 \times 2^{i-1}$ times in σ_i, we get,

$$R_i \geq 2^i. \tag{3}$$

Thus, from the construction of run σ_{n-1} where all the n processes participate, we get,

$$R_{n-1} \geq 2^{n-1}. \tag{4}$$

We have proved that there is an extension of σ where the number times, that process p_n has to scan the array $T[1..n]$ before it becomes the first enabled process is at least 2^{n-1}. Each such scan involves n accesses to shared memory location. Thus, we conclude that the time complexity the FLMS transformation is at least of order $2^{n-1} \times n$.   □

4   The Main Transformation

We now present our main transformation. It has $O(1)$ time complexity, and uses n atomic single-writer registers and a single compare-and-swap object which supports also a read operation. The other transformations, presented later, are variants of this transformation. One important strength of all the transformations is their simplicity.

To understand how the transformation works, let us start by assuming a fault-free model in which no process ever crashes. In such a model, we can design a simple transformation by using a single (mutual exclusion) lock. To avoid interference between different operations, a process performs steps of the original obstruction-free algorithm, denoted ALG, only inside its critical section (after it has acquired the lock), within which the process is guaranteed exclusive access with no interference to the original algorithm shared objects.

Using a single lock to prevent interference between different operations of ALG may degrade the performance, as it enforces processes to wait for a lock to be released, and thus, does not allow several processes with non-interfering operations to proceed concurrently. Furthermore, when there is no contention, acquiring the lock introduces additional overhead.

To overcome these limitations, before a process tries to acquire the lock, it first tries to complete its operation of ALG without holding the lock. If there is no contention or if the contention manager is effective the process will complete its operation without any overhead. Otherwise if the process, after taking many steps, does not succeed in completing its operation, it tries to acquire the lock.

Of course, as a result of such an approach, a process that is already holding the lock may experience interference. However, either *some* process will manage to complete its operation (without holding the lock), or this interference will vanish after some finite time.

Going back to our original model where processes may crash, using locks is problematic as a process may crash while holding the lock, preventing *all* other processes from ever completing their operations. Resolving this problem, is the main difficulty in designing efficient transformations, and is done as follows: The *winner* – the process that is currently holding the lock – is required to increment a (single-writer) counter, denoted $W[winner]$ every few steps, of ALG. A process p that fails to acquire the lock, reads the value of the winner's counter and delays itself for $W[winner]$ time units. Then, p checks $W[winner]$ again, and if the value was updated p delays itself again, and so on. Otherwise, if $W[winner]$ has not been changed, p assumes that the *winner* has crashed and releases the lock.

Releasing the lock by a process p, which is not the *winner*, is a very delicate issue, since the *winner* might be alive but very slow, and as a result: (1) the winner will notice that the lock has been released although it is interested in holding it further; (2) we might end up with two or more processes holding the lock at the same time; and (3) process p might be suspended just before releasing the lock, and may release the lock at some unexpected time later on.

We address these problems as follows: when a winner process, say p_i, notices that the lock has been released p_i tries to acquire the lock again. However, before doing so, p_i waits long enough so that other processes that have mistakenly concluded that p_i has crashed, will have enough time to release the lock (again) before p_i tries to acquire it again. Ensuring that eventually at most one correct process will hold the lock, has to do with the fact that the value of the counter of a winning process $W[winner]$ keeps on increasing over time. Thus, forcing processes that fail to acquires the lock to delay themselves for increasingly longer periods, and eventually – by the unknown-bound assumption, the waiting time is long enough to guarantee that only one process will hold the lock and that some process will complete its operation of ALG.

The code of our main transformation, Transformation 1, is given in Figure 1. Transformation 1 converts an arbitrary obstruction-free algorithm, denoted ALG, which may include a contention manager, into a non-blocking algorithm.

Process p_i first tries to execute X steps (for some predetermined constant X) of the original obstruction-free algorithm ALG (line 1). If p_i succeeds to complete its operation, it returns (line 2), otherwise p_i tries to acquire the lock. The lock is implemented by a compare-and-swap object, named T. $T = 0$ means that the lock is free, $T = i$ means that process p_i has acquired the lock. So process p_i tries to acquire the lock by setting the value of T to i (line 5). If p_i succeeds it tries to complete its operation by taking steps of the original algorithm ALG (lines 6 – 12). Every X such steps p_i increments its counter $W[i]$ by 1. It continues doing so until it either completes its operation and releases the lock (line 9) or finds that it is no longer holding the lock (line 12).

shared
    T: CAS/read object, initially 0   /* "the lock" */
    $W[1..n]$: array of atomic single-writer registers   /* initial values immaterial */
local   /* initial values immaterial */
    $winner$: ranges over $\{0, ..., n\}$; $wait$: integer; b: boolean

invoke(op)
```
1   execute up to X steps of ALG              /* ALG is the original algorithm */
2   if op is completed then return response fi
3   W[i] := 1                                  /* contention possible – set initial delay */
4   repeat                                     /* tries to execute op without interference */
5       if CAS(T, 0, i) then                   /* tries to acquires the "lock" */
6           repeat                             /* p_i is enabled */
7               execute up to X steps of ALG   /* original algorithm */
8               if op is completed then
9                   CAS(T, i, 0)               /* release "lock" */
10                  return response
11              else W[i] := W[i] + 1 fi       /* increase delay */
12          until read(T) ≠ i                  /* equivalent to ¬CAS(T, i, i) */
13          delay(2 × W[i])                    /* flash out processes waiting in lines 16–22 */
14      else                                   /* loser */
15          winner := read(T)                  /* tricky to imp. efficiently using CAS only */
16          if winner ≠ 0 then                 /* "lock" is captured by winner */
17              repeat                         /* wait for the winner to proceed */
18                  wait := W[winner]          /* delay time */
19                  delay(wait)                /* wait as requested */
20                  b := read(T) = winner      /* b := CAS(T, winner, winner) */
21              until wait = W[winner] ∨ ¬b    /* winner crashed? */
22              if wait = W[winner] ∧ b then CAS(T, winner, 0) fi fi fi  /*release */
23  until op is completed
```

Fig. 1. Transformation 1. Program for process p_i which invokes operation op.

In line 13, process p_i delays itself, so that other processes that may have concluded that p_i has crashed (lines 16–21), will have enough time to release the lock (line 22) before p_i tries to acquire the lock again. After executing the delay (line 13), process p_i tries to acquire the lock again. We notice that p_i may decrease the value of $W[i]$ only after it completes its operation of ALG.

If p_i fails to acquire the lock (line 5), it executes the code at lines 15 – 22. It finds out the identity of the winner (line 15), and waits for $W[winner]$ time units. Then, p_i checks $W[winner]$ again, and if the value has been updated (meaning the winner is alive) p_i delays itself again, and so on. p_i does so until it notices that either $W[winner]$ has not been changed or that the lock has been released (line 21). If $W[winner]$ has not been changed, p_i assumes that the $winner$ has crashed, releases the lock (line 22), and tries to acquire the lock (line 5).

Theorem 2. *Transformation 1 converts any obstruction-free algorithm into a non-blocking algorithm when analyzed in the unknown-bound semi-synchronous model.*

Proof. Assume to the contrary that there exists an obstruction-free algorithm, ALG, such that the transformation does not convert ALG into a non-blocking algorithm when analyzed in the unknown-bound semi-synchronous model. Thus, there exists a suffix, σ_0, of an infinite run σ in which (1) no process succeeds to complete an operation of ALG; and (2) no process executes line 1 or line 2. Let P denotes the set of all correct processes that do no succeed to complete their operations in σ_0.

Clearly, there must be at least one process $p_i \in P$, which succeeds to capture the "lock" in line 5 infinitely often (that is, its compare-and-swap operation in line 5 is successful infinitely often) and hence it executes the repeat loop in lines 6–12 infinitely often. This implies that the value of $W[i]$ grows without bound in σ_0. Thus, there exists a suffix σ_1 of σ_0, in which the value of $W[i]$ is big enough such that immediately after p_i executes the delay statement $delay(2 \times W[i])$ in line 13, no correct process is in the middle of executing any of the lines 16 – 22 while having its local variable *winner* set to i. In particular, no process can successfully execute the statement $CAS(T, i, 0)$ in line 22 (without p_i taking further steps).

Let us denote by r an upper bound on the number of time units required for p_i to go through the repeat loop at lines 6 – 12 *once* regardless of the activity of the other processes (such a bound exists by the properties of the unknown-bound semi-synchronous model). Let σ_2 be a suffix of σ_1 where (1) p_i succeeds in capturing the "lock" in line 5, and starts executing the repeat loop at lines 6 – 12, (2) $W[i] \geq r$, and (3) no correct process is in the middle of executing any of the lines 16 – 22 while having its local variable *winner* set to i.

Clearly, in σ_2, no process p_j will ever be able to successfully executes the statement $CAS(T, i, 0)$ in line 22, because each time p_j will execute the delay statement in line 19, p_i will go through the loop at least once and increment $W[i]$. Thus, (1) from that point on the value of T forever equals i, and (2) process p_i will never leave the repeat loop at lines 6 – 12. Thus, in σ_2, every other process that is in the middle of executing the repeat loop at lines 6 – 12 will eventually execute line 12 and exits the repeat loop. Thus, there exists a suffix σ_3 of σ_2 where p_i forever executes the loop at lines 6 – 12 alone. This implies that in σ_3 processes p_i will execute its operation on ALG continuously without interference and hence this operation must eventually be completed. A contradiction   □

Theorem 3. *Transformation 1 has $O(1)$ time complexity, and uses n atomic single-writer registers and one CAS/read object.*

Proof. Assume that process p_i becomes enabled. Lets examine what is the maximum number of steps which involve access to the shared memory that p_i may need to take until it becomes enabled since the last time some process has been enabled. Process p_i can becomes *enabled* in one of three ways: (1) when it starts it execution (line 1); (2) immediately after it succeeds to set the value of the CAS object T to its id (line 5), and (3) starting to execute another round of the repeat loop after executing lines 11 and 12. Option 1 requires 0 steps by p_i. Option 3 requires 2 steps by p_i since p_i was last enabled. So, lets assume that p becomes enabled as a result of option 2. Process p_i succeeds in setting the value of T to its id (line 5) only when $T = 0$. As soon as the value of T is 0 it will take p_i at most 5 steps (which involve access to the shared memory) to reach line 5. Finally, if $T = j$ and process p_j crashes or is slow, it will take p_i or some other process at most 8 steps until they set T to 0 in line 22. The result about the space complexity is obvious.   □

5   Transformation 2: Using a CAS Object with n Atomic Registers

Our second transformation is a modified version of Transformation 1, in which the three $read(T)$ operations from Transformation 1 (in lines 12, 15, and 20), are

shared
T: CAS object, initially 0   /* "the lock" */
$W[1..n]$: array of atomic single-writer registers   /* initial values immaterial */
local   /* initial values immaterial */
$winner$: ranges over $\{-1, 0, ..., n\}$; $wait$, t: integer; b: boolean

invoke(op)
```
1    execute up to X steps of ALG              /* ALG is the original algorithm */
2    if op is completed then return response fi
3    W[i] := 1                                 /* contention possible – set initial delay */
4    repeat                                    /* tries to execute op without interference */
5        if CAS(T, 0, i) then                  /* tries to acquires the "lock" */
6            repeat                            /* p_i is enabled */
7                execute up to X steps of ALG  /* original algorithm */
8                if op is completed then
9                    CAS(T, i, 0)              /* release "lock" */
10                   return response
11               else W[i] := W[i] + 1 fi      /* increase delay */
12           until ¬CAS(T, i, i)
13           delay(2 × W[i])                   /* flash out processes waiting in line 22 */
14       else                                  /* loser */
15.1         j := 0; winner := −1
15.2         repeat                            /* find the winner's id*/
15.3             if j (mod n) + 1 ≠ i then
                     j := j (mod n) + 1 else j := j + 1 (mod n) + 1 fi
15.4             if CAS(T, j, j) then winner := j fi    /* is j the winner? */
15.5             if CAS(T, 0, 0) then winner := 0 fi    /* "lock" is released ? */
15.6         until winner ≠ −1                 /* winner found */
16           if winner ≠ 0 then                /* "lock" is captured by winner */
17               repeat                        /* wait for the winner to proceed */
18                   wait := W[winner]         /* delay time */
19                   delay(wait)               /* wait as requested */
20                   b := CAS(T, winner, winner)
21               until wait = W[winner] ∨ ¬b   /* winner crashed? */
22               if wait = W[winner] ∧ b then CAS(T, winner, 0) fi fi fi  /*release */
23   until op is completed
```

Fig. 2. Transformation 2. Program for process p_i which invokes operation op.

type
    lock: record {*id*: integer ; $W[1..n]$: array of integers}
shared
    T: CAS/read object of type *lock* , initially $T.id = 0$ /*. "the lock" */
local   /* initial values immaterial */
    $temp, temp_1, temp_2$: of type *lock*; *winner*, *wait*: integer; b: boolean

invoke(op)
1   execute up to X steps of ALG /* ALG is the original algorithm */
2   **if** *op* is completed **then return** response **fi**
3   *setW*(1)   /* set $W[i]$ to 1 */
4   **repeat**   /* tries to execute *op* without interference */
5   **if** $setTid(0,i)$ **then**   /* tries to acquires the "lock" */
6   **repeat**   /* p_i is enabled */
7   execute up to X steps of ALG /* original algorithm */
8   **if** *op* is completed **then**
9               $setTid(i,0)$ /* release "lock" */
10   **return** response
11   **else** $temp := read(T); setW(temp.W[i] + 1)$ **fi** /* increment $W[i]$ */
12   **until** $temp.id \neq i$ /* until p_i does not hold the lock */
13        $delay(2 \times temp.W[i])$ /* flash out processes waiting in lines 16–22 */
14   **else**   /* loser */
15        $temp := read(T); winner := temp.id$
16   **if** $winner \neq 0$ **then**   /* "lock" is captured by winner */
17   **repeat**   /* wait for the winner to proceed */
18            $wait := temp.W[winner]$ /* delay time */
19            $delay(wait)$ /* wait as requested */
20            $temp := read(T); b := temp.id = winner$
21   **until** $wait = temp.W[winner] \vee \neg b$ /* winner crashed? */
22   **if** $wait = temp.W[winner] \wedge b$ **then** $setTid(winner,0)$ **fi fi fi**/*rel.*/
23 **until** *op* is completed

function *setW* (*val*: integer)   /* $W[i] := val$ */
1   **repeat**
2      $temp_1 := read(T); temp_2 := temp_1; temp_2.W[i] = val$
3   **until** $CAS(T, temp_1, temp_2)$
end

function *setTid* (*old*:integer, *new*:integer) **return**: boolean   /* $CAS(T, old, new)$ */
1   $temp_1 := read(T); b := false$
2   **while** $temp_1.id = old$ **do**
3      $temp_2 := temp_1; temp_2.id = new$
4      $b := CAS(T, temp_1, temp_2)$
5      $temp_1 := read(T)$ **od**
6   **return**(b)
end

Fig. 3. Transformation 3. Program for process p_i which invokes operation *op*.

implemented without using an implicit read operations of T. Transformation 2 has $O(1)$ time complexity, and uses n atomic single-writer registers and a single compare-and-swap object (which *does not* support a read operation). The code of Transformation 2, is given in Figure 2.

The $read(T)$ operations in lines 12 and 20 are easy to implement, as we are only interested in knowing whether the value of T equals some specific value. Implementing the $read(T)$ operation in line 15, while preserving the $O(1)$ time complexity of the transformation is slightly more complicated. The easiest way to implement $read(T)$ is to check, for each value $i \in \{0, ..., n\}$, whether the operation $CAS(T, i, i)$ returns true. However, such an implementation would increase time complexity of the transformation to $O(n)$. This can be easily fixed. First, we observe that as long as the value of T (in Transformation 1) is different from 0, some process is enabled; and that only steps that are taken while no process is enabled are counted. Thus, after each time we check whether the value of T equals i for $i \neq 0$ (by executing $CAS(T, i, i)$) we check whether the value of T equals 0 (by executing $CAS(T, 0, 0)$). The final implementation can be seen in lines 15.1 to 15.6. Correctness follows from that of Transformation 1.

6   Transformation 3: Using a Single CAS/Read Object

Our third transformation is also a modified version of Transformation 1, in which the values of the atomic registers $W[1..n]$ are encoded as part of the state of the CAS/read object T. Transformation 3 has $O(1)$ time complexity, and uses a single compare-and-swap/read object (with no atomic registers).

Using only a single shared object may degrade the performance, as it forces all processes to reference the same shared memory location. Thus, under contention, the average waiting time to access the shared object would be high. The code of Transformation 3, is given in Figure 3. The correctness of Transformation 3 follows from that of Transformation 1.

7   Discussion

We have introduced a new complexity measure and presented three transformations which are shown very efficient according to this measure. The transformations convert any obstruction-free algorithm into a non-blocking algorithm when analyzed in the unknown-bound semi-synchronous model.

As we have shown, the FLMS transformation has exponential time complexity. It is an open question whether achieving wait-freedom must require exponential time complexity when using only atomic registers and fetch-and-increment objects. It would be interesting to find tight bounds also when using other base objects. In particular, in what cases obstruction-free to non-blocking transformations have better time complexity than obstruction-free to wait-free transformations? Are transformations to wait-free implementations are inherently expensive?

References

1. Alur, R., Attiya, H., Taubenfeld, G.: Time-adaptive algorithms for synchronization. SIAM Journal on Computing 26(2), 539–556 (1997)
2. Chandra, T.D., Toueg, S.: Unreliable failure detectors for reliable distributed systems. Journal of the ACM 43(2), 225–267 (1996)
3. Dolev, D., Dwork, C., Stockmeyer, L.: On the minimal synchronism needed for distributed consensus. Journal of the ACM 34(1), 77–97 (1987)
4. Dwork, C., Lynch, N., Stockmeyer, L.: Consensus in the presence of partial synchrony. Journal of the ACM 35(2), 288–323 (1988)
5. Fich, E.F., Luchangco, V., Moir, M., Shavit, N.: Obstruction-free algorithms can be practically wait-free. In: Fraigniaud, P. (ed.) DISC 2005. LNCS, vol. 3724, pp. 78–92. Springer, Heidelberg (2005)
6. Guerraoui, R., Herlihy, M., Pochon, B.: Towards a theory of transactional contention managers. In: Proc. 24th Symposium on Principles of Distributed Computing, pp. 258–264 (2005)
7. Guerraoui, R., Kapalka, M., Kouznetsov, P.: The weakest failure detectors to boost obstruction-freedom. In: Dolev, S. (ed.) DISC 2006. LNCS, vol. 4167, pp. 376–390. Springer, Heidelberg (2006)
8. Herlihy, M.P.: Wait-free synchronization. ACM Trans. on Programming Languages and Systems 13(1), 124–149 (1991)
9. Herlihy, M.P., Luchangco, V., Moir, M.: Obstruction-free synchronization: Double-ended queues as an example. In: Proc. of the 23rd International Conf. on Dist. Computing Systems, p. 522 (2003)
10. Herlihy, M.P., Luchangco, V., Moir, M., Scherer III, W.N.: Software transactional memory for dynamic-sized data structures. In: Proc. 22nd ACM Symp. on Principles of Distributed Computing, pp. 92–101. ACM Press, New York (2003)
11. Herlihy, M.P., Wing, J.M.: Linearizability: a correctness condition for concurrent objects. ACM Trans. on Programming Languages and Systems 12(3), 463–492 (1990)
12. Raynal, M., Taubenfeld, G.: The notion of a timed register and its application to indulgent synchronization. In: Proc. 19th ACM Symp. on Parallelism in Algorithms and Architectures. ACM Press, New York (2007)
13. Scherer III, W.N., Scott, M.L.: Advanced contention management for dynamic software transactional memory. In: Proc. 24th Symposium on Principles of Distributed Computing, pp. 240–248 (2005)
14. Taubenfeld, G.: Computing in the presence of timing failures. In: Proc. 26th Int'l IEEE Conference on Distributed Computing Systems (ICDCS'06) (2006)
15. Taubenfeld, G.: Synchronization Algorithms and Concurrent Programming. Pearson / Prentice-Hall, p. 423 (2006) ISBN 0-131-97259-6
16. Valois, J.D.: Implementing lock-free queues. In: Proc. of the 7th International Conference on Parallel and Distributed Computing Systems, pp. 212–222 (1994)

Automatic Classification of Eventual Failure Detectors

Piotr Zieliński

Cavendish Laboratory, University of Cambridge, UK
piotr.zielinski@cl.cam.ac.uk

Abstract. Eventual failure detectors, such as Ω or $\Diamond P$, can make arbitrarily many mistakes before they start providing correct information. This paper shows that any detector implementable in a purely asynchronous system can be implemented as a function of only the order of most-recently heard-from processes. The finiteness of this representation means that eventual failure detectors can be enumerated and their relative strengths tested automatically. The results for systems with two and three processes are presented.

Implementability can also be modelled as a game between Prover and Disprover. This approach not only speeds up automatic implementability testing, but also results in shorter and more intuitive proofs. I use this technique to identify the new weakest failure detector *anti-Ω* and prove its properties. Anti-Ω outputs process ids and, while not necessarily stabilizing, it ensures that some correct process is eventually never output.

1 Introduction

In purely asynchronous systems, messages between processes can take arbitrarily long to reach their destinations. It is therefore impossible to distinguish a faulty process from a very slow one [8], which causes many practical agreement problems, such as consensus or atomic commit, to be unsolvable [5].

One method of dealing with this impossibility is by equipping the system with failure detectors [3, 11]. A failure detector is an abstract distributed object that processes can query to get information about failures in the system. Different kinds of failure detectors provide different sorts of information, with different reliability guarantees. For example, the eventually perfect detector ($\Diamond P$) returns a set of "suspected" processes, and guarantees that *eventually* it will equal the set of faulty processes. The eventual leader detector (Ω) returns a single process, and guarantees that eventually it will keep returning the same correct process.

Both $\Diamond P$ and Ω are reliable only *eventually*. They can make mistakes for an arbitrarily long but finite period of time, which is unknown to the application. Such detectors are attractive because algorithms using them are *indulgent*; they never fully "trust" the detector, therefore they never violate safety, even if the detector violates its specification [6]. This paper focuses exclusively on such detectors.

A. Pelc (Ed.): DISC 2007, LNCS 4731, pp. 465–479, 2007.
© Springer-Verlag Berlin Heidelberg 2007

Different distributed problems require different failure detectors. A detector is *implementable* if there is an algorithm that implements it, in a given model. A considerable amount of research has focused on determining the implementability relationships both between problems and failure detectors, and between failure detectors themselves [3, 4, 7, 9, 11]. For example, $\Diamond P$ can implement Ω, by outputting the non-suspected process with the smallest id. As a result, every problem solvable with Ω is solvable with $\Diamond P$, but not vice versa [3].

Despite a number failure detectors identified in the literature, no comprehensive exploration of their design space has yet been attempted. As a result, identifying new failure detectors is difficult, and their properties must typically proved from scratch. This paper presents a method that greatly simplifies these tasks: an efficient and fully mechanical procedure for determining the implementability relationship between eventual failure detectors in a system with a given number of processes. The overall strategy to arrive at this result consists of the following steps:

- Section 2 shows that, under reasonable assumptions, all eventual failure detectors can be completely specified by the list of allowed sets of symbols output infinitely often. For Ω, this list consists of singleton sets, each containing a single correct process.
- Section 3 shows that, assuming immediate reliable broadcast, any implementable failure detector can be implemented as a function operating solely on the sequence of past process steps.
- Section 4 shows that only the order of last occurrences of processes in the above sequence matters. With finitely many possible such orderings, this opens the door to automatic enumeration of failure detectors.
- Section 5 shows that any failure detector implementable in the immediate reliable broadcast model remains so in the purely asynchronous model. In particular, all results from Section 3 and 4 still apply.
- Section 6 generalizes the above results to automatically comparing relative strengths of different failure detectors.
- Section 7 introduces a more intuitive, game-theoretic interpretation of the results from previous sections. It also identifies the weakest non-implementable failure detector *anti-Ω*, and proves its properties.
- Section 8 presents the results of automatic enumeration of failure detectors and their relative implementability in a three-process system. Game-solving techniques are used to speed up the search.

The theorems and proofs referred to in this paper can be found in the extended version [14].

2   System Model and Failure Detector Specifications

The system consists of a fixed set $P = \{1, 2, \ldots, n\}$ of processes, which communicate using asynchronous reliable channels: messages between correct processes eventually get delivered, but there is no bound on message transmission delay.

Processes can fail by crashing. In any run, the *failure pattern* is a function $alive(t)$, which returns the set of non-crashed processes at any given time $t \in \mathbb{N}$. Crashed processes do not recover, therefore $alive(t) \supseteq alive(t+1)$. Processes that never crash ($C = \bigcap_t alive(t) \neq \emptyset$) are called *correct*, the others are *faulty*. Runs are *fair*: correct processes perform infinitely many steps.

The system may be equipped with a failure detector. When queried, the detector returns a *symbol*, for example, a process id (Ω) or a set of processes ($\Diamond$P). The *failure detector history* is a function $hist(p, t)$, which gives the symbol returned by the detector at process p at time t. A *failure detector specification* $\mathcal{H}$ is a function that maps each failure pattern $alive$ into a set of allowed functions $hist$. For example, for Ω, we have

$$\mathcal{H}_\Omega(alive) = \{ \, hist \mid \exists_{t \in \mathbb{N}} \, \exists_{p \in (\bigcap_t alive(t))} \, \forall_{p' \in P} \forall_{t' > t} \, hist(p', t') = p \, \}. \tag{1}$$

2.1   Failure Detector Assumptions

The standard failure detector specification method [3] described above is very general, but this results in complicated specifications (1). This section simplifies this specification method by making the following assumptions:

1. The detector can behave arbitrarily for any finite amount of time.
2. The set of possible symbols output by the detector is finite.
3. The detector cannot distinguish otherwise indistinguishable runs.

For example, a detector that "eventually keeps outputting the process that crashed first" violates Assumption 3: even knowing the entire infinite sequence of system states in a given run is not enough to determine any upper bound on processes' crash times. This is because we cannot distinguish between a process that crashed and one that simply does not take steps.

On the other hand, the set of correct processes, provided by $\Diamond$P, is deducible from such an infinite sequence of states. Detector $\Diamond$P and others are useful because they provide information about the entire infinite run at a finite time.

This paper additionally assumes that the detector is *querier-independent*, that is, function $hist$ depends only on time t, not on the querying process p. I do not list this with other assumptions, because detectors not satisfying this assumption can be emulated by ones that do (Section 3.1, (6)).

2.2   Failure Detector Specification

Assumptions 1–3 allow us to considerably reduce both the space of considered failure detectors as well as the complexity of their descriptions. First, Thm. 3 shows that $\mathcal{H}$ depends only on the set $C = \bigcap_t alive(t)$ of correct processes, not on the exact form of $alive$. This simplifies (1) to

$$\mathcal{H}_\Omega(C) = \{ \, hist \mid \exists_{t \in \mathbb{N}} \, \exists_{p \in C} \, \forall_{t' > t} \, hist(t') = p \, \}. \tag{2}$$

Theorem 4 shows that whether "$hist \in \mathcal{H}(C)$" depends only on the set of values that $hist(t)$ takes infinitely often, not on the exact form of $hist$. Therefore, we

	Ω	$\Diamond S$	$\Diamond P$	$\Diamond ?P$
$infset(1)$	1	▆	▆	▮
$infset(2)$	2	▃	▃	▮
$infset(12)$	1,2	▆▃, ▃▆	▯	▯

▆: only process 1 is correct
▃: only process 2 is correct
▮: either 1 or 2 faulty
▯: no failures

Fig. 1. Specifications $infset(C)$ for various failure detectors in a system with two processes 1 and 2 (left), and the interpretation of the output symbols (right)

can specify a failure detector as the set $infset(C)$ of allowed sets of symbols output infinitely often. The description (2) simplifies to

$$infset_{\Omega}(C) = \{\, \{p\} \mid p \in C \,\}. \tag{3}$$

In general,

$$infset(C) \stackrel{\text{def}}{=} \{\, inf(s_1 \ldots) \mid s_k = hist(k),\ hist \in \mathcal{H}(C) \,\}. \tag{4}$$

where $inf(s_1 \ldots) = \bigcap_{k=1,2,\ldots} \{s_k, s_{k+1}, \ldots\}$ is the set of symbols s_k's that occur infinitely often in $s_1 \ldots$, for example, $inf(32413512212122 \ldots) = \{1, 2\}$. Since a failure detector can behave better than required, $S \subseteq T \in infset(C)$ implies $S \in infset(C)$ (Thm. 5). All free set variables in this paper, such as S, T, C in the previous sentence, are implicitly assumed to be non-empty.

Examples. Figure 1 shows the specifications of several known detectors, in a two-process system. Detectors Ω and $\Diamond P$ have already been introduced. Anonymous $\Diamond ?P$ eventually detects whether all processes are correct (▯) or not (▮), without revealing the identities of faulty processes. Detector $\Diamond S$ is similar to $\Diamond P$: it also outputs a set of suspected processes, however, $\Diamond S$ can forever suspect some, but not all, correct processes [3]. Figure 1 represents a set of suspected processes as a vertical bitmap (eg. ▆), with one entry per process; black entries mean "suspected", white entries "not suspected".

For each detector, Figure 1 shows the value of $infset(C)$ for $C = \{1\}$, $\{2\}$, $\{1, 2\}$. For brevity, sets $\{a, b, \ldots\}$ are abbreviated to $ab \ldots$, non-maximal elements of $infset(C)$ removed (Thm. 5), and external braces omitted. For example,

$$infset_{\Diamond S}(\{1, 2\}) = \{\{▆\}, \{▃\}, \{▯\}, \{▆, ▯\}, \{▆, ▯\}\} \quad \Longrightarrow \quad infset_{\Diamond S}(12) = ▆▃, ▃▆. \tag{5}$$

This de-cluttering convention is used throughout the paper.

3   Implementability in the Immediate Broadcast Model

Our goal is to determine whether a given failure detector, as specified by its *infset*, is implementable. Sections 3 and 4 will investigate this question in the *immediate broadcast model*. This model is significantly stronger than the purely asynchronous model, for example, its basic broadcast primitive of implements atomic broadcast, which in non-implementable in the asynchronous model [3, 5]. Surprisingly, however, as far as implementability of (eventual) failure detectors is concerned, these two models are equivalent (Section 5).

In the *immediate broadcast model*, all messages are transmitted instantaneously and reliably. Processes take steps in any fair order: correct processes take infinitely many steps, faulty ones finitely many steps. Processes never fail in the middle of a step.

3.1   Failure Detector Implementations

Immediate and reliable broadcast ensures that each process always knows the complete state of the system: the sequence $p_1 \ldots p_k$ of processes that have taken steps until this moment. For example, the state at the end of

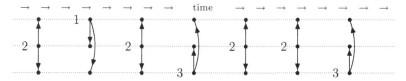

is $p_1 \ldots p_7 = 2123223$. Assuming determinism, all other state information can be inferred from $p_1 \ldots p_k$ (the initial state is fixed). Therefore, the complete state of any algorithm in this model depends only on $p_1 \ldots p_k$. In particular, any failure detector implementation can be modelled as a function *output* from sequences of processes $p_1 \ldots p_k$ to output symbols s_k.

A failure detector sensitive to the identity of the querying process has n functions: $output_1, \ldots, output_n$, one per process. However, these can be transformed into a single, querier-independent function outputting a composite symbol:

$$output(p_1 \ldots p_k) = [s_{k1} \ldots s_{kn}], \quad \text{where } s_{ki} = output_i(p_1 \ldots p_k). \quad (6)$$

The original detector output at process i is the s_{ki} in the composite symbol $[s_{k1} \ldots s_{kn}]$. Thus, for any failure detector implementation $output_1, \ldots, output_n$, there is a querier-independent detector implementation *output* that can emulate it. For this reason, this paper focuses on querier-independent detectors.

3.2   Failure Detector Specifications

From (4), an implementation *output* is consistent with a specification *infset* iff, for any infinite sequence $p_1 \ldots$ of processes, we have:

$$inf(s_1 \ldots) \in infset(C), \quad \text{where } s_k = output(p_1 \ldots p_k) \text{ and } C = inf(p_1 \ldots). \quad (7)$$

For example, consider a trivial failure detector:

$$infset_{\text{trivial}}(C) = \{ X \mid X \subseteq C \} \quad \text{for all } C \subseteq P, \quad (8)$$

which eventually outputs only correct processes. It can be implemented by returning the most recent process to take a step, that is, $output(p_1 \ldots p_k) = p_k$.

Similarly, returning the least recent process, for example, $output(2123223) = 1$, will eventually keep outputting one stable *faulty* leader, if it exists:

$$infset_{\text{faulty}}(C) = \{\, \{p\} \mid p \notin C \,\} \quad \text{for all } C \subset P. \tag{9}$$

(Compare with (3).) By convention, the undefined case $C = P$ allows arbitrary behaviour.

For any set X, let $perms(X)$ be the set of all permutations of elements of X. Let $order(p_1 \ldots p_k) \in perms(12 \ldots n)$ be obtained from $p_1 \ldots p_k$ by retaining only the last occurrence of each process (eg. $order(312233143433131) = 2431)$[1]. The implementations of failure detectors (8) and (9) can be succinctly written as

$$\begin{aligned}
output_{\text{trivial}}(p_1 \ldots p_k) &= \text{last element of } order(p_1 \ldots p_k) \\
output_{\text{faulty}}(p_1 \ldots p_k) &= \text{first element of } order(p_1 \ldots p_k)
\end{aligned} \tag{10}$$

Note that both implementations ignore all information in $p_1 \ldots p_k$, except for $order(p_1 \ldots p_k)$. Theorem 1 shows that all implementable failure detectors can be implemented this way, with $s_k = output(p_1 \ldots p_k) = map(order(p_1 \ldots p_k))$ for some function map from $perms(12 \ldots n)$ to output symbols. For example,

$$map_{\text{trivial}}(q_1 \ldots q_n) = q_n, \qquad map_{\text{faulty}}(q_1 \ldots q_n) = q_1. \tag{11}$$

With a fixed number n of processes, the number such functions map is finite, which enables us to automate implementability testing (Section 8).

In any run, as the sequence of steps $p_1 \ldots p_k$ grows, $order(p_1 \ldots p_k)$ keeps changing. Since faulty processes take finitely many steps, eventually the prefix of $order(p_1 \ldots p_k)$ consisting of all faulty processes will stabilize, while the rest, consisting of correct processes, will keep changing. Therefore, the implementation map is consistent (7) with the specification $infset$ iff for any order $q_1 \ldots q_k$ of faulty processes

$$\bigcup \{\, map(q_1 \ldots q_k r_1 \ldots r_{n-k}) \mid r_1 \ldots r_{n-k} \in perms(C) \,\} \in infset(C), \tag{12}$$

where $C = P \setminus \{q_1 \ldots q_k\}$.

For example, we can show that Ω is not implementable. To obtain contradiction, assume that it is. By Theorem 1, there is an implementation

$$output_\Omega(p_1 \ldots p_k) = map_\Omega(order(p_1 \ldots p_k)).$$

For any order $q_1 \ldots q_n$, we must have $map_\Omega(q_1 \ldots q_n) = q_n$ because q_n might be the only correct process (12). In other words, this implementation of Ω always outputs the last process to take a step. However, if more than one process is correct, the output may never stabilize, violating the properties of Ω.

---

[1] To ensure that $order(p_1 \ldots p_k)$ always contains all processes, even if some do not occur in $p_1 \ldots p_k$, I implicitly prefix each $p_1 \ldots p_k$ with $12 \ldots n$.

```
1   function update(q₁ ... qₙ) is
2     simulate qₙ taking a step
3     set map(q₁ ... qₙ) ← failure detector output in the simulation
4   function update(q₁ ... q_{k<n}) is
5     repeat
6       for each q ∉ q₁ ... qₖ do
7         update(q₁ ... qₖq)
8       until (12) holds for q₁ ... qₖ
9   task construct map is
10    update(ε), where ε is the empty sequence
```

Fig. 2. Generating a *map* for a given failure detector implementation using failure detector outputs in a specially constructed simulated run

4   Order Map Theorem

Section 3 used the fact that any implementable failure detector can be implemented using some function *map* acting solely on the order of recent process steps. This section proves this theorem. It is important because it restricts the originally infinite number of possible functions *output* to those induced by one of the functions *map*, whose number is finite.

Theorem 1. *Any implementable detector has an implementation of the form* $output(p_1 \ldots p_k) = map(order(p_1 \ldots p_k))$ *for some function map.*

Proof. Figure 2 presents an algorithm that, for any implementable failure detector, constructs a *map* that implements it, that is, is consistent (12) with the detector's *infset*. It takes the algorithm implementing the failure detector, and collects its outputs in a simulated run. This run is constructed by function $update(q_1 \ldots q_i)$, which also updates *map* so that (12) holds for all $q_1 \ldots q_k$ starting with $q_1 \ldots q_i$. Therefore, $update(\varepsilon)$ in line 10 produces a *map* that satisfies (12) for all $q_1 \ldots q_k$.

The implementation of $update(q_1 \ldots q_i)$ covers two cases. For $q_1 \ldots q_n$ consisting of all processes, *update* makes the last process step, queries the detector, and sets $map(q_1 \ldots q_n)$ to its output (lines 1–3). It trivially satisfies (12) because no valid sequence of faulty processes can contain all processes.

For shorter $q_1 \ldots q_k$, function *update* recursively ensures that (12) holds for all extensions of $q_1 \ldots q_k$, and then tests whether (12) holds for $q_1 \ldots q_k$ itself. If not, the process is repeated **until** success (lines 5–8). This cannot go on forever, because $update(q_1 \ldots q_k)$ makes only processes in $C = P \setminus \{q_1 \ldots q_k\}$ take steps. Therefore, any implementable detector will eventually start outputting symbols from some $S \in infset(C)$, passing the test in line 8.

Example. Consider the faulty-leader detector (9) implemented by returning the process that took least steps (not the least recent one to step), favouring lower ids to break ties. This results in the following run of the algorithm in Figure 2 on page 471:

	→ → → → → → time → → → → → →	
q_1	11**111**1112222222222222**222**2**2**233333333333**33**3**33**33	+: line 8 succeeded
q_2	2**2**23**3**3 11133333 1**1**13**3**3 11111222 1**1**12**2**2	−: line 8 failed
q_3	**3** **2** 3 1 1 **3** **1** 2 2 1 **2** **1**	← step (line 2)
map	**1**+ **1**++ 1+ 1-2+- **2**+ **2**++ 2-1+ 2+- **3**+ **3**+++	← det output (line 3)

Function $update()$ calls $update(1)$, $update(2)$, and $update(3)$. The recursion in $update(1)$ eventually makes processes 2 and 3 step. In both cases, the detector outputs 1, which results in mappings $map(123) = map(132) = 1$, which pass the line 8 test in $update(12)$, $update(13)$, and then $update(1)$.

Function $update(2)$ encounters more problems. It first calls $update(21)$, which produces $map(213) = 1$, and then $update(23)$. Function $update(23)$ recursively calls $update(231)$, which produces $map(231) = 1$. Since $1 infset(1)$, line 8 in $update(23)$ fails and $update(231)$ is called again. It sets $map(231) = 2$, which passes the test in $update(23)$, but (together with $map(213) = 1$) fails the test in $update(2)$ because $12 infset(13)$. Calling $update(231)$ and $update(213)$ again results in $map(213) = map(231) = 2$, which passes the test in $update(2)$.

Similarly, $update(3)$ results in $map(312) = map(321) = 3$. The algorithm in Figure 2 on page 471 has therefore transformed the original least-often-stepping implementation of (9), into the least-recent-to-step implementation map, ██████████ above (11).

5   Implementability in the Asynchronous Model

This section shows that any failure detector implementable in the immediate broadcast model (Sections 3 and 4) remains so in the purely asynchronous model. (The opposite implication is obvious.) This result implies, for example, that for any implementable failure detector, there is a querier-independent, implementable failure detector that can emulate it (Section 3.1).

Consider a failure detector implementable in the immediate broadcast model. Section 4 showed that there is a map consistent with it (12), which acts on the process order $q_1 \ldots q_n$. This process order must satisfy (12): (i) faulty processes precede correct ones, and (ii) the order of faulty processes is fixed. Let $Order$ $Oracle$ be an abstraction that, when queried, outputs an order that eventually satisfies (i) and (ii). It is sufficient to show that Order Oracle is implementable in purely asynchronous settings.

As an example, consider a four-process system with only processes 3 and 4 correct. Order Oracle can keep switching between 1234 and 1243 or between 2134 and 2143 in the same run. However, outputting both 1234 and 2134 infinitely often in the same run would violate (ii), and 2314 would violate (i).

In the algorithm in Figure 3 on page 473, processes reliably broadcast a message whenever they take a step. Each process keeps track of steps taken by others by storing the highest-numbered step for each process in the vector $maxstep$. When the algorithm is asked for an order on processes, it returns them in the increasing order of $maxstep$.

1    $maxstep[i] \leftarrow 0$ for all processes i

2   **when** process i takes its k-th step **do**

3   reliably broadcast "process i, step k"

4   **when** reliably receive "process i, step k" **do**

5        $maxstep[i] \leftarrow \max\{k, maxstep[i]\}$

6   **when** queried **do**

7   **return** the list of all processes i, ordered wrt increasing $maxstep[i]$

8   (ties broken deterministically)

Fig. 3. An implementation of Order Oracle in an asynchronous system

This simple algorithm is similar to the heartbeat failure detector [1], with one important difference: it uses reliable broadcast [10] rather than ordinary broadcast. This ensures that not only $maxsteps$ of correct processes keep increasing without limit (i), but also that eventually $maxsteps$ corresponding to faulty processes will be the same at all correct processes (ii). Note that the agreement on the order of faulty processes is only "eventual" in the same sense as reliable broadcast makes correct processes agree on the set of broadcast messages. In particular, it does not contradict FLP [5].

Conclusion. By taking the results from Section 4 and this section together, we can conclude that a failure detector is implementable in the purely asynchronous system iff there is a *map* consistent (12) with its specification *infset*.

6   Comparing Relative Strengths of Failure Detectors

This section shows that the theory developed in previous sections allows us not only to mechanically test implementability, but also to compare relative strength of failure detectors. In other words, we can test whether a given failure detector (eg. $\Diamond P$) is implementable in the asynchronous system equipped with another detector (eg. Ω).

For any failure detector S, consider a *purely asynchronous* system consisting of real processes P and virtual processes R_S, one for each possible output of S (its *range*). For example, with a two-process $\Diamond P$, we have processes $P = \{1, 2\}$ and $R_{\Diamond P} = \{\blacksquare, \blacksquare, \boxminus\}$. In general, the set of processes is the *disjoint union* $[P, R_S]$, in which members of P and R_S keep separate identities[2], even if they have identical names (eg. $R_\Omega = P$).

The scheduler ensures that virtual processes behave according to the detector specification, that is, the set $[C, S] \subseteq [P, R_S]$ of correct processes satisfies $S \in infset(C)$. (A process is correct iff it takes infinitely many steps.) Given this assumption, real processes $p \in P$ can emulate the failure detector by always outputting the most-recently heard-from virtual process $s \in R_S$ (Thm. 6).

---

[2] Formally, $[A_1 \ldots A_k] = \{(a, i) \mid a \in A_i\}$. Then, $[A, B] \subseteq [A', B'] \Leftrightarrow A \subseteq A' \wedge B \subseteq B'$.

To check whether a failure detector S can implement another detector T, we need to test whether T is implementable in the system $[P, R_S]$. The specification of T in this system is

$$infset_T([C, S]) = infset_T(C) \qquad \text{for all } S \in infset_S(C). \tag{13}$$

By convention (9), the undefined cases $[C, S]$ with $S \notin infset_S(C)$ allow arbitrary behaviour: $infset_T([C, S]) = \{ X \mid X \subseteq R_T \}$.

Example 1. Consider a two-process system equipped with $\lozenge?P$ (Figure 1). To show that $\lozenge P$ is implementable in such a system, consider the requirements (13):

$$infset_{\lozenge P}([1, \blacksquare]) = \square, \quad infset_{\lozenge P}([2, \blacksquare]) = \blacksquare, \quad infset_{\lozenge P}([12, \boxminus]) = \boxminus.$$

To implement $\lozenge P$, output $\boxminus$ if $\lozenge?P$ outputs $\boxminus$. Otherwise output $\square$ or $\blacksquare$, depending whether the most recently heard-from process is 1 or 2. This strategy corresponds to the following *map*, which satisfies (12):

$$\boxminus 21\blacksquare, \boxminus 2\blacksquare 1, \boxminus\blacksquare 21, 2\boxminus\blacksquare 1, 2\boxminus 1\blacksquare, 21\boxminus\blacksquare \mapsto \square \qquad \boxminus 12\blacksquare, \boxminus 1\blacksquare 2, \boxminus\blacksquare 12, 1\boxminus\blacksquare 2, 1\boxminus 2\blacksquare, 12\boxminus\blacksquare \mapsto \blacksquare$$
$$\blacksquare 12\boxminus, \blacksquare 1\boxminus 2, \blacksquare 21\boxminus, \blacksquare 2\boxminus 1, \blacksquare\boxminus 12, \blacksquare\boxminus 21 \mapsto \boxminus \qquad 12\blacksquare\boxminus, 1\blacksquare 2\boxminus, 1\blacksquare\boxminus 2, 21\blacksquare\boxminus, 2\blacksquare 1\boxminus, 2\blacksquare\boxminus 1 \mapsto \boxminus$$

Example 2. To show that Ω cannot implement $\lozenge?P$, consider the requirements

$$infset_{\lozenge?P}([1, \hat{1}]) = \blacksquare, \quad infset_{\lozenge?P}([2, \hat{2}]) = \blacksquare,$$
$$infset_{\lozenge?P}([12, \hat{1}]) = infset_{\lozenge?P}([12, \hat{2}]) = \boxminus.$$

(I use $\hat{1}, \hat{2}$ for Ω outputs to avoid name collisions with processes $1, 2$.) First, $infset([12, \hat{2}]) = \boxminus$ and (12) imply that $map(\hat{1}12\hat{2}) = \boxminus$. However, $infset([2, \hat{2}]) = \blacksquare$ implies $map(\hat{1}12\hat{2}) = \blacksquare$, which contradicts $map(\hat{1}12\hat{2}) = \boxminus$.

7 Game-Theoretic Interpretation of Implementability

Two players, YES and NO, play the following game. In the k-th turn, NO chooses a set $C_k \subseteq P$, and YES chooses $S_k \in infset(C_k)$. The sets must satisfy $C_1 \supset C_2 \supset \cdots \neq \emptyset$, and $S_1 \supseteq S_2 \supseteq \cdots \neq \emptyset$. The first player unable to make a move loses. Theorem 7 shows that YES has a winning strategy iff the failure detector is implementable.

Figure 4 (left) shows the game tree for the two-process Ω. Each path C_1, S_1, ..., starting at the root, represents a sequence of moves. For example, "12, $\hat{1}$, 1, $\hat{1}$" is a victory for YES, and "12, $\hat{2}$, 1" for NO. White nodes are wins for YES, black ones for NO. The colour of a node can be easily computed using the minimax algorithm [12]: C_k (resp. S_k) nodes are black iff all (resp. some) of their children are black. Since $C_1 = 12$ is black, NO has a winning strategy, so the two-process Ω is not implementable. As Fig. 4 (right) suggests, similar reasoning works for general $n > 2$ (Thm. 9).

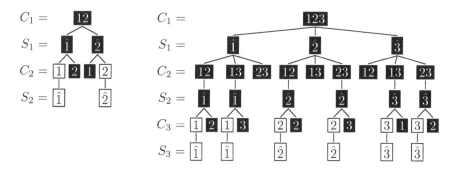

Fig. 4. Game trees for Ω with two processes (left), and three process (right)

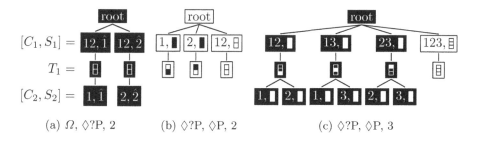

(a) Ω, $\Diamond$?P, 2   (b) $\Diamond$?P, $\Diamond$P, 2   (c) $\Diamond$?P, $\Diamond$P, 3

Fig. 5. Game trees corresponding to implementing detector T in a system equipped with detector S in an n-process systems, for three different (S, T, n)

7.1 Comparing Relative Detector Strengths Using Game Theory

With the modifications described in Section 6, the game-theory approach can also be used to check whether one failure detector S can implement another detector T. Since the system is now equipped with S, player NO chooses $[C_1, S_1] \supset [C_2, S_2] \supset \cdots \neq \emptyset$. YES chooses $T_1 \supseteq T_2 \supseteq \cdots \neq \emptyset$ with $T_k \in infset_T([C_k, S_k])$.

We can assume that $S_k \in infset_S(C_k)$ and $C_{k-1} \supset C_k$, because otherwise YES could always repeat its previous move, which cannot benefit NO (Lemma 8). With (13), this implies $T_k \in infset_T(C_k)$.

Figure 5 shows game trees corresponding to implementing detector T in a system equipped with detector S in an n-process systems, for three different (S, T, n). Case (a) shows that Ω cannot implement $\Diamond$?P in a two-process system. Detector $\Diamond$?P can implement $\Diamond$P with two processes (b), but not with three (c).

7.2 Anti-Ω: The Weakest Failure Detector

The anti-Ω failure detector is specified as

$$infset_{\text{anti-}\Omega}(C) = \{\, S \mid C \not\subseteq S \subseteq P \,\}. \tag{14}$$

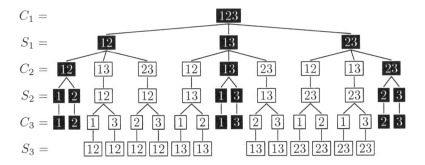

Fig. 6. Game tree for the three-process anti-Ω

It outputs process ids, and ensures that some correct process id will eventually *never* be output. Note that the classic Ω ensures that such an id will eventually *always* be output.

Theorem 10 shows that anti-Ω is not implementable: NO can win by playing $C_1 = P$ and then always copying YES's last move $C_{k+1} = S_k$. This strategy corresponds to the black nodes in the three-process anti-Ω game-tree shown in Figure 6 on page 476. In this tree, each S_k-node has exactly one black child; the minimax rule therefore implies that whitening any black node would make the game winnable by YES. In a sense, anti-Ω is therefore a "locally weakest detector".

Theorem 12 uses the method from Section 7.1 to prove a stronger result: anti-Ω is the (globally) weakest non-implementable eventual failure detector in the sense that it can be implemented by any non-implementable detector. In particular, anti-Ω is strictly weaker than Υ, the weakest *stable* detector [9]:

$$infset_\Upsilon(C) = \{ \{T\} \mid C \neq T \subseteq P \}. \tag{15}$$

(A detector is stable iff it eventually outputs the same symbol, that is, all *infset(C)*'s consist of singleton sets only.) As a by-product, this shows that some failure detectors, such as anti-Ω, have no stable equivalents.

Anti-Ω is also the weakest detector that solves set agreement [13].

8   Automatic Failure-Detector Discovery Results

Section 6 introduced a mechanical procedure for comparing failure detector strength in a system with a given number of processes. The game-theoretic approach of Section 7 dramatically improved the efficiency by using standard game solving techniques (eg. alpha-beta cutting [12], proof-number search [2]). This section gives a glimpse at the failure detector specification space by enumerating eventual failure detectors and their relationships in systems with two and three processes.

8.1 Two Processes, All Detectors

This section enumerates and compares all failure detectors with two processes and at most three outputs. The sets $infset(1)$, $infset(2)$, and $infset(12)$ can each take 18 possible values, giving the total of $18^3 = 5832$ failure detectors. Computer testing shows that they all fall into 5 equivalence classes, shown below (left) with several members (right).

	imple-mentable	Ω	$\Diamond?1$	$\Diamond?2$	$\Diamond P$		$\Diamond S$	$?\Omega$	$\Diamond?12$	$\Diamond?21$	$\Diamond?P$
$infset(1)$	1	1	⊟	■	▪		▪	1■	■⊟	■	■
$infset(2)$	2	2	■	⊟	▪		▪	2■	■	■⊟	■
$infset(12)$	12	1,2	⊟	⊟	⊟		▪⊟, ▪⊟	1⊟, 2⊟	⊟	⊟	⊟
		equivalent to $\longrightarrow$					Ω	Ω	$?1$	$?2$	$\Diamond P$

The implementability relationship between these classes is

implementable $< \Omega < \Diamond?1 < \Diamond$ P
implementable $< \Omega < \Diamond?2 < \Diamond$ P

Detectors $\Diamond?1$ and $\Diamond?2$, which eventually detect whether process 1 (resp. 2) is correct, are of incomparable strength.

8.2 Three Processes, Symmetric Detectors

The number of three-process failure detectors with three outputs is $18^7 \approx 6 \times 10^8$. For this reason, this section considers only *symmetric* failure detectors, which treat all processes equally, that is, do not favour any particular permutation of processes or group of such permutations. Such detectors fall into two categories: (i) those that output process-independent symbols, such as $\Diamond?P$, and (ii) those that output process ids, such as Ω. There are 6024 such detectors, grouped into 28 equivalence classes shown in Figure 7.

Figure 7 contains several known failure detectors, such as Ω, anti-Ω, and $\Diamond?P$. The strongest detector in Figure 7 on page 478 eventually outputs the number k of correct processes. It is equivalent to $\Diamond P$, which it can emulate by suspecting the $n - k$ least recently heard-from processes.

The 28 equivalence classes in Figure 7 on page 478 do not contain all symmetric detectors. Detectors that behave as class (i) or (ii), depending on the number of correct processes, form 654 such classes. Allowing non-symmetric detectors and/or more output symbols might increase this number even more. Based on the relatively few failure detectors identified in the literature, such a high number is rather unexpected (and we are only considering systems with three processes here!).

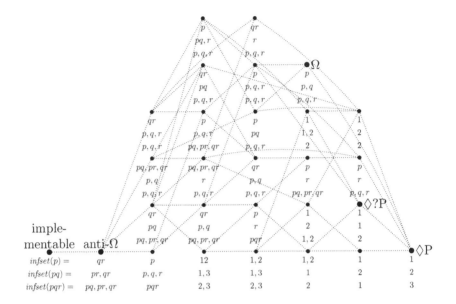

Fig. 7. Three-process failure detectors with three outputs

9   Conclusion

This paper investigated the space of eventual failure detectors. The key result is Theorem 1: every implementable detector is a function of the order of recently heard-from processes. By emulating failure detectors with virtual processes corresponding to their outputs, we can use the same technique to compare the strengths of different detectors.

Implementability is also equivalent to a winning strategy in a particular two-player game. The advantage of this approach is that it has more structure and a more intuitive visual representation. This makes failure detectors easier to analyse, and leads to more succinct, intuitive, and elegant proofs, using existing results from game theory. As an example, this paper identified the weakest eventual failure detector *anti-Ω*. Every query returns a single process; the detector might not stabilize, but there is a correct process that eventually will never be output.

Both approaches produce a finite number of failure detectors, thereby making comprehensive computer search possible. Such a search, applied to three-process detectors with three outputs, generated many known detectors, but also revealed an unexpected richness of non-equivalent failure detector classes. I hope that a similar methodology can be used to explore the space of distributed problems such as consensus, renaming, etc.

The benefits of computer search extend to theoretical results as well, many of which would have been difficult to derive without it. For example, the ability of quick implementability verification was very valuable in identifying anti-*Ω* and proving its properties. I believe that using computer search as a tool for developing and testing one's intuition about a problem is a useful and productive technique that should become more popular in distributed-computing research.

References

[1] Aguilera, M.K., Chen, W., Toueg, S.: Heartbeat: A timeout-free failure detector for quiescent reliable communication. In: Mavronicolas, M. (ed.) WDAG 1997. LNCS, vol. 1320, pp. 126–140. Springer, Heidelberg (1997)

[2] Allis, L.V.: Searching for Solutions in Games and Artificial Intelligence. PhD thesis, University of Limburg, the Netherlands (September 1994)

[3] Chandra, T.D., Hadzilacos, V., Toueg, S.: The weakest failure detector for solving Consensus. Journal of the ACM 43(4), 685–722 (1996)

[4] Delporte-Gallet, C., Fauconnier, H., Guerraoui, R., Hadzilacos, V., Kouznetsov, P., Toueg, S.: The weakest failure detectors to solve certain fundamental problems in distributed computing. In: 23rd PODC, St. John's, Newfoundland, Canada, pp. 338–346 (2004)

[5] Fischer, M.J., Lynch, N.A., Paterson, M.S.: Impossibility of distributed Consensus with one faulty process. Journal of the ACM 32(2), 374–382 (1985)

[6] Guerraoui, R.: Indulgent algorithms. In: Proceedings of the 19th Annual ACM Symposium on Principles of Distributed Computing, pp. 289–298. ACM Press, New York (2000)

[7] Guerraoui, R., Kouznetsov, P.: Finally the weakest failure detector for Non-Blocking Atomic Commit. Technical Report LPD-2003-005, EPFL, Lausanne, Switzerland (December 2003)

[8] Guerraoui, R., Hurfin, M., Mostéfaoui, A., Oliveira, R., Raynal, M., Schiper, A.: Consensus in asynchronous distributed systems: A concise guided tour. In: Krakowiak, S., Shrivastava, S.K. (eds.) Advances in Distributed Systems. LNCS, vol. 1752, pp. 33–47. Springer, Heidelberg (2000)

[9] Guerraoui, R., Herlihy, M., Kouznetsov, P., Lynch, N., Newport, C.: On the weakest failure detector ever. In: 26th PODC, Portland, OR, US (August 2007)

[10] Hadzilacos, V., Toueg, S.: Fault-tolerant broadcast and related problems. In: Mullender, S. (ed.) Distributed Systems, 2nd edn., ch. 5, pp. 97–146. ACM Press, New York (1993)

[11] Raynal, M.: A short introduction to failure detectors for asynchronous distributed systems. ACM SIGACT News 35(1), 53–70 (2005)

[12] Russell, S., Norvig, P.: Artificial Intelligence: A Modern Approach. Prentice-Hall, Englewood Cliffs (1995)

[13] Zieliński, P.: Anti-Ω: the weakest failure detector for set agreement. Technical Report UCAM-CL-TR-694, Computer Laboratory, University of Cambridge (July 2007)

[14] Zieliński, P.: Automatic classification of eventual failure detectors. Technical Report UCAM-CL-TR-693, Computer Laboratory, University of Cambridge (July 2007)

When $3f + 1$ Is Not Enough: Tradeoffs for Decentralized Asynchronous Byzantine Consensus*

Alysson Neves Bessani, Miguel Correia, Henrique Moniz,
Nuno Ferreira Neves, and Paulo Verissimo

LaSIGE, Faculdade de Ciências da Universidade de Lisboa, Portugal

1 Context and Motivation

Recently, we challenged the belief that randomized Byzantine agreement protocols are inefficient, by designing, implementing and assessing the performance of a stack of protocols of that type [3]. That assessment lead us to a set of properties desirable for Byzantine asynchronous binary consensus protocols: (1) Strong validity – if all correct processes propose the same value v, the decision is v (values proposed by Byzantine processes are often useless); (2) Asynchrony – no time assumptions are made (systems are often prone to arbitrary delays); (3) Decentralization – there is no leader (leader elections have a great impact on performance); (4) Optimal resilience – $n \geq 3f + 1$ processes to tolerate f Byzantine (extra processes are costly); (5) Optimal message complexity – $O(n^2)$ (high impact on throughput); (6) Signature freedom (high impact of signatures based on public-key cryptography on the performance); (7) Early decision – in "nice" runs the protocol should decide in a few communication steps (good latency in the "normal" case).

The main characteristic of the decentralized protocols we are interested in this paper is that they can not require any reliable certificate from a process p_i, obtained in phase k or less, in order to justify a message sent in phase $k + 1$. This is the case because, in our system model, this kind of certificate can only be build with digital signatures (violating signature freedom) or reliable multicast (that can not be executed by all processes maintaining a message complexity $O(n^2)$). Moreover, given the validity condition we stipulated (1), we require that all correct processes communicate their proposals to each other (a process can not trust another process to correctly communicate its value to a third process, since there are no signatures).

2 The Tradeoff

Is it possible to design such a Byzantine asynchronous binary consensus protocol? The main results in the paper are given by the following theorems:

---

* Work supported by project IST-4-027513-STP (CRUTIAL) and LaSIGE.

A. Pelc (Ed.): DISC 2007, LNCS 4731, pp. 480–481, 2007.

Theorem 1 (Impossibility result). *There is no decentralized algorithm that solves asynchronous binary Byzantine consensus with $n \leq 5f$, $O(n^2)$ message complexity and without signatures.*

Given this impossibility and several other results and protocols already described in the literature, it is possible to define in which conditions a binary decentralized Byzantine consensus protocol can exist:

Theorem 2 (Tradeoff). *Decentralized algorithms that solve asynchronous binary Byzantine consensus can be build with and only with:*

1. ***More Processes:*** $n \geq 5f + 1$, $O(n^2)$ *message complexity and signature freedom;*
2. ***More Messages:*** $n \geq 3f + 1$, $O(o)$ *message complexity ($n^2 < o \leq n^2f$) and signature freedom;*
3. ***Signatures:*** $n \geq 3f + 1$, $O(n^2)$ *message complexity and using signatures.*

Notice that the bound established by Theorem 2 regarding *more messages* is not tight: we do not know if it is possible to solve Byzantine consensus without signatures and optimal resilience with message complexity lower than $O(n^2f)$, but greater than $O(n^2)$.

3 Discussion

An interesting consequence of the theorems above is that decentralized protocols are inherently more costly in terms of the three properties considered (resilience, message complexity, signature) than leader-based Byzantine consensus protocols. For instance, the CL-BFT state machine replication protocol, that can be trivially adapted to solve consensus, is not subject to the tradeoff in Theorem 2 [2]. However, this protocol does not ensure the strong validity condition that we are interested in and requires synchrony to be able to terminate.

Theorem 1 implies that a consensus protocol with all the desired properties listed above can not be designed. However, we developed an improved protocol based on Bracha's Byzantine consensus [1], an algorithm that we believe is close enough to the desired characteristics that we envisage. This protocol improves the original Bracha's protocol in two main points: *(1.)* its message complexity is $O(n^2f)$ instead of $O(n^3)$; and *(2.)* it can terminate in one communication step if some optimistic conditions hold (no faults and unanimity).

References

1. Bracha, G.: An asynchronous $\lfloor (n-1)/3 \rfloor$-resilient consensus protocol. In: PODC'84. Proceedings of the 3rd ACM Symposium on Principles of Distributed Computing, pp. 154–162. ACM Press, New York (August 1984)
2. Castro, M., Liskov, B.: Practical Byzantine fault-tolerance and proactive recovery. ACM Transactions Computer Systems 20(4), 398–461 (November 2002)
3. Moniz, H., Neves, N.F., Correia, M., Veríssimo, P.: Randomized intrusion-tolerant asynchronous services. In: DSN 2006. Proceedings of the International Conference on Dependable Systems and Networks. LNCS, vol. 4615, pp. 568–577 (June 2006)

On the Complexity of Distributed Greedy Coloring[*]

Cyril Gavoille[1], Ralf Klasing[1], Adrian Kosowski[2], and Alfredo Navarra[1,3]

[1] LaBRI - Université Bordeaux - CNRS, 351 cours de la Liberation,
33405 Talence, France
{gavoille,klasing,navarra}@labri.fr

[2] Department of Algorithms and System Modeling, Gdańsk University of Technology,
Narutowicza 11/12, 80952 Poland
kosowski@sphere.pl

[3] Dipartimento di Matematica e Informatica, Universitá degli Studi di Perugia,
Via Vanvitelli 1, 06123 Perugia, Italy
navarra@dipmat.unipg.it

Abstract. Distributed Greedy Coloring is an interesting and intuitive variation of the standard Coloring problem. It still consists in coloring in a distributed setting each node of a given graph in such a way that two adjacent nodes do not get the same color, but it adds a further constraint. Given an order among the colors, a coloring is said to be *greedy* if there does not exist a node for which its associated color can be replaced by a color of lower position in this order without violating the coloring property. We provide lower and upper bounds for this problem in Linial's model and we relate them to other well-known problems, namely *Coloring, Maximal Independent Set (MIS)*, and *Largest First Coloring*. Whereas the best known upper bound for Coloring, MIS, and Greedy Coloring are the same, we prove a lower bound which is strong in the sense that it now makes a difference between Greedy Coloring and MIS.

We discuss the vertex coloring problem in a *distributed network*. Such a network consists of a set V of processors and a set E of bidirectional communication links between pairs of processors. It can be modeled by an undirected graph $G = (V, E)$. We denote $n = |V|$, $m = |E|$ and for each vertex v define its *neighborhood* $N_v = \{u : \{u, v\} \in E\}$ and *vertex degree* $\deg_G v = |N_v|$. The set of neighbours of high degree is denoted by $N_v^\geq = \{u \in N_v : \deg u \geq \deg v\}$.

To *color* the vertices of G means to give each vertex a positive integer color value in such a way that no two adjacent vertices get the same color. If at most k colors are used, the result is called a k-*coloring*. In many practical considerations, such as code assignment in wireless networks [1], it is desirable to minimise the number of used colors. The smallest possible positive integer k for which there exists a k-coloring of G is called the *chromatic number* $\chi(G)$. This value is bounded from above by $\Delta + 1$, where Δ denotes the maximal vertex degree of the graph; consequently, a graph always admits a $(\Delta + 1)$-coloring.

[*] The research was partially funded by the European projects COST Action 293, "Graphs and Algorithms in Communication Networks" (GRAAL) and, COST Action 295, "Dynamic Communication Networks" (DYNAMO).

A. Pelc (Ed.): DISC 2007, LNCS 4731, pp. 482–484, 2007.
© Springer-Verlag Berlin Heidelberg 2007

The problems discussed in this paper can be formulated using a local definition: the goal is to achieve a state of the system in which the local state variables associated with each node fulfill certain constraints with respect to the local state variables of its neighbours.

Definition 1. *The problems are defined by the following constraints on the local variable[1] c at vertex v:*

$(\Delta + 1)$-*Coloring (*COL*):*	$c(v) \in \{1, \dots, \Delta + 1\} \setminus c(N_v)$
*Greedy Coloring (*G-COL*):*	$c(v) = \min\{1, \dots, \Delta + 1\} \setminus c(N_v)$
*Largest-First Coloring (*LF-COL*):*	$c(v) = \min\{1, \dots, \Delta + 1\} \setminus c(N_v^{\geq})$
*Maximal Independent Set (*MIS*):*	$c(v) \neq 0 \Leftrightarrow c(N_v) = \{0\}$

We provide lower and upper bounds on the deterministic distributed (Linial's model) time complexity of *Greedy Coloring* (G-COL) with respect to *Coloring* (COL), *Maximal Independent Set* (MIS) and *Largest First Coloring* (LF-COL). A summary of the results is contained in Table 1, where (*) indicates the new results obtained in this paper. In particular, we derive new upper bounds for G-COL and LF-COL and a new lower bound for G-COL. Whereas the upper bounds for the COL, MIS, and G-COL are the same, we prove a strong lower bound in the sense that our lower bound now makes a difference between G-COL and MIS.

Table 1. The time complexity of Greedy Coloring with respect to other well-known problems in the distributed setting. The table can be read also vertically as $(\Delta + 1)$-Coloring $\leq$ Maximal Independent Set $\leq$ Greedy Coloring $\leq$ LF-Coloring.

Problem	Lower Bound	Upper Bound
$(\Delta + 1)$-Coloring (COL)	$\Omega(\log^* n)$ [2]	$2^{O(\sqrt{\log n})}$ [3,4]
Maximal Independent Set (MIS)	$\Omega\left(\sqrt{\frac{\log n}{\log \log n}}\right)$ [5]	$2^{O(\sqrt{\log n})}$ [3,4] $O(\Delta + \text{COL})$
Greedy Coloring (G-COL)	$\Omega\left(\frac{\log n}{\log \log n}\right)$ (*)	$2^{O(\sqrt{\log n})}$ (*) $O(\Delta + \text{COL})$ (*) $O(\Delta^2 + \log^* n)$ [2]
Largest-First Coloring (LF-COL)	$\Omega(\sqrt{n})$ [6]	$O(\sqrt{n})$ (*) $O(\Delta \cdot \text{MIS})$ [6]

References

1. Battiti, R., Bertossi, A.A., Bonuccelli, M.A.: Assigning codes in wireless networks: bounds and scaling properties. Wireless networks 5(3), 195–209 (1999)
2. Linial, N.: Locality in distributed graph algorithms. SIAM J. Comput. 21, 193–201 (1992)

---

[1] This variable represents the color or the characteristic function of the MIS.

3. Awerbuch, B., Goldberg, A.V., Luby, M., Plotkin, S.A.: Network decomposition and locality in distributed computation. In: FOCS, pp. 364–369. IEEE Computer Society Press, Los Alamitos (1989)
4. Panconesi, A., Srinivasan, A.: On the complexity of distributed network decomposition. J. Algorithms 20(2), 356–374 (1996)
5. Kuhn, F., Moscibroda, T., Wattenhofer, R.: What cannot be computed locally! In: Chaudhuri, S., Kutten, S. (eds.) PODC, pp. 300–309. ACM Press, New York (2004)
6. Kosowski, A., Kuszner, Ł.: On greedy graph coloring in the distributed model. In: Nagel, W.E., Walter, W.V., Lehner, W. (eds.) Euro-Par 2006. LNCS, vol. 4128, pp. 592–601. Springer, Heidelberg (2006)

Fault-Tolerant Implementations of the Atomic-State Communication Model in Weaker Networks⋆

Colette Johnen[1] and Lisa Higham[2]

[1] LRI, Univ. Paris-Sud, CNRS, F-91405 Orsay, France
`colette@lri.fr`
[2] Computer Science Department, University of Calgary, Canada
`higham@ucalgary.ca`

There is a proliferation of models for distributed computing, consisting of both shared memory and message passing paradigms. Different communities adopt different variants as the "standard" model for their research setting. Since subtle changes in the communication model can result in significant changes to the solvability/unsolvability or to the complexity of various problems, it becomes imperative to understand the relationships between the many models. The situation becomes even more complicated when additional requirements such as fault-tolerance are added to the mix. This motivates us to determine exactly under what circumstances a program designed for one model and delivering some set of additional guarantees can be converted into an "equivalent" programs for a different model while delivering comparable guarantees. Once these relationships are understood, they can be exploited in system design.

Our work addresses this question for networks of processors that communication by locally shared registers. A network that uses locally shared registers can be modelled by a graph where nodes represent processors and there is an edge between two nodes if and only if the corresponding processors communicate directly by reading or writing registers shared between them. Two variants are defined by specifying whether the registers are single-writer/multi-reader and located at the nodes (called state models) or single-writer/ single-reader and located on the edges (called link models).

The shared registers used by the communicating processors further distinguishes possible models. Lamport [4] defined three models of single-writer/multi-reader registers, differentiated by the possible outcome of read operations that overlap concurrent write operations. These three register types, in order of increasing power, are called safe, regular, and atomic. Program design is easier assuming atomic registers rather than weaker registers but the hardware implementation of an atomic register is costlier than the implementation of one of the weaker ones.

By specifying either state or link communication, via shared registers that are either regular, atomic, or safe we arrive at six different network models that use

---

⋆ This work was partially supported by the program ACI 'security and dependability' FRAGILE and by the NSERC (Canada) Discovery Grant.

A. Pelc (Ed.): DISC 2007, LNCS 4731, pp. 485–487, 2007.

locally shared registers. For example, the atomic-state model has atomic registers located at the nodes of the network. The other models are named similarly. An algorithm for any one of these networks could provide some fault tolerance. So, we consider a third parameter, namely, wait-freedom, which captures tolerance of stopping failures of components of the network, or self-stabilization, which captures recovery of the network from transient errors of its components.

We seek to determine under what conditions it is possible to transform a wait-free (respectively, self-stabilizing) solution to a given problem under one of these models into a wait-free solution (respectively, self-stabilizing) solution under another of the six models.

In an earlier paper [2], we proved that a wait-free compiler from atomic-state systems to atomic-link systems requires that if two processors, a and b, each share a register with a third processor c, then a and b must themselves share a register. But, in a network, processors that are not neighbours cannot share a register. A consequence of this essential distinction between networks and globally shared memory systems is the impossibility: "There is no wait-free compiler from atomic-state systems to regular-state systems for the same network graph for any network graph that is not complete". We also presented a self-stabilizing compiler from network graphs where neighbours communicate via atomic-state registers to systems where neighbours communicate via atomic-link registers [2]. This compiler, however, had some shortcomings. It is not a silence-preserving compiler; it requires that each processor in the atomic-state system being implemented executes an atomic-state read operation infinitely often; the implementation of the atomic-state write operation is not wait-free; the implementation of the atomic-state read operation is not even obstruction-free. Furthermore, the proof of correctness failed to characterize the legitimate configurations: instead it only established that all computations of the compiled algorithm are *eventually* linearizable.

Contributions. Our principal result is a self-stabilizing compiler from the atomic-state model to the regular-state model. This compiler is also *silent.* That is, if, once registers are stabilized, the atomic-state algorithm does not require the participation of neighbours, then the transformed regular-state algorithm also does not require the participation of neighbours. As a consequence, our compiler does not add significant overhead to communication. The code and the self-stabilization proof is presented in a technical report [3]. Our compiler has some additional appealing properties: The size of each shared regular register used by the compiled algorithm is $log(M) + 1 + log(B)$ bits where M is the number of processor states of the initial algorithm and B is greater than the network degree. The compiled algorithm has strong progress guarantees. Specifically, the implementation of any write operation is wait-free. The implementation of a read is not wait-free, but it is obstruction-free.

For all the remaining relationships (both possibilities and impossibilities) among the four models that use atomic and regular registers under either self-stabilizing and wait-free requirements, we either observe that they have been answered by existing research or we show how they can be derived from combinations of

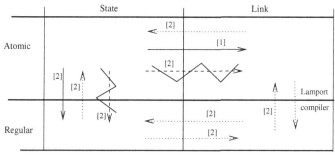

Fig. 1. Transformations between network models

earlier results. Thus, our compiler closes the proposed questions among four of the six models. These results are summarized in the following figure.

What remains open is whether or not there is a self-stabilizing compiler from networks (state or link) with regular registers, to the corresponding network with only safe registers. Interestingly, Lamport's construction of single-writer single-reader single-bit regular registers from single-writer single-reader single-bit safe registers [4] fails to be self-stabilizing [1]. We conjecture that this shortcoming can be rectified at the expense of wait-freedom.

References

1. Hoepman, J.H., Papatriantafilou, M., Tsigas, P.: Self-stabilization of wait-free shared memory objects. Journal of Parallel and Distributed Computing 62(5), 818–842 (2002)
2. Higham, L., Johnen, C.: Relationships between communication models in networks using atomic registers. In: IPDPS'2006, the 20th IEEE International Parallel & Distributed Processing Symposium. IEEE Computer Society Press, Los Alamitos (2006)
3. Higham, L., Johnen, C.: Self-stabilizing implementation of atomic register by regular register in networks framework. Technical Report 1449, L.R.I (2006)
4. Lamport, L.: On interprocess communication. Distributed Computing 1(2), 77–101 (1986)

Transaction Safe Nonblocking Data Structures*

Virendra J. Marathe, Michael F. Spear, and Michael L. Scott

Department of Computer Science, University of Rochester
Rochester, NY 14627-0226 USA
{vmarathe,spear,scott}@cs.rochester.edu

This brief announcement focuses on interoperability of software transactions with ad hoc nonblocking algorithms. Specifically, we modify arbitrary nonblocking operations so that (1) they can be used both inside and outside transactions, (2) external uses serialize with transactions, and (3) internal uses succeed if and only if the surrounding transaction commits. Interoperability enables seemless integration with legacy code, atomic composition of nonblocking operations, and the equivalent of hand-optimized, closed nested transactions.

The key to transaction safety is to ensure that memory accesses of operations called from inside a transaction occur (or appear to occur) if, only if, and when the surrounding transaction commits. We do this by making writes manifestly speculative, with their fate tied to that of the transaction, and by logging reads for re-validation immediately before the transaction commits. (Because correct nonblocking code is designed to tolerate races, additional, intermediate validation is not required.) When called from outside a transaction, operations behave as they did in the original nonblocking code, except that they aggressively abort any transaction that stands in their way. Operations inside a transaction similarly abort transactional peers. They are unaware of nontransactional peers.

We provide nonblocking objects with "transaction aware" versions of references and other basic primitive types such as integer, long, etc. These provide Get, Set, and CAS operations, which the programmer uses instead of conventional accesses. If called inside a transaction, Get logs the target location for later validation; Set and CAS speculatively modify the target location. Changes become permanent at transaction commit time. If called outside a transaction, all three operations "clean up" any encountered speculative updates, aborting conflicting transactions if necessary. Given correct nonblocking code, the changes required to create a transaction-safe version are mechanical.

To make a type transaction-aware, we must be able to distinguish between real and speculative values. For some types (e.g., pointers in C) we may be able to claim an otherwise unused bit, or use features such as *runtime type identification* in strongly typed languages such as Java. For others we may use a sentinel value to trigger address-based lookup in a separate metadata table. With support for transaction aware primitives, we expect that construction of transaction safe versions of nonblocking algorithms would require little or no

* This work was supported in part by NSF grants CNS-0411127 and CNS-0615139, equipment support from Sun Microsystems Laboratories, and financial support from Intel and Microsoft.

A. Pelc (Ed.): DISC 2007, LNCS 4731, pp. 488–489, 2007.

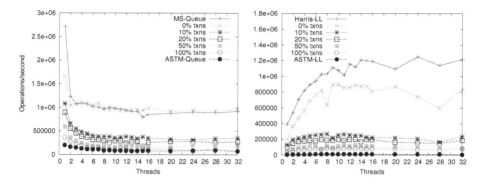

Fig. 1. Performance of transaction safe nonblocking objects with varying percentage of transactional and nontransactional invocations (50% inserts and 50% deletes). Experiments on a 16-processor 6800 SunFire cache coherent multiprocessor machine. Comparison with original nonblocking algorithms, and a natural transactional implementation.

additional programming effort, particularly if these primitives are supported in standard libraries.

Our preliminary implementation is in the context of the ASTM [3] system, where we extended the AtomicReference Java library class with a transaction aware version TxAtomicRef. We leveraged ASTM's transactional metadata structure (which consists of an indirection object called the *locator* that determines the current consistent version of the data, and its current writer transaction) to represent speculative values of TxAtomicRefs.

We implemented several nonblocking algorithms using TxAtomicRef including Michael and Scott's lock-free queue [4] and Harris' lock-free linked list [1] (results in Figure 1). In all cases we simply replaced the AtomicReferences in the original algorithms with TxAtomicRefs in our constructions. Our results suggest that while transaction safety makes nonblocking data structures somewhat slower, the resulting constructs interoperate smoothly with transactions, and can significantly outperform the natural "fully transactional" alternatives.

References

[1]   Harris, T.L.: A Pragmatic Implementation of Non-Blocking Linked-Lists. In: 15th Intl. Symp. on Distributed Computing, Lisboa, Portugal (October 2001)

[2]   Herlihy, M., Moss, J.E.: Transactional Memory: Architectural Support for Lock-Free Data Structures. In: 20th Intl. Symp. on Computer Architecture, San Diego, CA (May 1993)

[3]   Marathe, V.J., Scherer III, W.N., Scott, M.L.: Adaptive Software Transactional Memory. In: 19th Intl. Symp. on Distributed Computing, Cracow, Poland (September 2005)

[4]   Michael, M.M., Scott, M.L.: Simple, Fast, and Practical Non-Blocking and Blocking Concurrent Queue Algorithms. In: 15th ACM Symp. on Principles of Distributed Computing, Philadelphia, PA (May 1996)

Long Live Continuous Consensus

Tal Mizrahi and Yoram Moses

Department of Electrical Engineering, Technion, Haifa, 32000 Israel

Fault-tolerant systems often require a means by which independent processes or processors can arrive at an exact mutual agreement of some kind. The work announced in this note studies the *continuous consensus* problem, which is a general tool for enabling actions that are performed at the same time at different sites of the system to be consistent with one another (e.g., mutual exlusion, firing squad etc). Suppose that we are interested in maintaining a simultaneously consistent view regarding a set of events $\mathcal{E}$ in the system. These are application-dependent, but will typically record inputs that processes receive at various times, values that certain variables have at a given time, and faulty behavior in the form of failed or inconsistent message deliveries. A continuous consensus (CC) protocol maintains at all times $k \geq 0$ a *core* $M_i[k]$ of events of $\mathcal{E}$ at every site i. In every run of this protocol the following three properties are required to hold, for all nonfaulty processes i and j.

Accuracy: All events in $M_i[k]$ occurred in the run;
Consistency: $M_i[k] = M_j[k]$ at all times k; and
Completeness: If the occurrence of an event $e \in \mathcal{E}$ is known to process j at any point, then $e \in M_i[k]$ must hold at some time k.

A CC protocol can replace the need for initiating separate instances of a consensus protocol. By monitoring a number of events, the protocol can automatically ensure consensus on a variety of issues. Continuous consensus was defined in [2], where it was studied in the crash and sending omissions failure models. We consider the continuous consensus problem in harsher failure models. More interestingly, since continuous consensus is a service that should operate indefinitely, we study it under the bounded failure interval assumption, which is parameterized by a pair (t, T). The assumption states that at most t processes act in a faulty manner over any interval consisting of T rounds. In particular, it may well be the case that no process behaves correctly throughout an execution. This model was introduced by Castro and Liskov [1], who termed the interval T a *Window of vulnerability*, and studied protocols for such failure behavior in the context of malicious Byzantine failures. Note that the standard assumption that at most t processes fail overall is represented by the (t, ∞) assumption. An important distinction between (t, T) and (t, ∞) is the fact that correct protocols in this model must provide facilities for recovery of the data of processes that were formerly faulty and have become rehabilitated. Since processes can alternate between being considered faulty and nonfaulty during the course of an execution, we need to refine the specification of the continuous consensus problem slightly. For the purpose of the definition, we consider a process *nonfaulty* at time k if it behaves correctly in the preceding T rounds, as well as in the following round $k + 1$.

A. Pelc (Ed.): DISC 2007, LNCS 4731, pp. 490–491, 2007.
© Springer-Verlag Berlin Heidelberg 2007

The current work provides the following advances regarding continuous consensus in the different models.

- We show that for pairs (t, T) with $t \geq T$, no CC protocol can guarantee to ever maintain a nonempty core, even in the crash failure or sending omissions failure model. Interestingly, however, there are "lucky" behaviors of the adversary in such models, in which the core *does* become nonempty. (In such runs it is possible, for example, to reach simultaneous consensus.)
- We present an *optimum* and efficient polynomial-time solution to CC in the crash and (sending) omissions failure models. For every pattern of failures, the core maintained by this protocol at any given time is a superset of the core that any given correct (even computationally unbounded) protocol for CC would provide. Based on the (t, T) failure assumption, failure information may become outdated, allowing the adversary new powers to fail processes. As a result, the time it takes information to enter the core may vary in both directions (increasing and decreasing) during a given execution. Nevertheless, we show that the core itself is never reduced in size. The protocol we design is a non-trivial modification of the uniform CC protocol presented in [2] under the (t, ∞) bound assumption.
- We study CC in the general omissions (see [3]) and authenticated Byzantine models ([4]). We modify a lower bound in [3] to prove that an optimum protocol for CC in these models requires NP-hard computations to be performed between rounds. This news is not detrimental, since optimum solutions are rare in general. For eventual consensus, for example, it has been shown in [3] that no optimum protocol exists at all. We first present continuous consensus protocols for (t, T) failures of both types in which the information of correct processes enters the core within $t + 1$ rounds. We then proceed to provide CC protocols that place data in the core faster than that in many runs. To this end, we present two types of protocols. One type consists of computationally efficient protocols that have good behavior in the best case, and more theoretical protocols that make use of an NP oracle and produce good performance much more often.

We believe that both the the use of a continuous consensus service and the (t, T)-bounded failures model are worthwhile abstractions that will find many uses in a variety of applications.

References

1. Castro, M., Liskov, B.: Proactive recovery in a Byzantine-fault-tolerant system. ACM Trans. on Computer Systems, 398–461 (2002)
2. Mizrahi, T., Moses, Y.: Continuous consensus via common knowledge, Distributed Computing. An early version appears. In: The Proceedings of TARK X, pp. 236–252 (2005) (to appear, 2008)
3. Moses, Y., Tuttle, M.R.: Programming simultaneous actions using common knowledge. Algorithmica 3, 121–169 (1988)
4. Pease, M., Shostak, R., Lamport, L.: Reaching agreement in the presence of faults. Journal of the ACM 27(2), 228–234 (1980)

Fully Distributed Algorithms for Convex Optimization Problems

Damon Mosk-Aoyama[1], Tim Roughgarden[1], and Devavrat Shah[2]

[1] Department of Computer Science, Stanford University
[2] Department of Electrical Engineering and Computer Science, MIT

Abstract. We describe a distributed algorithm for convex constrained optimization in networks without any consistent naming infrastructure. The algorithm produces an approximately feasible and near-optimal solution in time polynomial in the network size, the inverse of the permitted error, and a measure of curvature variation in the dual optimization problem. It blends, in a novel way, gossip-based information spreading, iterative gradient ascent, and the barrier method from the design of interior-point algorithms.

1 Problem Description

We consider an undirected graph $G = (V, E)$, with $V = \{1, \ldots, n\}$, in which each node i has a non-negative decision variable x_i. Our goal is to solve convex optimization problems of the following form.

$$
\begin{aligned}
\text{minimize} \quad & f(x) = \sum_{i=1}^{n} f_i(x_i) \quad &(1) \\
\text{subject to} \quad & Ax = b \\
& x_i \geq 0, \quad i = 1, \ldots, n
\end{aligned}
$$

We assume that each function f_i is twice differentiable and strictly convex, with $\lim_{x_i \downarrow 0} f_i'(x_i) < \infty$ and $\lim_{x_i \uparrow \infty} f_i'(x_i) = \infty$. The elements of the $m \times n$ matrix A and the vector $b \in \mathbf{R}^m$ are non-negative.

Although we seek a solution to the primal problem (1), instead of directly enforcing the non-negativity constraints, we introduce a logarithmic barrier. For a parameter $\theta > 0$, we replace the objective function in (1) by $\sum_{i=1}^{n}(f_i(x_i) - \theta \ln x_i)$, and we remove the constraints $x_i \geq 0$ to obtain a primal barrier problem. The associated Lagrange dual problem is the following optimization problem, for which a feasible solution is any vector $\lambda \in \mathbf{R}^m$.

$$
\text{maximize} \quad g_\theta(\lambda) = -b^T \lambda + \sum_{i=1}^{n} \inf_{x_i > 0} \left(f_i(x_i) - \theta \ln x_i + a_i^T \lambda x_i \right) \quad (2)
$$

We assume that the primal barrier problem is feasible; that is, there exists a vector $x \in \mathbf{R}^n$ with $x_i > 0$ such that $Ax = b$. As a result, the optimal value of

A. Pelc (Ed.): DISC 2007, LNCS 4731, pp. 492–493, 2007.

the primal barrier problem is finite, and Slater's condition implies that the dual problem (2) has the same optimal value, and there exists a dual solution λ^* that achieves this optimal value. Since (2) is an unconstrained maximization problem with a strictly concave objective function, the optimal solution λ^* is unique.

2 Algorithm Description

Our approach to solving the primal problem (1) is to apply gradient ascent for the dual barrier problem (2). The algorithm generates a sequence of feasible solutions $\lambda^0, \lambda^1, \lambda^2, \ldots$ for (2), where λ^0 is an initial vector provided as input. To update λ^{k-1} to λ^k in an iteration k, the algorithm uses the gradient $\nabla g_\theta \left(\lambda^{k-1} \right)$ to determine the direction of the difference $\lambda^k - \lambda^{k-1}$.

For a dual solution λ, the gradient $\nabla g_\theta(\lambda)$ is given by $\nabla g_\theta(\lambda) = Ax(\lambda) - b$, where the vector $x(\lambda) \in \mathbf{R}^n$ is defined by $x_i(\lambda) = h_i^{-1} \left(-a_i^T \lambda \right)$. Here, the function h_i is defined as $h_i(x_i) = f_i'(x_i) - \theta/x_i$, and a_i is the ith column of the matrix A. To compute a component $j \in \{1, \ldots, m\}$ of the gradient, the nodes estimate the sum $\sum_{i=1}^n A_{ji} x_i(\lambda)$ using a distributed summation algorithm by Mosk-Aoyama and Shah (PODC, 2006). This is a randomized algorithm that takes an error parameter ϵ_1 as input, and is said to succeed if the output value it produces is within a factor of $1 \pm \epsilon_1$ of the actual sum.

Based on the formula above for $\nabla g_\theta(\lambda)$, the norm of the gradient measures how far the vector $x(\lambda)$ is from satisfying the equality constraints in (1). The nodes continue to execute iterations of gradient ascent until the ℓ_2-norm $\|\nabla g_\theta(\lambda)\|$ goes below a threshold determined by an input error parameter, where λ is the current dual solution. At this point, the algorithm terminates with the vector $x(\lambda)$ as the output. The number of iterations required for the algorithm to terminate can be bounded in terms of the following quantity.

$$R = \frac{\left(\max_{i=1,\ldots,n} \max_{\lambda \in B(\lambda^*, \|\lambda^0 - \lambda^*\|)} \left(h_i^{-1} \right)' \left(-a_i^T \lambda \right) \right) \sigma_{\max} \left(A^T \right)^2}{\left(\min_{i=1,\ldots,n} \min_{\lambda \in B(\lambda^*, \|\lambda^0 - \lambda^*\|)} \left(h_i^{-1} \right)' \left(-a_i^T \lambda \right) \right) \sigma_{\min} \left(A^T \right)^2} \quad (3)$$

Here, $B(\lambda^*, r) = \{\lambda \mid \|\lambda - \lambda^*\| \leq r\}$, and $\sigma_{\min} \left(A^T \right)$ and $\sigma_{\max} \left(A^T \right)$ denote the smallest and largest singular values, respectively, of the matrix A^T.

Given an error parameter ϵ as input, the nodes set the parameters used in the gradient ascent so that, provided that every invocation of the summation subroutine succeeds, the number of iterations executed is bounded as follows.

Theorem 1. *After $O \left(R^2 \log \left(\|Ax \left(\lambda^0 \right) - b\| / (\epsilon \|b\|) \right) \right)$ iterations, the gradient ascent terminates with a solution $x(\lambda)$ such that $\|Ax(\lambda) - b\| \leq \epsilon \|b\|$. The objective function value of the solution satisfies $f(x(\lambda)) \leq \mathrm{OPT} + \epsilon \|b\| \|\lambda\| + n\theta$, where OPT is the optimal value of the primal program (1).*

Some of the parameters in the gradient ascent are set by the nodes using quantities, such as R, whose values would be unknown to the nodes. A complete algorithm for computing an approximate solution to the primal problem (1) with high probability can be obtained by adding an outer loop to the algorithm that executes gradient ascent for different possible values of these quantities.

On the Power of Impersonation Attacks*

Michael Okun

Weizmann Institute of Science
mush@weizmann.ac.il

Background. In the standard message passing models it is assumed that the identity of a sender is known to the receiver. In practice, this often is not the case, due to impersonation attacks by malicious adversaries. Various impersonation attack schemes have been extensively investigated in the context of network security or cryptography, in particular for peep-to-peer and sensor networks [4,5]. Here, we study this problem in the context of distributed computing theory.

Consider a set of n processors, $p_1, ..., p_n$, communicating by means of point-to-point message passing between every pair of processors. Assume that the message sender is identified by including its id in the message. For simplicity the communication is assumed to be synchronous. The adversary is an external entity capable of injecting messages with arbitrary content into the network (but it is incapable of preventing the processors from receiving each other's messages). The ids of the processors are assumed to be fixed and known a priori, thus injecting messages that impersonate the real processors is the only way by which the adversary can interfere with the computation. Adversarial behavior of this kind is known as *stolen identities Sybil attack* [4,5]. For the purpose of formal analysis, the strength of the adversary is quantified by the number of messages it is able to send to each processor in every round. A k-*adversary* can generate up to k messages for every processor, so that a processor can receive up to $n+k$ messages in a round, instead of just n correct messages. This formulation includes the particular cases of an adversary that in every round can impersonate some specific k processors, or of a system with $n + k$ processors, k of which are Byzantine, capable of sending messages with arbitrary ids and content.

When a processor receives several messages tagged by p_i, it might be impossible to know which one of them is correct, in which case it is reasonable to drop these messages altogether. If all the messages having a "fake twin" are handled this way, we end up with a synchronous mobile failures model [7] in which the number of transmission failures with respect to every receiver is bounded by k. This is known to be equivalent to the standard asynchronous crash failure model [6]. The opposite direction, however, is not true - the k-adversary model is strictly stronger than the asynchronous model with k failures, because all the messages sent in every round by the processors are received. For example, in the impersonation model each processor is able to compute (in a single round) an upper bound on the input values of all the processors, which is impossible in the asynchronous case even with a single failure. Thus the question of the relative power of the impersonation model remains.

---

* This research was partially supported by Sir Charles Clore fellowship and the Ministry of Defence.

A. Pelc (Ed.): DISC 2007, LNCS 4731, pp. 494–495, 2007.
© Springer-Verlag Berlin Heidelberg 2007

Results. To answer the above question we have considered the k-set agreement problem (and consensus in particular) and the renaming problem in the impersonation model.

There exists a simple bivalency proof, similar to [1], which shows that deterministic consensus is impossible even in the presence of 1-adversary. For the k-set agreement problem, there exists an algorithm in the presence of $(k-1)$-adversary, but no deterministic algorithm resilient against a k-adversary. The proof of the latter result uses the combinatorial topology machinery from [3].

For the renaming problem[1] there exists a simple order-preserving algorithm resilient against a k-adversary, that has a target namespace of size $n + k$, which is optimal. In the asynchronous case, the minimum possible size of the target namespace of any order-preserving algorithm resilient to t failures is $2^t(n - t + 1) - 1$ [2]. Whereas for asynchronous order-preserving renaming, the large target namespace is a result of complete uncertainty about the input values of some processors, in the impersonation model this uncertainty is reduced (eventually the input of each processor is known to belong to a small set of possible values), and as a result the size of the target namespace is significantly smaller.

In summary, our results show that the effects of an impersonation attack, mobile failures and the loss of synchrony are very much alike. The subtle difference in the computational power of the models is not evident for k-set agreement. On the other hand, renaming, which is the easier among the coordination problems, reveals that the models are not equivalent.

References

1. Aguilera, M.K., Toueg, S.: Simple Bivalency Proof that t-Resilient Consensus Requires $t + 1$ Rounds. Inf. Proc. Lett. 71(3-4), 155–158 (1999)
2. Attiya, H., Bar-Noy, A., Dolev, D., Peleg, D., Reischuk, R.: Renaming in an Asynchronous Environment. J. ACM 37(3), 524–548 (1990)
3. Chaudhuri, S., Herlihy, M., Lynch, N.A., Tuttle, M.R.: Tight Bounds for k-set Agreement. J. ACM 47(5), 912–943 (2000)
4. Douceur, J.R.: The Sybil Attack. In: Druschel, P., Kaashoek, M.F., Rowstron, A. (eds.) IPTPS 2002. LNCS, vol. 2429, pp. 251–260. Springer, Heidelberg (2002)
5. Newsome, J., Shi, E., Song, D.X., Perrig, A.: The Sybil Attack in Sensor Networks: Analysis & Defenses. In: Proc. 3rd International Symposium on Information Processing in Sensor Networks (IPSN), pp. 259–268 (2004)
6. Raynal, M., Roy, M.: A Note on a Simple Equivalence between Round-based Synchronous and Asynchronous Models. In: Proc. 11th IEEE Pacific Rim International Symposium on Dependable Computing (PRDC), pp. 387–392 (2005)
7. Santoro, N., Widmayer, P.: Time is Not a Healer. In: Cori, R., Monien, B. (eds.) STACS 89. LNCS, vol. 349, pp. 304–313. Springer, Heidelberg (1989)

---

[1] To avoid a trivial solution, processor ids can be considered as entities that can be tested for equality but not compared, while renaming has to be performed using a unique private input provided to each processor.

Perfectly Reliable and Secure Communication in Directed Networks Tolerating Mixed Adversary[*]

Arpita Patra[1], Ashish Choudhary[1,**], Kannan Srinathan[2],
and Chandrasekharan Pandu Rangan[1]

[1] Dept of Computer Science and Engineering
IIT Madras, Chennai India 600036
{arpita,ashishc}@cse.iitm.ernet.in, rangan@iitm.ernet.in
[2] International Institute of Information Technology
Hyderabad India 500032
srinathan@iiit.ac.in

We characterize *Perfectly Secure Message Transmission* (PSMT) between two nodes **S** and **R** in *directed wire* model, assuming that n wires are directed from **S** to **R** (also termed as *top band*) and u wires are directed from **R** to **S** (also termed as *bottom band*). A *mixed* adversary (t_b, t_f) controls t_b wires in Byzantine fashion and t_f in *fail-stop* fashion among these $u + n$ wires with *unbounded* computing power. **S** wishes to send a message m from a finite field $\mathbb{F}$ in a *perfectly secure* manner to **R** such that the adversary gets no information whatsoever on m, though he has unbounded computing power. Our characterization is the first ever characterization for PSMT considering mixed adversary and reveals more fault tolerance than the existing results [1]. Our protocols terminates in constant number of phases[1], performs polynomial computation and have polynomial communication complexity. The values n, u, t_b and t_f are system parameters and known publicly. The characterization for the PSMT depending upon the value of u, t_b and t_f is as follows:

Theorem 1. *Let $G = (V, E)$ be a digraph and* **S**, **R** $\in V$ *with u wires in the bottom band and n wires in the top band such that the wires in the top band and bottom band are disjoint. Let G be under the influence of a mixed adversary (t_b, t_f). Then depending upon the value of u, the following holds:*

1. *If $1 \leq u \leq t_f$, then PSMT is possible iff $n = max\{3t_b + t_f + 1 - u, 2t_b + t_f + 1\}$.*
2. *If $t_f + 1 \leq u \leq t_b + t_f$ then PSMT is possible iff $n = max\{3t_b + 2t_f + 1 - 2u, 2t_b + t_f + 1\}$.*
3. *If $u > t_b + t_f$ then PSMT is possible iff $n \geq 2t_b + t_f + 1$.*

Due to space constraint, we only consider the first case[2].

---

[*] The Full Version of this paper is available at [2].

[**] Work Supported by Project No. CSE/05-06/076/DITX/CPAN on Protocols for Secure Communication and Computation Sponsored by Department of Information Technology, Government of India.

[1] A phase is a communication from **S** to **R** or vice-versa.

[2] The complete proof is available at [2].

A. Pelc (Ed.): DISC 2007, LNCS 4731, pp. 496–498, 2007.

Proof: <u>*Necessity:*</u> Any PSMT protocol should also be reliable for which there should exist $2t_b + t_f + 1$ wires in the *top band*[3].

<u>*Sufficiency:*</u> We design a three phase PSMT protocol which securely sends m from **S** to **R** provided there exists $n = 2t_b + t_f + 1$ wires $F_i, 1 \le i \le n$ in the *top band* and $u > t_b + t_f$ wires $B_j, 1 \le j \le u$ in the *bottom band*. We summarize the properties of the protocol. Any adversary controlling at most $t_b + t_f$ wires among $n + u$ wires gets *no* information about m. If **S** correctly receives the original *conflict graph* through at least one wire in the *bottom band*, then **S** and **R** will identify all F_i over which $Q(x, i)$ had been changed during **Phase I**. The communication complexity of the protocol is $O(n^4)$ field elements[4].

Phase I: S to R

• **S** selects bivariate polynomial $Q(x, y) = \sum_{i=0}^{t_b} \sum_{j=0}^{t_b} r_{ij} x^i y^j$, where r_{ij}'s are randomly chosen from $\mathbb{F}$ which are independent of m where $r_{00} = Q(0, 0) = m$. **S** evaluates $Q(x, y)$ at $y = 1, 2, \ldots, n$ where each $Q(x, i)$ is a polynomial in x of degree t_b and sends over $F_i, 1 \le i \le n$ the polynomial $Q(x, i)$ and the values $Q(x, j), 1 \le j \le n$ at $x = i$, denoted by v_{ji}. The n tuple $[v_{j1} v_{j2} \ldots v_{jn}], 1 \le j \le n$ corresponds to the Reed-Solomon codeword of $Q(x, j), 1 \le j \le n$.

Phase II: R to S

• During **Phase I** at most t_f wires may fail to deliver any values. However, **R** will receive information over at least $2t_b + 1$ wires. Let **R** receives information over $F_{i_1}, F_{i_2}, \ldots, F_{i_\alpha}$ where $2t_b + 1 \le \alpha \le 2t_b + t_f + 1$. Suppose **R** receives over $F_{i_k}, 1 \le k \le \alpha$ the polynomial $Q'(x, i_k)$ and the values $v'_{ji_k}, 1 \le j \le n$. The received codeword (possibly shortened) $[v'_{ji_1} v'_{ji_2} \ldots v'_{ji_\alpha}]$ can differ from corresponding the actual (shortened) codeword $[v_{ji_1} v_{ji_2} \ldots v_{ji_\alpha}]$ in at most t_b locations.

• **R** creates a directed graph $H = (\mathcal{W}, E)$, called *conflict graph* such that $\mathcal{W} = \{F_{i_1}, F_{i_2}, \ldots, F_{i_\alpha}\}$ and $(F_{i_j}, F_{i_k}) \in E$ if $Q'(x, i_j) \ne v'_{i_j i_k}, 1 \le i_j, i_k \le \alpha$. Thus there exists an arc from F_{i_j} to F_{i_k} in H if the value of $Q'(x, i_j)$ received over F_{i_j} when evaluated at $x = i_k$ does not match the corresponding value $v'_{i_j i_k}$ received over F_{i_k} implying that either F_{i_j} or F_{i_k} or both are corrupted. Corresponding to each arc $(F_{i_j}, F_{i_k}) \in H$, **R** adds a four tuple $(F_{i_j}, F_{i_k}, Q'(i_k, i_j), v'_{i_j i_k})$ to a list X. **R** finally broadcasts the list X to **S** through the *bottom band*.

Phase III from S to R

• During **Phase II**, the adversary might block the communication over at most t_f wires in the *bottom band* and change X to some arbitrary list X'. In the worst case, **S** may receive at most $t_b + 1$ different lists. Let **S** receives distinct lists $L_1, L_2, \ldots, L_\beta$ through the *bottom band*, where $1 \le \beta \le t_b + 1$. For each such list L_p, **S** does the following: **S** creates a fault list denoted by $L_{P_{fault}}$ which is initialized to $\emptyset$. For each four tuple $(F_{i_j}, F_{i_k}, Q'(i_k, i_j), v'_{i_j i_k})$ present in the list L_p, **S** locally checks $Q'(i_k, i_j) \stackrel{?}{=} Q(i_k, i_j)$ and $v_{i_j i_k} \stackrel{?}{=} v'_{i_j i_k}$. Depending upon the outcome of the test, **S** concludes that either **R** had received incorrect $Q(x, i_j)$ through wire F_{i_j} or **R** had received the value of the polynomial $Q(x, i_j)$ at $x = i_k$ incorrectly through wire F_{i_k} (or both) and hence accordingly add F_{i_j} or F_{i_k} (or both) to $L_{P_{fault}}$. After performing the above steps for each received list L_p, **S** broadcasts to **R** the pairs $(L_p, L_{P_{fault}})$.

Message Recovery by R

R correctly receives the pairs $(L_p, L_{P_{fault}})$ and checks for the original X which it had sent during **Phase II**. Since $u > t_b + t_f$, even if during **Phase II** the adversary had blocked communication over t_f wires and changed the original list X to X' over t_b wires, **S** will correctly receive X through at least one wire. Hence after **Phase III**, **R** always finds the original list X in the received pairs $(L_p, L_{P_{fault}})$. Let the received pair corresponding to list X be $(L_z, L_{z_{fault}})$. From $L_{z_{fault}}$, **R** comes to know the identity of all incorrect $Q(x, i_j)$'s out of the $2t_b + 1 \le \alpha \le 2t_b + t_f + 1$ $Q(x, i)$'s that **R** had received during **Phase I**, neglects them, interpolates $Q(x, y)$ using the remaining $Q(x, i_j)$'s and recovers $m = Q(0, 0)$.

---

[3] This is a necessary condition for reliable communication between **S** and **R** [2].
[4] Full details can be found in [2].

References

1. Desmedt, Y., Wang, Y.: Perfectly secure message transmission revisited. Cryptology ePrint Archive, Report 2002/128 (2002), http://eprint.iacr.org
2. Patra, A., Choudhary, A., Srinathan, K., Rangan, C.P.: Perfectly Reliable and Secure Communication in Directed Networks Tolerating Mixed Adversary. Available at http://www.cs.iitm.ernet.in/~ashishc/ashish_pub.html

A Formal Analysis of the Deferred Update Technique[*]

Rodrigo Schmidt[1,2] and Fernando Pedone[2]

[1] École Polytechnique Fédérale de Lausanne, Switzerland
[2] University of Lugano, Switzerland

Introduction. In the deferred update technique for database replication, a number of database replicas are used to implement a single serializable database interface. Its main idea consists in executing all operations of a transaction initially on a single database replica. Transactions that do not change the database state can commit locally to the replica they executed, but other transactions must be globally certified and, if committed, have their update operations submitted to all replicas. Despite its wide use, we are not aware of any work that explored the inherent limitations and characteristics of deferred update database replication, ours being the first attempt in this direction.

We specify a general abstract deferred update algorithm that embraces all the protocols we know of. This general specification allows for a better understanding of the technique, including its requirements and limitations and can be used to ease designing and proving specific protocols.

The Deferred Update Abstraction. Due to the space limitation, we present only the general idea of our approach and results in this brief announcement. In our extended technical report [1], we present complete specifications and explain the results in detail. We start with a general serializable database specification, later used to prove our abstraction correct, and gradually move towards an abstract deferred update algorithm. All our specifications have been translated into the TLA$^+$ specification language [2] and model checked.

From our initial specification of a serializable database, we formalize the notion of *order-preserving serializability*, introduced by Beeri et al. in the context of nested transactions [3], for its use in deferred update replication. While previous works assumed replicas should satisfy *order-preserving serializability* to ensure global serializability, we show that serializability is guaranteed if replicas satisfy the weaker notion of *active order-preserving serializability* that we introduce. Some multiversion concurrency control mechanisms [4], for example, are active order-preserving but not strict order-preserving; yet, our results show that they can be used in deferred updated protocols.

Our specification of serializability also allows us to reason better about the actions required to implement it using a number of internal database replicas. From that, we could specify the atomic actions that abstract the deferred update technique, that is, the actions implemented by all deferred update protocols. The abstract deferred update algorithm we present allows us to isolate the properties

---

[*] The work presented in this paper has been partially funded by the SNSF, Switzerland (project #200021-170824).

A. Pelc (Ed.): DISC 2007, LNCS 4731, pp. 499–500, 2007.

of the *termination protocol*, responsible for certifying and propagating update transactions to the replicas. We specify three safety properties, namely *Nontriviality*, *Stability*, and *Consistency*, and discuss their necessity. This discussion brings out the result that update transactions cannot be propagated to replicas in different orders, even if they operate (read or write) on completely disjunct subsets of the data items, for it can break serializability. This is rather counterintuitive since serializability would allow such transactions to be scheduled in any order. Our properties imply that the termination protocol must ensure something stronger than just the serializability of the update transactions, which means that proving only that does not suffice.

By extending the termination protocol with a simple liveness property that ensures propagation of committed transactions, we were able to show that its properties necessarily implement, for committed transactions, the Sequence Agreement problem explained in [5]. Briefly, in the sequence agreement problem, a set of processes agree on an ever-growing sequence of values, built out of proposed ones. This problem is a sequence-based specification of the celebrated Atomic Broadcast problem. Our result implies that implementations of the termination protocol are free to abort transactions, but they must atomically broadcast the transactions they commit. As a consequence, any lower bound or impossibility result for atomic broadcast and consensus applies to the termination protocol.

Conclusion. We have formalized the deferred update technique for database replication and stated some intrinsic characteristics and limitations of it. Previous works have only considered new algorithms, with independent specifications, analysis, and correctness proofs. To the best of our knowledge, our work is the first effort to formally characterize this family of algorithms and establish its requirements. Our general abstraction can be used to derive other lower bounds as well as to create new algorithms and prove existing ones correct. Some algorithms can be easily proved correct by a refinement mapping to ours. Others may require an additional effort due to their extra assumptions, but the task seems easier than with previous formalisms. In our experience, we have successfully used our abstraction to obtain interesting protocols and correctness proofs.

References

1. Schmidt, R., Pedone, F.: A formal analysis of the deferred update technique. Technical report, EPFL (2007)
2. Lamport, L.: Specifying Systems: The TLA+ Language and Tools for Hardware and Software Engineers. Addison-Wesley Longman Publishing Co., Inc., Boston, MA, USA (2002)
3. Beeri, C., Bernstein, P.A., Goodman, N.: A model for concurrency in nested transaction systems. Journal of the ACM 36(2), 230–269 (1989)
4. Bernstein, P., Hadzilacos, V., Goodman, N.: Concurrency Control and Recovery in Database Systems. Addison-Wesley, Reading (1987)
5. Lamport, L.: Generalized consensus and paxos. Technical Report MSR-TR-2005-33, Microsoft Research (2004)

DISC at Its 20th Anniversary (Stockholm, 2006)

Michel Raynal[1], Sam Toueg[2], and Shmuel Zaks[3]

[1] IRISA, Campus de Beaulieu, 35042 Rennes, France
[2] Department of Computer Science, University of Toronto, Toronto, Canada
[3] Department of Computer Science, Technion, Haifa, Israel

Prologue

DISC 2006 marked the 20th anniversary of the DISC conferences. We list below the special events that took place during DISC 2006, together with some information and perspectives on the past and future of DISC.

Special 20th Anniversary Events

The celebration of the 20th anniversary of DISC consisted in four main events: invited talks by three of the brightest figures of the distributed computing community, and a panel involving all the people who were at the very beginning of DISC (the abstracts of the invited talks appear independently in these proceedings).

- An invited talk *"Time, clocks and the ordering of my ideas about distributed systems"* by Leslie Lamport.
- An invited talk *"My early days in distributed computing theory: 1979-1982"* by Nancy Lynch.
- An invited talk *"Provably unbreakable hyper-encryption using distributed systems"* by Michael Rabin.
- A panel that discussed the contributions of the WDAG/DISC community to distributed computing from a historical perspective. The panelists (Eli Gafni, Jan van Leeuwen, Nicola Santoro, Shmuel Zaks) and the moderator (Michel Raynal) were the members of the program committee of the second DISC (called WDAG at that time), held in Amsterdam. The panel reviewed the status of many contributions to network protocol design and to the understanding of distributed computing in general. It also discussed the possible ways in which DISC may evolve in the future.

Past: A Short History

The *Workshop on Distributed Algorithms on Graphs* (WDAG) was initiated by Eli Gafni, Nicola Santoro and Jan van Leeuwen in 1985. It was intended to provide a forum for researchers and other interested parties to present and discuss recent results and trends in the design and analysis of distributed algorithms on communication networks and graphs.

Then, more than 10 years later, the acronym WDAG was changed to DISC (the international symposium on DIStributed Computing). This change was made to reflect the

A. Pelc (Ed.): DISC 2007, LNCS 4731, pp. 501–503, 2007.

expansion from a workshop to a symposium as well as the expansion of the research areas of interest. So, following 11 successful WDAGs, DISC'98 was the 12th in the series.

Since 1996 WDAG/DISC has been managed by a Steering Committee consisting of some of the most experienced members of the distributed computing community. The main role of this committee is to provide guidance and leadership to ensure the continuing success of this conference. To do so, the committee oversees the continuous evolution of the symposium's research areas of interest, it forges ties with other related conferences and workshops, and it also maintains contact with Springer-Verlag and other professional or scientific sponsoring organizations (such as EATCS). The structure and rules of the DISC Steering Committee, which were composed by Sam Toueg and Shmuel Zaks, and approved by the participants at the the 1996 WDAG business meeting in Bologna, can be found at *http://www.disc-conference.org*. This site also contain information about previous WDAG and DISC conferences.

The location, program chairs, and proceedings of the WDAG/DISC meetings are summarized in Table 1, and the Steering Committee Chairs are listed in Table 2.

Table 1. The past (and present) Wdag/Disc

Year	Location	Program Chair(s)	Proceedings
1985	Ottawa	N. Santoro and J. van Leeuwen	Carleton Scientific
1987	Amsterdam	J. van Leeuwen	LNCS 312
1989	Nice	J.-Cl. Bermond and M. Raynal	LNCS 392
1990	Bari	N. Santoro and J. van Leeuwen	LNCS 486
1991	Delphi	S. Toueg and P. Spirakis	LNCS 579
1992	Haifa	A. Segall and S. Zaks	LNCS 647
1993	Lausanne	A. Schiper	LNCS 725
1994	Terschelling	G. Tel and P. Vitányi	LNCS 857
1995	Le Mont-Saint-Michel	J.-M. Hélary and M. Raynal	LNCS 972
1996	Bologna	Ö. Babaoglŭ and K. Marzullo	LNCS 1151
1997	Saarbrücken	M. Mavronicolas and Ph. Tsigas	LNCS 1320
1998	Andros	S. Kutten	LNCS 1499
1999	Bratislava	P. Jayanti	LNCS 1693
2000	Toledo	M. Herlihy	LNCS 1914
2001	Lisbon	J. Welch	LNCS 2180
2002	Toulouse	D. Malkhi	LNCS 2508
2003	Sorrento	F.E. Fich	LNCS 2848
2004	Amsterdam	R. Guerraoui	LNCS 3274
2005	Cracow	P. Fraigniaud	LNCS 3724
2006	Stockholm	S. Dolev	LNCS 4167
2007	Cyprus	A. Pelc	This issue

Table 2. Steering committee chairs

1996-1998	1998-2000	2000-2002	2002-2004	2004-2007
Sam Toueg	Shmuel Zaks	André Schiper	Michel Raynal	Alex Shvartsman

Epilogue, and Future

Together with the whole DISC community, we congratulate DISC for its 20th anniversary. We feel proud to have taken part in this important and successful activity of our research community, and are confident that DISC will continue to play a central role in years to come.

We wish to thank all those who contributed over the years to the success of DISC. Each played an essential role, and each forms a vital link in the DISC chain:

- The local organizers, and their teams, who did everything to ensure a smooth and successful conference,
- The program committee chairs, program committee members, and external referees, who ensured the high academic level of the conference,
- The participants of the WDAG and DISC conferences,
- The steering committee members,
- The sponsor organizations, for their generous support over the years,
  and - last but not least -
- All the members of the distributed computing community who submitted papers to WDAG and DISC.

We are confident that the DISC community will continue to play a central role within the distributed computing and communication networks research communities for many years to come.

HAPPY ANNIVERSARY TO DISC!

This photo is from DISC 2005 in Cracow, Poland, and was taken during the banquet at *Wierzynek 1364* restaurant (one of the oldest restaurants in Europe). It shows the first five chairs of the DISC steering committee (from left to right: Shmuel Zaks, Alex Shvartsman, Michel Raynal, André Schiper and Sam Toueg).

DISC 20th Anniversary: Invited Talk
Time, Clocks, and the Ordering of My Ideas About Distributed Systems

Leslie Lamport

Microsoft Corporation
1065 La Avenida
Mountain View, CA 94043
U.S.A.
http://lamport.org

Abstract. A guided tour through the labyrinth of my thoughts, from the Bakery Algorithm to arbiter-free marked graphs. This exercise in egotism is by invitation of the DISC 20th Anniversary Committee. I take no responsibility for the choice of topic.

A. Pelc (Ed.): DISC 2007, LNCS 4731, p. 504, 2007.

DISC 20th Anniversary: Invited Talk
My Early Days in Distributed Computing Theory: 1979-1982

Nancy Lynch

CSAIL, MIT
Cambridge, MA 02139
U.S.A.
lynch@theory.csail.mit.edu

Abstract. I first became involved in Distributed Computing Theory around 1978 or 1979, as a new professor at Georgia Tech. Looking back at my first few years in the field, approximately 1979-1982, I see that they were tremendously exciting, productive, and fun. I collaborated with, and learned from, many leaders of the field, including Mike Fischer, Jim Burns, Michael Merritt, Gary Peterson, Danny Dolev, and Leslie Lamport.

Results that emerged during that time included space lower bounds for mutual exclusion; definition of the k-exclusion problem, with associated lower bounds and algorithms; the Burns-Lynch lower bound on the number of registers needed for mutual exclusion; fast network-wide resource allocation algorithms; the Lynch-Fischer semantic model for distributed systems (a precursor to I/O automata); early work on proof techniques for distributed algorithms; lower bounds on the number of rounds for Byzantine agreement; definition of the approximate agreement problem and associated algorithms; and finally, the Fischer-Lynch-Paterson impossibility result for consensus.

In this talk, I will review this early work, trying to explain how we were thinking at the time, and how the ideas in these projects influenced later work.

A. Pelc (Ed.): DISC 2007, LNCS 4731, p. 505, 2007.

DISC 20th Anniversary: Invited Talk
Provably Unbreakable Hyper-Encryption
Using Distributed Systems

Michael O. Rabin

DEAS Harvard University
Cambridge, MA 02138
rabin@deas.harvard.edu

Abstract. Encryption is a fundamental building block for computer and communications technologies. Existing encryption methods depend for their security on unproven assumptions. We propose a new model, the Limited Access model for enabling a simple and practical provably unbreakable encryption scheme. A voluntary distributed network of thousands of computers each maintain and update random pages, and act as Page Server Nodes. A Sender and Receiver share a random key K. They use K to randomly select the same PSNs and download the same random pages. These are employed in groups of say 30 pages to extract One Time Pads common to S and R. Under reasonable assumptions of an Adversary's inability to monitor all PSNs, and easy ways for S and R to evade monitoring while downloading pages, Hyper Encryption is clearly unbreakable. The system has been completely implemented.

Modern encryption methods depend for their security on assumptions concerning the intractability of various computational problems such as the factorization of large integers into prime factors or the computation of the discrete log function in large finite groups. Even if true, there are currently no methods for proving such assumptions. At the same time, even if these problems will be shown to be of super-polynomial complexity, there is steady progress in the development of practical algorithms for the solution of progressively larger instances of the problems in question. Thus there is no firm reason to believe that any of the encryptions in actual use is now safe, or an indication as to how long it will remain so. Furthermore, if and when the current intensive work on Quantum Computing will produce actual quantum computers, then the above encryptions will succumb to these machines.

At present there are three major proposals for producing provably unbreakable encryption methods. Quantum Cryptography employs properties of quantum mechanics to enable a Sender and Receiver to create common One Time Pads (OTPs) which are secret against any Adversary. The considerable research and development work as well as the funding invested in this effort are testimony to the need felt for an absolutely safe encryption technology. At present Quantum Cryptography systems are limited in range to a few tens of miles, are sensitive to noise or disturbance of the transmission medium, and require rather expensive special equipment.

The Limited Storage Model was proposed by U. Maurer. It postulates a public intensive source of random bits. An example would be a satellite or a system of satellites containing a Physical Random Number Generator (PRNG) beaming

A. Pelc (Ed.): DISC 2007, LNCS 4731, pp. 506–508, 2007.

down a stream a of random numbers, say at the rate of 100GB/sec. S and R use a small shared key, and use those bits and the key to form OTPs which are subsequently employed in the usual manner to encrypt messages. The Limited Storage Model further postulates that for any Adversary or group of Adversaries it is technically or financially infeasible to store more than a fraction, say half, as many bits as there are in a. It was proved by Aumann, Rabin, and Ding and later by Dziembowski-Maurer, that under the Limited Storage Model assumptions, one can construct schemes producing OTPs which are essentially random even for a computationally unbounded (but storage limited) Adversary. The critique of the Limited Storage Model is three-fold. It requires a system of satellites, or other distribution methods, which are very expensive. The above rate of transmission for satellites is right now outside the available capabilities. More fundamentally, with the rapid decline of cost of storage it is not clear that storage is a limiting factor. For example, at a cost of $ 1 per GB, storing the above mentioned stream of bytes will cost about $ 3 Billion per year. And the cost of storage seems to go down very rapidly.

The Limited Access Model postulates a system comprising a multitude of sources of random bytes available to the Sender and Receiver. Each of these sources serves as a Page Server Node (PSN) and has a supply ofrandom pages. Sender and Receiver initially have a shared key K. Using K, Sender and Receiver asynchronously in time access the same PSNs and download the same random pages. The Limited Access assumption is that an Adversary cannot monitor or compromise more than a fraction of the PSNs while the Sender or Receiver download pages. After downloading sufficiently many pages, S and are make sure that they have the same pages by employing a Page Reconciliation Protocol. They now employ the common random pages according to a common scheme in groups of, say, 30 pages to extract an OTP from each group. Let us assume that the extraction method is simply taking the XOR of these pages. The common OTPs are used for encryption in the usual manner.

A crucially important point is that a Page Server Node sends out a requested random page at most twice, then destroys and replaces it by a new page. Opportunity knocks only twice!

Why is this scheme absolutely secure? Assume that we have 5,000 voluntary participants acting as PSNs. Assume that a, possibly distributed, Adversary can eavesdrop, monitor or corrupt (including by acting as imposter) no more than 1000 of these nodes. Thus the probability that in the random choice of the 30 PSNs from which a group of 30 pages are downloaded and XORed, all 30 pages will be known to the Adversary is smaller than $(1/5)30$, i.e., totally negligible. But if an Adversary misses even one page out of the 30 random pages that are XORed into an OTP then the OTP is completely random for him.

The send at most twice, then destroy policy, prevents a powerful Adversary from asking for a large number of pages from each of the PSNs and thereby gain copies of pages common to S and R. The worst that can happen is that, say, S will down load a page P from PSNi and the Adversary (or another user of Hyper-Encryption) has or will download the same page P from PSNi. When R now requests according to the key K the same page from PSNi, he will not get it. So R and S never have a page P in common if P was also downloaded by a third party. The only consequence of an Adversary's down-loading from too many PSNs is denial of service to the legitimate users of the system. This is a problem for any server system and there are ways of dealing with this type of attack.

What if an Adversary eavesdrops onto the Sender and or Receiver while they are downloading pages from PSNs. Well, S and R can go to an Internet caf or one of those establishments allowing a customer to obtain an Internet connection. They can use a device that does not identify them and download thousands of pages from PSNs within a short time. The salient point is that S and R need not time-synchronize their access to the PSNs. Once S and R have common OTPs, they can securely communicate from their fixed known locations with immunity against eavesdropping or code breaking.

The initial key K is continually extended and updated by S and R using common One Time Pads. Each pair of random words from K is used to select a PSN and a page from that PSN only once and then discarded. This is essential for the absolute security of Hyper Encryption.

With all these provisions Hyper Encryption in the Limited Access Model also provides Ever Lasting Secrecy. Let us make a worst case assumption that the initial common key K or its later extensions were lost or stolen after their use to collect common random pages from PSNs. Those pages are not available any more as a result of the send only twice and destroy policy. Thus the extracted OTPs used to encrypt messages cannot be reconstructed and the encryption is valid in perpetuity. By contrast, all the existing public or private key encryption methods are vulnerable to the retroactive decryption attack if the key is lost or algorithms come up that break the encryption algorithm.

We shall also describe an additional scheme based on the use of search engines for the generation of OTPs and of unbreakable encryption.

Our systems were fully coded in Java for distribution as freeware amongst interested users. All the protocols described below are running in the background on the participating computers and impose negligible computational and storage overheads on the host computer.

Author Index

Lecture Notes in Computer Science

Sublibrary 1: Theoretical Computer Science and General Issues

For information about Vols. 1– 4431
please contact your bookseller or Springer